Welfare Economics and Second-Best Theory

Richard S. Markovits

Welfare Economics and Second-Best Theory

A Distortion-Analysis Protocol
for Economic-Efficiency Prediction

 Springer

Richard S. Markovits
University of Texas School of Law
Austin, TX, USA

ISBN 978-3-030-43359-8   ISBN 978-3-030-43360-4   (eBook)
https://doi.org/10.1007/978-3-030-43360-4

This Springer imprint is published by the registered company Springer Nature Switzerland AG
The registered company address is: Gewerbestrasse 11, 6330 Cham, Switzerland

Appreciation

I thank my wife and colleague Inga Markovits and our five children—Daniel, Stefanie, Benjamin, Julia, and Rebecca—for making it easy to keep what follows in an appropriate perspective. I also thank my personal assistant Sally Zaleski both for her friendliness, patience, and diligence and for the vision, intelligence, diagrammatic abilities, and (I admit) cartographic skills that enabled her to convert a complicated, difficult, and hard-to-decipher manuscript into a publishable document.

Contents

Acronyms and Symbols

General

ARDEPPS   Acronym for "(somewhat-)" arbitrarily-defined portion of product-space (substituted for the conventional expression "economic market")

Δ Indicates that the specific resource-use referenced by the category-of-resource-use symbol (see below) it precedes is either economics-marginal or economics just-extra-marginal

Symbols that Reference the Allocative or Private Benefits, Allocative or Private Costs, Allocative Efficiency, or (Private) Profits Associated with Particular Resource-Uses or Resource Allocations

LB   Allocative benefits
LC   Allocative cost
LE   Allocative efficiency
PB   Private benefits
PC   Private cost
Pπ (Private) profits

Symbols that Reference a Category of Resource-Uses or a Way of Using Resources

PPR   A production-process-research project or a production-process-research-executing resource-use

QV   A quality-or-variety-increasing investment (that creates a new product variant, a new distributive outlet, additional capacity, or additional inventory and which may or may not discover knowledge) or a QV-investment-creating resource-use

UO   A unit of output or a unit-output-producing resource-use

Symbols that Reference Functional Categories of Resource Allocations (Which Ignore Whether the Resource-Uses Sacrificed/Executed Are Economics Just-Extra-Marginal/Economics-Marginal)

inter-ARDEPPS PPR-to-PPR	An allocation of resources from the execution of one or more PPR projects in one or more ARDEPPSes to the execution of a PPR project in a different specifiable ARDEPPS
intra-ARDEPPS PPR-to-PPR	An allocation of resources from the execution of one or more PPR projects in a given ARDEPPS to the execution of a different PPR project in the same ARDEPPS
inter-ARDEPPS QV-to-QV	An allocation of resources from the creation of one or more QV investments in one or more ARDEPPSes to the creation of a QV investment in another ARDEPPS
intra-ARDEPPS QV-to-QV	An allocation of resources from the creation of one or more QV investments in a given ARDEPPS to the creation of a different QV investment in the same ARDEPPS
inter-ARDEPPS UO-to-UO	An allocation of resources from the production of one or more units of extant products in one or more ARDEPPSes to the production of a unit of a product in a different ARDEPPS
intra-ARDEPPS UO-to-UO	An allocation of resources from the production of one or more units of one or more products in a given ARDEPPS to the production of a unit of a different product in the same ARDEPPS
UO/QV/PPR-to-UO	A "three-to-one" allocation of resources from UO production, QV-investment creation, and PPR execution to the production of a unit of a particular product
UO/QV/PPR-to-PPR	A "three-to-one" allocation of resources from UO production, QV-investment creation, and PPR execution to the execution of a PPR project
UO/QV/PPR-to-QV	A "three-to-one" allocation of resources from UO production, QV-investment creation, and PPR execution to the creation of a QV investment

Symbols that Reference Approaches to Allocative-Efficiency (Economic-Efficiency) Analysis, Magnitudes of Parameters that Those Approaches Imply Are Economically Efficient, and Conclusions About the Identity of the Choices that Those Approaches Imply Are Economically Efficient

FBLE	First-best-allocative-efficiency or first-best-allocatively-efficient
SBLE	Second-best-allocative-efficiency or second-best-allocatively-efficient
TBLE	Third-best-allocative-efficiency or third-best-allocatively-efficient

Pareto-Imperfection-Related Symbols

BS   Buyer surplus
CX   Real consumption externalities
KCRX   Real knowledge-creation-related externalities
M   Monopoly (more precisely, imperfections-in-seller-competition)
        Pareto imperfections
MS   Monopsony (imperfections-in-buyer-competition-related) Pareto
        imperfections
NM   Resource-allocator non-maximization
NS   Resource-allocator non-sovereignty
oPp   otherwise-Pareto-perfect
PX   Real production externalities
T   Taxes on the margin of income
X   Real externalities

Symbols that Reference Categories of Distortions (D) in the Private Figures (PB, PC, Pπ) Associated with a To-Be-Specified Resource Allocation—More Specifically, that Reference PB–LB, PC–LC, or Pπ–LE for a To-Be-Specified Resource Allocation

$oPp(...)D(P...._{.../...})$

The symbol for the distortion (D) in a to-be-specified (by the letter B, C, or π that replaces the ellipsis that follows the second P in the symbol) private figure in an otherwise-Pareto-perfect (oPp) economy that would be generated by all extant exemplars of the one to six types of Pareto imperfections to be specified by the entry that replaces the ellipsis that precedes "D" in the symbol (if the entry surrounded by the first parentheses in the symbol contains no forward-slash, the referent is to the distortion that would be generated in an oPp economy by all exemplars of the one type of Pareto imperfection whose symbol replaces the ellipsis in the first parentheses; if the entry that is surrounded by the first parentheses contains one-to-five forward-slashes, the referent is to the distortion that would be generated by all exemplars of the two to six types of Pareto imperfections whose symbols appear between the parentheses in an "oPp" economy where the private figure in question is associated with the resource allocation to be specified in the subscript of the symbol

	[a subscript whose first ellipsis is replaced by symbols that indicate the category of use (or functionally-related pair of categories of use) to which the relevant resource allocation devotes resources—usually QV, PPR, or UO—sometimes preceded by (C) for "creation," (U) for "use," or (C+U) for "creation and use"—and the ARDEPPS to which it allocates resources and whose second ellipsis is replaced by symbols that indicate the category or categories of use (usually (C+U) PPR, (C+U) QV, (C+U) UO, or (C+U) PPR, QV, and UO) and ARDEPPS or ARDEPPSes from which the relevant resource allocation withdraws resources])
oPp(M)D(P……/…)	The symbol for the distortion in a to-be-specified private figure associated with a to-be-specified resource allocation that would be generated in an otherwise-Pareto-perfect economy by all extant exemplars of imperfections in seller competition (somewhat misleadingly symbolized by "M" for "monopoly")
oPp(MS)D(P……/…)	The symbol for the distortion in a to-be-specified private figure associated with a to-be-specified resource allocation that would be generated in an otherwise-Pareto-perfect economy by all extant exemplars of imperfections in buyer competition (symbolized by "MS" for "monopsony")
oPp([PX]D)(P……/…)	The oPp production-externalities ("PX") distortion in the to-be-specified private figure
oPp([CX]D)(P……/…)	The oPp consumption-externalities ("CX") distortion in the to-be-specified private figure
oPp([KCRX]D)(P……/…)	The oPp knowledge-creation-related-externalities ("KCRX") distortion in the to-be-specified private figure
oPp(XD)(P……/…)	The oPp distortion in the to-be-specified private figure that would be generated by all exemplars of all types of externalities ("X")
oPp(TD)(P……/…)	The oPp taxes-on-the-margin-of-income ("T") distortion in the to-be-specified private figure
oPp([NS]D)(P……/…)	The oPp resource-allocator-non-sovereignty ("NS") distortion in the to-be-specified private figure
oPp([NM]D)(P……/…)	The oPp resource-allocator-non-maximization ("NM") distortion in the to-be-specified private figure
oPp([BS]D)(P……/…)	The oPp buyer-surplus ("BS") distortion in the to-be-specified private figure

oPp([M/X]D)(P..._.../...)	The oPp distortion in the to-be-specified private figure that would be generated "jointly" by all extant imperfections in seller competition and all extant externalities of all types
ΣD(P..._.../...)	The aggregate distortion in the to-be-specified private figure for the to-be-specified resource allocation that was generated by all extant exemplars of all seven types of Pareto imperfections
(1E)ΣD(P..._.../...)=	The onesy formula for the referenced ΣD(P..._.../...) figure—the ([M/MS/X/T/NS/NM/BS]D) formula for the to-be-specified aggregate distortion, which takes simultaneous account of the ways in which all exemplars of each relevant type of Pareto imperfection affect the to-be-specified ΣD(P..._.../...) figure not only "directly" but also "indirectly" by affecting the incidences and magnitudes of all other relevant Pareto imperfections and of any other parameter that is relevant
(SW[...]D)(P..._.../...)	The step-wise distortion in a to-be-specified private figure to be specified by an entry that replaces the ellipsis following "P" that is associated with the resource allocation to be specified by the entries that replace the subscript-ellipses in the symbol that would be generated by all exemplars of the type of Pareto imperfections referenced by the entry that replaces the bracketed ellipsis—the distortion in that private figure that all extant exemplars of the referenced Pareto imperfections would be deemed to have generated if the calculation ignored both the distorting effects of the extant exemplars of all other types of Pareto imperfections and of the other relevant parameters in the economy and the impacts that the extant exemplars of the referenced type of Pareto imperfections had on the distortion in question by altering the incidences and magnitudes of the other types of Pareto imperfections and/or of other relevant parameters
(SW)ΣD(P..._.../...)=	The step-wise-distortion formula for the aggregate distortion in a to-be-specified private figure for a to-be-specified resource, which equals (SW[M])D(P..._.../...) + (SW[MS])D(P..._.../...) + (SW[X])D(P..._.../...) + (SW[T])D(P..._.../...) + (SW[NS])D(P..._.../...) + (SW[NM])D(P..._.../...) + (SW[BS])D(P..._.../...)

Symbols for Curves or Points on Curves

DD   Demand curve

MC   Marginal-cost curve or the marginal cost of a particular (usually
              the economics-marginal) unit of output

MLC   The marginal-allocative-cost curve for a relevant product or the
              marginal allocative cost of a particular unit (usually the
              economics-marginal) unit of output of that product

MLP   The marginal-allocative-product curve for a to-be-specified factor
              of production or the marginal allocative product of a particular
              unit (usually the economics-marginal unit) of a to-be-specified
              factor of production

MLV   The marginal-allocative-value curve for a to-be-specified product
              or the marginal allocative value of a to-be-specified unit (usually
              the economics-marginal unit) of a to-be-specified product

MR   The marginal revenue curve for a to-be-specified product or the
              marginal revenue yielded by the sale of a to-be-specified (usually
              the economics-marginal) unit of a to-be-specified product

MRP   The marginal-revenue-product curve for a to-be-specified factor
              of production or the marginal revenue product that would be
              yielded by the sale of the output that would be produced by a
              particular unit (usually the economics-marginal unit) of a
              to-be-specified factor of production

RAMLC   Resource-allocation (RA) marginal allocative cost (MLC)—the
              allocative cost of a to-be-specified economics-marginal resource
              allocation

RAMLC$_{.../...}$ Resource-allocation (RA) marginal-allocative-cost (MLC) curve
              —a curve whose height I assume is always $1 in a diagram
              whose vertical axis measures dollars and whose horizontal axis
              measures in dollars the total allocative cost of the resources
              devoted to the to-be-specified resource allocation from uses and
              ARDEPPSes to be specified by entries that replace the second
              ellipsis in the symbol's subscript to uses and an ARDEPPS to be
              specified by entries that replace the first ellipsis in the symbol's
              subscript

RAMLP   Resource-allocation (RA) marginal-allocative product (MLP)—
              the highest allocative value that resources whose allocative cost
              was $1 could generate if devoted to a specifiable category of use
              or pair of related uses in a specifiable ARDEPPS if all
              intrinsically-more-allocatively-efficient resource allocations to
              that category of use or pair of related uses in that ARDEPPS had
              already been executed

RAMLP.../...   Resource-allocation (RA) marginal-allocative-product (MLP) curve—a curve in a diagram whose vertical axis measures dollars and whose horizontal axis measures in dollars the total allocative cost of the resources devoted to a series of resource allocations each of whose exemplars has an allocative cost of $1 from uses or pairs of related uses in ARDEPPSes all of which are specified by entries that replace the second ellipsis in the symbol's subscript to a use or pair of related uses in an ARDEPPS all of which are specified by entries that replace the first ellipsis in the symbol's subscript that indicates the allocative value that would be generated by the successive resource-uses of the to-be-specified type in the to-be-specified ARDEPPS whose allocative cost was $1

RAMLP$_{\Delta.../\Delta...}$ A point on a RAMLP.../... curve that indicates the marginal allocative product of the resource-use or pair of related resource-uses secured by the resource allocation that brings RATLC.../... for a to-be-specified category of resource allocation to an indicated quantity (when the resource allocation that would bring RATLC.../... to a particular quantity would not be mathematics-marginal, the average marginal allocative product for the resource allocation that brought/would bring RATLC.../... to that quantity is the average height of the relevant RAMLP.../... curve between the RATLC.../... quantity that would prevail absent the allocation that brought RATLC.../... to the quantity in question and the RATLC.../... quantity that would have prevailed had the last allocation not been executed)

RATLC.../...   The total allocative cost (TLC) of a to-be-specified category of resource allocation (RA) from uses or pairs of related uses and ARDEPPSes all of which are specified by entries that replace the second ellipsis in the symbol's subscript to a use or pair of related uses in an ARDEPPS all of which are specified by entries that replace the first ellipsis in the symbol's subscript

---

Symbols that Reference Causes of Imperfect QV-Investment or PPR Competition

L   Retaliation barrier to QV-investment/PPR entry or expansion
M   Monopolistic QV-investment/PPR disincentives or incentives
O   Natural oligopolistic QV-investment/PPR disincentives
R   Risk barrier to QV-investment/PPR entry or expansion
S   Scale barrier to QV-investment/PPR entry or expansion

Introduction to The General Theory of Second Best, Its Central Implications, and the Appropriate Way to Respond to It

Abstract

Section 1.1 explains that, when the optimum is "maximizing economic efficiency"[1] and the set of sufficient conditions for that optimum's achievement is the Pareto-optimal conditions,[2] The General Theory of Second Best[3] concludes that, if one or more of the Pareto-optimal conditions will not be fulfilled, increasing the fulfillment of the remaining conditions will not in general even tend to increase economic efficiency (because individual departures from those conditions [individual Pareto imperfections] will in general be as likely to counteract the misallocative tendencies of the remaining departures to any given extent as to compound them to that extent). Section 1.2 explains why economists use an economic-efficiency-analysis protocol that ignores and is invalidated by The General Theory of Second Best. Section 1.3 lists some of the standard economic-efficiency conclusions this General Theory undermines. Section 1.4 outlines the protocol for economic-efficiency analysis that I claim responds economic-efficiently to this General Theory—a protocol that focuses both on the impact of a choice on the relevant economy's Pareto imperfections and resource allocations and on the different ways in which such imperfections interact to cause or not cause the various categories of economic inefficiency an economy can generate (most of which conventional economic-efficiency analyses ignore).

This book analyzes the implications of The General Theory of Second Best for economic-efficiency analysis. More specifically, after stating the conclusion of The General Theory of Second Best and explaining that conclusion's basic rationale, this book examines that conclusion's negative implications (1) for the protocol welfare economists have traditionally used to predict/post-dict the economic efficiency of any choice[4] and (2) for the conclusions that welfare economists have traditionally reached about the economic efficiency both of eliminating or reducing particular Pareto imperfections and of decreasing/increasing the Pareto-imperfectness of an economy in general. *Inter alia*, this book describes and assesses the economics

© Springer Nature Switzerland AG 2020

R. S. Markovits, *Welfare Economics and Second-Best Theory*,

https://doi.org/10.1007/978-3-030-43360-4_1

profession's various responses to The General Theory of Second Best (argues that welfare economists have not made the adjustments to either the general protocol they use to analyze the economic efficiency of choices or to the concrete economic-efficiency conclusions they claim are correct that The General Theory of Second Best implies are warranted). More positively, this book develops a protocol for economic-efficiency analysis that (it argues) responds appropriately to The General Theory of Second Best (the protocol whose use would be *ex ante* economically efficient). The book also investigates a number of standard economic-efficiency issues—delineates the respects in which the conventional analyses of these issues do not take appropriate account of The General Theory of Second Best, contrasts the conventional analyses with the analyses that The General Theory of Second Best implies are warranted, and explains why the conclusions that the conventional analyses yield are unlikely to be accurate.

I first encountered The General Theory of Second Best when assigned Lipsey and Lancaster's famous article of that title (Lipsey and Lancaster 1956) in the winter of 1964 in a course at the London School of Economics. I had two immediate reactions. First, how could I have failed to grasp the theory's central point on my own? Second, I must abandon the Ph.D. dissertation I had planned to write on the economic efficiency of various actual and proposed transportation policies: the approach I had intended to use took no account of The General Theory of Second Best, and I did not know how to respond appropriately to this General Theory. I chose instead to write a dissertation on pricing theory and competition theory— Potential Competition, Investment, and Pricing (Markovits 1966, whose most important theoretical contributions appear in Markovits 1975a).

Since obtaining my Ph.D. from the LSE, I have devoted a considerable portion of my research to developing a protocol for economic-efficiency analysis that responds *ex ante* economic efficiently to The General Theory of Second Best (to doing what I call "theoretical Welfare Economics" or "Second-Best Theory"[5]) and to using that protocol to analyze the economic efficiency of specific government and non-government choices and to criticize other scholars' analyses of the economic efficiency of such choices (to doing what I call "applied Welfare Economics"). More specifically, I have published (1) 10 theoretical-Welfare-Economics articles on Second-Best Theory (Markovits 1975b, 1976a, 1986b, 1992b, 1998b, d, 2011a, b, 2016, 2017a, b), (2) 18 applied-Welfare-Economics articles that use a protocol that takes account of The General Theory of Second Best to analyze the economic efficiency of particular government policies or non-government conduct or to address various, more general economic-efficiency-related issues (Markovits 1976b, c, d, 1979, 1980a, b, 1983, 1985a, b, 1986a, 1992a, 1996, 1998c, 2002a, 2005, 2006, 2011a, 2018), and (3) a book that executes both theoretical-Welfare-Economics and applied-Welfare-Economics analyses that attempt to respond *ex ante* economic efficiently to The General Theory of Second Best (Markovits 2008). The book you are now reading extends and improves my previous Welfare Economics scholarship.

1.1 The Conclusion and Basic Rationale of The General Theory of Second Best

According to The General Theory of Second Best, in a situation in which one or more members of a set of sufficient conditions for the achievement of an optimum cannot be or will not be fulfilled (henceforth "in a situation in which the relevant system will always contain one or more 'imperfections'—i.e., departures from the relevant set of sufficient conditions for the achievement of the specified optimum"), the elimination or reduction of any individual imperfection or set of imperfections will be as likely to worsen the relevant outcome by any given amount as it will be to improve the outcome by that amount. The basic rationale for this conclusion is that, in the absence of a correct general argument to the contrary (which has never been made for the case in which the relevant optimum is "maximum economic efficiency" and whose existence for that case I doubt), one must assume that, in general, the imperfection(s) that would be removed or reduced by an imperfection-reducing choice that would not eliminate all relevant imperfections would be as likely to have counteracted the relevant net-optimum-disserving effects of the remaining imperfections in the system to any given extent as they would be to have compounded the net-optimum-disserving effects of the remaining imperfections in the system to the same extent.[6] The General Theory of Second Best applies both when the relevant maximand (objective function) is economic efficiency and when it is a maximand in which economic efficiency (1) is not valued at all or is not the only *desideratum* and (2) is not monotonically related to the relevant maximand (objective function). However, as previously indicated, this book focuses exclusively on the implications of The General Theory of Second Best for the *ex ante* economically-efficient approach to take to the analysis of the economic efficiency of a choice.

I acknowledge that the central conclusion of and basic rationale for The General Theory of Second Best should be obvious to anyone with a mathematical background or sound mathematical intuitions. Nevertheless, I consider this General Theory to be one of the most important ever to be developed by an economist.[7]

Sections 1.2, 1.3, and 1.4 establish the basis of this claim—respectively explain why The General Theory of Second Best totally undermines the protocol for economic-efficiency prediction/post-diction that welfare economists used prior to the publication of the article that bears that title and overwhelmingly continue to use today, state some of the most important standard Welfare-Economics economic-efficiency conclusions that this General Theory undermines, and outline the protocol for economic-efficiency prediction/post-diction that I believe is *ex ante* economically efficient—is warranted by The General Theory of Second Best.

1.2   The Reason Why The General Theory of Second Best Has Such Important Implications for the Protocol for Predicting/Post-dicting the Economic Efficiency of a Choice that Is *Ex Ante* Economically Efficient

Admittedly, The General Theory of Second Best would not have much bearing on the protocol for economic-efficiency analysis that is *ex ante* economically efficient if the *ex ante* most-economically-efficient way to predict/post-dict the impact of a choice on economic efficiency were either (1) to identify all of the choice's winners and losers and estimate and sum these parties' respective equivalent-dollar gains and losses or, less ambitiously, (2) to identify a random sample of the choice's winner and losers, estimate their respective equivalent-dollar gains and losses, and derive a final estimate of the choice's economic efficiency by multiplying the difference between the sums of the studied parties' equivalent-dollar gains and losses by the ratio of (the total number of winners and losers in the relevant society) to (the total number of winners and losers identified and studied). In fact, however, for three reasons or sets of reasons, such an approach would not be *ex ante* economically efficient: (1) the incentives that the beneficiaries/victims of any choice have respectively to exaggerate the magnitude of the equivalent-dollar gains/losses it would confer/impose on them (to the extent that their doing so increases the probability that any government choice in question will be made/rejected or any non-government choice in question will be allowed/prohibited) would make it impracticable to estimate relevant winners'/losers' equivalent-dollar gains/losses by asking them to testify to them even if they could estimate them accurately, (2) the winners and losers of many choices will often not be well-placed to predict or even post-dict their equivalent-dollar effect on them, and (3) at least in my judgment, no method of estimating a choice's winners'/losers' equivalent-dollar gains/losses that does not rely on their "testimony" would be acceptably accurate or *ex ante* economically efficient. I am therefore not surprised that, to my knowledge, no concrete analysis of the economic efficiency of any choice (no "applied Welfare Economics" analysis) has ever proceeded by identifying all or a random sample of its winners and losers and estimating their equivalent-dollar gains and losses.

As I have already indicated, welfare economists have in fact always based their predictions/post-dictions of the impact of a choice on economic efficiency on their estimates of the choice's impact on the Pareto-imperfectness of the economy in question. Unfortunately, however, as I have also previously indicated, with extremely-limited exceptions, welfare economists have proceeded on a false and economically-inefficient assumption (which contravenes The General Theory of Second Best) about the economic-efficiency implications of a choice's impact on the Pareto-imperfectness of an economy—viz., have assumed that any choice that decreases/increases the Pareto-imperfectness of an economy (say, by reducing/increasing a given target Pareto imperfection) will increase/decrease economic efficiency on that account. Although this assumption (1) would almost always be true[8] if the choice in question reduced the magnitude of the only Pareto imperfection in an otherwise-Pareto-perfect economy and (2) would be *ex ante* economically efficient to make if it were *ex ante* economically efficient to assume either that the economy in question was otherwise-Pareto-perfect or that, acting together, the other Pareto imperfections the relevant economy contained would not critically affect the economic efficiency of reducing the target Pareto imperfection, economies in which one or more particular Pareto imperfections can be reduced or eliminated are never otherwise-Pareto-perfect, and no-one has ever justified the conclusion that it will be *ex ante* economically efficient to ignore the non-target Pareto imperfections all actual economies always contain when predicting/post-dicting the economic efficiency of increasing or decreasing a particular target Pareto imperfection (to ignore The General Theory of Second Best's demonstration that Pareto imperfections can combat as well as compound each other's tendencies to generate economic ineffi- ciency in an otherwise-Pareto-perfect economy). Hence, even if (contrary to the position that this book takes) The General Theory of Second Best did imply the impossibility of identifying any protocol for predicting/post-dicting the economic efficiency of a choice in a way that is *ex ante* economically efficient, this General Theory would perform an extremely valuable function by revealing the ground- lessness and unreliability of all economic-efficiency predictions/post-dictions that are generated by protocols that ignore its central conclusion. This revelation would be valuable even if The General Theory of Second Best did imply the impossibility of executing *ex ante* economically-efficient economic-efficiency analyses not only because it would prevent us from executing allocatively-costly *ex ante* economically-inefficient economic-efficiency analyses and relying on the inaccurate economic-efficiency conclusions such analyses would generate but also because it would tend to induce analysts/decision-makers to focus their analyses/base their choices on relevant considerations other than the choice's impact on economic efficiency—e.g., on the justness (as conceived in different ways) of the choice's consequences, on the choice's impact on the moral good (as conceived in different ways), and on the fairness of the political process that was used to make it. And, of course, in my view, as Sect. 1.4 argues and the rest of this book seeks to establish, The General Theory of Second Best is valuable because the relationships whose salience the theory establishes can be used to ground a protocol for economic-efficiency prediction/post-diction that is *ex ante* economically efficient.

1.3   The Negative Economic-Efficiency-Conclusion-Related Implications of The General Theory of Second Best

Sections 1.1 and 1.2 focus on The General Theory of Second Best's negative implications for the protocol that can be used *ex ante* economic efficiently to predict/post-dict the economic efficiency of a choice. This section focuses on The General Theory of Second Best's negative implications for various concrete economic-efficiency conclusions that welfare economists have traditionally endorsed and generally continue to endorse.

The General Theory of Second Best implies that the fact that the 7 Pareto-optimal conditions belong to a set of sufficient conditions for the maximization of economic efficiency does not imply that a choice that did or would reduce (1) the incidence and/or magnitudes of the imperfections in seller competition the relevant economy contains, (2) the incidence and/or magnitudes of the imperfections in buyer competition the relevant economy contains, (3) the incidence and/or magnitudes of the real externalities generated in the economy in question, (4) the incidence and/or magnitudes of the taxes on the margin of income (effectively) levied in the economy in question, (5) the incidence and/or magnitudes of any imperfections in the relevant information available to the economy's resource allocators, (6) the incidence and/or magnitudes of resource-allocator non-maximization in the economy in question, (7) the amount of buyer surplus generated in the economy in question, and (8) most comprehensively, the Pareto-imperfectness of an economy *will in general even tend to favor the conclusion that the choice did or would increase economic efficiency if the relevant economy did/would remain Pareto-imperfect post-choice.*

1.4   The Protocol for Economic-Efficiency Analysis that Responds *Ex Ante* Economic Efficiently to The General Theory of Second Best: A Somewhat-Detailed but Far-From-Comprehensive Account

Finally, something positive. This section delineates, explains, and comments on the protocol for economic-efficiency prediction/post-diction that I claim is *ex ante* economically efficient—a "distortion-analysis" protocol that builds on the relationships whose salience The General Theory of Second Best establishes. Because this section devotes far less attention to various concepts and economic-efficiency-analysis-protocol components than they will receive later in this book, I am concerned that it may discourage some who would be satisfied by these concepts' subsequent treatment from reading the rest of this study. I have included this summary of the protocol for economic-efficiency analysis I claim is *ex ante* economically efficient nevertheless not only because I suspect that many readers will find such an overview valuable in itself but also because this overview renders more comprehensible some of the criticisms Chap. 2 makes of various responses that different economists have made to The General Theory of Second Best.

Section 1.4 has four sections. Section 1.4.1 defines 10 concepts or sets of related concepts that the protocol or my discussion of the protocol references. Section 1.4.2 discusses in broad terms the *ex ante* economically-efficient protocol for determining whether it would be *ex ante* economically efficient to do any work that could produce conclusions that would bear on the *ex ante* economic efficiency of a choice. Section 1.4.3 defines 11 categories of resource allocations, each of which (obviously) is associated with a category of economic inefficiency (resource misallocation) an economy can generate. Section 1.4.4 provides a more-than-superficial but far-from-comprehensive account of the protocol for predicting/post-dicting the economic efficiency of a choice that I believe is *ex ante* economically efficient.

1.4.1   10 Concepts or Sets of Related Concepts that Play an Important Role in the Protocol for Economic-Efficiency Prediction/Post-diction I Claim Is *Ex Ante* Economically Efficient

The protocol for economic-efficiency analysis I claim is *ex ante* economically efficient references 10 concepts or sets of related concepts:

(1)   the first is the concept of a (somewhat-) arbitrarily-defined portion of product-space: (acronym, "ARDEPPS"): I substitute the concept of an ARDEPPS for the standard expression "economic market" because I believe that, regardless of whether the referent of the word "market" is a "classical economic market" or an "antitrust market," market definitions are inevitably arbitrary, not just at their peripheries but comprehensively (Markovits 2002b, 2012, and 2014, pp. 165–181);

(2)   the second is the concept of "a functional category of resource-use": 11 functional categories of resource-use are distinguished—(A) unit-output-producing (UO-producing) resource-uses in which resources are devoted to producing units of a given product or service (defined expansively to include as part of a given product or service such *desiderata* as warranties of the product's proper performance), (B) quality-or-variety-investment-creating (QV-investment-creating) resource-uses in which resources are devoted to executing an investment that (i) creates a new product or product variant or a new distributive outlet (either of which may or may not replace a pre-existing alternative) or (ii) creates additional capacity or inventory (which enables its owner to supply the relevant good or distributive or non-distributive service at a higher average speed throughout a fluctuating-demand cycle), (C) production-process-research-executing (PPR-executing) resource-uses in which resources are devoted to discovering privately and/or allocatively cheaper ways of producing relevant quantities of an existing product (research that seeks to discover a new product that is cheaper to produce than its extant alternatives is both QV-investment-creating and PPR-executing), (D) known-production-process-effectuating resource-uses (choice-among-known-production-process-effectuating resource-uses where the expression "production process" is defined to include (i) the process of producing goods and the process of supplying non-distributive services, (ii) acts of communicating to potential buyers information about a product's or service's attributes, uses, usefulness, methods of use, and/or durability, (iii) the choices that producers and distributors make between having production-process functions performed by employees or by independent contractors, (iv) the choices that firms that hire employees to perform various

production-process functions make among the various sorts of employee-selection processes, employee-training processes, and employee-reward systems, and (v) the choices that firms that use independent contractors to perform various production-process functions make among the contractual clauses and hiring and renewal-of-contract criteria they could employ to increase the extent to which the independent contractors with whom they contract make production-process choices that maximize the firm's profits, (E) the resource-uses that are associated with (i) individual firms' employing particular pricing-techniques to convert what might be buyer surplus into seller surplus (non-discriminatory "single pricing," in which the firm charges the same per-unit price and no lump-sum fee to all its potential customers for each unit of its product they purchase, perfect price discrimination in one or the other of its possible forms, pricing in which the buyer is charged a combination of a lump-sum fee for the right to purchase up to a certain quantity or an unlimited quantity of the seller's product for a specified per-unit price that exceeds the marginal cost the seller would have to incur to produce the unit of its output at which the demand curve it believes it faces cuts its marginal-cost curve from above, conventional price discrimination, tie-in pricing (in which a seller that may or may not also be charging a lump-sum fee conditions its agreeing to supply the relevant buyer with a stated quantity of one [so-called tying] product at a specified per-unit price or with as many units of the tying product as the buyer wishes to purchase at the specified per-unit price on the buyer's agreeing to purchase a specified quantity or its full requirements of a second [so-called tied] product at a specified per-unit price), reciprocal-trade-agreement pricing (in which a firm that may or may not also be charging the buyer in question a lump-sum fee conditions its agreeing to supply that buyer with a stated quantity of its product or with as many units of its product as the buyer wants to purchase at the specified per-unit price on the buyer's agreeing to supply the former firm with a specified quantity, as many units as the former firm wants to purchase, or the firm's full requirements of a second good [or an analogous reciprocity arrangement in which the relevant initiative is taken by a firm that is acting initially in its capacity as a buyer]), (ii) individual firms' trying to prevent their independent distributors from making sales of rival products whose consummation is against the joint interest of the producer and the distributor in question, (iii) individual firms' trying to induce their independent distributors to place mutually-profitable advertisements, to set up mutually-profitable in-store promotional displays, to make mutually-profitable shelf-space decisions, to make mutually-profitable salesmanship efforts, to communicate to the producers mutually-profitable sales-techniques, to provide mutually-profitable post-sale repair and maintenance services perhaps to fulfill warranty obligations (by subsidizing distributor advertising; by contractually obligating distributors to provide specified advertisements, in-store promotional-displays, and/or shelf-space; or by communicating to distributors its intention not to renew their distributorships if they do not make advertising/promotional-display/shelf-space/sales-effort decisions that are in the distributor's and the producer's joint interest), and (iv) individual firms' trying to deter their distributors from charging lower prices for the producer's product than is in the interest of the producer and all its distributors taken all together (e.g., by including vertical-territorial-restraint clauses, other sorts of vertical-customer-allocation clauses, and resale-price-maintenance clauses in their distributorship contracts), (F) the resource-uses that are associated with potential buyers' considering the purchases they will choose to make, with government entities' supplying final consumers with product-information (or banning certain products altogether), with private entities' supplying final consumers with product-information and product-recommendations, and with individual producers' trying to prevent their customers from combining the producer's products with inferior complements when the buyers' doing so would reduce the basic-product-producer's profits by leading its customers to be dissatisfied and/or by tarnishing the reputation of the basic-product-producers' products because the customers and third-party observers attribute the resulting poor performance of the producer's product to the producer's product rather than to the complement with which it was combined (by contractually obligating their distributors/their products' final consumers to sell exclusively/purchase their full requirements of complements produced by the firm itself or by other suppliers the producer names or by contractually obligating [their distributors to sell]/[their customers to use] complements that have specified attributes [and monitoring their distributors'/customers' complement-choices and legally enforcing the complement-obligations in question]), (G) the use of resources to commit (liberal) moral-rights-violating acts or illegal acts of other sorts—for example, to commit (i) acts that would be economically inefficient in an oPp economt that are motivated by specific anticompetitive intent (acts whose perpetrator[s] would not have found them *ex ante* profitable but for its/their belief that the conduct would or might increase its/their profits by reducing the absolute attractiveness of the best offers against which it/they would have to compete (price-fixing, predatory conduct of all kinds, some mergers and acquisitions, some joint ventures or functionally-related collaborative arrangements of other kinds, etc.), (ii) deceptive or fraudulent (sometimes competition-distorting) acts, (iii) libel and slander, (iv) assault or battery, (v) murder, (vi) kidnapping, (vii) theft or conversion, (viii) regulatory violations, and (ix) illegal tax-evasion, or lawful tax-evasion, (H) the use of resources by non-government and government actors (i) to prosecute, defend, participate in plea negotiations, and decide criminal cases and (ii) to initiate, settle, mediate, arbitrate, litigate, and officially resolve private disputes or disputes about alleged administrative-regulation violations, (I) the use of resources by private actors to participate in electoral politics and legislative or administrative-regulation-promulgative processes, (J) the use of resources by governments to devise and pass legislative/administrative regulations, and (K) the use of resources by governments to detect violations of the law, identify law-breakers, collect taxes, and execute government transfers.

(3) the third is the "concept" of a "pair of functionally-related resource-uses": (A) producing and "using"—i.e., consuming—a unit of output, (B) creating and using a QV investment—e.g., creating a new product variant and

combining that QV investment with additional resources (incurring variable costs) to produce units of that new product variant (which are then consumed), and (C) executing a production-process-research project and using the discovered production process;

(4) the fourth concept is the conventional concept of a "resource allocation," which refers to the withdrawal of resources from one or more uses or pairs of functionally-related uses in one or more specified ARDEPPSes and their devotion to a specified use or pair of functionally-related uses in a specified ARDEPPS (more specifically, I distinguish two sets of resource allocations: [A] the members of the first set are distinguished by the number of functional categories of use or pairs of functionally-related categories of use from which the referenced resource allocation withdraws resources ("three-to-one resource allocations" are allocations that withdraw resources from three functional categories of use or pairs of functionally-related categories of use [in practice, UO-producing or UO-producing-and-using, QV-creating or QV-creating-and-using, and PPR-executing or PPR-executing-and-using uses] and devote them to one functional category of use or one pair of functionally-related categories of use while "one-to-one resource allocations" are allocations that withdraw resources from one functional category of use or one pair of functionally-related categories of use and devote them to one functional category of use or one pair of functionally-related categories of use)—I should add that in some instances in which the actual resource allocation is a three-to-one resource allocation, it may be *ex ante* economically efficient to decompose that resource allocation into its three one-to-one components and analyze their economic efficiency separately; I should also note that my failure to consider the possibility that the resources devoted to UO-producing/UO-producing-and-consuming, QV-creating/QV-creating-and-using, or PPR-executing/PPR-generated-discovery-using uses or pairs of functionally-related categories of use may have been withdrawn from up to 11 categories of use or pairs of functionally-related categories of use manifests my contestable assumption that the percentages of the resources devoted to the categories of use referenced in Items (2)(E) and (2)(F) of this list of concepts are too low for it to be *ex ante* economically efficient to take account of the reality that some of the resources devoted to any such use or pair of functionally-related pairs of uses may have been withdrawn from these categories of use—and [B] the members of the second set of resource allocations are distinguished by the amount of information provided about the ARDEPPSes from which the resource allocation in question withdraws resources and the ARDEPPS to which it devotes resources ["purely"-functional categories of resource allocation identify the categories of use from/to which the referenced resource allocation withdraws/devotes resources but do not specify anything about the ARDEPPS(es) from which/the ARDEPPS to which the resource allocation in question withdraws/devotes resources, "functional *plus* destination" resource allocations indicate the ARDEPPS to which the allocation allocates resources as well as the functional category/categories of use from/to which the referenced resource allocation withdraws/devotes resources, and "fully-specified" resource

allocations specify both the category/categories of use from/to which the referenced resource allocation withdraws/devotes resources and the ARDEPPSes/ARDEPPS from/to which the referenced resource allocation withdraws/devotes resources];

(5)   the fifth "concept" is actually a pair of related concepts—the concepts of an "economics-marginal resource-use or pair of functionally-related resource-uses" and the concept of "an economics-marginal resource allocation": an "economics-marginal resource-use or pair of functionally-related resource-uses" is the least-profitable but not-unprofitable exemplar of the specified category of resource-use or pair of functionally-related resource-uses in the specified ARDEPPS, and an "economics-marginal resource allocation" is the least-profitable but not-unprofitable resource allocation in the specified functional category from the specified ARDEPPSes to the specified ARDEPPS (N.B., economics-marginal resource-uses/pairs of functionally-related resource-uses and economics-marginal resource allocations may or may not be mathematics-marginal [infinitesimally small]);

(6)   the sixth set of concepts contains parameters that are components of the economic efficiency of an economy other than the economic inefficiency generated by economically-inefficient decisions to execute or not to execute resource allocations—the allocative transaction costs that non-government actors and the government generate when making the various categories of choices specified in Item (2)(G) of this list (which I am saying reduce economic efficiency even when they are generated by choices to participate in electoral or government-policy-creating processes that increase economic efficiency by increasing the economic efficiency of government decisions because the conventional conception of maximum economic efficiency assumes that no allocative transaction costs will be generated by the electoral and government policy-creating processes that result in the government's making decisions that eliminate [or reduce] economic inefficiency), the risk costs borne by members of the relevant society (which are simultaneously private and allocative), the allocative costs resource allocators generate to reduce the private risk costs they bear, the allocative costs (economic-efficiency losses) that economic-efficiency analysis may generate by delaying government decisions, and the economic inefficiency generated by the government's financing of any research executed to determine the economic efficiency of a choice, of any efforts to consider the implications of available information for the economic efficiency of a choice, and of the implementation of any choice that is made;

(7)   the seventh concept is "a distortion in any private figure"—on my definition, a private cost is "distorted" if it differs from its allocative-cost counterpart, a private benefit (say, marginal revenue) is "distorted" if it differs from its allocative counterpart (say, the net equivalent-dollar gain generated when the relevant unit of output is consumed rather than being destroyed in some allocative-costless manner), and a profit-figure is "distorted" if it differs from the allocative-efficiency gain generated by the resource allocation that yielded the profits in question;

(8) the eighth concept is related to the seventh—"the aggregate distortion in the profits yielded by any resource allocation" (the difference between the profits and economic-efficiency gain yielded by the resource allocation in question that is generated by the interaction of all relevant exemplars of all relevant types of Pareto imperfections and [in some instances] by one or more other parameters as well);

(9) the ninth "concept" is actually three concepts that define different categories of protocols for economic/allocative-efficiency analysis and three associated different categories of economic-efficiency analyses—first-best-allocative-efficiency (FBLE) analyses of the economic efficiency of a choice proceed on the assumption that The General Theory of Second Best can be ignored (that the economic efficiency of altering the magnitude of a single Pareto imperfection can be predicted/post-dicted perfectly accurately on the assumption that this "target" Pareto imperfection is the only Pareto imperfection in the economy in question [regardless of whether that assumption is empirically accurate]), second-best-allocative-efficiency (SBLE) analyses of the impact of a choice on economic efficiency are executed through a protocol that would predict/post-dict the choice's economic-efficiency perfectly accurately if the protocol were executed with absolute precision (a protocol whose use would be *ex ante* economically efficient if all relevant theoretical and empirical work could be done perfectly accurately at no allocative cost and if the implications of all known theoretical and empirical information for the economic efficiency of any choice could be ascertained perfectly accurately at no allocative cost), and third-best-allocative-efficiency (TBLE) analyses of the economic efficiency of a choice are analyses that are *ex ante* economically efficient (analyses in which those but only those theoretical and empirical research-projects are executed and those but only those efforts to derive the implications of what is known for the economic efficiency of the choice under review are made whose *ex ante* allocative benefits exceed their *ex ante* allocative costs); and

(10) the tenth and final "concept" is two pairs of concepts—on the one hand, the privately-best-placed and the privately-worse-than-best-placed (privately-second-placed, privately-third-placed, etc.) potential supplier of a given buyer and, on the other hand, the allocatively-best-placed and the allocatively-worse-than-best-placed (allocatively-second-placed, allocatively-third-placed, etc.) potential supplier of a given buyer: (1) in my terminology, a seller is said to be "privately-best-placed" to supply a particular buyer if it can profit by supplying the buyer on terms contained in the offer it would find most profitable to make if the firm could not profit by charging the relevant buyer an oligopolistic, retaliatory, or predatory price[9] which offer no other supplier would find profitable to match if the matching offer were to be accepted and if none of its rivals could profit by charging that buyer an oligopolistic, retaliatory, or predatory price, given the relevant buyer's perception of the relative attractiveness of the goods in question and of the cost of purchasing these goods and assuming that the buyer in question would maximize, and a seller is

said to be "privately-worse-than-best-placed" to supply a particular buyer (or to be a privately-inferior potential supplier of that buyer") if the seller would not find it profitable to supply that buyer on terms contained in an offer that the buyer would perceive to be equally attractive as the offer the buyer's privately-best-placed supplier would find most profitable to make to that buyer on the assumptions just delineated, whereas (2) in my terminology, a seller is said to be "allocatively-best-placed" to supply a particular buyer if the seller's supplying that buyer would be more economically efficient than any other potential supplier of that buyer's supplying the buyer, and a supplier is said to be "allocatively-worse-than-best-placed" to supply a particular buyer ("to be an allocatively-inferior potential supplier of that buyer") if economic efficiency would be reduced if it rather than the buyer's allocatively-best-placed supplier supplied the buyer in question.

1.4.2 The Protocol for Determining Whether It Would Be *Ex Ante* Economically Efficient (TBLE) to Execute Any Task that Could Inform One's Assessment of the Economic Efficiency of a Choice

This section explains in very broad terms how an economic-efficiency analyst should determine the *ex ante* economic efficiency of doing any work that would bear on the economic efficiency of the choice under review. The protocol for economic-efficiency analysis that I am recommending (that I claim is TBLE) instructs the analyst (1) to estimate and sum the estimates of all the allocative costs of any work he or she could do—the allocative benefits that the resources that any such work would use up would have generated in their alternative uses *plus* the allocative transaction costs the government would generate to finance the work *plus* any economic inefficiency that the public financing of the work would generate (related allocative transaction costs aside) *plus* any economic inefficiency the work would generate by delaying the government decision on the choice under review, (2) to estimate and sum the allocative benefits any such work would generate—any increase in economic efficiency the work would generate by altering the government's decision on the choice under review *plus* any increase in economic efficiency the work would generate by yielding information and/or information-relevance insights that increase the economic efficiency of other government and non-government decisions, and (3) to compare the two sums just referenced and do work if and only if the sum of the predicted allocative benefits exceeds the sum of the predicted allocative costs. Before proceeding, an admission that relates to this pervasive feature of the protocol for economic-efficiency analysis that I claim is TBLE: As decision-theorists have long recognized, the instruction I have just delineated creates an infinite-regress problem that cannot really be overcome—an analyst who has been instructed to do that work and only that work he or she concludes is *ex ante* economically efficient must ask not only whether it would be *ex ante* economically efficient to do some specified work but also whether it would be *ex ante* economically efficient to think about whether it would be *ex ante* economically efficient to do that work and whether it would be *ex ante* economically efficient to think about whether it would be *ex ante* economically efficient to think about whether it would be *ex ante* economically efficient to do that work and so on and so forth. My somewhat-lame response is an *assertion* that at some point the analyst will intuit that it is not *ex ante* economically efficient to dive deeper into this rabbit-hole and that differences in the relevant intuitions of different analysts are unlikely to make a significant difference in their research-choice/information-consideration decisions or *a fortiori* in their economic-efficiency conclusions.

1.4.3   16 Categories of Resource Allocations (and Related Categories of Economic Inefficiency)

The protocol for economic-efficiency analysis I claim is TBLE instructs the analyst to focus on 16 categories of resource allocations (more precisely, on the impact that the choice whose economic efficiency is at issue had or would have on the amounts of economic inefficiency the economy in question generated/would generate by executing economically-inefficient exemplars of each of these 16 categories of resource allocations and/or by failing to execute economically-efficient exemplars of each of these 16 categories of resource allocations). As I indicated in Item 4 of Section 1.4.1's list of 10 concepts or sets of related concepts that play an important role in the protocol for economic-efficiency prediction/post-diction I claim is TBLE, my decision to focus on these categories of resource allocations reflects my contestable judgment that the amounts of resources allocated to the categories of resource-use referenced in Items (2)(E) through (2)(K) of that list are too low for it to be TBLE to take account of the possibility that some resources that are devoted to UO-producing, QV-creating, PPR-executing, choice-among-known-production-process-executing, and consumer-choice-among-final-products resource-uses will be withdrawn from those categories of use. In any event, here is the list of categories of resource allocations on which the distortion-analysis protocol for economic-efficiency prediction/post-diction that I claim is TBLE will primarily focus:

(1)   allocations of resources from specified UO-producing-and-using, QV-investment-creating-and-using, and PPR-executing-and-using pairs of related resource-uses in one or almost always more than one specified ARDEPPS to a UO-producing-and-using (consuming) use in a specified ARDEPPS or vice versa;

(2)   allocations of resources from specified UO-producing-and-using, QV-investment-creating-and-using, and PPR-executing-and-using pairs of related resource-uses in one or almost always more than one specified ARDEPPS to a QV-investment-creating-and-using related pair of uses in a specified ARDEPPS;

(3)   allocations of resources from specified UO-producing-and-using, QV-investment-creating-and-using, and PPR-executing-and-using related pairs of uses in one or almost always more than one specified ARDEPPS to a PPR-executing-and-using related pair of uses in a specified ARDEPPS;

(4)   intra-ARDEPPS UO-to-UO resource allocations;

(5)   intra-ARDEPPS QV-to-QV resource allocations;

(6)   intra-ARDEPPS PPR-to-PPR resource allocations;

(7)   resource allocations from the use of one known production process to another (where goods/services and hence "production processes" are defined in the expansive way in which I previously defined them)—resource allocations that may yield misallocations that entail departures from the production optimum in that they create a situation in which more of one good could have been produced without reducing the output of another good;

(8)   resource allocations from various specified uses in one or usually more-than-one specified ARDEPPS to uses in which specified producers use them to (A) implement pricing-techniques designed to convert into seller surplus what would otherwise be buyer surplus, (B) try to prevent their independent distributors from selling rival products, (C) try to induce their independent distributors to place mutually-profitable advertisements, set up mutually-profitable in-store promotional displays, make mutually-profitable shelf-space decisions, make mutually-profitable sales-efforts, communicate to the relevant producer mutually-profitable sales-techniques, and provide mutually-profitable post-sale repair-and-maintenance/warranty services, and (D) try to deter its distributors from driving down the price charged for the producer's product to an "organizationally"-unprofitable level by competing against each other;

(9)   resource allocations from various alternative uses in one or usually more-than-one specified ARDEPPS to uses in which (A) final consumers try to identify the consumption-choice that is privately-best for them, (B) governmental or non-governmental entities supply consumers with relevant product-information or recommendations, (C) the government bans certain products altogether, and (D) producers try to prevent their customers from combining their respective products with inferior complements whose use by the buyers in question disserves the joint interest of the respective buyers and basic-product producers;

(10)   resource allocations in which final goods that have been produced are allocated to one final consumer rather than to another (when the allocation that is made does not affect the extent of poverty or resource-ownership inequality the relevant economy generates)—i.e., that can cause conventional consumption-optimum-related misallocation;

(11)   resource allocations from various specified uses in one or usually more-than-one ARDEPPS to uses in which they execute the following categories of conduct: (A) conduct by private entities that is motivated by specific anti-competitive intent (conduct that would not have been perceived to be *ex ante* profitable by its perpetrator[s] had the perpetrator[s] not believed that it would

or might increase its [their] profits by reducing the absolute attractiveness of the offers against which it [they] would have to compete in one or more ways that would render profitable conduct that would be *ex ante* economically inefficient in an otherwise-Pareto-perfect economy—most often, contrived oligopolistic and predatory conduct and mergers, acquisitions, joint ventures, and other types of collaborative conduct when they are motivated by specific anticompetitive intent,[10] (B) conduct by private entities that violate the law because it is prohibited by statutes that deem such conduct illegal if it "lessens competition" in the sense of imposing a net equivalent-dollar loss on the combination of its perpetrator's or perpetrators' customers and the customers of its (their) product-rivals by reducing the absolute attractiveness of the best offer they respectively receive from any worse-than-privately-best-placed supplier (at least if this outcome was not critically affected by the conduct's driving a perpetrator-rival out or deterring a perpetrator-rival from making a QV investment by increasing the organizational allocative efficiency of the perpetrator[s]), and (C) conduct by private entities that distort competition (give its perpetrator[s] a private advantage that does not reflect its [their] allocative superiority by persuading buyers that the perpetrator's product [perpetrators' products] has [have] good qualities that they do not possess or that their rivals' products have bad qualities that they do not possess or by misleading buyers into underestimating the lifetime costs of their products or overestimating the lifetime cost of their rivals' products);

(12) resource allocations from various specified uses in one or usually more-than-one ARDEPPS to uses in which they execute various types of liberal-moral-rights-violating conduct not delineated in Item (11) of this list or tax or regulation avoidance or evasion;

(13) resource allocations from various specified uses in one or usually more-than-one ARDEPPS to uses by government to devise and promulgate legislation/administrative regulations/Presidential or Prime Ministerial decrees that have the force of law and to detect violations of these "laws";

(14) resource allocations from various specified uses in one or usually more-than-one ARDEPPS to prosecuting alleged criminal offenses, defending those accused of criminal wrongdoing, negotiating plea-deals, adjudicating criminal cases, penalizing those found guilty of criminal behavior, making civil-law claims, defending those accused of civil-law violations, negotiating civil-law settlements, using mediation or arbitration to resolve or help the parties to settle civil-law disputes, adjudicating civil-law cases, executing settlements, and enforcing civil-law judgments;

(15) resource allocations from various specified uses in one or usually more-than-one specified ARDEPPS to uses in which the government transfers money to claimants eligible for the transfer; and

(16) resource allocations from various specified uses in one or usually more-than-one ARDEPPS to uses by the government to devise and implement the various revenue-raising measures it adopts to finance its operations.

1.4.4 A Somewhat-Detailed but Far-From-Comprehensive Account of the Protocol for Predicting/Post-dicting the Economic Efficiency of a Choice that I believe Is TBLE

The approach to economic-efficiency analysis I claim is TBLE instructs economic-efficiency analysts to predict/post-dict the impact of any choice on the amounts of economic inefficiency generated in the whole economy by following a protocol that has 6 major components and a pervasive feature. The pervasive feature of the protocol is that it instructs the analyst to perform all exemplars of the work specified in the 6 components of the protocol to be delineated below but only those exemplars of that work whose performance is *ex ante* economically efficient.

The first major component of the protocol for economic-efficiency analysis I claim is TBLE focuses on the impact of the choice under review on 7 of the 16 categories of economic inefficiency an economy can generate—in particular, on those categories of economic efficiency that are associated with categories (1)–(6) and (10) in the preceding list of categories of resource allocations and economic inefficiency. This major component of the protocol instructs the economic-efficiency analyst to analyze the impact of the choice under review on any of the 7 categories of economic inefficiency in question by taking the following 7 steps:

(1) define a random subset of the economy's ARDEPPSes that is third-best-allocatively-efficient large—i.e., whose definition and use in this protocol would be TBLE;

(2) identify the private cost and more specific characteristics of each of the exemplars of the resource allocations in the functional categories on which this component of the protocol is focusing to or in each of the ARDEPPSes defined in Step (1) that the choice under review would/did deter/induce;

(3) estimate the profits that were/would be generated by each of the resource allocations in the fully-specified categories on which this component of the protocol is focusing that Step (2) concludes the choice did/would induce and the losses that would have been/would be generated by each of the fully-specified resource allocations on which this component of the protocol is focusing that Step (2) concludes the choice did/would deter;

(4) estimate the aggregate distortion in the profits/losses that the analyst estimated were/would be yielded by each resource allocation in the category on which this component is focusing to each ARDEPPS being studied that the analyst predicted the choice under review did/would induce/deter by combining the different correct formulas (which this book attempts to derive) for the aggregate distortion in the profits yielded by any exemplar of each of the relevant functional categories of resource allocations with estimates of the post-choice magnitudes of the parameters in the formulas in question (estimates that are themselves generated from information that the analyst possesses ab initio and information that the analyst obtains by doing TBLE research into the post-choice magnitudes of the parameters in question [when the choice under

review has already been made, the relevant research will be empirical research on the post-choice magnitudes of the parameters; when the choice under review has not yet been made, the relevant research may include additional empirical research on the pre-choice magnitudes of the parameters in question, theoretical research to identify the determinants of the impact of the choice on the relevant parameters and the way in which those factors interact to change the parameters in question, and empirical research on the magnitudes of those factors]);

(5) for each functional category of resource allocations to or in each ARDEPPS that is being studied, combine the conclusions generated in Steps (2)–(4) to yield estimates of the impacts that the choice under review would have on the quantity of the associated functional category of economic inefficiency each studied ARDEPPS contains (note that the definition that equates "the aggregate distortion in the profits yielded by a specified resource allocation" with the difference between the profits yielded by and the economic efficiency of that resource allocation implies that the allocative efficiency of any resource allocation equals the profits it yielded *minus* the aggregate distortion in those profits);

(6) sum the conclusions reached in Step (5) for each studied ARDEPPS to yield an estimate of the impact that the choice under review did/would have on the total amount of each of the categories of economy inefficiency on which this portion of the protocol is focusing that was/would be generated *in all the studied ARDEPPSes combined* by decisions to execute economically-inefficient resource allocations in the relevant functional category to or in them and decisions not to execute economically-efficient resource allocations in the relevant functional category to or in them; and

(7) estimate the impact of the choice under consideration on the amounts of economic inefficiency generated in the whole economy by decisions to execute economically-inefficient resource allocations and decisions not to execute economically-efficient resource allocations in each referenced category of resource allocations by multiplying (the Stage (6) estimates of the impacts of the choice under review on the total amount of resource misallocation in each such functional category in all studied ARDEPPSes) by (the respective ratios of [the private cost of the resource allocations in that category the choice did/would induce/deter in the economy as a whole] to [the private cost of the resource allocations in that category the choice did/would induce/deter in the studied ARDEPPSes]).

Even at this juncture, it may be worthwhile to make 6 general points about this first major component of the protocol for economic-efficiency analysis I claim is TBLE. First, in some situations, it may be analytically convenient (TBLE for "practical reasons") to decompose the first three categories of resource allocations in the preceding list of categories of resource allocations (and the associated categories of economic inefficiency) into their inter-ARDEPPS UO-to-UO, inter-ARDEPPS QV-to-QV, inter-ARDEPPS PPR-to-PPR, UO-to-QV or QV-to-UO, UO-to-PPR or PPR-to-UO, and QV-to-PPR or PPR-to-QV components.

Second, the members of the set of economic-inefficiency categories listed whose economic efficiency will be affected by a given choice will vary from choice to choice. Third, even those choices that affect the magnitudes of the same categories of economic inefficiency may affect those magnitudes not only by different amounts and by different percentages but also in different directions. Fourth, I am assuming that economic-efficiency analysts will have allocatively-costless access to perfectly-accurate formulas for the aggregate distortion in the profits yielded by any exemplar of any category of resource allocations, to all pre-existing data on the pre-choice magnitudes of any parameter that appears in any of the aggregate-profit-distortion or choice-impact formulas in question (as well as to any known information that relates to the accuracy of that data), to any theoretical or empirical work that has been done that bears on the impact of the choices whose economic efficiency they are predicting/post-dicting will have on the parameters whose magnitudes will affect the choice's effect on any relevant aggregate-profit-distortion figure, and on any theoretical or empirical work that has been done on any parameter that affects the impact that a choice under review will have on the amount of resources devoted to the categories of resource allocations (and economic inefficiency) on which this first component of the protocol for economic-efficiency analysis I am recommending focuses—categories (1)–(6) and (10) in the preceding list of categories of resource allocations. Fifth, the third-best allocative efficiency of the economic-efficiency analyst's collecting additional data on any relevant parameter will depend *inter alia* on the contribution that the additional data would make to the accuracy of the analyst's prediction/post-diction of the impact that the choice under review and all other choices that will be at issue would/did have on each of the categories of economic inefficiency to whose analysis that data are relevant: thus, even if it would not be TBLE to collect additional data on the externalities generated pre-choice by the production and consumption of two same-ARDEPPS products between whose production the choice whose economic efficiency is at issue allocates resources (say, a choice that would accurately internalize the externalities in question) if that data's only relevance were to the impact the choice would have on intra-ARDEPPS UO-to-UO misallocation in the instant "case," it might well be TBLE to collect additional data on such externalities if such data were also relevant (say) (1) to the instant choice's impact on the amounts of economic inefficiency generated by economically-inefficient allocations of resources between or among known production processes, (2) by the instant choice's impact on the amount of economic inefficiency generated by economically-inefficient allocations of resources between UO-producing-and-using uses and QV-investment-creating-and-using uses, and/or (3) by other choices' impacts on economic efficiency. Sixth and finally, a point that I hesitate to include both because it would be expositionally inadvisable to justify it at this juncture and because it is disfavored by its immediate predecessor in this list: I suspect that it will be TBLE to do more empirical research on more types of Pareto imperfections when predicting/post-dicting the impact of choices on the 3 categories of economic inefficiency associated respectively with the first 3 categories of resource allocations that appear in the preceding list of categories of resource allocations than when analyzing the impact of choices on the other categories of economic inefficiency associated respectively with the last 13 categories of resource allocations in that list—thus, although intra-ARDEPPS UO-to-UO misallocation can be caused by differences in the externalities generated by the production and consumption of units of same-ARDEPPS product variants between whose production a choice whose economic efficiency is at issue may allocate resources, by differences in the taxes levied on the sale of such product variants, and by errors that buyers make when choosing between such product variants (by consumer non-sovereignty and/ or non-maximization), I would not be surprised if it turned out to be TBLE for analysts of the impact of a choice on intra-ARDEPPS UO-to-UO allocation to concentrate overwhelmingly or even exclusively on whether the choice in question increases or decreases such misallocation by increasing or decreasing conduct that results in sales being made by privately-worse-than-best-placed suppliers that are also allocatively-worse-than-best-placed (specifically, on whether the choice increases or decreases [1] predatory pricing and [2] price-fixing [what I call contrived-oligopolistic pricing], which leads to sales being made by privately-worse-than-best-placed potential suppliers that are also allocatively-worse-than-best-placed when the contrived oligopolistic offer of the privately-best-placed firm is beaten by a non-cooperating competitive inferior, when the price-fixer retaliates against the privately-worse-than-best-placed rival that has taken the price-fixer's customer, and when the rival against which the price-fixer has retaliated engages in defensive retaliation against the retaliating price-fixer).[11]

The second major component of the protocol for economic-efficiency analysis I claim is TBLE focuses on the impact of the choice under review on the amount of economic inefficiency the relevant economy generated by using less-economically-efficient, known production processes rather than more-economically-efficient, known production processes—i.e., by generating economic inefficiency in the category that is associated with category of resource allocations (7) in the preceding list of categories of resource allocations. I should state at the outset that the 7-step protocol for economic-efficiency predication/post-diction that I argued is TBLE to follow when analyzing the impact of choices on those categories of economic inefficiency that are associated with categories of resource allocations (1)–(6) and (10) in the preceding list could also be TBLE when the goal is to determine the impact of a choice on choice-among-known-production-process-generated misallocation. I distinguish the current component of the overall protocol for economic-efficiency prediction/post-diction from its predecessor because choice-among-known-production-process-generated misallocation is far more likely than the categories of economic inefficiency on which the preceding component focuses to be generated by government prohibitions and regulations, a possibility that merits separate treatment. Thus, choice-among-known-production-process-generated misallocation is often caused (1) by government prohibitions of mergers, acquisitions, joint ventures, and other types of collaborative arrangements, which prohibitions preclude firms from using production processes that would involve their combining resources owned by different firms that are complementary for scale or non-scale reasons, (2) by fair-rate-of-return public-utility-pricing regulations that set the highest price the regulated firm can charge for any regulated product to be the price that will yield it just a "fair" (in practice, somewhat supernormal) rate-of-return on its investment ("rate-base"), thereby giving regulated utilities whose conventional profit-maximizing prices are higher than their highest originally-allowed regulated price an incentive to make otherwise-unprofitable decisions to expand their rate-bases (*inter alia*, to make intrinsically-unprofitable decisions to use known, more-privately-and-allocatively-expensive, more-capital-intensive production processes rather than known, less-privately-and-allocativley-expensive, less-capital-intensive production processes in order to expand their rate-bases and thereby put themselves in a position to persuade the regulatory authority to grant them permission to charge the higher prices they would find more profitable [the higher prices that would enable them to realize the allowed "fair rate-of-return" on their expanded rate-base]), and (3) by government prohibitions of firms' using various types of contractual arrangements (resale-price-maintenance clauses, vertical territorial restraints or customer-allocation clauses, single-brand exclusive-dealership arrangements, slotting/shelf-space-specifying/advertising-specifying clauses, tie-ins and reciprocity agreements) or related sales-policies to control their independent distributors or customers (e.g., to induce their independent distributors to supply customers with repair and maintenance services or make good on warranty clauses as allocative-efficiently as possible). I acknowledge that some of these sorts of government prohibitions and policies can also cause the categories of economic inefficiency on which the first major component of the protocol I claim is TBLE focuses: thus, merger prohibitions can prevent economically-efficient QV-investment or PPR projects from being executed by preventing mergers that would create merged firms that could execute more-economically-efficient QV and PPR investments, and fair-rate-of-return public-utility-pricing regulation can generate QV-investment-related misallocation by making it profitable for the regulated firm to execute inherently-unprofitable QV investments that are also allocatively inefficient and can generate PPR-related misallocation by making it profitable for regulated firms to execute less-inherently-profitable/less-economically-efficient PPR projects that are designed to discover more-capital-intensive production processes rather than more-inherently-profitable/more-economically-efficient PPR projects that are designed to discover less-capital-intensive production processes. However, although I do think that it will sometimes be TBLE for analysts to consider such possibilities when analyzing the impact of choices on the categories of economic inefficiency on which the first component of my protocol focuses, my intuition is that these possibilities are sufficiently more important when choice-among-known-production-process-generated misallocation is at issue to justify my delaying my discussion of this source of misallocation until I addressed choice-among-known-production-process misallocation.

The third major component of the distortion-analysis protocol for economic-efficiency prediction/post-diction that I think is TBLE focuses on the TBLE way for analysts to predict/post-dict the impact that a choice will have on economic efficiency by altering the extent of poverty and/or material inequality the economy in question generates. I should admit at the outset that (1) most of the categories of economic inefficiency whose magnitudes are affected by poverty and material inequality are categories on which the previous components of this account focuses and (2) to avoid double-counting, I should amend my previous account of the first two major components of the protocol I am proposing and recommending by acknowledging that the approaches I argued would be TBLE to use to predict/post-dict the impact of choices on the categories of economic inefficiency on which these components of my protocol focus are deficient in that they ignore the impacts that choices have on those categories of resource misallocation by changing the amounts of poverty and material inequality the economy in question generates. This third major component of my proposed protocol is designed to remedy this omission. This component of the protocol instructs the analyst (1) to identify the various ways in which poverty and/or material inequality can increase economic inefficiency—*inter alia*, by increasing the amount of economic inefficiency generated (A) by failures to make economically-efficient investments in human capital (in pre-natal and post-natal nutrition and medical care, in clothing and housing, in parenting, in formal and informal education, in job-training etc.), (B) by economically-inefficient consumption-choices caused by (i) consumer non-sovereignty and/or consumer non-maximization that result in the buyers' making consumption choices against their individual interest that are also economically efficient and (ii) the fact that poor consumers find it individually advantageous to purchase or rent cheap goods (say, ugly, breakdown-prone, noise-and-air-polluting, accident-prone cars or ugly and disease-and-fire spreading housing-units) whose consumption is more prone to generate external costs than is the consumption of their more-privately-expensive alternatives when the relevant external-cost differences render their privately-advantageous consumption-choices economically inefficient, (C) by choices to commit economically-inefficient crimes (poverty and material inequality increase such crime by increasing poor individuals' non-sovereignty and non-maximization and social alienation [which increases the extent to which they fail to internalize the equivalent-dollar losses their possible criminal acts would impose directly on others] and by reducing the difference between the attractiveness to poor potential criminals of life inside prison and the life they could lead outside prison if they did not engage in crime), (D) by economically-inefficient decisions to perform non-criminal, dangerous labor (increases in poverty increase the number of such decisions that are made both because increases in poverty increase relevant potential-worker non-sovereignty and non-maximization and because, in societies in which the incidence and magnitude of government transfers to poor individuals who are injured or killed at work and/or to their families are higher than the incidence and magnitude of such transfers to the better-off and their families [and because in some societies increases in poverty increase government subsidization of dangerous labor]), (E) by economically-inefficient government-decisions (because government decision-makers place less weight per person on the equivalent-dollar effects of their choices on the poor and relatively-less-well-off and more weight per person on the equivalent-dollar effects of their choices on the wealthy and relatively-better-off [since for a variety of reasons, the per-person political power of better-off individuals exceeds the per-person political power of worse-off individuals]), and (F) by increasing the net equivalent-dollar losses the society's distributions of income and wealth generate by dissatisfying the "external preferences" of its members and participants (their non-parochial preferences for others' having resources and opportunities)—I acknowledge that this last claim may reflect my unwarranted optimism about the extent to which the relevant society's members and participants share my distributive values, (2) to estimate/guesstimates the impact of the choice under consideration on poverty and/or material inequality, and (3) to estimate/guesstimate the effect that the choice's estimated/guesstimated impact on poverty and material inequality would have on economic efficiency in each of the ways in which it could affect economic efficiency if the government did nothing to combat the effects in question.[12]

The fourth major component of the protocol for economic-efficiency analysis I claim is TBLE instructs the analyst (1) to estimate/guesstimate the impact of the choice on the private costs that final consumers incur to determine the purchases that best promote their respective goals, the "private" cost to the government of supplying information about products (or banning some products), the private cost to non-government actors of supplying product descriptions and evaluations, and the private cost to producers of controlling the complements their customers combine with their products and (2) to analyze and estimate/guesstimate the magnitudes of the factors that determine the ratios of the above private costs to their allocative counterparts.

The fifth major component of the protocol for economic-efficiency analysis I claim is *ex ante* economically efficient instructs the analyst (1) to consider the impact of the choice on allocative transaction costs—i.e., both (A) the choice's impact on the private transaction costs that non-government actors incur to implement pricing-techniques designed to convert what would otherwise be buyer surplus into seller surplus, to induce their employees and the independent contractors they use to make choices in the actor's interest, to engage in and conceal various types of illegal conduct, and to respond to civil and criminal claims made against them and that government actors incur to promulgate and implement laws and regulations, to adjudicate criminal and civil cases, and to raise the resources required to finance government operations and (B) all those factors that affect the ratio of (the impact of the choice on the *allocative* transaction costs associated with these private costs) to (its impact on the private transaction costs in question)—*inter alia*, the proportions of the resources used up as transaction costs that are withdrawn respectively from UO-producing-and-using, QV-investment-creating-and-using, and PPR-executing-and-using uses, the Pareto imperfections that distort the private benefits those resources would have generated for their alternative users in each of the pairs of functionally-related uses from which they would be withdrawn, and the different ways in which those Pareto imperfections interact to distort the private benefits that those resources would have generated respectively in their alternative pairs of functionally-related uses, (2) to estimate/guesstimate the choice's impact on risk-cost-related allocative costs—i.e., both on (A) the risk costs the members of and participants in the relevant society incur and the private costs such actors incur to reduce such risk costs and (B) the factors that influence the ratio of the allocative cost of any choice-induced or choice-deterred allocative risk-cost-avoidance moves to their private counterparts and the ways in which those factors interact to determine that ratio (which vary with the nature of the alternative uses from which the resources devoted to risk-cost avoidance are withdrawn), (3) to estimate/guesstimate the non-allocative-transaction-cost-related allocative costs or benefits the choice would generate by increasing/decreasing moral-rights-violating conduct (e.g., the allocative cost of the injuries/deaths the choice would cause/deter, the allocative cost that the libel/slander the choice would cause/deter would generate/would have generated [both by causing/deterring direct harm to its target and those who value the target's welfare and indirectly by deterring/causing economically-efficient transactions/relationships with the target], the non-allocative-transaction-cost allocative cost of the thefts the choice would/did cause/deter by generating/deterring transfers of goods from their higher-dollar-valuing owners to their lower-dollar-valuing "transferees" and by inducing/deterring potential victims of theft to make/from making otherwise-allocatively-inefficient choices to protect themselves against theft [to install burglar alarms, to place valuables in safe-deposit boxes, to purchase goods that are less-hard rather than more-hard to steal, to work less and consume more leisure), and (4) when the choice in question affects government expenditures, to estimate the resource misallocation the choice would generate on this account even if no allocative transaction costs had to be generated to finance relevant government expenditures —i.e., (A) analyze the ways in which the government will respond to that fiscal reality (*inter alia*, by raising various taxes, increasing the prices it charges for various government-supplied goods and services, increasing government debt and/or inflation, and eliminating other expenditures) and (B) analyze the economic efficiency of each of these predicted responses (by using a protocol that responds *ex ante* economic efficiently to The General Theory of Second Best).

The sixth and final component of the protocol for economic-efficiency prediction/post-diction that I claim is TBLE instructs the analyst to add together all of his or her estimates of the impacts of the choice on the categories of economic inefficiency and other allocative costs the preceding components of this protocol reference to generate a prediction/post-diction of the overall impact of the choice under review on economic efficiency. I want to close this account of the protocol for economic-efficiency prediction I claim is *ex ante* economically efficient by reiter-ating the pervasive feature of the protocol that renders it *ex ante* economically efficient—i.e., *third-best* economically efficient. At each stage of the associated analysis, the protocol instructs the analyst to consider whether, everything con-sidered, it would be *ex ante* economically efficient to execute additional empirical or theoretical research-projects or to devote additional attention to the implications of the available information and to continue to do such additional work until the analyst concludes that it is TBLE to stop.

Notes

1. In this book, the economic efficiency of a choice is defined to equal the difference between the (equivalent-) dollar gains it confers on its beneficiaries and
   the (equivalent-) dollar losses it imposes on its victims where the gains and
   losses in question equal properly-elaborated versions of the equivalent variations (as opposed to the compensating variations) in the relevant parties'
   wealths. For the relevant elaborations, the justification for this definition, and
   explanations of its superiority to the various alternative operationalizations of
   the concept "the impact of a choice on economic efficiency" that other economists propose and use, see Chap. 3. I should point out that the first sentence of
   this footnote refers to equivalent-dollar gains and losses rather than to dollar
   gains and losses because many of the relevant effects not only are not direct
   monetary effects but, in some instances, cannot be capitalized by the person that
   experiences them. Take, for example, the equivalent-dollar gain that the owner
   of swampland who values it positively (for sentimental reasons) despite the fact
   that its market value is zero obtains from an environmental policy that cleans up
   the water in the swamp and/or the air over the swamp. If the policy does not
   improve the property sufficiently for it to have a positive market value
   post-policy, this winner will not be able to capitalize any equivalent-dollar gain
   the policy confers on him. In this book, the phrases "economic efficiency" and
   "economically efficient" are used respectively interchangeably with the phrases
   "allocative efficiency" and "allocatively efficient."

2. On my understanding, the Pareto-optimal conditions are: no imperfection in
   seller competition, no imperfection in buyer competition, no (real) externality,
   no tax on the margin of income, all resource allocators are sovereign (possess
   all the information relevant to their identifying the choice that best satisfies their
   preferences, given their "financial" position), all resource allocators maximize,
   and no choice generates any (critical) buyer surplus. Two related points should
   be made. First, the preceding list of Pareto-optimal conditions substitutes a "no
   critical buyer surplus" Pareto-optimal condition for the standard "no public
   good" Pareto-optimal condition: I have made this substitution because buyer
   surplus can generate economic inefficiency in an otherwise-Pareto-perfect
   economy even if no relevant good is a "public good" (is a good [1] whose
   marginal cost is lower than its average total cost at the output at which its
   demand curve cuts its marginal-cost curve from above and [2] whose average
   total cost at that output is lower than the average allocative value of the
   output-units in question [which approximately equals the average height of the
   demand curve for the good between output zero and the output in question])—
   for example, can cause a less-economically-efficient rather than a
   more-economically-efficient product-creating investment to be made if the
   buyer surplus that would be generated by the sale of units of the product that
   would be created by the more-economically-efficient investment exceeds the
   buyer surplus that would be generated by the sale of units of the product that
   would be created by the less-economically-efficient product-creating

investment by more than the economic efficiency of the former investment exceeds the economic efficiency of the latter. Second, it might be argued that the full set of Pareto-optimal conditions includes an eighth condition—viz., that the 7 conditions just listed can be fulfilled without generating any conventional allocative transaction costs, any organizational economic inefficiency (by precluding firms from combining assets that are complementary for scale or non-scale reasons), any increase in risk costs or any allocative costs by inducing resource allocators to adjust their choices to reduce the risk costs they bear, any delay-in-government-decision-generated economic-efficiency losses, or any public-financing-of-government-operations-generated misallocation (see Calabresi 1991).

3. The expression "The General Theory of Second Best" is the title of a famous article (Lipsey and Lancaster 1956), whose authors are generally credited with developing the theory. This article illustrates the theory's implications through a more-thorough mathematical analysis of the causes of a particular category of economic inefficiency than anyone had previously provided (see also Lipsey 2007). However, as Bohm and Woo have separately pointed out (Bohm 1987; Woo 2017, p. 229), both the argument of The General Theory of Second Best and its central conclusion were anticipated in earlier scholarship (by Pareto 1909; Hicks 1940, pp. 114–116; Samuelson 1947, pp. 252–253; Viner 1950, p. 133; Little 1951, pp. 577–584; Corbett and Hague 1953, pp. 21–30; Meade 1955, p. 8).

4. This focus is not peculiar. Historically, economists who analyzed the implications of The General Theory of Second Best also focused on its implications for the economically-efficient way to analyze the economic efficiency of a choice or its implications for the economic efficiency of particular choices. Indeed, most contemporary studies that attempt to take account of The General Theory of Second Best continue to assume that the relevant maximand is economic efficiency. Admittedly, however, some theoretical-Welfare-Economics analyses of the appropriate way to respond to The General Theory of Second Best and some applied-Welfare-Economics analyses focus on this General Theory's implications respectively for the appropriate way to analyze the impact of a choice on "social welfare" and for the most social-welfare-promotive response to make to a particular "problem." (I should add that these studies usually define "social welfare" by a crudely-specified function whose value is assumed not to increase monotonically with economic efficiency and that ignores the possibility that the relevant society may be committed to instantiating a particular conception of justice—that the society's pursuit of the *desiderata* that its social-welfare function references is constrained by the society's moral-rights [justice] commitments.) (Markovits 1998a, pp. 343–362).

5. The text's account of my definition of "theoretical Welfare Economics" is somewhat underinclusive. On my actual definition, "theoretical Welfare Economics" is the branch of Welfare Economics that is concerned not only with (1) developing the protocol for economic-efficiency analysis that is *ex ante*

most-economically-efficient (or for social-welfare analysis that is *ex ante* most-morally-desirable) and, relatedly, (2) identifying the conditions under which a choice will increase or decrease economic efficiency (or social welfare on various conceptions of that concept) but also with (3) articulating the definition of "the impact of a choice on economic efficiency" that is correct in the sense of being most useful and most congruent with popular and professional understanding and (4) determining the relevance of the economic efficiency of a choice to its justness (its securing and not violating moral rights) and its instantiating various morally-defensible conceptions of the moral good. The distinction between "justice" and "the moral good" is salient in societies that are committed to instantiating a conception of justice that leaves room for conceptions of the moral good to play an important role in their prescriptive-moral discourse. Thus, conceptions of the moral good can play an important role in the prescriptive-moral discourse of societies that are committed to instantiating a "liberal" conception of justice (according to which all concrete moral rights derive from a fundamental moral duty to treat all creatures that have the neurological prerequisites for taking their lives morally seriously with appropriate, equal respect and concern in part for their "welfare" in the utilitarian sense in which economists understand that concept but pre-eminently for their having a meaningful opportunity to lead a life of moral integrity [to take their liberal moral obligations seriously and to take seriously as well the dialectical task of developing a personal conception of the moral good and making choices that instantiate that conception]). To see why the liberal conception of justice leaves room for conceptions of the moral good to perform an important role in prescriptive-moral discourse, note that, although the liberal conception of justice implies that all moral-rights holders have a moral right to the resources, nurturing, education, etc. that contribute significantly not only to their survival but also to their ability to take their lives morally seriously, once that moral right is secured, moral evaluations of the desirability of securing different degrees of equality would be based on different, morally-defensible conceptions of the moral good (according to which the moral good is best promoted by distributions of income and wealth that, respectively, maximize the total utility of all creatures whose utility counts, that equalize the utility of all creatures whose utility counts, that give all creatures that are relevant the same amount of resources [measured by their allocative cost], that give all creatures that count an equal opportunity to do an X other than leading a life of moral integrity that is morally defensible, etc.). By way of contrast, if I continue to assume *ad arguendo* that utilitarianism can be operationalized (that all affective states can be mapped into units of utility —utils) and that utilitarianism is morally defensible, the distinction between justice and the moral good would play no role in the prescriptive-moral discourse of societies that are committed to instantiating a utilitarian conception of justice. In such societies, justice requires that the total utility of all creatures whose utility counts always be maximized, and this normative commitment leaves no room for any other consideration to play a role in the society's pertinent prescriptive-moral discourse. See Markovits (1998a), *id.* and pp. 410–412.

6. A non-economic example may make the Second-Best-Theory argument more comprehensible. Assume that there is an ideal way to drive a car around a corner (I will not specify the associated maximand or objective function [whatever it is that would ideally be maximized])—viz., to drive the car 15 miles per hour and turn the steering wheel in the appropriate direction 40° per second. If the car is being driven 15 miles per hour, the optimal rate at which to turn the steering wheel will be 40° per second because, if one turns the steering wheel 40° per second in the appropriate direction, both (all) of the optimal conditions will be fulfilled and the optimum will be achieved. However, what if the accelerator is jammed, the car is moving 85 miles per hour, and nothing can be done about those facts? Will it be (second-best) optimal to turn the steering wheel 40° per second in the direction that would be optimal in the absence of any imperfections? Almost certainly not. Although it might turn out that fulfilling the second optimal condition (turning the steering wheel 40° per second in the direction that a first-best analysis would recommend) is second-best optimal, any such reality will be fortuitous in the sense that it will not follow from the fact that turning the steering wheel 40° per second in the direction that a first-best analysis would recommend is an optimal condition (belongs to a set of sufficient conditions for the achievement of the relevant optimum). To determine the best way to turn the steering wheel when the car is traveling 85 miles per hour, one would have to examine how departures from the two optimal conditions interact to cause suboptimal outcomes both in general and in the particular relevant context—for example, the presence of a steel-reinforced concrete wall 50 yards from the road may play an important role in the relevant analysis even if it would play no role in determining the optimal way to drive the car around the corner in question. The pertinent points are: (1) once one of two optimal conditions is not fulfilled, there is no general reason to believe that fulfilling or more closely approximating the second optimal condition will even tend to improve the outcome, and (2) in order to determine whether to fulfill or more closely approximate the fulfillment of the second of two optimal conditions when the first is not fulfilled (or, more generally, what to do about a second of two outcome-determinants when the magnitude of the first outcome-determinant is not first-best), one must combine an appropriate theoretical analysis with context-specific empirical findings.

7. Admittedly, as footnote 1 indicated, the central claim of The General Theory of Second Best was stated or intimated by several economists before Lipsey and Lancaster's famous 1956 article.

8. I write "almost always" because the amount of economic inefficiency in an economy that contains only one Pareto imperfection may depend not only on the magnitude of that imperfection but also on the distributions of income and wealth in the economy in question and a choice that reduces the magnitude of the only Pareto imperfection in a given economy could increase the amount of economic inefficiency it contains if it alters the distributions of income and/or wealth in that economy in a way that increases the amount of resource

misallocation that would be generated by a Pareto imperfection of the relevant kind of different relevant magnitudes.

9. In my terminology, a seller is said to have initiated an oligopolistic-pricing sequence (perhaps *inter alia*) by charging an oligopolistic price if its perception that the price it charged would be (most) profitable was influenced by its belief that one or more of its rivals' responses to its price would or might be affected by their perception that the seller would or might react to their respective responses. When the rival anticipates such a reaction because the initiator has communicated to the rival its intention to react to a cooperative response by foregoing inherently-profitable opportunities to beat one or more offers the rival makes to buyers the rival is (usually) privately-best-placed to supply and/or to react to the rival's beating the initiator's oligopolistic offer by making inherently-unprofitable decisions (charging sub-marginal-cost prices to the rival's customers, executing inherently-unprofitable advertising campaigns that target the rival's customers, blowing up the rival's factory or distributive out-lets) to punish the non-cooperator to deter non-cooperation by it and others in the future, I denominate the initiator's oligopolistic pricing "contrived oligopolistic pricing," but when the rival anticipates the initiator's reacting to any non-cooperative response the rival would otherwise find profitable in a way that would render that response unprofitable because the rival realizes that the initiator will or may have the opportunity to react to the rival's response and will or may find it inherently profitable to react in a way that renders the rival's otherwise-profitable response unprofitable (because the buyer in question will or may give its privately-best-placed potential supplier an opportunity to rebid and the privately-best-placed potential supplier will or may find it inherently profitable to beat any offer a privately-inferior potential supplier would other-wise find profitable to make), I denominate the initiator's oligopolistic pricing "natural oligopolistic pricing." In my terminology, a competitive move is said to be "retaliatory" if it is inherently unprofitable but rendered profitable overall (in its maker's *ex ante* perception) because, by inflicting losses on a non-cooperator, it will deter the target of the retaliation and others from not cooperating in the future: thus, a contrived oligopolistic pricer may retaliate against a rival's beating its contrived oligopolistic offer (from a privately-inferior competitive position), and (by extension) a "non-cooperator" against which such retaliation has been practiced may practice defensive retaliation against a retaliating contriver. In my terminology, a competitive move is said to be predatory when it is inherently-unprofitable but its perpe-trator perceives it to be *ex ante* profitable overall because the perpetrator believes that it will or may reduce the absolute attractiveness of the offers against which it will have to compete in the future by driving a target out (that will not be immediately replaced by an equally-competitive rival), deterring a potential competitor from entering or an established rival from making an additional QV investment in the relevant area of product-space, or inducing an

existing rival or potential investor in its area of product-space to change the product-space location of its investment/planned investment to one that is less competitive with the predator's projects.

10. Conduct that is motivated by specific anticompetitive intent uses up resources because it is allocative-transaction-costly. The relevant allocative transaction costs include the allocative transaction cost of communicating contrived-oligopolistic threats and offers, the allocative transaction cost of negotiating joint contrivance, the allocative transaction cost of "price-fixers'" determining whether anyone is "cheating" and identifying the cheater, the allocative transaction cost of retaliating against non-cooperators, the allocative transaction cost that "cheaters" incur to engage in defensive retaliation against contrivers that have retaliated against them, the allocative transaction cost of communicating predatory threats, the allocative transaction cost of negotiating and coordinating joint predation, the allocative transaction cost of executing predatory moves, the allocative transaction cost generated by any defensive retaliation in which targets of predation engage, the allocative transaction cost of negotiating and executing mergers, acquisition, joint ventures, and related collaborative arrangements that are motivated by specific anticompetitive intent, the allocative transaction costs that the perpetrators of exemplars of all conduct motivated by specific anticompetitive intent generate to conceal it, to defend themselves in related civil and criminal litigation, the allocative transaction costs that private plaintiffs and the State generate when bringing associated civil and criminal suits and negotiating settlements or pleas, and the allocative transaction costs the State incurs to adjudicate associated suits and to penalize (say, imprison) offenders.

11. I acknowledge that the non-cooperative conduct of the privately-and-allocatively worse-than-best-placed potential supplier that results in its supplying the price-fixer's customer will reduce intra-ARDEPPS UO-to-UO misallocation only if the increase in intra-ARDEPPS UO-to-UO economic inefficiency it generates both directly and indirectly by inducing the price-fixer to retaliate against it and by inducing it to engage in defensive retaliation against the retaliating contriver is smaller than the decrease in intra-ARDEPPS UO-to-UO economic inefficiency it generates by deterring future contrived oligopolistic pricing. The same point applies to any defensive retaliation in which a non-cooperator engages in reaction to the price-fixer's retaliation against it. I also acknowledge that—if one ignores the fact that competitive inferiors' making superior offers to buyers will cause economic inefficiency equal to the allocative transaction cost of their making such offers if they would not otherwise have bid for the relevant buyers patronage—competitive inferiors' making superior offers to buyers will cause economic inefficiency only if (1) it results in their supplying the buyers in question and they are allocatively as well as privately worse-than-best-placed to supply those buyers or (2) it causes the buyers' privately-best-placed suppliers to make allocative-transaction-costly rebids to retain the relevant buyers' patronage.

12. Two related points need to be made. First, the magnitude of many of the effects that choices can have on economic efficiency by altering poverty and inequality in the society in which they are made depends on the content of the society's laws—e.g., on whether the society offers its members and participants free health-care, on the social services it offers pregnant women and parents of young children, on the pre-kindergarten (say, Head Start) programs it provides the children of the poor, on the quality of its K-12 public education, on its motor-vehicle safety-and-pollution inspection-programs and their implementation, on its housing codes and their implementation, on the product-information it supplies consumers or requires sellers to provide consumers (including information on maintenance and repair costs), on whether it requires retailers to post price-per-ounce information, on its criminal-law sentencing-policies and prison-regimes, etc. Second and relatedly, the text assumes that the government-choices that are under consideration do not contain components that are designed to reduce any economic inefficiency they would otherwise generate by increasing poverty and/or inequality. If a government-choice that is under consideration does have one or more such components, the economic-efficiency-analysis protocol I am claiming is economically efficient will instruct the analyst to consider both the allocative cost of any such choice-components and the economic-efficiency gains such components would yield by reducing the economic inefficiency generated by poverty and inequality if they were allocatively-costless.

References

Bohm, P. (1987). Second best. In Eatwell, J., Milgate, M., & Newsome, P. (Eds.), *The New Palgrave: A dictionary of economics* (Vol. 4 Q to Z, pp. 280–284). London: Macmillan.

Calabresi, G. (1991). The pointlessness of Pareto. *Yale Law Journal, 100,* 1211–1238.

Corbett, W., & Hague, D. (1953). Complementarity and the excess burden of taxation. *Review of Economic Studies, 21,* 21–30.

Hicks, J. R. (1940). The rehabilitation of consumers' surplus. *Review of Economic Studies, 8,* 108–116.

Lipsey, R. (2007). Reflections on the general theory of second best at its golden jubilee. *International Tax and Public Finance, 14,* 349–364.

Lipsey, R., & Lancaster, K. (1956). The general theory of second best. *Review of Economic Studies, 24,* 11–32.

Little, I. M. D. (1951). Direct & indirect taxes. *Economic Journal, 61,* 577–584.

Markovits R. (1966). *Potential competition, investment and pricing* (doctoral dissertation submitted to the University of London).

Markovits, R. (1975a). Potential competition, limit price theory, and the legality of horizontal and conglomerate mergers under the American antitrust laws. *Wisconsin Law Review, 1975,* 658–695.

Markovits, R. (1975b). A basic structure for micro-economic policy analysis in our worse-than-second-best world: A proposal and related critique of the Chicago approach to the study of law and economics. *Wisconsin Law Review, 1975,* 950–1080.

Markovits, R. (1976a). The causes and policy significance of Pareto resource misallocation: A checklist for micro-economic policy analysis. *Stanford Law Review, 28,* 1–44.

Markovits, R. (1976b). The allocative efficiency and overall desirability of oligopolistic pricing suits. *Stanford Law Review, 28,* 45–59.

Markovits, R. (1976c). Oligopolistic pricing, the Sherman Act, and economic welfare: A response to Professor Posner. *Stanford Law Review, 28,* 919–956.

Markovits, R. (1976d). The distributive impact, allocative efficiency, and overall desirability of ideal housing codes: Some theoretical clarifications. *Harvard Law Review, 89,* 1815–1846.

Markovits, R. (1979). Monopolistic competition, second best, and *The antitrust paradox*: A review article. *Michigan Law Review, 77,* 567–640.

Markovits, R. (1980a). Tie-Ins and reciprocity: A functional, legal (competitive impact), and policy analysis. *Texas Law Review, 58,* 1363–1445.

Markovits, R. (1980b). Legal analysis and the economic analysis of allocative efficiency. *Hofstra Law Review, 8,* 811–901.

Markovits, R. (1983). Legal analysis and the economic analysis of allocative efficiency: A response to Professor Posner's *Reply. Hofstra Law Review, 11,* 667–689.

Markovits, R. (1985a). An ideal antitrust law regime. *Texas Law Review, 64,* 251–352.

Markovits, R. (1985b). The functions, allocative efficiency and legality of tie-ins: A comment. *Journal of Law and Economics, 28,* 387–404.

Markovits, R. (1986a). Monopolistic competition and second best: Some new conceptual schemes. In K. Tucker (Ed.), *Firms and markets* (pp. 181–198). London and Sydney: Croom Helm.

Markovits, R. (1986b). Cost-benefit analysis and the determination of legal entitlements: A reply to Professor Carlson. *Cardozo Law Review, 8,* 75–83.

Markovits, R. (1992a). Second-Best theory and the standard analysis of monopoly rent seeking: A generalizable critique, a "sociological" account, and some illustrative stories. *Iowa Law Review, 77,* 327–369.

Markovits, R. (1992b). The case for "business as usual" in law-and-economics land: A critical comment. *Iowa Law Review, 77,* 387–395.

Markovits, R. (1996). Monopoly and the allocative inefficiency of first-best-allocatively-efficient tort law: The whys and some therefores. *Case Western Reserve Law Review, 46,* 313–448.

Markovits, R. (Ed.) (1998a). Symposium on second-best theory and law & economics. *Chicago-Kent Law Review, 73,* 1–274.

Markovits, R. (1998b). Second-best theory and law & economics: An introduction. *Chicago-Kent Law Review, 73,* 3–10.

Markovits, R. (1998c). The allocative efficiency of shifting from a "negligence" system to a "strict liability" regime in our highly-Pareto-imperfect economy: A partial and preliminary third-best-allocative-efficiency analysis. *Chicago-Kent Law Review, 73,* 11–134.

Markovits, R. (1998d). Second-best theory and the obligations of academics: A reply to Professor Donohue. *Chicago-Kent Law Review, 73,* 267–274.

Markovits, R. (2002a). On the economic efficiency of using law to increase research and development: A critique of various tax, antitrust, intellectual property, and tort law rules and policy proposals. *Harvard Journal on Legislation, 39,* 63–120.

Markovits, R. (2002b). On the inevitable arbitrariness of market definitions. *Antitrust Bulletin, 2002,* 571–601.

Markovits, R. (2005). Why Kaplow and Shavell's "double-distortion argument" articles are wrong. *George Mason Law Review, 13,* 511–619.

Markovits, R. (2006). On the economic inefficiency of a liberal-corrective-justice-securing law of torts. *Illinois Law Review, 2006,* 525–569.

Markovits, R. (2008). *Truth or economics: On the definition, prediction, and relevance of economic efficiency.* New Haven and London: Yale Univ. Press.

Markovits, R. (2011a). Background (fixed-cost) avoidance-choices, foreground (variable-cost) avoidance-choices and the economically efficient approach for courts to take to accident cases:

A marine-salvage example and related critique of Landes and Posner's classic study. *Buffalo Law Review, 59,* 57–140.

Markovits, R. (2011b). How American legal academics' beliefs about economic-efficiency analysis, moral philosophy, and valid legal argument disserve law & society empirical research. In R. Gordon and M. Horowitz (Eds.), *Law, society, and history: essays on themes in the legal history and legal sociology of Lawrence M. Friedman* (pp. 395–430), New York: Cambridge University Press.

Markovits, R. (2012). Why one should never define markets or use market-oriented approaches to analyze the legality of business conduct under U.S. antitrust law: My arguments and a critique of Professor Kaplow's. *Antitrust Bulletin, 57,* 747–885.

Markovits, R. (2014). *Economics and the interpretation and application of U.S. and E.U. antitrust law Vol. I Basic concepts and the economics-based legal analysis of oligopolistic and predatory conduct.* Heidelberg, New York, Dordrecht, London: Springer.

Markovits, R. (2016). The general theory of second best and economic-efficiency analysis: The theory, its negative corollaries, the appropriate response to it, and a coda on the economic efficiency of reducing poverty and/or income/wealth inequality. *Akron Law Review, 49,* 437–469.

Markovits, R. (2017a). A third-best-allocatively-efficient distortion-analysis protocol for analyzing economic efficiency (article manuscript under submission).

Markovits, R. (2017b). second-best theory and the analysis of the impact of choices on "social welfare" and on more specific objectives that the legal system, lawyers, and legal academics value (article manuscript under submission).

Markovits, R. (2018). "Public utility" regulation: Some economic and moral analyses. *Yale Journal on Regulation, 35,* 875–907.

Meade, J. (1955). *The theory of customs unions.* Amsterdam: North-Holland Press.

Pareto, V. (1909). *Manuel d'economie politique.* Paris: Gerard et Brière.

Samuelson, P. (1947). *Foundations of economic analysis.* Cambridge, MA: Harvard University Press.

Viner, J. (1950). *The customs union issue.* New York: Carnegie Endowment for Universal Peace.

Woo, W. C. (2017). The way we teach public economics: A rationalization using the theory of third best. *Pacific Economic Review, 22,* 229–248.

The Economics Profession's Responses to The General Theory of Second Best: Descriptions and Critiques

Abstract

This chapter argues that the economics profession has not responded appropriately to The General Theory of Second Best (Lipsey and Lancaster in Rev Econ Stud 24:11–32, 1956). Section 2.1 explains the deficiencies both of two influential arguments for the economic efficiency of ignoring Second Best and of the arguments for the economic efficiency of 6 decision-rules that are alleged to respond appropriately to Second Best. Section 2.1 also argues that—although many articles that do respond to Second Best establish relationships that can inform the protocol for economic-efficiency analysis that is economically efficient—taken as a whole, this valuable literature is deficient in that it (1) ignores most of the categories of economic inefficiency whose magnitudes choices can affect and most of the Pareto imperfections that affect these categories of economic inefficiency and (2) largely ignores the inaccuracy and allocative cost of relevant theoretical and empirical research. Section 2.2 criticizes in broad terms various subsets of the applied-Welfare-Economics literature. Section 2.3 explains that (with only a few limited exceptions) the substantial number of theoretical-and-applied-Welfare-Economics textbooks that I and others have examined either totally ignores Second Best or references and then largely disregards it. Section 2.4 delineates and criticizes 7 additional arguments that economists have claimed justify their and our profession's ignoring Second Best. Section 2.5 recounts a number of instances in which economists responded not only incorrectly but in doubtful good faith to Second-Best-Theory talks I gave. Finally, Sect. 2.6 delineates 6 reasons that may account for the economics profession's failure to respond appropriately to Second Best.

© Springer Nature Switzerland AG 2020
R. S. Markovits, *Welfare Economics and Second-Best Theory*,
https://doi.org/10.1007/978-3-030-43360-4_2

2.1   The Theoretical-Welfare-Economics Literature that Does Address The General Theory of Second Best

As I have already indicated, welfare economists have done disappointingly-little research on the protocol for economic-efficiency prediction or post-diction that is second-best-allocatively-efficient or third-best-allocatively-efficient. This subsection, which relies to a considerable extent on Lipsey's critiques of some of the relevant scholarship (Lipsey 2007, 2012, 2017a, b; Lipsey and Ng 2017a, b), claims that the post-1956 theoretical-Welfare-Economics literature supports my conclusion that the economics profession has not responded appropriately to The General Theory of Second Best. Its argument for this conclusion has two components.

The first focuses on individual pieces of theoretical-Welfare-Economics scholarship. It argues that these individual articles and books do not respond appropriately to The General Theory of Second Best for at least one and up to 7 reasons: (1) some proceed on explicit assumptions that their authors claim are frequently or almost always fulfilled that are, in fact, rarely if ever fulfilled; (2) some claim incorrectly to have established conclusions that would not follow from their (unrealistic) assumptions even if (contrary to fact) their additional implicit assumption that the economy contains no Pareto imperfections other than the imperfection on whose reduction's economic efficiency they focus were accurate; (3) all ignore the vast majority of the Pareto imperfections that economies contain that will affect the quantity the economy generates of each category of economic inefficiency they consider; (4) all ignore many of the categories of economic inefficiency whose magnitudes will be affected by the choices whose economic efficiency they analyze; relatedly (5) all ignore the different ways in which the Pareto imperfections they consider and the Pareto imperfections they ignore interact to cause or not cause the categories of economic inefficiency they disregard; relatedly (6) none attempts to identify the protocol for economic-efficiency analysis that is second-best-allocatively-efficient; (7) none investigates the implications of (A) the facts that (i) theoretical and empirical research-projects are imperfect, (ii) theoretical and empirical research-projects use up resources that would generate allocative benefits in their sacrificed uses, (iii) efforts to analyze the implications of what is known for the economic efficiency of the choice at issue are imperfect and resource-consuming, (iv) even the *ex ante* allocatively-efficient execution and use of research may generate allocative "costs" by delaying government decisions, (v) the government will usually generate economic inefficiency when financing the execution of relevant research and the consideration of all available information's implications for the economic efficiency of the choice at issue, and (vi) research findings may increase the economic efficiency of choices other than the choice immediately under consideration for (B) both the ways to investigate the difference between and the actual difference between third-best and second-best-allocative-efficiency analysis/concrete allocative-efficiency analyses.

The second component of my argument for my conclusion that the post-1956 theoretical-Welfare-Economics literature has not responded appropriately to The General Theory of Second Best seeks to respond to the perfectly-justifiable claim that it is unreasonable to demand that individual pieces of scholarship do everything that needs to be done. I acknowledge that progress comes in small steps—that progress is progressive. The second component responds to this objection to my criticism of the theoretical-Welfare-Economics literature by pointing out that, taken as a whole, the corpus of post-1956 theoretical-Welfare-Economics scholarship (1) ignores many types of Pareto imperfections and categories of economic inefficiency, relatedly (2) fails to analyze the different ways in which all exemplars of all types of Pareto imperfections interact to cause or not cause each of the different categories of economic inefficiency it is *ex ante* economically efficient to distinguish and consider separately, and (3) pays almost no attention to the protocol that would be *ex ante* economically efficient for economic-efficiency analysts to use to decide whether to execute an additional, relevant theoretical or empirical research-project or whether to devote additional time and effort to examining the implications of the information at the analyst's disposal for the economic efficiency of the choice whose economic efficiency is at issue (and of other individual choices or classes of choices).

The first individual theoretical-Welfare-Economics article that attempts to respond constructively to The General Theory of Second Best that I will discuss is E.J. Mishan's 1962 article *Second Thoughts on Second Best* (Mishan 1962). In this article, Mishan argues that The General Theory of Second Best has less bearing than it initially appeared to have on the economically-efficient way to analyze the economic efficiency of choices because (1) in many situations, resources do not flow from other sectors of the economy (say, Sectors Z1...n) into the sector of the economy in which a "target Pareto imperfection" (the Pareto imperfection that the choice under review would alter) is located (say, Sector T) or vice versa and (2) when that is the case, it is not only correct to ignore any Pareto imperfections in a Sector Z of the economy when analyzing the economic efficiency of reducing or eliminating a target Pareto imperfection in Sector T but also (in my terminology) it is third-best allocatively efficient to execute a first-best-allocative-efficiency analysis of the economic efficiency of decreasing or increasing the target Pareto imperfection in Sector T. Mishan's article caused welfare economists to breathe a huge sigh of relief. Unfortunately, for three reasons, I do not think that Mishan's argument was correct or that this reaction was justified:

(1) even if (contrary to my belief) economies could be divided up into different sectors non-arbitrarily, the vast majority of resource allocations would involve flows of resources from other sectors into the target sector and/or vice versa;

(2) even if resources did not flow directly from a particular non-target sector (say, Sector Z) to the target sector (Sector T) or vice versa, Pareto imperfections in Sector Z would affect the economic efficiency of reducing or eliminating a Pareto imperfection in Sector T if resources flowed from Sector Z to another non-target sector (say, Sector Y) and from Sector Y to Sector T or vice versa

and one or more Pareto imperfections in Sector Z distorted the private benefits that relevant resource-uses in Sector Y would or did generate; and

(3) even if all resource allocations to uses in Sector T involved allocations exclusively from alternative resource-uses in Sector T, The General Theory of Second Best would still have to be taken into account (first-best-allocative-efficient analysis would not be second-best-allocatively-efficient and would be highly unlikely to be third-best-allocatively-efficient) because, in addition to the target Pareto imperfection, Sector T will always or almost always contain many other Pareto imperfections whose presence will affect the economic efficiency of reducing or increasing the target Pareto imperfection.

I hasten to add that Mishan's later work suggests that he was not convinced of the empirical importance of his 1962 argument. Thus, Mishan's 1971 Welfare Economics textbook executes analyses of a variety of policy choices that take account of the central insights of The General Theory of Second Best (Mishan 1971, pp. 90–99).

The second post-1956 theoretical-Welfare-Economics scholarship I will discuss consists of a series of articles and books published by Y.-K. Ng from 1977 through 2017 (Ng 1977, 1984, 1987a, b, 2000, 2004a, b, 2017a, b; Lipsey and Ng 2017a, b). Like Mishan's 1962 article, this scholarship by Ng claims that, when a specified set of conditions is fulfilled that Ng believes is frequently if not usually fulfilled, it is (in my terminology) third-best-allocatively-efficient to execute first-best-allocative-efficiency analyses.[1]

I will devote considerable attention to Ng's argument despite the fact that, for a variety of reasons I will proceed to explain, I—like Richard Lipsey (Lipsey 2007, 2017a, b; Lipsey and Ng 2017a, b)—find it unpersuasive. I will do so because (1) Ng continues to believe his position is correct (Lipsey and Ng 2017a, b; Ng 1984, 1987a, b, 2000, 2004a, b, 2017a, b), (2) several other economists or government institutions have endorsed it in print (Woo 2010, pp. 287–288; Australian Government Productivity Commission 2008, p. 21; Maks 2005, p. 217; Ebert 1985, p. 264; Brennan and Buchanan 1980, p. 213), (3) even when a particular supporter of Ng's position has read Lipsey's analyses of its deficiencies, the Ng supporter insists that, although Ng's argument/conclusion does not apply/is not correct when the policy choice in question involves "a drastic deviation" from the "first-best rule," Ng's argument and conclusion are correct when the relevant policy choice involves a "non-drastic" deviation from that rule (see Woo 2010, p. 290 ; Woo 2017, pp. 237–240 and Lipsey's critique of this position of Woo in Lipsey 2017b, pp. 174–176; Lipsey 2017a, p. 196), and (4) of the 6 articles in the May 2017 issue of the *Pacific Economic Review,* which was devoted exclusively to Second and Third Best Theories: Criticisms and Applications, 4 (including a reprint of Ng's 1977 article) were devoted exclusively or primarily to Ng's argument and one (Woo's) contained a substantial section on Ng's argument (which it claimed justified the public-finance textbooks' it usefully reviewed either totally or overwhelmingly ignoring The General Theory of Second Best) (Woo 2017, pp. 239–240).

Ng begins by defining what he denominates "the relation curve"—the curve that "relates the value of the objective function (I am assuming that the maximand is economic inefficiency" and he, that it is "social welfare"[2]) to the direction and divergence from the first-best rule of the variable under consideration (in my terms, of the Pareto imperfection whose magnitude the policy analyst is considering altering—for example, crudely put, to the direction and magnitude of the divergence between P and MC) (Ng 2017c, p. 156). Ng assumes that this relation curve is (in "most cases") concave (Ng 2017c, p. 156) and that the objective function is maximized when the parameter that can be directly controlled (which he calls "the variable under consideration" and I call "the target parameter") has its first-best value (in the case in which the objective function is economic efficiency, the target parameter will be a Pareto imperfection and the first-best value of that parameter will be zero) (Ng 2017c, p. 156 Fig. 1). It is important to recognize that this last assumption presumes (when the maximand is economic efficiency) totally unrealistically either that the economy contains no other Pareto imperfections or that the other Pareto imperfections the economy contains leave unaffected the impact that small changes in the target imperfection will have on economic efficiency (at least when the pre-choice magnitude of the target imperfection is infinitesimally small).

Ng next distinguishes three types of informational situations:

(A) *Informational Poverty* where the available information is insufficient to provide a reasonable probabilistic judgment regarding: (i) the direction and extent of the divergence of the second-best optimum [in my terms, the magnitude of the Pareto imperfection that the policymaker could affect that would be second-best-allocatively-efficient] from that resulting from the application of the first-best rule in the presence of the second-best distortion and (ii) the shape and skewness of the relation curve apart from its general concavity
(B) *Informational Scarcity* where the information is sufficient for such purposes but is not perfect
(C) *Information Abundance* (i.e., perfect information).

Although Ng recognizes that, in some situations, information will be merely scarce—will be sufficiently available to make it TBLE to adopt policies that would be deemed economically inefficient by a FBLE analysis (Lipsey and Ng 2017a, p. 220)—he and his followers clearly believe that the usual situation is one of Informational Poverty.

Ng then argues that, in situations of Informational Poverty when the relation curve is concave, it will be TBLE to base economic-efficiency predictions/post-dictions on FBLE economic-efficiency analysis—i.e., it will be TBLE to eliminate or reduce to the greatest extent possible the Pareto imperfection whose magnitude the analyst is assuming can be controlled. According to Ng, this conclusion is correct because (1) what I call non-target (Pareto) imperfections alter the position of the relation curve for the target Pareto imperfection, (2) under conditions of *Informational Poverty*, the analyst has no information that will justify the rejection of the assumption that the non-target Pareto imperfections will be as likely to move the relation curve to the left as to the right and no reason to believe that the relation curve will be skewed in any particular way, and (3) under these conditions, the concavity of the relation curve implies that any choice that would convert a situation in which there was no imperfection of the target type (no Pareto imperfection of the target type) into one in which the magnitude of the target (Pareto) imperfection was non-zero would have a negative weighted-average-expected impact on the magnitude of the objective function (on economic efficiency).

I have 4 objections to this argument or its significance. My first objection is that (1) Ng's argument (Ng's construction of his relation curve—in particular, his assumption that the objective function is maximized when the target imperfection is eliminated) implicitly assumes either (A) that the target Pareto imperfection is the only Pareto imperfection in the economy or (B) that the interaction of the other Pareto imperfections in the economy leaves unaffected the impact of the target imperfection on the objective function (at least when the target imperfection has been eliminated or rendered infinitesimally small) and (2) both these assumptions are empirically ridiculous. Lipsey makes this objection to Ng's argument as well: in Lipsey's words, Ng's argument is based on "a critical assumption…that the rest of the economy…obeys first-best rules"—an assumption that he clearly considers to be obviously unrealistic (Lipsey 2017a, p. 198, b, p. 170). (Lipsey's position differs from mine in that he does not reference the admittedly-remote possibility that Ng's assumption that the objective function will be maximized if the target imperfection is eliminated will also be correct if the other imperfections that the relevant system contains perfectly counteract each other when the target imperfection is eliminated.) My second objection to Ng's argument is that (1) it assumes that the relation curve is concave and (2) this assumption seems likely to be sufficiently false sufficiently often to significantly undermine the empirical relevance of Ng's argument and conclusion even if no other objection could be made to it (Lipsey makes these points as well in Lipsey 2017a, pp. 173–176). My third objection to Ng's argument is that, in an economy that is not oPp, even if the relation curve were concave, eliminating the target imperfection (making the choice that FBLE economic-efficiency analysis would commend) would not be *ex ante* economically efficient in a situation of Informational Poverty: given the fact that changes are allocative-transaction-costly to execute and allocative-costly to finance, the *ex ante* economically-efficient response to Informational Poverty is to do nothing. Lipsey makes this objection too: in Lipsey's words, on the assumptions Ng makes, the *ex ante* economically-efficient choice is "to maintain [ ] the policy status quo" (Lipsey 2017a, p. 172). Here is Lipsey's explanation for this conclusion: "The case for doing nothing depends on not having sufficient information to know in which direction to move" (Lipsey 2017b, p. 198). Fourth, unlike Ng, I think that policymakers are rarely in a position of Informational Poverty and that, even if (as I doubt will often be true) they confront a situation of Informational Poverty when they start their analysis, it will usually be *ex ante* economically efficient for them to obtain additional information before reaching their economic-efficiency conclusion. Of course, to do that, the policymakers would have to do more than collect additional data on the pre-choice and post-choice magnitudes of most if not all of the various types of Pareto imperfections an economy may contain—viz., (1) would have to be supplied with or to create themselves a list of the various categories of economic inefficiency and other sorts of allocative costs relevant choices can generate that are *ex ante* economically efficient to distinguish and analyze separately and (2) would have to generate conclusions about (A) the different ways in which the various types of Pareto imperfections any economy contains interact to generate or not generate respectively each such category of economic inefficiency and (B) the determinants of the other sorts of allocative costs a choice can affect. Ng's theory of third best does not address any of these issues, though (to be fair) when Ng himself addresses concrete economic-efficiency issues, he proceeds in a way that takes as many of these possibilities and parameters into account as do most other welfare economists who address concrete economic-efficiency issues (Ng 1987a, 2000, 2004a, b).

The third theoretical-Welfare-Economics scholarship I will address is Arnold Harberger's *Three Basic Postulates for Applied Welfare Economics* (Harberger 1971). I address this article (1) because Harberger has a deservedly-high reputation, (2) because the article itself is widely regarded to be a "classic" (see Lipsey 2007, p. 358), and (3) because Richard Lipsey has singled it out for special separate consideration (Lipsey 2007, pp. 358–359). However, I must admit that I comment on Harberger's conclusions and the arguments he made for them somewhat reluctantly because—although Lipsey seems to understand Harberger's conclusion and argument—I am not confident that I do.

Harberger appears to be focused on two issues: (1) are there situations in which the standard deadweight-loss-diagram analysis of the economic efficiency of a choice that would increase or decrease a Pareto imperfection (in his terms, "a distortion") is sufficiently inaccurate for that analysis to be (in my terms) third-best-allocatively-inefficient and (2) in those cases in which the standard deadweight-loss analysis (which equates the economic efficiency of a choice with the choice's impact on the sum of the buyer and seller surplus realized by the buyers and sellers whose respective dollar product valuations and dollar costs determine the demand and marginal-cost curves in the deadweight-loss-analysis diagram) is third-best-allocatively-inefficient, is there an alternative protocol for predicting or post-dicting the economic efficiency of Pareto-imperfection-altering choices that is third-best-allocativley-efficient or, in such cases, is the effort to increase allocative efficiency by making economic-efficiency predictions or post-dictions "effectively hopeless" (Harberger 1971, p. 791)?

Before proceeding to delineate Harberger's answers to these questions and the reasons (I think: I am not sure) he gives for those answers, I want to make 8 preliminary points or sets of related points. First, my discussion of Harberger will ignore those parts of his article that reflect the fact that he is assuming that the operative maximand is total utility rather than economic efficiency (Harberger 1971, pp. 787, 791, and 795) and those parts of his article that are concerned with the difference between the impact of a choice on an economy's GNP, NNP, or national income and its impact on economic efficiency (Harberger 1971, p. 787).

Second, I will assume that Harberger's self-reported "motivation" for writing this article—his desire to "secure professional consensus in the area of applied welfare economics" (Harberger 1971, p. 786)—did not cause him to take any position he would not otherwise have taken. (I must add, however, that I find this motive peculiar, especially for someone like Harberger who recognizes that, in his words, "there is no complete correspondence between what is traditional and what is right" (Harberger 1971, p. 796).)

Third, Harberger appears to believe that the effects of the choices whose economic efficiency is to be analyzed that usually have the greatest impact on economic efficiency are their substitution effects (Harberger 1971, p. 793). I agree.

Fourth, although Harberger recognizes that the income-effects of choices significantly affect not only their impact on total utility but also their impact on economic efficiency when those income-effects are substantial (Harberger 1971, p. 794), I suspect that he and I disagree about the ways in which a choice's income-effects affect its economic efficiency, regardless of whether those income-effects have an impact on the extent of income/wealth inequality and poverty in the society in question. To begin, I suspect that we disagree about the reasons why a choice's income-effects will influence its economic inefficiency even if those income effects have no impact on poverty or income-wealth inequality. Admittedly, we both believe that such income-effects will affect economic efficiency by creating or extending lives (on my more precise account, by creating or extending wrongful or non-wrongful lives lived by moral-rights holders who would or could properly be deemed to place positive or negative dollar values on the extra days of life or lives in question). However, Harberger attributes the other impacts that a choice's income-effects will have on economic efficiency even if those income-effects do not affect poverty or income/wealth inequality to the income-effects' altering relevant demand and possibly marginal-cost curves (though he does not reference the general-equilibrium relationships that may yield the marginal-cost effects in question) whereas I attribute such income-effects' impacts on economic efficiency to their altering relevant marginal-allocative-value (MLV) curves, average-fixed-allocative-cost (AFLC) curves, and marginal-allocative-cost (MLC) curves by altering not only these allocative curves' private counterparts but also the incidences and magnitudes of the relevant economy's Pareto imperfections and derivatively the impact that the choice-changed operative Pareto imperfections have on the divergences between any pair of DD and MLV curves, AFC (average-[private-]fixed-cost) and AFLC issues, and MC and MLC curves. Moreover, I also suspect that Harberger and I disagree about the impact that a choice's income-effects have on economic efficiency by altering (if it does alter) the extent of poverty and/or income/wealth inequality in the society in question. Section 1.4 listed the large number of ways in which a choice's impact on poverty and income/wealth inequality can affect its impact on economic inefficiency: it seems reasonable to assume that Harberger ignored these relationships, given that, in 1971, no economist wrote about the possibility or, I think, recognized the reality that poverty and inequality might/will cause economic inefficiency.

Fifth, Harberger recognizes both (1) that economies may contain a wide variety of Pareto imperfections—his "brief list [ ]" includes taxes on the margin of income, imperfections in what I call QV-investment competition (in his account: seller supernormal profits), imperfections in seller price-competition (prices that exceed marginal costs), monopsony profits (realized by buyers because they have power as buyers), monopsony-generated positive differences between the marginal cost of a unit of a product to a buyer and that unit's price (generated by the combination of the buyer's monopsony power and its not being able to engage in perfect price discrimination as a buyer either at all or without incurring special costs to do so), and externalities of many different sorts (Harberger 1971, pp. 794–795), (2) that economic-efficiency analysts are often asked to predict or post-dict the economic efficiency of increasing or decreasing a Pareto imperfection (which he denominates "a distortion" and Lipsey denominates "a source") in an economy that contains one or more other Pareto imperfections "over whose presence neither… [the economic-efficiency analyst] nor his client have [sic] control" (Harberger 1971, p. 795), (3) that individual Pareto imperfections or sets of Pareto imperfections can either compound or counteract (in his terms "neutralize") each other (Harberger 1971, p. 795), and (4) that the goal of an economic-efficiency analysis in a situation in which it is not possible (or economically efficient) to eliminate all Pareto imperfections is to identify the choice "that entails the minimum cost of [what some analysts—not I—term] distortions" (Harberger 1971, p. 795).

Sixth, Harberger appears to recognize that (except rarely and fortuitously) in an economy that is not oPp the non-target Pareto imperfections the economy contains will render inaccurate the conclusions of any analysis that assumes that the economic efficiency of a choice equals its impact on the sum of the buyer surplus and seller surplus realized by the buyers and sellers whose dollar valuations and dollar cost realities determine respectively the demand and supply curves in a traditional deadweight-loss-analysis diagram. Moreover, there is every reason to believe that Harberger realizes that, to secure accurate conclusions about the impact of choices on the magnitudes of those categories of economic inefficiency an economy contains to whose analysis deadweight-loss diagrams can contribute, one will have to replace the traditional deadweight-loss analysis with an analysis that equates the economic-efficiency impact of the choice with (1) the area between the pre-choice marginal-allocative-value and marginal-allocative-cost curves for the product in question between that product's pre-choice actual and economically-efficient outputs *minus* (2) the area between the post-choice marginal-allocative-value and marginal-allocative-cost curves for the product in question between that product's post-choice actual and economically-efficient outputs where (1) the marginal-allocative-value (MLV) curves in question can and probably should be derived by adjusting the associated pre-choice and post-choice demand curves (DD) for the product to take account of sales taxes and the difference that the operative Pareto imperfections generate between the marginal allocative values of successive units of any good and the highest dollar value to any potential consumer of successive units of the good in question, (2) the marginal-allocative-cost (MLC) curves in question can and probably should be derived by adjusting the associated pre-choice and post-choice supply curves for the product (the pre-choice and post-choice marginal-cost [MC] curves for the product) to reflect the differences that, taken together, the operative Pareto imperfections generate between the marginal allocative cost and marginal private cost to its producer of the successive units of the good in question that could be produced, and (3) the pre-choice allocatively-efficient output is the output at which the pre-choice MLV curve cuts the pre-choice MLC curve from above and the post-choice allocatively-efficient output is the output at which the post-choice MLV curve cuts the post-choice MLC curve from above.

Seventh, Harberger's article suggests that he mistakenly assumes that the adjustments just described will always be the adjustments that are associated with the substitution of a general-equilibrium analysis of the relevant issue for a partial-equilibrium analysis of that issue (Harberger 1971, pp. 786, 789, 790, and 791). This association claim is mistaken because, although general-equilibrium analyses, unlike partial-equilibrium analyses, will recognize that Pareto imperfections that are located in a different sector from the sector in which the target sector is located can cause MLV curves to diverge from DD curves and MLC curves to diverge from MC curves, both partial-equilibrium analyses and general-equilibrium analyses will recognize that Pareto imperfections that are located in the same sector as the target imperfection can cause a relevant MLV curve to diverge from the associated DD curve and a relevant MLC curve to diverge from an associated MC curve. (This Harberger mistake is worth pointing out *inter alia* because it is one of the errors that undermines Mishan's claim that, in more modern terminology, in many cases, it will be TBLE to take no account of The General Theory of Second Best.)

Eighth, Harberger does not seem to appreciate the fact that the deadweight-loss-diagram approach cannot be used economic efficiently to analyze the economic efficiency of a choice's impact on the allocative cost of the resources that are devoted to QV-investment creation or PPR execution. The protocol for economic-efficiency analysis I claim is TBLE covers the categories of economic inefficiency that can be generated by resource allocations from and/or to QV-investment-creating and PPR-executing uses.

I turn next to Harberger's conclusions and his reasons for those conclusions. On my reading, Harberger is claiming that (1) applied welfare economists can increase economic efficiency by predicting or post-dicting the economic efficiency of increasing or decreasing a Pareto imperfection (in his terms, "a distortion") when the change in the Pareto imperfection that the choice did/would effectuate was/would be small—more specifically, in more modern terminology, that it will be third-best allocatively efficient to use an appropriately-adjusted deadweight-loss analysis to assess the economic efficiency of choices that effectuate only a small change in a target Pareto imperfection—but (2) applied welfare economists cannot increase economic efficiency by predicting or post-dicting the economic efficiency of increasing or decreasing a Pareto imperfection when the choice in question did/would have a large effect on the Pareto imperfection it targets (Harberger 1971, pp. 791–792). It appears to me that Harberger offers two justifications for this pair of conclusions: (1) (A) choices that did/would effectuate large changes in the magnitudes of exemplars of the type of Pareto imperfection they target but not choices that did/would effectuate small changes in the magnitudes of exemplars of the type of Pareto imperfection they target may have large income-effects (e.g., may save or cost human lives), (B) these income-effects will often have a critical impact on the economic efficiency of the choices that generate them (not only on the impact those choices have on the total utility of all creatures whose utility counts), and (C) no TBLE protocol can be devised to identify the income-effects and the related (total utility or) economic-efficiency effects of choices that would effectuate a large change in the magnitudes of the type of Pareto imperfection they respectively target and (2) (A) one or more other mathematical functions whose attributes may critically affect the economic efficiency of a choice that will be well-behaved over the range of parameter values that will be implicated by a choice that effectuates a small change in the magnitudes of the type of Pareto imperfection it targets may not be well-behaved over the range of parameter values that will be in play for a choice that effectuates a large change in the magnitude of the type of Pareto imperfection it targets (Harberger 1971, p. 792), and (B) no TBLE protocol can be devised to estimate/guesstimate the mathematical functions in question. I am not persuaded by either of these arguments. I believe that, even in a world in which the theoretical relationships and empirical realities that underlie The General Theory of Second Best prevail, a third-best-allocatively-efficient protocol can be devised for predicting/post-dicting the economic efficiency both of choices that did/would have small income-effects because they did/would have a small impact on the magnitudes of the Pareto imperfections they did/would respectively target and of choices that did/would have large income-effects because they did/would have a large impact on the magnitudes of the Pareto imperfections they did/would respectively target. Indeed, I see no reason to believe either that the probability that it will be *ex ante* economically efficient to take account of the economic-efficiency impact of a choice's income-effects will be lower than the probability that it will be *ex ante* economically efficient to take account of the presence of all or any subset of the non-target Pareto imperfections in the economy (i.e., to identify MLV curves that accurately reflect the way in which the economy's various Pareto imperfections interact to cause the relevant MLV curves to diverge from the DD curves in standard deadweight-loss diagrams and to identify the relevant MLC curves that accurately reflect the way in which the economy's various Pareto imperfections interact to cause those MLC curves to diverge from the MC curves in the standard deadweight-loss diagram) or that, if it proves to be *ex ante* economically inefficient to estimate the economic-efficiency impact of a choice's income-effects (to estimate the choice's income-effect and predict that effect's impact on economic efficiency), that reality will preclude the analyst from increasing economic efficiency by making economic-efficiency prediction/post-dictions that ignore the impact that the choice under review has on economic efficiency by generating income-effects. My inability to explain Harberger's failure to address the preceding two claims lies behind my previously-articulated concern that I may have failed to fully understand his argument. (As I have already indicated, I do recognize the difficulty of determining the impact that a choice has on economic efficiency by altering the number of creatures whose experiences of life count in any economic-efficiency calculation and/or the duration and quality of the lives of any such creatures. For my position on these issues and comments of the positions that others have taken on them, see Markovits 2008, pp. 38–41).

So far, I have focused on Harberger's discussion of the ability of analysts to use deadweight-loss-diagram analyses to generate TBLE predictions/post-dictions of the impact of choices on the functional category of economic inefficiency on which those sorts of diagrams have focused—viz., UO-to-UO (in practice, inter-ARDEPPS UO-to-UO) misallocation. Obviously, the deadweight-loss diagram would have to be "adjusted" substantially to be used to analyze the impact of choices on functional categories of resource allocations that involve the net withdrawal of resources from or the net devotion of resources to uses that are associated with fixed-cost expenditures—QV-to-UO or UO-to-QV resource allocations, UO-to-PPR or PPR-to-UO resource allocations, and (QV + PPR + UO) creation-and-use pairs of functionally-related uses to a (QV, PPR, or UO) creation-and-use pair of functionally-related uses. I also do not think that it would be TBLE to use an adapted variant of the standard deadweight-loss diagram to analyze the impact of choices on a wide variety of other categories of economic inefficiency or economic-efficiency-impact-relevant allocative costs. Of course, my doubts about the TBLE of using an adapted deadweight-loss-diagram approach to predict/post-dict the impact of choices on economic efficiency do not undercut my confidence that it will be TBLE to use some more-or-less-refined variant of the approach I am recommending to predict/post-dict the economic efficiency of choices.

For balance, I conclude this discussion of Harberger's position with Richard Lipsey's assessment, which concludes that Harberger errs in the opposite direction from the direction in which I claim he errs—specifically, that concludes or at least seems to imply that it will not be possible to devise a TBLE protocol for predicting/post-dicting the economic efficiency of any choice, regardless of the size of the change(s) it effectuates in the magnitude(s) of the Pareto imperfection(s) it targets. I quote Lipsey (2007), pp. 358–359:

> Harberger…argues that second best policies are easier to establish than…[Lancaster and Lipsey] maintained. In a space for the set of all (economic) activities he plots the subset of those that are affected by significant distortions and the subset of activities that would be affected if public policy alters one of these. He argues that the interaction of these sets is all that matters for small changes in public policy because a marginal policy-induced change in any non-distorted activity has no significant effect on welfare [for my purposes, on economic efficiency]. He states that the area of this intersection is small enough "…to dispel any thoughts that the job of incorporating general equilibrium aspects [in my view, a mischaracterization] is so big as to be effectively hopeless." My response is twofold. First, I am skeptical of Harberger's judgment that the proportion is small. As a first approximation, I would say it was close to 100%. Second, I know of no evidence that the space of activities affected by the typical new policy is small. After all, sectors everywhere can be affected by a 'distortion' anywhere and to say that only a few markets will be affected by changing a *source* in one is an empirical judgment whose substantiation requires evidence gathered case by case.

I turn now to theoretical-Welfare-Economics scholarship that makes two general sorts of claims or pairs of related claims. The first general sort of claim is that a specified general decision-rule either (1) is second-best-allocatively-efficient (SBLE) in that its application will always increase economic efficiency or (2) is third-best-allocatively-efficient (TBLE) in that it will always be *ex ante* most economically efficient for it to be implemented even if one or more of its applications does not turn out to increase economic efficiency. The theoretical-Welfare-Economics literature contains articles that make one or both of these claims for 6 general decision-rules. (I am ignoring the fact that the actual claims that are made focus on the specified decision-rules' impact on social welfare rather than economic efficiency. I am also ignoring the fact that the relevant articles' authors do not clearly distinguish between the second-best-allocative-efficiency-oriented and third-best-allocative-efficiency-oriented variants of these claims.) The second general sort of claim is that decisions to implement a particular specified decision-rule will "generally" increase economic efficiency—a claim that is not a SBLE claim and is not accompanied by an explicit TBLE claim, though I assume that anyone who claims that the implementation of a particular rule will generally increase economic efficiency (social welfare) does so to convince readers that the implementation of this rule will be third-best-allocatively-efficient (will be best from the perspective of social welfare).

I will now delineate each of the 6 decision-rules in question and criticize the claims that their implementation will be SBLE or TBLE. I should acknowledge at the outset that in one respect the criticisms I will make of the 6 decision-rules to which I will now turn are expositionally premature. They would be better-grounded and probably more convincing if I could rely on this book's subsequent analyses of the way in which an economy's various Pareto imperfections interact to cause or not cause the profits yielded by an allocation of resources from the production of just-extra-marginal units of some product Y to the production of a marginal unit of another product X to diverge from the economic efficiency of that allocation—*inter alia*, (1) on the ways in which different Pareto imperfections cause (A) marginal cost to diverge from marginal-allocative cost and marginal revenue to diverge from marginal-allocative value and, relatedly, (B) MC_X/MC_Y to diverge from the marginal rate of transformation of Y into X and P_X/P_Y to diverge from the marginal rate of substitution of Y for X and (2) on the various reasons why it will not be *ex ante* economically efficient to assume that the Pareto imperfections that are present in the area of product-space to which a relevant resource allocation devotes resources will equal their economy-wide weighted-average counterparts.

The first decision-rule in question instructs the decision-maker to make any choice that reduces the magnitude of the absolutely-largest exemplar of any type of Pareto imperfection toward but not below the magnitude of the average Pareto imperfection of that type in the relevant economy. (I have added the part of this account of the decision-rule in question that begins with "toward": some supporters of "the rule" do not include this language).

I have 6 objections to the specification of this rule or the claims that it is SBLE and/or TBLE. My first objection is to the specification (actually, to the lack of specification) of this rule. Proponents of this rule have never specified their definition of the magnitude of any exemplar of any type of Pareto imperfection. For example, they have never stated whether the magnitude of an imperfection in seller price-competition is an increasing function of $(P - MC)$, $(P - MC)/P$, or $(P - MC)/MC$ or whether the magnitude of an externality (say external cost [XC]) imperfection is an increasing function of the external cost generated by the production of a marginal unit of a relevant product, the ratio of that external cost to the (internal) marginal cost of producing that unit, the ratio of that external cost to the average-total cost of producing that unit, etc.

My second objection to "the claim" that has been made for the first rule is directed at the variant of that claim that asserts that the first rule is second-best-allocatively-efficient and, derivatively, that its implementation will always be third-best-allocatively-efficient: even if the relevant economy is oPp, the choice under consideration does not change the "sign" of the Pareto imperfection (e.g., does not reduce a price that originally exceeded marginal cost below marginal cost or does not overinternalize what was originally an external marginal cost), the various exemplars of the target type of Pareto imperfection counteract each other, and a choice that reduces a target Pareto imperfection that was originally the largest exemplar of that type of Pareto imperfection to or toward the average or economy-wide weighted-average magnitude of that type of Pareto imperfection may not reduce economic efficiency if the relevant set of other extant exemplars of the target type of Pareto imperfections is not a random sample of such imperfections but is a sample of those imperfections whose weighted-average magnitude is greater than the economy-wide weighted-average magnitude of that type of Pareto imperfection. Thus, in an oPp economy, a choice that reduces the P/MC ratio of a product whose P/MC ratio was originally the highest in the economy toward the weighted-average P/MC ratio in the economy (when the weights attached to different products' P/MC ratios are proportionate to the allocative value of the resources devoted to the respective products' production) will not reduce (say) UO-to-UO misallocation if the pre-choice weighted-average P/MC ratio of the competitors of the product whose P/MC ratio is targeted (where the weights assigned to the P/MC ratios of the respective individual competitors of the product whose price is being targeted are [roughly speaking] proportionate to the allocative benefits that the resources that would be withdrawn from the production of the respective competitors in question would have yielded in that competitor's employ when the target product's price was reduced) is higher than the economy-wide weighted-average P/MC ratio and (put crudely) the ratio of (the weighted-average P/MC ratio of the target product's competitors) to (the target product's post-choice P/MC ratio) *exceeds* the ratio of (the target product's pre-choice P/MC ratio) to (its competitors' weighted-average P/MC ratio). (I am ignoring *inter alia* the P/MC ratios of complements of the target product and the complements of its competitors and not directly addressing the possibility that the choice may change the P/MC ratios of its competitors.)

My third objection is that the claim that the first decision-rule is SBLE (and TBLE) ignores the fact that the relevant economy will contain exemplars of other types of Pareto imperfections. Even if the immediately-preceding objection is not critical (even if the effectuation of the rule would always bring the P/MC ratio of the target product closer to the weighted-average P/MC ratio of its competitors), the application of the rule would not increase economic efficiency if (in the case of UO-to-UO misallocation) the interaction of the exemplars of the non-target types of Pareto imperfections the economy contained pre-choice and the pre-choice target Pareto imperfection (which is by assumption the largest exemplar of its type of Pareto imperfection in the economy pre-choice) generated less misallocation than would be generated by the interaction of the non-target types of Pareto imperfections the economy would contain post-choice and the post-choice, smaller target imperfection (regardless of whether the choice would indirectly affect the magnitudes of the economy's non-target types of Pareto imperfections).

My fourth objection is that the claim that the implementation of the first rule will always be SBLE ignores the possibility that, even if the choice that reduces the magnitude of the largest Pareto imperfection of the target type to or toward the weighted-average magnitude of the relevant economy's Pareto imperfections of that type does reduce the absolute magnitude of the aggregate distortion in the profits yielded by the economics-marginal resource allocations whose aggregate-profit-distortions it affects, it may not decrease economic inefficiency on that account if it changes the sign of the operative aggregate-profit-distortion because in so doing it may increase the absolute difference between the allocative cost of the resources actually devoted to the functional category of resource allocations in question and the amount of resources measured by their allocative cost that would be economically efficient to devote to that functional category of resource allocations.

My fifth objection is that the claim that the implementation of the first rule will always be SBLE ignores the possibility that, even if the implementation of the rule reduces the absolute magnitudes of the aggregate distortions in the profits yielded by the economics-marginal exemplars of the categories of resource allocations it affects without changing the sign of those distortions, it may not increase economic efficiency if it changes the distributions of income and wealth in ways that increase economic inefficiency.

My sixth and final objection is that no one has ever made any argument to establish the conclusion that it would be TBLE to implement the rule now under consideration when its implementation would not be SBLE and I see no reason to believe that the implementation of this rule would be TBLE when it would not be SBLE.

The second general decision-rule that has been proposed is: "It will always increase economic efficiency or it will always be TBLE to assume that it will be economically efficient to substitute two smaller Pareto imperfections of any type for one larger Pareto imperfection of that type whose magnitude equals the sum of the replaced Pareto imperfections or to substitute (what I call) two smaller absolute aggregate distortions in the profits yielded by two economics-marginal resource allocations for one larger absolute distortion in the profits yielded by one economics-marginal resource allocation when the sum of the absolute values of the two smaller distortions equals the absolute value of the larger distortion." My objections to this second general rule are similar to my objections to its predecessor:

(1) the variant that focuses on Pareto imperfections is ill-specified in that it does not specify how the magnitude of any type of Pareto imperfection is to be measured;

(2) the claim that the variant of this decision-rule that focuses on Pareto imperfections is SBLE is wrong because it ignores the possibilities that (A) even if the choice does not change the "sign" of the Pareto imperfections it affects, non-target Pareto imperfections may critically affect the economic efficiency of the recommended "substitution" by causing it not to "substitute" two smaller aggregate-profit-distortions of a given sign for one larger absolute aggregate-profit-distortion of the same sign whose magnitude equals the sum of the two smaller distortions, (B) even if the choice in question does substitute two smaller absolute aggregate-profit-distortions for one larger absolute aggregate distortion whose absolute magnitude equals the sum of the absolute magnitudes of the two smaller distortions, the choice may not increase economic efficiency if it changes the sign of the aggregate-profit-distortions in question, (C) even if the choice in question does substitute two smaller absolute aggregate-profit distortions for one larger absolute aggregate-profit distortion that equals the sum of the absolute values of the two smaller aggregate profit-distortions without changing those profit distortions' signs, it may not increase economic efficiency if it affects the distributions of income and wealth in ways that increase the amount of economic inefficiency that is generated; and

(3) if, for one or more of the above reasons, the rule now under consideration is not SBLE, no argument has been made for the claim that and I see no reason to suspect that its implementation will be TBLE.

The third general decision-rule that has been proposed (Hoff 2001) is: "Always reduce to a small magnitude rather than eliminate a Pareto imperfection or distortion." I have three objections to the claim that this decision-rule is either SBLE or TBLE. First, the variant of this claim that focuses on Pareto imperfections ignores the fact that the impact that either eliminating a Pareto imperfection or reducing a Pareto imperfection to make it small without eliminating it will have on the aggregate distortions in the profits yielded by various economics-marginal resource allocations and thereby on economic efficiency will be affected by the other Pareto imperfections the economy in question will contain respectively when the target Pareto imperfection is small and when it is zero. Second, if the variant of this claim that references "distortions" is defining this word in the way in which I define it as opposed to defining it to refer to what I call Pareto imperfections and Lipsey calls "sources" of non-optimal outcomes, the claim for the greater economic efficiency of making distortions small as opposed to eliminating them (1) would be wrong if one assumed (A) that all resource allocators were sovereign maximizers and (B) that eliminating the distortion would *not* be (i) more allocative-transaction-costly, (ii) more prone to increase risk costs and the allocative costs that resource allocators generate to reduce the risk costs they bear, (iii) more allocative-efficiency-costly to publicly finance, or (iv) more prone to generate allocative-efficiency losses by preventing complementary resources from being controlled by single entities and (2) would also be wrong if the conditions listed after "(1)(B)" in this sentence were fulfilled unless the combination of the errors that resource allocators would make if there were small distortions and those small distortions would always yield less misallocation than would be yielded by the combination of the errors that resource allocators would make if there were no distortions and no distortions were present (a condition in whose fulfillment there is no reason to believe). Third, once more, if this third decision-rule is not SBLE, no argument has been made for its third-best-allocative-efficiency, and I see no reason to believe that it would be TBLE.

The fourth decision-rule that has been proposed is: "Make all choices that will reduce the aggregate distortion in the profits yielded by an economics-marginal resource allocation (presumably if one can do so without generating allocative transaction costs, risk costs, risk-cost-avoidance-move allocative costs, and public-finance-of-decision-implementation-generated misallocation that are collectively prohibitive)." The argument that, under the conditions just specified, this decision-rule will be SBLE is wrong for three reasons: (1) regardless of whether the incidence and character of the errors that relevant resource allocators make are altered by decisions that satisfy this rule, the interaction of the larger distortion and the errors that resource allocators will make when it is generated may yield less economic inefficiency than the combination of the smaller distortion and the errors that resource allocators will make when the smaller distortion is generated; (2) if the choice that reduces the aggregate distortion in the profits yielded by an economics-marginal resource allocation changes the sign of that distortion, it may not increase economic efficiency; (3) even if the choice that reduces the absolute magnitude of a relevant aggregate-profit distortion does not change that distortion's sign, the choice may not increase economic efficiency if it increases economic inefficiency by altering the distributions of income and wealth. Moreover, no argument has been made for the claim that, under the conditions specified, it will always be TBLE to implement this fourth decision-rule if the rule is not SBLE, and this latter claim seems extremely unlikely to be correct.

The fifth decision-rule that has been recommended is: "When one can do so, always make the two-part decision of reducing the largest Pareto imperfection of any type toward the weighted-average Pareto imperfection of that type and increasing the smallest Pareto imperfection of that type toward the weighted-average Pareto imperfection of that type." (Admittedly, this claim was not explicitly made for all types of Pareto imperfections: it was made for tax rates when the tax-rate changes raise revenue and the taxed goods are substitutes for the aggregate of all goods. However, I see no reason why the argument would not apply to all other types of Pareto imperfections if it were correct for taxes on the margin of income.) Once more, this general rule is ill-specified in that it does not indicate the metric for the magnitude of any type of Pareto imperfection. The claim that this decision-rule is SBLE is wrong because (1) it ignores the fact that the relevant economy will contain exemplars of many non-target types of Pareto imperfections that will affect the impacts of the target Pareto imperfection on relevant aggregate-profit-distortion figures and thereby on economic efficiency, (2) it ignores the possibility that relevant resource allocators may make errors, and (3) it ignores the possibility that the choice in question may affect economic efficiency by changing the distributions of income and wealth. Moreover, no one has ever made an argument for the conclusion that it will be TBLE to implement this decision-rule when the rule is not SBLE, and it seems highly unlikely that it will be TBLE to do so in such cases.

The sixth and final general rule that has been proposed that I will discuss is: "Starting from a tax-distorted situation, always execute proportional reductions in all 'distortions'." According to Lipsey (Lipsey 2007, p. 360), the proponents of this decision-rule (Atkinson and Stiglitz 1976) claimed not that it was SBLE but that implementing it would "generally" increase "social welfare" (for which I am substituting "economic efficiency"). Before criticizing this decision-rule, I want to make two preliminary comments. First, I assume that its proponents are using the term "distortions" to refer to what I call Pareto imperfections (and Lipsey calls "sources" [of non-optimal outcomes]). Second, I find it difficult to assess whether the implementation of this rule will generally increase economic efficiency (or some conception of social welfare) not just because of the non-specificity of the word "generally" but also because I would need to have a lot more empirical data to estimate the percentage of cases in which the implementation of this rule would increase economic efficiency or social welfare. I will now make 6 observations about this rule. First, if the word "distortion" is a synonym for "Pareto imperfection," the rule is ill-specified because no metric is proposed for the magnitude of any type of Pareto imperfection. Second, if "distortion" is being used as a synonym for "Pareto imperfection," it will not be SBLE to secure proportional reductions in all taxes on the margin of income (or in all exemplars of any other type of Pareto imperfection), regardless of how one measures the magnitude of each type of Pareto imperfection): (A) even in an oPp economy, proportional reductions in all exemplars of a particular type of Pareto imperfection will not always increase economic efficiency, and (B) when the relevant economy contains exemplars of other types of Pareto imperfections, proportional reductions in all exemplars of a target type of Pareto imperfection will not always increase economic efficiency, regardless of the impact those reductions have on the magnitudes of the other types of Pareto imperfections the relevant economy contains. Third, I suspect that, in an oPp economy, proportional reductions in the magnitudes of all exemplars of a single type of Pareto imperfection will probably tend to (will "generally"?) increase economic efficiency (if one ignores the other allocative costs and economic-efficiency losses the implementation of such a rule might generate) because, at least in relation to several categories of economic inefficiency, the exemplars of any one type of Pareto imperfection will counteract each other's tendency to distort relevant profit-figures and proportional reductions in their size will tend to reduce the absolute differences between them and in so doing increase how completely they offset each other. Fourth, in an economy that is not oPp, I see little reason to believe that proportional reductions in the magnitudes of the exemplars of a particular type of Pareto imperfection will "generally" increase economic efficiency. Fifth, although the following conclusion is disfavored by the fact that resource-allocator errors may be made both when relevant aggregate-profit distortions are higher and when they are proportionally lower, I suspect that proportional reductions in distortions in the above sense (indeed, any reductions in aggregate-profit distortions) will generally increase economic efficiency. Sixth, I see no reason to believe that in our actual, otherwise-Pareto-imperfect economy it will be TBLE to implement a decision-rule that instructs the decision-maker always to execute proportional reductions in either Pareto imperfections or aggregate-profit-distortions.

To summarize: I am not persuaded by the theoretical-Welfare-Economics literature that claims that the particular decision-rules it claims are SBLE, TBLE, or "generally" economically efficient are SBLE (or always social-welfare-enhancing), TBLE, or "generally" economically efficient. In my judgment, these attempts to respond appropriately to The General Theory of Second Best have not succeeded.

No discussion of the theoretical-Welfare-Economics literature that takes account of and attempts to respond appropriately to The General Theory of Second Best should conclude without commenting on Drèze and Stern's excellent article *The Theory of Cost-Benefit Analysis* (Drèze and Stern 1987). Although this study is primarily directed at identifying the optimal protocol for government decision-makers who are seeking to maximize "social welfare" to use when evaluating public-sector investment-projects, most of its analyses apply equally well when the objective function is economic efficiency and, as they say (Drèze and Stern 1987, p. 90), "the theory we develop also offers clear guidelines for the evaluation of government decisions in such varied fields as tax, trade or incomes policies, the provision of public goods, the distribution of rationed commodities, or the licensing of private investment." Indeed, I would say that the relevant parts of Drèze and Stern's analysis apply to the prediction/post-diction of the economic efficiency of all government and non-government choices.

Drèze and Stern's article has a substantial number of virtues that are not solely related to the fact that it is a highly-skilled response to The General Theory of Second Best. For example, (1) it takes great care to define precisely the key verbal expressions it uses, (2) it incorporates usefully general-equilibrium mathematical models whose value is not restricted to the contribution they can make to the development of Second-Best Theory and the analysis of the economic efficiency of particular government or non-government choices, and, more generally, (3) it clearly exposits the mathematical models whose use it recommends. For the purposes of this study, Drèze and Stern's article is particularly notable and praiseworthy because it (1) explicitly references and recognizes the importance of The General Theory of Second Best (Drèze and Stern 1987, pp. 920–923), (2) incorporates instructive scholarship by others that takes useful account of this General Theory (Drèze and Stern 1987, pp. 937–953), (3) develops mathematical models that advance significantly our understanding of the SBLE way to respond to The General Theory of Second Best (Drèze and Stern 1987, *passim*.), (4) as I previously indicated, recognizes (at Drèze and Stern 1987, p. 910) that one must take account of The General Theory of Second Best not only when analyzing the impact of choices on UO-to-UO misallocation (which is the type of economic efficiency on which they primarily focus) and the misallocation caused when, given the total allocative cost of the resources devoted to investment, too many or too few resources are devoted to public investment relative to the amount of resources that are devoted to private investment from the perspective of economic efficiency (a concern that is understandable for theorists who are primarily focusing on the evaluation of public investment-projects) but also on the misallocation that can be generated by government decisions to create or secure the creation of public goods or to secure the execution of investments that would create products that are not public goods, (5) recognizes (Drèze and Stern 1987, pp. 913 and 919) that imperfections in the information available to particular government decision-makers may affect the optimal way for them to respond to questions they are asked to answer (that the approach and answer to a question that is TBLE will often be quite different from their SBLE counterparts), (6) recognizes that taxes on the margin of income, imperfections in seller-competition, and externalities can cause marginal rates of transformation to diverge from marginal-cost ratios (Drèze and Stern 1987, p. 917), and (7) recognizes that much more work needs to be done on the ways in which various Pareto imperfections interact to generate the categories of economic inefficiency on which their article focuses (Drèze and Stern 1987, p. 984).

On the other hand, from my perspective, it is important to point out as well that the Drèze and Stern article and the valuable Second-Best-Theory scholarship by others that it profits from using are deficient in several respects. Specifically, these pieces of valuable scholarship (1) do not identify or analyze the impact of choices on most of the categories of economic inefficiency whose magnitudes can be affected by the government decisions on which they are focusing, (2) do not identify all the types of Pareto imperfections that can cause marginal rates of transformation to diverge from marginal-cost ratios or the way in which the relevant Pareto imperfections interact to cause or not cause such divergences, (3) do not consider the possibility that Pareto imperfections (except perhaps for consumer non-sovereignty and non-maximization) may cause marginal rates of substitution to diverge from price ratios, (4) do not take account of the fact that any public or private investment will withdraw resources from some UO-producing, some QV-creating, and some PPR-executing uses and therefore that any such investment's private cost will almost certainly be distorted by the different interactions of the various Pareto imperfections that would individually respectively distort in an oPp economy the private benefits that the relevant sacrificed UO-producing, QV-creating, and PPR-executing resource-uses would have conferred on their respective alternative potential users, (5) do not analyze in any detail the protocol a decision-maker should use to identify the differences between the second-best-allocatively-efficient (welfare-maximizing) and the third-best-allocatively-efficient (welfare-maximizing) protocols for predicting or post-dicting the economic efficiency (social-welfare impact) of any choice, and relatedly (6) do not develop a protocol for economic-efficiency prediction/post-diction whose use would be third-best-allocatively-efficient.

The preceding discussion has revealed that, although no theoretical-Welfare-Economics article makes a serious attempt to work out a protocol for economic-efficiency analysis whose use would be second-best-allocatively-efficient or third-best-allocatively-efficient, a significant number of such articles do execute analyses that generate useful conclusions that can contribute to the development of a protocol for economic-efficiency analysis whose use would be TBLE. I acknowledge the obvious fact that it is not reasonable to judge individual pieces of scholarship by whether they do everything that is required: progress comes in small steps, and each step that leads to the desired goal should be valued and praised. Still, it does seem fair to ask whether, taken as a whole, the corpus of post-1956 theoretical-Welfare-Economics literature has responded appropriately to The General Theory of Second Best. Does a balanced review of this body of the literature support or disfavor the conclusion of one theoretical welfare economist who has done much valuable work that "Second-Best Theory…[Is] Ageing Well at Sixty" (Boadway 1977) or is my and I think Lispey's far-less-positive assessment (Lipsey 2007; 2017a, b; Lipsey and Ng 2017a, b) closer to the mark? I do not think that this disagreement can be attributed to the favorable assessor's perceiving the glass to be half-full and the disappointed assessor's perceiving it to be half-empty.

In my judgment, an on-balance negative assessment of the corpus of post-1956 theoretical-Welfare-Economics literature is warranted by the fact that, taken as a whole, it has the following 7 deficiencies. First, it does not identify many of the categories of economic inefficiency an economy can generate. Second, it does not establish the different ways in which all exemplars of all types of Pareto imperfections interact to cause or not cause both the categories of economic inefficiency it does identify and consider separately and (of course) the categories of economic inefficiency it fails to identify (A) by distorting the profits yielded by or that would have been yielded by relevant exemplars of the various categories of resource allocations that are associated with categories of resource misallocation that it is *ex ante* economically efficient to identify and consider separately and/or (B) by causing resource allocators to execute/(fail to execute) unprofitable/profitable resource allocations in each relevant category. Third, it does not examine the determinants of the allocative costs and benefits of doing the various theoretical and empirical research that can inform economic-efficiency analyses and of devoting additional time to considering the economic-efficiency implications of what is known (i.e., has not examined the issues one must resolve to identify the difference between the protocol for executing the analysis of one or more economic-efficiency issues that would be second-best-allocatively-efficient and the protocol that is third-best-allocatively-efficient)—*inter alia*, it does not develop an approach to determining the conditions under which it will be third-best-allocatively-efficient to pay some attention to all types of Pareto imperfections and the conditions under which it will be third-best-allocatively-efficient to ignore altogether certain types of Pareto imperfections when analyzing the impact of a choice on the amount of a particular category of economic inefficiency the economy in question contains and therefore does not analyze the third-best economic efficiency of executing more-complete or less-complete analyses of the impact of a choice on the amount of specific categories of economic inefficiency. Fourth, it does not develop a protocol for executing either the more-complete or the less-complete analyses of the impact of a choice on a particular category of economic inefficiency just referenced. Fifth, it does not pay any attention to the various ways in which choices can affect economic efficiency by increasing or decreasing poverty and/or inequality and therefore does not develop any protocol for analyzing the impact that choices will have on economic efficiency by altering the distributions of income and wealth or by affecting the parameters that determine the amount of economic inefficiency that is generated by relevant given degrees of poverty and inequality. Sixth, it does not analyze the determinants of (1) a choice's impact on private transaction costs, risk costs, or the private costs that actors generate to reduce the risk costs they bear or (2)(A) the ratio of the relevant allocative transaction costs to the relevant private transaction costs or (B) the ratio of the allocative to the private cost of risk-cost-avoidance moves. Seventh, although some of the relevant scholarship recognizes that government choices that increase/decrease government expenditures will (usually) increase/decrease economic inefficiency on that account because the decisions government makes to finance its operations are (usually) *ceteris paribus* misallocative, none of the relevant scholarship analyzes the determinants of the amount of misallocation government will generate when raising various relevant amounts of revenue.

Perhaps, I should be embarrassed. Basically, I have just argued that the post-1956 theoretical-Welfare-Economics literature does not as a whole respond appropriately to The General Theory of Second Best because the corpus of this literature does not do what this book does (what I think should be done). But even if the preceding list of deficiencies is too tightly tied to my recommended protocol for analyzing the economic efficiency of choices, it should be clear that a more generic set of criticisms of the corpus of post-1956 theoretical-Welfare-Economics litera-ture would be warranted.

I hope that the preceding critique of the post-1956 theoretical-Welfare-Economics literature is convincing by itself. However, even if it is not, the com-bination of the preceding arguments and the discussions in the following subsec-tions of Chap. 2 may persuade you that the overall response of the economics profession to The General Theory of Second Best has been both disappointing and inappropriate.

2.2   The Failure of the Bulk of Applied-Welfare-Economics Scholarship to Respond *Ex Ante* Economic-Efficiently to The General Theory of Second Best

Chapter 1 argues that, to be *ex ante* economically efficient, economic-efficiency analyses (1) must focus separately on the impact that the choices under investigation would/did have on the quantities of a large number of categories of economic inefficiency the relevant economy contains and (2) must execute analyses of each of these impacts that take appropriate account of the different ways that the extant exemplars of each type of Pareto imperfection interact to cause or not cause the respective relevant categories of economic inefficiency (the categories that are *ex ante* economically efficient to distinguish and consider separately). In my judgment, most applied-Welfare-Economics analyses fail on both these accounts. For reasons of both space and time, I will not provide a systematic, comprehensive survey of individual exemplars of the applied-Welfare-Economics literature. However, I will point out what appears to me to be the basic deficiencies of the different subsets of this applied literature (subsets that respectively focus on one type of Pareto imperfection and the policies that are designed to reduce the economic inefficiency that is generated by each such type of Pareto imperfection).

I start with the literature on imperfections in seller-competition and pro-competition policies. The vast bulk of the scholarship on both the economic inefficiency generated by imperfections in seller competition and the economic efficiency of prohibiting particular categories of competition-reducing conduct has three striking deficiencies: (1) the relevant studies focus exclusively on price-competition (ignore quality-or-variety-increasing-investment [QV-investment] competition—the competition through which firms in an ARDEPPS compete away their potential supernormal profits by introducing into the ARDEPPS additional [perhaps superior] product variants, opening up additional [perhaps superior] distributive outlets, or creating additional capacity and inventory)—admittedly, a competition theory as opposed to a pure-Welfare-Economics deficiency; (2) (A) virtually all of the relevant studies focus exclusively on inter-ARDEPPS UO-to-UO misallocation, the misallocation that results when assets are not owned by a single entity when it would be economically efficient for them to be so owned, and the impact of relevant choices on *private* transaction costs (which they mistakenly assume always equal *allocative* transaction costs), and (B) the exceptions expand the set of possibilities considered only to include either the possibility that a relevant imperfection in seller competition might cause goods to be produced at a higher cost than was necessary by generating so-called X inefficiency (the inefficiency that monopolies and regulated firms allegedly generate because they face less pressure to and therefore do not operate proficiently) or the possibility that the relevant conduct or choice might increase what I call QV investment (which they assume creates no allocative value), and (3) the relevant studies' analyses of the categories of economic inefficiency that imperfections in seller competition could cause or whose magnitudes pro-competition policies could reduce are FBLE—(A) assume almost-always-incorrectly that the demand curve a seller faces coincides with the marginal-allocative-value curve for its product, that the marginal-cost curve a seller faces coincides with the marginal-allocative-cost curve it faces, derivatively *inter alia* that the amount of economic inefficiency that an imperfection in seller price-competition generates by reducing the relevant seller's unit output equals the area between the demand and marginal-cost curves it faces between its actual output and the output it would sell if its price equaled its marginal cost, that the economic-efficiency gain that a pro-price-competition policy generates by increasing the directly-affected sellers' unit outputs equals the sum of the areas between their demand and marginal-cost curves between the outputs they would respectively have produced absent the policy in question and the outputs they produced post-policy, and that a competition policy that causes its addressee to make a QV investment/execute a PPR project it would not otherwise have made/executed will on that account generate an increase in economic efficiency that equals the profits the induced investment yields the investor, (B) assume that any change in the amount of private transaction costs generated will be associated with an identical change in allocative transaction costs, (C) assume that any increase in private production or investment costs that a pro-competition policy generates by preventing one or more individual firms from owning assets that are complementary for scale or non-scale reasons (e.g., by breaking up an existing firm or prohibiting or deterring internal growth) will be associated with an identical increase in allocative costs, and (D) assume that any increase in private production or investment costs that an imperfection in seller competition generates by yielding "X inefficiency" will be associated with an identical increase in allocative costs. The scholarship I am referencing includes (1) the traditional analysis of the deadweight loss of monopoly and the economic-efficiency costs of monopoly—often misdenominated the "social costs" of monopoly (see Harberger 1954; Stigler 1956; Schwartzman 1960; Kamerschen 1966; Carson 1973; Posner 1975; Bergson 1975; Cowling and Mueller 1978; Masson and Shannon 1984, and, for my critiques, Markovits 2008, pp. 272–277 and 283–286), (2) Oliver Williamson's analysis of the economic efficiency of a pro-competition policy that would prohibit a series of horizontal mergers that would convert a perfectly-competitive industry into a pure monopoly while creating a merged firm that faced lower marginal, average-variable, and average-total costs than the merger partners would have faced (see Williamson 1968 and, for my critiques, Markovits 2008, pp. 277–281 and Sect. 9.1.1.2 of this book), (3) the standard analysis of the economic efficiency of prohibiting oligopolistic pricing (or the subset of oligopolistic pricing I call "contrived-oligopolistic pricing": oligopolistic pricing in which anticompetitive threats and/or promises have been communicated), whose analysis of the impact of such pricing on inter-ARDEPPS UO-to-UO misallocation makes the same mistakes that the standard analysis of the deadweight loss of monopoly makes, that ignores the tendency of contrived-oligopolistic pricing (more specifically, of the under-cutting from positions of inferiority and the retaliation against such undercutters it spawns) to generate *intra*-ARDEPPS UO-to-UO misallocation as well as the practice's impacts on UO-to-QV or QV-to-UO, UO-to-PPR or PPR-to-UO, and

QV-to-PPR or PPR-to-QV misallocation, and that contains analyses of the private transaction-cost consequences of such prohibitions that are simplistic and that ignore the difference between private and allocative transaction costs (for my critique, see Markovits 2008, pp. 242–250, Markovits 1976b, and Sect. 9.1.2.1 of this book), and (4) analyses of the economic efficiency of prohibiting predatory conduct, horizontal mergers that lessen competition, and various categories of vertical conduct, which have many of the same deficiencies as does the standard analysis of prohibiting price-fixing (see Markovits 1985, 2008, pp. 206–210 and pp. 231–237 and Sect. 9.1.2 of this book).

I move now to the bulk of the literature on the economic efficiency of eliminating or internalizing costs or internalizing benefits that would otherwise be external—*inter alia*, the literature on the economic efficiency of accident-and-pollution-loss-focused tort law, environmental policy, and intellectual-property (IP) policy. Almost all of the relevant tort-law literature has the same two deficiencies that undermine the bulk of the competition-policy literature: (1) it focuses exclusively on only a subset of the categories of economic inefficiency whose magnitudes the relevant tort law affects—in this case, on inter-ARDEPPS and intra-ARDEPPS UO-to-UO misallocation, on choice-among-known-production-processes misallocation, and on the misallocation caused when economically-efficient research projects into less-accident-and-pollution-prone production processes and products are not executed (see Shavell 1980)—and (2) it analyzes the impact that choices that would eliminate or internalize what would otherwise be external costs would have on the magnitudes of these categories of economic inefficiency on the assumption that the economy in question is otherwise-Pareto-perfect (for a study that makes this mistake, see Shavell 1980). Thus, all standard Law & Economics analyses of the private cost and private benefits (to potential victims) of accident-and-pollution-loss-avoidance-moves and, relatedly, of the Hand formula for negligence (according to which a failure to make a particular accident-or-pollution-loss [AP-loss] avoidance-move is deemed negligent if the private cost or burden of avoidance [symbolized by "B"] is lower than the weighted-average benefits that the avoidance-move should be predicted to generate [symbolized simplistically as $\downarrow$ (PL) where "$\downarrow$" stands for "reduction in," "P" stands for the probability of the loss that might result if the avoidance-move is not made, "L" stands for the magnitude of the loss that might be avoided, and the formula assumes simplistically[3] that the avoidance-move will eliminate the possibility of the loss' occurring]) assume that the *private* cost of avoidance equals the *allocative* cost of avoidance and that the weighted-average-expected private benefits of avoidance to the prospective victims with whose losses the law is concerned equal the allocative benefits of avoidance. Both these assumptions will almost always be wrong because they ignore the facts that the economy is not oPp and that the interaction of its extant Pareto imperfections will almost always generate imperfectly-offsetting or compounding distortions in the private cost of avoidance-moves (to potential injurers) and important components of the private benefits (to the conventionally-recognized potential victims of relevant accidents and pollution) of accident-and-pollution-loss-avoidance-moves. Thus, the relevant economy's other Pareto imperfections will almost always jointly distort the private benefits that the resources that would be devoted to any resource-consuming avoidance-move would generate in their alternative UO-producing, QV-creating, and PPR-executing uses (which private benefits equal the private cost of the resources in question to the avoider) and the distortions in question will perfectly counteract each other only rarely and fortuitously. Similarly, the relevant economy's other Pareto imperfections will almost always distort the private benefits that an AP-loss-avoidance move will confer on potential victims who would be prevented from working by any injuries or illnesses they sustain because the interaction of those imperfections will almost always distort the private benefits that such prospective victims' labor would confer on their prospective employers (and hence on the lost-wage component of the victims' prospective losses) (see Markovits 1996 for more detailed discussions). Relatedly, all standard Law & Economics analyses ignore the vast majority of the reasons why the profitability of avoidance to both potential injurers and potential victims will be distorted under a negligence/contributory-negligence regime, a comparative-negligence regime, and a strict-liability regime (regardless of whether, contrary to common-law reality, strict liability is combined with a contributory-negligence or a comparative-negligence doctrine) (for detailed explanations, see Markovits 2008, pp. 253–270). The tort-law (and more general environmental-policy) literature also fails to take account of the impact of externality-internalizing policies on the magnitudes of many of the categories of economic inefficiency whose magnitudes they are likely to affect—e.g., on the magnitude of UO-to-QV misallocation. To see why this omission is salient, note that choices that eliminate or internalize what would otherwise be the external costs generated by the production and/or consumption of goods seem likely to increase UO-to-QV misallocation because (1) as I have explained elsewhere (Markovits 2008, pp. 172–201), the other types of Pareto imperfections the relevant economies contain (most importantly, imperfections in seller price-competition) inflate the profits of withdrawing resources from UO-producing uses and devoting them to QV-creating uses and (2) it seems likely that the ratio of (the external marginal costs of production and consumption that the tort-law doctrine in question would eliminate or internalize) to (the relevant producers' already-internalized marginal costs) is higher than the ratio of (the external fixed costs of creating relevant QV investments that the tort-law doctrine in question would eliminate or internalize) to (the relevant QV investors' already-internalized fixed costs of QV-investment creation)—i.e., because the non-internalization of the externalities that tort law would eliminate or internalize seems likely to cause resources to be allocated from QV creation to UO production and thereby to counteract the net tendency of the economy's other Pareto imperfections to cause too many resources to be allocated from UO production to QV creation from the perspective of economic efficiency.

To my knowledge, the only exception to my claim that the literature on the economic efficiency of tort law ignores The General Theory of Second Best is Steven Shavell's argument (Shavell 1987) that (1) the fact that, in cases in which cause-in-fact cannot be determined in any other way, the common law finds a defendant to be the legal cause of a loss if the defendant's activity contributed more than 50% of the *ex ante* probability of the loss' occurring (and deems the defendant liable for the whole loss [absent contributory negligence] if the defendant is found to be the cause-in-fact of the loss and all other conditions for liability are satisfied) while finding the defendant not to be the legal cause of the loss and therefore not liable if the defendant's activity contributed 50% or less of the *ex ante* probability of the loss' occurring implies that (2) it will be more economically efficient to dismiss cases on the ground that, for some reason related to the low probability or "unforeseeability" of the defendant's failure to avoid causing the particular loss that resulted, the resulting loss should be deemed not to fall within the defendant's "scope of liability" when the defendant is strictly liable than when the defendant is liable only for those losses it has caused negligently. I will now explain (1) why, although Shavell does not couch his argument in Second-Best-Theory terms, it is a Second-Best-Theory-based argument and (2) why, although Shavell is making a valid Second-Best-Theory-related point, his argument does not justify his conclusion.

Here is the Second-Best-Theory-related account of Shavell's argument:

(1)   in an oPp economy, decisions to find tort defendants not liable because the loss for which they were found to be the legal cause was not within the scope of their liability would deflate the profits that AP-loss-avoidance moves would yield them;

(2)   under the common law, in all cases in which cause-in-fact cannot be established in any other way, a defendant will be found to be the cause-in-fact and legal cause of a loss if its activity contributed more than 50% of the *ex ante* probability of the loss' occurring but not to be the cause-in-fact of the loss if its activity contributed 50% or less than 50% of the *ex ante* probability of the loss' occurring;

(3)   in an oPp economy, in all cases in which the just-articulated common-law cause-in-fact rule is operative, the rule will inflate the private benefits that will be conferred on a strictly-liable potential injurer by an avoidance-move that will reduce the contribution that its activity makes to the *ex ante* probability of a loss' occurring from over 50 to 50% or less than 50% because (A) in an oPp economy, a strictly-liable potential injurer will have to compensate its victims for all the losses but only the losses for which it is deemed to have been the cause-in-fact and (B) (if I assume for simplicity that no AP-loss-contingency-related risk costs are generated, that the size of any loss that might be generated is certain, and that no avoidance-move will alter the magnitude of any loss that results) the private benefits that such an avoidance-move will confer on a strictly-liable potential injurer (by reducing the losses it causes for all of which it will be liable)—(the probability that the loss will occur, absent the potential injurer's avoidance) *times* (the magnitude of the loss that will result if the loss does eventuate)—will exceed the allocative benefits that such avoidance-moves will generate—on oPp assumptions, (the absolute amount by which the

avoidance-move will reduce the probability of the loss' occurring) *times* (the magnitude of the loss that will result if the loss does eventuate);

(4) in an oPp economy, the just-articulated common-law cause-in-fact rule will critically inflate the profitability of a strictly-liable injurer's making an avoidance-move that reduces the contribution that its activity makes to the *ex ante* probability of a loss' occurring from over 50 to 50% or less than 50% if the private benefits that the avoidance-move will yield the avoider exceed its private cost while its private cost (which equal its allocative cost on oPp assumptions) exceeds the allocative benefits it generates;

(5) in an oPp economy, the just-articulated common-law cause-in-fact rule will not inflate much less critically inflate the private benefits a potential injurer that will be liable only if found negligent for causing the loss can secure by making an allocatively-inefficient avoidance-move that reduces the contribution its activity makes to the *ex ante* probability of a loss' occurring from over 50 to 50% or less than 50% because, even though that cause-in-fact rule will result in a potential injurer that has failed to make such an avoidance-move being found to be the legal cause of any relevant loss that eventuates, that rule will not change the fact that it will not be negligent for a potential injurer to reject an avoidance-move that is economically inefficient—in an oPp economy, the private cost of every avoidance-move will equal its allocative cost, the private benefits that every avoidance-move will confer on the potential injurer's potential victims will equal the avoidance-move's allocative benefits, and every avoidance-move whose allocative cost exceeds its allocative benefits (whose execution would be economically inefficient) will be an avoidance-move whose private cost (B in the Hand formula) exceeds its private benefits ($\downarrow$PL in the Hand formula)—i.e., will be an avoidance-move whose rejection would not be negligent); therefore

(6) even if (in an oPp economy) the just-articulated common-law cause-in-fact (legal-cause) rule would favor the economic efficiency of dismissing cases on scope-of-liability grounds when the potential injurer is strictly liable because, in such a liability regime, the cause-in-fact rule would generate an inflation in the private benefits of making the specified category of avoidance-moves that would counteract the deflation in the private benefits of such avoidance that scope-of-liability dismissals generate, the cause-in-fact rule in question would not favor the economic efficiency of dismissing cases on scope-of-liability grounds in an oPp economy if the defendant is liable only for losses it causes negligently because under a negligence regime the cause-in-fact rule in question will not inflate the private benefits to potential injurers of making the relevant category of avoidance-moves.

I turn now to the four reasons why Shavell's Second-Best-Theory-related point does not justify his conclusion that it is more economically efficient to dismiss cases on scope-of-liability grounds when defendants are strictly liable than when they are liable only for the consequences of their negligence. The first two reasons have no connection to The General Theory of Second Best. The first is that, at most,

Shavell's argument favors his conclusion only in a small percentage of accident-or-pollution-loss cases—viz., in those cases in which (1) the court bases its cause-in-fact (legal-causation) conclusion on whether the defendant's activity contributed more than 50% of the *ex ante* probability of the loss' occurring and (2) the defendant has the option of making an avoidance-move that would reduce its activity's contribution to the *ex ante* probability of the loss' occurring from over 50% to 50% or less than 50%. The second reason relates to Shavell's grounds for believing that scope-of-liability rulings in favor of tort defendants may sometimes be economically efficient. Shavell believes that this may be the case because he thinks that resolving cases by ruling that the loss does not fall within the defendant's scope of liability will reduce transaction costs (litigation costs). (Shavell does not distinguish private from allocative transaction costs, but that mistake is not salient in this context.) Shavell's transaction-cost (litigation-cost) conclusion appears to be based on the assumption that decisions to resolve cases on scope-of-liability grounds will obviate the litigation of all the issues that tort cases involve other than the issue of whether the defendant is strictly liable or liable at most for the consequences of its negligence (an issue that Shavell assumes must be resolved to determine whether the loss should be deemed not to fall within the defendant's scope of liability)—in particular, obviates the litigation of the cause-in-fact issue, any contributory-negligence or comparative-negligence issues that arise in non-strict-liability cases, and actual and punitive damage issues. In fact, however, tort trials are not run that way. The scope-of-liability issue is not tried and resolved first (before the other issues are litigated): one does not obtain a summary judgment on the scope-of-liability issue. The only transaction-cost savings that scope-of-liability case resolutions generate are the savings that will result if a decision by the trier-of-fact to resolve the case on scope-of-liability grounds obviates the trier-of-fact's devoting (additional) time to the above issues post-trial. In fact, even if the scope-of-liability issue were always litigated and resolved before any other issue, the possibility of resolving cases on scope-of-liability grounds might not reduce (allocative) litigation costs: whether it will depends on (1) the percentage of cases in which the scope-of-liability issue was litigated that were resolved on scope-of-liability grounds and (2) the relative cost of trying the scope-of-liability issue and of trying the other issues whose litigation scope-of-liability case resolutions (I am now assuming, contrary to fact) would obviate. In cases in which the defendant was strictly liable, it is not at all clear to me that it would be cheaper to try the scope-of-liability issue (whose trial might involve such issues as the probability and foreseeability of the loss) than the other issues whose litigation I am now assuming *ad arguendo* that scope-of-liability case resolutions would obviate (since in strict-liability cases, one does not have to determine the probability or foreseeability of the loss).

The third and fourth reasons why Shavell's Second-Best-Theory-related point does not establish his conclusion do relate to The General Theory of Second Best. The third reason is that in strict-liability cases the interaction of the scope-of-liability-doctrine imperfection and the previously-described common-law cause-in-fact-doctrine imperfection may create a positive distortion in the private benefits that relevant avoidance-moves would generate that is absolutely larger than the negative distortion in those private benefits that the scope-of-liability doctrine would generate in an oPp economy.

The fourth reason is that Shavell's argument ignores not only the fact that the economies of common-law countries are not oPp but also the fact that any shift from negligence to strict liability will change the distortion in the private benefits (and profits) that will be yielded by the avoidance-moves on which his argument focuses in a large number of other ways than by affecting the distortion that the relevant cause-in-face rule generates and that, taken together, these other effects may (indeed, I suspect, will) make it less-economically-efficient to resolve cases on scope-of-liability grounds when the defendant is strictly liable than when the defendant is liable only for the consequences of its negligence (see Markovits 2008, pp. 253–265). For example, a shift from negligence to strict liability may well reduce the deflation in the private benefits of potential-injurer avoidance generated by entitled victims' decisions not to try to obtain redress (by reducing the cost of the associated litigation and removing an issue [negligence] that they think is more likely to be resolved against them than it actually will be), by reducing the extent to which settlements fall below actual losses (by reducing victims' litigation costs [which are higher] by absolutely more than they reduce [repeat-player] injurers' litigation costs [which are lower]), by eliminating the possibility that the trier-of-fact may make a false-negative finding on the negligence issue, and in a large number of other ways I will not recount here.

I turn now to the environmental-economics/policy literature. In my judgment, this scholarship has the same three deficiencies that the Law & Economics literature on AP-loss externality-internalizing tort law has. First, much of this scholarship executes FBLE analyses—i.e., ignores the fact that the externality on which it is focusing is not the only Pareto imperfection the relevant economy contains that would cause the category of economic inefficiency with which the study in question is concerned if the economy were oPp. Second, studies that correctly analyze the impact that an exemplar of a non-externality Pareto imperfection will have on the effect that internalizing an externality will have on the category of economic inefficiency on which the relevant analysis is focusing ignore the fact that the economy contains many other exemplars of the non-externality imperfection in question and of other types of Pareto imperfections that will affect the impact that the internalization of the externality will have on the category of economic inefficiency on which the study is focusing. For example, articles that point out that a choice to internalize the external marginal costs of production a producer generates might not reduce UO-to-UO misallocation if the producer faces imperfections in seller price-competition do not recognize that such a policy's impact on UO-to-UO misallocation will also be affected by any imperfections in price-competition faced by the producers from whose unit-output production the target producer would withdraw resources, any externalities that would be generated by the production and/or consumption of the latter producer's products, any sales/consumption/value-added/excise taxes that would be levied on the sale of the target producer's and the latter producer's products, and any errors that consumers of the products in question would make when choosing which of them to purchase. Third, much of the environmental-economics/policy literature does not take account of the important impacts that the externalities-internalization policies being considered will have on the magnitudes of a variety of categories of economic inefficiency. Thus, although this literature does consider the fact that externalities-internalization policies can affect (1) the amount of UO-to-UO misallocation that is generated, (2) the amount of misallocation that is generated because producers choose known, less-allocatively-efficient, more-external-cost-prone production processes rather than known, more-allocativley-efficient, less-external-cost-prone production processes, and (3) the amount of misallocation that is generated because no one executes economically-efficient PPR projects that seek to discover more-allocatively-efficient because less-external-cost-prone production processes, they ignore the impacts that externalities-internalization policies may have on the amounts of (4) inter-ARDEPPS and intra-ARDEPPS QV-to-QV misallocation, (5) inter-ARDEPPS and intra-ARDEPPS PPR-to-PPR misallocation, (6) UO-to-QV or QV-to-UO misallocation, and (7) UO-to-PPR or PPR-to-UO misallocation that are generated.

I want to close this discussion of the environmental-economics/policy literature with a story I find illuminating. Over the past 10 to 15 years, I have had several conversations with environmental economists who argued that—even if Environmental Economics had in the past largely ignored The General Theory of Second Best—a large number of more recent studies do take substantial account of Second Best. Unfortunately, although the studies that they cited were better than their predecessors in that they substituted more-useful general-equilibrium analyses for less-useful partial-equilibrium analyses, they did not in any way take account of The General Theory of Second Best: they focused on the effects of externality-internalization policies on parameters other than economic efficiency such as unit output—i.e., did not focus at all on Pareto imperfections or the different ways such imperfections interact to cause the different categories of economic inefficiency that externalities would generate in an oPp economy.

The third subset of standard externality-related efficiency analyses I will describe and criticize focuses on the effect of various types of externalities and externality-internalization policies on the economic efficiency of the relevant economy's R&D decisions. The extant literature focuses almost exclusively on (1) the fact that research will yield external benefits to the extent that actors use the discovery it yields without paying the discoverer for the right to do so, (2) the fact that the non-internalization of such external benefits will always deflate the private benefits and profits of executing the research that yields them, (3) the fact that (implicitly, in an oPp economy) the non-internalization of such external benefits will cause some economically-efficient research projects not to be executed by rendering their execution unprofitable, (4) the fact that policies that are designed to induce the execution of economically-efficient research projects by giving discoverers intellectual-property rights over their discovery will simultaneously generate economic inefficiency by causing the discoveries that are made to be underutilized from the perspective of economic efficiency by making it profitable for discoverers to set a price for the right to use their discoveries that exceeds the allocative cost (usually zero) of their being used, and (5) the implications of the underutilization possibility for the substance of the IP policy that would be most economically efficient.[4] In my view, this literature has 5 major deficiencies: (1) it ignores the fact that imperfections in seller price-competition inflate the profits yielded by *product* R&D and deflate the profits yielded by *production-process* R&D and the associated possibility that, for these reasons, from the perspective of economic efficiency, economies may devote too many resources to product research and not enough to PPR; relatedly (2) it fails to consider the possibility that it may be economically efficient to provide longer and broader IP protection to production-process discoveries and shorter and narrower IP protection to product discoveries or to give tax subsidies to PPR but not to product research (see Markovits 2008, pp. 172–202 and 212–228, 2002, 2018a, and Sect. 9.3 of this book); (3) it fails to take account of the fact that, when two or more research-projects seek to make the same discovery, each project almost always generates a real external cost by reducing the probability that the others will make the discovery first; (4) it fails to take account of the fact that, in societies in which some individuals value owning "the latest thing," product R&D will generate external costs to the extent that the existence of discovered products reduces the dollar value to their owners of pre-existing product variants; and (5) it fails to consider the possibility that the most-economically-efficient way for the government to promote economically-efficient non-basic-science-research decisions may be to subsidize research on condition that any resulting discoveries be made available for use without charge rather than to devise and implement intellectual-property regimes—an approach that the government does use to support "basic science" research but has not used when the research in question is "applied."

The third subset of applied-Welfare-Economics studies I want to discuss focuses on the economic efficiency of various taxes on the margin of income. Admittedly, starting already in the 1960s, public-finance scholars made more of an effort than the scholars in any other applied-Welfare-Economics specialty to respond constructively to The General Theory of Second Best (for relatively-early efforts of this kind, see Green 1961; Davis and Winston 1965; Dixit 1970; Mirrlees 1971; Diamond and Mirrlees 1971a, b; Stiglitz and Dasgupta 1971; Atkinson and Stiglitz 1972). Indeed, as Boadway shows in his 2017 article *Second-Best Theory: Aging Well at Sixty* (Boadway 2017, pp. 252 and 257–263), public-finance economists continue to execute tax-focused economic-efficiency analyses that establish important results, which I acknowledge a TBLE protocol for economic-efficiency analysis should take into account. However, I must also point out that even those contemporary analyses of the economic efficiency of particular taxes that make valuable contributions to the development of a defensible protocol for economic-efficiency analysis have many of the deficiencies that I claim undermine other branches of the applied-Welfare-Economics literature: (1) fail to recognize that many non-tax Pareto imperfections that in an oPp economy would cause the categories of economic inefficiency on which the relevant studies focus affect the impact that the taxes whose economic efficiency they are investigating have on those categories of economic inefficacy, relatedly (2) fail to examine how the non-tax Pareto imperfections they ignore interact with the taxes on the margin of income on which they focus to generate or not generate the categories of economic inefficiency on which they focus, and (3) ignore many of the categories of economic inefficiency whose magnitudes the taxes on the margin of income on which they focus can increase or decrease. The first two or these deficiencies are manifest in the failure of contemporary analyses of the impact of income and commodity taxes on labor/leisure misallocation to consider the fact that imperfections in seller price-competition (indeed, probably, the interaction of all non-tax Pareto imperfections) inflate the private benefits that QV-creating labor confers on its employer (and hence the gross wage of QV-investment-creating workers) while deflating the private benefits that unit-output-producing labor and PPR-executing labor confer on their employers (and hence the gross wage of UO-producing and PPR-executing workers). The third of these deficiencies is manifest by the failure of the public-finance literature to consider the possibilities that (1) a tax regime that imposed appropriately-different effective tax-rates on the income generated by QV investments or PPR projects in different ARDEPPSes might reduce respectively inter-ARDEPPS QV-to-QV misallocation and inter-ARDEPPS PPR-to-PPR misallocation, (2) a tax regime that imposed higher effective tax-rates on the income generated by product research than on the income generated by PPR could reduce the amount of economic inefficiency generated by the allocation of resources between product research and PPR (if I am correct in concluding that, from the perspective of economic efficiency, too many resources are allocated to product research and not enough to PPR), and (3) a tax regime that imposes a higher effective tax-rate on the profits yielded by the creation and use of new QV investments than on the profits yielded by the use of old QV investments (by the production of extant products) may reduce the amount of economic inefficiency the economy generates by allocating too many resources to QV creation and not enough to the production of extant products from the perspective of economic efficiency.[5]

I turn now to the behavioral economics, behavioral Law & Economics, and more-old-fashioned literature that focuses on the realities that resource allocators are sometimes imperfectly informed and fail sometimes to maximize. I want to make two points about this literature: the analyses of scholars that are concerned with the tendency of such non-sovereignty and non-maximization to cause economic inefficiency fail to consider both (1) that non-sovereignty and non-maximization can counteract as well as compound each other and (2) that the other Pareto imperfections the relevant economy contains can make any unprofitable decisions to which non-sovereignty and/or non-maximization lead more economically inefficient than unprofitable, less-economically-inefficient than unprofitable but still economically inefficient, or economically efficient though unprofitable.

The last body of applied-Welfare-Economics literature on which I want to comment focuses on buyer surplus. This small body of literature has the same deficiencies as the applied-Welfare-Economics literature on the other types of Pareto imperfections already discussed. My first objection to this literature relates to the conventional analysis of public goods (which should be defined not in the conventional way to be goods whose marginal cost is zero or whose consumers cannot be excluded if they do not pay for the good in question but to be goods for which [1] the demand curve cuts the marginal-cost curve from above at a height that is lower than the height of the good's average-total-cost curve at the associated output when [2] the average height of the demand curve between output zero and the output just referenced equals or exceeds the height of the average-total-cost curve for the product in question at the referenced output—i.e., to be goods whose creation and production in the quantity that would be economically efficient on oPp assumptions would be economically efficient on oPp assumptions even though it would be rendered unprofitable by the buyer surplus the sale of the oPp economically-efficient output of the good would yield if it had to be priced by charging for each unit sold the single per-unit price at which its demand curve cut its marginal-cost curve from above). This first objection is that the conventional analysis of the economic-efficiency problem posed by public goods is based on oPp assumptions (ignores the fact that, in actual economies, which are not oPp, the extant Pareto imperfections will almost certainly cause the demand curve for the public good to differ from the marginal-allocative-value curve for the public good [the Pareto imperfections that are most relevant to this point are sales/consumption/value-added/excise taxes] and cause the marginal-cost and average-total-cost curves for the public good to differ respectively from the marginal-allocative-cost and average-total-allocative cost curves for the public good) (see Markovits 2008, pp. 109–112; Markovits 2018c, pp. 881–884). My second objection to this literature relates to the failure of its authors to take account of inter-ARDEPPS QV-to-QV misallocation, intra-ARDEPPS QV-to-QV misallo-cation, intra-ARDEPPS PPR-to-PPR misallocation, inter-ARDEPPS PPR-to-PPR misallocation, and QV-to-PPR or PPR-to-QV misallocation. This omission has precluded these scholars from realizing that, even if there are no public goods, (1) in an oPp economy, buyer surplus can cause each of these categories of misallocation and (2) in an economy that is not oPp, buyer surplus can critically affect the aggregate distortion in the profits yielded by the various exemplars of the resource allocations associated with each of these categories of economic inefficiency. Thus, even if there are no public goods, in an oPp economy, buyer surplus will cause inter-ARDEPPS or intra-ARDEPPS QV-to-QV misallocation whenever the dif-ference between the economic efficiencies of two potentially-rivalrous QV invest-ments only one of whose creation would be economically efficient (when each QV investment's economic efficiency is measured relative to the situation that would prevail if neither were created) is smaller than the amount by which the buyer surplus that would be generated by the use of the more-economically-efficient QV investment exceeds the buyer surplus that would be generated by the use of the less-economically-efficient QV investment (see Markovits 2008, pp. 112–113).

So far, I have based my claims on my reading of an admittedly non-random, relatively-small sample of academic-journal articles. The last set of findings I want to report relates to a somewhat-more-comprehensive set of readings. In 2006, to put myself in a better position to write a Book Proposal for my 2008 study TRUTH OR

Economics (Markovits 2008), I examined all the Welfare Economics books reviewed in the *Journal of Economic Literature* over the preceding decade to determine the extent to which they took account of The General Theory of Second Best. None did so to any extent whatsoever.

I hope that this account of the bulk of the applied-Welfare-Economics literature rings true and that you are persuaded at least to take seriously my claims that most concrete economic-efficiency analyses (1) ignore the impact of the choices whose economic efficiency they investigate on a wide variety of categories of economic inefficiency whose magnitudes the relevant choices are likely to significantly affect and (2) either totally ignore The General Theory of Second Best when analyzing the impact of the choices under consideration on the categories of resource misallocation they do consider or take account of only one exemplar of one other type of Pareto imperfection when analyzing the economic efficiency of reducing or eliminating a target Pareto imperfection.

2.3   The Failure of Undergraduate and Graduate Textbooks on Theoretical and Applied Welfare Economics to Respond Appropriately to The General Theory of Second Best

This subsection reviews in the following order a non-random sample of textbooks on Welfare Economics, Law & Economics, Environmental Economics, the Economics of Regulation, and Public Finance to assess the extent to which they take account of The General Theory of Second Best. The books in each category will be discussed in the order of their first edition's year of publication.

The earliest Welfare Economics textbook I will discuss is E.J. Mishan's Cost-Benefit Analysis: An Informal Introduction (Mishan 1971). This book focuses primarily on UO-to-UO misallocation and takes The General Theory of Second Best into account by referencing it not only explicitly at page 117 note 3 when discussing the economic efficiency of internalizing external costs but also implicitly when discussing (at pages 90–99) the conditions under which imperfections in seller price-competition will generate UO-to-UO misallocation—i.e., more specifically (1) by stating that a full analysis of the conditions under which UO-to-UO misallocation will be eliminated will have to take account not only of the P/MC ratio of any product whose unit-output quantity's economic efficiency is of concern but also of the weighted-average P/MC ratio of the products with which each such good is competitive (which he misdenominates each product's "*substitutes*," which is wrong because the substitutability of goods depends solely on consumer preferences among them whereas the competitiveness of goods [which is what is relevant] depends not only on differences in the dollar values of the respective goods to relevant buyers but also on differences in the marginal costs of those goods' production), the externalities that are generated by the production of the marginal/just-extra-marginal units of the goods in question, and any taxes that would be levied on the sale of the marginal units of the good in question and (2) by stating that the claim that UO-to-UO misallocation will be eliminated (in the absence of externalities and taxes on relevant sales) if all goods have the same supracompetitive P/MC ratio ignores the fact that the price of one good—leisure—equals its marginal cost (as well as the fact that it would be neither economically nor politically feasible to render all other products' P/MC ratios equal). This Mishan book also recognizes (at page 182) that buyer surplus may cause misallocation related to what I denominate QV investment. For "*An Informal Introduction*," not a bad start, though the book does not try to provide a comprehensive account of the categories of economic inefficiency economies can contain, to analyze the different ways in which all exemplars of all types of Pareto imperfections interact to cause or not cause respectively each category of economic inefficiency an economy may contain, or to propose a general, *ex ante* economically-efficient approach to predicting or post-dicting the impact of choices on economic efficiency.

The next Welfare Economics textbook to be discussed—Boadway and Bruce's WELFARE ECONOMICS (1984)—also pays considerable attention to The General Theory of Second Best: (1) states (at pages 22–23) that policymakers who seek to increase economic efficiency must respond appropriately to The General Theory of Second Best, (2) devotes a chapter—Chap. 4—to "Market Failure and the Theory of Second Best," (3) examines the way (at page 136) in which imperfections in seller price-competition and external costs of production interact to cause or not cause what I denominate UO-to-UO misallocation, (4) considers (at pages 241–245 and 254–255) the difficulty of developing measures for changes in economic efficiency (which it misdenominates "welfare changes") in an economy that contains Pareto imperfections ("in a distorted economy"), and (5) references (at page 265) the literature on The General Theory of Second Best. However, once more, although this book in no way ignores The General Theory of Second Best, it has the same three deficiencies I claim Mishan's (1971) textbook has.

The third Welfare Economics textbook I will discuss is Per-Olov Johansson's INTRODUCTION TO MODERN WELFARE ECONOMICS (Johansson 1991), a text for undergraduates and non-specialists. This book focuses exclusively on what I call UO-to-UO misallocation and totally ignores The General Theory of Second Best.

The fourth Welfare Economics textbook to be considered is Yew-Kwang Ng's WELFARE ECONOMICS: TOWARD A MORE COMPLETE ANALYSIS (2004). Not surprisingly, given the multiplicity of articles Ng has written on Second-Best Theory, this book devotes a considerable amount of attention to The General Theory of Second Best. Indeed, its Chap. 9 (pp. 187–229) is entitled "First Second or Third Best." Equally unsurprisingly, given the position to which Ng has subscribed since 1977 (Ng 1977), this book argues that under certain conditions that it implicitly assumes will often be fulfilled it will be TBLE to execute FBLE analyses—i.e., to ignore The General Theory of Second Best. Section 2.1 of this chapter explained why I and Lipsey find Ng's argument for this conclusion unpersuasive in all realistic situations.

The fifth Welfare Economics textbook I will discuss is Chris Jones' APPLIED WELFARE ECONOMICS (2005). Although this text's subject index makes no reference to The General Theory of Second Best and its author index makes no reference to Lancaster or Lipsey, the book (1) does reference (on p. xxi) the article by Drèze and Stern (1987) I discussed in Sect. 2.1 of this chapter, which not only takes Second Best seriously but contains analyses that the protocol for economic-efficiency analysis I think is TBLE would incorporate and (2) does recognize (at pages 42–44) that the economic-efficiency effects of different Pareto imperfections can either compound or counteract each other. However, like the other texts I have discussed, this text (1) does not contain anything like a comprehensive account of the various categories of economic inefficiency an economy may generate, (2) does not attempt to delineate the different ways in which different Pareto imperfections interact to generate or not generate respectively each of these categories of economic inefficiency, (3) does not attempt to delineate a SBLE or TBLE protocol for economic-efficiency analysis, and (4) does not even provide accounts of the different approaches to economic-efficiency analysis that various economists have proposed or used.

The sixth and final Welfare Economics textbook I will consider is Massimo Florio's APPLIED WELFARE ECONOMICS (2014). This text contains (on pages 62–65) a correct general discussion of The General Theory of Second Best, presents (on pages 73–74) a useful account of Drèze and Stern's valuable (1987) Second-Best-Theory-based analysis, and (on pages 82–84) further develops the Drèze and Stern analysis. However, although Florio's text deserves credit on these accounts, it has the same 4 deficiencies the last sentence of the immediately-preceding paragraph claims the Jones text has.

To summarize: one of the 6 Welfare Economics textbooks I considered completely ignores The General Theory of Second Best, one considers it but concludes that in most situations it will be economically efficient to ignore it, 4 recognize its importance and execute or report some analyses that take it into account to some extent, and none identifies the wide variety of categories of economic inefficiency economies contain, analyzes the different ways in which all exemplars of all types of Pareto imperfections interact to generate or not generate respectively each category of economic inefficiency an economy can contain, discusses the various protocols that different economists have respectively argued would be economically efficient (morally desirable) to use to analyze the economic efficiency (moral desirability) of choices, or delineates and attempts to justify the protocol for economic-efficiency analysis its author(s) consider best.

I turn now to textbooks and readers in Law & Economics (a field that is in part interested in the economic efficiency of judicially-announced doctrines, statutory law, constitutional law, legal-dispute-resolution procedures and institutions, and governmental processes more generally). Once more, I will start with the books that were published earliest (though, when those books have multiple editions, I will discuss the various editions of a given book in the same paragraph).

I begin with Richard Posner's Economic Analysis of Law, whose first edition was published in 1972. That edition largely ignores The General Theory of Second Best but does reference it at pages 112–113 while claiming that the conclusion (to which, it seems to be implying supporters of this General Theory subscribe) that the economic inefficiency of the "output effects" of "monopolizing" is "completely indeterminate" is "a rather extreme inference to draw from the existence of second-best problems." In the book's fifth (1998) edition, Posner writes when discussing the same issue (at note 2 of page 302): "The empirical significance of… the problem of second best…is dubious." The book's ninth (2014) edition makes no reference to The General Theory of Second Best. All of the applied-economic-efficiency analyses these books execute ignore The General Theory of Second Best.

The first edition (1983) of Mitch Polinsky's textbook An Introduction to Law and Economics makes no reference to The General Theory of Second Best and ignores its central implication (e.g., at page 87, by asserting that the outcomes that will result when price exceeds marginal cost will be economically inefficient). The General Theory of Second Best receives no more attention in the fourth (2011) edition of Polinsky's book: neither the theory nor any of the literature that deals with it is discussed, and the claim that "efficient outcomes" will result if price equals (marginal) cost of production is repeated (at pages 7–11, 59, and 105–106).

The General Theory of Second Best is also completely ignored in Mercuro and Medema's (1997) textbook Economics and the Law: From Posner to Post-Mod-ernism. The book's extensive bibliography does not reference Lancaster and Lip-sey's article The General Theory of Second Best or any other scholarship that focuses on or applies this General Theory but does reference many articles that execute FBLE economic-efficiency analyses. Moreover, the book's discussion of Welfare Economics (at pages 137–144) does not reference The General Theory of Second Best and takes no account of it.

The 1998 reader Foundations of the Economic Approach to Law edited by Avery Katz does not contain any article that delineates or discusses The General Theory of Second Best or that attempts to respond defensibly to it and does contain several articles that execute or reference economic-efficiency analyses that ignore The General Theory of Second Best.

The various editions of Jeff Harrison's Law and Economics in a Nutshell do a much better job of communicating the importance of The General Theory of Second Best. Thus, the 2000 (2d) edition states at pages 54–56 that the fact that "[t]he theory of second best has received scant attention in the literature…" (citing at note 13 Markovits 1975b as an exception) "is unfortunate, as its implications are important and have the potential to undermine a great deal of modern analysis." The second edition (at pages 54–55 and 244–245) explains why The General Theory of Second Best undermines the traditional (in my terms, "UO-to-UO") economic-efficiency argument for pro-price-competition policies (the possible implication of The General Theory of Second Best that Richard Posner references but then calls into question [in reality, dismisses]). However, the second edition of Harrison's Law and Economics in a Nutshell ignores Second Best elsewhere and (under-standably, given the book's scope and brevity) does not attempt to develop a comprehensive list of categories of economic inefficiency, to analyze the different ways in which all exemplars of all types of Pareto imperfections interact to cause or not cause each category of economic inefficiency, to delineate a protocol for economic-efficiency analysis that would be SBLE or TBLE, or to delineate and comment on the protocols for economic-efficiency analysis that other Law & Economics scholars recommend or use. Subsequent editions of this Harrison book also explain The General Theory of Second Best and illustrate it by criticizing the standard (first-best) argument that imperfections in seller price-competition cause the producers that face them to produce too few units of their products from the perspective of economic efficiency (see the 2003 [3rd] edition at 31–33, 257, and 260–261; the 2011a [5th] edition at 32–34, 289, and 292–293; and the 2011b [6th] edition at 33–35, 296–299, and 301–302). However, these later editions also do no more than state the theory and indicate and illustrate its importance. The same comments apply to Harrison's textbook LAW AND ECONOMICS: POSITIVE, NORMATIVE AND BEHAVIORAL PERSPECTIVES (see the 2007 [2d] edition at 58–59 and *passim*).

All the articles in Eric Posner's (2000) reader CHICAGO LECTURES IN LAW AND ECONOMICS that are concerned with economic efficiency ignore The General Theory of Second Best, and none of the articles in question cites any scholarship that uses or tries to respond to this General Theory.

Steven Shavell's (2004) textbook FOUNDATIONS OF ECONOMIC ANALYSIS OF LAW pays no attention to The General Theory of Second Best. This book does not mention the theory by name, does not cite the Lancaster and Lipsey article or any other theoretical-Welfare-Economics or applied-Welfare-Economics article that addresses this General Theory, and presents many analyses that take no account of it.

The LAW AND ECONOMICS textbook authored by Bob Cooter and Tom Ulen (e.g., its 2012 sixth edition) also totally ignores The General Theory of Second Best, though it does contain a discussion (on pages 37–43) of "General Equilibrium and Efficiency Theories," which I would have thought would have provided a segueway to a discussion of this General Theory. (Admittedly, Second-Best problems can also arise in the context of a partial-equilibrium analysis since two or more Pareto imperfections can be operative even when the relevant analysis focuses exclusively on the conditions facing an individual resource allocator or the firms in a given "market" or sector.)

Jim Leitzel's (2015) textbook CONCEPTS IN LAW AND ECONOMICS: A GUIDE TO THE CURIOUS makes no reference to and pays no attention to The General Theory of Second Best, even though it makes many references to economic efficiency and specific economic-efficiency analyses.

I also do not believe that The General Theory of Second Best plays any role in any of the articles in any of the three volumes of the 2017 reader THE OXFORD HANDBOOK OF LAW AND ECONOMICS edited by Francesco Parisi, though somewhat surprisingly the bibliography of the article by David Driesen and Robin Malloy it contains—*Critiques of Law and Economics*, Chap. 15 (pages 300–320 of Volume I: METHODOLOGY AND CONCEPTS)—does reference the Lancaster and Lipsey (1956) article on page 315. (Richard Zerbe's Chap. 17 of Volume I [pages 355–380], entitled *Cost-Benefit Analysis in Legal Decision-Making*, takes no account of The

General Theory of Second Best and makes no reference either to the Lancaster and Lipsey article or to any other scholarship that tries to respond appropriately to The General Theory of Second Best.)

Finally, to my knowledge, none of the editions (including the 2017 third edition) of Thomas Miceli's textbook THE ECONOMIC APPROACH TO LAW takes account of The General Theory of Second Best or cites Lancaster and Lipsey's article of that title or any other scholarship that references, uses, or attempts to respond appropriately to this General Theory.

In sum, Jeff Harrison's claim that The General Theory of Second Best has received scant attention in the scholarly Law & Economics literature applies fully to Law & Economics textbooks and readers. Indeed, no Law & Economics textbook or reader that I could find other than Harrison's textbooks recognizes that this General Theory has important implications for (1) the appropriate protocol to use to analyze the economic efficiency of judge-announced legal doctrines, legislation, constitutional provisions, legal-dispute-resolution processes, and political and governmental decision processes more generally or (2) the economic efficiency of particular exemplars of any of these phenomena.

I will now discuss Environmental Economics textbooks (including successive editions of individual textbooks). The earliest textbook in this category I will consider is Baumol and Oates' THE THEORY OF ENVIRONMENTAL POLICY, whose first edition was published in 1975 and whose second edition was published in 1988. Both these editions (1) discuss the general importance of The General Theory of Second Best (in the first edition at pages 71–78), (2) illustrate its salient negative corollary by analyzing a case in which the tendency of the external costs generated by a producer's production of its marginal and intra-marginal units of output to cause it to produce too many units of its product from the perspective of economic efficiency is counteracted by the tendency of the imperfection in seller price-competition the producer faces to cause it to produce too few units of its product from the perspective of economic efficiency (see pages 92–93 of the second edition), (3) fail to point out that the economic efficiency of the relevant producer's unit-output decision will also be affected by any imperfections in price-competition faced by any producer from which the producer in question withdraws the resources it uses to produce its output, by any external costs that would have been generated by the production of the sacrificed units of the product from whose production the resources used to produce the product in question would have been withdrawn, by any taxes that were levied on the "target producer's" sales or that would have been levied on the sale of the sacrificed units of output, etc., (4) fails to allude to the fact that the interaction of external costs of production and exemplars of other types of Pareto imperfections can also affect the magnitudes of a number of categories of economic inefficiency other than UO-to-UO misallocation and, more specifically, that, for reasons I discussed previously, the non-internalization of external costs of production may very well reduce UO-to-QV misallocation, and perhaps most importantly (5) after illustrating the fact that The General Theory of Second Best has important implications for the conditions under which a producer that faces an imperfection in price-competition will produce too few units of its product from the perspective of economic efficiency, proceeds to ignore this General Theory throughout the rest of the text.

Turner, Pearce, and Bateman's (1993) textbook ENVIRONMENTAL ECONOMICS: AN ELEMENTARY INTRODUCTION makes no reference to The General Theory of Second Best, fails to cite any literature that tries to respond appropriately to this General Theory, and ignores the insights and implications of this theory when discussing particular issues such as how markets fail (at pages 65–78) and how green taxes succeed (at pages 166–179).

The Hanley et al. (1997) textbook ENVIRONMENTAL ECONOMICS IN THEORY AND PRACTICE also does not reference The General Theory of Second Best, also fails to cite any literature that attempts to respond appropriately to this General Theory, and, with one exception (at page 64, it considers the possible relevance of regulator misperceptions), ignores the implications of this General Theory for the economic efficiency of environmental policies.

The preceding criticisms also apply to Gilpin's (1999) textbook ENVIRONMENTAL ECONOMICS: A CRITICAL OVERVIEW. For example, its Chap. 1 on "Economics and the Environment" pages 1–34) and its more specific discussion of "The Optimization of Pollution Abatement" (pages 24–28) do not reflect at all the relevant corollaries of The General Theory of Second Best.

The fifth edition (2007) of Tom Tietenberg's textbook ENVIRONMENTAL ECONOMICS & POLICY is equally deficient. Thus, its Chap. 7 (pages 122–134)—"Natural Resource Economics: An Overview"—totally ignores The General Theory of Second Best.

Stephen Smith's (2011) textbook ENVIRONMENTAL ECONOMICS: A VERY SHORT INTRODUCTION also pays no attention to The General Theory of Second Best. Thus, the text's discussions (on pages 9–13) of why an unregulated market will damage the environment and (on pages 14–27) of "The Economic Theory of Efficient Pollution Control" do not consider either the possibility that, at least in relation to some categories of economic inefficiency, multiple exemplars of externalities may counteract (or compound) each other's distorting effects or the possibility that an economy's exemplars of other types of Pareto imperfections can either counteract or compound the distorting effects of its externalities.

From the perspective of The General Theory of Second Best, Ross McKitrick's (2012) textbook ECONOMIC ANALYSIS OF ENVIRONMENTAL POLICY is no better. Thus, its claim (on page 55) that "a competitive equilibrium is economically efficient" ignores the fact that types of imperfections other than imperfections in seller competition can cause economic inefficiency, and all its analyses of the tendency of externalities to generate economic inefficiency ignore both the possibility that two or more externalities may counteract each other and the fact that the extant exemplars of the other types of Pareto imperfections the relevant economy contains can counteract (or compound) the distorting effects of its externalities.

The final Environmental Economics textbook I will consider is Barry Field's 1979 textbook ENVIRONMENTAL ECONOMICS: AN INTRODUCTION. Regrettably, it also pays no attention to The General Theory of Second Best. Thus, the economic-efficiency analyses it executes or describes on pages 64–77 and 181–183 totally ignore the basic point of this General Theory.

In short, with the significant but extremely-partial exception of Baumol and Oates' THE THEORY OF ENVIRONMENTAL POLICY, the Environmental Economics textbooks I reviewed pay no attention whatsoever to The General Theory of Second Best.

In turn now to textbooks on the Economics of Regulation, I am pleased to report that the three (early) textbooks on the Economics of Regulation I considered all recognize the importance of The General Theory of Second Best (though they do not develop a comprehensive list of the categories of economic inefficiency whose magnitudes will be affected by the types of regulation they consider, do not analyze how all exemplars of all types of Pareto imperfections interact to cause or not cause each category of economic inefficiency an economy can contain, and do not attempt to devise an *ex ante* economically-efficient protocol for predicting the impact of such regulations on even those categories of economic inefficiency on which they focus).

The first Economics of Regulation textbook I will discuss is Crew and Kleindorfer's (1986) textbook THE ECONOMICS OF PUBLIC UTILITY REGULATION. This textbook contains (at pages 14–22) an intelligent account of The General Theory of Second Best and an intelligent discussion of its general implications. It also makes use of various academic articles (e.g., at pages 77–79, Davis and Winston's (1965) piece in *The Review of Economic Studies*) that bear on the economic-efficiency issues it addresses.

Alfred E. Kahn's (1970) two-volume textbook/treatise THE ECONOMICS OF REGULATION not only cites the Lancaster and Lipsey article (at pages 69–70 of Volume I) in the context of evaluating the claim that it is economically efficient for a producer to equate its price with its marginal cost but also repeatedly acknowledges and accurately identifies the relevance of The General Theory of Second Best. Thus, Volume I discusses "The Problem of Second Best" quite generally at pages 69–70 and recognizes (1) the implications of this General Theory for the claim that a seller will produce the economically-efficient quantity of its output if and only if its price equals its marginal cost when (A) other products' prices exceed their marginal costs (at page 44) or (B) when the production of the marginal units of the good in question generates external costs (at page 198) and (2) the relevance of "regulatory imperfections" for economic-efficiency analysis (at page 53). Similarly, Volume II recognizes the fact that taxes on the margin of income will affect the pricing rules that will be economically efficient (at pages 241–243 in a section entitled "Offsetting Imperfections and the Problem of Second Best").

F.M. Scherer's (1970) textbook/treatise MARKET STRUCTURE AND ECONOMIC PERFORMANCE also pays some attraction to The General Theory of Second Best. Thus, at page 26, Scherer states: "On the positive side, if we have absolutely no prior information concerning the direction in which second-best solutions lie, eliminating avoidable monopoly power is as likely statistically to improve welfare as to reduce it." And at pages 77–79, after executing a FBLE variant of a stochastic model of peak-load pricing, Scherer discusses Second-Best Theory's implications for the protocol one should use to analyze the relevance of a minimum-profit constraint for the economic efficiency of various price regulations.

Of course, as the parenthetical at the end of the paragraph that introduces this account of Economics of Regulation textbooks states, the textbooks surveyed do not by any means adjust their content to The General Theory of Second Best in the way that I think is warranted. Still, these textbooks/treatises give students/readers far more reason to keep The General Theory of Second Best in mind than do the Law & Economics and the Environmental Economics textbooks I have already described or the public-finance (public economics) textbooks to which I will now turn.

Rather than surveying the undergraduate and graduate textbooks on public finance (public economics) myself, I will rely substantially on (though I will also supplement) Wai Chiu Woo's perspicuous account of the extent to which The General Theory of Second Best is referenced and considered in eight major public-finance textbooks (Woo 2017, pp. 232–234). I start by quoting Woo's conclusion:

> …[M]y survey of major textbooks in…[public finance] give[s] me the impression that the second-best considerations are only a side issue. The first-best policies represent core concerns and are emphasized everywhere. The second-best considerations are only rarely mentioned, most commonly through only one or two examples. One cannot but conclude that, if one reads these textbooks, second best is not a central feature of policy-making.

I will now summarize Woo's account of the eight public-finance textbooks he considered. According to Woo, "Rosen and Gayer's (2014) very popular textbook [PUBLIC FINANCE] with 10 editions published already, introduces the theory of Second Best only briefly (no more than 3 pages in this book of 588 pages) when discussing the excess burden of taxation (p. 334 together with a chapter appendix at pp. 345–[34]6). There is one example illustrating that preexisting distortions are a constraint extra to the original first-best problem and so a second-best problem exists. The remaining parts of this book, however, are based on the traditional welfare economics framework [i.e., FBLE analysis].… Second-best considerations are normally not mentioned when designing policies to cope with…[market] failures. For example, [the book] ignores the fact that if the financing [of] the provision of a public good…involves using distortionary taxation, the marginal [allocative] cost of [a \$1 public expenditure is] more than \$1 [and hence recommends what Woo terms] a first-best policy…."

On Woo's account, Joseph Stiglitz's ECONOMICS OF THE PUBLIC SECTOR (2000), "another famous textbook, introduces the idea of second best only when discussing (optimal) taxation in a one-paragraph section on page 551. This book, however, gives a better account of the theory as it states more generally the consequence of introducing second-best considerations: when some irremovable distortions [what I would call "Pareto imperfections"] exist, it may no longer be desirable to remove other distortions. Stiglitz is also more willing to handle second-best policies in the book, although the brand of 'second best' is generally not mentioned except in the paragraph referred to above. ...[A]lthough the policy of public goods is still framed more in a line with the first-best case where...[in my terms the demand curve is assumed to coincide with the marginal-allocative-value curve and the marginal cost curve is assumed to coincide with the marginal allocative-cost curve], the author provides some discussion of the second-best case when distorting taxes must be used to finance public goods [which, I should add, represents an advance on Rosen and Gayer's treatment of this issue]." I should also point out that Stiglitz's book does not provide a comprehensive list of the categories of economic efficiency whose magnitudes public-financing decisions may affect or attempt to identify the TBLE protocol for analyzing the economic efficiency of public-finance choices.

According to Woo, Hyman's (2008) PUBLIC FINANCE: A CONTEMPORARY APPLICATION OF THEORY TO POLICY (1) "mentions the theory of second best explicitly only in one short paragraph (the last paragraph of p. 109)," (2) characterizes "the theory more or less as an 'ad hoc' consideration that economists should tackle when dealing with a specific problem," and (3) "uses the example [that I have indicated others such as Baumol and Oates and Kahn have also used] of a monopolist who generates pollution to illustrate that two opposing distortions [in my terminology, two opposing Pareto imperfections) can offset each other...[i.e., to illustrate what is] said to be an essential point of the theory." I would add that Hyman's textbook ignores Second-Best Theory in many other contexts, does not identify many of the categories of economic inefficiency whose magnitudes public-finance decisions can affect, and makes no attempt to develop a TBLE protocol for analyzing the economic efficiency of public-finance decisions.

According to Woo, even though Boadway and Wildasin's (1984) textbook PUBLIC SECTOR ECONOMICS (1) does "provide an extensive discussion of the theory of second best" and (2) illustrates it with examples that are "not limited to taxation" (e.g., examines the economically-efficient price for a public enterprise to charge when its production withdraws resources from an industry whose prices are "set below marginal cost" [not, to my mind, an empirically-important situation]), (3) its "treatment of second best is still quite brief," (4) it executes FBLE analyses of many "market failure cases, such as public goods and externalities," and (5) "it has been out of print for a long time."

Woo states that Bruce's (1998) textbook PUBLIC FINANCE AND THE AMERICAN ECONOMY (1) "provides a more detailed introduction (pp. 54–55) to the theory [of second best]" than any of the other books he considers, (2) discusses "typical scenarios" in which the theory is salient, (3) lists three reasons why some Pareto imperfections (which he calls "constraints") are irremovable ("political, property rights, and information"), and (4) uses the theory (at page 614) to argue against the claim that the consumption tax is more economically efficient than the income tax. However, Woo also points out that this textbook does not use the theory to criticize the conventional analysis of the public-good problem or to examine the economic efficiency of internalizing externalities. Once more, I would add that the book contains no comprehensive account of the categories of economic inefficiency whose magnitudes public-finance decisions can affect, no significant analyses of the different ways in which all exemplars of all types of Pareto imperfections interact to cause or not to cause respectively each such category of economic inefficiency, and no discussion of the protocol for economic-efficiency analysis that would be TBLE.

Woo proceeds to state that Hillman's (2009) textbook PUBLIC FINANCE AND PUBLIC POLICY: RESPONSIBILITIES AND LIMITATIONS OF GOVERNMENT and Hindricks and Myles' (2006) textbook INTERMEDIATE PUBLIC ECONOMICS—both intermediate-level textbooks—"provide only minimal discussion of the theory of second best." Although both books point out that the theory implies that reducing the number of Pareto imperfections in an economy that will remain Pareto-imperfect may not increase economic efficiency (Hillman in a footnote on page 347 and Hindricks and Myles at page 25)—a conclusion that is weaker than the conclusion that The General Theory of Second Best actually establishes—and both give an example (Hillman on page 200 and Hindricks and Myles on page 82) that illustrates the point of this General Theory, most of these textbooks' economic-efficiency analyses and claims ignore The General Theory of Second Best.

Finally, Woo comments on whether David Gruber's (2011) textbook PUBLIC FINANCE AND PUBLIC POLICY pays appropriate attention to The General Theory of Second Best:

> Gruber (2011), now a very popular textbook among top-ranked universities, seemingly wants to shun completely the complications due to the theory of second best. It does not even mention the term 'second best' in any chapter titles, subtitles or index. The closest encounter of the theory can only be found in a short subsection (p. 596) where preexisting distortions are shown to affect the efficiency implications resulting from taxes. This discussion is carried out, again, without mentioning the theory of second best or giving more generalized statements. The book shows a very strong inclination towards sticking to a first-best policy framework.

I began this discussion of the extent to which public-finance textbooks respond appropriately to The General Theory of Second Best by quoting Woo's discouraging, negative conclusions. My assessment is even more negative than Woo's because I think that applied-Welfare-Economics textbooks should devote considerable attention to the task of identifying the protocol for economic-efficiency analysis that is *ex ante* economically efficient. I am not surprised by the following Lipsey comment: "I find that when graduate students trained in general theory are asked for policy advice with regards to a taxed market, they typically suggest removing the 'distortion' [I would say: "the Pareto imperfection that would be a cause or source of the distortion"] with no consideration of second best ramifications" (Lipsey 2007, p. 356).

2.4 The Inadequacy of the Arguments that Various Economists Have Made to Justify Ignoring The General Theory of Second Best

Economists have made 10 arguments of which I am aware to justify their ignoring The General Theory of Second Best. The first 8, all of which have been made to me many times orally, were put into print by John Donohue in his article *Some Thoughts on Law and Economics and the General Theory of Second Best* (Donohue 1998)—a contribution to the 1998 symposium on this topic I organized and edited (Markovits 1998a). These arguments, to which I responded in an article in this symposium (Markovits 1998b), respectively claim that it is justifiable to ignore The General Theory of Second Best because this General Theory

(1) is "paralyzing in that it does not offer a clear replacement for what it purports to destroy" (Donohue 1998, pp. 257 and 263);

(2) implies our "inability to make…guesses" about economic-efficiency-prediction-relevant micro economic effects—for example, about the effects of "deregulation in the phone company and airline industry" on product quality and production costs (Donohue 1998, p. 268);

(3) ignores the importance of making "simplifying assumptions" (Donohue 1998, pp. 263–264);

(4) and Second-Best Theory are respectively too "arcane" and "abstruse" to be useful (Donohue 1998, pp. 259 and 263);

(5) cannot provide the basis for developing a protocol for assessing the economic efficiency of any policy that is as economically efficient as drawing inferences from empirical analyses of the actual consequences of similar policies that have been implemented in the past (Donohue 1998, pp. 258–259);

(6) and Second-Best Theory may yield conclusions that turn out to be wrong ("even the conclusions of nuanced and sophisticated analyses may well be overturned by yet more nuanced and sophisticated approaches") (Donohue 1998, p. 260);

(7) disserves the public interest because, by "weakening…reliance on law and economics[,] …[its consideration] might lead to reliance on even less beneficial modes of analysis" (Donohue 1998, p. 266); and

(8) disserves the public interest because (I am filling in some gaps) the third-best-allocatively-efficient protocol for economic-efficiency analysis that can be derived from it instructs economic-efficiency analysts to base their conclusions in part on imperfectly-informed "guesstimates" of the magnitudes of various parameters and on that account can be misused ("invoked opportunistically") by the bad guys to achieve bad results (Donohue 1998, p. 258).

Donohue adds that the approach that The General Theory of Second Best calls into question (what I call first-best-allocative-efficiency analysis) "has been largely successful" at "organiz[ing] our thinking" but admits that that approach has been much less successful at generating "accurate predictions and policy assessments" (Donohue 1998, p. 263).

None of Donohue's arguments against the importance of The General Theory of Second Best can bear scrutiny (Markovits 1998b):

(1) (A) although The General Theory of Second Best does not itself directly indicate how to deal with the complications whose salience it establishes, I believe that one can—as I hope my previous work does and this book will—derive from this General Theory a protocol that will enable its applier to increase economic efficiency by generating economic-efficiency predictions (Markovits 1998b, pp. 267–268), and (B) even if, contrary to fact, The General Theory of Second Best does imply the impossibility of increasing economic efficiency by generating economic-efficiency predictions, that dismal "reality" would not render The General Theory of Second Best unimportant: even on that assumption, The General Theory of Second Best would still reveal to policy evaluators that they should ignore economic efficiency and base their recommendations on other (say distributive-norm or political-process-norm) considerations (Markovits 1998b, pp. 270–271);

(2) The General Theory of Second Best (A) has no bearing whatever on our ability to predict the impact of choices on the sort of micro-economic parameters that the second argument references and (B) in no way relies on any claim that such effects cannot be reliably predicted—it simply reveals that and why predicted micro-economic effects have less economic-efficiency relevance than economists tend to assume (e.g., that increases in product quality and decreases in private production costs cannot be assumed to be associated with increases in economic efficiency) (Markovits 1998b, pp. 268 and 273);

(3) although The General Theory of Second Best pays no attention to the importance of making simplifying assumptions, the Second-Best Theory it informs can and does do so (Markovits 1998b, p. 269);

(4) I do not think that Second-Best Theory is too arcane and abstruse to be positively practicable and, even if it were, for the reason stated in Item (1)(B) in this list, that reality would not justify ignoring The General Theory of Second Best or render that theory unimportant (Markovits 1998b, pp. 270–271);

(5) the empirical studies that the fifth argument claims will produce more-economically-efficient economic-efficiency assessments of policies are micro-economic as opposed to economic-efficiency analyses—i.e., do not reveal the economic efficiency of the policies in question, and it is not practicable to predict the economic efficiency of a current policy option by estimating the economic efficiency of similar past policies by identifying an appropriately-large random sample of their winners and losers, estimating their respective equivalent-dollar gains and losses, summing these figures, and

multiplying the resulting difference by the ratio of all affected parties to the number of affected parties in the random sample or by following any other protocol that would be superior to the protocol for economic-efficiency analysis this book proposes (Markovits 1998b, pp. 271–272);

(6) the fact that some decisions that are justifiably deemed to be economically efficient *ex ante* turn out to be economically inefficient *ex post* does not in itself imply the economic inefficiency of using the protocol for economic-efficiency prediction that is justifiably deemed to be most economically efficient *ex ante* or of deriving that protocol from The General Theory of Second Best—predictions that were *ex ante* economically efficient are not rendered less so by the fact that they turned out to be inaccurate *ex post* (the predictions that were made were equally likely to have underestimated as to have overestimated the economic efficiency of the choice under review by any given number of dollars [on the weighted average]) (Markovits 1998b, p. 272);

(7) I doubt that The General Theory of Second Best disserves the public interest by inducing the government to substitute for first-best-allocative-efficiency analyses decision-protocols that pay less attention to economic-efficiency consequences (in part because the economic-efficiency conclusions generated by first-best analyses are highly inaccurate and in part because *desiderata* other than economic efficiency that do not increase monotonically with economic efficiency are relevant to the moral desirability of choices), and even if The General Theory of Second Best would disserve the public interest for this reason, that reality would not relieve academics in liberal, moral-rights-based societies of their moral duty to speak the scientific truth (Markovits 1998b, pp. 272–273); and

(8) (A) a full specification of the third-best-allocatively-efficient protocol for economic-efficiency analysis would include provisions that relate to the qualifications, recruitment, and remuneration of government economic-efficiency evaluators, the emoluments they may and may not receive from others when employed by the government, the jobs they may take and the emoluments they may receive from non-government sources after their government employment ends, and the procedures they must follow when executing their government economic-efficiency analyses (the identities of the parties that have the right to submit evidence to them, the amount and nature of the evidence that entitled parties can submit and the time-period during which such parties may submit such evidence, the duties of government economic-efficiency analysts to respond to such evidence and, more generally, to explain the basis of their decisions, etc.), (B) such provisions will significantly reduce the incidence of the misfeasance on which Donohue's eighth argument focuses, (C) even if some such misfeasance occurs, I doubt that its incidence is sufficient to render *ex ante* economically inefficient the protocol for economic-efficiency analysis I claim would be third-best–allocatively-efficient, and (D) even if proposition (8)(C) in this list is wrong, the negative implications of The General Theory of Second Best would still be very important (Markovits 1998b, p. 273).

Section 2.1 of this chapter has already delineated and criticized the ninth and tenth arguments that economists have made for ignoring The General Theory of Second Best (under specified conditions that the authors of these arguments thought when they made their respective arguments are often fulfilled and [in one case] continue to believe are usually fulfilled). The ninth argument is Mishan's claim (Mishan 1962) (in essence) that FBLE analysis will be TBLE when the question is the economic efficiency of increasing or decreasing a Pareto imperfection in a sector of the economy that is isolated in the sense that no resources flow from other sectors to the sector in question or from the sector in question to other sectors. As Sect. 2.1 of this chapter argued, (1) this argument would be far less important than Mishan suggested it was and many economists took it to be even if it were correct because no or virtually no sector of an economy is isolated in the above sense, and (2) Mishan's argument is also incorrect even for isolated sectors because (A) even isolated sectors will almost always contain Pareto imperfections other than the target imperfection and (B) it will almost always be *ex ante* economically efficient to take account of the "target sector's" other Pareto imperfections when analyzing the economic efficiency of increasing or decreasing a target imperfection.

The tenth and final argument for the economic efficiency of ignoring The General Theory of Second Best (i.e., for the conclusion that it will be TBLE to execute FBLE economic-efficiency analyses) is Y.-K. Ng's argument that this conclusion is justified under conditions of "Informational Poverty" when the curve that relates the economic efficiency of the outcome to the size and sign of the target Pareto imperfection is concave. As I stated in Sect. 2.1, Ng's claim that his argument demonstrates that it will often be third-best-allocatively-efficient to execute first-best-allocative-efficiency analyses is unpersuasive because (1) Informational Poverty is less pervasive than Ng asserts and it will often be *ex ante* economically efficient for economic-efficiency analysts to increase the information on which they base their conclusions, (2) the relation curve on which he focuses will be concave less often than he claims, (3) contrary to Ng's claims, his argument depends on one of two unrealistic implicit assumptions—(A) that the target Pareto imperfection is the only relevant Pareto imperfection in the economy or (B) the non-target Pareto imperfections the relevant economy would contain if the target Pareto imperfection were eliminated would perfectly counteract each other (would have no impact on the extent to which the outcome was non-optimal) if the target Pareto imperfection were eliminated, and (4) even if the first two of the above three objections were incorrect, the third objection implies that Ng's argument implies the third-best allocative efficiency (or third-best social-welfare desirability) of doing nothing as opposed to making the choice that would be commended by a first-best analysis.

2.5 Some Personal Anecdotes

This subsection is risky because it is anecdotal. I include it because, in my judgment, the personal experiences it recounts are revealing.

My initial exposures to economists' reactions to The General Theory of Second Best occurred in 1964 and 1965 at the LSE and in 1965–1968 at Yale. (After leaving London, I took a law degree at Yale and, during my second and third years at the law school, taught a full load of courses as a Lecturer in the Yale Economics Department.) At LSE, several graduate students and faculty members with whom I raised issues related to The General Theory of Second Best responded by saying that it was entirely appropriate to ignore The General Theory of Second Best. Many attempted to justify their responses by citing E.J. Mishan's argument in his 1962 article *Second Thoughts on Second Best* (Mishan 1962), which for reasons that Sect. 2.1 of this chapter discusses and Mishan's own subsequent applied-Welfare-Economics scholarship implicitly recognizes does not justify this response. (Mishan is an Englishman who taught at the LSE, and the article was published in an English academic economics journal—*Oxford Economics Papers.*) Others attempted to justify this response (to my mind, both incorrectly and bewilderingly) by saying that "If that theory is right, we have nothing to say about economic efficiency." With one exception, the colleagues and graduate students at Yale with whom I discussed The General Theory of Second Best also claimed it was appropriate to ignore it, once again on the ground that, if it is right, economists cannot say anything useful about economic efficiency. The exception was an economics professor whose graduate course on applied Welfare Economics (micro-economic-policy analysis) I audited during my second semester at Yale Law School (before receiving my appointment as a Lecturer in the Economics Department). At the end of one of the early classes in this course, I raised my hand and offered a somewhat-halting Second-Best-Theory-based critique of the analysis the professor had executed. After the next class, I approached the professor and said that I could make a similar critique of that lecture but thought it was not my place to do so. The professor responded in a friendly way, indicating that he understood my position and had no objection to my critiquing his analyses. In fact, on several subsequent occasions, toward the end of class, the professor turned toward me and said: "Markovits, please tell us what you think I have ignored and why it matters."

Over the next 30 years or so, in numerous casual conversations at conferences and in other settings, economists used all the arguments. Sect. 2.4 of this chapter delineates and criticizes to "justify" their individual and our profession's ignoring The General Theory of Second Best and executing FBLE economic-efficiency analyses. I had an unusually-large number of such conversations in 1996 and 1997 when inviting about two dozen well-known economists who specialized in theoretical and applied Welfare Economics to contribute to a special issue of an academic journal I was assembling and editing. The issue was published in 1998 under the title *Symposium on Second-Best Theory and Law & Economics* (Markovits 1998a). The vast majority of the economists whose participation I solicited turned me down. Several said they knew nothing about The General Theory of Second Best. Others articulated The General Theory of Second Best correctly but said that the profession had decided to ignore it and that they saw no reason to behave differently.

I can tell one other story that seems to me to reinforce this account of the profession's reaction to The General Theory of Second Best. In the early 1990s, I had a revealing exchange with a deservedly-highly-regarded economist who edited an applied-Welfare-Economics journal to which I had submitted a manuscript that explained The General Theory of Second Best and proposed a protocol for executing economic-efficiency analyses that I claimed responded economic-efficiently to this General Theory (a protocol that was a prototype of the protocol this book delineates). The editor responded promptly and politely, indicating that he would not send out my manuscript for review because it was concerned with "methodology" and his journal was (in this book's terminology) an applied-Welfare-Economics and not a theoretical-Welfare-Economics journal. I responded equally promptly and (I hope) equally politely that I recognized that he was the editor and that the choice he made fell within his editorial discretion but that I thought that the criterion he was applying was unwise. To demonstrate my point, I added a number of Second-Best-Theory-based critiques of several of the articles his journal had published in the recent past. The response I received was rapid but anything but polite—could best be described as vituperative.

I hasten to acknowledge that conversations I have had with economists about The General Theory of Second Best over the last 10 years have been more encouraging. Although the vast majority of my interlocutors did not themselves take account of The General Theory of Second Best when executing economic-efficiency analyses and some conflated analyses that take appropriate account of The General Theory of Second Best with general-equilibrium analyses that focus on non-economic-efficiency outcomes and their determinants, most were not defensive—indeed, most seemed interested and more than willing to consider the possibility that the profession's economic-efficiency-analysis practices would have to be substantially altered in light of this General Theory.

I turn finally to the experiences I have had when giving Welfare Economics talks in the USA, England, Germany, and Switzerland to Economics conferences, Economics Departments, or Law & Economics Workshops (which are attended by economists and academic lawyers who are conversant with economics). All of these talks were precursors or mini-versions of this book. The talks began by delineating The General Theory of Second Best and its central negative corollaries, then gave an outline of the protocol for economic-efficiency analysis that I argued responded economic-efficiently to this General Theory, and concluded by using this approach to analyze particular concrete economic-efficiency issues (sometimes the issues on which the relevant conference focused) and to criticize others' analyses of these issues.

From 1970 until about 2010, with one important qualification and one important exception, my audiences responded to these talks either by simply asserting that my applied-economic-efficiency-analysis conclusions were wrong and arguing that my protocol for economic-efficiency analysis must therefore be wrong as well or by arguing that my concrete economic-efficiency conclusions (and therefore my protocol for economic-efficiency analysis) had to be wrong because my conclusions were inconsistent with another conclusion they specified that they knew was right.

On each of these occasions, I responded to the latter argument by (1) articulating the argument that yielded the economic-efficiency conclusion my critics were certain is right, (2) pointing out that this latter argument implicitly assumes that a critical private-benefit, private-cost, and/or profit figure equals its allocative counterpart, (3) explaining that the relevant private and allocative figures would equal each other only if (A) the economy contains no non-target Pareto imperfection of any type or (B) the non-target Pareto imperfections the economy contains perfectly counteract each other in the relevant contexts, (4) suggesting that, for good reason, my critics did not believe that either of the two conditions specified in Item (3) of this list is satisfied, and (5) explaining (A) that my analysis differs from the argument on which they were (implicitly) relying in that my analysis takes account of the Pareto imperfections that the argument on which they were relying ignores and (B) that my economic-efficiency conclusion is inconsistent with the conclusion they are certain is right because, unlike their conclusion, my conclusion reflects the effects of the Pareto imperfections they were ignoring. Although, on most of these occasions, my response induced the objectors to drop their initial argument against my conclusion and analysis, it did not get them to accept my position: they simply shifted to arguing that my economic-efficiency conclusion and analysis must be wrong because my conclusion is inconsistent with a different economic-efficiency conclusion they specified that they knew is right. My response to this second argument paralleled my response to the first. There were often multiple iterations of this interchange. Regrettably, even on those occasions on which the objections stopped before the end of the relevant session, I did not leave with the impression that I had convinced the other participants. In several instances, my perception was confirmed when attendees who had stopped objecting during the session or who had made no objection during the session came up to me an hour or so later and made a variant of one of the arguments against my position that I had addressed during my presentation—a variant that was not critically different from (indeed, in some cases, was coincident with) an "argument" against my position that had been voiced during the session.

I wrote earlier that the preceding account of my 1970–2005 experience needs to be qualified. On three occasions, after a number of the exchanges I have just described took place, a mathematical economist in the audience responded to yet another argument of the same type that a colleague was making against my position by cutting in and saying: "Don't you see? That argument does not work. He is going to say..., and that response is correct." Unfortunately, these interventions did not seem to persuade the other participants any more than did my own counterarguments.

I also wrote earlier that there was an exception to the talk experiences I have just described. In 1974, I gave what amounted to a job-talk to the Economics Department of Cal Tech. The audience (primarily, mathematical economists) immediately grasped the point, asked for more details, and speculated insightfully about those details. They were skeptical of or resistant to only that part of my proposal that rendered it third-best-allocatively-efficient as opposed to second-best-allocatively-efficient: they were disinclined to endorse any approach that generates conclusions from estimates and *a fortiori* from guesstimates of the magnitudes of relevant parameters.

I am pleased to report that since about 2005 my talks have not met with such resistance. The audience may not have agreed with everything I said, and some participants may have expressed their belief that in many circumstances (which they did not specify) for some reason (which they also did not articulate) it will (in my terminology) be third-best-allocatively-efficient to execute first-best-allocative-efficiency analyses. But they were more than willing to listen and were interested in the details of what I am proposing.

2.6   The Reasons Why Economists Have Resisted The General Theory of Second Best

The preceding sections of this chapter have presented a considerable amount of evidence to support my claim that the economics profession as a whole has been less willing than it should have been to accept and attempt to respond constructively to The General Theory of Second Best. I recognize the legitimacy of readers' questioning my stories and the representativeness of the samples of economics scholarship and textbooks that I have described and criticized. I will close this chapter by delineating six reasons why economists might fail to respond appropriately to The General Theory of Second Best in the hope that the plausibility of these explanations may make you more willing to accept my conclusion that the profession has not responded properly to this General Theory.

First, a failure by the economics profession to respond appropriately to The General Theory of Second Best might at least partially be explicable by the general human reluctance to admit that one has made mistakes and to accept ideas or empirical claims that are inconsistent with one's long-held beliefs: the latter cognitive-dissonance-based reaction is likely to be particularly strong when the beliefs in question were instilled through lengthy, comprehensive professional training.

Second, economists might be reluctant to accept and properly respond to The General Theory of Second Best because of a combination of (1) individual economists' desires for professional success and (2) the fact that the relevant professional gatekeepers (journal editors, journal referees, tenured faculty members, department chairs) tend to be senior welfare economists who are convinced of the correctness of the prevailing paradigm, have personal professional stakes in its continuing acceptance, and are inclined to preserve the acceptance of the existing paradigm by denying jobs and promotions to those who question it and by rejecting manuscripts that attack it explicitly or that propound and/or apply theories that are inconsistent with it.

Third, economists might not respond appropriately to The General Theory of Second Best because of the combination of (1) individual economists' desires to have their profession and their skills highly valued and (2) their fear that an admission that welfare economists have been making a fundamental logical mistake (which, at least in hindsight, is obvious) that invalidates the arguments they used to generate all the economic-efficiency conclusions they reached would injure the reputation of and respect given to welfare economists and perhaps to economists more generally.

Fourth, economists might be reluctant to accept or respond appropriately to The General Theory of Second Best because they fear that this General Theory would reduce their ability to get consulting jobs, their opportunities to give testimony before legislative, administrative, and judicial decision-makers, and their power to influence public policy in other ways either (1) because the economists in question mistakenly believe that, if The General Theory of Second Best is correct, it will not be possible for anyone to say anything reliable or useful about the economic efficiency of policies or (2) because they (A) recognize that Second-Best Theory implies that the analyses that must be executed and explained to justify any economic-efficiency conclusion are far more complicated than the first-best-economic-efficiency analyses The General Theory of Second Best invalidates and (B) believe (perhaps correctly) that government decisionmakers and the policy audience are not disposed to devote the time and effort required to listen to and assess correct analyses.

Fifth, at least some economists might fail to accept or adequately respond to The General Theory of Second Best because they believe that (1) public acceptance of this General Theory would disserve the public interest (defined through a morally-acceptable decision process), their personal values, and/or their material interests because it would reduce the role that economic-efficiency conclusions play in public decision-making by revealing that such conclusions are less reliable than they are currently perceived to be and (2) the government's substituting the kind of economic-efficiency-analysis protocol that Second-Best Theory commends for first-best-allocative-efficiency analysis would disserve the public interest, their own values, and/or their material interests (A) because (as we shall see) that protocol will reveal that government choices that reduce poverty and/or inequality (which choices these economists believe are morally unwarranted or against their material interests) will increase economic efficiency on that account, (B) because that protocol may well lead to the conclusion that economic efficiency would be promoted by selective government interventions, which first-best-allocative-efficiency analysis never favors, and these economists subscribe to a certainly-contestable and probably-indefensible conception of liberty that they believe (contestably) selective interventions disserve, and (C) because the protocol for economic-efficiency analysis that Second-Best Theory commends creates more opportunities for manipulation and corruption than does the simpler decision-rule commended by first-best-allocative-efficiency analysis by instructing analysts to base their economic-efficiency predictions and post-dictions on (some) parameter-estimates that are not so accurate as they might be.

Sixth and finally, I will offer a negative reason why the economics profession might not have accepted The General Theory of Second Best or responded to it in the way that seems to me to be appropriate. Although natural scientists often continue to subscribe to theoretical paradigms long after they should have been led to reject them by the combination of empirical findings that are inconsistent with the paradigm and alternative theories that fit the extant relevant empirical results better than the established paradigm fits them (see Kuhn 1962), eventually enough empirical evidence against the accepted paradigm accumulates for it to come crashing down. Welfare economists might have continued to do first-best-allocative-efficiency analysis when they should not have done so in part because Welfare Economics has not produced and cannot produce empirical research on the equivalent-dollar gains and losses that particular non-government or government choices generated that would reveal the economic inefficiency (efficiency) of choices that first-best-allocative-efficiency analysis implies would be economically efficient (economically inefficient).

Notes

1. Mishan's and Ng's arguments that, in the different sets of situations they respectively specify, it will be third-best-allcoativley-efficient to execute FBLE economic-efficiency analyses are not the only arguments of this sort that have been made. For other arguments in this category (which I also do not find convincing), see Santoni and Church 1972, Dusarsky and Walsh 1976, and Rapanos 1980. These references are taken from Bohm 1987, p. 283.

2. More specifically, Ng's argument assumes that the relevant maximand is a social-welfare function that he does not specify that may or may not be monotonically related to economic efficiency—i.e., in which economic efficiency may be the only *desideratum*, may be one of many *desiderata* that may or may not increase monotonically with it, or may play no role whatsoever and in which one or more other constraints may be operative. I will ignore this feature of Ng's analysis here, which is irrelevant to whether his argument justifies the conclusion that, under the conditions he specifies (which he seems to assume will at least frequently be satisfied), it will be TBLE to execute FBLE analyses of the economic efficiency of choices. Ng's failure to specify the relevant "social-welfare" function is important because it prevents commentators from assessing the likely accuracy of his assumption that the amount by which a relevant outcome is non-optimal increases at an increasing rate with the difference between the actual and first-best magnitudes of any determinant of "social welfare." The "social-welfare function" that Ng assumes to be in play is also problematic in that, like the "social welfare" functions that all or virtually all other welfare economists consider (see Harberger 1978), it fails to take account of the "fact" that, in moral-rights-based societies such as the USA, the member-nations of the EU, and many other countries, moral rights (considerations of justice) act as a moral constraint on the securing of the (other) *desiderata* in the "social-welfare" function. (Moral-right-based societies are societies whose members and governments engage in a bifurcated

prescriptive-moral discourse in which [1] a strong distinction is drawn between the analysis of moral rights [the analysis of justice] and the analysis of what morally ought to be done when moral-rights commitments are not determinative [the analysis of the moral good] and [2] a lexically-higher value is placed on the securing of moral rights than on the instantiation of even a universally-subscribed-to conception of the moral good—i.e., in which moral-rights conclusions trump moral-ought conclusions when the two favor different decisions.)

3. It would be easy enough to alter the Hand formula for negligence to take account of the fact that, regardless of whether a relevant avoidance-move was made, the loss contingency would most accurately be represented by a probability distribution of losses of different magnitudes. It is not so easy (indeed, in certain classes of situations, it is not possible) to alter the Hand formula for negligence to take account of the facts that (1) both the potential injurer and the potential victims face loss-contingency-related risk costs, which will vary in part with the identity of the parties that will be liable for any loss that results, which will depend *inter alia* on the applicable rule of tort-law liability, and (2) avoidance-moves will alter not only weighted-average-expected accident-losses but also the sum of potential-injurer and potential-victim accident-and-pollution-loss-related risk costs (Markovits 2004).

4. Admittedly, the literature on the economic efficiency of providing intellectual-property protection to creators of literary, musical, and visual-art works also takes account of the related fact that some art works may reduce the value of their predecessors by rendering them trite or just contaminating or altering their social meaning.

5. The text ignores three general deficiencies and one specific deficiency of the conventional economic-efficiency-focused public-finance literature, only one of which (admittedly) relates to The General Theory of Second Best. The deficiency that is connected to this General Theory is the general failure of the relevant analyses to recognize that the private transaction cost of devising, collecting, and paying taxes or other government charges will equal their allocative counterpart only rarely and fortuitously. The two other general deficiencies of this literature are its failure (1) to specify the other fiscal decisions that will inevitably be combined with any revenue-increasing or revenue-decreasing tax-decision or (2) to analyze the economic efficiency of these other fiscal decisions. The specific deficiency is the failure of public-finance experts to recognize that (on implicit oPp assumptions) taxes on the margin of income will not cause labor/leisure misallocation if the supply of labor is inelastic over the relevant range—i.e., if the relevant tax does not affect the quantity of labor supplied. On oPp assumptions, taxes on the margin of income will also cause too few units of labor to be supplied from the perspective of economic efficiency when they do not affect the quantity of labor supplied because in such cases the taxes will increase the quantity of labor whose supply would be economically efficient. To see why, note that (1) taxes on the margin of income will have no

effect on the quantity of labor supplied only when the negative substitution effect of the tax is perfectly offset by its equally-absolutely-large positive wealth effect (which will increase the quantity of labor whose supply is economically efficient) and (2) the relevant wealth effects of the tax are irrelevant to its economic efficiency.

References

Atkinson, A., & Stiglitz, J. (1972). The structure of indirect taxation and economic efficiency. *Journal of Public Economics, 1,* 97–119.

Atkinson, A., & Stiglitz, J. (1976). The design of tax structure: Direct versus indirect taxation. *Journal of Public Economics, 6,* 55–75.

Australian Government Productivity Commission. (2008). *Promoting better environmental outcomes: Roundtable proceedings* (p. 2008). Melbourne, Australia: Australian Government Productivity Commission.

Baumol, W., & Oates, W. (1975). *The theory of environmental policy* (1st ed.). Englewood Cliffs, NJ: Prentice-Hall.

Baumol, W., & Oates, W. (1988). *The theory of environmental policy* (2d ed.). Cambridge and New York: Cambridge University Press.

Bergson, A. (1975). On monopoly welfare losses: A reply. *American Economic Review, 65,* 1024–1031.

Boadway, R. (2017). Second-best theory: Ageing well at sixty. *Pacific Economic Review, 22,* 249–270.

Boadway, R., & Bruce, N. (1984). *Welfare economics.* Oxford and New York: Basil Blackwell.

Boadway, R., & Wildasin, D. (1984). *Public sector economics.* Boston: Little Brown.

Bohm, P. (1987). Second best. In Eatwell, J., Milgate, M., and Newman, P. (Eds.), *The new Palgrave: A dictionary of economics*—Vol. 4, *Q to Z* (pp. 280–284). London: Macmillan.

Brennan, G., & Buchanan, J. (1980). *The power to tax: Analytical foundations of a fiscal constitution.* Cambridge, England and New York: Cambridge University Press.

Bruce, N. (1998). *Public finance and the American economy* (1st ed., p. 2001). Reading, MA: Addison-Wesley.

Bruce, N. (2001). *Public finance and the American economy* (2nd ed.) Reading. MA: Addison-Wesley.

Bruce, N., & Waldman, M. (1991). Transfers in kind: Why they can be efficient and nonpaternalistic. *American Economic Review, 81,* 1345–1351.

Carson, R. (1973). On monopoly welfare losses: A comment. *American Economic Review, 63,* 853–870.

Cooter, R., & Ulen, T. (2012). *Law and economics* (6th ed.). Boston, MA: Pearson Prentice Hall.

Cowling, K., & Mueller, D. (1978). The social costs of monopoly. *Economics Journal, 88,* 724–748.

Crew, M., & Kleindorfer, P. (1986). *The economics of public utility regulation.* Basingstoke and London: Palgrave Macmillan.

Davis, O., & Winston, A. (1965). Welfare economics and the theory of second best. *The Review of Economic Studies, 32,* 1–14.

Diamond, P., & Mirrlees, J. (1971a). Optimal taxation and public production II. *American Economic Review, 61,* 261–278.

Diamond, P., & Mirrlees, J. (1971b). Optimal taxation and public production. *American Economic Review, 61,* 8–27, 261–278.

Dixit, A. (1970). On the optimum structure of commodity taxes. *American Economic Review, 60,* 295–301.

Donohue, J. (1998). Some thoughts on law and economics and the general theory of second best. *Chicago-Kent Law Review, 73,* 257–266.

Drèze, J., & Stern, N. (1987). The theory of cost-benefit analysis. In A. J. Auerbach & M. Feldstein (Eds.), *Handbook of public economics* (Vol. II, pp. 909–989). Amsterdam, New York, Oxford, Tokyo: North Holland.

Driesen, D., & Malloy, R. (2017). Critiques of law and economics. In F. Parisi (Ed.), *The Oxford handbook of law and economics methodology and concepts,* (Vol. I, pp. 300–320). New York: Oxford University Press.

Dusansky, R., & Walsh, J. (1976). Separability, welfare economics, and the theory of second best. *Review of Economic Studies, 43,* 49–51.

Ebert, U. (1985). On the relationship between the Hicksian measures of change in welfare and the Pareto principle. *Social Choice and Welfare, 1,* 263–272.

Faith, R., & Thompson, E. (1981). A paradox in the theory of second best. *Economic Inquiry, 19,* 235–244.

Field, B. (1979). *Environmental economics: An introduction.* New York: McGraw Hill.

Florio, M. (2014). *Applied welfare economics.* London and New York: Routledge.

Gilpin, A. (1999). *Environmental economics: A critical overview.* Chichester, NY: Wiley.

Green, H. (1961). The social optimum in the presence of monopoly and taxation. *Review of Economic Studies, 29,* 68–78.

Gruber, J. (2011). *Public finance and public policy.* New York: Worth Publishers.

Hanley, N., Shogren, J., & White, B. (1997). *Environmental economics in theory and practice.* Oxford and New York: Oxford University Press.

Harberger, A. (1954). Monopoly and resource allocation. *American Economic Review, 44,* 77–87.

Harberger, A. (1971). Three basic postulates for applied welfare economics. *Journal of Economic Literature, 9,* 785–797.

Harberger, A. (1978). On the use of distributive weights in social cost-benefit analysis. *Journal of Political Economy, 86,* S87–S120.

Harrison, J. (2000). *Law and economics in a nutshell* (2d ed.). St. Paul, Minn.: West Group.

Harrison, J. (2003). *Law and economics in a nutshell* (3d ed.). St. Paul, Minn.: Thomson West.

Harrison, J. (2007). *Law and economics: Positive, normative and behavioral perspectives* (2d ed.). St. Paul, Minn.: Thomson West.

Harrison, J. (2011a). *Law and economics in a nutshell* (5th ed.). St. Paul, Minn.: Thomson West.

Harrison, J. (2011b). *Law and economics in a nutshell* (6th ed.). St. Paul, Minn.: West Academic Publishing.

Hillman, A. (2009). *Public finance and public policy: Responsibilities and limitations of government.* Cambridge, England and New York: Cambridge University Press.

Hindricks, J., & Myles, G. D. (2006). *Intermediate public economics,* Cambridge, MA: MIT Press.

Hoff, K. (2001). Second and third best theories. In J. Michie (Ed.), *Readers guide to the social sciences* (pp. 1463–1464). London: Fitzroy Dearborn.

Hyman, D. (2008). *Public finance: A contemporary application of theory to policy.* Mason, OH: Thomson South-Western.

Johansson, P.-O. (1991). *An introduction to modern welfare economics.* Cambridge, England and New York: Cambridge University Press.

Jones, C. (2005). *Applied welfare economics.* Oxford and New York: Oxford University Press.

Kahn, A.E. (1970). *The economics of regulation*—Vol. I, *Principles* and Vol. II, *Institutional Issues.* New York, London, Sydney, and Toronto: Wiley.

Kamerschen, D. (1966). An estimation of the "welfare losses" from monopoly in the American economy. *Western Economic Journal, 4,* 221–236.

Katz, A. (Ed.). (1998). *Foundations of the economic approach to law*. New York: Oxford University Press.

Kuhn, T. (1962). *The structure of scientific revolutions*. Chicago: University of Chicago Press.

Leitzel, J. (2015). *Concepts in law and economics: A guide for the curious*. Oxford and New York: Oxford University Press.

Lipsey, R. (2007). Reflections on the general theory of second best at its golden jubilee. *International Tax and Public Finance, 14*, 349–364.

Lipsey, R. (2012). Prof. Ng's third-best theory (Working Paper, Department of Economics, Simon Fraser University) 1–12.

Lipsey, R. (2017a). Economic policy with and without maximizing rules. *Pacific Economic Review, 22*, 189–212.

Lipsey, R. (2017b). Generality versus context specificity: First, second, and third best in theory and policy. *Pacific Economic Review, 22*, 167–177.

Lipsey, R., & Lancaster, K. (1956). The general theory of second best. *Review of Economic Studies, 24*, 11–32.

Lipsey, R., & Ng, Y.-K. (2017a). Concluding comments to the debate. *Pacific Economic Review, 22*, 213–228.

Lipsey, R., & Ng, Y.-K. (2017b). Editor's introduction. *Pacific Economic Review, 22*, 147–154.

Maks, J. (2005). New-Austrian, industrial and ordo-Austrian competition policy. In J. G. Backhaus (Ed.), *Modern applications of Austrian thought* (pp. 209–222). New York: Routledge.

Markovits, R. (Ed.) (1998a). Symposium on second-best theory and law & economics. *Chicago-Kent Law Review, 73*, 1–274.

Markovits, R. (1998b). Second-best theory and the obligations of academics: A reply to Professor Donohue. *Chicago-Kent Law Review, 73*, 267–274.

Markovits, R. (2008). *Truth or economics: On the definition, prediction, and relevance of economic efficiency*. New Haven and London: Yale University Press.

Markovits, R. (2018a). On the economic efficiency and/or antitrust legality of R&D, R&D-related policies, and R&D-affecting conduct. (article manuscript under submission.).

Masson, R., & Shannon, J. (1984). Social costs of oligopoly and the value of competition. *Economics Journal., 94*, 520–535.

McKitrick, R. (2012). *Economic analysis of environmental policy*. Toronto, Buffalo, and London: University of Toronto Press.

Mercuro, N., & Medema, S. (1997). *Economics and the law: From Posner to post-modernism*. Princeton, NJ: Princeton University Press.

Miceli, T. (2017). *The economic approach to law* (3d ed.) Stanford, CA: Stanford University Press.

Mirrlees, J. (1971). An exploration in the theory of optimum income taxation. *Review of Economic Studies, 38*, 175–208.

Mishan, E.J. (1962). Second thoughts on second-best. *Oxford Economic Papers*, N.S. *14*, 205–217.

Mishan, E. (1971). *Cost-benefit analysis: An informal introduction*. London: George Allen and Unwin.

Ng, Y.-K. (1977). Toward a theory of third-best. *Public Finance, 32*, 1–15.

Ng, Y.-K. (1984). Quasi-Pareto social improvements. *American Economic Review, 74*, 1033–1050.

Ng, Y.-K. (1987a). Equity, efficiency and financial viability: Public-utility pricing with special reference to water supply. *Australian Economic Review, 20*, 21–35.

Ng, Y.-K. (1987b). "Political distortions" and the relevance of second and third-best theories. *Public Finance, 42*, 137–145.

Ng, Y.-K. (2000). The optimal size of public spending, and the distortionary cost of taxation. *National Tax Journal, 53*, 253–272.

Ng, Y.-K. (2004a). *First, second or third-best?, Welfare economics: Towards a more complete analysis*. New York: Palgrave Macmillan.

Ng, Y.-K. (2004b). *Welfare economics: Toward a more complete analysis*. Basingstoke, England and New York: Palgrave Macmillan.

Ng, Y.-K. (2017a). Theory of third best: How to interpret and apply. *Pacific Economic Review, 22,* 178–188.

Ng, Y.-K. (2017b). Towards a theory of third-best (reprint of Ng 1977). *Pacific Economic Review, 22,* 150–166.

Parisi, F. (Ed.) (2017). *The Oxford handbook of law and economics*: Vol. I *Methodology and concepts*; Vol. II *Private and commercial law*; Vol. III *Public law and legal institutions.* Oxford and New York: Oxford University Press.

Polinsky, A. M. (1983). *An introduction to law and economics* (1st ed.). Boston and Toronto: Little Brown and Company.

Polinsky, A. M. (2011). *An introduction to law and economics* (4th ed.). New York: Walter Kluwers.

Posner, E. (Ed.). (2000). *Chicago lectures in law and economics*. New York: Foundation Press.

Posner, R. (1972). *Economic analysis of law* (1st ed.). Boston and Toronto: Little Brown and Company.

Posner, R. (1975). The social costs of monopoly and regulation. *Journal of Political Economy, 83,* 807–828.

Posner, R. (1977). *Economic analysis of law* (2nd ed.). Boston and Toronto: Little Brown and Company.

Posner, R. (1998). *Economic analysis of law* (5th ed.). New York: Walter Kluwers (Aspen).

Posner, R. (2014). *Economic analysis of law* (9th ed.). New York: Walter Kluwers (Aspen).

Rapanos, V. (1980). A comment on the theory of second best. *Review of Economic Studies, 47,* 817–819.

Rosen, H., & Gayer, T. (2014). *Public finance*. New York: McGraw-Hill Higher Education.

Santoni, G., & Church, A. (1972). A comment on the general theorem of second best. *Review of Economic Studies, 39,* 527–530.

Scherer, F. M. (1970). *Market structure and economic performance*. Chicago: Rand McNally.

Schwartzman, D. (1960). The burden of monopoly. *Journal of Political Economy, 68,* 627–630.

Shavell, S. (1980). An analysis of causation and the scope of liability in the law of torts. *Journal of Legal Studies, 9,* 463–516.

Shavell, S. (1987). *Economic analysis of accident law*. Cambridge, MA and London: Harvard University Press (1987).

Shavell, S. (2004). *Foundation of economic analysis of law*. Cambridge, MA and London: Harvard University Press.

Smith, S. (2011). *Environmental economics: A very short introduction*. Oxford and New York: Oxford University Press.

Stigler, G. (1956). The statistics of monopoly and merger. *Journal of Political Economy, 64,* 33–40.

Stiglitz, J. (2000). *Economics of the public sector*. New York: W. W. Norton.

Stiglitz, J., & Dasgupta, P. (1971). Differential taxation, public goods, and economic efficiency. *Review of Economic Studies, 38,* 151–174.

Tietenberg, T. (2007). *Environmental economics & policy* (5th ed.). Boston: Pearson Addison Wesley.

Turner, R. K., Pearce, D., & Bateman, I. (1993). *Environmental economics: An elementary introduction*. Baltimore, MD: The John Hopkins University Press.

Williamson, O. (1968). Economies as an antitrust defense: the welfare trade-off. *American Economic Review, 58,* 18–36.

Woo, W. C. (2010). The theory of second best and third best. In M. Blaug & P. Lloyd (Eds.), *Famous figures and diagrams in economics* (pp. 286–291). Cheltenham, England: Edward Elgar.

Woo, W. C. (2017). The way we teach public economics: A rationalization using the theory of third best. *Pacific Economic Review, 22,* 229–248.

Zerbe, R. (2017). Cost-benefit analysis in legal decision-making. In F. Parisi (Ed.), *Oxford handbook of law and economics methodology and concepts* (Vol. I, pp. 355–380). Oxford and New York: Oxford University Press.

The Concept of the Impact of a Choice (or Natural Event) on Economic Efficiency

3

Abstract

This chapter has two sections. After claiming that definitions of such concepts as "the impact of a choice on economic efficiency" should be evaluated by their conformity to professional and popular understanding and their ability to contribute to the analyses in which they will be used, Sect. 3.1 articulates and elaborates on an equivalent-variation-oriented definition of the concept that it argues best satisfies these criteria. Section 3.2 then contrasts this definition with and explains its superiority to the Pareto-superior/Pareto-inferior definition of increases/decreases in economic efficiency and to the definitions of "the impact of a choice on economic efficiency" implicit in the Kaldor-Hicks test for economic efficiency, the Scitovsky test for economic efficiency, and the potentially-Pareto-superior test for economic efficiency.

3.1 The "Correct" Definition of "The Impact of a Choice on Economic Efficiency"

Two criteria should be used to evaluate definitions of such concepts as "the impact of a choice on economic efficiency": the conformity of the definition to professional and popular understanding and the ability of the concept as defined to contribute to the analyses in which it plays a role. In my judgment, the definition of "the impact of a choice on economic efficiency" that best satisfies these criteria is a monetized definition that equates that impact with the difference between the equivalent-monetary (henceforth, equivalent-dollar) gains the choice confers on its beneficiaries (the winners) and the equivalent-dollar losses it imposes on its victims (the losers). In this formulation, a winner's equivalent-dollar gain equals the number of dollars that would have to be transferred to him to leave him as well-off as the choice would leave him if

© Springer Nature Switzerland AG 2020
R. S. Markovits, *Welfare Economics and Second-Best Theory*,
https://doi.org/10.1007/978-3-030-43360-4_3

(1) he did not agree to the transfer;
(2) he either was intrinsically indifferent to the substitution of the transfer for the choice in question or was unaware of the linkage between the transfer and the relevant choice's rejection;
(3) his distributive attitude toward such transfers, non-parochial distributive preferences, or normative distributive commitments gave him no reason to prefer the transfer to the choice or vice versa; and
(4) the financing of the transfer would not benefit or harm him indirectly by changing the conduct of others by altering their incomes and/or wealths (or by satisfying or dissatisfying his external preferences—i.e., his non-parochial preferences for or against specified others' obtaining resources or having opportunities).

Similarly, in this formulation, a loser's equivalent-dollar loss equals the number of dollars that would have to be withdrawn from him to leave him as poorly-off as the choice would leave him under the loser-counterparts of the four assumptions just delineated.

In essence, this definition of the impact of a choice on economic efficiency incorporates elaborated versions of what economists denominate the "equivalent-variation" as opposed to the "compensating-variation" operationalizations of, respectively, a choice's winners' equivalent-dollar gains and a choice's losers' equivalent-dollar losses: (1) it measures the winners' equivalent-dollar gains by the number of dollars that would have to be transferred to them (on appropriate assumptions) to make them as well-off as the choice would make them as opposed to by the number of dollars whose withdrawal from them on appropriate assumptions would leave them as well-off with the choice's being made as they would have been had neither the withdrawal nor the choice been made, and (2) it measures the losers' equivalent-dollar losses by the number of dollars whose withdrawal from them would (on appropriate assumptions) leave them as poorly-off as the choice would leave them as opposed to by the number of dollars whose transfer to them would (on appropriate assumptions) leave them as well-off with the choice being made as they would have been had neither the transfer nor the choice been made. Basically, the equivalent-variation measures of a choice's winners' equivalent-dollar gains and a choice's losers' equivalent-dollar losses are correct because they are consistent with the reality that the winners have won and the losers have lost. I believe that the definition I have proposed of "the impact of a choice on economic efficiency" conforms to the intuitive understanding of this concept not only of economists but also of members of the policy-audience and the public in general. Moreover, because my definition correctly measures the equivalent-dollar gains of a choice's winners and the equivalent-dollar losses of the choice's losers, it operationalizes the concept in the way that it enables it to contribute most to the evaluation of choices from normative perspectives that deem relevant (even if indirectly) a choice's equivalent-dollar impacts on its beneficiaries and victims.

I acknowledge that, as Sect. 3.2 discusses, other economists recommend and use (or at least purport to use) definitions of "the impact of a choice on economic efficiency" that are different from the definition I claim is "correct"—in particular, propose or use the Pareto-superior/Pareto-inferior definition and the definitions implicit in, respectively, the Kaldor-Hicks test for economic efficiency (Hicks 1940), the Scitovsky test for economic efficiency (Scitovsky 1941), and the potentially-Pareto-superior test for economic efficiency. However, although I admit that, on a few occasions, economists have actually used a monetized version of the Kaldor-Hicks test when analyzing the economic efficiency of large public investments (by basing their assessments of the economic efficiency of dams or airports on the answers that prospective winners and losers give to the questions from whose answers the Kaldor-Hicks test for economic efficiency derives its economic-efficiency conclusions), I do not think that the definition implicit in that test or in any of the other tests referenced in the preceding sentence conforms with these economists', the policy audience's, or the general public's intuitive understanding of "the impact of a choice on economic efficiency." All such individuals believe that the concept references the difference between the actual (equivalent-) dollar gains the relevant choice confers on its beneficiaries and the actual (equivalent-) dollar losses it imposes on its victims, and, as Sect. 3.2 explains, none of these alternative definitions operationalizes the concept in a way that conforms to that understanding.

For related reasons, I also think that my definition creates a concept that can contribute most to the analyses in which it plays a role. Economic-efficiency conclusions play a role in two categories of analyses. The first contains moral evaluations of choices. I acknowledge that, regardless of whether the concept of "the impact of a choice on economic efficiency" is given a monetized or non-monetized definition, economic efficiency is not a moral value in itself. Thus, if "the impact of a choice on economic efficiency" is given a monetized definition according to which a choice is deemed to increase/decrease economic efficiency if the equivalent-dollar gains it confers on its winners exceed/are lower than the equivalent-dollar losses it imposes on its losers, a choice's "economic efficiency" will have no intrinsic moral significance because net equivalent-dollar (greenback) effects have no moral salience in themselves: net greenback gains/losses are not intrinsically morally desirable/morally undesirable. Similarly, if "the impact of a choice on economic efficiency" is given a non-monetized definition according to which a choice is said to increase economic efficiency if and only if it makes somebody better-off and nobody worse-off—i.e., if it moves the economy to a Pareto-superior position—and a choice is said to decrease economic efficiency if and only if it makes somebody worse-off and nobody better-off—i.e., if it moves the economy to a Pareto-inferior position—the economic efficiency of a choice is not directly relevant to its moral desirability from all defensible normative perspectives for two reasons. First, even if one assumes *ad arguendo* that utilitarianism is coherent (that one can measure all affective experiences by units of utility) and morally defensible and that all moves to Pareto-superior/ Pareto-inferior positions increase/decrease the total utility of all creatures whose utility counts (that these conclusions will never be rendered false by the disutility that a Pareto-superior move causes some individuals who value *desiderata* other than utility to experience or by the utility that some Pareto-inferior moves cause some individuals who value *desiderata* other than utility to experience [see below]), utilitarianism is not the only morally-defensible normative position. And second, from many defensible non-utilitarian normative perspectives, it is not morally desirable to make one or more particular individuals better-off even if one can do so without making anyone worse-off, and it is not morally undesirable to make one or more particular individuals worse-off even if doing so does not enable you to make anyone better-off. Thus, from some morally-defensible non-utilitarian normative perspectives, it may not be morally desirable to make a brutal child-murderer better-off even if one can do so without making anyone worse-off. Indeed, one need not conjure up such an extreme case to illustrate this point. For example, from the (admittedly-dubious[1]) moral perspective of the variant of libertarianism that asserts that individuals should receive resources whose allocative cost equals the respective individuals' allocative products (the contribution they make to the total allocative value the relevant economy generated)—i.e., that does not value increases in total utility at all, that values only individuals' being allocated an amount of resources (measured by their allocative cost) equal to the individuals' allocative products defined in the above way, a choice that would confer a gain or impose a loss on an individual who was already being allocated resources whose allocative cost equaled or exceeded his allocative product would be morally undesirable.[2]

I hasten to add, however, that the fact that the economic efficiency of a choice (defined in either the monetized or the non-monetized sense just delineated) is not directly relevant to its moral desirability is perfectly consistent with the conclusion that the economic efficiency of a choice defined in the monetized sense I claim is correct—more specifically, information about the equivalent-dollar gains and losses a choice will confer/impose on its beneficiaries/victims—can perform a useful role in analyses of its moral desirability from a variety of normative perspectives. Indeed, the fact that my definition of "the impact of a choice on economic efficiency" will lead those who use it to supply choice-evaluators with the "equivalent-dollar gain and loss" figures they find relevant is part of my argument for the "correctness" of my definition of "the impact of a choice on economic efficiency."

Let me be more specific. The fact that utilitarians believe that the moral desirability of a choice depends on its impact on the total utility of all creatures whose utility counts will make them value correct estimates of the equivalent-dollar gains and losses a choice generates if I am correct in concluding that the protocol for evaluating choices from the above utilitarian perspective that utilitarianism commends will proceed by (1) estimating the equivalent-dollar gains and losses the choice did/would generate, (2) identifying the characteristics of any individual and of his or her original position that will affect the average per-dollar marginal utility/disutility to that person of any equivalent-dollar gain/loss he or she did/would experience, (3) identifying a random sample of the choice's winners and losers, (4) estimating the marginal-utility-of-money-relevant characteristics and positions of the affected parties being studied, (5) combining steps (2), (3), and (4) to determine the average marginal utility of the equivalent-dollar gains and losses of the winners and losers that were being studied, (6) calculating from this information the average marginal utility of the equivalent-dollars gained by the choice's studied winners and the average marginal utility of the equivalent-dollars lost by the choice's studied losers, (7) multiplying the estimated total-equivalent-dollar-gain and total-equivalent-dollar-loss figures for the studied individuals by the estimates of the average-utility value to the studied winners of the equivalent-dollars they did/would gain and the average-utility value to the studied losers of the equivalent-dollars they did/would lose, (8) calculating the difference between the two multiplicands just referenced, and (9) multiplying that difference by the ratio of the combined number of winners and losers in the whole economy to the combined number of winners and losers in the studied random sample.

Non-utilitarians who think that the amount of resources (measured by their allocative cost) that any individual should receive depends on his or her history (say [morally-dubiously] on the amount by which the individual increased the allocative value generated by the operation of the economy in question and/or on the moral attractiveness of other aspects of the individual's conduct) will also want to know the actual equivalent-dollar gains and losses that the choice in question did/would generate (information that my definition will lead the analyst to provide) because, in conjunction with their conclusions about the allocative cost of the resources that different individuals should receive and their estimates of the allocative cost of the resources relevant individuals would be allocated absent the choice under review, this information will enable them to evaluate the moral desirability of the choice from their respective distributive-norm perspectives if they conclude that, from their normative perspective, the most-morally-desirable way for them to proceed is (1) to estimate the equivalent-dollar gains and losses the choice in question generates, (2) to combine their values and the information they possess about the winners' and losers' value-relevant characteristics, behaviors, and pre-choice positions to determine the weights that their values imply should be assigned to the average equivalent-dollar gained by the choice's winners and the average equivalent-dollar lost by the choice's losers, (3) to multiply their estimates of the equivalent-dollar gains and losses that were/would be generated by the choice to be evaluated by their estimates of the weights that should be assigned to the estimated equivalent-dollar gain and loss figures, and (4) to compare the weighted equivalent-dollar gains and weighted equivalent-dollar-losses.

A second category of analyses to which economic-efficiency conclusions are relevant contains three kinds of legal analyses: (1) analyses of whether administrative officials are legally obligated to cancel or renew (or should cancel or renew) particular administrative regulations when that determination is to be based on a cost-benefit analysis that focuses either exclusively on the economic efficiency of the regulation is question (the criterion that US President Reagan instructed his officials to use) or a more complicated conception of the relevant costs and benefits in which allocative costs and allocative benefits play an important role (the approach that US President Clinton instructed his officials to take); (2) analyses of the interpretations of constitutional provisions, statutes and ordinances, administrative regulations, and judge-announced legal doctrines that are correct as a matter of law or that judges and relevant administrative officials should make in general or in the case at hand (if one believes that legal "interpretations" that are "correct as a matter of law" either never exist or do not exist in the case at hand) in those cases in which (A) the text of the relevant constitutional provision, statute or ordinance, administrative regulation, or judicially-announced doctrine explicitly states that it was designed to promote economic efficiency either exclusively or together with other *desiderata* or (B)(i) such a conclusion is warranted by the relevant source of law's history (the events that led to a statute's promulgation, comments made by its promulgators about the way in which they thought it would be interpreted, and statements made by its promulgators about the reasons for their voting for it, etc.) and (ii) in the legal system in question, information about promulgator-intent is deemed relevant to legal interpretation even when the relevant text does not reveal the intent; and (3) analyses of the applications of a constitutional provision, statute or ordinance, administrative regulation, or judicially-announced doctrine that are, respectively, correct as a matter of law or that judges/relevant administrative officials should make. In the USA, many pollution-focused statutes, ordinances and regulations, many land-use statutes, ordinances, and regulations, and many intellectual-property statutes and regulations are clearly designed at least in substantial part to increase economic efficiency. (I reject the claim of most US Law and Economics scholars that US antitrust law promulgates or should be interpreted to promulgate an economic-inefficiency test of illegality as well as the claim of many Law and Economics scholars that economic-efficiency analysis is an algorithm for determining the responses to common-law legal-rights claims that are correct as a matter of law, the responses to such claims that judges should make, or the responses to such claims that judges will increasingly make over time.) In any event, to the extent that the conclusions that relevant decision-makers should reach on these sorts of legal issues should at least partially be influenced by the relative economic efficiency of the available options, my definition of economic efficiency will lead economic-efficiency analysts to supply the legal decision-makers in question with the relevant information.[3]

3.2   The Alternative Definitions of "The Impact of a Choice on Economic Efficiency" that Other Economists Have Proposed and Used and Why These Alternatives Are Either Useless or Inaccurate

This section delineates and criticizes four definitions of "the impact of a choice on economic efficiency" that differ from the definition I have proposed. The first is the (non-monetized) Pareto-superior/Pareto-inferior definition of an increase/decrease in economic efficiency that economists often claim to be using even though, when they actually get down to analyzing the economic efficiency of the choices on which their respective articles focus, they abandon this definition in favor of some usually-unarticulated monetized definition because they realize that the choices in question produce both winners and losers.

According to the Pareto-superior/Pareto-inferior definition of the impact of a choice on economic efficiency, (1) a choice is said to have increased economic efficiency if and only if it made at least one-person better-off and no-one worse-off (effectuated a move to a so-called Pareto-superior position), and (2) a choice is said to have decreased economic efficiency if and only if it made at least one person worse-off and no-one better-off (effectuated a move to a so-called Pareto-inferior position). Although I recognize the advantage of using a non-monetized definition of "the impact of a choice on economic efficiency" (doing so avoids the problem that introducing money into the model creates for solving any general-equilibrium system of equations), this definition neither comports with the way in which economists, members of the policy-audience, or the public in general understands the concept nor creates a concept that can play a useful role in any analysis: the Pareto-superior/Pareto-inferior definition is useless because, as I have already indicated, all or virtually all choices whose economic efficiency is at issue will make some individuals better-off and some, worse-off so that, on the Pareto-superior/Pareto-inferior definition, the economic efficiency of all or virtually all such choices will be indeterminate. I should add that, as I have also previously indicated, the usefulness of the Pareto-superior/Pareto-inferior definition is under-mined as well by the fact that—from various defensible, non-utilitarian normative perspectives—the moral desirability of a choice is not guaranteed by its Pareto-superiority and the moral undesirability of a choice is not guaranteed by its Pareto-inferiority.

The second alternative to my definition that economists have proposed and continue to use is the Kaldor-Hicks test (Hicks 1940). According to this test, a choice increases economic efficiency if and only if its winners could profit by paying its losers enough for granting their respective essential consents to it to leave each loser indifferent to accepting the (hypothetical) "bribe" in question. This test and its implicit definition of "the impact of a choice on economic efficiency"—in the test's monetized variant, the difference between the sum of the dollar-amounts the winners would be indifferent to paying if the alternative were the choice's rejection and the sum of the dollar-bribes the losers would be indifferent to accepting in exchange for granting their respective critical assents to the choice's being made—are wrong for three reasons. First, the Kaldor-Hicks test is incorrect because it uses the compensating-variation rather than the equivalent-variation measures, respectively, of a choice's winners' equivalent-dollar gains and a choice's losers' equivalent-dollar losses. Its adoption of the compensating-variation measure is wrong for two reasons. First, successive monetary units have dimin-ishing marginal value and on this account (A) the number of dollars whose with-drawal from a winner will inflict a given value-loss (say, utility-loss) on the winner will be lower than the number of dollars whose transfer to the winner will confer the same amount of value (e.g., the same utility-gain) on him and (B) the number of dollars whose withdrawal from a loser will inflict a given value-loss (say, utility-loss) on the loser will be lower than the number of dollars whose transfer to the loser will confer an equal value-gain (e.g., utility-gain) on the loser—i.e., on this account, the Kaldor-Hicks test will tend to underestimate each winner's equivalent-dollar gain and overestimate each loser's equivalent-dollar loss if one grants (as I think one must) that a winner's equivalent-dollar gain equals the number of dollars whose transfer to him would (on appropriate assumptions) leave him as well-off as the choice would leave him and that a loser's equivalent-dollar loss equals the number of dollars whose withdrawal from him would (on appropriate assumptions) leave him as well-off as the choice would leave him. Second, the compensating-variation measure is wrong because (1) the equivalent-dollar gain that some choices confer on their winners and the equivalent-dollar loss that some choices confer on their losers depend on these parties' wealths at the time at which the choice is implemented and (2) the Kaldor-Hicks test proceeds on counterfactual assumptions about the wealth-positions of the choice's winners and losers at the time the choice will be made—viz., assumes that the choice's winners' wealths will (counterfactually) be reduced by the (hypothetical) bribe they would have to pay its losers to leave the losers as well-off with the choice being made as they would have been had it not been made and that the choice's losers' wealths will (counterfactually) be increased prior to the choice's being made by the hypothetical bribe in question. The following example illustrates the point made in the preceding sentence. Assume that the quantity demand that those beneficiaries of an antitrust policy that would reduce the price of a good they purchase have for that good at any relevant price increases (decreases) with their wealths at the time of the choice's implementation. Because the Kaldor-Hicks test measures the equivalent-dollar gains that such a policy will confer on such winners on the counterfactual assumption that their wealths will be reduced (by the bribe they are asked to assume they will be paying the policy's losers) prior to the policy's adoption and implementation, this test's estimates of the equivalent-dollar gains the policy will confer on these winners will on this account be too low in positive-wealth-elasticity-of-demand cases because the test will measure each winner's dollar gain on the assumption that the winner will be poorer than he or she actually will be when the policy is implemented (that, counterfactually, each winner's wealth will be reduced by the Kaldor-Hicks hypothetical bribe prior to the policy's implementation)—a false assumption that will lead (1) any winner whose demand for the relevant product is positively wealth-elastic to base his/her response to the Kaldor-Hicks question on the assumption that he will buy fewer units of the product in question than he in fact will buy post-policy and therefore will gain less from the price-reduction the policy secures than he actually will gain from it and (2) will lead any winner whose demand for the relevant product is negatively-wealth-elastic to base his/her response to the Kaldor-Hicks question on an assumption that he/she will buy more units of the product in question post-policy than he/she in fact will buy and therefore will gain more from the price-reductions the policy secures than he actually will gain from it. The Kaldor-Hicks test will also on this account mis-estimate the equivalent-dollar loss a policy that imposes an effluent tax on a producer will impose on consumers of the good the taxed producer produces by increasing the marginal costs the producer must incur to produce the relevant product and hence the price it charges for that product if the relevant buyers' demands for this product are wealth-elastic because the test will measure those losses on the counterfactual assumption that the losers' wealths will be increased prior to the policy's implementation by the bribe they will hypothetically but counterfactually be paid to secure their critical acquiescence to the policy's adoption and implementation—i.e., on counterfactual assumptions about the quantities of the good in question the relevant buyers will purchase at various prices. I should point out that this error can cause the Kaldor-Hicks test either to overestimate or to underestimate the economic efficiency of a choice, depending on whether the winners' and losers' dollar-valuations of the choice are positively or negatively wealth-elastic.

Second, the Kaldor-Hicks test is also incorrect because it measures the winners' equivalent-dollar gains and the losers' equivalent-dollar losses on the assumption that the parties in question have agreed to the choice's being made in a voluntary market transaction. This assumption is at least sometimes distorting because (1) it is always inaccurate—no bribes are ever offered or paid—and (2) in some cases, engaging in voluntary market transactions will be intrinsically costly or beneficial— e.g., agreeing to a choice that compromises your or your spouse's, child's, or friend's health or agreeing to a choice that compensates someone you consider to be a wrongdoer for not engaging in wrongdoing may be intrinsically costly to the agreer or agreeing to sell one of your kidneys to obtain money to finance your child's education may have an intrinsic positive value for the agreer.

Third, the Kaldor-Hicks test is incorrect as well because it ignores the fact that the hypothetical bribes it posits (1) could confer an equivalent-dollar gain or impose an equivalent-dollar loss on the choice's winners by altering the wealth-positions of the choice's losers (the recipients of the bribes) and thereby their consumption and labor decisions—e.g., by causing them to buy a less-polluting car, which they drive in the winners' neighborhood—and (2) could confer an equivalent-dollar gain or impose an equivalent-dollar loss on the choice's losers (the bribes' recipients) by altering its winners' (the bribes' payors') wealth-positions and thereby their consumption and labor decisions. This third mistake of the Kaldor-Hicks test renders the test inaccurate because the mistake leads the choice's winners to base their calculations of the highest bribe they would be willing to pay *inter alia* on their estimate of the equivalent-dollar impact that the hypothetical, counterfactual bribe would have on them by altering the choices of those bribed by altering their wealths and because it will lead the choice's losers to base their calculations of the lowest bribe that would make them whole *inter alia* on their estimate of the equivalent-dollar impact on them that the hypothetical, counterfactual bribe in question would have by altering the bribe-payors' choices by altering the bribe-payors' wealths.

The third alternative to my definition that economists use is the definition implicit in the Scitovsky test for economic efficiency (Scitovsky 1941). In a 1941 article, Scitovsky used an Edgeworth Box to demonstrate that the indifference curves (now called "revealed preference curves") for two relevant products could have attributes that would create a situation in which both a choice and its immediate reversal would pass the Kaldor-Hicks test. This Scitovsky Paradox is obviously problematic because it reveals that, under certain conditions, according to the definition of the impact of a choice on economic efficiency that is implicit in the Kaldor-Hicks test, the choices that give rise to Scitovsky Paradoxes are simultaneously economically efficient (because they pass the Kaldor-Hicks test) and economically inefficient (because their reversals are economically efficient in that they would pass the Kaldor-Hicks test). Rather than trying to identify the conditions under which the Scitovsky Paradox will arise[4] and, derivatively, the mistake in the Kaldor-Hicks test that Scitovsky's analysis reveals, economists responded to the Scitovsky Paradox by proposing a new (so-called) Scitovsky test for economic efficiency that, in more-modern terminology, merely puts a patch on the Kaldor-Hicks test. According to this Scitovsky test, a choice increases economic efficiency if and only if (1) the choice passes the Kaldor-Hicks test and (2) the choice's immediate reversal does not pass the Kaldor-Hicks test. Unfortunately, the Scitovsky test is still incorrect: (1) since its first component is the Kaldor-Hicks test, its use of the compensating-variation rather than the equivalent-variation measure of the choice's winners' and losers' equivalent-dollar gains and losses will continue to result in its failing to deem economically efficient some economically-efficient choices that fail the Kaldor-Hicks test, and (2) both its first component and its second component have all the other deficiencies of the Kaldor-Hicks test.

   The fourth and final alternative definition of "the impact of a choice on economic efficiency" I will discuss is the definition implicit in the potentially-Pareto-superior test for economic efficiency. According to this test, a choice is said to increase economic efficiency if and only if the combination of the choice and an allocative-transaction-costless money-transfer policy that could be financed without generating any economic inefficiency (I am elaborating on and improving this test) would move the economy to a Pareto-superior position. The definition of "the impact of a choice on economic inefficiency" that is implicit in this potentially-Pareto-superior test for economic efficiency (I assume: the net equivalent-dollar gain that would be generated by a policy-package that consists of the choice and the money transfer whose combination with it would produce a Pareto-superior policy-package) is incorrect because this test ignores the fact that—even if the hypothesized money transfer would not generate any allocative transaction costs or public-financing-generated misallocation—in economies that would contain some Pareto imperfections at some distributions of wealth and income (though not in economies that would always be Pareto-perfect) the hypothesized money-transfer could increase or decrease economic efficiency by changing the wealth and derivatively the nature and/or economic efficiency of the choices of the transfer-recipients. For this reason, in realistically-Pareto-imperfect economies, (1) a choice that could be combined with an allocative-transaction-costless government-transfer program whose implementation would not generate any economic-efficiency losses in any other way to form a Pareto-superior choice/transfer-policy-package might be economically inefficient—in particular, would be economically inefficient if the government transfer-program in question increased economic efficiency by more than the choice decreased economic efficiency—and (2) a choice that could not be combined with an allocative-transaction-costless government transfer-policy whose implementation would not cause economic inefficiency in any other way to form a Pareto-superior choice/transfer policy-package would still be economically efficient if it was economically efficient and all otherwise-suitable government transfer-programs would decrease economic efficiency by altering the wealths and therefore the decisions and/or the economic efficiency of the decisions of the payors and payees by more than the choice under review increased economic efficiency. The error that renders the potentially-Pareto-superior definition of economically-efficient choices false (the failure to realize that in economies that may contain Pareto imperfections at some distributions of wealth) is one of the errors that renders the Kaldor-Hicks test false (its failure to take account of the fact that in actual, Pareto-imperfect economies the hypothetical bribe it posits may affect not only the winners' and losers' equivalent-dollar-gains but also economic efficiency by changing the distribution of wealth).

Notes

1. This norm is morally dubious *inter alia* because it is based on an implicit assumption that individuals are morally responsible for their respective allocative products when in fact an individual's allocative product is substantially affected by many factors over which he or she had no control (*inter alia*, his or her genetic endowments, the individual's mother's nutrition and psychological state when the individual was in utero, the nutrition/clothing/housing/medical care/parental nurturing the individual received when growing up, the quality of the formal education he or she received, the tastes of members of the society in question and the distributions of income and wealth in that society [both of which determine the allocative value of the most-allocatively-efficient and personally-advantageous labor the individual could supply], the number of other members of the society who had the abilities/education/skills the individual in question possessed, the number of other members of the society who would find it profitable to supply for different wages labor that would yield goods or services that are complements to the good or service the individual in question could produce, the incidences and magnitudes of those of the relevant economy's Pareto imperfections that distort the value of the individual's labor to prospective employers, etc.). For a more detailed account of this argument and a partially-related critique of the claim that government redistributions of income are morally undesirable from a libertarian perspective, see Markovits (2008), pp. 358–359, 442 note 10, and 448 note 11.
2. For a more general discussion of the moral relevance of a choice's impact on economic efficiency, see Markovits (2008), pp. 344–362 and pp. 378–397.
3. For a more-detailed account of the relevance to (1) the correctness as a matter of law of a decision to renew or cancel a regulation or to interpret or apply a constitutional provision, statute or ordinance, regulation, or judge-announced doctrine in a particular way of (2) that decision's/interpretation's/application's economic efficiency, see Markovits (2008), pp. 362–375 and pp. 397–401.

4. If I ignore complications associated with the Kaldor-Hicks test's and the Scitovsky test's assumptions that the relevant actors are engaging in voluntary market transactions and other complications related to my elaboration of the correct equivalent-variation-oriented definition of "the impact of a choice on economic efficiency," the Scitovsky Paradox will arise when (1) the choice in question is economically inefficient (as shown by the fact that its reversal passes the Kaldor-Hicks test) but (2) it passes the Kaldor-Hicks test because (for example) the absolute magnitude of the choice's victims' negative dollar-valuation of the choice is sufficiently negatively-wealth-elastic to cause their responses to the question to which the Kaldor-Hicks test asks them to respond to underestimate their equivalent-dollar loss sufficiently to lead the Kaldor-Hicks test to yield the conclusion that an economically-inefficient choice was economically efficient. For a detailed example illustrating this conclusion, see Markovits (2008), pp. 54–55.

References

Hicks, J. R. (1940). The rehabilitation of consumer surplus. *Review of Economic Studies, 8,* 108–116.
Markovits, R. (2008). *Truth or economics: On the definition, prediction, and relevance of economic efficiency.* New Haven and London: Yale University Press.
Scitovsky, T. (1941). A note on welfare propositions in economics. *Review of Economic Studies, 9,* 77–88.

"First-Best," "Second-Best," and "Third-Best": Definitions, Elaborations, and Other Economists' Usages

4

Abstract

Section 4.1 states that, on my definition, first-best-allocative-efficiency (FBLE)-analysis protocols and concrete FBLE economic-efficiency analyses proceed on the assumption that the Pareto imperfection whose alteration's economic efficiency is at issue is the only Pareto imperfection in the relevant economy. Section 4.1 also points out that the FBLE magnitude of any Pareto imperfection is zero. Section 4.2 explains that, on my definitions, second-best-allocative-efficiency (SBLE)-analysis protocols and concrete SBLE analyses are the protocols and analyses that would be economically efficient if all theoretical and empirical research could be executed perfectly accurately and financed at no allocative cost. Section 4.2 also indicates that the SBLE magnitude of any Pareto imperfection is the magnitude of that imperfection that minimizes the amount of economic inefficiency generated in the relevant situation. Section 4.3 states that, on my definitions, third-best-allocatively-efficient (TBLE) protocols for economic-efficiency analysis and TBLE concrete economic-efficiency analyses are, respectively, the protocols and analyses that are ex ante economically efficient, given the inaccuracy of relevant research and the allocative cost and benefits of executing and financing it and assessing its economic-efficiency implications. Section 4.3 also states that the TBLE magnitude of any Pareto imperfection is the magnitude that a TBLE concrete analysis will deem economic-inefficiency-minimizing. Section 4.4 contrasts my definitions of "first-best," "second-best," and "third-best" with the usages of two other prominent Second-Best theorists.

© Springer Nature Switzerland AG 2020
R. S. Markovits, *Welfare Economics and Second-Best Theory*,
https://doi.org/10.1007/978-3-030-43360-4_4

4.1 First-Best-Allocatively-Efficient (FBLE) Economic-Efficiency-Analysis Protocols, FBLE Concrete Economic-Efficiency Analyses, and the FBLE Magnitude of Any Pareto Imperfection

In my terminology, a protocol for economic-efficiency analysis is FBLE if it instructs the analyst to assume that each Pareto imperfection the analyst is assuming can be changed is the only Pareto imperfection in the relevant economy. Relatedly, any concrete economic-efficiency analysis is a FBLE economic-efficiency analysis if its analysis of the impact on economic efficiency of increasing or decreasing the magnitude of each Pareto imperfection whose magnitude the past/proposed choice under review did/would change assumed that that Pareto imperfection was the only Pareto imperfection in the relevant economy. And, again relatedly, the magnitude of any Pareto imperfection that is FBLE is the magnitude that would be economically efficient for that Pareto imperfection to have (namely, zero) if the economy in question were oPp and would remain oPp post-choice and no allocative transaction costs and no economic inefficiency of any type would have to be generated to eliminate the Pareto imperfection in question. The last clause of the preceding sentence is included in recognition of the fact that choices that eliminate a particular Pareto imperfection might generate (what might be called) another Pareto imperfection (e.g., choices to secure perfect price competition by breaking up firms that charged supra-competitive prices pre-choice and not allowing them to reintegrate might cause economic inefficiency by creating firms that cannot take advantage of economies of scale—i.e., by prohibiting firms from making what would otherwise be their profit-maximizing choice [to reintegrate to take advantage of economies of scale]).

Five points should be made about FBLE analysis. First, any claim that FBLE analysis always yields accurate economic-efficiency conclusions (in effect, is second-best-allocatively-efficient—see below) because the Pareto imperfection the decision-maker can directly control (the "target Pareto imperfection") is the only Pareto imperfection in the economy is based on an obviously false empirical assumption. Second, any claim that FBLE analysis always yields accurate economic-efficiency conclusions because—although relevant economies do contain non-target Pareto imperfections—acting individually, none of the individual non-target Pareto imperfections that actual economies contain would render the economic-efficiency conclusions of FBLE analyses inaccurate (or critically inaccurate) is wrong—i.e., it is clear that, in all or virtually all cases, acting individually, one or more than one of the non-target Pareto imperfections that actual economies contain will affect the impact of increasing or decreasing the target Pareto imperfection on economic efficiency (inter alia, will affect the most-allocatively-efficient magnitude[s] of the target Pareto imperfection[s]). Third, any claim that FBLE analysis always yields accurate economic-efficiency conclusions because the non-target Pareto imperfections that any economy contains will always interact in ways that result in their collectively having no impact (or no critical impact) on the effect that increasing or decreasing the target imperfection has on economic efficiency is wrong: at least, no one has ever demonstrated that this claim is correct, and there is no reason to believe that the conditions that would have to be satisfied for this claim to be true for all sets of non-target Pareto imperfections that actual economies contain will always be satisfied. Fourth, those that claim that FBLE analysis will always yield accurate economic-efficiency conclusions ignore the facts that, even if all relevant economies were oPp pre-choice, a choice that reduces a target Pareto imperfection (1) might cause the economy to contain one or more non-target Pareto imperfections and (2) the combination of the relevant economy's resulting non-target Pareto imperfections and the post-choice target Pareto imperfection (whose magnitude may be zero) may yield more economic inefficiency than was generated pre-choice by the pre-choice target Pareto imperfection in an oPp economy. Some explanation of this last point may be instructive. Thus, a choice to reduce a supra-competitive price could substitute for a situation in which no external costs were generated by the production of any units of the product in question a situation in which significant external costs were generated by the production of the marginal and some intra-marginal units of the good in question by increasing the unit output of that good. Or a choice to impose a pollution tax that would internalize what was originally an external cost of production might cause external costs to be generated by the consumption decisions of buyers of the product whose production generated external costs pre-choice by causing the price of that good to rise, thereby inflicting a loss on that product's consumers, thereby inducing them to make economically inefficient because external-cost-generating consumption decisions (to live in cheaper, uglier, more-disease-and-fire-spreading housing units or to buy and drive cheaper cars that are more accident-prone, more breakdown-prone, more air-polluting, and more noise-polluting than the cars they would otherwise have purchased and driven) by making these buyers worse-off and thereby making it in their individual interests to purchase the cheaper, more-externality-prone product. Fifth, and relatedly, those that claim that FBLE analysis will always yield accurate economic-efficiency conclusions ignore the fact that, in an economy that is not oPp pre-choice, (1) a choice that increases a target Pareto imperfection might decrease or eliminate a non-target Pareto imperfection and (2) the combination of the higher post-choice target Pareto imperfection and the lower post-choice non-target Pareto imperfection may yield less economic inefficiency than was yielded by the combination of the lower pre-choice target Pareto imperfection and the higher pre-choice non-target Pareto imperfection. For example, such commentators ignore the possibility that a choice that will increase the supra-competitiveness of prices (e.g., by allowing a merger between competitors) may increase economic efficiency by preventing the generation of external costs of production by reducing the unit outputs of the merged firm's two divisions (one for each merger partner's operations) below the unit outputs that the merger partners would otherwise have produced when the production of the lower unit outputs generates no external costs while the production of the "eliminated" output did generate external costs pre-merger in a situation in which the post-choice combination of more-supra-competitive prices and lower external costs of production is less misallocative than the pre-choice combination of less-supra-competitive prices and higher external costs of production.

4.2 Second-Best-Allocatively-Efficient (SBLE) Economic-Efficiency-Analysis Protocols, SBLE Concrete Economic-Efficiency Analyses, and the SBLE Magnitude of Any Pareto Imperfection

In my terminology, (1) a protocol for economic-efficiency analysis is SBLE if its perfect execution would yield completely accurate conclusions about the economic efficiency of choices, (2) a concrete economic-efficiency analysis is SBLE if it was carried out in the way that would yield completely-accurate economic efficiency conclusions, and (3) the magnitude of any Pareto imperfection that would be SBLE in a given situation is the magnitude of that Pareto imperfection that would minimize economic inefficiency in the situation in question.

I want to make two points or sets of points about SBLE economic-efficiency analyses. First, such analyses are the analyses that would be *ex ante* economically efficient if they could be executed perfectly accurately at no allocative cost. Second, it is important to recognize that at least two specific types of economic-efficiency-analysis protocols could be second-best-allocatively-efficient. One would instruct the analyst (1) to identify all of the relevant choice's winners and losers, (2) to determine perfectly accurately (through some protocol I will not and cannot delineate) each such creature's equivalent-dollar gain or loss, and (3) to sum the accurate determinations of those equivalent-dollar gains and losses. The other would be the SBLE variant of the distortion-analysis protocol for economic-efficiency analysis this book proposes.

4.3 Third-Best-Allocatively-Efficient (TBLE) Economic-Efficiency-Analysis Protocols, TBLE Concrete Economic-Efficiency Analyses, and the TBLE Magnitude of Any Pareto Imperfection

In my terminology, a protocol for economic-efficiency analysis is TBLE if its use is *ex ante* allocatively efficient, given all the allocative costs and the allocative benefits of executing any relevant theoretical or empirical research-project and of devoting additional attention to the implications of what is known for the economic efficiency of any choice. Relatedly, a concrete economic-efficiency analysis is TBLE if it is *ex ante* economically efficient, given the just-referenced allocative costs and benefits. Relatedly again, the magnitude of a Pareto imperfection is TBLE if and only if it would be deemed to be the most *ex ante* economically-efficient magnitude for that Pareto imperfection by a TBLE economic-efficiency analysis.

I have two points or sets of points to make about third-best-allocatively-efficient concrete economic-efficiency analyses. First, although, like SBLE concrete economic-efficiency analyses, TBLE concrete economic-efficiency analyses always proceed on the accurate assumption that it is impossible or economically inefficient to remove all Pareto imperfections, unlike SBLE concrete economic-efficiency analyses, TBLE concrete economic-efficiency analyses take account of the facts that (1) theoretical research, empirical research, and the consideration of the implications of what was known ab initio and the conclusions of the research the analyst has done for the economic efficiency of the choice under consideration (and other choices) use up resources that would have generated net allocative benefits in their sacrificed uses (resources whose use is allocatively costly), (2) the *ex ante* economically-efficient execution and use of such research may cause economic inefficiency by delaying government decisions, (3) the government's financing of such research and its use may generate allocative transaction costs and may generate various categories of economic inefficiency, (4) research and its use may be imperfect, and (5) the allocative benefits that research generates equals the amount by which it increases the economic efficiency not only of the choice under consideration but also of other choices whose economic efficiency its conclusions illuminate. In my judgment, the preceding account of the protocol for third-best-allocatively-efficient economic-efficiency analysis is extremely important. Indeed, one of my basic criticisms of the theoretical-Welfare-Economic literature is that it does not devote any attention to the protocol that would be *ex ante* economically efficient for economic-efficiency analysts to use to decide whether it would be *ex ante* economically efficient to devote additional resources to executing particular theoretical or empirical research projects or to devote additional attention to considering the implications of what they know for the economic efficiency of the choice whose economic efficiency is at issue (that it assumes that economic-efficiency analysts cannot alter the information at their disposal and ignores the allocative cost of economic-efficiency analysts' considering the implications of what they know for the economic efficiency of the choices whose economic efficiency they are assessing as well as the economic-efficiency gains that research that is originally designed to illuminate the economic efficiency of one choice can generate by improving the prediction/post-diction of the economic efficiency of other choices).

Second, I want to repeat the standard decision-theory point I made in Sect. 1.3. To provide a complete account of the economic-efficiency-analysis protocol that would be TBLE, one would have to resolve the following infinite-regress problem, which seems to me to be unresolvable: how can an analyst determine whether it would be *ex ante* economically efficient to consider whether it would be *ex ante* economically efficient to consider whether it would be economically efficient to consider whether it would be economically efficient…to execute a particular research project that might be relevant to determining the economic efficiency of a choice whose economic efficiency is at issue or to devote additional resources to analyzing the implications of the information at the analyst's disposal for the economic efficiency of that choice? As I said earlier, my only response is the somewhat-lame claim that at some point the analyst will intuit that it will not be economically efficient to proceed further down this rabbit-hole and that intra-analyst differences in such intuitions are unlikely to affect significantly the set of research-projects that is executed, the time devoted to considering the implications of the information at the analyst's disposal, or a fortiori the analyst's economic-efficiency conclusion.

4.4 The Differences Between My Use of the Expressions "First-Best," "Second-Best," and "Third-Best" and the Ways in Which These Expressions Are Used by Other Economists—In Particular, by Y.-K. Ng and Richard Lipsey

The final points I wish to make in this chapter relate to the difference between (1) my use of "first-best," "second-best," and "third-best" as modifiers of economic-efficiency-analysis protocols, concrete economic-efficiency analyses, and the magnitude of some Pareto imperfection that would be economically efficient in the situation in question and (2) other economists'—in particular, Richard Lipsey's and Y.-K. Ng's—use of "first-best," "second-best," and "third-best" terminology. The first such point is that these other economists do not explicitly use the expressions "first-best," "second-best," and "third-best" to describe categories of protocols for economic-efficiency (or social-welfare) analyses or particular concrete economic-efficiency (or social-welfare) analyses. They use them instead to characterize (1) magnitudes of "distortions" (Ng's term for what I denominate "Pareto imperfections" or "departures from a set of optimal conditions") or "sources" (Lipsey's term for what I denominate "Pareto imperfections" or "departures from a set of sufficient optimal conditions") that are first-best-economically-efficient or most-promotive-of-social welfare, second-best-economically-efficient or most-promotive-of-social welfare, or third-best-economically-efficient or most-promotive-of-social welfare [I will omit the words following "or" in the text that follows], (2) policy choices or government decision-rules that are "first-best" (economically efficient), "second-best" (economically efficient), or "third-best" (economically efficient), and (3) in Ng's case, states of the world that (he argues) make the first-best decision-rule *ex ante* most-economically-efficient (third-best-economically-efficient). I am tempted to say that this difference in usage is revealing in that it suggests that, like other economists, these scholars do not make any attempt to identify the protocol for economic-efficiency analysis that is *ex ante* economically efficient in the real world. I admit, however, that that inference is disfavored by the fact that Ng is arguing that, under particular conditions he thinks will often be fulfilled (when what he calls the "relation curve" is concave and the analyst is operating under conditions of "Informational Poverty"), the conclusions of what I call first-best-economically-efficient economic-efficiency analyses will be *ex ante* economically efficient.

The second difference in usage I want to point out relates to my and Lipsey's or Ng's description of the states of the world that call for "second-best" and "third-best" analyses. Thus, according to Lipsey: "A 'second best situation' refer[s] to *any* situation in which the first best ... [is] unachievable" and "[t]he 'second best optimum setting' for any *source* (what I would denominate "Pareto imperfection" or "departure from a set of optimal conditions") refer[s] to the setting of that *source* that maximizes the value of the objective function, given settings on all the other existing sources" (Lipsey 2007, p. 35, summarizing and confirming his continuing adherence to the position he and Lancaster took in 1956—Lancaster and Lipsey 1956). I disagree with the part of Lipsey's statement that begins with "given": that component of Lipsey's account ignores the fact that, as I explained in Sect. 4.1, changes in the magnitude of one "source" (one Pareto imperfection) may affect the magnitudes of one or more other "sources" (Pareto imperfections) and hence the extent to which the actual outcome is non-optimal. I also disagree with Ng's accounts of the defining characteristics of what he calls "a third-best world": (1) the combination of what he denominates "distortions" (which I call "Pareto imperfections" or "departures from a set of optimal conditions") and "information costs" (Ng 2017, p. 157) or (2) "the existence of some second-best constraints [in my terms, 'Pareto imperfections that cannot be removed either at all or economic-efficiently'] plus the presence of informational and administrative costs" (Ng 2017, p. 181). I think that my usages are more informative than Ng's. Thus, I think it more informative to attribute economic inefficiency to Pareto imperfections (more accurately, to the interaction of Pareto imperfections) than to "distortions." I acknowledge that (1) in ordinary language, in an economic-efficiency-analysis context, a private figure would be said to be "distorted" if it differs from its allocative counterpart—for example, the profits yielded by a resource allocation would be said to be distorted if they differ from the economic efficiency of that allocation—and (2) profit distortions cause economic inefficiency (or at least will do so if [A] they cause economically-efficient resource allocations to be unprofitable or economically-inefficient resource allocations to be profitable and [B] the resource allocator is a sovereign maximizer). Nevertheless, I still find it more informative to attribute economic inefficiency to Pareto imperfections or their non-perfectly-counteracting interaction, given that (1) non-perfectly-counteracting Pareto imperfections are the cause of profit distortions and (2) profit distortions may not cause economic inefficiency if they do not critically affect the profitability of the relevant resource allocation and/or if the relevant resource allocator makes the economically-efficient choice despite the fact that the operative profit distortion rendered it unprofitable (because he or she is not a sovereign maximizer and his or her ignorance and miscalculations interact to cause him or her to make a mistake). I also think that my specification of the reasons why TBLE economic-efficiency analyses differ from SBLE economic-efficiency analyses is far more informative than Ng's attribution of this difference to "informational and administrative costs." But I should keep my eye on the ball: for current purposes, the relative informativeness of my and Ng's different statements of the cause of economic inefficiency and different definitions of "third-best" analyses and "third-best world" is less important than readers' keeping in mind my specification of the defining characteristics of any third-best-economically-efficient economic-efficiency-analysis protocol when considering the arguments that follow.

References

Lipsey, R., & Lancaster, K. (1956). The general theory of second best. *Review of Economic Studies, 24*, 11–32.

Lipsey, R. (2007). Reflections on the general theory of second best on its golden jubilee. *International Tax and Public Finance, 14*, 349–364.

Ng, Y.-K. (2017). Towards a theory of third-best. *Pacific Economic Review, 22*, 150–166.

The Symbols for Various Pareto Imperfections, Private and Allocative Concepts, Categories of Resource-Uses, and Categories of Resource Allocations

5

Abstract

This chapter has five sections. Section 5.1 specifies the symbols I use to reference, respectively, each of the seven types of Pareto imperfections an economy may contain. Section 5.2 specifies the symbols I use to reference, respectively, private-benefit, private-cost, (private) profit, allocative-benefit, allocative-cost, and allocative-efficiency figures. Section 5.3 specifies the symbols I use to reference, respectively, three categories of resource-uses. And Sect. 5.4 specifies the symbols I use to reference, respectively, particular categories of resource allocations.

5.1 The Symbols I Use to Reference, Respectively, Each Type of Pareto Imperfections

In an oPp economy, an exemplar of any of the seven types of Pareto imperfections can cause economic inefficiency.[1] One type of Pareto imperfections is imperfections in seller competition. Three variants of imperfect seller competition can be distinguished—imperfections in seller price-competition, imperfections in quality-or-variety-increasing-investment (QV-investment) competition, and imperfections in production-process-research (PPR) competition. Imperfect seller price-competition is manifest in one or more sellers' obtaining a price for its (their) product(s) in excess of the product's (products') marginal cost(s). Imperfections in QV-investment competition/PPR competition are manifest in one or more sellers' realizing a supernormal profit-rate on a QV investment it created/a PPR project it executed in a relevant area of product-space. I use the letter "M" to stand for an imperfection in seller competition. This symbol (which calls to mind the word "monopoly") is somewhat misleading because imperfections in seller price-competition or QV-investment or PPR competition can be attributable to the seller's

© Springer Nature Switzerland AG 2020

R. S. Markovits, *Welfare Economics and Second-Best Theory*,

https://doi.org/10.1007/978-3-030-43360-4_5

oligopoly power and/or to its rivals' monopoly and oligopoly power as well as or instead of to the seller's monopoly power.

The second type of Pareto imperfections is imperfections in buyer competition. Conventionally, a buyer is said to have monopsony power if it faces an upward-sloping supply curve. However, it also seems appropriate to say that a buyer has monopsony power if it is engaging in a one-on-one negotiation with an individual potential supplier and its power as a buyer enables it to secure more favorable terms from this supplier. I use the symbol "MS" to stand for monopsony.

The third type of Pareto imperfections is (real) externalities—real costs/benefits that one actor's choice imposes/confers on other actors. Three types of externalities can be distinguished. Production externalities are generated by the production of units of output, the process of creating QV investments (regardless of whether those investments are knowledge-creating), and the process of executing PPR projects. Consumption externalities are generated by the consumption of goods. And knowledge-creation-related externalities are generated by the creation of knowledge and attempts to create knowledge. Many variants of each of these subcategories of externalities can be distinguished. Production externalities include air-pollution, water-pollution, noise-pollution, visual-aesthetic, olfactory, road-congestion, and accident/disease/fire-generated externalities. Consumption externalities can include visual-aesthetic, olfactory, sound-related, envy-related, road-congestion, store-congestion, air-pollution, water-pollution, and accident/disease/fire-generated externalities. Knowledge-creation-related externalities include the real external costs that a researcher's research generates by lowering the probability that the research-efforts of others will make the relevant discovery (first), the external cost that the introduction of a newly-discovered product imposes on owners of pre-existing products who value owning "the latest thing," and the external costs that new literary, visual, or musical creations generate by rendering trite or contaminating the meaning and social value of pre-existing characters/stories/visual representations/melodies/orchestrations, etc. One might also include in the category of knowledge-creation-related externalities the dollar gains that users of discoveries who do not pay the discoverer for the right to use its discovery obtained by using the discovery. I symbolize externalities with an upright "X," which contrasts with the italicized "X" I use to stand for product X. I use "PX" to stand for production externalities, "CX" to stand for consumption externalities, and "KCRX" to stand for knowledge-creation-related externalities.

The fourth type of Pareto imperfections is taxes on the margin of income (taxes that vary with income). Such taxes include taxes on individual earned income, taxes on individual unearned income, taxes on the purchase or consumption of goods, estate taxes, and taxes on business income. I symbolize "tax on the margin of income" Pareto imperfections with the letter "T."

The fifth type of Pareto imperfections is resource-allocator non-sovereignty. A resource allocator is not a sovereign to the extent that he or she does not possess information about the attributes of a good (including its durability), the dollar value to him/her of goods with specified attributes, the cost to him/her of goods with specified attributes (including the good's price per ounce and the long-run cost of servicing and repairing a durable good) that is relevant to his/her identifying the good whose purchase would best serve his/her possibly-not-totally-parochial perceived interest. I use the letters "NS" to stand for the non-sovereignty Pareto imperfection.

The sixth type of Pareto imperfections is resource-allocator non-maximization. A resource allocator fails to maximize if the resource allocator makes a choice that the information at his or her disposal implies does not maximize the satisfaction of his or her preferences. Resource allocators can fail to maximize because they do their maths wrong or because they make a resource-allocating choice non-thinkingly (manifest what economists call "acrazia"). I use the letters "NM" to stand for the non-maximization Pareto imperfection.

The seventh type of Pareto imperfections I distinguish is buyer surplus, the positive difference between the price a buyer could have paid for a good and have remained equally well-off and the price the buyer actually paid for the good.[2] I use the letters "BS" to stand for buyer surplus.

5.2 The Symbols I Use to Reference, Respectively, the Private-Benefit, Private-Cost, (Private) Profit, Allocative-Benefit, Allocative-Cost, and Allocative-Efficiency Figures Associated with a Specified Resource-Use or Resource Allocation

When predicting or post-dicting the economic efficiency of a choice, it is often *ex ante* economically efficient to determine the private benefits that a particular resource-use (say, to produce a unit of an existing product) yields the resource-user, the private cost to a resource-user of the resources that he, she, or it used to perform a particular function, the profits that a resource allocation yielded a resource allocator, the allocative benefits generated by a particular resource-use or resource allocation, and/or the allocative efficiency of a particular resource allocation. In this study, I use the symbols PB, PC, Pπ, LB, LC, and LE to refer, respectively, to the above private-benefit, private-cost, (private) profit, allocative-benefit, allocative-cost, and allocative-efficiency figures. The PB, PC, Pπ, LB, LC, and LE symbols in question will often be followed by subscripts that identify the resource-use or resource allocation that is associated with the referenced private or allocative figure. These subscripts will be discussed in Sect. 5.4.

5.3   The Symbols I Use to Reference, Respectively, Three Functional Categories of Resource-Uses

Section 1.4 argued that it is *ex ante* economically efficient to distinguish and take account of 11 more-or-less-broad categories of resource-uses when predicting/post-dicting the economic efficiency of a choice. Section 1.4 also indicated that (1) I employ the symbol "UO" to refer not only to "unit output" but also to uses in which resources are devoted to increasing the unit output of an existing product, (2) I employ the symbol "QV" to refer not only to "a quality-or-variety-increasing investment" but also to uses in which resources are devoted to creating a quality-or-variety-increasing investment—i.e., a new (different and perhaps superior) product, a new (different and perhaps superior) distributive outlet, or additional capacity or inventory (which enable their owner to offer buyers faster average speed of supply through a fluctuating-demand cycle), and (3) I employ the symbol "PPR" to refer not only to "production-process research" but also to uses in which resources are devoted to executing a production-process-research project—a research-project aimed at discovering a production process whose use will lower the average private total cost (and usually the average allocative cost) of producing a relevant quantity of an existing product.[3]

I sometimes combine the UO, QV, and PPR symbols with other symbols that provide additional information about the resource-use being referenced. Specifically, I place an upper-case delta—Δ—before UO, QV, or PPR to indicate that the referenced resource-use is economics-marginal (i.e., is the least-profitable but not-unprofitable resource-use in the indicated category in the ARDEPPS in which it did or would take place) or is economics-just-extra-marginal and a letter after UO, QV, or PPR to indicate the ARDEPPS in which the indicated resource-use would or did take place. When the UO, ΔUO, QV, ΔQV, PPR, or ΔPPR symbol appears in a subscript to a PB, PC, Pπ, LB, LC, or LE symbol (i.e., is used to identify the resource-use or resource allocation that is associated with the referenced private or allocative figure), I place (1) an upper-case "C" before the UO, ΔUO, QV, ΔQV, PPR, or ΔPPR symbol to indicate that the referenced private or allocative figure is associated with the "creation" (hence "C") (actually, respectively production, creation, or execution) of the referenced unit of input, QV investment, or PPR project, (2) an upper-case "U" before the UO, ΔUO, QV, ΔQV, PPR, or ΔPPR symbol to indicate that the referenced private or allocative figure is associated with the "use" (hence "U") of the created thing of value (the consumption of the unit of output that was produced, the use of the created product variant or distributive outlet [the production, sale, and consumption of units of the created product variant or the operation of the created distributive outlet and the consumption of the goods or services it distributed], or the use of the production process that the executed PPR project discovered), (3) an upper-case "(C + U)" before the UO, ΔUO, QV, ΔQV, PPR, or ΔPPR symbol to indicate that the referenced private or allocative figure is associated with the creation and use of the referenced marginal or non-marginal unit of output, QV investment, or PPR project and (4) (once more) a letter after the UO,

ΔUO, QV, ΔQV, PPR, or ΔPPR symbol to identify the ARDEPPS in which the referenced resource-use did or would take place. Thus, the symbol ΔUOi stands for the marginal unit produced in ARDEPPS i, and the symbol $PB_{U\Delta QVi}$ stands for the private benefits that the QV investor that created the marginal QV investment in ARDEPPS i obtained by using it. (In most situations, merely creating a QV investment generates no private benefits for the creator, though I can imagine situations in which the creation of a QV investment benefits the creator by enabling him, her, or it to learn things that will enable it to earn additional profits by making other allocative choices or by giving the creator a reputation for ingenuity, which will enable it to earn additional profits by making other allocative choices.)

5.4   The Symbols I Use to Reference, Respectively, Six Functional Categories of Resource Allocations

As Sect. 1.4.1 stated, I define the concept of a "resource allocation" in the standard economic way to refer to the withdrawal of resources from one or more categories of use in one or usually more-than-one ARDEPPS and their devotion to a single category of use in a single ARDEPPS. As Sect. 1.4.1 also indicated, I distinguish three general subcategories of "resource allocations." "Purely-functionally-defined resource allocations" are resource allocations that are defined solely by the functions that the resources they involve performed in the category or categories of use or functionally-related pairs of use (e.g., the production and consumption of a unit of output, the creation and use of a QV investment, or the creation of a PPR project and the use of the production-process discovery it yields) from which the referenced resource allocation withdrew them and the category or pair of functionally-related categories of use to which the referenced resource allocation devoted them. "Purely-functionally-defined" resource allocations do not specify the area or areas of product-space from which the referenced resource allocation withdrew resources or the area of product-space to which the referenced resource allocation allocated resources. "Functionally-plus-destination-defined" resource allocations specify not only the categories of use from which/to which resources are being withdrawn/devoted but the area of product-space to which resources are being allocated. "Fully-specified resource allocations" are resource allocations whose definition identifies the areas of product-space from which/to which the referenced resource allocation withdrew/allocated resources as well as the functional category or categories of uses from/to which the referenced resource allocation withdrew/allocated resources.

Section 1.4.3 identified 16 categories of purely-functionally-defined resource allocations whose economic efficiency I believe it is sometimes *ex ante* economically efficient to consider separately when predicting/post-dicting the economic efficiency of a choice. I think it is expositionally beneficial to use symbols to stand for some of these categories of resource allocations both when referencing the resource allocation itself and as subscripts to indicate the resource allocation with which a PB, PC, Pπ, LB, LC, LE, or specified distortion-figure is associated. When used by themselves to refer simply for a particular category of resource allocations,

(1) the symbol "UO/QV/PPR-to-UO" references a resource allocation from UO-producing-and-using, QV-creating-and-using, and PPR-executing-and-using uses to the production and consumption of a single unit of an individual product, and the symbol "UO-to-UO/QV/PPR" references a resource allocation from the production and consumption of a single unit of a single product to UO-producing-and-using, QV-creating-and-using, and PPR-executing-and-using uses;

(2) the symbol "UO/QV/PPR-to-QV" references a resource allocation from UO-producing-and-using, QV-creating-and-using, and PPR-executing-and-using resource-uses to the creation and use of a single QV investment, and the symbol "QV-to-UO/QV/PPR" references the "reverse" allocation of resources;

(3) the symbol "UO/QV/PPR-to-PPR" references a resource allocation from UO-producing-and-using, QV-creating-and-using, and PPR-executing-and-using resource-uses to the execution and use of a single project, and the symbol "PPR-to-UO/QV/PPR" references the reverse allocation of resources;

(4) the symbol "UO-to-UO" references a resource allocation from the production of less-than-one, one, or more-than-one unit of one or more products to the production of a single unit of one product: when the products between whose productions resources are allocated are located in the same ARDEPPS, the resource allocation is denominated an intra-ARDEPPS UO-to-UO resource allocation, and when the product between whose productions resources are allocated are located in different ARDEPPSes, the resource allocation is denominated an inter-ARDEPPS UO-to-UO resource allocation (a given UO-to-UO resource allocation may be a component of a UO/QV/PPR-to-UO resource allocation);

(5) the symbol "QV-to-QV" references a resource allocation from the creation and use of less-than-one, one, or more-than-one QV investment to the creation and use of another QV investment: when the QV investments between whose creations resources flow are located in the same ARDEPPS, the resource allocation is denominated an intra-ARDEPPS QV-to-QV resource allocation and when the QV investments between whose creations resources are allocated are located in different ARDEPPSes, the resource allocation is denominated an inter-ARDEPPS QV-to-QV resource allocation (a given QV-to-QV resource allocation may be a component of a UO/QV/PPR-to-QV resource allocation); and

(6) the symbol "PPR-to-PPR" references a resource allocation from the execution and use of less-than-one, one, or more-more-than-one PPR project to the execution and use of a different PPR project: when the PPR projects between whose executions resources flow relate to the production processes used to produce products in the same ARDEPPS, the resource allocation is denominated an intra-ARDEPPS PPR-to-PPR resource allocation, and when the PPR

projects between whose executions resources flow relate to the production processes used to produce products in different ARDEPPSes, the resource allocation is denominated an inter-ARDEPPS PPR-to-PPR resource allocation (a given PPR-to-PPR resource allocation can be a component of a UO/QV/PPR-to-PPR resource allocation).

The symbols just explained are sometimes supplemented with additional symbols that provide additional information about the referenced resource allocation. For example, (1) the presence of a "Δ" before any UO, QV, or PPR symbol that appears before the word "to" indicates that the referenced executed UO-producing, QV-creating, or PPR-executing resource-use is economics-marginal, and the presence of a "Δ" before any UO, QV, or PPR symbol that appears after the word "to" indicates that the specified sacrificed resource-use is just-extra-marginal, and (2) the presence of a letter following any UO, QV, or PPR symbol that precedes the word "to" indicates the ARDEPPS in which the referenced use to which the referenced resource allocation devotes resources is located and the presence of one or more letters after any UO, QV, or PPR symbol that follows the word "to" indicates the ARDEPPS or ARDEPPSes whose indicated resource-uses were/would be sacrificed by the referenced resource allocation (although a complete specification of any exemplar of any of the categories of resource allocation in the preceding list would have to indicate the quantity of resources withdrawn from each specified category of sacrificed uses in each ARDEPPS from which they were/would be withdrawn, I never use a symbol that provides such information because, in my judgment, it would be self-defeatingly expositionally-cumbersome to do so).

The symbols I have just delineated also have analogues that appear as subscripts to PB, PC, Pπ, LB, LC, or LE, and related distortion-symbols and indicate the resource-uses or resource allocations associated with private, allocative, or distortion figures to which they are attached. When these symbols are used as subscripts, the word "to" is omitted, the first symbol indicates the resource-use (and perhaps the ARDEPPS) to which resources have been devoted by the resource-use or resource allocation in question, the next symbols (which appear only in the case of resource allocations) appear after a forward-slash and indicate the resource-use or resource-uses and perhaps the ARDEPPSes from which the indicated resource allocations withdraw resources: when more than one type of resource-use is sacrificed the symbols indicating each separate type of sacrificed resource-use are separated by commas.

Notes

1. It may well be that an eighth Pareto-optimal condition should be added to this list—viz., that the standard 7 Pareto-optimal conditions can be fulfilled without generating any allocative transaction costs or any economic inefficiency of any type (e.g., without preventing complementary resources from being placed under the control of a single entity). See Calabresi (1991).

2. The standard Welfare Economics list of Pareto imperfections substitutes "public goods" for "(critical) buyer surplus." For my reasons for substituting a "no critical buyer surplus" Pareto-optimal condition for the standard "no public good" Pareto-optimal condition, see note 3 of Chap. 1 and Markovits (2008), pp. 249–307.

3. I acknowledge that individual research-projects can be designed to discover a new product or distributive outlet that is simultaneously different (or even superior) from the perspective of some buyers and cheaper to produce or build and operate than existing alternatives—i.e., that individual resource-uses can be simultaneously   quality-or-variety-increasing-investment-creating   and production-process-research-executing. The analysis of the economic efficiency of the allocative benefits generated by any such dual-purpose resource-uses and of the allocative efficiency of any resource allocation from and/or to any such dual-purpose resource-use will take account of both functions the resource-use performs.

References

Calabresi, G. (1991). The pointlessness of Pareto. *Yale Law Journal, 100,* 1211–1238.
Markovits, R. (2008). *Truth or economics: On the definition, prediction, and relevance of economic efficiency.* New Haven and London: Yale University Press.

The Vocabulary and Symbols of Distortion Analysis

6

Abstract

Section 6.1 defines the general concept of a "distortion" in a private-benefit, private-cost, or profit figure, the concept of the "aggregate distortion" in such a private figure, and the concept of the "aggregate percentage-distortion" in such a private figure. Section 6.2 defines three basic categories of profit-distortion formulas: conventional, otherwise-Pareto-perfect (oPp) profit-distortion formulas, onesy (1E) formulas for the "aggregate distortion in the profits yielded by a specified resource allocation," and step-wise-distortion—(SW)D—and step-wise aggregate profit-distortion—$(SW)\Sigma D(P\pi)$—formulas. Section 6.3 indicates the symbols that stand for each of the categories and subcategories of distortions that Sects. 6.1 and 6.2 define. Section 6.4 concretizes the concept of the 1E formula for the aggregate distortion in the profits yielded by a specific category of resource allocation. Section 6.5 concretizes the concept of the (SW)D formula for the aggregate distortion in the profits yielded by any resource allocation by deriving such a formula for the same category of resource allocation on which Sect. 6.4 focuses. Section 6.6 outlines the way in which the 1E and (SW)D formulas previously derived would have to be revised to take account of various complications previously ignored. Section 6.7 explains why the study will assume that it will prove to be TBLE for economic-efficiency analysts to use (SW)D rather than (1E) formulas for any aggregate profit-distortion.

© Springer Nature Switzerland AG 2020
R. S. Markovits, *Welfare Economics and Second-Best Theory*,
https://doi.org/10.1007/978-3-030-43360-4_6

6.1 The "Distortion Analysis" Definitions of "a Distortion," "the Aggregate Distortion," or "the Aggregate Percentage-Distortion" in a Relevant Private-Benefit, Private-Cost, or (Private-) Profit Figure

6.1.1 The Distortion in a Private-Benefit, Private-Cost, or (Private-) Profit Figure

In my terminology, a private figure is said to be "distorted" if it differs from its allocative counterpart. Thus, the private benefits a resource allocator has obtained/would obtain by using resources in a specified way or by executing a particular resource allocation (PB) are said to be "distorted" to the extent that they diverge from the allocative benefits the resource-use or resource allocation in question will yield (LB)—i.e., the net equivalent-dollar gain that will result from the resources' in question being used in the indicated way as opposed to their being destroyed in some allocative-costless manner. (N.B., in my terminology, the PBs a resource allocation yields are distinguished from the profits that a resource allocation yields, which equal the difference between the private benefits yielded by and the private cost of the resource allocation in question); the private cost of a resource allocation to a resource allocator [PC] is said to be "distorted" to the extent that it diverges from the allocative cost of the resource allocation [LC]—i.e., the allocative value that the resources the resource allocation "consumes" [in the sense of using up] would have yielded in the alternative use[s] from which they were withdrawn; and the [private] profits a resource allocation confers on the resource allocator [$P\pi$] are said to be "distorted" to the extent that they diverge from the resource allocation's allocative efficiency [LE]. Note as well that, in this study, the lower-case pi—π—stands for "profits" while the upper-case pi—Π—stands for profit-rate.) Obviously, since $P\pi = PB–PC$ and $LE = LB–LC$, $P\pi$ will be distorted when either PB or PC is distorted unless both are distorted and the two distortions perfectly offset each other. Somewhat more specifically, in my terminology, a PB, PC, or $P\pi$ figure is said to be "inflated" if it exceeds its allocative counterpart and "deflated" if it is lower than its allocative counterpart.

6.1.2 The Aggregate Distortion in Any Private-Benefit, Private-Cost, or (Private-) Profit Figure

The aggregate distortion in any private figure is the distortion in that figure that is generated by all exemplars of all types of Pareto imperfections the economy in question contains. The aggregate distortion in a private figure should, therefore, be contrasted with the distortion in that figure that would be generated in an otherwise-Pareto-perfect economy by a subset of the Pareto imperfections the economy contains—for example, with the distortion in some private figure that would be generated by the interaction of all imperfections in seller competition if the economy were oPp or with the distortion in that figure that would be generated by all exemplars of the imperfections in seller competition and all externalities of production the economy in question contains if that economy contained no other Pareto imperfections.

6.1.3 The Aggregate Percentage-Distortion in Any Private-Benefit, Private-Cost, or (Private-) Profit Figure

The aggregate percentage-distortion in any private-benefit figure equals (the distortion in the private benefits that the specified resource allocation yields the resource allocator that is generated by all exemplars the relevant economy contains of all types of Pareto imperfections) *divided by* (the private benefits that the relevant resource allocation confers on the resource allocator) *times* 100%. The aggregate percentage-distortion in any private-cost figure equals (the distortion in the private cost to the resource allocator of the specified resource allocation that is generated by all exemplars the relevant economy contains of all types of Pareto imperfections) *divided by* (the private costs in question) *times* 100%. The aggregate percentage-distortion in the profits yielded by any resource allocation equals (the distortion in the profits yielded by the specified resource allocation by all exemplars the relevant economy contains of all types of Pareto imperfections) *divided by* (the private profits yielded by that that resource allocation) *times* 100%.

6.2 The Three Basic Categories of Profit-Distortion Formulas that This Study References and Their Various Subcategories

This study references three basic categories of profit-distortion formulas. Although each profit-distortion formula has private-benefit and private-cost counterparts— indeed, although any profit-distortion figure equals the sum of the associated private-benefit-distortion and private-cost-distortion figures, to shorten the exposition, I will ignore the private-benefit-distortion and private-cost-distortion counterparts to the categories of profit-distortion formulas that will be defined and discussed.

6.2.1 Conventional, Otherwise-Pareto-Perfect (oPp) Profit-Distortion Formulas

The expression "the conventional, otherwise-Pareto-perfect formula for the distortion in the profits yielded by a specified resource allocation" references any formula for the distortion in such a profit figure that would be generated *in an otherwise-Pareto-perfect economy* by a specified subset of the Pareto imperfections that economy contains. I characterize this category of profit-distortion formula "conventional" because, frequently in conversation and sometimes in print, theoretical and applied welfare economists use this category of profit-distortion formula and seem to assume that such formulas and the figures associated with them can play a useful role in analyses of the economic efficiency of choices. I should state at the outset that—although such formulas can contribute to the development of the TBLE distortion-analysis protocol for economic-efficiency analysis by revealing how an individual exemplar of a particular type of Pareto imperfection, all exemplars of a particular type of Pareto imperfection, or all exemplars of two-to-six types of Pareto interactions would interact to cause or not cause profit distortions in an oPp economy—the profit-distortion figures that such formulas yield cannot play a useful role in any protocol for economic-efficiency analysis that is TBLE.

This study considers four subcategories of conventional, otherwise-Pareto-perfect profit-distortion formulas—viz., formulas that indicate the distortion in the profits that would be yielded by a specified resource allocation in an otherwise-Pareto-perfect economy (1) by an individual exemplar of a single type of Pareto imperfection, (2) by two or more than two but fewer than all (relevant) exemplars of a particular type of Pareto imperfection, (3) by all exemplars of a particular type of Pareto imperfection, and (4) by all exemplars of two-to-six types of Pareto imperfection. As the name I have given this category of profit-distortion formula indicates, the defining feature of this category of formula is that such formulas proceed on the assumption that the economy is otherwise-Pareto-perfect— i.e., all such formulas ignore (more fairly, do not purport to take account of) the impacts that the Pareto imperfections the relevant formula does consider may have on the magnitudes of the Pareto imperfections that the relevant formula assumes do not exist and vice versa and the way or ways in which those other Pareto imperfections would in any event interact with the Pareto imperfection(s) the formula does take into account to generate the aggregate distortion in the profits yielded by the resource allocation in question.

Each of these four subcategories of conventional, otherwise-Pareto-perfect (oPp) profit-distortion formulas can perform a useful, heuristic role. Thus, the conventional, oPp distortion formula for the distortion that would be generated in the profits yielded by a specified category of resource allocation by an individual exemplar of a specified single type of Pareto imperfection in an otherwise-Pareto-perfect economy can provide significant insight into the way in which an individual exemplar of that type of Pareto imperfection distorts the profit figure in question, and the conventional, oPp distortion formula for the distortion that would be generated in an oPp economy in the profits that a specified resource allocation would yield by multiple exemplars of an individual type of Pareto imperfection or by one or more exemplars of two-to-six types of Pareto imperfections can provide significant insight into how these different Pareto imperfections interact to cause or not cause a distortion in the profits yielded by the specified category of resource allocation. However, the profit-distortion figures that are associated with conventional, oPp distortion-formulas in any subcategory do not play a role in the distortion-analysis protocol for predicting or post-dicting the economic efficiency of a choice that I claim is *ex ante* economically efficient. This conclusion reflects the fact that, for the two reasons I previously delineated, the profit-distortion figures any such conventional, oPp profit-distortion formula yields will not equal the dollar impact that the Pareto imperfections the particular conventional, oPp formula takes into account have on the relevant aggregate profit distortion: (1) the Pareto imperfections they consider may affect the magnitudes of the Pareto imperfections they ignore and vice versa, and (2) the Pareto imperfections that any conventional, oPp profit-distortion formula ignores may (will usually) influence the distorting impact of the Pareto imperfections such formulas consider.

In any event, in my terminology, the expressions/symbols "oPp monopoly distortion—oPp(MD)," "oPp monopsony distortion—oPp ([MS]D)," "oPp externality distortion—oPp (XD)," "oPp tax-on-the-margin-of-income distortion—oPp (TD)," "oPp non-sovereignty distortion—oPp([NS]D)," "oPp non-maximization distortion —oPp ([NM]D)," and "oPp buyer-surplus distortion—oPp ([BS]D)" refer to the conventional, oPp distortion that all exemplars of the referenced type of Pareto imperfection would generate in an otherwise-Pareto-perfect world in a referenced private figure for a referenced resource allocation and the expressions/symbol "oPp monopoly/externality distortion—oPp ([M/X]D)" and its other two-to-six-Pareto-imperfection-referencing counterparts refer to the conventional, oPp distortion that would be generated in the referenced private figure for a referenced resource allocation by all exemplars of the referenced two-to-six types of Pareto imperfections. I should add that each of the above symbols may be supplemented with subscripts (to be explained below) that identify the resource allocation with which the indicated distortion figure is associated.

6.2.2   The Onesy Formula for the Aggregate Distortion in the Profits Yielded by a Resource Allocation—i.e., for the Distortion in Those Profits Generated by All Exemplars the Relevant Economy Contains of All Seven Types of Pareto Imperfections—(1E)ΣD(P$\pi_{.../...}$)

The "onesy formula" for the aggregate distortion in the profits yielded by a specified exemplar of any specified category of resource allocation is an extension of the various conventional, oPp formulas for the distortion that all exemplars of six of the seven types of Pareto imperfections would generate in the profits that specified exemplars of that specified category of resource allocation would yield if the economy contained no exemplars of the non-covered type of Pareto imperfection (if the economy were oPp). I denominate this category of formula a "onesy formula" because a "onesy" is a type of clothing (usually infant-clothing) that combines into one article all components (bottoms and tops, pants and shirts) of the relevant outfit and, unlike the step-wise-distortion distortion formulas that Sect. 6.2.3 defines, onesy formulas calculate the aggregate profit distortions in question in one sense "in one go"—more specifically, do not proceed by calculating separately and summing seven, admittedly-somewhat-peculiarly-defined, individual-Pareto-imperfection-oriented figures. I should add that the entries that replace the ellipses in the subscript in the symbol that appears in the heading of this subsection provide information that identifies the resource allocation with which the distortion figure in question is associated.

6.2.3 The Step-Wise-Distortion Formula for the Distortion that All Exemplars of All Seven Types of Pareto Imperfections Will Generate in the Profits Yielded by a Specified Resource Allocation—(SW)ΣD(Pπ.../...)

In my vocabulary, the step-wise-distortion formula for the aggregate distortion in the profits that were or would be generated by a specified resource allocation by all exemplars of all seven types of Pareto imperfections is defined to equal the sum of the seven single-type-of-Pareto-imperfection-oriented distortions in the relevant profit figure (respectively by all exemplars of each of the 7 types of Pareto imperfections) when each of these separate distortions is calculated on the realistic assumptions about the magnitudes of the other types of Pareto imperfections in the economy and the magnitudes of any other determinants of the profit distortion in question, ignoring both (1) the impact that the extant exemplars of the other types of Pareto imperfections and other relevant parameters have on the relevant profit-distortion and the impact that the exemplars of the type of Pareto imperfection in question has on the relevant profit-distortion by changing the incidences and magnitudes of the other types of Pareto imperfections and of these other parameters. "Step-wise-distortion" aggregate-profit-distortion formulas differ from "onesy" aggregate-profit-distortion formulas because, rather than calculating the relevant figure in one sense "in one go," they calculate seven, somewhat-peculiarly-defined individual-Pareto-imperfection-oriented distortion-figures and then sum those figures. The entries that will replace the ellipses in the subscript of the (SW)ΣD(Pπ.../...) symbol that appears in the heading of this subsection identify the resource allocation that is associated with the referenced aggregate-profit-distortion figure.

6.3   The Symbols that Reference Various Distortion-Concepts

6.3.1   The Symbol for the Aggregate Distortion in Some To-Be-Specified Private Figure Associated with a To-Be-Specified Marginal or Non-Marginal Allocation—$\Sigma D(P\ldots_{(\ldots)\Delta\ldots/(\ldots)\Delta\ldots})$ or $\Sigma D(P\ldots_{(\ldots)\ldots/(\ldots)\ldots})$

In this study, the symbol for the aggregate distortion in a specified or to-be-specified private figure for a specified or to-be-specified economics-marginal allocation of resources will be $\Sigma D(P\ldots_{(\ldots)\Delta\ldots/(\ldots)\Delta\ldots})$ or $\Sigma D(P\ldots_{(\ldots)\ldots/(\ldots)\ldots})$. In this notation, the upper-case Greek letter sigma (Σ) stands for "aggregate"; the letter D stands for "distortion"; the letter P stands for "private" (as contrasted with "allocative"); the forward-slash in the subscript of the symbol separates information that relates to the resource-use to which the relevant resource allocation devotes resources (which is provided by symbols that precede the forward-slash) from information that relates to the uses from which the indicated resource allocation withdrew resources (which is provided by symbols that follow the forward-slash); the symbol in question contains two or more "Δ"s in its subscript, the first Δ indicates that the executed resource-use in the to-be-specified category (see below) in the to-be-specified area of product-space to which resources have been allocated by the resource allocation to which the distortion-information in question relates is an economics-marginal resource-use, and the subsequent Δ or Δs indicate that the to-be-specified category (categories) of resource-use(s) it precedes (the to-be-specified category or categories of resource-use[s] that the to-be-specified resource allocation sacrifices) are the successively-least-unprofitable resource-uses in the to-be-specified category or categories in the to-be-specified area or areas of product-space from which resources would be withdrawn (are the first, second,... nth extra-marginal resource-uses in the to-be-specified category or categories in the to-be-specified areas of product-space from which resources would be withdrawn to enable the economics-marginal resource-use in question to be executed). (I hasten to point out that the definition of the second Δ in any subscript that contains two Δs is somewhat inconsistent with the definition of the first Δ in any such subscript in that the resource-use[s] to which the second Δ refers is [are] economics-extra-marginal use[s] whereas the resource-use to which the first Δ refers is an economics-marginal resource-use.) When the resource allocation in question withdraws resources from more than one category of use, the symbols following the forward-slash, which indicate the respective uses from which the relevant resource allocation withdrew resources, are separated by commas.

I will now explain the five ellipses in the symbol for the aggregate distortions being referenced. The letter (B, C, or π) that replaces the first ellipsis, which follows the letter "P," indicates whether the private figure whose distortion the symbol references is a private-benefit, private-cost, or profit figure. (If the first ellipsis is replaced by a capital pi [Π], the private figure whose distortion the symbol refer-ences is a profit-*rate* figure.)

Like the symbol in the above heading, the following account assumes that the referenced resource allocation withdrew resources from only one category of use. The letter or letters that replace the second ellipsis in the above symbol (the first ellipsis in its subscript)—a "C," a "U," or a "(C+U)" where "C" stands for creation, "U" stands for use, and "(C+U)" stands for creation and use—indicates or indicate whether the private figure indicated by the entry that replaces the first ellipsis is associated with the creation, use, or creation and use of the unit of output, QV investment, or PPR project to whose production, creation, or execution the entry that replaces the third ellipsis in the symbol (the second ellipsis in its subscript) indicates the relevant resource allocation devotes the resources it involves. The letter or letters that replace the fourth ellipsis in the above symbol (again [C], [U], or [(C+U)]) indicate whether the resource-uses from which the referenced resource allocation withdrew resources are "creation," "use," or "creation and use" resource-uses, and the letters that replace the fifth ellipsis in the above symbol— UO, QV, or PPR—indicate the category of resource-use or pairs of related resource-uses that was or were sacrificed by the resource allocation in question— unit-output-production (creation) and use, QV-investment creation and use, or PPR-execution (creation) and use.

Because the previous paragraph is quite a mouthful, some concretization may be helpful. The expression "the *creation* of a unit of output" refers to the act of producing and/or distributing that unit. The expression "the use of a marginal unit of output" refers to the sale, possible resale, and consumption of that unit of output as opposed to its allocative-costless destruction.

The conduct that is covered by the expression "the creation of a QV investment" varies with the nature of the QV investment in question. When the QV investment is an investment in capacity or inventory, its creation consists of the construction of the capacity or the production of the inventory. When the QV investment is an investment that yields a new product variant, its creation entails preliminary market research, product-design efforts, the production of prototypes, the market-testing of proposed variants or actual prototypes, the construction and operation of pilot plants (to determine the feasibility of producing the product in commercially-viable quantities, the cheapest way to produce the product, the most profitable approaches to quality-control, and the cost of producing the product in needed quantities), the construction of the plant that will be used to produce the new product, and the execution of the promotional campaign that is run to launch the product. When the QV investment is an investment in a new distributive outlet, its creation involves market research into the geographic location and other attributes of the outlet that would be most profitable, the construction of the outlet, and the execution of the promotional campaign that is run to launch the outlet.

The conduct that is covered by the expression "the use of a QV investment" also varies somewhat with the nature of the QV investment. When the QV investment creates inventory, the expression "the use of the QV investment" refers to the sale of the inventory. When the QV investment creates capacity, the expression "the use of the QV investment" refers to the use of the capacity in question. When the QV investment creates a new product variant, the expression "the use of the QV investment" refers to the production and sale of units of the product the QV investment created by combining inputs whose cost are variable costs with the relevant QV investment. When the QV investment creates a new distributive outlet, the expression "the use of the QV investment" refers to the operation of the distributive outlet the QV investment created.

The expression "the creation—i.e., execution—of a PPR project" refers to the act of doing the production-process research the project entails. Relatedly, the expression "the use of a PPR project" refers to the project-owner's use of the information or production process the project discovered in its own production facilities, the use of that information or discovery by others to whom the project-owner sold any associated patents or whom the project-owner licensed to use the protected information, and (when the issue is the allocative benefits the use of the PPR project generates or the distortion in the private benefits generated by the use of a PPR project) the use of that information or discovery as well by free-riders who use it without paying for the right to use it.

The letters that appear instead of the third ellipsis in the symbol for the aggregate distortion in any private figure—the second ellipsis in the subscript of the symbol, which follows the first Δ in that symbol if the symbol contains Δs—indicate the category of resource-use that has generated the private benefits, private cost, or profits to whose possible distortion the symbol in question refers. In this study, the letters UO, QV, or PPR will always replace this third ellipsis. As already indicated, UO, QV, and PPR indicate respectively that the resource-use in question is unit-output-producing, QV-investment-creating, and production-process-research-executing. Any letter that appears immediately after a UO, ΔUO, QV, ΔQV, or PPR, ΔPPR symbol in the third ellipsis indicates the ARDEPPS-location of the product that the referenced non-marginal or marginal unit-output-producing resource-use produced, of the non-marginal or marginal QV investment it created, or of the non-marginal or marginal PPR project it executed. (A more complete analysis would also take account of allocations of resources to and partially from modernizing existing plants using exclusively known technology, constructing new plants using exclusively known technology, and selecting and training a relevant workforce [to the use of one known production process from the use of another known production process] and/or to and partially from the other categories of uses Sect. 1.4.1 identified. My protocol for analyzing the impact of choices on the amount of economic inefficiency generated by decisions to execute or not execute resource allocations to UO-producing, QV-creating, and PPR-executing uses ignores the possibility that some of the resources that were/(would have been) involved were/(would have been) withdrawn from such uses reflects my admittedly-contestable assumption that this simplification is TBLE.)

Finally, the letters that appear in the fourth ellipsis in the symbol for any aggregate distortion—the ellipsis that follows the forward-slash in the subscript and any "Δ" that appears in the subscript after this forward-slash—indicate the category or categories of resource-use(s) and sometimes the ARDEPPSes from which it is being assumed the resources devoted to the resource-use previously specified are being withdrawn. The fourth ellipsis will, therefore, be replaced by the symbols

UO, QV, and PPR supplemented occasionally by a symbol to indicate the ARDEPPS(es) from which the relevant resources are being withdrawn.

Some examples may be helpful. In my system, $\Sigma D(P\pi_{(C+U)\Delta UOX/(C+U)\Delta UOY})$ stands for the aggregate distortion (the distortion generated by the interaction of all the Pareto imperfections of all types the economy contains) in the (private) profits the producer of a marginal unit of product X did or would earn by producing and selling or using in some other way the marginal unit of X with resources withdrawn from the production and use of just-extra-marginal units of product Y. For simplicity, I will usually substitute the symbol $\Sigma D(P\pi_{\Delta UOX/\Delta UOY})$ for $\Sigma D(P\pi_{(C+U)\Delta UOX/(C+U)\Delta UOY})$. $\Sigma D(PC_{(C+U)\Delta QVX/(C+U)\Delta UOY1...n})$ stands for the aggregate distortion in the private cost of creating and using the economics-marginal QV investment in ARDEPPS X with resources withdrawn from the production and use of just-extra-marginal units of products $Y1...n$.

6.3.2   The Symbols for the Conventional oPp Distortions that All Exemplars of One-to-Six Types of Pareto Imperfections Would Generate in a To-Be-Specified or Specified Private Figure Associated with a To-Be-Specified or Specified Resource Allocation (in an Otherwise-Pareto-Perfect Economy)

With one exception, the symbol I will use to reference any such distortion is the same as the symbol for the aggregate distortion in the private figure in question—$\Sigma D(P...{(...)...}/{...})$. The exception is that the letter Σ that appears before the D in the aggregate-distortion symbol will be replaced by the letters oPp followed by either an ellipsis or one symbol or two-to-six symbols in parentheses that indicate the type or types of Pareto imperfections all of whose exemplars are "jointly" causing the referenced distortion in the otherwise-Pareto-perfect economy. Thus, if oPp(M) replaces the Σ at the beginning of the aggregate-distortion symbol just explained, the symbol will reference the oPp monopoly (imperfection in seller competition) distortion in the referenced private figure for the to-be-specified or specified resource allocation in the to-be-specified or specified ARDEPPS—the distortion that all exemplars of imperfections in seller competition would generate in the relevant private figure in an otherwise-Pareto-perfect economy. Similarly, if the symbol oPp(M/X) replaces the Σ at the beginning of the aggregate-distortion symbol just explained, the symbol will reference the oPp distortion that would be generated in the to-be-specified or specified private figure for the to-be-specified or specified resource allocation in the to-be-specified or specified ARDEPPS by all imperfections in seller competition and all externalities acting "in concert" in an otherwise-Pareto-perfect economy.[1]

6.3.3 The Symbol for the Onesy Formula for the Aggregate Distortion in the Profits Yielded by Any Specified or To-Be-Specified Economics-Marginal or Economics-Non-Marginal Resource Allocation

Although I could use the symbols $(M/MS/X/T/NS/NM/BS)D(P\pi_{(C+U)\Delta...{/}(C+U)\Delta...})$ and $(M/MS/X/T/NS/NM/BS)\Delta(P\pi_{(C+U)...{/}(C+U)...})$ to stand for the onesy formula for the aggregate distortion in the profits yielded respectively by any economics-marginal or economics-non-marginal resource allocation that is generated by all extant exemplars of all seven types of Pareto imperfections, I will let the symbols $(1E)\Sigma D(P\pi_{(C+U)\Delta...{/}(C+U)\Delta...})$ and $(1E)\Sigma D(P\pi_{(C+U)...{/}(C+U)...})$ stand for these formulae where the symbol "Σ" stands for "aggregate." Similar formulas could be used to stand for the onesy formula for the aggregate distortion in the private benefits or private cost of any economics-marginal or economics-non-marginal resource allocation that is generated by all extant exemplars of all seven types of Pareto imperfections.

6.3.4 The Symbols for the Individual-Pareto-Imperfection-Oriented Step-Wise Distortion in a Specified or To-Be-Specified Private Figure Associated with a Specified or To-Be-Specified Economics-Marginal or Economics-Non-Marginal Resource Allocation to a To-Be-Specified or Specified ARDEPPS

The symbol I use to refer to an individual-type-of-Pareto-imperfection-oriented step-wise distortion in any category is (SW[...])D(...) where the first ellipsis is replaced by letter(s) that indicate the relevant types of Pareto imperfection, the second ellipsis is replaced by letters that indicate the type of private figure that is distorted, and the third (subscript) ellipsis indicates the resource-use or resource-allocation that is associated with the private figure that is distorted. Thus, the step-wise monopoly-distortion symbol is (SW[M])D: by contrast, the conventional oPp monopoly distortion would begin with the letters MD. The text that follows will also sometimes use a symbol to refer to the sum of the individual-type-of-Pareto-imperfection-oriented step-wise distortions for two-to-six types of Pareto imperfections. The symbol for that sum, which equals the sum of the step-wise distortions for each of the covered types of Pareto imperfections, will begin with the letters (SW[.../...]) where the number of forward-slashes is one number below the number of referenced types of Pareto imperfections and the ellipses are to be replaced by symbols for the respective types of Pareto imperfections being covered.

6.3.5   The Symbol for the Step-Wise-Distortion Formula for an Aggregate Distortion in a Specified or To-Be-Specified Private Figure Associated with a Specified or To-Be-Specified Economics-Marginal or Economics-Non-Marginal Resource Allocation

The symbol for the step-wise-distortion formula for any $\Sigma D(P\ldots_{(\ldots)\Delta\ldots/(C+U)\Delta\ldots})$ or $\Sigma D(P\ldots_{(\ldots)\ldots/(C+U)\ldots})$ figure is the relevant symbol preceded by (SW).

6.4   An Illustration of the Onesy Formula for the Aggregate Distortion in the Profits Yielded by Any Resource Allocation

This section illustrates the concept of a "onesy formula" for the aggregate distortion in the profits yielded by any resource allocation by deriving that formula for an allocation of resources from the production of less-than-one, one, or more-than-one just-extra-marginal units of a single product Y to the production of a marginal unit of a single product X on the assumption that neither Y nor X has any complements. (Resources could flow from the production of Y to the production of X either or both because X and Y are product-rivalrous or because they are input-rivalrous—i.e., because the production of X and Y use the same inputs.) The derivation that follows proceeds on five simplifying assumptions that do not critically affect the points I want to make: (1) the standard assumption that marginal revenue equals marginal cost, (2) the assumptions that the producer of the marginal unit of X does not practice price discrimination when selling that unit and that the producer of the sacrificed units of Y would not have practiced discrimination when selling those units, (3) the standard assumption that the private benefits that the producer of X obtained by producing its marginal unit of X and that any producer of a sacrificed unit of Y would have obtained by selling that sacrificed unit equals the change in its conventional total revenue (the sale of the marginal unit did yield it)/(the sale of the sacrificed unit would have yielded it)—that the production of the marginal unit of X did not and the production of the sacrificed units of Y would not have yielded their respective producers profits by increasing their future sales or by giving them production/distribution experience that did enable/would have enabled them to reduce their future costs, (4) the assumptions that if any allocative costs were generated by the consumption of the marginal unit of X those costs would be external to the consumer and that if any allocative costs would have been generated by the consumption of the sacrificed units of Y those costs would have been external to their consumers, and (5) the assumption that, if more than one unit of Y will be sacrificed to the production of the marginal unit of X, the price of each sacrificed unit of Y, the allocative value of each sacrificed unit of Y, the marginal revenue that would have been yielded by the sale of each sacrificed unit of Y, the marginal cost of each sacrificed unit of Y, and the marginal allocative cost of each sacrificed unit of Y would respectively be the same for each sacrificed unit of Y. (This fifth assumption obviates my replacing P_Y, MLV_Y, MR_Y, MC_Y, and MLC_Y in the following derivation respectively with AP_Y, $AMLV_Y$, AMR_Y, AMC_Y, and $AMLC_Y$ where the "A" stands for "average" [for the sacrificed units of Y].)

On the above assumptions, here is the derivation of the onesy formula for the aggregate distortion in the profits the producer of a marginal unit of X would obtain by bidding away the resources it used to create a marginal unit of X from an alternative user of those resources that would have employed them to create less-than-one, one, or more-than-one units of Y:

1. $(1E)\Sigma D(P\pi_{(C+U)\Delta UOX/(C+U)\Delta UOY}) = (1E)\Sigma D(PB_{(C+U)\Delta UOX/(C+U)\Delta UOY})-$
   $(1E)D(PC_{(C+U)\Delta UOX/(C+U)\Delta UOY})\equiv$
2. $(PB_{U\Delta UOX}-LB_{U\Delta UOX})-(PC_{C\Delta UOX/(C+U)\Delta UOY}-LC_{C\Delta UOX/(C+U)\Delta UOY}])=$
3. $(MR_{U\Delta UOX}-MLV_{U\Delta UOX})-(MC_{C\Delta UOX}-MRT_{Y/X}[MLV_{U\Delta UOY}])=$
4. $\left(MR_X - P_X^*\right) - \left(MC_X - \left[MC_X^*/MC_Y^*\right)P_Y^*\right)=$
5. $-P_X^* + \left(MC_X^* MC_Y^*\right)P_Y^*=$
6. $MC_X^*\left(\left[P_Y^*/MC_Y^*\right] - \left[P_X^* MC_X^*\right]\right).$

In this derivation, (1) $(1E)\Sigma D$ stands for the onesy formula for the relevant aggregate distortion, (2) (the subscript $_{(C+U)\Delta UOX/(C+U)\Delta UOY}$) specifies the resource allocation in question, (3) $MLV_{U\Delta UOX}$ and $MLV_{U\Delta UOY}$ stand respectively for the net allocative value that is generated by the use (i.e., consumption) of the marginal unit of X and the net allocative value that would have been generated by the use (i.e., consumption) of each of the sacrificed units of Y (which in a Pareto-perfect economy would respectively equal P_X and P_Y), (4) $MRT_{Y/X}$ indicates the rate at which at the margin Y can be transformed into X (which in a Pareto-perfect economy would equal MC_X/MC_Y), (5) P_X^* and P_Y^* stand respectively for the adjusted (*) price of X and the adjusted price of Y—adjusted in each case so that $P_X^* = MLV_X$ and $P_Y^* = MLV_Y$ regardless of whether, in the actual, Pareto-imperfect economy, $P_X = MLV_X$ and $P_Y = MLV_Y$, and (6) MC_X^* and MC_Y^* stand respectively for the adjusted (*) marginal cost of X and the adjusted marginal cost of Y—adjusted in each instance so that $(MC_X^*/MC_Y^*) = MRT_{Y/X}$ regardless of whether in the actual, Pareto-imperfect economy $(MC_X/MC_Y) = MRT_{Y/X}$.

Step (1) in the preceding derivation simply indicates that the aggregate profit-distortion equals the distortion in the private benefits the producer of X obtains by selling its marginal unit of X *minus* the distortion in the private cost to the producer of X of producing its marginal unit of X. Step (2) of the derivation is also definitional—simply indicates that the distortion in the private benefits the producer of X obtains by selling its marginal unit of X equals the difference between the private and allocative benefits generated by the sale/consumption of the marginal unit of X and that the distortion in the private cost of producing the marginal unit of X equals the difference between the private cost to the producer of X of producing that unit and the allocative cost of its doing so. Step (3) indicates that

$PB_{U\Delta UOX}$ equals the conventional marginal revenue of selling a marginal unit of X, substitutes the symbol MLV (marginal allocative value) for the symbol LB (allocative benefits), substitutes the symbol $MC_{C\Delta UOX}$ for $PC_{C\Delta UOX/\Delta UOY}$, indicates that the allocative cost of producing the marginal unit of X equals (the number of units of Y that must be sacrificed to do so—the marginal rate of transformation of Y into X [$MRT_{Y/X}$]) *times* (the [average] allocative value of the sacrificed units of Y). Step (4) substitutes the symbol P_X^* for the symbol $MLV_{U\Delta UOX}$, substitutes the symbol MC_X for the symbol $MC_{C\Delta UOX}$, substitutes the symbol (MC_X^*/MC_Y^*) for the symbol $MRT_{Y/X}$, and substitutes the symbol P_Y^* for the symbol $MLV_{U\Delta UOY}$. Step (5) simply eliminates the MR_X and $(-MC_X)$ terms (because $MR_X = MC_X$) and converts $(-[-(MC_X^*/MC_Y^*)P_Y^*])$ into $(+[MC_X^*]MC_Y^*]P_Y^*)$. And Step (6) simply divides each term in Step (5) by MC_X^* and multiplies the resulting sum by MC_X^*.

Obviously, it will not be easy to use the 1E formula of Step (6) to determine the numerical value of $\Sigma D(P\pi_{(C+U)\Delta UOX/(C+U)\Delta UOY})$. It would be difficult enough to generate that figure from the Step (6) formula if one could do so solely from correct estimates of P_X, MC_X, P_Y, and MC_Y. But the task is made far more complex by the need to adjust the P and MC figures in question—to create P_X^* and P_Y^* figures that equal respectively MLV_X and MLV_Y (or whose ratio equals the marginal rate of substitution of Y for X) and to create MC_X^* and MC_Y^* figures whose ratio (MC_X^*/MC_Y^*) equals $MRT_{Y/X}$—say, by adjusting MC_X to create an adjusted-MC_X figure (MC_X^*) that equals MLC_X and by adjusting MC_Y to create an adjusted-MC_Y figure (MC_Y^*) that equals MLC_Y. I will now discuss each of these sets of adjustments in turn.

To start, to derive a $P_X^* = MLV_X$ figure from P_X where P_X stands for the before-tax price the seller of X obtains for its marginal unit, one will have (1) to adjust P_X upward by the amount of any monopsonistic rents the buyer of the marginal unit of X has to pay to purchase it, (2) to adjust P_X upward by any external benefits the consumption of the marginal unit of X generated or downward by any external costs the consumption of that unit generated, (3) to adjust P_X upward by any sales/excise/VAT/consumption taxes the consumer of the marginal unit of X paid to purchase it, (4) to adjust P_X upward by any amount by which the consumer of the marginal unit of X underestimated its dollar value to him or her or downward by any amount by which that buyer overestimated the unit's value to him or her, (5) to adjust P_X upward by any amount by which the buyer of the marginal unit of X overestimated the price he or she was paying for that unit (including the cost of maintaining and repairing it if it was a durable good) or downward by any amount by which that buyer underestimated the price he or she was paying to buy that unit, and (6) to adjust P_X upward by the amount of any buyer surplus the buyer of the marginal unit of X realized on its purchase. Obviously, to derive a $P_Y^* = MLV_Y$ figure from P_Y, one would have to make the same adjustments in P_Y that had to be made to P_X to create an adjusted-P_X figure that equaled MLV_X.

I turn to the adjustments one would have to make to convert MC_X into an adjusted–MC_X figure that equals MLC_X. In the simple case on which I am now focusing—in which all the resources that are devoted to producing the marginal unit of X are withdrawn from the production of less-than-one, one, or more-than-one units of a single product Y, the difference between $MLC_X = MC_X^*$ and MC_X will equal the difference between (1) the allocative value of the sacrificed units of Y, which, on my simplifying assumption that each sacrificed unit of Y has the same allocative value, equals MLV_Y *times* Q_{SY} where Q_{SY} stands for "the quantity of sacrificed units of Y" and (2) the private benefits that the producer of Y would have obtained by selling the sacrificed units of Y, which equal the private value of those units of Y to the producer of Y, hence the private value to the producer of Y of the resources it would have used to produce the sacrificed units of Y, hence the private cost to the producer of X (perhaps infinitesimally less than this private cost) of the resources it bid away from the producer of the sacrificed units of Y to use them to produce the marginal unit of X. Therefore, to adjust MC_X to create a MC_X^* that equals MLC_X (which I am assuming equals MC_X^*, though one could create MC_X^* and MC_Y^* figures that do not respectively equal MLC_X and MLC_Y but still have values such that $[MC_X^*/MC_Y^*] = MRT_{Y/X}$), one would have to raise MC_X by every amount by which some Pareto imperfection causes MLV_Y for a sacrificed unit of Y to exceed MR_Y for that sacrificed unit of Y and lower MC_X by every amount by which some Pareto imperfection causes MR_Y for a sacrificed unit of Y to exceed MLV_Y for that sacrificed unit of Y. Hence, to derive a MC_X^* figure that equals MLC_X from MC_X, one would have (1) to add to MC_X the number of dollars by which the sum of the before-tax prices that the prospective purchasers of the sacrificed units of Y would have paid for those units exceed the marginal revenue their sale would have generated for their possible producers, (2) to add to MC_X all monopsony rents the prospective purchasers of the sacrificed units of Y would have had to pay for other units of Y they purchased if they had purchased the sacrificed units of Y, (3) to add to MC_X any external benefits that would have been generated by the production and consumption of the sacrificed units of Y and to subtract from MC_X any external costs that would have been generated by the production and consumption of the sacrificed units of Y, (4) to add to MC_X any sales/excise/consumption/VAT taxes the prospective buyers of the sacrificed units of Y would have had to pay to purchase those units, (5) to add to MC_X the number of dollars by which the prospective buyers of the sacrificed units of Y would have underestimated their value to them or to subtract from MC_X the number of dollars by which the prospective buyers of the sacrificed units of Y would have overestimated their dollar value to them, and (6) to add to MC_X the number of dollars by which the prospective purchasers of the sacrificed units of Y would have overestimated their cost to them or made a mathematical error that resulted in their paying less for those units than they thought they were paying for them or subtract from MC_X the number of dollars by which the prospective purchasers of the sacrificed units of Y would have underestimated the price they would have paid for those units, and (7) to add to MC_X the amount of buyer surplus the prospective buyers of the sacrificed units of Y would have realized on their purchases of those units (buyer surplus that could be generated even though I am assuming that DD_Y is horizontal over the relevant range if the purchases would have been made in individual negotiations and one or more buyers had buyer power).

Finally, I discuss the adjustments that must be made to MC_Y to create an adjusted-MC_Y that equals MLC_Y (recall: I am assuming that the MC for each sacrificed unit of Y is the same and that the MLC for each sacrificed unit of Y is the same). In the simple case now under consideration, all the resources that would have been used to produce the sacrificed units of Y would have been withdrawn from the production of the marginal unit of X. Hence, to adjust MC_Y to create an adjusted-MC_Y (MC_Y^*) that equals MLC_Y, one would have to add to and subtract from MC_Y the Y-oriented counterparts of all the X-oriented numbers of dollars that the previous paragraph indicated would have to be added to and subtracted from MC_X to create a MC_X^* that equaled MLC_X.

6.5 An Illustration of the Step-Wise-Distortion Formula for the Aggregate Distortion in the Profits Yielded by a Particular Resource Allocation

This section illustrates the step-wise-distortion formula for the aggregate distortion in the profits yielded by any resource allocation initially by deriving that formula for the same resource allocation for which Sect. 6.4 derives the onesy formula—an allocation of resources from the production of less-than-one, one, or more-than-one just-extra-marginal units of product Y to the production of a marginal unit of product X on the assumption that neither Y nor X has any complements—and then by deriving the step-wise-distortion formula for the aggregate distortion in the profits that would be yielded by a UO-to-UO resource allocation from the production of just-extra-marginal units of multiple products that have complements to the production of a marginal unit of a single product that has complements. This section's analysis continues to assume that (1) $MR_X = MC_X$ and $MR_Y = MC_Y$, (2) the producer of X does not practice and the producer(s) of the sacrificed units of Y would not have practiced price discrimination when selling the marginal unit of X/the sacrificed just-extra-marginal units of Y (or $Y1...n$), and (3) the production of the marginal unit of X and the production of the sacrificed just-extra-marginal unit(s) of Y (or $Y1...n$) respectively did not and would not have yielded their respective producers profits by increasing their future sales or giving them production/distribution experience that did enable/would have enabled them to reduce their future costs. However, this section's analysis relaxes Sect. 6.4's assumption that if the resource allocation in question reduces the unit output of Y or one or more members of the set of products $Y1...n$ by more than one unit, the P, MR, MLV, MC, and MLC of each of the sacrificed units will respectively be the same. This section will place the symbol A (for average) before P, MR, MLV, MC, and MLC to indicate that the referenced figure is an average for the sacrificed units of Y or $Y1...n$ and a subscript SY below any AP, AMR, AMLV, AMC, or AMLC symbol to indicate that the average figure in question refers to the sacrificed (S) units of Y. The section uses the symbol Q_{SY} to refer to the quantity (Q) of any product Y that was sacrificed (S).

I will now delineate and explain the formulas for each of the seven individual-Pareto-imperfection-oriented SW-distortion components of the SW-distortion formula for the distortion that would be generated by an allocation of resources from the production of just-extra-marginal units of Y to the production of a marginal unit of X on the above assumptions. The symbol (SW[...])D will be used to stand for each such individual-type-of-Pareto-imperfection-oriented component of the (SW)D in the referenced private figure: the entry that replaces the ellipsis in the symbol—M, MS, X, T, NS, NM, or BS—will indicate the referenced type of Pareto imperfection. I want to remind you of the peculiar but defining feature of each of these derivations. Each equates the SW single-type-of-Pareto-imperfection-oriented component of the aggregate distortion in a PB, PC, or Pπ figure with the change that the extant exemplars of that type of Pareto imperfection would make in the specified aggregate-distortion figure, given the other Pareto imperfections in the relevant economy, if one ignores the possibilities that (1) the exemplars of the type of Pareto imperfection being referenced might affect the incidences and magnitudes of one or more of the other types of Pareto imperfections the relevant economy contains, (2) the changes in the incidences and magnitudes of these other types of Pareto imperfections might affect the specified aggregate distortion, and (3) regardless of whether the extant exemplars of any referenced type of Pareto imperfection affect the incidences and magnitudes of the other types of Pareto imperfections the relevant economy contains, the extant exemplars of other types of Pareto imperfections might affect the impact that the extant exemplars of the referenced type of Pareto imperfection has on the relevant aggregate distortion.

On this understanding of the definition of the step-wise-distortion components of the step-wise-distortion formula for the aggregate distortion in the profits yielded by any resource allocation and with the reminders that (1) any imperfection that inflates/deflates the private benefits that the prospective producer of the sacrificed units of Y would have realized by producing and selling (or using) those units will deflate/inflate the profits the producer of X realizes by withdrawing resources from the production of Y and using them to produce a marginal unit of X (by inflating/deflating the cost of those resources to the producer of X) and (2) any imperfection that inflates/deflates the private benefits that the producer of the marginal unit of X obtains by selling that unit inflates/deflates the profits that the producer of the marginal unit of X secures by withdrawing resources from the production of Y and using them to produce a marginal unit of X, I will now analyze the seven individual-Pareto-imperfection-oriented step-wise-distortion components of the step-wise-distortion formula for $\Sigma D(P\pi_{\Delta UOX/\Delta UOY})$.

The (SW[M])D component of $\Sigma D(P\pi_{\Delta UOX/\Delta UOY})$ equals $(AP_{SY}-AMR_{SY})Q_{SY}-(P_X-MR_X)$. This conclusion reflects the fact that since the tendencies of the exemplars of the other types of Pareto imperfections the economy contains to make P_Y diverge from MLV_Y and P_X diverge from MLV_X are taken into account in the calculation of the components of the (SW)D formula for $\Sigma D(P\pi_{\Delta UOX/\Delta UOY})$ that are respectively oriented to these other types of Pareto imperfections, one can calculate the (SW[M])D of $\Sigma D(P\pi_{\Delta UOX/\Delta UOY})$ on the assumptions that $P_Y = MLV_Y$ and $P_X = MLV_X$.

Economists use the expressions "monopsony power" or "buyer power" to refer to two overlapping but distinct phenomena. The more-narrowly-defined, more-traditional concept of monopsony power refers to the power that the only buyer of some resource or product has when it faces an upward-sloping supply curve. The more-broadly-defined concept of "monopsony power" or "buyer power" refers to the ability of a buyer to secure price-concessions or other-terms-of-sale concessions from a non-perfectly-competitive supplier because it is sufficiently irreplaceable as a customer to be able to do so. It may be worth pointing out that "monopsony power" in either of the above two senses cannot exist in the absence of imperfections in seller competition. Thus, because one cannot have an upward-sloping supply curve for a resource or product whose sales exceed one unit without one or more suppliers being able to secure supra-competitive prices for the intra-marginal units that are sold, monopsony power in the single-buyer/upward-sloping-supply-curve sense cannot exist without one or more relevant suppliers' facing imperfections in price-competition. And because (at least in equilibrium) a buyer's irreplaceability cannot enable it to secure more-favorable terms-of-purchase unless the supplier would otherwise have been able to secure supra-competitive prices or other terms of sale, monopsony or buyer power in the ability-to-secure-concessions sense cannot exist unless the relevant seller is a non-perfect competitor.

In any event, a complete step-wise-distortion-analysis of the distortion in the profits yielded by a UO-to-UO resource allocation will have to take account of the step-wise distortions that monopsony power in each of the above two senses will generate in those profits both (1) when the monopsony power is possessed by a buyer of X and/or a buyer of Y and (2) when the monopsony power is possessed by the producer of X and/or the sacrificing producer of the sacrificed unit(s) of Y as purchasers or prospective purchasers of the resources they respectively used to produce the marginal unit of X or would have used to produce the sacrificed unit(s) of Y.

I start by analyzing the (SW[MS])D component of the step-wise formula for $\Sigma D(P\pi_{UOX/UOY})$ that is generated by any monopsony power in the (possibly-) single-buyer/upward-sloping-supply-curve sense possessed by the buyer of the marginal unit of X and the buyer(s) of the unit(s) of Y sacrificed to the production of the marginal unit of X. I will assume that any such buyer that possesses monopsony power will purchase the X or Y it purchases by offering a single per-unit price for X or Y and purchasing all units of the product in question that its potential suppliers are willing to supply at that price. The essential point is that, on these assumptions, the marginal kost ("kost" with "k" when the reference is to the cost of buying) a monopsonist must incur to purchase all but the first unit of the monopsonized product it purchases exceeds the price it pays for each unit including the last unit of the product it purchases because the marginal kost includes the sum of the extra amounts it paid for the intra-marginal units it purchased when it raised the price it paid for all units of the product in question to elicit the supply of the marginal unit of that product it purchased: (MK–P) for the marginal unit equals the increase in economic rents ($\uparrow$ER) the buyers paid the suppliers of the intra-marginal units of the good in question it purchased as a result of its raising the price it paid for each unit of that good in order to elicit the supply of the marginal unit of that good it purchased. The fact that the marginal kost (MK) the buyer incurred to buy the marginal unit of the product it purchased exceeds the price (P) it paid for that unit is relevant in the current context because, on the assumptions of step-wise analysis, MK equals both the dollar value of the unit in question to its purchaser and the allocative value generated by the supply of that unit of the product to its purchaser, whereas P equals the private benefits that the supplier of the unit in question obtained by supplying it or that the sacrificing supplier of that unit would have obtained by supplying it. These conclusions imply that any upward-sloping-supply-curve type of monopsony power possessed by any single-pricing purchaser of the marginal unit of X will generated a negative (SW[MS]) distortion in $PB_{\Delta UOX}$ and $P\pi_{\Delta UOX/\Delta UOY}$ equal to $(MK_{\Delta UOX}-P_{\Delta UOY})$, which in turn equals the increase in the economic rents obtained by the suppliers of the intra-marginal units of X that resulted from the monopsonist's purchases of the marginal unit of X. The preceding conclusions also imply that any upward-sloping-supply-curve type of monopsony power possessed by one or more single-pricing prospective purchasers of the sacrificed units of Y will generate a positive (SW[MS]) distortion in $P\pi_{\Delta UOX/\Delta UOY}$ by generating a negative distortion in PB_{SUOY} (equal to $[AMK_{SY}-AP_{SY}]Q_{SY}$ where "AMK" stands for the average marginal kost that the prospective buyers of the sacrificed units of Y would have had to incur to purchase them, "AP_{SY}" stands for the average price that the prospective buyers of the sacrificed units of Y could have paid for those units and remained equally-well-off, and "Q_{SY}" stands for the quantity of Y that would be sacrificed to the production of the marginal unit of X), hence an equal negative distortion in $MC_{\Delta UOX}$, hence an absolutely-equal positive distortion in $P\pi_{\Delta UOX/\Delta UOY}$. I hasten to add that the qualitative variants of all the preceding conclusions will be justified if the relevant monopsonist(s) are implementing more-complicated buyer-pricing schemes so long as the scheme they employ does not result in MK's equaling P for the unit(s) of output in question (as would the practice of perfect price discrimination "against" each supplier if it could be carried out perfectly without generating any private transaction costs).

I move now to the (SW[MS])D component of the step-wise formula for the $\Sigma D(P\pi_{UOX/UOY})$ that is generated by any bilateral-monopoly-related monopsony power possessed by the buyer of the marginal unit of X and the prospective buyer(s) of the units of Y sacrificed to the production of the marginal unit of X (the power that these buyers had to obtain price or other-term-of-supply concessions in the bilateral-monopoly situation in which they found themselves). Two sets of points are salient. The first is that even though these buyers' possessions of this second type of monopsony power will affect $\Sigma D(P\pi_{UOX/UOY})$, it would be incorrect to include any such effect in the (SW[MS]) component of the step-wise-distortion formula when calculating the numerical value of the step-wise-distortion formula for $\Sigma D(P\pi_{UOX/UOY})$ because doing so would involve double-counting: all such effects will already have been counted when calculating the (SW[M]) component of the step-wise-distortion formula for $\Sigma D(P\pi_{UOX/UOY})$. The second point or pair of points is that (1) any bilateral-monopoly-related monopsony power that the buyer of the marginal unit of X possessed will have decreased the absolute magnitude of the negative (SW[M]) distortion in $PB_{\Delta UOX}$ and hence increased the positive (SW[M]) distortion in or decreased the negative (SW[M]) distortion in $P\pi_{UOX/UOY}$ not only by lowering P_X but by making it more likely that the contract of sale for X allowed the buyer of the marginal unit of X to purchase as many units of X as it wished at a stipulated per-unit (probably supra-marginal-cost) price, in which case $P_X = MR_X$ and (2) any bilateral-monopoly-related monopsony power that the buyer(s) of any sacrificed unit(s) of Y possessed will have decreased the absolute magnitude of the (SW[M]) distortion in PB_{SY}, hence decreased the absolute magnitude of the negative (SW[M]) distortion in $PC_{\Delta UOX}$, hence had a negative impact on (SW[M])$D(P\pi_{\Delta UOX/\Delta UOY})$.

I turn now to the impact that any "monopsony power" the producer of the marginal unit of X possessed when purchasing the resources it used to produce the marginal unit of X and that any "monopsony power" that the producer(s) of the sacrificed unit(s) of Y would have possessed when purchasing the resources it (they) would have used to produce the sacrificed unit(s) of Y will have on the (SW[MS]) component of the step-wise-distortion formula for $\Sigma D(P\pi_{UOX/UOY})$. I should acknowledge at the outset my concern that I may be about to analyze the contents of an empty economic box: although it does seem possible for both the producer of the marginal unit of X and the prospective producer(s) of the sacrificed unit(s) of Y to have monopsony power in the bilateral-monopoly-related sense, I am less convinced that both the producer of the marginal unit of X and the sacrificing producers of the sacrificed units of Y could have traditional upward-sloping-supply-curve-oriented monopsony power as purchasers of the resource they would respectively have used to produce the marginal unit of X and the sacrificed units of Y. But I will now proceed to ignore these qualms.

I start by addressing the traditional, upward-sloping-supply-curve-monopsony possibilities. If the producer of X were a traditional monopsonist of any of the resources (or intermediate products: hereinafter "resources") it used to produce the marginal unit of X and its purchase-pricing policy resulted in the MK to it of purchasing the units of a resource it monopsonized and used to produce its marginal unit of output, its traditional-monopsony power over those resources would generate a positive (SW[MS]) distortion in $PC_{\Delta UOX}$ equal to (AMK–AP)Q for the monopsonized resources it used and an absolutely-equal negative (SW[MS]) distortion in $P\pi_{UOX/UOY}$ if it did not practice perfectly accurately perfect price discrimination when purchasing multiple units of the relevant resource or intermediate product from an individual supplier and conventional price discrimination perfectly accurately when dealing with different suppliers. If the sacrificing producer(s) of Y were traditional monopolists of any of the resources it (they) would have used to produce the sacrificed unit(s) of Y, any traditional-monopsony power each such sacrificing producer of Y possessed over those resources would generate a positive (SW[MS]) distortion in $P\pi_{\Delta UOX/\Delta UOY}$ equal to the negative (SW[MS]) distortion it would generate in $PC_{\Delta UOX/\Delta UOY}$ by generating a negative distortion in the price the producer of the marginal unit of X has to pay for the resources it bid away from the producer(s) of the scarified unit(s) of Y that had traditional-monopsony power in relation to those resource (because the sacrificing producers' monopsony power would reduce the price[s] the sacrificing producers would be willing to pay for the resources in question [which is (are) infinitesimally below the price(s) the producer of the marginal unit of X paid for them] below the marginal revenue products the resources would have yielded the sacrificing producers of Y [which would equal those resources' marginal allocative products in the sacrificing producer(s) of Y's employ on the assumptions of the step-wise-distortion analysis]).

I turn finally to any bilateral-mononpoly-oriented monopsony power that the producer of the marginal unit of X and/or the sacrificing producer(s) of the sacrificed unit(s) of Y had when buying resources they would respectively use to produce the marginal unit of X or a sacrificed unit of Y. The same two points that I made about the effect of bilateral-monopoly-related monopsony power when the monopsonists were the buyer of the marginal unit of X and the prospective buyers of the sacrificed unit(s) of Y will be applicable when the relevant monoposists are the producer of the marginal unit of X and the sacrificing producer(s) of the sacrificed unit(s) of Y and the monopsonized resource (or intermediate product) is a resource (or intermediate product) that was used to produce the marginal unit of X or that would be used to produce the sacrificed unit(s) of Y: (1) even though these producers' possession of this type of monopsony power will affect $\Sigma D(P\pi_{\Delta UOX/\Delta UOY})$, it would be incorrect to include this effect in the (SW[MS])-distortion figure that is a component of the step-wise-distortion formula for $\Sigma D(P\pi_{\Delta UOX/\Delta UOY})$ because that effect will already be reflected in the magnitude of the (SW[M])-distortion component of the step-wise-distortion formula for $\Sigma D(P\pi_{\Delta UOX/\Delta UOY})$ and (2)(A) any bilateral-monopoly-type monopsony power that the producer of the marginal unit of X possesses when purchasing resources from a non-perfectly-competitive supplier will reduce the positive (SW[M]) distortion in the private kost of the monopsonized resource to the producer of the marginal unit of X by reducing the amount by which that resource's price exceeds its marginal cost and hence will generate a positive distortion in $P\pi_{\Delta UOX/\Delta UOY}$ while (B) any bilateral-monopoly-type monopsony power that the producer(s) of the sacrificed unit(s) of Y possessed when purchasing any of the resources it (they) would have used to produce the sacrificed unit(s) of Y from a non-perfectly-competitive supplier will have no effect on the distortion in $P\pi_{\Delta UOX/\Delta UOY}$: although such bilateral-monopoly-related monopsony power will reduce the positive (SW[M]) distortion in the prospective private kost of the relevant resources to them, hence the positive distortion in the marginal cost that sacrificing producers of the sacrificed units of Y would have had to incur to produce the sacrificed unit(s) of Y, hence the private benefits that the sale of the sacrificed units of Y would have conferred on the sacrificers (which are just below their private marginal costs), they will not in so doing affect the distortion in those private benefits or derivatively the distortion in the private cost of producing the marginal unit of X or the aggregate distortion in $(P\pi_{\Delta UOX/\Delta UOY})$.

I have devoted more attention to the step-wise-monopsony distortion in $P\pi_{\Delta UOX/\Delta UOY}$ than the incidence of the two variants of monopsony power that should be distinguished may warrant. I have done so in one sense against interest because monopsony poses problems for my step-wise-distortion approach to which I am not confident I have responded appropriately and I wanted to expose these difficulties in the hope that others might be able to deal with them more satisfactorily than I have managed to do.

The third component of the (SW)D formula for $\Sigma D(P\pi_{\Delta UOX/\Delta UOY})$ I will discuss is the externality-component—(SW[X])D(P$\pi_{\Delta UOX/\Delta UOY}$) = (SW[PX])D(P$\pi_{\Delta UOX/\Delta UOY}$) + (SW[CX])D(P$\pi_{\Delta UOX/\Delta UOY}$) where "PX" stands for production externality and "CX" stands for consumption externality. If I let "AXC$_{SY}$" stand for the average net external costs (external costs *minus* external benefits) that would have been generated by the production and consumption of the sacrificed units of Y and XC$_{\Delta UOX}$ stand for the net external costs (external costs *minus* external benefits) that were generated by the production and consumption of the marginal unit of X, (SW[X])D(P$\pi_{\Delta UOX/\Delta UOY}$) = $-$(AXC$_{SY}$)(Q$_{SY}$) + XC$_{\Delta UOX}$ since the net external costs that would have been generated by the production and consumption of the sacrificed units of Y deflate P$\pi_{\Delta UOX/\Delta UOY}$ by inflating the private value of the sacrificed units of Y to their prospective producers and hence the private cost to the producer of the marginal unit of X of the resources it bid away from the prospective producers of the sacrificed units of Y that they would have used to produce those units and any net external costs that were generated by the production and consumption of the marginal unit of X will inflate P$\pi_{\Delta UOX/\Delta UOY}$. I hasten to add that when the external benefits generated by the production and consumption of Y or X exceed the external costs the XC figures in the preceding expression will be negative.

I turn now to the (SW[T])D component of the (SW)D formula for $\Sigma D(P\pi_{\Delta UOX/\Delta UOY})$. Four types of taxes on the margin of income can generate such a (SW[T])D. The first are the sales/excise/VAT/consumption taxes that would have been levied on the sales of the sacrificed units of Y. If I let "ST%$_Y$" stand for the sales-tax rate that would have been applied to the sales of the sacrificed units of Y, this sales tax will inflate P$\pi_{\Delta UOX/\Delta UOY}$ (by deflating PB$_{SY}$ for those units' prospective producers and hence the PC to the producer of the marginal unit of X of the resources it would have withdrawn from the production of Y) by (ST%)(AP$_{SY}$)(Q$_{SY}$) where AP$_{SY}$ stands for the average before-tax price the prospective producers of the sacrificed units of Y would have received for those units. The second are the sales taxes that were levied on the sale of the marginal unit of X. If I let "ST%$_X$" stand for the sales-tax rate that was applied to the sale of the marginal unit of X, this sales tax would change the (SW[T])D(P$\pi_{\Delta UOX/\Delta UOY}$) by ($-$[ST%$_X$]P$_X$) where P$_X$ stands for the before-tax price the seller of the marginal unit of X obtains for that unit since the application of the sales tax on X reduces the private benefits the producer of X obtains by selling its marginal unit below that unit's allocative value, which on the assumptions on which the (SW[T])D(P$\pi_{\Delta UOX/\Delta UOY}$) figure is calculated equals the post-tax price of X, the after-tax price that that unit's buyer actually pays for it. The third tax on the margin of income that affects the (SW[T]D) component of the (SW)D formula for $\Sigma D(P\pi_{\Delta UOX/\Delta UOY})$ are the sales taxes that are levied on any inputs that the producer of the marginal unit of X uses to produce that unit. If I let "WAST%$_{TIX}$" stand for the weighted-average (WA) sales-tax rate (ST%) applied to the taxed inputs used to produce the marginal unit of product X (TIX)—weighted by the dollar cost of each taxed input used to produce the marginal unit of X—that the producer of the marginal unit of X paid and $V$$_{TIX}$ stand for the dollar value of the taxed inputs used to produce the marginal unit of X, this subcomponent of the (SW[T]) component of the (SW)D formula for $\Sigma D(P\pi_{\Delta UOX/\Delta UOY}) = -(WAST\%_{TIX})(\$V_{TIX})$ because, on the assumptions made in the calculation of the (SW[T])D component of the (SW)D formula for $\Sigma D(P\pi_{\Delta UOX/\Delta UOY})$, the input taxes that the producer of the marginal unit of X pays for those inputs it uses to produce that unit on whose sale/purchase such taxes are levied inflate MC_X. The fourth and final tax on the margin of income that affects the (SW[T])D component of the (SW)D formula for $\Sigma D(P\pi_{\Delta UOX/\Delta UOY})$ are the taxes that are levied on the income that those workers who forego leisure to produce the marginal unit of X earn by doing so. These taxes deflate $P\pi_{\Delta UOX/\Delta UOY}$ by inflating the cost of this labor to the producer of the marginal unit of X since, on the assumptions on which the (SW[T]) D distortion is calculated, the post-tax wages those workers secure for foregoing leisure to produce the marginal unit of X equal the allocative cost of the labor they devoted to producing the marginal unit of X (the allocative value of the leisure they forewent to do so). If my consideration of such taxes is not invalidated by the fact that it presupposes that the relevant resource allocation is from the production not only of just-extra-marginal units of Y but from the production of just-extra-marginal units of Y and leisure to the production of a marginal unit of X (which it probably is), this subcomponent of the (SW[T])D component of the (SW)D formula for $\Sigma D(P\pi_{\Delta UOX/\Delta UOY}) = -(YT\%_{RWY})(RWY)$ where YT% stands for the effective tax rate (T%) applied to the relevant (pre-tax) income (non-italicized Y) and "RWY" stands for the relevant worker's (RW) pre-tax income (Y).

Next to be considered is the non-sovereignty component of the (SW)D formula for $\Sigma D(P\pi_{\Delta UOX/\Delta UOY})$—(SW[NS])D. The possible non-sovereignty of four resource allocators or sets of resource allocators are relevant—the prospective buyers of the sacrificed units of Y, the suppliers of the produced unit of X, the buyer of inputs to the producer of the marginal unit of X, and the prospective producers of the sacrificed units of Y. The non-sovereignty of the producer of the marginal unit of X cannot distort the profitability of the resource allocation on which I am now focusing. (Of course, it can cause [1] prospective producers of an additional unit of X not to produce that unit even though it would have been profitable for them to do so despite the economic inefficiency of their doing so or [2] a prospective producer of an additional unit of X to produce that unit even when it was unprofitable for it to do so despite the economic efficiency of its doing so.) If the prospective buyers of the sacrificed units of Y overestimate/underestimate the dollar value of those units to them or underestimate/overestimate the cost to them of buying those units, the price they would have been willing to pay for those units will exceed/be lower than the allocative value of those units on the assumptions that any (SW)D analysis makes—on the assumptions that the (SW[NS])D analysis makes, the dollar cost to the producer of the marginal unit of X of the resources it withdraws from the production of just-extra-marginal units of Y will exceed/be exceeded by the allocative cost of its using those resources and $P\pi_{\Delta UOX/\Delta UOY}$ will be deflated/inflated on that account. Hence, if the prospective buyers of the sacrificed units of Y would have overvalued these units by $\$\alpha$, (SW[NS])D($P\pi_{\Delta UOX/\Delta UOY}$) will be ($-\$\alpha$), and if they would have undervalued those units by \$α, (SW[NS])D($P\pi_{\Delta UOX/\Delta UOY}$) will be (+\$α). It should be obvious that (1) if the buyer of the marginal unit of X overvalues it by \$β or underestimates the cost of buying (and maintaining and repairing) it by \$β, his or her non-sovereignty will cause the (SW[NS])D component of the (SW)D formula for $\Sigma D(P\pi_{\Delta UOX/\Delta UOY})$ to be (−\$β) and (2) if the buyer of the marginal unit of X undervalues it by \$β or overestimates the cost of buying (and repairing and maintaining) it by \$β, his or her non-sovereignty will cause the (SW[NS])D component of the (SW)D formula for $\Sigma D(P\pi_{\Delta UOX/\Delta UOY})$ to be (+\$β). If the prospective suppliers of inputs to the producer of the marginal unit of X overesti-mate/underestimate the cost to them of doing so by a total of \$ε, their non-sovereignty will add respectively a (−\$ε) and (+\$ε) subcomponent of the (SW[NS])D component of the (SW)D formula for $\Sigma D(P\pi_{\Delta UOX/\Delta UOY})$ if these input-supplier errors affect dollar-for-dollar the price that the producer of the marginal unit of X must pay for the relevant inputs. And if the prospective pro-ducers of the sacrificed units of Y overestimate/underestimate the private benefits they would obtain by selling the sacrificed units of Y by \$ʏ and any such error would affect dollar-for-dollar the (before-tax) price the producer of the marginal unit of X paid for the resources it used to produce that unit, these producers' non-sovereignty would add a subcomponent respectively of (−\$ʏ) and (+\$ʏ) to the (SW[NS])D component of the (SW)D formula for $\Sigma D(P\pi_{\Delta UOX/\Delta UOY})$.

The analysis of the non-maximization (NM) component of the (SW)D formula for $\Sigma D(P\pi_{\Delta UOX/\Delta UOY})$—(SW[NM])D—is perfectly analogous to the analysis of that formula's (NS) component (which is just as well, given the contestability of my classification of overestimates of the cost of buying something as manifestations of non-sovereignty rather than of non-maximization). If non-maximization by the prospective buyers of the sacrificed units of Y would lead them to pay more/less for the sacrificed units of Y than their preferences should have led them to be indifferent to paying, the prospective overpayment (say, of \$α) would generate a (−\$α) subcom-ponent of the (SW[NM])D component of the (SW)D formula for $\Sigma D(P\pi_{\Delta UOX/\Delta UOY})$ component if such actors' non-maximization would somehow enable them to pay \$α less than they should have been indifferent to paying for the sacrificed units of Y (as it might be in an individual-bargaining [bilateral-monopoly] situation), the prospective "underpayment" would generate a (+\$α) subcomponent of (SW[NM])D($P\pi_{\Delta UOX/\Delta UOY}$). If the non-maximization of the prospective producer or producers of the sacrificed units of Y would have led them to charge \$β less than they could have obtained for those units, this non-maximization would have generated a (+\$β) subcomponent of the (SW)(NM)D component of the (SW)D formula for $\Sigma D(P\pi_{\Delta UOX/\Delta UOY})$. If the non-maximization of input-suppliers to the producer of the marginal unit of X had led them to accept remuneration that was \$ε less than the amount of money they should have been indifferent to accepting for the inputs they supplied, their non-maximization would have generated a (+\$ε) subcomponent of the (SW[NM])D component of the (SW)D formula for $\Sigma D(P\pi_{\Delta UOX/\Delta UOY})$. If the non-maximization of the producer of the marginal unit of X led it to accept \$ʏ less for that unit than it should have been indifferent to accepting for that unit that non-maximization will have generated a (–$ȳ) subcomponent of the (SW)(NM)D component of the (SW)D formula for $\Sigma D(P\pi_{\Delta UOX/\Delta UOY})$.

I turn finally to the buyer-surplus-oriented (SW)D component of the (SW)D formula for $\Sigma D(P\pi_{\Delta UOX/\Delta UOY})$. To avoid double-counting, I will define this component to cover only that buyer surplus that is not attributable to non-sovereignty and/or non-maximization. If the prospective buyers of the sacrificed units of Y would have realized $\$\alpha$ in buyer surplus on those purchases, that BS would generate a (+$\$\alpha$) subcomponent of the (SW[BS])D component of the (SW)D formula for $\Sigma D(P\pi_{\Delta UOX/\Delta UOY})$ by deflating by $\$\alpha$ the private cost to the producer of X of the resources it withdrew from the production of the sacrificed units of Y, and if the sale of the marginal unit of X generated $\$\beta$ in buyer surplus for reasons unrelated to anyone's non-sovereignty or non-maximization that buyer surplus would generate a (–$\$\beta$) subcomponent of the (SW)(BS)D component of the (SW)D formula for $\Sigma D(P\pi_{\Delta UOX/\Delta UOY})$.

As I have already indicated, the (SW)D formula for $\Sigma D(P\pi_{\Delta UOX/\Delta UOY})$ simply adds together the formulas for each of the seven, individual-Pareto-imperfection-oriented (SW)D component-formulas. Obviously, the required analysis is complicated.

6.6 The Ways in Which the (1E) and (SW)D Formulas for the Aggregate Distortion in the Profits that Would Be Yielded by an Economics-Marginal UO-to-UO Resource Allocation Will Have to Be Altered When that Allocation Is from the Production of Just-Extra-Marginal Units of Two or More Products Y1…n to the Production of a Marginal Unit of One Product (X) and When Both Y1…n and X Have Complements (Respectively, YC and XC)

6.6.1 The Revision in the 1E Formula and the (SW)D Formula for the Aggregate Distortion in the Profits Yielded by a UO-to-UO Resource Allocation to the Production of Product X When that Allocation Involves the Withdrawal of Resources from the Production of Just-Extra-Marginal Units of a Set of Products Y1…n Rather Than from the Production of Just-Extra-Marginal Units of a Single Product Y

When the relevant UO-to-UO resource allocation is from the production of $Y1…n$ to the production of X rather than from the production of Y to the production of X, (1) the P_Y^* and MC_Y^* symbols in Sect. 6.4's derivation of the 1E formula for the aggregate distortion in the profits yielded by the referenced UO-to-UO resource allocation will have to be replaced by symbols that refer respectively to the sums of the adjusted prices and adjusted marginal costs of the units of output that are sacrificed to the production of the marginal unit of X—to $\sum_{i=1}^{n} P_i^*$ and $\sum_{i=1}^{n} MC_i^*$ or, if I relax Sect. 6.5's assumption that the adjusted prices and adjusted marginal costs of each unit of sacrificed output are respectively the same, to $\sum_{i=1}^{n} AP_{SYi}^*$ and $\sum_{i=1}^{n} AMC_{SYi}$—and (2) the same substitutions will have to be made for the AP_{SY}, AMR_{SY}, Q_{SY}, AXC_{SY}, $ST\%_Y$, $YT\%_{RWY}$, and RWY figures that appear in the (SW)D formula for the aggregate distortion in the profits yielded by the referenced UO-to-UO allocation.

6.6.2   The Revisions in the 1E Formula and the (SW)D Formula for the Aggregate Distortion in the Profits Yielded by a UO-to-UO Resource Allocation When that Allocation Involves the Withdrawal of Resources from the Production of Just-Extra-Marginal Units of One or More Goods *and Their Complement(s)* and Their Devotion to the Production of a Marginal Unit of Another Good *and Its Complement(s)*

If I let XC stand for the complement of X and YC stand for the complement of Y and the relevant UO-to-UO resource allocation is from the production of just-extra-marginal units of Y or $Y1...n$ and its/their complements to the production of a marginal unit of X and its complement(s), both the onesy formula and the step-wise-distortion formula for the aggregate distortion in the profits yielded by the referenced resource allocation will have to be altered to reflect that fact. For example, in the simple case in which the allocation is from the production of a single product Y and its complement YC to the production of a marginal unit of X and its complement XC, the $(AP_Y^*)(Q_{SY})$ figure in the more-realistic 1E formula will have to be replaced with a $\left(\left[AP_Y^* \right] \left[Qsy \right] + \left[AP_{YC}^* \right] \left[Q_{SYC} \right] \right)$ figure. Analogous changes will have to be made when relevant to the formulas for the subcomponents of the relevant (SW)D figure. An admission: to simplify and shorten the expositions, virtually all of the analyses that follow implicitly assume that the products whose production and creation or to whose production and/or creation the studied resource allocation withdraws or devotes resources have no complements.

6.7   The Relative Economic Efficiency of Using 1E and (SW)D Formulas for the Aggregate Distortion in the Profits Yielded by Any Resource Allocation

This study uses (SW)D formulas rather than 1E formulas for the aggregate profit distortions that play a role in the distortion-analysis protocol for economic-efficiency analysis that I claim is TBLE. It does so despite the fact that (unsurprisingly) the two categories of formulas manifest the salience of the same Pareto imperfections and other relevant parameters because I think that economic-efficiency analysts will be able to apply (SW)D formulas more-economic-efficiently —that it will be more allocatively-cost-effective for analysts to make the calculations that the use of (SW)D formulas require them to make than the adjustments in P and MC figures they would have to make to apply the 1E formula. I want to emphasize that in my judgment, this choice is not critical—i.e., the economic efficiency of the distortion-analysis protocol for economic-efficiency analysis does not critically depend on the assumption that it will be more economically efficient for economic-efficiency analysts to use SW(D) than 1E formulas for relevant aggregate profit distortion.

Note

1. In Markovits (2008), pp. 157–162, I generate a series of oPp distortion formulas to illustrate the fact that in a world that contains exemplars of one or more other types of Pareto imperfections, the contribution that all exemplars of a particular type of Pareto imperfection an economy contains (say Type α) makes to the distortion in a relevant profit figure that would be generated by the interaction of the extant exemplars of that type of Pareto imperfection (Type α) and the exemplars of the other types of Pareto imperfections the economy contains will equal the distortion that all exemplars of the Type α Pareto imperfection would generate in the relevant profit figure in an oPp economy only rarely and for-tuitously because, as I indicated previously, (1) in an economy that is not oPp, Type α Pareto imperfections may also affect the relevant profit-distortion by changing the incidences and magnitudes of the other types of Pareto imper-fections the economy contains and (2) regardless of whether Type α imper-fections have such effects, the exemplars of the other types of Pareto imperfections contained by an economy that is not oPp will usually affect the contribution that Type α Pareto imperfections make to the relevant aggregate profit-distortion.

Reference

Markovits, R. (2008). *Truth or economics: On the definition, prediction, and relevance of economic efficiency*. New Haven and London: Yale University Press.

Analyses of Various Step-Wise-Monopoly Distortions

Abstract

Section 7.1 analyzes the step-wise-monopoly (imperfections-in-seller-price-competition-generated and imperfections-in-QV-investment-competition-generated) distortion in the private benefits that a specifiable unit-output (UO) producer did obtain/would have obtained by selling a specified unit of output it produced/could have produced, that a specifiable QV investor did obtain/would have obtained by using a specified QV investment it created/could have created, and that a specifiable production-process researcher did obtain/would have obtained by using the production-process discovery its specified PPR project did make/would have made. Section 7.1 also analyzes the step-wise-monopoly (SW[M]) distortion that the combination of imperfections in seller (price and QV investment) competition and traditional fair-rate-of-return public-utility-pricing regulation can generate in the private benefits yielded by the creation of some QV investments and the execution of some PPR projects. Section 7.2 analyzes the (SW[M])D in the profits yielded by various categories of economics-marginal resource allocations.

This chapter analyzes (1) the step-wise monopoly distortion in the private benefits that a resource-user that uses resources to produce and sell a unit of output it produced, to use a QV investment it created, or to use the production-process discovery yielded by a production-process-research project it executed obtains by doing so (and concomitantly the step-wise-monopoly distortion in the private cost to a resource-user of any resources it withdraws from any UO production-and-sale, QV creation-and-use, or PPR execution-and-use pairs of functionally related resource-uses) and (2) the step-wise-monopoly distortion in the profits that were/would be yielded by ten categories of resource allocations that involve the withdrawal of resources from and/or the devotion of resources to at least one of the just-referenced resource-uses or pairs of related resource-uses. This chapter's analyses are relevant to what I claim is the third-best-allocatively-efficient protocol for predicting/post-dicting the economic efficiency of any choice because (1) that protocol generates its conclusions in

© Springer Nature Switzerland AG 2020

R. S. Markovits, *Welfare Economics and Second-Best Theory*,

https://doi.org/10.1007/978-3-030-43360-4_7

substantial part from TBLE estimates/guesstimates of the pre-choice and post-choice magnitudes of the aggregate distortions in the profits that were/would be yielded by the resource allocations the choice did/would deter and elicit, (2) there is good reason to believe that the formula for the aggregate distortion in such profit figures that is TBLE to use is the step-wise-distortion formula for that aggregate-profit distortion, and (3) that step-wise-distortion formula equals the sum of the formulas, respectively, for the step-wise monopoly, monopsony, externality, tax-on-the-margin-of-income, resource-allocator-non-sovereignty, resource-allocator-non-maximization, and buyer-surplus distortions in the relevant profit figure. Chapter 8 will comment on these six other individual-type-of-Pareto-imperfection-oriented step-wise profit distortions.

7.1 The Step-Wise-Monopoly Distortion in $PB_{(U)UO}$, $PB_{(U)QV}$, and $PB_{(U)PPR}$

7.1.1 The Step-Wise Imperfections-in-Seller-*Price*-Competition-Generated Monopoly Distortions in $PB_{(U)UO}$, $PB_{(U)QV}$, and $PB_{(U)PPR}$

7.1.1.1 The Imperfections-in-Seller-Price-Competition-Generated Step-Wise-Monopoly Distortion in $PB_{(U)UO}$

I will focus first on the step-wise imperfections-in-seller-price-competition-generated (SW[M]) distortion in $PB_{(U)UO}$. The text will focus on the simplest and (probably) the most common case—viz., the case that assumes that the sale of the relevant unit of output does not alter the demand curve the seller faces for the product in question or for any other product it produces. (All future analyses of the (SW[…]) distortion in any private-benefit or private-cost figure for any resource-use that did or would have withdrawn resources from one or more UO-producing resource-uses will be based on the same assumption.) Appendix B will delineate the various reasons why the sale of a unit of output may alter the future demand curves the seller faces when selling the good to which the price applies and other products it will sell in the future as well any private-benefit and profit distortions associated with these effects.

In the simple case on which the text focuses, $(SW[M]D)PB_{(U)UO}$ equals the difference between the pre-tax-price the seller did/would obtain for the unit in question and the marginal revenue the seller did/would obtain by selling that unit at that price. I hasten to add that this $(P - MR)$ difference depends not just on the demand and marginal-cost curves the seller faces but also on the pricing-technique the seller did/would use when pricing the relevant good (i.e., on all the other determinants of the profitability of using different pricing-techniques and on the private cost to the seller of using each such pricing-technique). Thus, $P = MR$ for each unit of output sold by a seller that faces a downward-sloping demand curve if that seller can and does practice perfect price discrimination perfectly accurately when selling the relevant product to each of its customers without incurring any pricing-costs.

7.1.1.2   The Imperfections-in-Seller-Price-Competition-Generated Step-Wise-Monopoly Distortion in PB$_{(U)QV}$

The step-wise distortions in PB$_{(U)UO}$ that Sect. 7.1.1.1 analyzed can be generated only by imperfections in seller price-competition. The step-wise-monopoly distortions in PB$_{(U)QV}$ and in PB$_{(U)PPR}$ that Sects. 7.1.1.2 and 7.1.1.3, respectively, analyze can be generated by imperfections in seller QV-investment competition, by the fair-rate-of-return public-utility-pricing regulation that is a traditional government response to the imperfections in seller price-competition and imperfections in QV-investment competition that result in sellers being classified as public utilities, and by imperfections in PPR competition. Sections 7.1.1.2 and 7.1.1.3 address the imperfections in seller price-competition that can generate (SW[M]) distortions, respectively, in PB$_{(U)QV}$ and PB$_{(U)PPR}$, Sect. 7.1.3 addresses the imperfections in seller investment competition that can generate (SW[M]) distortions, respectively, in PB$_{(U)QV}$ and PB$_{(U)PPR}$, and Sects. 7.1.3.1 and 7.1.3.2 address the imperfections-in-seller-price-and-investment-competition-generated fair-rate-of-return public-utility regulation (SW[M]) distortion, respectively, in PB$_{(U)QV}$ and PB$_{(U)PPR}$.

I will assume for simplicity that the use of the QV investments to be analyzed will not increase the profits their owners realize in the future when selling other products they produce, operating other distributive outlets they own, or selling additional units of the products whose inventories the QV investments in question increased that were not supplied out of the inventory created by the QV investment in question. On that assumption, the private benefits that the use of a QV investment generates for its owner equal the conventional operating profits its use generates—the difference between the total revenue its use generates and the private variable cost of its use. Section 7.1.2.1 analyzes the (SW[M]) distortion that imperfections in seller price-competition generate in the (conventional) operating profits the use of a QV investment yields.

The imperfections in seller price-competition faced by four sets of sellers generate (SW[M]) distortion in the private benefits (i.e., the operating profits) yielded by the use of any QV investment (including the QV investment "of ultimate interest"—the QV investment whose creation and use was either elicited or deterred by a choice whose economic efficiency is to be predicted/post-dicted). I will now proceed to identify each of these four sets of sellers, to describe the imperfections in seller price-competition the members of each set may face, and to analyze the (SW[M]) distortion that each such imperfection in seller price-competition generates in the operating profits that was or would have been yielded by any QV investment of ultimate interest.

To simplify the exposition, the text that follows assumes that "any QV investment of ultimate interest" is a QV investment that the choice whose economic efficiency is at issue elicited/would elicit and that "any QV investor of ultimate interest" is a QV investor whose QV investment a relevant choice elicited—i.e., the following text ignores the reality that some of the QV investments of ultimate interest are QV investments whose creation (and use) the choice whose economic efficiency is at issue deterred/would deter. Nevertheless, the analysis that follows is regrettably complex. I see no way to reduce its complexity: to be TBLE, the relevant analysis must be a general-equilibrium analysis, such analyses are inevitably complex, and I am trying to execute the relevant general-equilibrium analysis verbally.

The first set of sellers whose facing imperfections in seller price-competition generates a (SW[M]) distortion in $PB_{(U)QV}$ for any QV investment of ultimate interest (indeed, for any QV investment) contains one seller—the QV investor that made the QV investment. At least if I attribute (as I will) any buyer surplus the use of a QV investment generates to the QV investor's facing imperfections in seller price-competition when selling the product the QV investment created,[1] the imperfections in seller price-competition the QV investor faces when using its QV investment will have generated a negative (SW[M]) distortion in $PB_{(U)QV}$ for the QV investment (i.e., in the total revenue and concomitantly the operating profits that the use of the QV investment generated) equal to the buyer surplus that was generated by its use.

The second set of sellers whose facing imperfections in seller price-competition will have generated (SW[M]) distortions in the operating profits yielded by the use of any QV investment of ultimate interest contains all those UO producers, QV investors, and production-process researchers from which the use of the QV investment of ultimate interest directly withdrew resources. The imperfections in seller price-competition that those directly-sacrificing alternative resource-users would have faced are relevant because these imperfections would have generated (SW[M]) distortions in the private benefits the directly-sacrificed resource-uses would have yielded the directly-sacrificing resource-users, hence an absolutely-equal and same-signed (SW[M]) distortion in the private cost to the QV investor of ultimate interest of the resources it withdrew from these directly-sacrificed employments to use the QV investment of ultimate interest, hence an absolutely-equal but oppositely-signed (SW[M]) distortion in $PB_{(U)QV}$ for the QV investment of ultimate interest (i.e., in the operating profits its use generated).

I will now discuss in turn the impacts that the imperfections in seller price-competition facing respectively (1) each UO producer, (2) each QV investor, and (3) each production-process researcher from which the QV investor of ultimate interest directly withdrew resources when using its QV investment would have on the imperfections-in-seller-price-competition-generated (SW[M]) distortion in the operating profits the use of that QV investments yielded the QV investor in question. I focus first on the imperfection in seller price-competition that would have confronted each prospective UO producer from whose UO production the QV investor of ultimate interest directly withdrew resources to use the QV investment of ultimate interest. If (as I always will) I attribute the additional buyer surplus that would have been generated had any directly-sacrificing UO producer made the sale of those units of its product whose production was directly sacrificed to the use of the QV investment of ultimate interest to the directly-sacrificing UO producer's confronting imperfections in seller price-competition,[2] those imperfections in seller price-competition will have generated a positive (SW[M]) distortion in the operating profits that the use of the QV investment of ultimate interest yielded equal to the additional buyer surplus that the directly-sacrificed sales would have caused the directly-sacrificing UO producer to generate by generating a negative (SW[M]) distortion in $PB_{U(UO)}$ to the directly-sacrificing UO producer whose units of output were directly sacrificed to the use of the QV investment of ultimate interest equal to that amount of buyer surplus and hence an equal negative (SW[M]) distortion in the private cost that the QV investor of ultimate interest incurred to use the QV investment of ultimate interest.

I address next the imperfections in seller price-competition that would have confronted each prospective QV investor whose QV-investment's creation and use was directly sacrificed to the use of the QV investment of ultimate interest. Such a directly-sacrificing QV investor could confront imperfections in seller price-competition that would generate (SW[M]) distortions in $PB_{(U)QV}$ for the QV investment of ultimate interest (1) in its capacity as (A) a licensor of the right to use any product-patent to whose issuance the directly-sacrificed QV investment would have led or (B) a franchisor of the right to operate a member of a chain of distributive outlets its QV investment designed, trademarked, and promoted (e.g., of a chain of distinctive restaurants, fast-food purveyors, food stores, bakeries, hardware stores, clothing stores, and kitchen-appliance stores) or (2) in its capacity as (A) a prospective seller of the good or service the directly-sacrificed QV investment would have created, (B) a prospective seller of the inventory the directly-sacrificed QV investment would have produced, (C) a prospective operator of the distributive outlet the directly-sacrificed QV investment would have created, or (D) a prospective seller of the units of "the good" that the production capacity the directly-sacrificed QV investment would have constructed would have been used to produce (I have enquoted the expression "the good" because increases in a seller's production capacity [and increases in its inventory] may increase the quality of "the good" the seller offers for sale if "that good" is defined comprehensively to include speed of supply by enabling the seller to supply the material good or service in question more quickly on the average through a fluctuating-demand cycle if the demand for it varies through time and sometimes exceeds inventory *plus* immediate-production capacity.). In any event, if (1) the directly-sacrificed QV investment belongs to the subset of QV investments that yield patentable product-discoveries or that design, brand, and promote distinctive, trademarked distributive outlets, (2) the sacrificing prospective QV investor would not have produced exclusively itself the product its QV investment would have created or would not have owned itself all the distinctive, branded distributive outlets its QV investment would have designed, branded, and promoted, and (3) the sacrificing prospective QV investor would have faced imperfections in seller price-competition when licensing others to produce the patented product its QV investment would have invented or to construct and/or operate (as a franchisee) one or more of the distributive outlets its QV investment would have designed, branded, and promoted, those imperfections in seller price-competition would have generated a negative (SW[M]) distortion in the private benefits the sacrificed QV investment would have enabled the directly-sacrificing QV investor to obtain by selling such licenses and franchises equal to the amount of buyer surplus its sales of such licenses and franchises would have generated (if I continue to attribute that buyer surplus to the direct sacrificer's facing a downward-sloping demand curve when selling such licenses and franchises), an equal negative (SW[M]) distortion in the private cost to the QV investor of ultimate interest of the resources it withdrew from such directly-sacrificing QV investors to use the QV investment of ultimate interest, and hence an equally-absolutely-large but oppositely-signed (positive) (SW[M]) distortion in $PB_{(U)QV}$ for the QV investment of ultimate interest.

The imperfections in seller price-competition that any QV investor whose prospective QV investment's creation and use were directly sacrificed to the use of the QV investment of ultimate interest would have faced as a seller of the goods or services the directly-sacrificed QV investment would have put it in a position to sell will also have generated a positive (SW[M]) distortion in $PB_{(U)QV}$ for the QV investment of ultimate interest by generating an equally-absolutely-large negative (SW[M]) distortion in $PB_{(U)QV}$ for the directly-sacrificed QV investment and hence in $PC_{(U)QV}$ for the QV investment of ultimate interest equal to the buyer surplus that the directly-sacrificing QV investor's use of its directly-sacrificed QV investment would have generated.

I address now the imperfections in seller price-competition that would have confronted each sacrificing production-process researcher whose PPR project's execution and use were directly sacrificed to the use of the QV investment of ultimate interest. The imperfections in seller price-competition that would have confronted a vertically-integrated (production-process researcher)/(producer of the product G to whose production process the relevant PPR project related) whose PPR project's execution and use were directly sacrificed to the use of the QV investment of ultimate interest would generate two categories of (SW[M]) distortions in $PB_{(U)QV}$ for the QV investment of ultimate interest: (1) those that would have confronted the directly-sacrificing production-process researcher in its capacity as a seller of licenses to sell the right to use the production process that the directly-sacrificed PPR project would have discovered[3] and (2) those that would have confronted the directly-sacrificing production-process researcher in its capacity as a seller of the product G to whose production process the directly-sacrificed PPR project would have related if it produced that good itself (and any other producers to which the directly-sacrificing PPR executer or those it would have licensed to sell the right to use its discovery would have licensed the right to use the production-process discovery the directly-sacrificed PPR project would have yielded). Each dollar of buyer surplus that would have been generated by the directly-sacrificing production-process researcher's licensing of the right to license others to use the production process its directly-sacrificed PPR project would have discovered will be associated with a one-dollar negative (SW[M]) distortion in

PB$_{(U)PPR}$ for the directly-sacrificed PPR project, hence a one-dollar negative (SW[M]) distortion in PC$_{(U)QV}$ for the QV investment of ultimate interest, and hence a one-dollar positive (SW[M]) distortion in the operating profits generated by the use of the QV investment of ultimate interest—*i.e.,* in PB$_{(U)QV}$ for that QV investment. Similarly, in what I take to be the typical case in which the directly-sacrificed PPR project would have discovered a production process whose use would have reduced the marginal cost that any of its users would have had to incur to produce one or more additional units of any product it would have been used to produce (*i.e.,* would have made it profitable for its user[s] to reduce their price[s] of the good[s] to whose production process it would have related and to expand their output[s] of the good[s] in question beyond the output[s] it [they] would have produced had they used the old production process),[4] the imperfections in seller price-competition that would have faced the production-process researcher in its capacity as a producer of the good *G* to whose production process the discovery that the directly-sacrificed PPR project would have yielded would have related if it produced that good itself and any independent producers of that would have been licensed to use the production process that the directly-sacrificed PPR project would have discovered (either by the directly-sacrificing production-process researcher or by any licensee that researcher would have licensed to sell such licenses) would yield a negative (SW[M]) distortion in PB$_{(U)PPR}$ for the sacrificed PPR project, hence an equal negative (SW[M]) distortion in PC$_{(U)QV}$ for the QV investment of ultimate interest, and hence an absolutely-equal positive (SW[M]) distortion in PB$_{(U)QV}$ for that QV investment equal to the additional buyer surplus that the use of the directly-sacrificed production process would have caused its user(s) to generate (because the user[s] of the sacrificed marginal-cost-reducing production-process discovery would have faced downward-sloping demand curves).

The third set of sellers whose facing imperfections in seller price-competition will have generated (SW[M]) distortions in the operating profits yielded by the use of any QV investment of ultimate interest contains those UO produces, QV investors, and production-process researchers whose prospective unit-output production and use, QV-investment creation and use, and PPR execution and use would have respectively been sacrificed to the "counterfactual" use of the QV investments that were directly sacrificed to the use of the QV investment of ultimate interest ("counterfactual" in that the QV investments to whose uses the resource-uses in question would have been sacrificed would themselves have been directly sacrificed to the use of the QV investment of ultimate interest). For reasons that I have just discussed, the imperfections in seller price-competition that these three subsets of counterfactually-sacrificing resource-users would have faced will have generated a negative (SW[M]) distortion in the private benefits these sacrificers would have obtained by selling the units of output, using the QV investments, and using the PPR discoveries that would have been sacrificed to the use of the QV investments that were sacrificed to the directly-sacrificed use of the QV investment of ultimate interest had that QV investment not been sacrificed, hence an equal negative (SW[M]) distortion in the "prospective" private cost to the QV investors whose QV investments were directly sacrificed to the use of the QV investment of ultimate interest of the resources the directly-sacrificing QV investor would have employed to use the directly-sacrificed QV investment, hence an absolutely-equal but positive (SW[M]) distortion in the operating profits the directly-sacrificing QV investor would have obtained by using its directly-sacrificed QV investment, hence an equal positive (SW[M]) distortion in the private cost to the QV investor of ultimate interest, hence an absolutely-equal but negative (SW[M]) distortion in the operating profits that the QV investor of ultimate interest obtained by using the QV investment of ultimate interest.

The fourth set of sellers whose facing imperfections in seller price-competition will have generated (SW[M]) distortions in the operating profits yielded by any QV investment of ultimate interest contains two (presumably-largely-overlapping) sets of resource-users whose facing imperfections in seller price-competition is relevant because the imperfections in seller price-competition they face would have generated (SW[M]) distortions in the private benefits that the PPR projects directly sacrificed to the use of the QV investment of ultimate interest would have generated for the production-process researchers whose PPR projects were directly sacrificed to the use of the QV investment of ultimate interest: (1) the set of actually-sacrificing UO producers, QV investors, and production-process researchers whose sacrificed resources were used to produce the actual outputs of the goods to whose production processes the PPR projects directly sacrificed to the use of the QV investment of ultimate interest would have related and (2) the set of "counterfactually-sacrificing" UO producers, QV creators, and production-process researchers whose counterfactually-sacrificed resources would have been used to produce the extra units of the goods to whose production processes the PPR projects directly sacrificed to the use of the QV investment of ultimate interest related that would have been produced had (counterfactually) those PPR projects not been sacrificed if the use of the discoveries that those directly-sacrificed PPR projects would have yielded would have reduced the marginal cost of producing additional units of those products (again, "*counterfactually*-sacrificing" and "*counterfactually*-sacrificed" because the PPR project whose execution would have led to the sacrifice in question was not in fact executed [was itself sacrificed]).

The imperfections in seller price-competition that these two sets of UO producers, QV investors, and production-process researchers would have faced are relevant (1) because they would have generated (SW[M]) distortions in the private benefits that the sacrificed units of output, QV investments, and PPR projects would have generated respectively for the sacrificing UO producers, QV investors, and production-process researchers, (2) because they generated on that account equal (SW[M]) distortions in the fixed and variable cost to the producers of the goods to whose production processes the above-referenced PPR projects would have related of producing with the old production processes the outputs of those goods they did produce with the old production processes and (B) would have generated (SW[M]) distortions in the variable cost to those producers of producing any extra units of these goods the use of any (sacrificed) production process would have led them to produce had the sacrificed PPR project not been sacrificed, had the sacrificed production-process discovery that the sacrificed PPR project would have yielded been made, had that sacrificed discovered production process been used, and had its use reduced the variable cost of producing one or more extra units of the products in question, and (3) because any (SW[M]) distortion in the private cost of producing any output of a good will be associated with an equal (SW[M]) distortion in the private-production-cost saving a production-process discovery will enable its user to obtain, hence in the private benefits that a production-process discovery would have yielded the production-process researcher that would have made it, hence with an equal (SW[M]) distortion in the private cost to a QV investor of withdrawing resources from PPR execution and use to use its QV investment, hence with an absolutely-equal but oppositely-signed (SW[M]) distortion in the operating profits yielded by the QV investment in question. Thus, if I assume for reasons that will be explained (far from fully satisfactorily) below that, all tolled, the relevant imperfections in seller price-competition generate a negative (SW[M]) distortion in the private cost to the producers of the good(s) to whose production process(es) any PPR project relates of the resources that those producers did use to produce the actual outputs of their products and any additional output they would have produced if they could have employed the production process the sacrificed PPR project in question would have discovered, those imperfections in seller price-competition would generate (1) negative (SW[M]) distortions in the private benefits the PPR project in question would have conferred on the user of the discovery it would have yielded (and hence on the sacrificing production-process researcher) (A) by enabling the user(s) of the discovery it would have yielded to produce more privately cheaply the output(s) of its (their) product(s) they did produce with the production process that the sacrificed PPR project would have replaced[5] and (B) by enabling them to profit by expanding their outputs in the latter case by generating a negative (SW[M]) distortion in the amount by which the [sacrificed] discovery would have reduced the variable cost of any output-expansion its use would have rendered profitable, hence (2) an equal negative (SW[M]) distortion in the private cost to the QV investor of ultimate interest of withdrawing resources from PPR execution to use the QV investment of ultimate interest, hence (3) an absolutely-equal but positive (SW[M]) distortion in the private benefits (i.e., the operating profits) that the QV investor of ultimate interest obtained by using the QV investment of ultimate interest.

7.1.1.3   The Imperfections-in-Seller-Price-Competition-Generated Step-Wise-Monopoly Distortion in PB$_{(U)PPR}$

Finally, some expositional good news: Sections 7.1.1.1 and 7.1.1.2 executed virtually all the analyses required to determine the imperfections-in-seller-price-competition-generated step-wise-monopoly distortion in PB$_{(U)PPR}$ for any PPR project that a choice whose economic efficiency is at issue elicited or deterred. Thus, those sections analyzed (1) the negative (SW[M]) distortion in PB$_{(U)PPR}$ for any PPR project of ultimate interest that would be generated by any imperfection in seller price-competition that the production-process researcher of ultimate interest faced when licensing others to license the use of its discovery, (2) the negative

(SW[M]) distortion in $PB_{(U)PPR}$ for any project of ultimate interest that would be generated by any imperfection in seller price-competition the production-process researcher faced when licensing the use of its discovery to produce the good(s) to whose production process it related or by any imperfection in seller price-competition any party the researchers licensed to license the use of the discovered production process faced when licensing the use of the production process, (3) the negative (SW[M]) distortion in $PB_{(U)PPR}$ for the PPR project of ultimate interest that would be generated by any imperfection in seller price-competition faced by the UO producers that would use the production process it discovered if the use of that process lowered the marginal cost of producing the units of the good(s) it would be used to produce that the producer(s) in question would not have found profitable to produce with the old production process, and (4) either (A) the negative (SW[M]) distortion in $PB_{(U)PPR}$ for the PPR project of ultimate interest that would be generated by the imperfections in seller price-competition faced by the UO producers, QV investors, and production-process researchers whose respective units of output, QV investments, and PPR projects were directly sacrificed to the production of the good(s) to whose production process the PPR project of ultimate interest related if (as I suspect—see below), all tolled, those imperfections generated negative (SW[M]) distortions in the average total cost of producing the units of the latter products that would have been produced had their producers not used the production process the PPR project of ultimate interest discovered and the total variable cost of producing any extra units of the latter product(s) to whose production the use of the discovery yielded by the PPR project of ultimate interest led or (B) a positive (SW[M]) distortion in $PB_{(U)PPR}$ for the PPR project of ultimate interest if (contrary to my expectations), all tolled, the imperfections in seller price-competition just referenced generated a positive (SW[M]) distortion in the average fixed cost and total variable cost just referenced.

As already indicated, Sects. 7.1.2.1 and 7.1.2.2 analyze respectively the (SW[M]) distortions that imperfections in QV-investment competition can generate in $PB_{(U)QV}$ for QV investments and imperfections in PPR competition can generate in $PB_{(U)PPR}$ for PPR projects of ultimate interest, and the various sections of Sect. 7.2 analyze the implications of Sect. 7.1 for the (SW[M]) distortion in the profits that will be yielded by a large variety of categories of resource allocations. Before proceeding, I want to comment on my far-from-perfectly-informed beliefs about four sets of "empirical" issues (enquoted because their resolution depends in part on a number of theoretical conclusions) that will inform Sects. 7.1 and 7.2 analyses (though the case for my general approach does not depend on their accuracy). The first of these sets of issues is (1) the sign of the (SW[M]) distortion that the imperfections in seller price-competition that face the UO producers, QV investors, and production-process researchers from which resources were/(would be) withdrawn to use any (QV investment of ultimate interest)/(any sacrificed QV investment) did/would generate in the private cost of using the QV investment in question, (2) the sign of the (SW[M]) distortion that the imperfections in seller price-competition that face the UO producers, QV investors, and production-process researchers from which resources were/(would be) withdrawn to produce the units of output of any good(s) to whose production process (a PPR project of ultimate interest related or would have related)/(a sacrificed PPR project would have related) that would have been produced had the referenced PPR project not been executed and used did/would generate in the average total cost of producing the output(s) in question, and (3) the sign of the (SW[M]) distortion that the imperfections in seller price-competition that face the UO producers, QV investors, and production-process researchers from which resources were/(would have been) withdrawn to produce the extra units of the product(s) to whose production the PPR project of ultimate interest or a relevant sacrificed PPR project related that were/(would have been) generated because the use of the PPR project in question (did reduce)/(would have reduced) the marginal cost of producing extra units of the good to whose production process the relevant PPR project related. The second of these sets of issues is the implications of my (admittedly-contestable) conclusions about the first set of issues for the sign of the imperfections-in-seller-price-competition-generated (SW[M]) distortions in PB$_{(U)QV}$ and PB$_{(U)PPR}$ for QV investments and PPR projects of ultimate interest. The third of these sets of issues is the sign of the (SW[M]) distortion that the imperfections in seller price-competition that would have faced the UO producers, QV investors, and production-process researchers whose prospective resource-uses (1) were/(would have been) directly sacrificed to the creation of a QV investment of ultimate interest or the execution of a PPR project of ultimate interest and (2) would have been sacrificed to the creation and use of any QV investments or to the execution and use of any PPR projects that were/(would have been) sacrificed to the creation of a QV investment of ultimate interest or the execution of a PPR project of ultimate interest did/(would have generated) in the private cost of creating a QV investment of ultimate interest or executing a PPR project of ultimate interest.

To resolve the first set of issues accurately, one would have to know (1) the weighted-average percentage-distortions in the private benefits that would have been yielded by the various (1) UO-producing-and-using, QV-creating-and-using, and PPR-executing-and-using uses that would be sacrificed to (2) the QV-creating-and-using, PPR-creating, and product-G-producing uses to which the sacrificed resource-uses would be sacrificed and the percentages of the resources allocated to each of the categories of use referenced after "(2)" in this sentence that would be withdrawn, respectively, from the UO-producing-and-using, QV-creating-and-using, and PPR-executing-and-using uses referenced after "(1)" in this sentence.

My beliefs about the signs of the (SW[M]) distortions that imperfections in seller price-competition generate in the private cost of creating a relevant QV investment, the private cost of using a QV investment, the private cost of executing a relevant PPR project, and the private cost of producing relevant outputs of the product G to whose production process a relevant PPR project relates are contestable because I do not know enough about these issues. More specifically, I have inadequate information about (1) the percentages of an economy's resources that are devoted, respectively, to UO-producing, QV-investment-creating, and PPR-executing uses, (2) the extent to which an economy's individual resources are better-suited to perform one of the above functions than the other functions, (3) the weighted-average P/MC ratio for the relevant economy's individual products and the mean deviation of the distribution of any economy's P/MC ratios, (4) the weighted-average percentage of the resources the production of units of each of any relevant economy's individual products withdraws from the production of products with which it is atypically competitive[6] and something like the mean deviation of the relevant economy's economy-wide distribution of the non-weighted percentages just referenced, (5) the correlation between the difference between the P/MC ratios of various pairs of products in any relevant economy and the extent to which they are competitive with each other, (6) the correlation between the P/MC ratio of each product in a relevant economy and the ratio of its sales to the private cost of the QV investment that created it, the economy-wide weighted-average sales-to-QV-investment ratio in the relevant economy, and something like the mean deviation of the economy's economy-wide distribution of (individual QV-investment-created-"product" sales)-to-(individual QV investment) ratios, (7) the correlation of the P/MC ratio of any product G in the relevant economy (the weighted-average P/MC ratio of the products $[G1...n]$ to whose production process a production-process discovery relates) and the percentage of the sales of G ($G1...n$) that a relevant production-process researcher makes, etc. I suspect that (1) the vast majority of any economy's resources (even any advanced economy's resources) are devoted to the production of units of existing products, that a quite low percentage of even such economies' resources are devoted to QV-investment creation (and that most of the QV investments in all economies are neither technologically nor commercially innovative [e.g., that most create such "products" as a pizzeria or gas station on 50th St. that are essentially physically identical to other pizzerias or gas stations on 20th St. and 80th St. or a bar of soap with green stripes that smell of mint in an economy that already produces bars of soap that contain purple stripes that smell of lavender, or a TV set with a 34-in. diameter or a fake rosewood case in an economy in which TV sets with 30-in. and 39-in. diameters and fake-oak and black chassis are already being produced]), and that a still lower percentage of even an advanced economy's resources are devoted to PPR; (2) with the exception of scientifically-or-technologically-innovative researchers who are likely to be better-suited to creating technologically-innovative QV investments or designing PPR projects than to performing other economic functions and economically-imaginative entrepreneurs (like the entrepreneurs who thought of creating launderettes in which one could buy beer and other drinks to consume on the premises—suds and suds, so to speak—or the "guys" who developed commercially-successful search-engines, browsers, websites, etc.) who are better at doing this kind of work than they would be at UO production or non-innovative-QV-investment creation, I suspect that the economy's human and certainly its non-human resources are not better-suited to performing one category of economic function than another; (3) I do not have much sense of the weighted-average P/MC ratio of any relevant economy's individual products or the mean deviation of the distribution of such ratios in any relevant economy; (4) I also do not have much sense of the percentages of the resources that are devoted to the production of units of any relevant economy's individual products that are withdrawn from the production of units of other existing products with which the individual products in question (to be crude) are respectively highly competitive, moderately competitive, and distantly competitive or the extent to which such "competitiveness distributions" vary from product to product in any relevant economy; (5) I am uncertain about the correlation between how competitive any pair of products a relevant economy produces are with each other and the similarity of their P/MC ratios: a highly-differentiated product whose attributes may enable its producer to obtain prices that substantially exceed its marginal costs from some buyers whose dollar preferences for the product substantially exceed the amount by which the marginal cost of its production exceeds the marginal cost of an undifferentiated rival product may also be privately-best-placed or privately-second-placed to obtain the patronage of other buyers who place a much lower-dollar value on its distinguishing attributes (other buyers whose privately-best-placed or privately-second-placed but far-better-placed-than-privately-third-placed supplier is a producer of an undifferentiated product that charges a price that is close to the undifferentiated product's marginal costs); (6) I am also uncertain about the relationship between the P/MC ratio of each product in any relevant economy and its sales-to-QV-investment ratio, about any relevant economy's economy-wide weighted-average sales-to-QV-investment ratio, and about the mean deviation of the distribution of such ratios for all of any relevant economy's QV investments; and, finally, (7)(A) I do not have much of a sense of the correlation between the share of the sales of the products G (or set of similar products G1...n) that given producers in a relevant economy make and the probability that the producer in question will do PPR into the production process used to produce G (G1...n) that is not designed to discover a production process whose use will reduce the private accident-and/or-pollution-related external costs that the production of relevant quantities of G or G1... n will generate; (B) there is reason to believe that the probability that any producer of some product G in any relevant economy whose tort-law liability for any accident-and/or-pollution-related (private) external costs it generates depends on its generation of such costs being found negligent will execute *ex ante* economically-efficient PPR projects that are designed to discover less-accident-and-pollution-loss-generating production processes is inversely related to the producer's share of the sales of G or G1...n that are made,[7] and (C) there is some evidence that firms whose research operations tend to be controlled by managers whose choices tend to be profit-motivated devote a higher percentage of their budgets to commercially-viable product and production-process R&D than do either small firms (that cannot take advantage of relevant economies of scale) or medium-sized firms (whose scientists are alleged to have a tendency to do more "pure research," which is less profitable).[8]

I recognize that it would be perfectly consistent with the character of the vast majority of the analyses this study executes to proceed without making any assumptions about the signs of the imperfections-in-seller-price-competition-generated (SW[M]) distortions in (1) the (private) marginal cost that any QV investor of ultimate interest and any sacrificing QV investor incurred or would have to incur to use its QV investment, (2)(A) the total cost that any producer of a good G to whose production process a PPR project of ultimate interest or any relevant sacrificed PPR project did relate or would have related incurred to produce the output of G it would produce if it could not use the production process the relevant PPR project did discover/would have discovered as well as (B) the variable costs that the producer(s) of any such product G incurred/would have incurred to produce any extra units of G that its (their) use of the production process that the PPR project of ultimate interest or the sacrificed PPR project (did discover)/(would have discovered) because the use of that discovered or discoverable production process (did reduce)/(would have reduced) the marginal cost of producing those extra units of G, (3) $PB_{(U)QV}$ for any QV investor of ultimate interest or for any sacrificing QV investor, (4) $PB_{(U)PPR}$ for any production-process researcher of ultimate interest or for any sacrificing production-process researcher, (5) $PC_{(C)QV}$ for any relevant QV investment (recall: the subscript "(C)" refers to "creation of"), and (6) $PC_{(C)PPR}$ for any relevant PPR project. I also recognize that my lack of knowledge about the magnitudes of many parameters that will affect such imperfection-in-seller-price-competition-generated (SW[M]) distortions counsels against my taking positions on the signs of these distortions—that not only mathematical purists (like the Cal Tech mathematical economists referenced in Sect. 2.5 [whose dispositions make them understandably-uncomfortable with *third*-best-economic-efficiency analyses]) but also economists who believe that it is appropriate to generate conclusions from parameter estimates or parameter guesstimates to whose accuracy one cannot attest so long as one points out the relevance of those empirical assumptions, explains their basis, and acknowledges their contestability will conclude that one should not rely on analyses that are based on such qualitative sign-assumptions. My defense is that (1) these assumptions seem to me to be more likely to be correct than incorrect, (2) I do not have the space to execute analyses that are based on all possible distortion-sign assumptions, (3) the analyses in question are intended to be purely illustrative, and (4) I will always point out the salience of any contestable empirical assumption I make—i.e., I will always indicate that any conclusion I reach that depends on the accuracy of any such assumption does so.

In the text that follows, I will frequently explicitly assume that the relevant imperfections in seller price-competition generate a negative (SW[M]) distortion (1) in the private cost that any QV investor incurs to use its QV investment, (2) in the total private cost of producing the output of any good G to whose production process a relevant PPR project relates that would be produced if that PPR project were not executed or the discovery it would yield was not used, and (3) in the variable cost of producing any additional units of any such good G that the use of the production process a relevant PPR project would discover would render profitable to produce by reducing the variable cost of producing the units in question. I will adopt these assumptions (1) because (as we have seen) the imperfections-in-seller-price-competition-generated (SW[M]) distortion in $PB_{(U)UO}$ is negative, (2) because (as we shall see) the imperfections-in-seller-price-competition-generated distortion in $PB_{(U)QV}$ is also negative, and (3) because—although (as we shall also see) the imperfections-in-seller-price-competition-generated distortion in $PB_{(U)QV}$ is positive—the percentages of the resources devoted to using QV investments and producing units of any good G to whose production process any relevant PPR project related/(would have related) that are withdrawn from QV-investment creation and use seem likely to me to be too low relative to the percentages withdrawn from UO production and use and PPR execution and use to overcome any likely positive difference between the weighted-average absolute (positive) imperfections-in-seller-price-competition-generated percentage-distortion in $PB_{(U)QV}$ for the relevant sacrificed QV-investment projects and the weighted-average absolute (negative) imperfections-in-seller-price-competition-generated percentage-distortion in the relevant $PB_{(U)UO}$ and $PB_{(U)PPR}$ figures for the sacrificed UO-producing and PPR-executing-and-using uses. As previously indicated, this guess reflects my beliefs that (1) the overwhelming majority of all economies' economically-productive resources are not intrinsically-better-suited to perform either UO-producing or QV-creating or PPR-executing uses, (2) the overwhelming majority of all economies' resources are devoted to UO production, (3) the vast majority of resources devoted to QV-investment creation are not technologically/scientifically-skilled human resources or commercially-innovative human resources (both because the overwhelming majority of QV investments are not innovative and because the majority of resources devoted to creating even innovative QV investments are not technologically/scientifically/economically-innovative human resources—are resources that are used to construct pilot plants, final production-facilities, physical distributive outlets, capacity, or inventory), and (4) for reasons to be discussed below, the imperfections-in-seller-price-competition-generated (SW[M]) percentage-distortion in $PB_{(U)PPR}$ is negative and may well be absolutely as large as or larger than the counterpart (SW[M]) percentage-distortion in $PB_{(U)UO}$.

Several future applied analyses will also proceed on the assumption that the imperfections-in-seller-price-competition-generated (SW[M]) distortion in the operating profits yielded by the use of any QV investment is positive—that the absolute magnitude of the negative imperfections-in-seller-price-competition-generated (SW[M]) distortion in the private cost of using any QV investment that I am assuming the referenced imperfections generate *exceeds* the negative buyer-surplus-related (SW[M]) distortion in $PB_{(U)QV}$ that the imperfection in price-competition the QV investor itself faces generates. I will first state an argument that establishes that this conclusion would be justified if the argument's admittedly-unrealistic empirical assumptions are correct and then explain why the admitted inaccuracy of the empirical assumptions on which this argument is based does not critically affect its conclusion. Here is the initial argument. Assume that (1) all the resources employed to use any QV investment are withdrawn from alternative UO-producing uses, (2) the demand curve for the product that would be created by any QV investment is linear and identical to each of the demand curves for the products whose respective unit outputs would be reduced if that QV investment was used, (3) the use of any QV investment would reduce by one unit the outputs of each product whose unit output it would reduce, (4) the marginal-cost curves for any QV investment and for each of the products whose output would be reduced when that QV investment was used were horizontal and identical, and (5) the relevant imperfections in seller price-competition generate equal negative (SW[M]) distortions in the marginal cost of producing each unit of the product that the relevant QV investment created and in the marginal cost of producing each unit of each product whose output would be reduced by the use of that created QV investment. On these assumptions, the (SW[M]) distortion in the private cost of using any QV investment that would be generated by the imperfections in seller price-competition that faced the UO producers whose unit outputs were reduced by the use of the QV investment would be negative, and its absolute magnitude would be twice the magnitude of the negative buyer-surplus-related (SW[M]) distortion that the imperfections in seller price-competition facing the QV investor in question would generate. These conclusions reflect the fact that the preceding assumptions imply that the average per-unit amount of buyer surplus generated by the sale of units of the product created by the relevant QV investment (the average gap between P and MR for the product created by the QV investment between output zero and the product's actual output [which, given linearity and single pricing, equals the distance between the demand and marginal-revenue curves for that product at the output that is half that product's actual output]) will be half the imperfections-in-seller-price-competition-generated negative distortions in the private marginal cost of producing each unit of the product created by the QV investment (the gap between P and MR for the sacrificed unit of output of each of the products whose output is reduced by one unit when the QV investment in question is used).

Diagram 7.1 illustrates the preceding argument. In Diagram 7.1, the subscript "n" indicates that the curve to whose symbolic representation it is attached provides information that relates to the new product, distributive outlet, capacity, or inventory ("n" for "new") created by a relevant QV investment and the subscript "o" indicates that the curve to whose symbolic representation it is attached provides information that relates to each and all of the old "products" ("o" for "old") whose output is reduced when a unit of the new product is produced. Although the output of more than one old product is reduced when the new "product" is produced (when the QV investment in question is used), Diagram 7.1 does not manifest this fact (does not indicate that the old products belong to a set of old products [say $o_{\alpha-r}$]) because the analysis that the diagram illustrates does not distinguish among the relevant old products (assumes that the demand [DD], marginal revenue [MR], marginal cost [MC], and marginal allocative cost [MLC] [more precisely, the marginal-allocative-cost curve that would be deemed to be operative if one took into account only private marginal costs and any imperfections-in-seller-price-competition-generated (SW[M]) distortion in those private marginal costs] curves for each old product are the same as their counterparts for each of the other old products and that the production of the new product reduces the output of each of the old products in question by one unit). Diagram 7.1 is constructed on the assumptions that (1) the QV investor that created the QV investment in question used the investment exclusively itself, (2) all the resources employed to use the QV investment that created product n are withdrawn from the production of units of old products o, (3) DD_n and DD_o for each of the relevant old products are identical and linear, (4) MC_n and MC_o for each of the old products are horizontal and identical at height BL, (5) the seller of the new product n and the sellers of the various old products o sell their respective products by setting a single per-unit price and allowing all buyers to purchase as

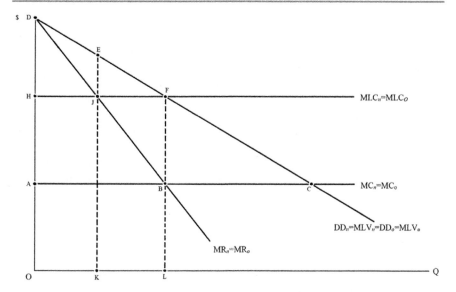

Diagram 7.1 A diagram that illustrates the analysis of the imperfections-in-seller-price-competition-generated (SW[M]) distortion in $PB_{(U)QV}$

many units of their respective products as they wish at that price (engage in what I call "single pricing") (an assumption that Diagram 7.1 manifests by constructing MR_n and MR_o so that their quantity at any height equals half the quantity of the DD curve with which they are respectively associated at that height—e.g., HJ = JF in Diagram 7.1),[9] (6) the equilibrium price for n and each o is FL (the price at which respectively MR_n cuts MC_n and MR_o cuts MC_o from above), (7) the equilibrium (P/MC) = (P/MR) ratio for n and each o is FL/BL, (8) DD_n = MLV_n (the marginal-allocative-value curve for n) and DD_o= MLV_o (the marginal-allocative-value curve for each o)—a result that reflects the fact that the relevant analysis ignores the distorting effects of all types of Pareto imperfections other than imperfections in seller price-competition, (9) (MLC_n/MC_n)= $([MC_n(MLC_n/MC_n)]/MC_n) = ([MC_n(Po/MC_o)]/MC_n) = ([BL(FL/BL)]/BL) = FL/BL$, and $(MLC_o/MC_o) = ([MC_o(MLC_o/MC_o)]/MC_o) = ([MC_o(P_n/MC_n)]/MC_o) = ([BL(FL/BL)]/BL = FL/BL$, (10) $(MLC_n- MC_n) = FL - BL = FB$—i.e., the per-unit negative distortion in the private cost of producing the actual output of n (the per-unit positive distortion in $PB_{(U)QV}$) that is generated by the imperfections in seller price-competition faced by the producers of o is FB, (11) the average per-unit amount of buyer surplus generated by the sale of the actual output of n (OL units)—the average per-unit negative distortion in $PB_{(U)QV}$ that the imperfection in seller price-competition faced by the creator of n when selling n generated by causing the sale of n to yield buyer surplus—equals EJ—the difference between P_n and MR_n at the output of n that is half the actual output of n (at output OK, which equals half output OL), and (12) FB = 2EJ because DD_n is linear and the QV investor that created n engages in single pricing when selling it.

Of course if the assumptions on which the construction of Diagram 7.1 are relaxed, the preceding conclusions will obtain only fortuitously. Thus, if each of the products whose outputs are reduced by the use of the QV investment has its output reduced by more than one unit, the absolute value of the negative imperfections-in-seller-price-competition-generated (SW[M]) distortion in the private cost of using the QV investment will be less than twice the absolute value of the negative imperfections-in-seller-price-competition (SW[M]) distortion in the revenues generated by the use of the QV investment (though the absolute value of the former distortion will still be higher than the absolute value of the latter). If the demand curves for the new and old products in question are identical but convex or concave to the origin, the ratios of the two negative distortions in question will respectively be smaller or greater than 2 if all the other assumptions continue to obtain. If the demand curves and marginal-cost curves for the new product and the products whose outputs are reduced by the new product's sales are different, the relevant differences could either increase or decrease the distortion ratio just referenced by causing the weighted-average P/MC ratio for the relevant os to be higher or lower than P_n/MC_n. Nevertheless, although I will not execute the relevant analyses here, for what it's worth, I would be confident that the imperfections-in-seller-price-competition-generated (SW[M]) distortion in the operating profits of using any QV investment would virtually always be positive if all the resources employed to use a QV investment were withdrawn from UO-producing uses even if I took into account (as the analysis that Diagram 7.1 illustrates does not) the possibility that the QV investor of ultimate interest might not use its QV investment itself and might face imperfections in seller price-competition when licensing others to use its QV investment as well as the possibility that one or more of the QV investors whose QV investments would have been sacrificed to the use of the QV investment of ultimate interest might have not used their sacrificed QV investments themselves and might have faced imperfections in seller price-competition when licensing others to use their sacrificed QV investments. Clearly, however, if some of the resources employed to use a QV investment were withdrawn from QV-investment-creating-and-using and/or PPR-executing-and-using uses, it would almost certainly be TBLE to take these realities into account when analyzing the imperfections-in-seller-price-competition-generated (SW[M]) distortion in $PB_{(U)QV}$ for any QV investment. The possibility that some of the resources that are employed to use a QV investment may be withdrawn from PPR-executing-and-using uses is less problematic because—for reasons that will shortly be discussed—the imperfections-in-seller-price-competition-generated (SW[M]) distortion in the private benefits of using production-process research discoveries is almost certainly negative (though the fact that the percentage-deflation in $PB_{(U)PPR}$ will equal its counterpart for $PB_{(U)UO}$ only rarely and fortuitously will render it TBLE to take account of any flow of resources from PPR execution and use to QV-investment use when analyzing the imperfections-in-seller-price-competition-generated (SW[M]) distortion in $PB_{(U)QV}$ for any QV investment of ultimate interest or, indeed, for any sacrificed QV investment whose $PB_{(U)QV}$ affects the imperfections-in-seller-price-competition-generated (SW[M]) distortion in the private benefits yielded by the use of any QV investment of ultimate interest).

Several future applied analyses will proceed on the assumption that the imperfections-in-seller-price-competition-generated (SW[M]) distortion in the profits yielded by the use of PPR projects is negative. Diagram 7.2 illustrates the argument for this conclusion that would apply even if the production-process researcher that executed the PPR project in question used the resulting discovery exclusively itself[10] if, for the same reasons that led me to reach these conclusions earlier, all tolled, relevant imperfections in seller price-competition generated a negative (SW[M]) distortion in (1) the total private cost of producing the output of the good G to whose production process the relevant PPR project related that would have been produced had the production process that project (did discover)/(would have discovered) not been used and (2) the variable cost of producing any extra units of G that the use of the discovered production process would have rendered profitable to produce if the new production process would lower the variable cost of producing each of the extra units of G in question.

Diagram 7.2 contains six curves. The first is a $DD_G = MLV_G$ curve for the good G to whose production process the relevant PPR project relates. The labeling of the MLV_G curve is actually misleading: the MLV_G curve that Diagram 7.2 contains is actually the MLV_G curve that would be operative if the unrealistic step-wise-monopoly-analysis practice of ignoring the distorting effects of all exemplars of all types of Pareto imperfections other than imperfections in seller price-competition made no difference. The fact that $DD_G = MLV_G$ is constructed to be convex to the origin plays no role in the analysis that follows.

The second curve in Diagram 7.2 is MR_G. It is constructed on the assumption that G is sold at a single per-unit price that applies to all units of the product and all potential buyers of the product. This single-pricing assumption does affect the quantitative conclusion the following analysis reaches because it guarantees that the use of any marginal-cost-reducing production process a relevant PPR project discoveries will yield a negative (SW[M]) distortion in $PB_{(U)PPR}$ by increasing the amount of buyer surplus generated by the sale of G.

The third and fourth curves in Diagram 7.2 are the $MC_{G/o}$ and $MC_{G/n}$ curves. These curves indicate the marginal cost of producing successive units of G using, respectively, (1) the new (hence subscript "n") production process the PPR project in question (did discover)/(would have discovered) and (2) the old (hence subscript "o") production process that (presumably) was/(would be) replaced by the new production process that the PPR project in question (did discover)/(would have discovered). $MC_{G/n}$ is lower than $MC_{G/o}$ in Diagram 7.2 (FO < CO) because the analysis that Diagram 7.2 illustrates assumes (as I believe is typically the case) that the use of the new production process will reduce the marginal cost of producing G.[11]

The fifth and sixth curves in Diagram 7.2—$MLC_{G/n}$ and $MLC_{G/o}$—indicate the marginal allocative cost of producing successive units of G using, respectively, the new production process that the PPR project in question (did discover)/(would have discovered) and the old production process that the new production process (did

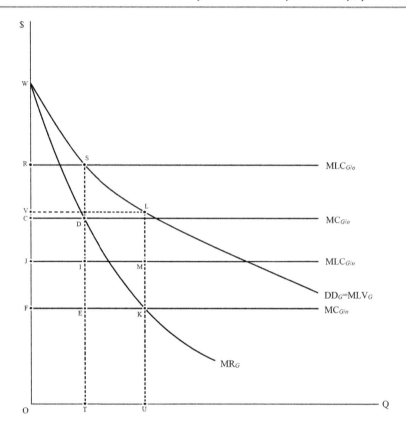

Diagram 7.2 A diagram that illustrates the analysis of the imperfections-in-seller-price-competition-generated (SW[M]) distortion in $PB_{(U)PPR}$

replace)/(would have replaced)—more precisely, the $MLC_{G/n}$ and $MLC_{G/o}$ curves that would be operative if the step-wise imperfections-in-seller-price-competition distortion-analysis protocol of ignoring the distorting effects of all exemplars of all types of Pareto imperfection other than imperfections in seller price-competition would not affect the relationship between $MLC_{G/n}$ and $MLC_{G/o}$. Diagram 7.2 constructs its $MLC_{G/n}$ curve below its $MLC_{G/o}$ curve on the assumption that the relevant imperfections in seller price-competition would generate negative (SW[M]) distortions in both the private marginal cost of producing each unit of the output of G that would be produced if the old production process were used (output OT—the output at which $MR_{G/o}$ cuts $MC_{G/o}$ from above at point D) and the extra units of G that the use of the new production process would make it profitable for the producer of G to produce (TU where OU is the output at which MR_G cuts $MC_{G/n}$ from above at point K). In Diagram 7.2, the height of the $MLC_{G/o}$ curve (RO) exceeds the height of the $MC_{G/o}$ curve (CO) by the same percentage as the height of the MLC$_{G/n}$ (JO) curve exceeds the height of the MC$_{G/n}$ curve (FO). This construction manifests an assumption that the relevant imperfections in seller price-competition will yield the same negative (SW[M]) distortion in MC both when the old production process is used and when the new production process is used—i.e., that (MLC$_{G/o}$/MC$_{G/o}$) = (MLC$_{G/n}$/MC$_{G/n}$) > 1.

Diagram 7.2 illustrates the fact that on the assumptions on which it is constructed and on the further assumption that the researcher that executed the relevant PPR project will/would use any discovery it will/would yield exclusively itself, the use of the discovered process will (1) increase the profits the production-process researcher would realize if it produced the output of G it would produce if it used the old production process (output OT) by area CDEF, (2) increase allocative efficiency by reducing the allocative cost of producing output OT by area RSIJ where area RSIJ *exceeds* area CDEF, (3) increase the profits that the production-process researcher can earn by expanding its unit output from OT to OU by area DKE (the area between MR$_G$ and MC$_{G/n}$ between outputs OT and OU), and (4) increase allocative efficiency by inducing the production-process researcher to increase its output of G from OT to OU by area SLUT (the allocative value of the extra units of output) *minus* area IMUT (the allocative cost of producing the extra TU units of G with the new production process), which equals area SLMI and is larger than area DKE (the area that equals the profits that the discovery will enable the production-process researcher to realize by expanding its unit output of G from OT to OU). To see why on the assumptions of Diagram 7.2[12] relevant imperfections in seller price-competition will generate a negative (SW[M]) distortion in the profits a vertically integrated (production-process researcher) (producer of the good G to whose production process its PPR relates) can realize by expanding its output of G if the production process it discovers reduces MC$_G$, note (1) that SI (the discovery-generated reduction in MLC$_G$) exceeds DE (the discovery-generated reduction in MC$_G$) and (2) that the average slope of DD$_G$=MLV$_G$ between outputs OT and OU is gentler than the average slope of MR$_G$ between outputs OT and OU. For current purposes, the important point is that, on the assumptions of Diagram 7.2, the relevant imperfections in seller price-competition will generate a negative (SW[M]) distortion in PB$_{(U)PP}$ for any marginal-cost-reducing PPR project both by generating a negative (SW[M]) distortion in the reduction in the private cost of producing G's pre-discovery output use of the discovered process yields and by increasing the amount of buyer surplus yielded by the sale of the product G.

7.1.2 The Step-Wise Imperfections-in-QV-Investment-Competition-Generated and Step-Wise Imperfections-in-PPR-Competition-Generated Monopoly Distortions in PB$_{(U)QV}$ and PB$_{(U)PPR}$

QV investors/production-process researchers can face and/or generate not only imperfections in price-competition but also imperfections in QV-investment competition/PPR competition. Imperfections in QV-investment competition enable a QV investor to realize supernormal profit-rates on one or more of the QV investments it owns in an arbitrarily-defined portion of product-space (ARDEPPS), and imperfections in PPR competition can enable a production-process researcher to realize supernormal profit-rates on one or more of the PPR projects it executes that are designed to discover privately-cheaper ways of producing relevant quantities of one or more products in an ARDEPPS. The extent to which QV-investment competition or PPR competition in a given ARDEPPS is imperfect[13] depends not only on the magnitudes of the various sources of imperfect QV-investment or PPR competition but on the way in which various subsets of these sources interact with each other.

I will begin by identifying the six possible sources of imperfect QV-investment competition/PPR competition. The first I will discuss is "the profit-differential (Π_D) barrier" to QV investment creation or PPR execution facing the QV investor/ production-process researcher that is privately-best-placed to raise QV investment/ PPR above its equilibrium quantity in a given ARDEPPS. These Π_D barriers, which can face an established firm in a given ARDEPPS that is contemplating expanding its QV investment in that ARDEPPS or a potential entrant into that ARDEPPS, are defined to equal the difference between the lifetime profit-rate (as opposed to supernormal profit-rate) that the most-supernormally-profitable QV investment/PPR project in the relevant ARDEPPS would be expected on the weighted average to generate and its counterpart for the most-supernormally-profitable QV investment/ PPR project the investor previously referenced could create/execute in the ARDEPPS in question. The second possible source of imperfections in QV-investment/PPR competition is "the risk barrier" to QV-investment creation or PPR execution (the "R" barrier) facing the just-referenced investor—the difference between the normal rate-of-return for the most-supernormally-profitable investment that any investor could add to the relevant ARDEPPS once investment had reached its equilibrium level and the normal rate-of-return for the most-supernormally-profitable QV investment/PPR project in the relevant ARDEPPS. To avoid double-counting, I calculate the normal rates-of-return just referenced on the sometimes unrealistic assumption that none of the relevant investments will induce rival retaliation. The third possible source of imperfections in QV-investment/PPR competition is the retaliation barrier to creating the referenced QV investment/ executing the referenced PPR project that the relevant potential expander or entrant faces (symbolized by the letter "L")—the difference between the amounts by which the lifetime supernormal profit-rates of the most-supernormally-profitable QV investment(s)/PPR project(s) in the relevant ARDEPPS and the most-supernormally-profitable (actually, least-subnormally-profitable) investment that could raise ARDEPPS investment above its equilibrium quantity are/would be reduced by retaliation or the prospect of retaliation against the relevant investment's creation/execution (by established rivals in the ARDEPPS in question that want to drive the investment in question out and/or deter future QV-investment creation/ PPR execution in the ARDEPPS in question). The fourth possible source of imperfect investment competition is the scale barrier to expansion or entry (symbolized by "S") that faces the incumbent or potential entrant that was privately-best-placed to expand ARDEPPS investment above its equilibrium quantity—the amount by which the expansion or entry in question would reduce the weighted-average-expected profit-rate of all QV investments/PPR projects in the relevant ARDEPPS (I am simplifying) by increasing the total quantity of QV investment/PPR in the ARDEPPS in question. The fifth and sixth possible sources of imperfections in QV-investment or PPR competition is the monopolistic or natural-oligopolistic investment disincentives (symbolized respectively by "M" and "O") that an incumbent QV investor or production-process researcher may face when contemplating creating a QV investment or executing a PPR project in an ARDEPPS in which it already owns one or more QV investments or patent/ secrecy-protected production processes. A prospective investor that already owns one or more QV investments or patent/secrecy-protected production processes in a given ARDEPPS will confront monopolistic investment-disincentives on a proposed QV/PPR investment in that ARDEPPS to the extent that the proposed investment will reduce the profit-yields of its existing investments in that ARDEPPS more by competing directly against them and inducing rivals to make non-retaliatory responses to its investment than any rival investment the investment in question would have deterred would have done. Such an investor will confront natural-oligopolistic investment disincentives to make a particular investment when the proposed investment would reduce its profits not only in the above ways but also by inducing a rival to make an investment it would not otherwise have made in the ARDEPPS in question by depriving that rival of the opportunity to deter the investor first referenced from making an investment by not making an investment.[14] (I should add that incumbents may also have a monopolistic incentive to make an additional investment in an ARDEPPS—in particular, will have such an incentive when the investment it is contemplating will reduce its pre-existing investment's or investments' profit-yields less by competing directly against it or them and inducing rival owners of existing investments to respond than would the rival investment[s] the contemplated investment would deter. Monopolistic investment-incentives will also be symbolized by "M," though when the investor has such an incentive the value of M will be lower than zero while it will exceed zero when the M references a monopolistic investment-disincentive.)

If one defines the intensity of QV-investment competition in any ARDEPPS or the intensity of the PPR competition that relates to the discovery of production processes to produce the good(s) located in any ARDEPPS to be inversely related to the highest supernormal profit-rate generated by any QV investment/PPR project in/(related to the production process used to produce the good[s] located in) that ARDEPPS, the relationship between the above possible sources of imperfect investment competition and the intensity of such competition depends on whether equilibrium investment in that ARDEPPS (1) exceeds the entry-preventing investment quantity in that ARDEPPS (because the entry-barred expansion-preventing investment quantity [the quantity of investment incumbents would make if entry were (perhaps counterfactually) precluded]) exceeds the entry-preventing investment quantity), (2) equals the entry-preventing investment quantity (either

[A] because the entry-barred expansion-preventing investment-quantity equals the entry-preventing investment quantity or [B] because the entry-barred expansion-preventing investment quantity is lower than the entry-preventing investment quantity and [i] incumbents find it profitable to make enough "limit" investments to prevent all entry—i.e., to raise ARDEPPS investment to the entry-preventing quantity (in my terminology, a "limit investment" is any investment whose *ex ante* predicted profitability was critically affected by its deterring a rival investment)—or [ii] the sum of the limit investments incumbents find it profitable to make and the investments that new entrants make equals the difference between the entry-preventing and entry-barred expansion-preventing investment-quantities), or (3) is lower than the entry-preventing investment quantity (because the entry-barred expansion-preventing investment quantity is lower than the entry-preventing investment quantity and the sum of any limit investments the incumbents make and the investments that entrants make is smaller than the investment-difference last referenced). When the ARDEPPS' equilibrium investment quantity exceeds its entry-preventing investment quantity, the (lifetime) supernormal profit-rate yielded by the ARDEPPS' most-supernormally-profitable investment will equal the barriers to expansion facing the privately-best-placed expander at the equilibrium investment quantity *plus* any monopolistic or natural-oligopolistic investment-disincentives it faced on its most-profitable (least-unprofitable) possible expansion or *minus* any monopolistic investment-incentive it had to make that investment. When the ARDEPPS' equilibrium investment quantity equals its entry-preventing investment quantity, the supernormal profit-rate yielded by the ARDEPPS' most-supernormally-profitable investment will equal either (1) the sum of the Π_D, R, S, and L barriers to entry facing the ARDEPPS' privately-best-placed potential entrant at the equilibrium investment-quantity or (2) the sum of the Π_D, R, S, and L barriers to expansion facing the incumbent that is privately-best-placed to add an investment to the ARDEPPS in question when its investment-quantity is its equilibrium investment-quantity *plus* any monopolistic or natural-oligopolistic investment-disincentive it would have to make that investment or *minus* any monopolistic investment-incentive it would have to make that investment where the totals indicated after "(1)" and "(2)" in this sentence are equal. When the ARDEPPS' equilibrium investment-quantity is lower than its entry-preventing investment quantity, the lifetime supernormal profit-rate yielded by its most-supernormally-profitable investment will equal the lower of (1) the sum of the Π_D, R, S, and L barriers to entry that would have faced the potential entrant that would have been privately-best-placed to make an investment when the ARDEPPS' investment quantity equaled its equilibrium investment-quantity or (2) the sum of the Π_D, R, S, and L barriers to expansion that would have faced the incumbent that was privately-best-placed to make an investment when the ARDEPPS' investment quantity equaled its equilibrium investment quantity *plus* any monopolistic or natural-oligopolistic investment-disincentive that incumbent would have had to make the investment in question or *minus* any monopolistic investment-incentive it would have had to make that investment.[15]

Only two of the five possible sources or related sets of possible sources of imperfect investment competition can yield (SW[M]) distortions in the private benefits yielded by a QV investment or PPR project (be it a QV investment or PPR project of ultimate interest or one that would be sacrificed to some other resource-use). The first is the set of possible sources of imperfect investment competition that contains monopolistic investment-disincentives, natural-oligopolistic investment-disincentivizes, and monopolistic investment-incentives. The analysis of the (SW[M]) distortion in the losses that an investment imposed/would impose on an investor (be it a QV investor or a production-process researcher) because the investor had/would have a monopolistic investment-disincentive to make it varies with whether the creation/execution of the investment in question deters an alternative investment of the same magnitude in the same functional category or withdraws resources from a broader set of sacrificed uses because the answer to that question determines whether the (SW[M]) distortion in the private cost of creating/executing the investment in question equals the (SW[M]) distortion in the deterred investment or the sum of the (SW[M]) distortions in the broader set of alternative resource-uses sacrificed to the investment in question. In what I take to be the standard case in which an investor faces a monopolistic investment-disincentive—namely, the case in which the investment in question (did not)/(would not) deter a rival investment ("standard" because, in situations in which a prospective investor knows that its investment will deter a rival investment, it will usually make an investment that is less-competitive with its pre-existing projects than the deterred investment would have been and less likely than the deterred investment would have been to induce its existing rivals to respond to the new investment by making moves that lower the investor's other investments' profit-yields—i.e., will usually have a monopolistic investment-*incentive* to make the investment it makes), the monopolistic investment-disincentive it faces will be associated with a negative (SW[M]) distortion in the private benefits the relevant investment yields the investor in question: (1) to the extent that the investor has a monopolistic investment-disincentive to make the investment in question because the investment did reduce or would reduce the sales of its other "products" (enquoted because in this context the term "product" also covers a production processes) either by taking sales from them itself or by inducing rivals to make responses that result in their taking sales from them, there will be a negative (SW[M]) distortion in the private benefits yielded by the investment in question because there will be a negative (SW[M]) distortion in the private variable cost of producing the units of the investor's other products whose sales were/would be lost (even when the "product" is a discovered production process, some variable sales costs will usually have to be incurred to sell the extra "units"), hence a positive (SW[M]) distortion in the profits those lost sales would have yielded the investor, and hence a negative distortion in the profits the investment in question yielded and (2) to the extent that the investor has a monopolistic investment-disincentive to make the investment in question because the investment (did reduce)/ (would reduce) the price it obtained or would obtain for units of its other "products'" it still sold or would still sell, the resulting loss in profits would be associated with an equal negative (SW[M]) distortion in the private benefits yielded by the investment in question since these losses would reflect a monetary transfer from the investor to its other "products'" buyers that would have no economic-efficiency consequences (if one assumes as I think the step-wise-distortion analysis requires that the transfer would not affect economic efficiency by altering the extent of material inequality and/or poverty in the society in question). Admittedly, the last sentence ignores the fact that the investment-induced reductions in the price(s) of one or more of the investor's other "products" that enabled it to prevent its investment from reducing each such "product's" unit sales might result in the investment's increasing the unit sales of the investor's other "products" (might cause the investor to sell one or more additional units of one or more of its other "products" for prices that exceed their marginal costs of production): if one views those sales in isolation (i.e., ignores the fact that they are associated with reductions in the prices the investor obtained for units of the relevant "product" it would have sold had it not made the investment), the relevant imperfections in seller price-competition would yield a positive (SW[M]) distortion in those "profits" by generating a negative (SW[M]) distortion in the private cost of producing and/or selling the units in question and hence an equal positive (SW[M]) distortion in the private benefits generated by the investment in question. Still, all things considered, the monopolistic investment-disincentives that face an investor on an investment will almost always be associated with a negative (SW[M]) distortion in the private benefits the investment in question yields the investor. In the unusual case in which an investor of ultimate interest or sacrificing investor of interest has a monopolistic investment-disincentive to make an investment that would reduce the profit-yields of the other investments of the former investor by more than the rival investment would have done, the relevant analysis will focus on (1) the (SW[M]) distortion in the difference between the sales of the investor in question's other "products" the investor in question's investment would cause the investor in question to lose and the sales of its other products the investor in question's other "products" that the deterred rival's investment would have caused the investor in question to lose, (2) the (SW[M]) distortion in the difference between the revenue-loss the investor in question's investment would cause the investor in question to sustain by reducing the prices it obtained on those units of one or more of its other "products" it retained by reducing their prices and the revenue-loss (relative to the *status quo ante*) that the deterred rival investment would have caused the investor in question to sustain by making it profitable for it to reduce the prices of one or more units of one or more of its other "products" to preserve their sales, and (3) the (SW[M]) distortion in the difference between any "profits" the investment of the investor in question caused it to earn at least normally on the extra units of any of its other "products" it sold as a result of its investment's making it profitable for the investor to reduce their prices and any "profits" the deterred rival investment would have caused the investor in question to realize in this way, but otherwise the relevant analysis and conclusions will be the same as its predecessor.[16]

An investor faces a natural-oligopolistic investment-disincentive to make a particular investment when that investment will induce a rival investment that will reduce its profits not only (1) by reducing the profits yielded by the other investments the first investor owns but also (2) by reducing the profits yielded by the inducing investment itself because the induced investment will compete against both "sets" of the inducing investor's investments and will induce responses by other investments that will reduce the profits yielded by both "sets" of the influencer's investments. The analysis of the (SW[M]) distortion in the first set of losses just referenced is the same as the analysis of those losses in the case in which the investment in question does not deter a rival investment. The second set of losses just referenced—the set of losses that are generated only in situations in which the investor has a natural-oligopolistic investment-disincentive to make the investment in question—has three components that are analogous to those the first set of losses contains: (1) the losses the investor sustains because the induced rival investment causes the investor to lose sales of its other "products" and of the "product" the investment in question created/would create, (2) the losses the investor sustains because the induced rival investment lowers the prices the investor in question obtains on sales of the "products" its other investments created as well as the prices it charges for the "product" the investment in question created/would create, and (3) the "profits" the investor in question nominally obtains on any additional sales it makes of its other "products" and of the "product" the investment in question created/would create insofar as the sum of the prices it obtains on these units exceeds the sum of the variable costs of their production. The preceding analyses of and conclusions about the signs of the (SW[M]) distortions in these three private figures and their total apply *mutatis mutandis* here as well.[17]

An investor/prospective investor had/has a monopolistic incentive to make a particular investment if (1) that investment would deter a rival investment and (2) the number of dollars by which that investment would reduce the profit-yields of the investor's other investments in the relevant ARDEPPS relative to the status quo ante by competing against the products/services those other investments created directly and by eliciting non-retaliatory responses from the investor's rivals in that ARDEPPS is lower than the number of dollars by which the rival investment the investment in question would deter would have reduced the profit-yields of the investor's other investments in the ARDEPPS in question in the same two ways. The analysis of the (SW[M]) distortion in the profits an investment did/would yield because the investor had a monopolistic investment-incentive to make it is[18] analogous to the analysis of the (SW[M]) distortion in the profits an investment did/would yield because the investor had a monopolistic or natural-oligopolistic investment-disincentive to make it. Let me be more specific: (1) imperfections in seller price-competition generate a positive (SW[M]) distortion in the private benefits that any investment confers on the investor by enabling it to retain sales of its other "products" at the price for which it would have sold them had neither the investor nor any rival made an investment in the relevant ARDEPPS by generating a negative (SW[M]) distortion in the private variable cost of producing the units in question and hence a positive distortion in the profits yielded by the sales the investment in question enabled or would enable the investor to retain at its other "products'" pre-investment prices; (2) the step-wise distortion in any benefits an investment confers on the investor by obviating its reducing the price of units of its other "products" it still sells post-investment is positive and equal to the benefits in question since those benefits manifest what is in essence a pure money-transfer from the relevant buyers to the investor in question and any economic-efficiency gain or loss that such a transfer would generate in the real world by affecting the extent of material inequality and poverty in the society in question must be ignored in a step-wise-distortion analysis; and (3) imperfections in seller price-competition will generate a positive (SW[M]) distortion in the nominal losses an investment imposes on the investor (will make those private losses higher than the associated allocative-efficiency losses) by obviating its making price reductions on its other products that would have yielded revenues that would have exceeded the private variable cost of producing the units in question by generating a negative (SW[M]) distortion in those private variable costs—i.e., will on this account generate a negative (SW[M]) distortion in the monopolistic investment-incentives any investor has to make an investment in relation to which it has such incentives, though this third distortion will clearly be absolutely smaller than the sum of the two distortions previously discussed.

The point of the preceding analyses of the (SW[M]) distortions in the monop-olistic investment-disincentives, natural-oligopolistic investment-disincentives, and monopolistic investment-incentives an investor may have to make a particular investment is that these (SW[M]) distortions are non-zero and would have to be taken into account in any TBLE analysis of the economic efficiency of a choice if they could be accurately determined at no allocative cost. Perhaps I should say no more. But it might be of interest to speculate about whether these (SW[M]) imperfections-in-investment-competition-related distortions will tend to compound or counteract the (SW[M]) distortions generated directly by imperfections in seller price-competition in $PB_{(U)QV}$ and $PB_{(U)PPR}$. The answer to these questions will depend not only on the accuracy of my conclusions about the signs of the four step-wise-monopoly distortions in question but also on the relative incidences of monopolistic and natural-oligopolistic investment-disincentives on the one hand and of monopolistic investment-incentives on the other as well as on whether their relative incidences varies with whether the investments in question are QV investments or PPR projects.

I offer three observations on these issues. First, I suspect that the conditions that must be fulfilled for two or more investors to face natural-oligopolistic investment-disincentives are rarely fulfilled and that, in the rare instances in which they are fulfilled, their fulfillment is evanescent (given that the magnitudes of the parameters that determine the profitability of any investment change through time)—i.e., I suspect that it will usually be TBLE to ignore the possibility that a relevant investor may face natural-oligopolistic investment-disincentives. Second, I am disposed to think that investors are more often in a position in which an investment they are contemplating making will deter a rival investment than in a position in which their contemplated investment will not deter a rival investment— i.e., I suspect that investors more often face monopolistic investment-incentives than monopolistic investment-disincentives. Third, I see no reason to believe that the relative incidences of such incentives and disincentives will be different for QV investments than for PPR projects. These observations (should I say: speculations?)

dispose me to conclude that, all tolled, the operative monopolistic investment-disincentives, natural-oligopolistic investment-disincentives, and monopolistic investment-incentives tend to be associated with positive (SW[M]) distortions in the private benefits yielded by both QV investments and PPR projects and tend on that account to increase the positive (SW[M]) distortions in the private benefits an economy's QV investments yield the investors that make them and to decrease the negative (SW[M]) distortions in the private benefits the economy's PPR projects yield the production-process researchers that execute them.

The second set of sources of imperfect investment competition that can generate (SW[M]) distortions in a relevant PB$_{(U)QV}$ or PB$_{(U)PPR}$ figure contains retaliation barriers to incumbent investment-expansions or potential-competitor new entries. Two subsets of retaliation barriers must be distinguished. The first contains any retaliation barriers to investment that any relevant investor intends its investment to erect. I do not think that incumbents often make investments to retaliate against rivals that have competed more intensely against them than the retaliator was willing to accept (to deter the target of the retaliation and others from competing as much against them in the future). However, although I believe that it will usually be more profitable to retaliate by making inherently-unprofitable price-cuts to their target's customers or by placing inherently-unprofitable advertisements that are directed at their target's customers, there are situations in which a retaliator will find it most cost-effective to retaliate by making an investment that will harm its target (e.g., by making an inherently-unprofitable decision to open up a "fighting store" next to a target-outlet or to introduce a product that is highly-competitive with one or more of a target's products). In such situations, the private benefits that the investment in question will confer on the investor by driving the target out and deterring the target and/or others from competing as intensively against the retaliator in the future (including by raising retaliation barriers to the retaliator's existing and potential competitors' making investments in any ARDEPPS in which the retaliator is operating or will operate in the future) will equal the allocative-efficiency gains the retaliation generates only rarely and fortuitously. The distortion in the private benefits that a retaliatory investment confers on the retaliator will depend on the type of competitive behavior the retaliation deters: (1) if the retaliatory investment deters price-cutting, I suspect that the resulting private gains will be associated with an economic-efficiency loss (since I suspect that price-cutting increases economic efficiency by lowering QV investment and increasing PPR)—i.e., the associated imperfection-in-investment-competition-related distortion will be a positive distortion equal to the sum of the private benefit to the retaliating investor and the economic-efficiency gain the deterred price-competition would have generated; (2) if the retaliatory investment deters competitive advertising, the associated imperfection-in-investment-competition-related distortion will depend *inter alia* on whether the deterred advertising would have (A) increased economic efficiency by providing allocatively-valuable information and/or creating positively-valued product images or (B) decreased economic efficiency by providing misleading information and/or creating personally-and-socially-harmful product images (we are entering deep waters)—viz., will equal the private benefit the investment confers on the investor *minus* any economic-efficiency gain the deterred advertising would have generated or *plus* any economic-efficiency loss the deterred advertising would have generated; (3) if the retaliatory investment reduces equilibrium QV investment in the ARDEPPSes in which it is effective by raising retaliation barriers to QV-investment expansions or entry, it will (if I am right) increase economic efficiency on that account so that the relevant distortion will equal the private benefits *minus* the QV-investment-related increase in economic efficiency; and (4) if the retaliatory investment reduces equilibrium PPR in the ARDEPPSes in which it is effective, it will (if I am right) decrease economic efficiency on that account so that (if I am right) the relevant distortion will be a positive distortion that equals the sum of the private benefits and the sacrificed economic-efficiency gain. I suspect that the (SW[M]) distortion in the private benefits that a retaliatory investment confers on the retaliator will almost always be positive.

The second subset of retaliation barriers that can yield imperfections-in-investment-competition-generated (SW[M]) distortions in relevant $PB_{(U)QV}$ and $PB_{(U)PPR}$ figures are the retaliation barriers that the investor in question can face. When the investor of interest is the target of the relevant retaliation, the negative (SW[M]) distortion in the private cost that those retaliation barriers impose on the target-investor of interest equals the private cost the retaliation barriers impose on the investor in question *minus* any allocative inefficiency generated by the erection of the relevant retaliation barriers or *plus* any allocative-efficiency loss generated by the moves that erected the retaliation barrier to investment the target-investor faces. I suspect that the retaliation barriers to investment a target-investor faces will virtually always be associated with a negative imperfections-in-investment-competition-generated (SW[M]) distortion in the private benefits the target-investor's investment did or would confer on it.

Once more, the point of the analysis of the (SW[M]) distortions in $PB_{(U)QV}$ and $PB_{(U)PPR}$ that are associated with the investor in question's executing a retaliation-barrier-to-investment-raising investment or facing a retaliation barrier to investment is that it may well be TBLE to consider these possibilities when analyzing the economic efficiency of a choice. Although it will almost certainly be TBLE to execute choice-specific analyses of these possibilities, it may also be worthwhile to speculate about whether these possibilities tend to increase or decrease the (SW[M]) distortion in the private benefits that an economy's QV investments/PPR projects yield the investors that create/execute them. The issues that must be resolved to answer this question are: (1) are the relevant investors more likely to be "sinning" investors (investors that make retaliatory investments) or "sinned-against" investors (investors that face retaliation barriers to investment) and (2) does the answer to the preceding question vary with whether the investments in question are QV investments or PPR projects. I see no reason to believe that the relative incidence of sinning and sinned-against QV investors is different from the relative incidence of sinning and sinned-against production-process researchers. I also think that both QV investors and production-process researchers are far more likely to face retaliation barriers to investment than to make retaliatory investments.

I therefore think that, across all cases, retaliation-barrier-to-investment sources of imperfect investment competition will tend to generate negative (SW[M]) distortions in the private benefits that both QV investments and PPR projects confer on the investors that create/execute them and that, on this account, retaliation-barrier-to-investment-related imperfections in investment competition will decrease the positive (SW[M]) distortion in the private benefits that QV investments confer on the investors that make them and increase the negative (SW[M]) distortion in the private benefits that PPR projects confer on the investors that execute them.

7.1.3   The Step-Wise-Monopoly Distortion that Imperfections in Seller Price-Competition and Investment-Competition Generate in the Profits Yielded by Some QV Investments and Some PPR Projects by Leading Governments to Classify Some Firms that Face Such Seller-Competition Imperfections to Be Public Utilities and to Subject the Pricing of the Products Such Firms Allegedly "Monopolize" to "Fair-Rate-of-Return" Pricing-Regulations

Firms that are assessed to have an unusually-large amount of what is conventionally called "market power" that is conventionally attributed to the existence of substantial economies of scale relative to the size of the "market" in question—i.e., to face imperfections in price and/or investment competition that are unusually high for this reason—when selling one or more goods in what is conventionally called a given "market" are sometimes deemed to be "public utilities" and are subjected to a variety of government regulations on that account.[19] One of the standard types of regulation to which public utilities are subjected is "fair-rate-of-return public-utility-pricing regulation." Under this regulatory scheme, a commission (1) determines the investment that the public utility has in the businesses that it operates as a public utility (i.e., determines the firm's "rate-base"), (2) determines the rate-of-return on the public utility's investment in the relevant area of product-space that would constitute a "fair-rate-of-return" on that investment, and then (3) calculates the maximum prices it will permit the public utility to charge for the products the public utility produces as a public utility by determining the set (actually, *a* set) of prices for these goods that would yield the public utility the decided-upon fair rate-of-return on its estimated rate-base in that area of product-space. In virtually all cases, the designated "fair rate-of-return" is in fact a supernormal profit-rate, and the maximum prices that any public utility is allowed to charge for its "regulated products" are lower than the prices the public utility would find most profitable to charge for them if it made no effort to work around this system of price-regulation by making inherently-unprofitable investments to expand its rate-base—i.e., result in the regulatee's facing what I call a "prevented-profit pool" (a quantity of potential profits it would be able to obtain if it were allowed to raise its regulated-products' prices to their profit-maximizing levels). In practice, public-utility commissions do not prevent any of their regulatees from securing the commission's permission to raise the prices the regulatee charges for products whose profit-potential the regulatee was previously precluded from fully exploiting by (1) making inherently-unprofitable investments that the commission includes in the public utility's rate-base and (2) arguing that since, post-investment, the public utility's overall rate-of-return on its now-enlarged rate-base falls below the rate-of-return the commission deems "fair" the public utility must be allowed to raise its prices sufficiently to enable it to secure the "fair" rate-of-return on its total rate-base: although most public-utility regulators are authorized to prevent this outcome by excluding "imprudent" investments from the public utilities' rate-bases, public-utility regulators virtually never exercise this authority. Economists denominate this tendency of "fair-rate-of-return public-utility-pricing regulation" to induce the regulated public utilities to make inherently-subnormally-profitable decisions to increase their rate-base the "AJW" effect of such pricing-regulations because this phenomenon was first pointed out by two articles written respectively and independently by Averch and Johnson (the AJ) and by Wellisz (the W).[20]

For current purposes, the salient points are that, when imperfections in seller price-competition and QV-investment or PPR competition lead the sellers that confront them to be classified as public utilities and to be subjected to "fair-rate-of-return public-utility-pricing regulation" of the kind just described by a public-utility commission that does not prevent its regulatees from gaining access to the prevented-profit pools its pricing-regulations would otherwise create by making subnormally-profitable QV investments or executing subnormally-profitable PPR projects, the imperfections in competition in question (1) will increase the private benefits and profits yielded by any AJW-effect-induced QV investment or PPR project the regulatee creates/executes by the amount of profits the QV investment/PPR project enables the regulatee to take out of its prevented-profit pool (*minus* the cost the public utility had to incur to secure the change in the prices it was allowed to charge for one or more of its other products), (2) on this account,[21] will generate a (SW[M]) positive distortion in the private benefits yielded by the induced investment equal to the AJW-effect-generated net profit-yield *plus* the allocative-efficiency loss generated by the resulting price-increases (or *minus* any economic-efficiency gain generated by the resulting price-increases), and (3) on this account,[22] will tend to generate a (SW[M]) positive distortion in the profits yielded by any additional QV investment made or PPR project executed because of AJW effects (since the positive AJW-effect-related private-benefit effect of any additional investment made for AJW reasons is likely to be larger than the positive AJW private-benefit effect that would have resulted from the creation of the additional QV investments and execution of the additional PPR projects sacrificed to [the creation of the QV investment in question]/[the execution of the PPR project in question] because most of the sacrificed resource-uses will be sacrificed UO-producing resource-uses ([that can yield no AJW-effect-related benefit-distortions] and most sacrificed QV-investment-creating and PPR-executing resource-uses would not have been generated by AJW effects).

7.2 The Step-Wise-Monopoly Distortion in the Profits Yielded by Various Categories of Economics-Marginal Resource Allocations

Section 7.2 has two sections. Section 7.2.1 analyzes the step-wise-monopoly distortion in the profits yielded by three categories of realistic resource allocations—resource allocations *from* specifiable UO-producing-and-consuming, QV-investment-creating-and-using, *and* PPR-executing-and-uses pairs of functionally-related categories of resource-use *to* a specifiable UO-producing-and-consuming, QV-creating-and-using, *or* PPR-executing-and-using pair of functionally-related categories of resource-use. Section 7.2.2 analyzes the step-wise-monopoly distortion in the profits yielded by exemplars of 12 other categories of resource allocations, some of which are policy-relevant components of the above three realistic categories of resource allocations and some of which are other realistic categories of resource allocations.

Let me begin by explaining once more how this section relates to the distortion-analysis approach to economic-efficiency prediction or post-diction I claim is TBLE. That approach proceeds (1) by identifying the resource allocations that any choice whose economic efficiency is to be predicted/post-dicted elicits/deters by increasing/decreasing the aggregate distortion in the profits yielded by economics-marginal and relevant economics-non-marginal exemplars of various categories of resource allocations (by changing the magnitudes of the determinants of the aggregate distortions in the profits the relevant resource allocations yield) and (2) by assessing the deterred and elicited resource allocations' economic efficiency by estimating (A)(i) the profits that the resource allocations the choice did or would elicit did or would yield and (ii) the aggregate distortions in those profits and (B)(i) the losses that the resource allocations the choice did or would deter would have yielded or would yield and (ii) the aggregate distortions in those losses. The analyses of this section play an important role in this approach because (1) (in my judgment) it will be TBLE to use step-wise-distortion formulas for the referenced aggregate-profit distortions and (2) the formulas for the step-wise-monopoly distortions in the (profits yielded by)/(losses that would have been yielded) by the resource allocations that the choice at issue (did or would elicit)/(did or would deter) are components of the step-wise-distortion formulas for the aggregate profit/loss distortions in question.

Section 7.2 analyses all make use of the following two relationships: (1) the step-wise-monopoly distortion in the profits yielded by any resource allocation equals the step-wise-monopoly distortion in the private benefits generated by the resource-use to which that resource allocation devotes resources *minus* the step-wise-monopoly distortion in the private cost to the resource-user to which the resource allocation devotes resources of the resources the resource allocation allocates to it and (2) the step-wise-monopoly distortion in the private cost of any resource-use equals the sum of the step-wise-monopoly distortions in the private benefits that would have been generated by the resource-uses sacrificed to the resource-use in question. To save space, to protect the writer's health, and to avoid taxing the readers' patience, all the analyses of Sect. 7.2 will reference rather than repeat the conclusions of Sect. 7.1 on which they rely.

7.2.1 The Step-Wise-Monopoly Distortion in the Profits Yielded by Resource Allocations from Specifiable UO-Producing-and Consuming, QV-Investment-Creating-and-Using, *and* PPR-Executing-and-Using Pairs of Resource-Uses to Individual Specifiable Pairs of Economics-Marginal UO-Producing-and Consuming, QV-Creating-and-Using, *or* PPR-Executing-and Using Resource-Uses

For convenience and because I suspect that it will often be TBLE to do so, this section ignores the possibility that some of the resources devoted to UO-producing-and-consuming, QV-creating-and-using, or PPR-executing-and-using uses may not be withdrawn from one of these three pairs of functionally-related categories of use—for example, may be withdrawn from government-uses (from legislative/administrative-agency efforts to pass legislation/promulgate regulations, from executive-branch efforts to implement legislation and apply regulations, from judicial-branch efforts to adjudicate cases, including cases involving legislation designed to finance the government's operations).

7.2.1.1 The Step-Wise-Monopoly Distortion in the Profits Yielded by Resource Allocations from Specifiable UO-Producing-and-Consuming, QV-Investment-Creating-and-Using, and PPR-Executing-and Using Resource-Uses to Individual Specifiable Pairs of Economics-Marginal UO-Producing-and Consuming Resource-Uses

This section will focus on the step-wise-monopoly distortion in the profits yielded by the economics-marginal exemplars of the categories of resource allocations its heading references. It will make four sets of points.

The first set relates to the TBLE of various generalizations one might make about what I will call the (SW[M]) distortion in the profits yielded by the UO-to-UO component of an economy's UO/QV/PPR-to-UO resource allocations to the production of the marginal units of the products it produces—i.e., to the third-best-allocative efficiency (TBLE) of making use of various generalizations one might make about the relative absolute magnitudes of the negative (SW[M]) percentage-distortion in the private benefits that the production of an economy's economics-marginal units of output confers on their producers (which is generated by the imperfections in seller price-competition that the producers of the units face) and the negative (SW[M]) percentage-distortion in the private cost to the producers of these economics-marginal units of output of the resources they withdrew from alternative UO-producing uses to produce them, which is generated by the imperfections in seller price-competition that the sacrificing unit-output producers would have faced when selling the sacrificed units of output: the absolute magnitudes of the two negative (SW[M]) percentage-distortions in question for a UO/QV/PPR-to-UO resource allocation to the production of the marginal unit of a particular product equal respectively $([P - MC])/MC) = ([P - MR]/MR)$ for that product and the weighted-average $([P - MC]/MC) = ([P - MR]/MR)$ ratio for the products from whose unit-output production the production of the economics-marginal unit of the relevant product withdraws resources.

The first generalization about the relative absolute magnitudes of these two negative percentage-distortions whose use's TBLE I want to consider is that these two negative percentage-distortions are always equal. This generalization would be accurate and its use would therefore be TBLE if (1) the production of the marginal unit of any product withdrew the resources it "consumed" exclusively from the production of products with which the former product was highly competitive and (2) the P/MC ratios of all highly-competitive products were the same. However, neither of these two conditions seems likely to be satisfied: (1) some of the resources used to produce any product's marginal unit are withdrawn from the production of products with which the product in question is only moderately competitive and some from the production of products with which it is distantly competitive (particularly when some relevant inputs are specialized and used to produce different products that are distantly competitive or not-at-all-competitive on the demand side), and (2) the fact that products are highly competitive does not imply that they have similar P/MC ratios (the P/MC ratio of a high-MC/high-quality [or at least strongly-differentiated] product may be much higher than the P/MC ratio of a low-MC/low-quality [or less-differentiated] product with which it is substantially competitive if [1] the dollar preferences of a substantial number of buyers for the high-marginal-cost product [put crudely] substantially exceeds the number of dollars by which its marginal cost is higher than the marginal cost of the lower-marginal-cost product, but [2] the dollar preferences of a substantial number of buyers for the high-marginal-cost product is approximately equal to the number of dollars by which the marginal cost of the high-marginal-cost-product exceeds the marginal cost of the low-marginal-cost product). I therefore do not think it would be TBLE to assume that the negative (SW[M]) percentage-distortion in the private benefits of producing a marginal unit of any product equals the weighted-average negative distortion in the private benefits that the production of the units of output sacrificed to the production of the marginal unit of the former product would have yielded its (their) producer(s).

The second generalization that some might think would be TBLE to use about the relative magnitudes of the two negative (SW[M]) percentage-distortions of interest is that the negative percentage-distortion in the private benefits the production of a marginal unit of a good confers on its producer will be absolutely larger than the weighted-average negative percentage-distortion in the private benefits that would have been conferred on the UO producers whose unit-output production is partially sacrificed to the production of the relevant marginal unit of output by their production of the sacrificed units of output if the P/MC ratio of the good whose private-benefit and private-cost (SW[M]) percentage-distortions are at issue is higher than the weighted-average P/MC ratio for the other goods in its ARDEPPS. This general assumption would be justified if the percentages of the resources that the production of the marginal unit of each good in any ARDEPPS withdrew from the production of each of the other goods in that ARDEPPS were proportionate to the amounts of resources devoted to the production of the respective other goods in that ARDEPPS. In fact, however, this condition is also not fulfilled: the individual members of each of the various pairs of the various goods that one might place in any ARDEPPS are not well-placed to secure the patronage of the same percentages of the buyers each of them is best-placed to supply (believe it or not: I am simplifying). It is therefore unlikely that this second generalization would be TBLE to use.

The third generalization that some might think would be TBLE to use focuses on the relative absolute magnitudes of the negative (SW[M]) percentage-distortion in the private cost to the relevant marginal-unit-output producer of the resources its production of that marginal unit withdrew from distant competitors. The generalization relies on what I take to be the more-than-plausible assumption that the weighted-average P/MC ratio of each product's distant competitors approximately equals the weighted-average P/MC ratio of all products in the economy (to be more precise, is slightly higher/lower than that weighted average when the P/MC ratio of the product in question is lower/higher than that economy-wide weighted average). The generalization is that the absolute magnitude of the negative (SW[M]) percentage-distortion in the private cost of those resources that any producer of a marginal unit of output withdraws from the production of units of products that are its product's competitors is higher/lower than the absolute magnitude of the negative (SW[M]) percentage-distortion in the private benefits that the production of a product's marginal unit of output confers on its producer when the P/MC ratio for the product whose marginal-unit-of-output percentage-distortions are at issue is lower/higher than the weighted-average P/MC ratio for all products in the economy in question. Although this generalization is probably accurate, it may not be TBLE to rely on it: it may be more economically efficient to identify each product's distant competitors and their P/MC ratios than to calculate the relevant economy's weighted-average P/MC ratio.

The fourth generalization on which it might be TBLE to rely is in one sense the least ambitions: it is that, with one exception, one should assume that, *across all cases*, the negative (SW[M]) percentage-distortion in the $PB_{(U)UO}$ figure for marginal units of output equals the negative (SW[M]) percentage-distortion in that component of the private cost of producing marginal units of output that relates to the private cost of withdrawing the resources from the UO-producing uses that were sacrificed to the production of marginal units of output—i.e., the economy-wide weighted-average P/MC ratio of the marginal units of output that are produced equal the economy-wide weighted-average P/MC ratio of the goods whose unit outputs are sacrificed to the production of the marginal units of output. The exception I previously referenced is the good "leisure," which is self-produced and therefore has an untaxed "price" (recall that this is a (SW[M])-distortion analysis) that equals its private marginal cost. Since the relevant P/MC ratio for leisure (1) is lower than the weighted-average P/MC ratio of the goods that are competitive with leisure, one should assume that the (SW[M]) percentage-distortion in the private benefits of producing and consuming leisure (zero) is absolutely lower than the negative (SW[M]) percentage-distortion in the private cost of producing leisure with time that would otherwise have been devoted to UO production-and-use, QV-investment creation-and-use, and PPR-execution-and-use. Of course, this analysis (like all its predecessors in this section) ignores the reality that leisure (and most other goods) is (are) consumed with complements (in the case of leisure, with sports equipment, gasoline, etc.) as are most of the goods whose unit outputs or creation would be sacrificed to the production of leisure. Obviously, this leisure analysis is relevant to the assessment of the economic efficiency of choices that shift resources from QV-investment creation and PPR execution to UO production (including the production of extra units of leisure). I should also note that this leisure analysis has a current-consumption analogue where the competitor of current consumption is future consumption and the possible imperfections-in-seller-competition source of profit distortions is the possible increase or decrease in the supra-competitiveness of prices through time.

The second set of points or claims I want to make in this section relates to the QV-to-UO and PPR-to-UO components of UO/QV/PPR-to-UO resource allocations. This set has four members. The first is that, for at least two reasons, the relevant QV-to-UO flows are likely to be larger than the relevant PPR-to-UO flows: (1) more of an economy's resources are devoted to QV-investment creation and use than to PPR execution and use (in part because the use of production-process discoveries usually saves resources) and (2) the percentage of the resources devoted to QV-investment creation and use that consists of technologically/scientifically-skilled human resources that are better-suited to QV-investment creation than to UO production is lower than the percentage of resources devoted to PPR execution and use that consists of technologically/scientifically-skilled human resources that are better-suited to PPR execution than to UO production. The second subset of this second set of claims contains three admittedly-contestable claims that relate to the absolute magnitudes of the economy-wide weighted-average (1) positive (SW[M]) percentage-distortion in $PB_{(U)QV}$ for the QV investments whose creation and use are sacrificed to the production of marginal units of output, (2) negative (SW[M]) percentage-distortion in $PB_{(U)PPR}$ for the PPR projects whose execution and use are sacrificed to the production of marginal units of output, and (3) negative (SW[M]) percentage-distortion in $PB_{(U)UO}$ for the economy's marginal units of output. I believe that (1) the absolute magnitude of the economy-wide weighted-average (SW[M]) positive percentage-distortion in the just-referenced $PB_{(U)QV}$ figure exceeds the economy-wide weighted-average (SW[M]) negative percentage-distortions in both the just-referenced $PB_{(U)PPR}$ and $PB_{(U)UO}$ figures, (2) that the absolute value of the negative economy-wide weighted-average (SW[M]) percentage-distortion in the just-referenced $PB_{(U)PPR}$ figure is probably higher than the absolute value of the negative economy-wide weighted-average percentage-distortion in the just-referenced $PB_{(U)UO}$ figure (at least for PPR projects that discover relevant-marginal-cost-reducing production processes whose respective uses increase the buyer surplus their employers generate when selling the goods to whose production processes the discoveries in question relate), but (3) that the absolute value of the negative economy-wide weighted-average percentage-distortion in $PB_{(U)PPR}$ for the PPR projects sacrificed to the production of an economy's marginal units of output is lower than the absolute value of the positive economy-wide weighted-average percentage-distortion in the $PB_{(U)QV}$ for the QV investments whose creation is sacrificed to the production of the economy's marginal units of output.

The third set of points I want to make about the (SW[M]) distortion in the profits yielded by three-to-one resource allocations from UO-related, QV-related, and PPR-related resource-uses to UO-related resource-uses focuses on the impact of AJW effects on this profit distortion. To the extent that AJW effects would have generated a positive (SW[M]) distortion in the profits that would have been yielded by the QV investments and PPR projects sacrificed to the production of a unit of output, those effects will generate a positive (SW[M]) distortion in the private marginal cost of producing the unit of output to whose production the relevant resource allocation devoted resources and hence a negative (SW[M]) distortion in the profits yielded by the resource allocation in question.

The fourth claim I want to make at this juncture is that, on the economy-wide weighted-average, the absolute value of the negative percentage-deflation in the private cost of marginal units of output produced with resources withdrawn from UO production and consumption, QV creation and use, and PPR execution and use is lower than the absolute value of the negative percentage-deflation in the private benefits of marginal units of output produced with resources withdrawn from these categories of use. This conclusion implies that, if all exemplars of all other types of Pareto imperfections could be ignored, too few resources would be devoted to UO production from the perspective of economic efficiency. Perhaps a numerical example would be useful. Assume that both the MR and the MC of all economics-marginal units of output were $100, that the percentage-distortion in the MC figures was (−20%), and that the percentage-distortion in the MR (i.e., PB) figures was (−18%). If these numbers were accurate, the allocative benefits generated by the production of the marginal unit of each product would be $120, and the allocative cost of producing the marginal unit of each product could be $118—i.e., the production of the marginal unit of each product would increase economic efficiency by $2 so that each product would be underproduced from the perspective of economic efficiency (since the production of some additional units of each product would increase economic efficiency—would generate allocative benefits slightly but increasingly below $120 and allocative costs slightly above $118). In an otherwise-Pareto-perfect economy, this conclusion (if correct) would have significant economic-efficiency implications (would favor the conclusion that all choices [including all government policies] that allocate resources to UO-producing-and-consuming uses from QV-investment-creating-and-using and PPR-executing-and-using uses will tend to increase economic efficiency on that account unless they [roughly speaking] change a situation in which the distortion in the profits yielded by UO/QV/PPR-to-UO resource allocations was positive to one in which it was negative and [probably] absolutely larger).

7.2.1.2 The Step-Wise-Monopoly Distortion in the Profits Yielded by Resource Allocations from Specifiable UO-Producing-and-Consuming, QV-Investment-Creating-and-Using, and PPR-Executing-and Using Related Pairs of Resource-Uses to Individual Specifiable Economics-Marginal QV-Creating-and-Using Related Pairs of Resource-Uses

This section makes four sets of points or claims. The first set relates to the imperfection-in-seller-competition step-wise distortions in the profits yielded by the UO-to-QV components of resource allocations from (the production and consumption of units of output, the creation and use of QV investments, and the execution and use of PPR projects) to (the creation and use of an economics-marginal QV investment). The first member of the first set of points is that the imperfections in seller price-competition that face the UO producers whose unit outputs are reduced when any economics-marginal QV investment is created generate a positive (SW[M]) distortion in $PB_{(U)QV}$ and hence a positive (SW[M]) distortion in $P\pi_{QV}$ for any economics-marginal QV investment by generating a negative (SW[M]) distortion in $PC_{(U)QV}$ and that the imperfections in seller price-competition that face the UO producers whose unit outputs are reduced when any economics-marginal QV investment is created generate a negative (SW[M]) distortion in $PC_{(C)QV}$ for any such QV investment and hence another positive (SW[M]) distortion in the private profits of creating and using any such QV investment (indeed, in creating and using any QV investment). The second member of this first set of points is that, for reasons previously discussed, although the imperfections in seller price-competition faced by the QV investor in question generate equal buyer-surplus-related negative (SW[M]) distortions in $PB_{(U)QV}$ and $P\pi_{QV}$ for the relevant QV investments, these negative (SW[M]) distortions in $P\pi_{QV}$ will always be lower than the positive distortions in $P\pi_{QV}$ just referenced. The third member of this first set of points is that, although the imperfections in QV-investment competition that the maker of an economics-marginal QV investment faces will generate a negative (SW[M]) distortion in $P\pi_{QV}$ both when the investor faces retaliation barriers on the investment and when it has a monopolistic QV-investment disincentive to make the relevant investment, I suspect that across all cases imperfections in QV-investment competition will tend to generate a positive (SW[M]) distortion in $P\pi_{QV}$ because creators of economics-marginal QV investments are more likely to have monopolistic QV-investment incentives to make them than to have monopolistic QV-investment disincentives to make them or face retaliation barriers in relation to them.

The second set of points relates to the fact that technologically-skilled/scientifically-skilled human resources are more privately and allocatively productive when devoted to creating technologically/scientifically-innovative QV investments and executing PPR projects than when devoted to UO production. More specifically, this second set of points focuses on the related (1) possible difference between the percentages of resources withdrawn, respectively, from UO producing-and-consuming, QV-investment creating-and-using, and PPR executing-and-using functionally-related pairs of resource-uses, respectively, by resource allocations to QV-investment creating-and-using uses on the one hand and to UO producing-and-consuming uses on the other and (2) to the difference any such difference makes to the overall (SW[M]) distortion in the private profits yielded by three-to-one resource allocations to the production and consumption of marginal units of output on the one hand and by three-to-one resource allocations to QV-investment creation and use. This second set of points or claims has six members.

The first is that, because technologically/scientifically-skilled human resources are better-suited to creating technologically/scientifically-innovative investments and to executing PPR projects than to creating QV investments that are not technologically/scientifically-innovative or to producing UO, the percentages of the resources devoted to creating technologically/scientifically-innovative QV investments that are withdrawn, respectively, from the creation of other technologically/scientifically-innovative QV investments and the execution of PPR projects exceeds the percentages of the economy's human resources that are technologically/scientifically-skilled whereas the percentages of the resources devoted to the creation of non-technologically-innovative QV investments that are withdrawn from the creation of technologically/scientifically-innovative QV investments and PPR execution that are withdrawn from such uses are far lower than the percentages of the economy's human resources that are technologically/scientifically-skilled. The second "point" in this second set is an admission: I cannot even guesstimate the ratio of the amounts of an economy's technologically/scientifically-skilled human resources that are devoted to creating technologically/scientifically-innovative QV investments to the amount that are devoted to executing PPR projects. I have already explained the (contestable) basis of the third point in this second set: I suspect that the positive (SW[M]) percentage-distortion in the private benefits yielded by technologically/scientifically-innovative QV investments and hence in the marginal revenue products and therefore the wages of technologically/scientifically-skilled workers who create QV investments is higher than the absolute magnitude of the negative (SW[M]) percentage-distortion in the private benefits yielded by the use of production-process discoveries and hence in the marginal revenue products and therefore the wages of workers who execute PPR. The fourth "point" in this second set is another admission: I cannot decide whether the appropriate response to the second and third "points" in this second set is to *bleib stumm* (remain silent) about the impact that the resource specializations the first point notes has on the relative magnitudes of the (SW[M[) percentage-distortions in the private cost of creating (economics-marginal) QV investments and the (SW[M]) percentage-distortion in the private cost of producing (economics-marginal) units of output or to speculate that the resource specialization in question will cause the weighted-average (SW[M]) percentage-distortion in $PC_{(C)QV}$ for any economy's (economics-marginal) QV investment to be less negative than the weighted-average (SW[M]) percentage-distortion in $PC_{(C)UO}$ for any economy's (economics-marginal) units of output. The fifth point in this set is that, regardless of how the issue to which the fourth point relates is resolved, I am confident that the relevant imperfections in seller competition generate a negative (SW[M]) percentage-distortion in $PC_{(C)QV}$ for all economics-marginal QV investments (indeed, for all QV investments) and hence a positive (SW[M]) percentage-distortion in the profits yielded by all three-to-one resource allocations to the creation of all economics-marginal (indeed, all) QV investments. The sixth and final point in this set is just a reminder: the first four points relate only to what I take to be the small subset of (economics-marginal) QV investments that are technologically/scientifically-innovative.

The third set of points relates to the fact that commercially-innovative human resources are more privately and allocatively productive when devoted to QV-investment creation than when devoted to UO production or PPR execution. This reality seems to me to warrant the conclusions that (1) the creation of economically-innovative QV investments withdraws a higher percentage of the relevant economy's commercially-innovative human resources from the creation of other commercially-innovative QV investments than from the production of units of extant products or the execution of PPR projects and (2) the absolute magnitude of the negative (SW[M]) percentage-distortion in the private cost of creating economics-marginal (and economics-non-marginal) commercially-innovative QV investments is on this account lower than it would otherwise be. However, I am still confident that the (SW[M]) percentage-distortion in the private cost of creating commercially-innovative QV investments is negative and *a fortiori* that the (SW[M]) percentage-distortion in the profits yielded by the creation and use of (economics-marginal) commercially-innovative QV investments is positive.

The fourth set of points relates to the impact of AJW-effect-generating (SW[M]) distortions in the private benefits yielded by those QV investments and PPR projects that are made by public utilities whose pricing is subjected to "fair-rate-of-return public-utility-pricing regulation" to put themselves in a position to secure profits from what I call their "prevented-profit pools." Since AJW-effect-related private benefits are associated with positive (SW[M]) distortions in the private benefits and profits yielded by any QV investments or PPR projects they elicited, the profits of most of the QV investments and PPR projects that are sacrificed by any three-to-one resource allocation to the creation of a QV investment would not otherwise have been (critically) increased by AJW effects, but the profits of a small percentage of the QV investments and PPR projects that are sacrificed by any three-to-one resource allocation to the creation of a QV investment that would otherwise have been increased by the profits they would have yielded for AJW-effect reasons, it seems reasonable to assume (1) that AJW effects (i.e., the imperfections in seller competition that play a critical role in their generation) will generate a positive (SW[M]) distortion in the profits yielded by any three-to-one resource allocation to the creation of a QV investment whose profitability was critically affected by AJW-effect-generated benefits and (2) that AJW effects will if anything generate a negative (SW[M]) distortion in the profits yielded by any three-to-one resource allocation to the creation of a QV investment whose profits were not enhanced by AJW effects.

7.2.1.3 The Step-Wise-Monopoly Distortions in the Profits Yielded by Resource Allocations from Specifiable UO-Producing-and-Consuming, QV-Investment-Creating-and-Using, and PPR-Executing-and-Using Functionally-Related Pairs of Resource-Uses to Specifiable Economics-Marginal PPR-Executing-and-Using Related Pairs of Resource-Uses

This section makes four sets of points or claims. The first relates to the sign of the $(SW[M])$ distortion in $PB_{(U)PPR}$. For reasons that Sect. 7.1 explained, I am certain that the $(SW[M])$ distortion in $PB_{(U)PPR}$ for not only economics-marginal PPR projects but for all PPR projects is negative.

The second set of points relates to the impact on the $(SW[M])$ percentage-distortion in $PC_{(C)PPR}$ of the fact that the technologically/scientifically-skilled labor that executes PPR projects is more productive when executing PPR projects or creating technologically/scientifically-innovative QV investments than when producing units of existing products or creating QV investments that are not technologically or scientifically innovative. The first point in this second set is that the preceding claim about the relative productivity of technologically/scientifically-skilled human resources is correct and significant. The second point in this second set is that, because technologically/scientifically-skilled human resources are better-suited to execute PPR projects and create technologically/scientifically-innovative QV investments than to produce units of existing products or to create non-technologically/scientifically-innovative QV investments, the execution of PPR projects withdraws higher percentages of the resources it uses from the execution of other PPR projects and the creation of technologically/scientifically-innovative QV investments than from UO production and the creation of QV investments that are not technologically or scientifically innovative. The third point in this second set is that, although I suspect that the positive $(SW[M])$ percentage-distortion in the wages paid to technologically/scientifically-skilled workers that create technologically/scientifically-innovative QV investments and hence in the private cost of withdrawing such labor from such uses to execute a PPR project is higher than the absolute magnitude of the negative $(SW[M])$ distortion in the private wages paid to technologically/scientifically-skilled workers that execute PPR projects and hence in the private cost of withdrawing such labor from such uses to execute a PPR project, my inability to even guesstimate the ratio of the number of technologically/scientifically-skilled workers who do technologically/scientifically-skilled product R&D to the number of such workers prevents me from guessing whether this resource-specialization reality makes the negative $(SW[M])$ percentage-distortion in $PC_{(C)PPR}$ higher or lower than it otherwise would have been. The fourth point in this second set is that, regardless of how the issue referenced in the third point in this set is resolved, I am certain that the $(SW[M])$ percentage-distortion in $PC_{(C)PPR}$ for all economics-marginal (indeed all) PPR projects is negative.

The third set of points I want to make at this juncture relates to the impact of AJW effects on the $(SW[M])$ distortion in the profits yielded by three-to-one resource allocations to PPR-related uses. This set of points parallels its counterpart for three-to-one resource allocations to QV-investment-related cases: the AJW-effect-related (SW[M]) distortion in the profits yielded by this category of resource allocation will be positive when the executed PPR project was rendered at least normally profitable by AJW-effect-generated private benefits and will, if anything, be negative when the executed PPR project did not enable its executer to take profits out of any "fair-rate-of-return public-utility-pricing-regulation"-generated prevented-profit pool since the benefits that would have been yielded by one or more of the sacrificed QV investments or PPR projects may have included profits the investment/project enabled its creator/executor to withdraw from a prevented-profit pool.

The fourth and final point I want to make about the (SW[M]) distortion in the profits yielded by three-to-one resource allocations to PPR-related resource-uses is that I am unable to make a defensible guess about the relative absolute magnitudes of the (SW[M]) negative percentage-distortions in $PB_{(U)PPR}$ and $PC_{(C)PPR}$ for economics-marginal PPR projects—i.e., about whether economics-marginal PPR projects would tend to be economically efficient or economically inefficient if, taken together, the extant exemplars of all types of Pareto imperfections other than imperfections in seller price-competition generated no (SW[M]) distortion in $P\pi_{PPR}$ for an economy's economics-marginal PPR projects (whether on the just-referenced assumption choices that increased or decreased the magnitudes of resource allocations from UO production and consumption and QV creation and use to PPR execution and use would increase or decrease economic efficiency on that account).

7.2.2 The Step-Wise-Monopoly Distortion in the Profits Yielded by Exemplars of 12 Categories of Resource Allocations Not Analyzed in Sect. 7.2.1

This section analyzes the (SW[M]) distortion in the profits yielded by (hopefully-heuristically-instructive) components of the three three-to-one categories of resource allocations that Sect. 7.2.1 considered and by several other categories of resource allocations that can have economically-inefficient exemplars whose total magnitudes choices can affect. Some of its analyses focus on the (SW[M]) distortions in the profits yielded by the economics-marginal exemplars of particular categories of resource allocations: all those that do will assume that the profits yielded by each such exemplar are zero (though, in fact, positive profits will often be yielded by resource allocations to economics-marginal QV-investment-creating-and-using uses, by resource allocations to economics-marginal PPR-executing-and-using uses, and by resource allocations to economics-marginal unit-output-producing-and-consuming uses when the marginal cost of producing the relevant marginal unit of output [and, more to the point, the first extra-marginal unit of the good in question] is substantial). All the analyses of this section will take advantage of the fact that the (SW[M]) distortion (percentage-distortion) in the private cost of any resource-use to which a relevant resource allocation devotes resources will equal the (SW[M]) distortion (the weighted-average percentage-distortion) in the private benefits that the resource-uses the relevant resource allocation sacrifices would have conferred on the sacrificing resource-users.

7.2.2.1 The Step-Wise-Monopoly Distortion in the Profits Yielded by Inter-ARDEPPS UO-to-UO Resource Allocations

If I assume for simplicity that the sale of no unit of any product involved in this analysis will alter the profits the seller earns on future sales of the product in question or of other products it will sell in the future, that none of the products in question has any complement, and that all products in any ARDEPPS have the same P/MC ratio, the (SW[M]) distortion in the profits yielded by inter-ARDEPPS UO-to-UO resource allocations to the production of the marginal units of all products in a given ARDEPPS will be negative if P/MC in that ARDEPPS is higher than the weighted-average P/MC ratio of the products in the other ARDEPPSes whose outputs are reduced when the respective economics-marginal units of the products in the ARDEPPS to which resources are being allocated are produced. Of course, because the resources that are being withdrawn from UO production else-where are not being withdrawn randomly from all other ARDEPPSes in the economy (are being withdrawn from other individual ARDEPPSes' UO production in amounts that reflect how competitive the other ARDEPPS in question is with the ARDEPPS to whose UO production resources are being allocated both as sellers of the goods in question and as buyers of any specialized inputs used to produce both sets of goods), the preceding conclusion does not imply that it will be accurate or even TBLE to assume that the (SW[M]) distortion in the profits yielded by the production and consumption of the goods produced by any ARDEPPS will be positive/negative when that ARDEPPS' P/MC ratio is lower/higher than the weighted-average P/MC ratio for all goods in the economy in question. The argument for the "accuracy-conclusion" would be strengthened to the extent that choices (policies) that shift resources from UO production in other ARDEPPSes to UO production in a particular ARDEPPS (say, by decreasing prices in the latter ARDEPPS) tend to withdraw resources from close substitutes of the receiving ARDEPPS if the difference between the P/MC ratios of products in two ARDEPPSes is inversely correlated with how competitive their products are with each other. In any event, it will virtually always be TBLE to devote some resources to identifying the ARDEPPSes whose unit outputs are sacrificed to the production of the marginal units of the goods produced by the ARDEPPS to which the relevant resource allocations allocate resources and to calculating the weighted-average P/MC ratio for the sacrificed units of output.

7.2.2.2 The Step-Wise-Monopoly Distortion in the Profits Yielded by Intra-ARDEPPS UO-to-UO Resource Allocations

To analyze the (SW[M]) distortion in the profits yielded by an intra-ARDEPPS UO-to-UO resource allocation, one will have to reject the previous section's unrealistic assumption that the P/MC ratio of each product in any given ARDEPPS is the same: (SW[M]) distortions in the profits yielded by intra-ARDEPPS UO-to-UO resource allocations are generated by differences in the P/MC ratio of the good whose economics-marginal units of outputs' (SW[M]) profit distortion is at issue and the weighted-average P/MC ratio of the good(s) from whose production resources are being withdrawn to secure the resources used to produce the former product's economics-marginal unit of output. I want to make two sets of points that relate to the circumstances in which the (SW[M]) distortion in the profits yielded by the production of a unit of output produced with resources withdrawn from the production of other products in its ARDEPPS are likely to be positive (the circumstances in which the production of the unit in question would be economically inefficient if the unit were an economics-marginal unit of output, all resources used to produce that marginal unit of output were withdrawn from the production of units of other goods produced in the same ARDEPPS, and, all tolled, all other exemplars of all other types of Pareto imperfections had no effect on the aggregate distortion in the profits yielded by the production of the economics-marginal unit of the good in question). The first set of circumstances in which the relevant (SW[M]) profit distortion is likely to be positive is when the sale of the unit in question was secured by the charging of a retaliatory or predatory, inherently-unprofitable price since in such cases the P/MC ratio of the seller (which will be lower than 1) will always be critically lower than the P/MC ratio of the product whose producer is the target of the retaliatory or predatory pricing in question ("critically" because the associated difference between the retaliator's predator's [P − MC] gap and that of its target led to the retaliator's/predator's taking the sale away from its target from a privately-inferior and, on step-wise-analysis assumptions, allocatively-inferior position). I admit the contestability of the second claim I will make about the second set of circumstances in which the (SW[M]) profit distortion in the profits yielded by the sale of a unit of output produced with resources withdrawn from the production of fewer-than-one, one, or more-than-one units of another product in its ARDEPPS will be positive: I suspect that this outcome will sometimes obtain when sales are made by producers of lower-quality/lower-marginal-cost/less-differentiated products in one ARDEPPS to buyers who would otherwise have purchased a higher-quality/higher-marginal-cost/more-differentiated product that is also located in the ARDEPPS in question because I suspect that not only is (P−MC) higher for the higher-marginal-cost product that lost the sale than for the lower-marginal-cost product that was sold but (more contestably) the (P/MC) ratio for the cheaper product is likely to be lower than the (P/MC) ratio for the more-expensive product (so that the negative percentage-deflation in the $PB_{(U)UO}$ for the cheaper product that was sold is likely to be lower than the negative percentage-deflation in the $PC_{(C)UO}$ for that cheaper product).

7.2.2.3 The Step-Wise-Monopoly Distortion in the Profits Yielded by Inter-ARDEPPS QV-to-QV Resource Allocations

The (SW[M]) distortion in the profits yielded by an inter-ARDEPPS QV-to-QV resource allocation equals the (SW[M]) distortion in the private benefits the use of the created QV investment yielded the investor that created it *minus* the (SW[M]) distortion in the private benefits that the use of the sacrificed QV investments would have yielded the sacrificing QV investors from whose QV-investment creations the relevant resource allocation withdrew resources (which equal the (SW[M]) distortion in the private cost of creating the created QV investment). The (SW[M]) distortion in the profits yielded by an inter-ARDEPPS QV-to-QV resource allocation could also be said to equal (1) (the imperfections-in-seller-*price-competition*-generated (SW[M]) distortion in the private benefits that the use of the created QV investment conferred on its creator *minus* the imperfections-in-seller-*price-competition*-generated (SW[M]) distortion in the private benefits that the use of the sacrificed QV investment[s] would have conferred on the sacrificing QV investor[s]) *plus* (2) (the imperfections-in-*QV-investment-competition*-generated (SW[M]) distortion in the private benefits that the use of the created QV investment conferred on the QV-investment creator *minus* the imperfections-in-*QV-investment-competition*-generated (SW[M]) distortion in the private benefits that the use of the sacrificed QV investment[s] would have conferred on the sacrificing QV investor[s]) *plus* (3) (the imperfections-in-seller-price-and-QV-investment-competition-generated AJW-effect-related positive (SW[M]) distortion in the private benefits that the use of the created QV investment conferred on its creator *minus* the AJW-effect-related positive (SW[M]) distortion in the profits that the sacrificed QV investments would have conferred on the sacrificing QV investors). This section will make six points/comments or sets of points that relate to the determinants of and/or the relative absolute magnitudes of these six (SW[M]) distortions.

The first is that the QV investments that are sacrificed in any inter-ARDEPPS QV-to-QV allocations are withdrawn from what might be called a random sample of those of the economy's ARDEPPSes that produce products that are distantly competitive with the products produced by the ARDEPPS in which the created QV investment is located. This pattern contrasts with the resource-flow pattern involved in inter-ARDEPPS UO-to-UO resource allocations where the resources that are devoted to the production of a unit of a product in one ARDEPPS will tend to be withdrawn from the production of products in ARDEPPSes whose products are atypically competitive with the products in the ARDEPPS in which the product to whose production the relevant resource allocations devoted resources is located. Thus, if an additional QV investment is created in a particular ARDEPPS because prices have risen in that ARDEPPS, the relevant increase in prices will tend to cause the equilibrium quantity of QV investment to rise not only in the ARDEPPS in question but also in ARDEPPSes that produce products that are atypically competitive with the products produced in the ARDEPPS in which the created QV investment is located: an increase in the prices in one ARDEPPS not only (1) increases the profits yielded by all QV investments in that ARDEPPS and hence its equilibrium-QV-investment quantity but also (2) increases the profits yielded by all products in ARDEPPSes that produce products that are atypically competitive with the products produced in the ARDEPPS whose prices have risen and hence in their equilibrium-QV-investment quantities. Contrastingly, if an additional unit of output is produced in one ARDEPPS because prices have fallen in that ARDEPPS, the reduction in the prices of that ARDEPPS' products will tend to be associated with a decrease in the unit outputs of the products in other ARDEPPSes that produce products that are atypically competitive with the products produced in the ARDEPPS in which the additional unit of output is being produced—*i.e.*, the inter-ARDEPPS resource allocations that involve the devotion of resources to the production of a unit of a product in one ARDEPPS are likely to involve the withdrawal of resources from the production of products that are atypically competitive with the products produced by the ARDEPPS in which the product whose output is increased is located. Admittedly, if an additional QV investment is created in a particular ARDEPPS because a QV-investment-deterring barrier to entry or QV-investment disincentive has been reduced in that ARDEPPS, the resources devoted to creating that QV investment that are withdrawn from QV-investment creation elsewhere will tend to be withdrawn from QV-investment creation in ARDEPPSes that produce products that are atypically competitive with the products produced by the ARDEPPS in which the created QV investment is located because the new QV investment will tend to reduce the profits yielded by all QV investments in ARDEPPSes whose products are atypically competitive with the ARDEPPS in which the new QV investment was created and hence their equilibrium-QV-investment quantities both directly by increasing the quality and variety of the products produced in the ARDEPPS in which the created QV investment is located and indirectly by decreasing prices in the ARDEPPS in which the created QV investment is located. However, although this latter possibility diminishes the magnitude of the difference that I am now pointing out, it does not eliminate that difference.

The second point or pair of points I want to make about the (SW[M]) distortion in the profits yielded by inter-ARDEPPS QV-to-QV resource allocations follows from the first: (1) because the QV investments whose creation is sacrificed to the creation of any QV investment created by an inter-ARDEPPS QV-to-QV resource allocation tend to be located in ARDEPPSes that are distantly competitive with the ARDEPPS in which the created QV investment is located, the weighted-average P/MC ratio of the products that would have been created by the sacrificed QV investments will tend to deviate from the weighted-average P/MC ratio of all products in the relevant economy in the opposite direction from the direction in which the created QV investment's product's P/MC ratio and the weighted-average P/MC ratio of all products in the created QV investment's ARDEPPS deviate from that economy-made weighted average and therefore the absolute magnitude of the imperfections-in-seller-price-competition-generated negative (SW[M]) percentage-distortion in the private benefits that would have been generated by the use of the QV investments that any inter-ARDEPPS QV-to-QV resource allocation sacrifices will tend to deviate from its weighted-average economy-wide counterpart in the opposite direction from the direction in which the absolute magnitude of the negative imperfection-in-seller-price-competition-generated (SW[M]) distortion in the profits generated by the created QV investment will deviate from its economy-wide weighted-average counterpart. This last conclusion implies that the imperfections-in-seller-price-competition-generated (SW[M])D yielded by an inter-ARDEPPS QV-to-QV resource allocation will tend to be positive/negative when the P/MC ratio of the goods in the ARDEPPS in which the created QV investment is located is higher/lower than the weighted-average P/MC ratio for all the relevant economy's goods because, when the weighted-average P/MC ratio in the created QV investment's ARDEPPS is higher/lower than the weighted-average P/MC ratio in the ARDEPPSes in which QV investments are sacrificed, the imperfections-in-seller-price-competition-generated positive (SW[M]) percentage-distortion in $PB_{(U)QV}$ for the created QV investment will tend to be higher/lower than the imperfections-in-seller-price-competition-generated positive (SW[M]) percentage-distortion in $PB_{(U)QV}$ for the sacrificed QV investments and hence in the imperfections-in-seller-price-competition-generated positive (SW[M])distortion in $PC_{(C)QV}$ for the created QV investment—i.e., the imperfections-in-seller-price-competition (SW[M]) distortion in the profits yielded by an inter-ARDEPPS QV-to-QV resource allocation will tend to be positive when the weighted-average P/MC ratio in the ARDEPPS in which the created ARDEPPS is located is higher than its weighted-average economy-wide counterpart and will tend to be negative when the weighted-average P/MC ratio in the ARDEPPS in which the created QV investment is located is lower than its weighted-average economy-wide counterpart.

The third set of points I want to make at this juncture focuses on the usefulness of the preceding conclusions. To be useful, these conclusions would have to be combined with sufficiently-accurate estimates of the weighted-average P/MC ratio of the products in various specific ARDEPPSes of interest and the weighted-average P/MC ratio of all of the relevant economy's products, and data on these parameters are admittedly not in long supply. However, it should be noted that most businesses do keep track of what they call the "direct costs" they incur to produce each of the products they produce (what economists call the total variable cost of producing each such product) and their unit outputs of each product they produce, and to the extent that the marginal cost of producing the last unit of any product that is produced equals the average-variable cost of producing that good, one would be able to estimate the relevant marginal-cost figures from company estimates of their product-by-product "direct costs" and unit outputs (unless, in the relevant legal system, companies are deemed to have proprietary property-rights in such information [which would entitle them to prevent the government from ordering them to provide such information] and companies choose to enforce those property-rights).

The fourth set of points/comments I want to make at this juncture relates to the possible positive correlation between the imperfections-in-seller-price-competition-generated (SW[M]) percentage-distortion in the profits yielded by inter-ARDEPPS QV-to-QV resource allocations and the imperfections-in-QV-investment-competition-generated (SW[M]) percentage-distortion in the profits yielded by inter-ARDEPPS QV-to-QV resource allocations. The argument for this correlation is that the larger the share that a QV investor owns of the total QV investment in its ARDEPPS)/(makes of the sales made of all products in its ARDEPPS) the larger the positive percentage-distortion in the profits yielded by the referenced resource allocation generated both by imperfections in QV-investment competition and by imperfections in seller price-competition. This argument is dubious because, although something can be said for each of its asserted correlations, both of them are questionable. Here is the argument for the positive correlation between the positive (SW[M]) percentage-distortion in the profits yielded by any QV investment created through an inter-ARDEPPS QV-to-QV resource allocation and the share that the QV investor that created the QV investment in question (owned of the QV investments its ARDEPPS contained)/(made of the sales of that ARDEPPS's products) prior to the creation of the created QV investment: (1) any monopolistic QV-investment incentive an investor has to make any QV investment it makes (including any economics-marginal QV investment it makes) in any ARDEPPS will generate a positive (SW[M]) distortion in $PB_{(U)QV}$ for that QV investment; (2) the magnitudes of the monopolistic QV-investment incentive an investor has to make a QV investment in an ARDEPPS in which it already owns one or more QV investments and of the related positive percentage-distortion in the profits that QV investment will yield the investor will increase with the amount of QV investment the investor owned in the relevant ARDEPPS prior to making the created QV investment and hence with the share the investor owned of the QV investment the relevant ARDEPPS contained prior to the investor's making the QV investment in question; (3) the probability that a firm that already owns one or more QV investments in a given ARDEPPS will make an economics-marginal QV investment in that ARDEPPS that is associated with an inter-ARDEPPS QV-to-QV resource allocation will increase with the firm's shares of the ARDEPPS' pre-existing QV investments and sales (in part because the monopolistic QV-investment incentives that different firms have to make an additional QV investment in one ARDEPPS in which they are already operating increases with their respective shares of the ARDEPPS' pre-existing QV investments and sales); (4) although the monopolistic QV-investment disincentive an investor faces on a particular QV investment will be associated with a negative (SW[M]) distortion in that investment's profitability, investors rarely have monopolistic QV-investment disincentives to make any QV investment they make; (5) although any retaliation barrier to investment an investor faces on a QV investment will be associated with a negative (SW[M]) distortion in the profits that investment yields the investor, I suspect that (A) the incidence of retaliation barriers to investment is much lower than the incidence of monopolistic QV-investment disincentives and (B) larger firms (which tend to have larger shares of the QV investments in the ARDEPPSes in which they are operating) are less likely to face retaliation barriers to investment than are smaller firms (because it is less likely to be profitable to retaliate against larger firms' QV investments since, I suspect, larger firms are less likely to be deterred from making QV investments or other competitive moves by retaliation both because larger firms are more likely to have the financial resources not only to survive retaliation but to continue to compete aggressively and because they are in a better position to take advantage of institutional economies of scale in building and maintaining a reputation for not being deterrable through retaliation). The argument for any positive correlation between the share that the firm that creates the QV investment to whose creation any inter-ARDEPPS QV-to-QV resource allocations devote resources has of its ARDEPPS' QV investment and sales and the P/MC ratio of that QV investor and of the other producers in its ARDEPPS is substantially weaker, to say the least. Any such argument would have to establish that a firm's ARDEPPS share is positively correlated with its and its in-ARDEPPS rivals' basic competitive advantages, natural-oligopolistic margins, and/or contrived-oligopolistic margins, and I doubt that any such connection can be established for the P/MC of the firm itself or *a fortori* for the P/MC ratios of its in-ARDEPPS rivals. Thus, the fact that the QV investor has a high share of the QV investment and sales of its ARDEPPS tells you little about its basic competitive advantages, natural-oligopolistic margins, or contrived-oligopolistic margins—i.e., about the number of sellers in the ARDEPPS, about the importance of product differentiation in the ARDEPPS, about the percentage of the buyers of the ARDEPPS' products that are repeat buyers that have an incentive not to allow privately-best-placed suppliers whose offers to them have been beaten to rebid and not to identify suppliers that have beaten their respective privately-best-placed suppliers' offers to them, about the cost to privately-best-placed sellers whose initial offers have been beaten of rebidding, about the public character of the prices that are being offered, about the ability of sellers to predict the sales to their old customers they will retain, the sales to established customers of their rivals they will secure, and the sales to new buyers they would make in each case if no-one fails to cooperate with their contrived-oligopolistic pricing, about the frequency with which sellers are privately-second-placed to obtain the patronage of customers of rivals that might otherwise beat their contrived-oligopolistic offers and the amounts by which such contrivers are better-placed than the third-placed suppliers of the buyers in question when the contriver is those buyers' second-placed supplier, *etc.*, and even less about its rivals' basic competitive advantages, natural-oligopolistic margins, or contrived-oligopolistic margins. All things considered, I see little reason to believe that there is any correlation between on the one hand (1) the P/MC ratio of a QV investor and the weighted-average P/MC ratios of its sales rivals and hence the imperfections-in-seller-price-competition-generated percentage-distortion in the profits yielded by any QV investment it makes with resources withdrawn from the creation of QV investments in other ARDEPPSes and, on the other hand, (2) the imperfections-in-QV-investment-competition-generated percentage-distortion in the profits yielded by any such QV investment. I therefore do not think that it will ever be TBLE to rely on any such general correlation when analyzing the impact of any choice on inter-ARDEPPS QV-to-QV misallocation.

The fifth and sixth sets of points I want to make about the (SW[M]) distortion in the profits yielded by inter-ARDEPPS QV-to-QV resource allocations relate to the possibility that a seller's facing imperfections in price-competition and QV-investment competition may result in its being classified as a public utility and subjected to fair-rate-of-return public-utility-pricing regulations that have AJW effects (that make it overall profitable for the firm to make an inherently-unprofitable QV investment that enables it to gain access to the prevented-profit pool such regulation would otherwise create). The fifth point is that any AJW-effect-related benefits a QV investor has to make a QV investment will be associated with a positive (SW[M]) distortion in both the private benefits the investment confers on it and the profits the investment yields it. The sixth point is that the AJW-effect-related positive (SW[M]) distortion in the private benefits that some QV investments confer on the investors that make them will be associated with a positive (SW[M]) distortion in the profits yielded by any inter-ARDEPPS QV-to-QV resource allocation to a public-utility QV investor that has an AJW-effect-related incentive to make the QV investment to which the resource allocation devoted resources and will be associated, if anything, with a negative (SW[M]) distortion in the profits yielded by any inter-ARDEPPS QV-to-QV resource allocation to a QV investor that had no such AJW-effect-related invest-ment incentive since one or more of the QV investments such a resource allocation sacrificed might otherwise have been made by a QV investor that would have had an AJW-effect-related incentive to make it.

7.2.2.4   The Step-Wise-Monopoly Distortion in the Profits Yielded by Intra-ARDEPPS QV-to-QV Resource Allocations

I can think of at least four reasons why the profits yielded by imperfections in seller competition can distort the profits yielded by intra-ARDEPPS UO-to-UO resource allocations—i.e., four imperfections-in-seller-competition-related reasons why intra-ARDEPPS QV-to-QV economic inefficiency might be generated if, taken together, all the exemplars of all other types of Pareto imperfections did not affect the distortion in the profits yielded by any intra-ARDEPPS QV-to-QV resource allocation. The first reason is a buyer-surplus-related reason that I have been contestably attributing to imperfections in seller price-competition. If, for sim-plicity, one controls for the average competitive advantage that (say) the seller(s) of two products each of which would be profitable to introduce if the other were not introduced but only one of which can be profitably introduced would enjoy when selling the products in question and the number of buyers whose patronage each of these products would be privately-best-placed to secure, differences in the shapes of the demand curves for and the marginal-cost curves for the two products may create a critical positive (SW[M]) distortion in the profits yielded by one of the products in question if these differences would result in the sale of the units of the product that would be more economically efficient to introduce that would be sold if it were introduced to yield critically more buyer surplus than would the sale of the product that would be less economically efficient to introduce (say, because the demand for the product that was more profitable but less economically efficient to introduce was highly concave to the origin whereas the demand for the product that was less profitable but more economically efficient to introduce was convex to the origin [more generally because the buyer surplus that would have been generated by the sale of the product that was less profitable but more economically efficient to introduce *exceeded* the buyer surplus that was generated by the sale of the product that was more profitable but less economically efficient to introduce by more than the economic-efficiency gain that would have been generated by the introduction of the product whose introduction would have been more economically efficient exceeded the economic-efficiency gain that was generated by the introduction of the product that was less economically efficient to introduce [where the two economic-efficiency gains just referenced are calculated on the assumption that the alternative to introducing the product in question is introducing no new product]).

The second imperfections-in-seller-competition-related reason why the (SW[M]) distortion in the profits yielded by an intra-ARDEPPS QV-to-QV resource allocation may be positive (i.e., may cause a less-economically-efficient QV investment rather than a more-economically-efficient QV investment to be created in a given ARDEPPS if, taken together, all exemplars of all other types of Pareto imperfections made no difference) is monopolistic QV-investment incentives: a potential QV-investment expander in a given ARDEPPS may find it profitable to make a less-economically-efficient rather than a more-economically-efficient QV investment in that ARDEPPS if the monopolistic QV-investment incentive it had to make the less-economically-efficient QV investment was critically larger than the monopolistic QV-investment incentive it had to make the more-economically-efficient QV investment or if the incumbent that faced the larger monopolistic QV-investment was not the same incumbent that faced the smaller monopolistic QV-investment incentive.

The third reason why there might be a positive (SW[M]) distortion in the profits yielded by an intra-ARDEPPS QV-to-QV resource allocation is the monopolistic or natural-oligopolistic QV-investment disincentive counterpart of the second reason. In this case, the positive distortion results because the monopolistic QV-investment disincentive or natural-oligopolistic QV-investment disincentive that is associated with the creation of the less-economically-efficient QV investment that could be added to a given ARDEPPS is critically smaller than its counterpart for the more-economically-efficient sacrificed QV investment that could have been created in the ARDEPPS in question.

The fourth imperfections-in-seller-competition-related "reason" why there might be a distortion in the profits yielded by an intra-ARDEPPS QV-to-QV resource allocation is that the investor that created the QV investment that was created (1) either obtained profits by creating the investment it created because that investment raised the retaliation barriers to investment that one or more of its rivals faced or (2) chose to create the QV investment it created rather than another QV investment it would otherwise have created in the ARDEPPS in question because it faced lower retaliation barriers on the QV investment it created than on the QV investment it could have created instead or because the QV investment that was created because the investor that created it faced lower retaliation barriers on that investment than the other investor that would otherwise have created a sacrificed QV investment would have faced on that sacrificed QV investment.

7.2.2.5 The Step-Wise-Monopoly Distortion in the Profits Yielded by Inter-ARDEPPS PPR-to-PPR Resource Allocations

The (SW[M]) distortion in the profits yielded by any inter-ARDEPPS PPR-to-PPR resource allocation equals the (SW[M]) distortion in the private benefits yielded by the use of the PPR project to which that resource allocation devotes resources *minus* the step-wise distortion that imperfections in seller competition would have generated in the private benefits that would have been generated by the use of the PPR project(s) the resource allocation in question sacrificed (which equal the step-wise-monopoly distortion in the private cost of executing the PPR project to whose execution the resource allocation in question devoted resources). If I assume for convenience that the executed PPR project is an economics-marginal PPR project, that its execution and use yielded zero-supernormal profits (that the private benefits that its use conferred on its executer equal the private cost its executer had to incur to execute it), and that imperfections in seller competition will generate a negative step-wise distortion in the private benefits yielded by each PPR project that was or might have been executed, the (SW[M]) distortion in the profits yielded by any inter-ARDEPPS PPR-to-PPR resource allocation to the execution of any such PPR project will be positive/negative if the absolute magnitude of the negative (SW[M]) percentage-distortion in the private benefits that the use of the executed PPR project conferred on the executer is lower/higher than the absolute magnitude of the negative (SW[M]) percentage-distortion in the private benefits that the use of the sacrificed PPR project(s) would have conferred on its (their) sacrificing exe-cuters: thus, if the absolute magnitude of the negative (SW[M]) percentage-distortion in the private benefits that the use of the executed zero-supernormal-profit-yielding economics-marginal PPR project would have conferred on its exe-cuter is higher than the absolute magnitude of the weighted-average negative (SW[M]) percentage-distortion in the private benefits that the use of the sacrificed PPR project(s) would have conferred on its (their) sacrificing executers, imper-fections in price-competition will have created a negative (SW[M]) distortion in $PB_{(U)PPR}$ for the executed PPR project that is lower than the negative (SW[M]) distortion in $PC_{(C)PPR}$ for that project—i.e., will have "deflated" the project's pri-vate benefits by less than it "deflated" its private cost and hence will have inflated the profits it yielded (generated a positive (SW[M]) distortion in the profits yielded by the resource allocation in question).

I will now identify and comment on four of the most important sets of deter-minants of the (SW[M]) distortion in $P\pi_{PPR}$ for an economics-marginal PPR project with the above characteristics that is executed with resources withdrawn exclusively from the execution of PPR projects in other ARDEPPSes. The first set of deter-minants is (1) the weighted-average P/MC and hence (P − MC)/MC ratios of the goods from whose production resources were withdrawn to produce the outputs of those goods to whose production processes the PPR project(s) that the resource allocation in question sacrificed would have related (which are important deter-minants of the negative (SW[M]) percentage-distortion in the private benefits that these sacrificed PPR projects would have conferred on their executers and hence of the negative (SW[M]) percentage-distortion in the private cost to its executer of the PPR project to whose execution the resource allocation in question devoted resources). If I ignore the role played by independent scientific/technological dis-coverers (i.e., discoverers that do not produce the goods to whose production processes their discoveries relate), resource allocations that devote additional resources to the PPR done in relation to the production process used to produce a particular product G (or a set of product variants $G1...n$ whose members are pro-duced with similar or the same production process) are most likely to be triggered (1) by reductions in the price of G (prices of $G1...n$), which make PPR that would discover a marginal-cost-reducing production process more profitable by increasing the unit output(s) of the good(s) any such resulting discovery could be used to produce, (2) (far less likely) by reductions in the monopolistic and natural-oligopolistic PPR-investment disincentives faced by potential researchers that previously found additional PPR "just unprofitable"—i.e., for which additional PPR would originally have yielded subnormal profits that were smaller than the decrease in the monopolistic or natural-oligopolistic PPR-investment disincentive it faced that triggered its PPR) (by a reduction in the share[s] of the PPR-ARDEPPS of one or more incumbents that previously found additional PPR just unprofitable), (3) (somewhat more likely) by increases in the monopolistic PPR-investment incentive an established member of the PPR-ARDEPPS had to execute a relevant PPR project that previously found additional PPR "just unprofitable"), and/or (4) (possibly but also improbably) by a critical decrease in the retaliation barrier to executing a PPR project a possible researcher faced or a critical increase in the profits a potential production-process researcher could realize by executing a PPR project to retaliate against a competitor. The reductions in the price(s) of G or $(G1...n)$ that can trigger increases in the PPR done on G's or $(G1...n)$'s production process will have an uncertain impact on the quantity of PPR done in ARDEPPSes that are atypically competitive with G or $(G1...n)$ because reductions in the price of G will have an uncertain impact on the outputs of the goods produced in ARDEPPSes that are atypically-competitive with G—will have an impact on G's rivals' outputs that depends on the ratio of the reduction in the prices charged for G's rivals' products to the triggering reduction in the price(s) of G $(G1...n)$. In the unlikely event that the increase in the PPR done in relation to G was triggered by a reduction in the PPR disincentives that faced a relevant researcher, the impact that the reduction in the relevant PPR disincentives will have on the amount of PPR executed in ARDEPPSes that produce goods that are atypically competitive with G $(G1...n)$ will depend (1) on whether the reduction in the disincentives in question was itself caused by a reduction in a relevant potential production-process researcher's share not only of the ARDEPPS for PPR into G's production process but also of the ARDEPPS in which G is produced, (2) on whether, if it is associated with a decrease in the relevant researcher's share of the G market, that change will be associated with a reduction in the price(s) of G $(G1...n)$, and (3) on whether any associated reduction in the prices of G or $G1...n$ will be associated with an increase in the sales of the products in ARDEPPSes whose products are atypically com-petitive with G or $G1...n$. Even if the answer to the first of these questions is "more likely than not," the connections on which the second and third of these questions focus seem insufficiently likely for there to be good reason to believe that any reduction-in-PPR-disincentive-triggered increase in the PPR done in relation to the production processes used to produce any product(s) G $(G1...n)$ will be associated with an increase or, for that matter, with a decrease in the amount of PPR done in ARDEPPSes whose products are atypically competitive with G $(G1...n)$. I will simply assert without explaining the basis for my conclusion that no tendency of increases in the PPR done into the production process used to produce G $(G1...n)$ to be associated with increases or decreases in the PPR done into the production processes used to produce products that are atypically competitive with G $(G1...n)$ can be attributed to the possibilities that the increase in the G-related PPR might be triggered by increases in the monopolistic PPR incentives a relevant researcher faced, decreases in the retaliation barriers to PPR a prospective relevant researcher faced, or any incentive a relevant researcher had to execute a PPR project to retaliate against a target. I therefore assume that the weighted-average P/MC ratio for the goods produced in any ARDEPPS to whose production process the PPR project whose execution is secured by any inter-ARDEPPS PPR-to-PPR resource allocation will differ slightly in the opposite direction from the relevant economy's weighted-average P/MC ratio than does the weighted-average P/MC ratio in the ARDEPPSes one or more of whose PPR projects are sacrificed by any inter-ARDEPPS PPR-to-PPR resource allocation—that on this account the (SW[M]) distortion in the profits yielded by inter-ARDEPPS PPR-to-PPR resource allocations will be negative/positive when the weighted-average P/MC ratio of the products to whose production process the executed PPR project relates is higher than its weighted-average economy-wide counterpart. Of course, the magnitude of any relevant profit distortion will depend on the extent to which the weighted-average P/MC ratio in the ARDEPPS to whose production process the executed PPR project relates deviates from the economy-wide weighted-average P/MC ratio.

The second set of determinants of the (SW[M]) distortion in the profits yielded by an inter-ARDEPPS PPR-to-PPR resource allocation contains the monopolistic PPR disincentives or monopolistic PPR incentives and the retaliation-barrier-to-PPR-related disincentives and/or incentives, respectively, that (1) the production-process researcher that executed the PPR project to which the relevant resource allocation devoted resources had to make the executed PPR project and (2) the production-process researchers whose PPR projects were sacrificed by the relevant resource allocations faced on the sacrificed PPR projects. Given that all such incentives are associated with positive distortions in the private benefits yielded by the PPR projects to which they relate, that all such disincentives are associated with negative distortions in those private benefits, and that the incentives and disincentives that face the sacrificing production-process researchers will deviate slightly from their weighted-average-economy-wide counterparts and in the opposite direction from their economy-wide counterparts as did the incentives and disincentives that faced the production-process researcher that executed the PPR project to which the resource allocation in question devoted resources, the following crude generalization might be in order (crude because it fails to reflect the possible difference between the percentage-distortions in the various categories of PPR incentives and disincentives): if as I suspect on the weighted average the sacrificing production-process researchers would have had a PPR incentive to execute their sacrificed PPR projects, the (SW[M]) distortion in the profits yielded by inter-ARDEPPS PPR-to-PPR resource allocations will be positive if the production-process researcher that executed the PPR project whose execution the relevant resource allocation secured had positive PPR incentives to do so that constituted a higher percentage of their $PB_{(U)PPR}$ figure than the sum of the positive PPR incentives the sacrificing researchers had to execute their sacrificed projects constituted of their total sacrificed $PB_{(U)PPR}$ figures and will be negative if the executer of the PPR project to which the relevant resource allocation devoted resources had net PPR incentives that constituted a lower percentage of its $PB_{(U)PPR}$ figure than the sum of the PPR incentives that the sacrificing production-process researchers had to execute their sacrificed PPR projects constituted of their sacrificed $PB_{(U)PPR}$ figures where the percentage for the sacrificers should be assumed to deviate slightly and in the opposite direction from its weighted-average economy-wide counterpart. Of course, it may well not be TBLE to devote any attention to this issue—to estimate the weighted-average economy-wide figures for any relevant economy's just-extra-marginal PPR projects.

The third set of determinants of the (SW[M]) distortion in the profits yielded by an inter-ARDEPPS PPR-to-PPR resource allocation contains (1) the percentage of the private benefits yielded by a PPR discovery's use that are attributable to the use's lowering the private cost discovery-users must incur to produce the outputs they would have produced of the relevant product(s) had they not used the discovered process (as opposed to the percentage of those private benefits that the use of the discovery conferred on its users by making it profitable for them to expand their unit outputs) and (2) the counterpart percentage for the sacrificing production-process researchers on their sacrificed projects. The ratio of these percentages is important because (I am convinced) the absolute magnitude of the negative (SW[M]) percentage-distortion in the profits a production-process discovery enables its user(s) to obtain by lowering the cost of the output it (they) would have produced without it is lower than the absolute magnitude of the negative (SW[M]) percentage-distortion in the profits that a (marginal-cost-reducing) production-process discovery enables its user(s) to obtain by expanding their unit outputs (indeed, as we saw, the latter percentage-distortion may even be positive). If my last, relative-absolute-magnitude claim is correct, the (SW[M]) distortion in the profits yielded by an inter-ARDEPPS PPR-to-PPR resource allocation will on this account tend to be negative/positive if the just-specified ratio is higher/lower for the PPR project to which the relevant resource allocation devotes resources than (collectively) for the PPR projects it sacrifices because when the ratio (exceeds one)/(is lower than one) the negative (SW[M]) distortion in $PB_{(U)PPR}$ for the executed PPR project will be absolutely higher/lower than the negative distortion in $PB_{(U)PPR}$ for the sacrificed PPR projects on this account.

The fourth set of determinants of the (SW[M]) distortion in the profits yielded by an inter-ARDEPPS PPR-to-PPR resource allocation relates to any difference between the AJW-effect-related profits that the production-process researcher that executed the PPR project to which the inter-ARDEPPS PPR-to-PPR resource allocation in question devoted resources earned by executing that PPR project and the AJW-effect-related profits that the sacrificing production-process researchers would have earned by executing the PPR projects the relevant resource allocation sacrificed. As Sect. 7.1.3 argued, AJW effects not only increase the profits yielded by the PPR projects they induce they also generate a positive (SW[M]) distortion in those profits. These conclusions have three implications for the AJW-effect-related (SW[M]) distortion in the profits yielded by any PPR project executed exclusively with resources withdrawn from the execution of PPR projects in other ARDEPPSes: (1) the (SW[M]) distortion in the profits yielded by any PPR project executed through any inter-ARDEPPS PPR-to-PPR resource allocation will be positive/ negative when the executer of the PPR project to which the inter-ARDEPPS PPR-to-PPR resource allocation in question devoted resources has an AJW-effect-related incentive to execute that project that was larger/smaller than the AJW-effect-related incentives that the prospective production-process researchers whose PPR projects were sacrificed by the resource allocation in question had to execute the sacrificed projects, (2) since most of the relevant sacrificed PPR projects would not have been executed by public utilities that would have had critical AJW-effect-related incentives to make them had the executed PPR project not competed against them for resources, the AJW-effect-related (SW[M]) distortion in the profits yielded by inter-ADREPPS PPR-to-PPR resource allocations to public utilities whose decisions to execute the executed PPR projects were critically affected by AJW-effect-related incentives will be positive; and (3) since across all cases some (admittedly a small percentage) of the PPR projects that are sacrificed by an inter-ARDEPPS PPR-to-PPR resource allocation would have been made by public utilities whose decisions to execute the sacrificed projects would have been critically influenced by AJW effects had the resource allocations in question not taken place, the AJW-effect-related (SW[M]) distortion in the profits yielded by those PPR projects executed through inter-ARDEPPS PPR-to-PPR resource allocations by production-process researchers that had no AJW-effect-related incentive to make them will if anything be negative (will be negative if one or more of the prospective productions-process researchers whose PPR projects the resource allocation sacrificed had an AJW-effect-related incentive to execute the sacrificed project[s] that would have been critical but for the resource-competition of the researchers that executed the PPR project to which the relevant resource allocation devoted resources).

I want to close this section with two observations that relate to the impact that imperfections in seller competition can have (1) on the step-wise-monopsony or buyer-surplus distortion in the private benefits and profits yielded by the use of a PPR project and (2) on the step-wise-externality distortion in the private benefits and profits yielded by a PPR project. If one defines "monopsony" to cover not only situations in which a buyer faces an upward-sloping supply curve but also situations in which a buyer and seller are operating in what is called a bilateral-monopoly situation (both have power in their respective roles), the monopoly power that a production-process researcher has when selling its intellectual property or the right to use its discovered production process to a buyer that has power may enable the discoverer to obtain higher prices than it would otherwise have been able to obtain and may therefore reduce what could be described as either the negative monopsony distortion or the negative buyer-surplus distortion in the private benefits and profits yielded by the PPR project in question.

Second, as I explained in footnote 7 of this chapter, in a legal regime in which (1) some potential generators of external costs are liable for only those external-accident-and-production costs they are deemed to have generated negligently, (2) decisions not to avoid such costs are deemed negligent only if (A) the decision not to avoid belongs to a category of such decisions whose rejection is assessed for negligence and (B) (put crudely) the private cost of a rejected avoidance-move to the potential avoider was lower than the amount by which the move should have been predicted to reduce the weighted-average-expected (private) accident or pollution losses traditional legal victims should have been predicted to suffer, and (3) decisions not to do production-process research are never assessed for negligence, the probability that a potential production-process researcher will fail to execute a PPR project whose execution would have been *ex ante* economically efficient will increase with the possible production-process researcher's share of the sales of the product to whose production process the PPR would have related—i.e., the likelihood that the benefits that the research will yield by reducing the amount of illnesses and injuries that are generated will be external to the researcher and will critically affect the research's profitability will increase with the researcher's ARDEPPS share. I hasten to add that this conclusion is operative regardless of whether the resources that would be used to execute the accident-and-pollution-loss-reducing PPR project in question would be withdrawn from PPR in other ARDEPPSes, PPR in the same ARDEPPS, or a combination of UO-producing-related, QV-creating-related, and PPR-executing-related uses.

7.2.2.6　The Step-Wise-Monopoly Distortion in the Profits Yielded by Intra-ARDEPPS PPR-to-PPR Resource Allocations

I will start by identifying three possible causes of (SW[M]) distortions in the profits yielded by intra-ARDEPPS PPR-to-PPR resource allocation that I do not think will often be salient and suspect will usually therefore not be TBLE to consider and then identify two possible causes of (SW[M]) distortions in the profits yielded by intra-ARDEPPS PPR-to-PPR resource allocations that I do think are both significant and TBLE to consider when analyzing the economic efficiency of some choices. The three possible causes that I suspect will usually be TBLE to ignore are (1) differences in the negative (SW[M]) percentage-distortions in the private cost of producing the different goods in a given ARDEPPS to whose production process relevant executed and sacrificed PPR projects would relate, (2) differences in the shapes of the demand and marginal-cost curves for the products in a given

ARDEPPS to whose production processes the relevant executed PPR project and the relevant sacrificed PPR project(s) would relate between the outputs of the goods in question that would be produced if the alternative discovered production processes were not used and the outputs of those goods that would be produced if the discovered and to-be-discovered production processes were used (when the use of the discoveries in question would reduce the marginal cost of producing the extra units of output in question), and (3) differences in the ratios for the executed PPR project and the sacrificed PPR project(s) in the ARDEPPS in question of (A) the private benefits the use of the discoveries they respectively (generated)/(would have generated) by lowering the private cost of producing the outputs of the products they respectively (would be)/(would have been) used to produce if the discoveries were not used to (B) the private benefits the use of the respective discoveries (did generate)/(would have generated) by making it profitable for their respective users to increase their unit outputs of the goods to whose production processes the discoveries related. *Inter alia*, I suspect that the first two of these possible causes of non-zero imperfections-in-seller-competition-generated step-wise distortions in the profits yielded by intra-ARDEPPS PPR-to-PPR resource allocations will rarely be operative because (I suspect) the use of the vast majority of production-process discoveries has a similar impact on the private cost of producing all or at least most of the product variants that would be placed (admittedly somewhat-arbitrarily) in any ARDEPPS.

Each of the two possible causes of non-zero (SW[M]) distortions in the profits yielded by (some) intra-ARDEPPS PPR-to-PPR resource allocations have the special characteristics of being operative only when other conditions are fulfilled. The first possible cause is externality-related. For reasons that footnote 7 of this chapter explains, in legal jurisdictions in which some accident-and-pollution-loss generators are liable for the accident-and-pollution losses they impose on others only if their failure to avoid is deemed negligent but such injurers' decisions not to do research into less-accident-and-pollution-loss-prone production processes is never assessed for negligence, the imperfection in seller competition associated with a firm's having a large share of the sales of the product(s) to whose production process an accident-and-pollution-loss-reducing PPR project would relate might generate a positive (SW[M]) distortion in the profits the firm can earn by substituting a PPR project that would not lead to a discovery whose use would (A) reduce accident-and-pollution losses by more than it would increase other production costs while (B) increasing non-accident-and-pollution-loss production costs for (2) a PPR project that would lead to the discovery of a production process whose use would have the above effects.

The second possible cause of non-zero imperfections-in-seller-competition-generated (SW[M]) distortions in the profits yielded by an intra-ARDEPPS PPR-to-PPR resource allocation is AJW-effect-related. The imperfections in seller price-competition that lead a firm to be classified as a public utility may lead the firm to substitute a less-inherently-profitable PPR project that is designed to discover a more-capital-intensive production process for a more-inherently-profitable

PPR project that is designed to discover a production process that is less-capital-intensive if the firm is subjected to "fair-rate-of-return public-utility-pricing regulation" by a regulatory commission that does not exclude from the regulators' rate-bases "imprudent"—i.e., inherently-unprofitable—investments. The imperfections in seller price-competition and investment competition that lead to firms being subjected to public-utility-pricing regulations that give them AJW-effect-related incentives may also generate a critical positive (SW[M]) distortion in the profits yielded by an intra-ARDEPPS PPR-to-PPR resource allocation if the firm that executed the PPR project to which the relevant resource allocation devoted resources had a larger AJW-effect-related incentive to execute the PPR project the relevant resource allocation executed than did the firm whose PPR project was sacrificed by the relevant resource allocation because the executing firm had more profits in its prevented-profit pool than did the sacrificing production-process researcher and therefore could outbid the sacrificer for the resources involved (a situation that would generate economic inefficiency if the executer's project was more-inherently-non-profitable than was the sacrificed PPR project and, taken together, all exemplars of all other Pareto imperfections did not affect the relative economic efficiency of the two projects).

7.2.2.7   The Step-Wise-Monopoly Distortion in the Profits Yielded by Allocations of Resources from Just-Extra-Marginal UO-Producing-and-Consuming and PPR-Executing-and-Using Uses to the Creation and Use of an Economics-Marginal QV Investment

I have previously argued that the step-wise-monopoly distortions in the private benefits that the "use" of any just-extra-marginal unit of output would confer on the UO producer and that the use of any just-extra-marginal PPR project would confer on the production-process researcher are negative and that the step-wise-monopoly distortion that would be generated by any allocation of resources from UO-producing and PPR-executing resource-uses to a QV-creating resource-use is positive. This last conclusion implies that if, taken together, all exemplars of all other types of Pareto imperfections would not cause the aggregate distortion in the profits yielded by such resource allocations to differ from the (SW[M]) distortion in those profits (though they might affect the (SW[M]) distortion in those profits) (1) the aggregate distortion in the profits yielded by the economics-marginal exemplars of this category of resource allocations would be positive, and (2) all such resource allocations in this category whose profit-yields were lower than the positive step-wise-monopoly and aggregate distortion in these profit-yields would be economically inefficient (would reduce economic efficiency by the difference between the positive distortion in their profits and the profits they yielded).[23]

7.2.2.8 The Step-Wise-Monopoly Distortion in the Profits Yielded by Allocations of Resources from the Production of Just-Extra-Marginal Units of Output and the Creation of Just-Extra-Marginal QV Investments to the Execution of an Economics-Marginal PPR Project

I have previously argued that the step-wise-monopoly distortion in the private benefits that the production of a just-extra-marginal unit of output would confer on its producer is negative, that the step-wise-monopoly distortion in the private benefits that the use of a just-extra-marginal QV investment would confer on its creator is positive, and that the step-wise-monopoly distortion in the private benefits that the use of any economics-marginal PPR project confers on the researcher is negative. These conclusions do not justify any qualitative conclusion about the size of the step-wise-monopoly distortion in the profits yielded by any economics-marginal allocation of resources from just-extra-marginal UO-producing and QV-creating uses to an economics-marginal PPR-executing use. Concomitantly, even if, taken together, all exemplars of all other types of Pareto imperfections would not cause the aggregate distortion in the profits yielded by such resource allocations to differ from the (SW[M]) distortion in those profits (though they might affect that (SW[M]) distortion), the conclusions I have reached about the signs of the (SW[M]) distortions in the relevant $PB_{(U)UO}$, $PB_{(U)QV}$, and $PB_{(U)PPR}$ figures would not justify any conclusions about the sign of the step-wise-monopoly distortion in the profits yielded by exemplars of the category of resources allocations with which this section is concerned or about the economic efficiency of those resource allocations.

7.2.2.9 The Step-Wise-Monopoly Distortion in the Profits Yielded by Allocations of Resources from Just-Extra-Marginal QV-Investment-Creating and Just-Extra-Marginal PPR-Executing Uses to Economics-Marginal Unit-Output-Producing Uses

I have previously argued that the step-wise-monopoly distortion in the private benefits that the use of any QV investment confers on its creator is positive, that the step-wise-monopoly distortion in the private benefits that the use of any PPR project confers on its executer is negative, and that the step-wise-monopoly distortion in the private benefits that the production and sale of any unit of output confers on the unit-output producer is negative. These conclusions do not justify any conclusion about the sign of the (SW[M]) distortion in the profits yielded by resource allocations from the creation of just-extra-marginal QV investments and the execution of just-extra-marginal PPR projects to the production of a marginal unit of output. However, my empirical beliefs (1) about the percentage of the resources devoted to producing a marginal unit of output that would be withdrawn respectively from QV-investment creation and PPR execution—viz., that far more of the resources devoted to such UO production are withdrawn from QV-investment creation than from PPR-execution, (2) about the relative absolute magnitudes of the percentage-distortions in the private benefits that the use of QV

investments confers on their creators and the use of PPR confers on its executers—
viz., that the absolute magnitude of the former positive percentage-distortion is
higher than the absolute magnitude of the latter negative percentage-distortion—
and (3) about the absolute magnitudes of the (SW[M]) percentage-distortions in the
relevant $PB_{(U)QV}$, $PB_{(U)PPR}$, and $PB_{(U)UO}$ figures—viz., that the absolute magnitude
of the positive (SW[M]) percentage-distortion in $PB_{(U)QV}$ exceeds the absolute
magnitude of the negative (SW[M]) distortion in $PB_{(U)UO}$ sufficiently to outweigh
the fact that some of the resources devoted to the relevant UO production will be
withdrawn from sacrificed PPR-executing uses for which the relevant (SW[M])
percentage-distortion is negative—lead me to suspect that the (SW[M]) distortion in
the profits that would be yielded by resource allocations from just-extra-marginal
QV-creating and PPR-executing resource-uses to an economics-marginal
UO-producing resource-use would be negative.

7.2.2.10 The Step-Wise-Monopoly Distortion in the Profits Yielded by Decisions to Substitute One Known Production Process for Another

I can think of two reasons why there may be a (critical) positive (SW[M]) distortion
in the profits yielded by a decision to use one known production process rather than
another to produce a particular good. The first is a general reason: imperfections in
seller competition can either (1) generate a larger positive step-wise distortion in the
private cost to the producer in question of the resources it must employ to use the
rejected production process than in the private cost to the producer in question of
the resources it must employ to use the selected production process or (more
likely in my judgment) (2) generate an absolutely smaller negative step-wise distortion in the private cost to the producer in question of the resources it must
employ to use the rejected production process than in the private cost to the producer in question of the resources it must employ to use the selected production
process. The second of these conditions might be fulfilled, for example, if the two
relevant production processes employed different resources, both sets of resources
would be withdrawn from the production of units of other products, and the
weighted-average P/MC ratio of those products from whose production resources
would be withdrawn if the selected production process were used was lower than
the weighted-average P/MC ratio of those products from whose production
resources would have been withdrawn had the rejected production process been
used. I have no doubt that in some instances the extant imperfections in seller
price-competition will for this reason generate what would be a critical step-wise
distortion in the profits yielded by the substitution of the selected for the rejected
production process if, all tolled, the extant exemplars of all other types of Pareto
imperfections would not alter the aggregate distortion in the profits yielded by the
relevant choice by altering the six other-type-of-Pareto-imperfection-oriented
step-wise-distortions in those profits. However, I doubt that it will ever be TBLE
to consider this possibility or any analogous possibility associated with the percentages of the resources that the use of the selected production process would have
caused to be withdrawn respectively from UO-producing, QV-investment-creating,

and PPR-executing uses' differing from the percentages of the resources that the use of the rejected production processes would have caused to be withdrawn from those alternative categories of alternative uses.

The second reason why there may be a (critical) positive (SW[M]) distortion in the profits yielded by a decision to use one known production process rather than another is related to AJW effects. If the relevant producer faces imperfections in seller competition that result in its being classified as a public utility and being subjected to "fair-rate-of-return public-utility-pricing regulation," it may have an AJW-effect-related incentive to adopt a more-capital-intensive but more-private-and-allocatively-costly production process rather than a less-capital-intensive but less-privately-and-allocatively-costly production process under conditions that generated a positive (SW[M]) distortion in the private benefits that this selection confers on the producer by enabling it to secure profits from what would otherwise be its prevented-profit pool.

7.2.2.11 The Step-Wise-Monopoly Distortion in the Profits Generated by Resource Allocations of a Final Good to One Final Consumer Rather Than to Another (by a Seller's Decision to Supply a Particular Unit of Its Product to One Buyer Rather Than to Another)

The imperfection in seller price-competition a seller faces will tend to result in its supplying one or more units of its product to buyers who place a lower dollar-value on it rather than to buyers who place a higher dollar-value on it—i.e., to generate conventional consumption-optimum misallocation—when the seller in question finds it profitable to engage in conventional price discrimination despite the fact that it does not find it profitable or possible to define the classes of buyers to whose respective members it is charging different prices "perfectly" (in particular, so as to avoid deterring any buyer who is being charged the higher price from purchasing the seller's good despite the fact that it would have been willing to purchase that good at the lower price the seller was charging some other potential buyer that actually purchased it). Assume, for example, that a seller that faces imperfect-price competition finds it most profitable to charge one subset of potential buyers $18 and another subset of potential buyers $12 despite the fact that some members of the former group place a lower-than-$18 value on the product and some members of the latter group place a higher-than-$12 value on the product. In such a situation, the seller may supply a unit of its product to a buyer to whom it is offering a $12 price who values it (say) at $13 rather than to a different buyer to whom it is offering an $18 price who values it (say) at $17. If, taken together, the exemplars of the other types of Pareto imperfections the relevant economy contains do not affect the resulting economic inefficiency, $4 in conventional consumption-optimum misallocation will have been generated by the imperfection in seller price-competition that led to the relevant seller's practicing price discrimination.

I have so far not used the distortion-analysis conceptual system to analyze this situation because, to be honest, I do not usually think it desirable to do so. However, this conceptual scheme could be used to describe the preceding situation. To do so, the relevant choice would be described as a seller's choice to sell a unit of its product that has already been produced to one buyer rather than to another when the alternative to selling it to one of the buyers in question would be to destroy it in some privately-and-allocatively-costless way. To simplify, I will assume that the sale of the unit for $12 to the lower-dollar-valuing buyer will not affect the profits the seller realizes by making other sales and that the sale of the relevant unit to the other buyer for $17 would not have affected the profits the seller would have realized by making other sales. On these assumptions, (1) the private benefits to the seller of making the sale for $12 are $12, (2) the buyer-surplus-related (SW[M]) distortion in those private benefits are (−$1), (3) the private cost to the seller of making the sale for $12 is $0 since the alternative to its making the sale is to destroy the relevant unit in a privately-costless way, (4) the allocative cost the seller generates by making the sale to one buyer for $12 when the unit could have been supplied to another buyer who would have valued it at $17 is $17, (5) the (SW[M]) distortion in the private cost of selling the unit to its actual purchaser is (−$17), (6) the profit the seller obtained by selling the unit in question for $12 rather than destroying it at zero private cost is $12, (7) the (SW[M]) distortion in those profits is (−$1) *minus* (−$17) or (+$16), and (8) the economic efficiency of the sale (if it is not affected by the interaction of all the other Pareto imperfections the relevant economy contains) is (−$4)—i.e., equals the profits it yielded (+$12) *minus* the (SW[M]) distortion in those profits, which equals ([the step-wise-monopoly distortion in its private benefits] *minus* [the step-wise-monopoly distortion in its private costs] or ([−$1]−[−$17] = $16). (I warned you that this account would not be particularly informative.)

7.2.2.12   The Economic Inefficiency that Imperfections in Seller Competition Will Generate, Given the Fact that the Economy in Question Will Contain Various Pareto Imperfections at Various Distributions of Income and Wealth, by Increasing Poverty and Income/Wealth Inequality

This section will not reference the distortion-analysis conceptual system, though that system could be used to explain its central conclusion. Its central point is that— because in all extant societies imperfections in seller price-competition and imperfections in investment competition increase poverty and income/wealth inequality—imperfections in seller-competition generate economic inefficacy in all the ways that Sect. 1.4.3 argued poverty and material inequality increase economic inefficiency.

*****

This chapter has executed exhaustive and exhausting analyses of the distortions in the private benefits conferred by, private cost imposed by, and profits yielded by all the most important categories of resource allocations. This chapter can serve as a template for analogous analyses of the step-wise-monopsony, externality, tax-on-the-margin-of-income, resource-allocator-non-sovereignty, resource-allocator-non-maximization, and buyer-surplus step-wise distortions in the private benefits, private costs, and profits associated with each of the categories of resource allocations the chapter addressed. Not to worry. I will not proceed to lumber you with six chapters replicating this chapter's analyses for a different type of Pareto imperfection. Considerations of publishing costs, reader patience, and writer endurance have persuaded me to substitute for six such chapters one chapter (Chap. 8) that will make what I take to be the most salient points about these other categories of single-type-of-Pareto-imperfection-oriented step-wise distortions.

Notes

1. Admittedly, a seller's facing imperfect price-competition is neither a sufficient nor a necessary condition for its sales' generating buyer surplus. Imperfect seller price-competition is not a sufficient condition for the relevant seller's sales' generating buyer surplus for two reasons: (1) a seller that faces imperfect seller price-competition (A) may face a demand curve (i) that is horizontal between the horizontal axis and the output at which the associated marginal-revenue curve cuts the seller's marginal-cost-curve from above, (ii) that is higher than its marginal-cost curve at that output, and (iii) that is associated with a marginal-revenue curve that is sufficiently discontinuous at this output for the seller's profit-maximizing single per-unit price to equal the height of the demand curve over its horizontal range and (B) may not find it profitable to engage price discrimination and (2) a seller that faces a downward-sloping demand curve may find it most profitable to practice perfect price discrimination when selling its product to each of its customers. At least in the short run, a seller's facing imperfect seller price-competition is not a necessary condition for its sales' generating buyer surplus because a seller that faces perfect seller price-competition may mistakenly set a price below its marginal costs (below its profit-maximizing price). I hasten to add that I will be careful not to double-count buyer-surplus-generated step-wise distortions: No buyer-surplus-oriented (SW) distortion that is attributed to the seller's facing imperfect price-competition will be counted again as a (SW[BS]) distortion. For a diagrammatic illustration of the argument for the conclusion articulated earlier in this footnote, see Markovits (2008), pp. 215–219 and its Diagram A.3.

2. For an explanation of why this attribution is not perfectly accurate, see note 1 of this chapter *supra*.

3. Two categories of production-process researchers may choose to license others to use the production process its PPR project discovers: (1) independent research-firms which by definition do not produce the product(s) to whose production process their discovery relates and (2) vertically-integrated firms that both execute PPR (say, into the production process that could be used to produce some product G they produce) and produce the product G to whose production process their PPR relates but find it profitable not only to use the discovered process themselves but to license other producers of G and/or of product-variants $G1...n$ that are competitive with G to use it as well.

4. For simplicity, I ignore the possibility that any sacrificed average-total-cost-reducing production-process discovery might have increased the marginal cost of producing not only additional units of product G but, more relevantly, the units of G whose production would have been marginal and intra-marginal had its producer or their producers been prohibited from using the production process the sacrificed PPR project would have discovered.

5. For example, assume (1) that the allocative variable cost of producing a given output of a sacrificed product is $1500, (2) that the private variable cost of doing so is $1000, and (3) that the use of a discovered production process will reduce by 10% the private and allocative variable cost of producing that output (the amount of resources required to produce that output). On these assumptions, the use of the discovered process will reduce the private variable cost the producer would have to incur to produce the relevant output of the product in question by 10% of $1000 or $100 but will generate 10% of $1500 or $150 in allocative-cost savings—i.e., the 50% negative distortion in the private variable cost of producing the relevant quantity of the relevant product with the old production process will translate into a 50% negative distortion in the private-cost savings the use of the discovered production process generates (when an X percent distortion in a private figure is defined to equal [the difference between the allocative figure and the private figure] divided by the private figure).

6. The concept of "the competitiveness of two products" requires detailed specification. In my usage, roughly speaking, in contexts in which sellers are setting individualized prices to each potential customer, the competitiveness of two products is defined to reference (1) the sum of the amounts by which each reduces the competitive advantages the other enjoys in its relations with those buyers it is "privately-best-placed" to supply or privately-equal-best-placed to supply (again, roughly speaking, the sum of its buyer-preference advantages and marginal-cost advantages in its relations with those buyers it can profit by supplying on terms contained in offers no rival would find profitable to match, strategic considerations aside) *plus* (2) the sum of the amounts by which each reduces the natural oligopolistic margins the other can obtain *plus* (3) the sum by which each reduces the contrived oligopolistic margins the other can (profitability) obtain. (In my usage, a seller initiates an oligopolistic-pricing sequence when it sets a price that it would not have found *ex ante* profitable but for its *ex ante* belief that its rivals' responses would or might be influenced by their perception that it would or might react to their responses. In my usage, oligopolistic pricing is said to be "natural" and the higher $(P - MC)$ margins it yields are said to be "natural-oligopolistic margins" when the rivals anticipate the initiator's relevant reactions because they believe that the relevant buyer will give the initiator an opportunity to beat their undercutting response and that the imitator will find it inherently profitable to do so. In my usage, oligopolistic pricing is said to be "contrived" and the higher $(P - MC)$ margins it yields are

said to be "contrived" when the rivals anticipate the initiator's relevant reactions because the initiator has communicated to them its intention to react to their undercutting or not undercutting in one or more ways that would render the undercutting unprofitable for them despite the reaction's inherent unprofitability for the initiator—i.e., to the imitator's promising to respond to their not undercutting by foregoing the opportunity to make profits by beating their contrived-oligopolistic offers to buyers they are privately-best-placed to supply and/or by threatening to retaliate against their undercutting (say) by making inherently-unprofitable offers to buyers the rivals are privately-best-placed to supply. For a discussion that illuminates the concept of "the competitiveness of two goods," see Markovits (2014b) at 54–70. The concept of the "competitiveness" of two goods should not be confused with the concept of their "substitutability." The latter concept references only the extent to which each good reduces the buyer-preference advantage the other enjoys (ignores the possible differences in the marginal cost of producing the two goods). For scholarly work that conflates the substitutability of two goods with their competitiveness, see Robinson (1933) at p. 17. For government antitrust guidelines that conflate the substitutability of two goods with their competitiveness, see United States Department of Justice and Federal Trade Commission (1992) Section 1.11 and 2010 at Section 4.1.1.4.

7. Some explanation is required. In a tort-law regime (such as the current common law of torts) in which (1) at least some injurers (namely, those whose activities are not deemed "utlrahazardous") are liable for the accident and/or pollution losses their conduct imposes on others only if (1) they are deemed to have caused those losses by negligently rejecting an avoidance-move that would have militated against their inflicting accident-and/or-pollution losses on their actual victim(s) which avoidance-move belongs to a category of avoidance-moves whose rejection is assessed for negligence, (2) the rejection of an avoidance-move that belongs to a category of avoidance-moves whose rejection is assessed for negligence is deemed negligent (I am simplifying) if and only if the private cost of the avoidance-move to the potential injurer is lower than the amount by which it should have been predicted to reduce the accident-and/or-pollution losses that the potential injurer would impose on others, and (3) decisions not to do research designed to discover production processes whose use would reduce the accident-and/or-pollution losses that the production of relevant quantities of the relevant good would impose on others are never assessed for negligence (even when the decisions are made by producers whose production generates the accident-and/or-pollution losses that could have been avoided), the negative distortion that this legal regime will generate in the private benefits that a PPR project that would lead to the discovery of a production process whose use would (1) reduce the accident-an/or-pollution external costs imposed on others by the production of relevant outputs of the goods in question, (2) reduce the sum of the internal production costs and the

accident-and/or-pollution costs imposed on others (on traditional legal victims) by the production of relevant outputs of these goods, but (3) increase the internal costs of production (accident-and/or-pollution-related external costs aside) that the production of the relevant output of those goods would generate will confer on the production-process researcher that executes it will increase with the quantity of the good(s) G $(G1...n)$ that the prospective researcher in question produced (and hence with that researcher/producer's share of the sales of good[s] G $[G1...n]$). Thus, the relevant legal regime would generate no negative distortion in the PB_{PPR} for that relevant category of PPR projects if the researcher was an independent research-firm (a firm that produced no G). If no producer of G had any monopsony power and nothing else caused such an independent research-firm to allow its licensees to obtain buyer surplus when purchasing the right to use its discovery, such an independent research-firm would sell the right to use its discovery to each producer of G for a price that equals the difference between the amount by which the use of the discovered process would reduce the accident-and/or-pollution costs that producer's production of G would generate and the extra production costs that producer would have to incur to use the discovered process, licensee-fees aside, since—once the production process described above was discovered—each producer of G's production of G with the old production process would be negligent (would render it liable for the accident-and/or-production costs it could have avoided generating by using the discovered process). Absent monopsony, pricing costs that prevent the discoverer from eliminating all buyer surplus, and production-process-researcher error in pricing the right to use its discovered process, the operating profits an independent researcher could earn by licensing the use of its discovery would therefore equal the amount by which the actual use of the discovery would increase economic efficiency in an oPp economy—the difference between the reduction in accident-and/or-pollution costs the process' use would generate and the added (non-licensee-fee) production costs its use would generate. By way of contrast, the legal regime in question would yield a negative distortion in $PB_{(U)PPR}$ for such a PPR project if it were to be executed by an integrated (production-process researcher)/(producer of G) that produced 100% of the G that was produced: in particular, far from yielding any such researcher/producer any benefits, the discovery would impose costs on such an actor equal to the amount of extra production costs it would have to incur to use the discovered process (since the discovery would make the integrated researcher/G-producer liable for the accident-and/or-pollution costs it could have avoided generating by using the discovered process by making its rejection of that process negligent whereas it would not have been liable for generating those accident-and/or-pollution external costs before the discovery was made if I assume as I will that, before the discovery was made, the firm's generation of those accident-and/or-pollution costs would not have been negligent). For such an integrated researcher/producer, the PPR project in question would be a lose/lose proposition: would involve the spending of money to do research whose successful execution would impose losses on the researcher/ producer in question. Obviously, the negative distortion in $PB_{(U)PPR}$ that the legal regime under consideration would generate for any producer/(potential discoverer) of the kind of production process described above will increase with the amount of G (the share of G's production) the relevant researcher produced in its capacity as a producer of G because it will equal the extra production costs the discovery would result in the integrated researcher/producer's incurring (which will increase with its sales of G) *plus* the increase in economic efficiency that the use of the discovered production process would generate. I want to close this footnote by making two additional points. The first may or may not be worth making. If it is appropriate to assume that there is a positive correlation between the (production-process researcher)/(producer of G's) share of the sales of G (or $G1...n$) and the imperfections of the price-competition it faces when selling G, this law-of-torts-generated negative distortion in the private benefits of executing some PPR projects that are designed to discover external-accident-and-pollution-loss-reducing production processes might also be said to be an imperfections-in-seller-price-competition-generated (SW[M]) distortion in $PB_{(U)PPR}$ for the PPR projects in question (though, admittedly, such a designation would be misleading in that the relevant imperfections in seller price-competition would not be causing the step-wise private-benefits distortion in question—would simply be correlates of the relevant causes). The second and final point is clearly worth making. All the analyses of this footnote apply *mutatis mutandis* to product R&D that is designed to discover new products whose production and consumption are less accident-and/or-pollution-loss-generating since the failure of an injurer (or anyone else) not to execute such research is also never assessed for negligence and many of the actors that could execute such research are not engaged in ultrahazardous activities (are liable only if found negligent).

8. Kamien and Schwartz (1975).
9. To see why this is the case when the relevant DD curve is linear and the seller prices its product by setting a single per-unit price and allowing buyers to purchase as much as they wish at that price, note that, under those conditions: (1) buyer surplus equals either area DFH or area DFB (the sum of the differences between the heights of the DD and MR curves between output zero and the actual output AB), (2) both these areas contain area DFJ, (3) area DFH also contains area DJH while area DFB contains area JFB, (4) both of these areas are right triangles whose angles have the same magnitudes (thus, angle BJF equals angle DJH), and (5) area DJH will equal area JFB (so that area DFH equals area DFB [in both cases, the buyer surplus generated]) if and only if HJ = JF (the bases of the two right triangles are equal).
10. Obviously, if the relevant production-process researcher did not use exclusively itself the production process the PPR project in question (did discover)/(would have discovered), any imperfection in seller price-competition if faced/(would have faced) when selling the right to license others to use the production

process the PPR project in question discovered/(would have discovered) and any imperfection in seller price-competition it faced/(would have faced) when licensing other producers of G (or $G1...n$) to use the discovered production process would generate negative (SW[M]) distortions in $PB_{(U)PPR}$ for the PPR project in question whose existences would strengthen the argument for the conclusion that the imperfections-in-seller-price-competition-generated (SW [M]) distortion in $PB_{(U)PPR}$ is negative.

11. For an analysis that considers the case in which the use of the discovered production process would increase MC_G, see Markovits (2008), pp. 220–222.

12. Namely, on the assumption that the relevant imperfections in seller price-competition deflate MC_G and therefore cause $(MLC_{G/n} - MLC_{G/o})$ to exceed $(MG_{G/n} - MC_{G/o})$.

13. Just as there is no universally-applicable non-arbitrary way to define the extent to which price competition is imperfect—for example, to decide whether to measure the imperfectness of price competition by $(P - MC)$, (P/MC), $([P - MC]/P)$, or $([P - MC]/MC)$ or how to take account of the fact that one or more sellers are charging different prices for different units of their respective products, are charging lump-sum fees as well as per-unit prices, or are using tie-ins or reciprocity agreements to sell their products, there is no universally-applicable non-arbitrary way to define the extent to which QV-investment competition or PPR competition in a given ARDEPPS in imperfect—for example, to decide whether to measure the imperfectness of such competition by the highest supernormal profit-rate generated by any (QV investment)/(PPR project) in the relevant ARDEPPS, by the weighted-average supernormal profit-rate generated by all QV investments/PPR projects in the relevant ARDEPPS, by the absolute difference between the quantity of QV investment/ PPR in a given ARDEPPS that would result in its most-supra-normally-profitable QV investments/PPR projects generating just a normal rate-of-return and the quantity of QV investments or PPR projects in the ARDEPPS in question in equilibrium, by the ratio of the former quantity to the latter, etc.

14. For further explanations, see Markovits (2014a) at pp. 47–49.

15. For a more detailed explanation of these conclusions and some diagrammatic illustrations of the relevant analyses, see *id.* at pp. 49–68.

16. Even at this juncture, it may be worth pointing out that, in the case in which the investment in question deters an equally-large investment in the same category, the fact that the investor that did or might make the investment in question had a monopolistic investment-disincentive to make it would be associated with a negative distortion in its profitability: (1) the fact that the investment in question would reduce the profit-yields of the investor's other investments by more than they would be reduced by the investment in question would deter because the investment in question was more competitive with the investor's other projects than the deterred investment would have been reducers the investment in question's profitability but has no bearing on the relative allocative efficiency of

the investment in question and the rival investment it would deter, which would "overlap" less with the investments of the investor in question by "overlapping" more with other investments in the relevant area of product-space, and (2) the fact that the investment in question would induce owners of extant rival investments to respond in ways that would be more costly to the investor in question than the responses they would make to the deterred rival investment would make the investment in question less profitable for the investor than it would otherwise be but would—if anything—make the investment in question more economically efficient than it would otherwise be (to the extent that I am right in concluding that pro-competitive pricing-moves tend to increase economic efficiency [by reducing the total amount of QV investment in the economy in question, by increasing total PPR in the economy in question, and by decreasing the amount of material inequality and poverty in the economy in question]).

17. Even at this juncture, it may be worth pointing out that natural-oligopolistic investment-disincentives that reduce the equilibrium quantity of investment in the relevant category in the ARDEPPS in which they are operative by deterring the established firms that face them from making investments they would otherwise have made will tend to increase economic efficiency when the relevant investments are QV investments. If I am correct in concluding that economies tend to have too much QV investment from the perspective of economic efficiency and will tend to decrease economics efficiency when the relevant investments are PPR investments if I am correct in concluding that economies tend to have too little PPR from the perspective of economic efficiency. The same conclusions will apply to monopolistic investment-disincentives that reduce equilibrium investment in the ARDEPPEes in which they are operative. Obviously, the opposite conclusions will apply to monopolistic investment-incentives that increase equilibrium investment in the ARDEPPSes in which they are operative. Admittedly, the preceding observations ignore the possible effects of such disincentives and incentives on inter-ARDEPPS QV-to-QV and inter-ARDEPPS PPR-to-PPR misallocation.

18. It may be worth noting that investments made by investors that would not have perceived them to be at-least-normally-profitable *ex ante* but for their belief that they had or might have a monopolistic investment-incentive to make them are properly deemed to be "predatory"—i.e., to violate the specific-anticompetitive-intent test of illegality that many antitrust or competition laws promulgate. According to that test of illegality, covered conduct is illegal if its perpetrator's *ex ante* perception that it was *ex ante* at least normally profitable was critically affected by the perpetrator's belief that it would reduce the absolute attractiveness of the offers against which it would have to compete in the future in one or more ways that would render the conduct profitable though economically inefficient if one ignored any profit-distortions generated by the other Pareto imperfections the economy in question contained. For more details, see Markovits (2014a) at pp. 582–605.

19. For analyses of a wide variety of issues relating to the historical and contemporary definitions of "public utilities," the ways in which their regulation has changed through time, the intellectual and political causes of these changes, and the economic efficiency and moral desirability of the various regulations that have been applied to "public utilities," see Symposium on Public Utilities 2018.

20. See Averch and Johnson (1962) and Wellisz (1963). The AJW effect includes not only making subnormally-profitable additional QV investment and executing subnormally-profitable additional PPR projects but also substituting more-privately-expensive more-capital-intensive production processes for less-privately-expensive less-capital-intensive production processes, executing less-profitable PPR projects designed to discover more-capital-intensive production processes for more-profitable PPR projects designed to discover less-capital-intensive production processes, putting managers or workers on annual salaries rather than hourly wages (if the former but not the latter are deemed to be part of the firm's rate-base), buying rather than leasing buildings, machinery, and motor vehicles. For a fuller discussion that covers possibilities that Averch & Johnson and Wellisz did not address, see Markovits (2018) at pp. 889–893.

21. I wrote "on this account" because the statement that follows ignores the (SW [M]) distortions in the profits that imperfections in seller competition generate in other ways in the profits yielded by the AJW-effect-induced additional QV investments and PPR projects in question.

22. I wrote "on this account" once again for the same reason that I did so after "(2)" in this sentence of the text. See note 21 *supra*.

23. Recall that, given the existence of economies of scale in creating any QV investment—i.e., the existence of scale barriers to incumbent QV-investment expansions and new entry, the economics-marginal QV investment in any ARDEPPS will often (indeed, will usually) generate some supernormal profits.

References

Averch, H., & Johnson, L. H. (1962). Behavior of the firm under regulatory constraint. *American Economic Review, 52,* 1052–1069.

Kamien, M. I., & Schwartz, N. L. (1975). Market structure and innovation: A survey. *Journal of Economics Literature, 13,* 1–37.

Markovits, R. (2008). *Truth or economics: On the definition, prediction, and relevance of economic efficiency*. New Haven and London: Yale University Press.

Markovits, R. (2014a). *Economics and the interpretation and application of U.S. and E.U. antitrust law* Vol. I *Basic concepts and oligopolistic and predatory conduct*. Heidelberg, Dordrecht, New York, London: Springer.

Markovits, R. (2014b). *Economics and the interpretation and application of U.S. and E.U. antitrust law* Vol. II *Economics-based legal analyses of mergers, vertical practices, and joint ventures*. Heidelberg, Dordrecht, New York, London: Springer.

Markovits, R. (2018). "Public utility" regulation: Some economic and moral analyses. *Yale Journal on Regulation, 35,* 875–907.

Robinson, J. (1933). *The theory of imperfect competition.* London: Macmillan & Co.

United States Department of Justice and Federal Trade Commission. (1992). *Horizontal merger guidelines.*

United States Department of Justice and Federal Trade Commission. (2010). *Horizontal merger guidelines.*

Wellisz, S. (1963). Regulation of natural gas pipeline companies: An economic analysis. *Journal of Political Economy, 71,* 30–43.

The Various Non-Monopoly Step-Wise Private-Benefit, Private-Cost, and Profit Distortions

8

Abstract

This chapter focuses on the six types of Pareto imperfections other than the imperfections in seller competition with which Chap. 7 is concerned. This chapter does not attempt to be as comprehensive as Chap. 7. Instead, each of its six sections makes some salient comments on (1) the step-wise distortions that all exemplars of one of the six types of Pareto imperfections other than imperfections in seller competition generate in the private benefits, private costs, and profits that members of various functionally-defined categories of resource allocations, respectively, confer on, impose on, and yield the resource-user to which the relevant category of resource allocations allocates resources and (2) the causal or correlational relationship between the magnitudes of the step-wise private-benefit, private-cost, and profit distortions for indicated resource allocations generated by all exemplars of the type of Pareto imperfections on which the section in question is focusing and the magnitudes of its counterparts for one or more of the same step-wise distortions that all exemplars of another type of Pareto imperfections generate.

The monopsonies, externalities, taxes on the margin of income, resource-allocator non-sovereignties, resource-allocator non-maximizations, and buyer surplus on which this chapter focuses can generate step-wise distortions in the private-benefit, private-cost, and profit figures associated with exemplars of all the various categories of resource allocations I have distinguished in all the same ways that the imperfections in seller competition on which Chap. 7 focuses can do so, and resource-allocator non-sovereignty and non-maximization can cause economic inefficiency not only by critically distorting the profits yielded by particular resource allocations but also by leading resource-users to execute resource-uses that are both unprofitable and economically inefficient and to reject resource-uses that would have been both profitable and economically efficient (though the human errors to which non-sovereignty and/or non-maximization lead when they do not

© Springer Nature Switzerland AG 2020
R. S. Markovits, *Welfare Economics and Second-Best Theory*,
https://doi.org/10.1007/978-3-030-43360-4_8

perfectly counteract each other may increase economic efficiency by causing resource allocators to execute unprofitable resource-uses whose execution was economically efficient and to reject profitable resource-uses whose execution would have been economically inefficient). However, the six sections of this chapter will not execute comprehensive analyses of all of these possibilities for the type of Pareto imperfection on which the section in question focuses. Instead, each section of this chapter will be limited to making what I take to be the most salient points about the step-wise distortions the type of Pareto imperfection on which it focuses generates. My decision to proceed in this way is favored by considerations of publishing cost, reader patience, and writer endurance.

8.1 The Step-Wise-Monopsony Distortions in the Private Benefits, Private Costs, and Profits that Exemplars of Various Functional Categories of Resource Allocations Respectively Confer on, Impose on, and Yield the Actors to Which Those Resource Allocations Allocate Resources: Some Comments

Section 8.1 makes six sets of monopsony-related points, some of which were made in Chap. 6 and some of which are extensions of points made in Chap. 6. The first is that the expressions "monopsony power" and "buyer power" are used to reference two related but distinct phenomena: (1) a buyer's facing an upward-sloping supply curve (paradigmatically because the buyer is the only potential purchaser of a resource or product whose [ARDEPPS-] supply curve is upward-sloping) and (2) a buyer's possessing the power to secure price-concessions (or other terms-of-trade concessions) from a non-perfectly-competitive potential supplier because it is sufficiently irreplaceable as a buyer to be able to do so.

Second, monopsony power in both these senses can exist only if one or more relevant suppliers could obtain supra-competitive prices if the relevant buyer did not possess monopsony power (only if [in the upward-sloping-supply-curve case] the suppliers of the intra-marginal units of the relevant resource or product enjoyed competitive advantages when selling the units in question or only if [in the bilateral-monopoly concession-securing case] the relevant supplier could give the buyer a concession without preventing itself from realizing a normal rate-of-return on its supply of the product in question).[1]

Third, at least seven subsets of relevant upward-sloping-supply-curve-facing monopsonists can be distinguished: (1) buyers of the unit of any extant product to whose production a resource allocation of interest devoted resources and prospective buyers of these units of extant products whose production was sacrificed by a resource allocation of interest, (2) unit-output producers to which/from which a resource allocation of interest devoted/withdrew resources in their capacities as buyers of resources or intermediate products they did use/would have used to produce the units of output to/from whose production that resource allocation devoted/withdrew resources, (3) buyers of any new product that was/would have been created by a QV investment whose creation a resource allocation of interest secured/sacrificed, (4) QV investors/sacrificing QV investors to which/from which a resource allocation of interest allocated/withdrew resources in their capacities as buyers of resources or intermediate products they did employ/would have employed to create or use their respective created/sacrificed QV investments, (5) buyers of any good whose cost of production would be reduced by the use of a production process that would be discovered by a PPR project whose execution a resource allocation of interest secured/sacrificed, (6) producers of any good whose cost of production would be reduced by the use of a discovery that would be yielded by a PPR project whose execution a resource allocation of interest secured/sacrificed in their capacities as buyers of any resources or intermediate products that would be used to produce the good the producers purchased, and (7) production-process researchers to whose/from whose PPR's execution a resource allocation of interest devoted/withdrew resources in their capacities as buyers of the resources or intermediate products they did employ/would have employed to execute a PPR project whose execution a resource allocation of interest secured/sacrificed.

Fourth, the set of bilateral-monopoly-participant concession-obtaining monopsonists contains at least nine subsets: seven that contain a counterpart to one of the upward-sloping-supply-curve-facing-monopsonist subsets of monopsonists, an eighth that contains buyers of any patents (yielded by)/(that would have been yielded by) a QV investment whose creation was secured/sacrificed by a resource allocation of interest and as well as buyers of any license to produce and sell or distribute any good (perhaps in specified quantities or in specified locations or to specified buyers) that was/(would have been) "discovered" by a QV investment whose creation a resource allocation of interest secured/sacrificed, and a ninth that contains buyers of any patents that were/would have been issued to a production-process researcher whose PPR project a resource allocation of interest secured/sacrificed as well as buyers of any licenses to use or sell the right to use any production process that (was yielded)/(would have been yielded) by any PPR project whose execution a resource allocation of interest secured/sacrificed.

I want to make four sets of points about the incidence, general step-wise-distortion-in-private-cost consequences, and step-wise-profit-distortion consequences of the individual-buyer-facing-an-upward-sloping-supply-curve variant of monopsony. I start with some "observations" about the incidence of this variant of monopsony. I acknowledge that I have no special expertise about the empirical importance of such monopsony or about the kinds of buyers that are more likely to possess this type of monopsony power. My suspicion is that this type of monopsony power is rare. The only firms of which I am aware that possess this type of monopsony power in the US own food-processing plants and canneries in small, geographically-isolated agricultural communities. Such firms are often the sole industrial employer in locales in which the only other jobs are farm labor, work as owners or employees of various sorts of distributive outlets (the local gas station, food store, bakery, department store, bank, insurance outlet), work as teachers or other sorts of civil servants, or work as suppliers of domestic services to the

better-off members of the communities in question. The owners of the sole
food-processing-plant/cannery in any such town may face an upward-sloping
supply curve of labor because the wage that will induce different locals to work for
them rather than moving away may vary from individual potential employee to
individual potential employee.[2] Next, I address the step-wise distortion that this
type of monopsony will generate in the cost of buying all but the first unit of the
monopsonized resource or product the monopsonist purchased. Assuming that the
relevant upward-sloping-supply-curve-facing monopsonist did not prevent this
outcome by practicing perfect price discrimination perfectly accurately when
buying the monopsonized resource or product from each of its potential suppliers,
this type of monopsony will always generate a positive step-wise-monopsony
distortion in the private kost to any such monopsonist that purchased more than one
unit of the monopsonized resource or product in question of buying all but the first
unit of that resource or product equal to the extra economic rents that the
monopsonist's decision to pay the higher price for all units of the monopsonized
"good" that it had to pay to elicit the supply of the last non-first unit it purchased of
that "good" enables suppliers of the earlier units of the "good" in question to
secure.[3] I turn now to the step-wise-monopsony distortion that this type of
monopsony power will generate in the profits yielded by exemplars of various
categories of resource allocations if four conditions are fulfilled: (1) the "good" in
relation to which the relevant monopsonist faces an upward-sloping supply curve is
labor of a given relevant quantity, (2) the monopsonist in question purchases more
than one unit of the monopsonized type of labor, (3) the monopsonist engages in no
form of price discrimination when purchasing the relevant labor, and (4) the
alternative employer of the labor in question (which might be the worker himself if
the worker would "produce leisure" or perform do-it-yourself labor [say, engage in
household production] if it did not work for the monopsonist]) was not a monopsonist. In such a case, the resource allocation in question will have allocated
resources *inter alia* from the alternative use to which the labor in question would
have been devoted (e.g., UO production [including leisure-production and
household-production], QV-investment creation, and/or PPR execution) to any
category of resource-use, and the sign of the step-wise-monopsony profit distortions
the relevant monopsony will generate will be negative regardless of the category of
use to which the relevant resource-user devoted the monopsonized resource:

1. if the labor in question was used to increase the unit output of an extant product,
   the employer's facing an upward-sloping supply curve of labor would on the
   above assumptions generate a positive step-wise-monopsony distortion in the
   private kost of successive units of the relevant labor to the employer, hence a
   positive step-wise-monopsony distortion in the private variable cost the labor's
   employer incurred to produce its marginal unit and almost all of its
   intra-marginal units of the product it used the labor in question to produce,
   hence a negative step-wise-monopsony distortion in the profits the relevant
   employer/producer obtained by producing the units of its product it used the
   relevant type of labor to produce (absolutely equal to the [usually-varying]

positive step-wise-monopsony distortions in the private variable cost it incurred to produce the marginal and various intra-marginal units of its product), and hence an identical negative step-wise-monopoly distortion in the profits yielded by any resource allocation that devoted resources to the production of relevant profits of the good in question;

2. (A) if the labor in question was used to create a QV investment (say, a food-processing plant/cannery), the QV investor's facing an upward-sloping supply curve for that labor would generate a positive step-wise-monopsony distortion in the private kost it had to incur to create the QV investment in question and hence an absolutely-equal negative distortion both in the profits it earned by creating and using the QV investment in question and (obviously) in the profits yielded by the resource allocation that devoted resources to the creation and use of the QV investment in question, and (C) if the labor in question was employed to use a newly-created QV investment, the QV investor's facing an upward-sloping supply curve for that labor would generate a positive step-wise-monopsony distortion in the private cost to the QV investor of using its QV investment and an absolutely-equal negative distortion in the operating profits yielded by the use of the QV investment, in the profits yielded by the creation and use of the QV investment, and in the profits yielded by the allocation of resources that devoted resources to the creation and use of the QV investment in question; and

3. (A) if a production-process researcher to which a resource allocation of interest allocated resources faced an upward-sloping supply curve when hiring labor to execute its PPR project (because part of any PPR project is the construction of pilot plants to try out the discovered process and it is most profitable to locate the pilot plant to be used to test out a food-processing/canning innovation by constructing a pilot plant in the isolated-small-town location near the farms in which the fruits and vegetables to be processed and canned are produced), its possession of upward-sloping-supply-curve-related monopsony power will have generated a positive step-wise-monopsony distortion in the private cost of executing the PPR project and hence an absolutely-equal negative step-wise-monopsony distortion in the profits yielded by the execution and use of the PPR project in question (and in the profits yielded by the resource allocation that allocated resources to the execution and use of the relevant PPR project), and (B) if the producer(s) (say, food-processors/canners) to whose production process(es) a PPR project of interest related were monopsonists of the labor it (they) used to produce its (their) product(s) and the PPR project in question was designed to discover a production process whose use would reduce the amount of monopsonized labor required to produce relevant quantities of the product(s) to whose production process the PPR project related, the relevant final-product producers' possession of upward-sloping-supply-curve monopsony power would generate a positive step-wise-monopsony distortion in the private kost to them of the monopsonized labor they used to produce the products to whose production process the relevant PPR project related, hence an equal positive step-wise-monopsony distortion in the private benefits the

final-product producers' use of the production-process discovery enabled them to secure by reducing the amount of labor they had to employ to produce relevant quantities of their final products, hence a positive step-wise-monopsony distortion in the private benefits the production-process researcher obtained by selling the right to use its discovery (i.e., by executing and using the PPR project), hence a positive step-wise-monopsony distortion in the profits yielded both by the execution and use of the PPR project and by the resource allocation that devoted resources to the execution and use of the PPR project.

The last members of this fifth set of points I want to make relate to my previous assumption that the alternative employer of the labor whose actual employer was an upward-sloping-supply-curve-facing monopsonist was not a monopsonist. I made this assumption for two reasons: (1) because it seems to me to be highly realistic— although the alternative employer of workers hired by a food processor/canner in one town that was a monopsonist of labor might be a food processor/canner in a geo-graphically distant similar town that also was a monopsonist of labor, I suspect that this will rarely be the case—and (2) to be honest, I am uncomfortable with my own analysis of the step-wise-monopsony distortions that would be generated by the alternative employers of the relevant workers' being upward-sloping-supply-curve-facing monopsonists. I believe that any such monopsony power that relevant workers' alternative employers possess would generate a negative step-wise-monopsony distortion in these workers' private kost to their actual employers by reducing the wage that these workers' alternative employers were willing to pay them below the kost their alternative employers would have had to incur to employ them, which on the assumptions of step-wise analyses would be infinitesimally below (in the case of the just-extra-marginal worker) not only the marginal revenue product but of the marginal allocative product that worker would have generated in his or her alternative employer's employ and hence a step-wise-monopsony positive distortion in the profits that were yielded by the resource allocation that involved these workers' being allocated to their actual employer (regardless of whether their actual employer used them to produce a unit of an extant product, to create and/or use a QV investment, or to execute a PPR project).

Sixth, I want to make some comments about bilateral-monopoly monopsony. To start, I suspect that many buyers possess this variant of monopsony power—are sufficiently irreplaceable as customers of non-perfectly-competitive suppliers to be able to obtain price-concessions or other terms-of-sale concessions. Next, I want to point out that at least three categories of actors can possess bilateral-monopoly concession-securing monopsony power whose exercise will affect the aggregate distortions in profits yielded by exemplars of various functional categories of resource allocations: (1) the resource-users to which relevant resource allocations allocate resources; (2) buyers of the products, intellectual property, or licenses to use the intellectual property to whose production, creation, and issuance relevant resource allocations devote resources; and (3) users of the production processes discovered by PPR projects to whose execution relevant resource allocations devote resources in their capacities as buyers of the resources that their use of the discovered production processes enables them to save. I also want to comment on the way in which the bilateral-monopoly-related monopsony power of each such category of actors will affect the aggregate distortion in the profits yielded by particular categories of resource allocations either by changing the magnitude of the step-wise-monopoly distortion in those profits or by generating step-wise-monopsony distortions in those profits: (1) the impact of the bilateral-monopoly-related monopsony power of an actor to which a relevant resource allocation allocates resources on the (M/MS) distortion in the cost of the product to the relevant resource-user and hence on the oppositely-signed (M/MS) distortion in the profits yielded by the relevant resource-use and resource allocation will depend on whether the lower price differs more or less from the marginal allocative cost of the product being bought than does the higher price; (2) the bilateral-monopoly-related monopsony power of buyers of any products produced by, of intellectual property created by, or of the right to license others to use the intellectual property created by the resource-use to which a relevant resource allocation devotes resources will generate a negative (SW[MS]) distortion in the private benefits and profits that a relevant resource-use confers on the resource-user equal to the additional buyer surplus the relevant buyer's monopsony power enables it to obtain; and (3) the (SW [MS]) distortion in the profits that will be yielded by a PPR project that will be generated by the bilateral-monopoly-related monopsony power of the producers to whose production processes the PPR project relates when those producers are acting as buyers of the resources they employ to produce their products that the use of the production process the project will discover will enable them to do without when producing relevant quantities of their products will depend on whether the price that their buying power enables them to pay for the saved resources is closer or further from the marginal allocative cost of their using those resources than the price they would have had to pay for them had they not had such monopsony power would have been: recall that any positive/negative difference between the cost of those resources to the discovered-production-process user and the marginal allocative cost of its using them will be associated with a positive/negative distortion in the private benefits and profits the relevant PPR project yields the researcher. Finally, I want to point out that if I am correct in claiming that, from the perspective of economic efficiency, all economies currently devote too many resources to QV-investment creation (including to the creation of scientifically/technologically innovative QV investments) and not enough to the execution of PPR projects because the Pareto imperfections they contain generate a positive aggregate distortion in the profits yielded by economics-marginal and economics-intra-marginal allocations of resources from UO production and PPR execution to QV creation and a negative aggregate distortion in the profits yielded by economics-marginal and economics-extra-marginal resource allocations from UO production and QV creation to PPR execution, the bilateral-monopoly monopsony power of buyers of product-R&D intellectual-property rights reduces the amount of (UO-and-PPR) to QV misallocation generated in all (market) economies by reducing the positive aggregate distortion in the profits yielded by such allocations and increases the amount of (UO-and-QV) to PPR misallocation generated in all (market) economies by increasing the negative aggregate distortion in the profits yielded by such allocations.

I may have devoted more attention to monopsony than its incidence warrants. My decision to do so is a choice against interest: I am far from comfortable with some of the analyses this section executes. I hope that my efforts will lead others to do a better job.

8.2   The Step-Wise-Externality Distortions in the Private Benefits, Private Costs, and Profits that Exemplars of Various Functional Categories of Resource Allocations Respectively Confer on, Impose on, and Yield the Actors to Which Those Resource Allocations Allocate Resources: Some Comments

Section 8.2 makes four externality-related points or externality-related sets of points. The first specifies many of the "sorts" of externalities that can be generated by QV-investment creation, by the production of units of products (be the products old or newly-created), by production-process research, by choice among known production processes, by shopping, and by consumption. QV-investment creation that entails the construction of pilot-plants, final production-facilities, and distributive outlets can generate air-and/or-water-pollution externalities, noise-pollution externalities, olfactory externalities, and road-congestion externalities. The execution of non-"artistic" QV investments that create new products can generate external costs by reducing the worth of already-produced units of pre-existing products to those of their owners and highest-valuing prospective buyers who value "owning the latest thing." The execution of "artistic" QV investments, which create music, art, architecture, or literature, can generate external costs by contaminating the meaning of or rendering trite pre-existing works of art. The operation of a QV-investment-created additional distributive outlet can yield (in essence) external benefits by reducing the in-store congestion costs that shoppers generate when shoppers generate lower congestion costs when patronizing the new store the QV investment created rather than the old store they would otherwise have patronized. The creation of a QV investment that makes a scientific, technological, or commercial discovery will generate external benefits if some user of the discovery it yielded do not pay for the right to use that discovery and will generate external benefits if the discovery it makes enables others that do not pay for the right to use the discovery to execute derivative, economically-efficient research. The creation of an artistic QV investment will generate external benefits if other musical composers, visual artists, architects, or writers make economically-efficient use of the "discovery" the relevant artistic QV investor made without paying for the right to do so. The operation of a QV-investment-created additional distributive outlet can either increase or decrease the amount of road-congestion, air-pollution, and accident-related external costs that buyers generate when traveling to do their shopping: if I ignore the possibility that the construction of a new, additional distributive outlet may affect the amount of such externalities generated (indeed, may affect economic efficiency) by inducing buyers and their potential employers to change their geographic locations, the net effect that the operation of a QV-investment-created distributive outlet will have on travel-generated externalities will depend *inter alia* on whether the outlet's operation reduces shopping-travel more by shortening the distance of each shopping-trip (by increasing shopping locational convenience) than it increases shopping-travel by increasing the number of shopping-trips that are made (once again, by increasing shopping locational convenience—i.e., by reducing the distance one must travel to make and hence the cost of making a shopping-trip). The production of new or old products can also generate air-and-water-pollution externalities and olfactory externalities. The execution of production-process research can generate external costs to the extent that it entails the external-cost-generating construction of research facilities and pilot plants. The use of any PPR project (i.e., of the production process it discovered or would have discovered had it not been sacrificed) can increase or decrease externalities, depending on whether the process that was or would have been discovered is/would have been more or less external-cost-prone than was the production process it replaced/would have replaced. Choices among known production processes can increase or decrease externalities, depending on whether the chosen production process generated higher or lower external costs than the rejected production process would have generated. Consumption choices (say, to wear an attractive/unattractive suit/dress or shirt/blouse, to use an attractive/unattractive cologne/perfume, to consume nice-smelling/fetid food) can generate external benefits/costs to the extent that the effects that such consumption-choices have on others are not perfectly internalized to the consumer by their impact on the way in which others interact with him or her. Finally, the execution of product research or PPR can generate external costs by reducing the probability that other researchers who are trying to make the same discovery will make it (first).

The second externality-related point I want to make is that the external effects of a particular choice that puts a known amount of a known pollutant into the air or water may be difficult to predict *inter alia* because (1) those effects may depend on the levels of other pollutants or chemicals or "undesirables" in the relevant medium and (2) we have little information about the incidence of the relevant "undesirables" in any medium or about how all relevant undesirables interact to cause equivalent-dollar losses. Thus, the health-related equivalent-dollar cost of putting a given carcinogen or a given amount of radiation into the air or water may vary substantially with the amounts and identities of the other carcinogens in the relevant medium or the amount of radiation that the relevant medium would in any event contain. At the extreme, something that would generate external costs in some environments may generate external benefits in others: take, for example, the case in which the dumping of unwanted car-parts into Lake Erie generated an external benefit because their decomposition yielded an acid that killed the algae that would otherwise have caused more damage to the relevant environment.

The third externality-related point I want to make is that the step-wise-externality distortion in the profits yielded by any resource-use (or by any resource allocation that devoted resources to the resource-use in question) depends not only on the externalities that were generated by the resource-use to which the resource allocation of interest devoted resources but also by the externalities that would have been generated by the resource-use the resource allocation of interest sacrificed. To save space, I will not examine all the possible externality combinations or the various step-wise benefit, cost, and profit distortions they would generate individually or in combination.

The fourth and final externality-related set of points I want to make relates to the impact of externalities on various categories of resource misallocation. To start, I suspect that the step-wise-externality distortion in the profits yielded by choices to use a more-externality-prone rather than a less-externality-prone, known production process will often play a critical role in the generation of choices-among-known-production-process economic inefficiency in cases in which the individual victims of the externality cannot obtain redress: find it difficult to identify the polluter whose production-process choice harmed them, suffered losses that were too low for it to be profitable for them to incur the cost of litigating any related claim, were deterred from suing by their ignorance of the law or their belief that their case would not be decided correctly, would find it profitable to settle any claims they made for less than their respective losses even if they would receive damages at trial equal to their respective losses, would be awarded damages at trial that were lower than their losses, etc. Next, I also suspect that the step-wise-externality distortion in the profits that would be yielded by PPR that would discover a less-accident-or-pollution-loss-generating production process will often render economically-efficient PPR of this type unprofitable (*i.e.,* will often cause economically-inefficient decisions not to do such PPR to be made when [1] the relevant possible researcher is a producer of the good to whose production process the PPR project in question would relate, [2] this actor is liable for the accident and pollution losses it generated only if its generation of them is deemed to have been negligent, [3] decisions not to do PPR are never assessed for negligence, and [4] the potential researcher in question makes a sufficiently-large percentage of the sales of the good to whose production process the rejected PPR project in question would have related to render unprofitable economically-efficient PPR into less-accident-and-pollution-loss-generating production processes.)[4] I should add that I doubt that the (SW[PX]) distortions that the non-internalization of external costs of production generates in the profits that would be yielded by inter-ARDEPPS UO-to-UO resource allocations counteract the (SW[M]) distortions in those profits—i.e., I doubt that the weighted-average P/MC ratios for the products in any economy's various ARDEPPSes are strongly positively correlated with their XMC/MC ratios. However, I do suspect that the (SW[PX]) distortions that the non-internalization of the external costs that result from the production of old products, the creation and use of QV investments, and the execution and use of PPR projects yield in the profits generated by resource allocations from   UO-producing-and-consuming   and   PPR-executing-and-using   uses   to QV-investment-creating-and-using uses is negative and counteracts the positive

(SW[M]) distortion that imperfections in seller competition generate in the profits that such resource allocations generate—i.e., I believe that the weighted-average external-cost to internal-cost ratio for the production and consumption of the units of output and the execution and use of the PPR projects that are sacrificed to the creation and use of economics-marginal and many economics-intra-marginal QV investments is higher than the external-cost to internal-cost ratio for those QV investments (and concomitantly that policies that internalize the externalities in question will tend to increase the amount of economic inefficiency generated by economically-inefficient resource allocations from UO production-and-consumption and PPR execution-and-use to QV-investment creation-and-use). Finally, I suspect that the non-internalization of consumption externalities does cause some traditional consumption-optimum misallocation because the externalities generated by the consumption of some units of some products will be significantly affected by the identity of the individual who consumes them (e.g., by whether the consumer is someone who consumes a product whose consumption generates external costs in an isolated situation or in the presence of others). However, I doubt that it will ever be economically efficient (or morally desirable) to prevent consumption externalities from generating this conventional category of consumption-optimum misallocation (though it may be possible to prevent consumption externalities from generating intra-ARDEPPS UO-to-UO resource misallocation [say, when the consumption of different same-ARDEPPS product variants would generate external costs that con-stitute different percentages of the dollar benefits the consumption of those products confers on their consumers] or even [though less likely] inter-ARDEPPS UO-to-UO resource misallocation [when the ratio of consumption externalities to dollar value to consumers is significantly different for the products in one ARDEPPS than for the weighted-average product in the economy as a whole or for the subset of the econ-omy's products with which the products in the ARDEPPS in question are atypically competitive]).

8.3   The Step-Wise-(Taxes-on-the-Margin-of-Income) Distortions in the Private Benefits, Private Costs, and Profits that Exemplars of Various Functional Categories of Resource Allocations Respectively Confer on, Impose on, and Yield the Actors to Which Those Resource Allocations Allocate Resources: Some Comments

Section 8.3 makes 12 sets of taxes-on-the-margin-of-income-related points. The first set identifies the categories of taxes on the margin of income that need to be considered when executing economic-efficiency analyses. Even if I ignore poll taxes (which can cause economic inefficiency by rendering "advantageous" suicides that are economically inefficient), eight categories of taxes on the margin of income should be distinguished: (1) taxes on individuals' or (married) couples' earned

incomes, (2) taxes on individuals' or (married) couples' "unearned" (i.e., investment) incomes—*inter alia*, taxes on interest, dividends, realized capital gains, and
unrealized capital gains (which are, admittedly, not now taxed), (3) taxes on purchases—*inter alia*, sales taxes, excise taxes, value-added taxes, and consumption
taxes, (4) gift taxes and estate taxes, (5) taxes on the wealth of individuals or
couples that are taxed as joint taxpayers, (6) real-estate taxes (which, in the UK are
called Council taxes) levied on individuals, couples that are treated as joint entities,
and businesses, and (7) taxes on business income.

   The second set of taxes-on-the-margin-of-income-related points focuses on the
step-wise-(taxes-on-the-margin-of-income) distortion—(SW[T])D—in the profits
yielded by allocations of time from market labor to leisure-"production" and/or
do-it-yourself (non-market) labor. Because taxes on individuals' or
married-couples' earned incomes, unearned incomes (yielded by the investment of
savings from earned income or other unearned income), purchases, owned assets
and wealth during life, gifts, and estates reduce the value to its earner of
market-labor-earned gross wages (reduce the *desiderata* he or she can secure as a
result of his or her being paid any given amount of gross wages), all such taxes will
generate a negative (SW[T]) distortion in the profits yielded by allocations of time
from leisure-production and/or non-market (do-it-yourself) labor to market labor. It
is important to emphasize that the effect that any such (SW[T]) distortion would
have on the magnitude of the aggregate distortion in the profits yielded by any such
resource allocation and hence the impact that such (SW[T]) distortions will have on
the amount of economic inefficiency generated by economically-inefficient decisions to allocate or not to allocate resources from leisure-production and/or
non-market labor to some functional category of market labor (if I assume that the
time-allocators in question are sovereign maximizers) will depend on (1) the
functional category of market labor that the workers in question would perform,
(2) the sum of the step-wise distortions that all exemplars of each of the other types
of Pareto imperfections will have on the aggregate distortion in the gross wages that
would be paid to workers that perform the relevant category of market labor, and
(3) the sum of the step-wise distortions that all exemplars of each of the other six
types of Pareto imperfections would generate in the private benefits that relevant
leisure-production and do-it-yourself labor would confer on the individuals that are
allocating their time among leisure-production-, do-it-yourself-labor performance,
and market-labor performance. It would probably be useful for me to be more
specific. I previously argued that the imperfections in seller competition that
economies contain generate negative (SW[M]) distortions in the private benefits
that UO production confers on unit-output producers, positive (SW[M]) distortions
in the private benefits that QV-investment creation confers on QV investors (positive distortions of this type in the operating profits yielded by the use of QV
investments), and negative (SW[M]) distortions in the private benefits that PPR
execution confers on production-process researchers (in the profits such researchers
will earn by using their production-process discoveries themselves, licensing others
to use them, or selling the patents to their discoveries). Since non-monopsonistic
employers pay workers in any category wages equal to the marginal revenue

product of the last worker in that category they hire, the preceding conclusions imply that the (SW[M]) distortion in the gross wage of unit-output-producing workers is negative, that the (SW[M]) distortion in the gross wage of QV-investment-creating workers is positive, and that the (SW[M]) distortion in the gross wage of PPR-executing workers is negative. If for simplicity I assume that the sum of the (SW[MS]) distortion, the (SW[X]) distortion, the (SW[NS]) distortion, the (SW[NM]) distortion, and the (SW[BS]) distortion in the gross wages paid to UO producers, QV-investment creators, and PPR executers is zero, the preceding conclusion has two sets of two related implications: (1)(A) the negative (SW[T]) distortions in the private benefits and "profits" or net gains that the performance of UO-producing and PPR-executing labor confers on the workers that perform such labor compounds the negative (SW[M]) distortions in those private benefits (gross wages) and gains—indeed, increase dollar for dollar the aggregate distortions in those private benefits and gains—and (B) the negative (SW[M]) distortions in those private benefits and gains increase substantially the amount of economic ineffi-ciency the relevant taxes on the margin of income generate by causing additional "time" to be withdrawn from the performance of UO-producing and PPR-executing market-labor and devoted to the production of leisure and performance of non-market labor (since the amount of misallocation that is caused by any given increase in the absolute value of the aggregate distortion in the profits yielded by any category of resource allocation increases with the pre-increase absolute value of that aggregate distortion [particularly when the change in question does not alter the sign of the relevant aggregate distortion]), and (2)(A) the negative (SW[T]) dis-tortion in the private benefits and "profits" or net gains that the performance of QV-investment-creating labor confers on the workers that perform such labor counteracts the positive (SW[M]) distortion in the private benefits (gross wages) and net gains that the performance of QV-investment-creating labor confers on the workers that perform such labor and (B) will reduce the absolute value of the aggregate distortion in those private benefits and net gains dollar for dollar if the relevant positive (SW[M]) distortion is lower than the absolute value of the relevant negative (SW[T]) distortion, will reduce the absolute values of the aggregate dis-tortions in those private benefits and net gains by |(SW[M])|D *minus* (|(SW[T])D|–(SW[M])D) when the absolute value of the negative (SW[T]) distortion exceeds the positive (SW[M]) distortion but is less than twice the magnitude of the (SW[M]) distortion, will increase the aggregate distortion in those private benefits and net gains only in what I take to be the extremely unlikely case in which the absolute value of the negative (SW[T]) distortion is more than twice the positive (SW[M]) distortion, and will therefore in my judgment tend to reduce the amount of eco-nomic inefficiency generated by economically-inefficient allocations of time from QV-investment creation to leisure-production- and non-market-labor performance. Admittedly, in many contexts, it would be TBLE to consider the impact that the extant exemplars of other types of Pareto imperfections have on the impact that taxes on the margin of income have on the amounts of economic inefficiency generated by economically-inefficient decisions by individuals to reduce the time they devote to performing UO-producing, QV-investment-creating, or

PPR-executing market labor and increase the time they devote to leisure-production- and/or non-market-labor performance. However, there can be no doubt about the empirical difficulties one would have to confront to do so. For example, to take relevant (SW[X]) distortions into account, one would have to estimate or guesstimate the external-cost to internal-cost ratios not only for market UO production, market QV-investment creation, and market PPR execution but also for the performance of relevant subcategories of non-market labor and for the consumption of leisure (which can yield either external benefits [as it will if it involves friendly interactions with family members and friends or coaching youth sports teams] or external costs [as it will if it involves hostile interactions with others or the external-cost-generating use of cars]).

Five final points, all of which relate to the literature on the alleged tendency of taxes on the margin of income to generate economic inefficiency by deterring the performance of market labor: (1) much of this literature ignores the possibility that taxes on the margin of income may induce relevant individuals to substitute non-market labor for market labor; (2) the literature ignores the fact that non-tax Pareto imperfections can affect the impact that taxes on the margin of income will have on this category of economic inefficiency; relatedly and more specifically, (3) the literature fails to recognize that these other types of Pareto imperfections (in particular, imperfections in seller price-competition) may affect differently the signs and magnitudes of the economic-efficiency effects that taxes on the margin of income have by deterring the performance, respectively, of UO-producing, QV-creating, and PPR-executing market labor; (4) the literature claims incorrectly that taxes on the margin of income will not affect the economic efficiency of the choices that are made to perform or not perform units of any particular type of market labor if those taxes do not affect the quantity of such labor that is performed (because the supply curve for that type of labor is inelastic over the relevant range): this claim would be incorrect even if one could assume away all the other com-plexities I have addressed because taxes on the margin of income will usually leave unaffected the quantity of market labor performed not when such taxes have no substitution effect but when the negative substitution effect they have on the quantity of labor informed is exactly offset by their positive income/wealth effect on that quantity (by the associated reduction in the relevant workers' real incomes' making it "profitable" or advantageous for them to perform more labor than would otherwise have been most-personally-advantageous for them to perform) and (if we ignore other Pareto imperfections) the relevant substitution effects will be misal-locative—i.e., on oPp assumptions, the tax on the margin of income will cause workers to make economically-inefficient decisions to substitute leisure-production and/or the performance of do-it-yourself non-market labor for the performances of market labor in the vast majority of cases in which such taxes have no impact on the quantity of market labor performed because in the vast majority of such cases the taxes on the margin of income will have increased the amount of market labor that is economically efficient for the relevant workers to perform; and (5) the literature does not consider or consider sufficiently the possibilities that one might prevent market-labor/non-market-labor/leisure misallocation in an economy in which taxes on the margin of income are levied by taxing the real income generated by non-market labor, by taxing the consumption of leisure (say, beyond some specified quantity), and/or by placing higher sales taxes on complements of leisure than on other goods (though admittedly all of these alternatives have economic-efficiency-related drawbacks).

The third set of taxes-on-the-margin-of-income-related points focuses on possible misallocative effects of taxes on unearned income, wealth taxes, and estate taxes. I will limit myself to six points:

1. in an oPp economy, taxes on unearned income, wealth, and estates would generate misallocation not only by inducing individuals to allocate more time to leisure production and do-it-yourself labor than to market labor than is economically efficient but also by generating a negative (SW[T]) distortion in the private benefits and "profitability" of saving—i.e., by inducing individuals to make economically-inefficient substitutions of current consumption for future consumption;

2. the amount of "future-consumption *versus* current-consumption" misallocation that given taxes on unearned income, wealth, and estates generate will be higher than it would otherwise be if (as I suspect) non-sovereignty and non-maximization lead individuals to save too little from their own respective perspectives;

3. the amount of "future-consumption *versus* current-consumption" misallocation that given taxes on unearned income, wealth taxes, and estate taxes generate will be lower if prices become increasingly supra-competitive through time (since such a price-trend will cause the step-wise-monopoly distortion in the "profits" of substituting future consumption for current consumption to be negative and will be higher if prices become increasingly monopolistic through time since such a price-trend will cause the step-wise-monopoly distortion in the profits of substituting future consumption for current consumption to be positive—*i.e.*, to counteract the distortion generated by the taxes on the margin of income in question;

4. if the tax-rates on dividends and interest-income are higher than the tax-rate on capital gains, that set of taxes may tend to cause economic inefficiency by making it profitable for a company's shareholders for it to retain its earnings even when the profits it can realize by using the funds in question are lower than the profits that other (say, new) companies could earn with those funds;

5. the amount of economic inefficiency that a tax regime that imposes a higher tax-rate on dividends and interest-income generate in the way specified in the preceding point will be increased if the managers of existing companies retain earnings even when it is not in their shareholders' interest for them to do so; and

6. if capital gains are taxed only when they are realized, this feature of the taxation of unearned income will generate a positive step-wise distortion in the profits that investors can obtain by holding on to existing investments whose value has increased since their date of acquisition as opposed to liquidating them and either consuming or reinvesting the proceeds.

The fourth set of taxes-on-the-margin-of-income-related points I will make is that if the earned-income tax regime in question does not take account of the shortness of an employee's work-week, the amount of vacation-time the employee receives, the pleasantness of the labor in question, the health-effects of the labor, the intrinsic satisfaction the job gives the person who does it, the attractiveness of the working environment (both of the physical facility and of each worker's co-workers), the medical benefits that the employee receives, the quality and price of the food that the employer offers its workers, the quality and price of any day-care facilities the employer provides its workers, the recreational facilities and/or vacation facilities the employer makes available to its employees, etc., it will generate step-wise-tax-on-the-margin-of-income distortions in the gains the employees can obtain by exchanging money wages—i.e., all those things that the employee could buy with money wages—for such untaxed (or lower-taxed) "non-monetary" employer-supplied benefits. Once more, of course, the impact of this step-wise-tax distortion on the aggregate distortion in the private benefits that employees can obtain by making such substitutions and hence on the amount of economic inefficiency that these sorts of substitutions generate will depend on the sum of the other six individual-type-of-Pareto-imperfection-oriented step-wise distortions in the gains such employees obtain by making the relevant trade-offs.

The fifth set of taxes-on-the-margin-of-income-related points I will make contains two investment-in-human-capital-oriented points: (1) all taxes on the margin of income generate a negative step-wise distortion in the gains that an individual can obtain by making investments in his or her human capital that will increase the individual's gross wages and/or overall income, and (2) the impact that this effect of taxes on the margin of income will have on the aggregate distortion in the gains that individuals obtain by making investments in their human capital that increase their gross wages and/or overall income will depend on the sum of the six other single-type-of-Pareto-imperfection-oriented distortion in the wages and incomes the relevant individuals would obtain (A) if they did not make the relevant investments in their human capital and (B) if they did make the relevant investments in their human capital. For reasons of space, I will not elaborate on the last observation here.

The sixth set of taxes-on-the-margin-of-income-related-points I will make focuses on the special distorting effects of progressive taxes on earned income. Such taxes not only will increase the earned-income-tax-related negative distortion in the profits or gains an individual can obtain by making investments in his or her human capital that raise the individual's ability to secure earned income and/or unearned income but also generate positive (SW[T]) distortions (1) in substituting known production processes whose use employs lower-wage-earning labor for known production processes whose use employs higher-wage-earning labor, (2) in executing PPR that is designed to discover production processes whose use employs lower-wage-earning labor rather than PPR that is designed to discover production process whose use would employ higher-wage-earning labor, (3) in creating and using QV investments whose creation and use would employ lower-wage-earning labor, and (4) in producing units of products whose production employs lower-wage-earning labor rather than units of products whose production employs higher-wage-earning labor.

The seventh set of taxes-on-the-margin-of-income-related points focuses on "purchase taxes." I will limit myself to making five points:

1. purchase taxes generate a positive (SW[T]) distortion in the profits yielded by decisions of individuals to devote their time to leisure-production and/or do-it-yourself (non-market) labor rather than to market labor;

2. if the "purchase-tax" regime applies a lower tax-rate to the purchase of "standard-quality" goods than to the purchase of unusually-high-quality (so-called luxury) goods—for example, if the normal "sales-tax" rate (which applies to the purchase of ordinary goods) is lower than the "excise-tax" rate (which applies to the sale of luxury goods), the regime will generate a positive step-wise-taxes-on-the-margin-of-income distortion in the profits that producers will obtain by producing ordinary goods rather than luxury goods both when the ordinary good and the luxury good in quotation are highly competitive (when any resulting economic inefficiency would be intra-ARDEPPS UO-to-UO misallocation) and when the ordinary good and luxury good in question are not particularly competitive (are in different ARDEPPSes)—when any resulting economic inefficiency would be inter-ARDEPPS UO-to-UO misallocation;

3. purchase-tax regimes that levy taxes on the purchase of some goods but not on the purchase of others will generate a positive (SW[T]) distortion in the profits yielded by allocations of resources to the production of goods whose purchase is not taxed from the production of goods whose purchase is taxed;

4. if different countries, different states in the same country, or different cities in the same state set different purchase-tax rates, the differences in question will generate a positive step-wise-taxes-on-the-margin-of-income distortion in the profits that are generated by withdrawing resources from the production of goods in jurisdictions in which the higher purchase-tax rate applies and allocating them to the production of goods in jurisdictions in which the lower purchase-tax rate applies;

5. purchase taxes generate a positive step-wise-taxes-on-the-margin-of-income distortion in the "profits" generated by making gifts and/or bequests rather than purchases, though obviously the overall step-wise-taxes-on-the-margin-of-income distortion in the profits of making such choices will depend on the difference between the operative purchase-tax rate, gift-tax rate, and estate-tax rate as well as on the extent to which taxpayers manage to conceal altogether or to reduce the detected magnitudes of their purchases, gifts, and bequests.

The eighth set of taxes-on-the-margin-of-income-related points I will make relates to gift and bequest (estate) taxes. I will make six points about the step-wise-"profit" distortions such taxes generate, the step-wise-"profit" distortions that various combinations of such taxes generate, and the impact that various combinations of such taxes have on the step-wise-tax distortions and the aggregate distortion in the "profits" yielded by giving gifts or bequests and relatedly on the amount of economic inefficiency generated by economically-inefficient decisions to make or not make gifts or bequests:

1. gift taxes and/or estate taxes will generate a negative step-wise distortion in the "profits" (net gains) that decisions to perform market labor or non-market labor that will produce *desiderata* that can be gifted or bequested rather than to produce leisure will confer on any individual that would otherwise and might anyway make gifts or bequests;
2. gift taxes and/or bequest (estate) taxes will generate a negative step-wise distortion in the "profits" (net gains) that decisions to save and invest rather than consume will confer on any individual that would otherwise and might anyway make gifts and/or bequests;
3. gift taxes and/or bequest (estate) taxes will generate a negative step-wise-tax distortion in the "profits" (net gains) that decisions by individuals to make investments in their human capital that will increase their respective earned incomes and investment incomes will confer on individuals that would otherwise and might anyway make gifts and/or bequests;
4. if in the relevant tax regime gifts are taxed at a lower rate than bequests or are not taxed when bequests are taxed, this tax regime will generate a positive step-wise-tax distortion in the "profits" (net gains) of substituting gifts for bequests;
5. if gifts to some donees (say, recognized charities) are exempt from taxation whereas gifts to other donees (say, political causes, political parties, political candidates, friends, family members) are taxed or are not tax-deductible, such a tax regime will create a positive step-wise-tax distortion in giving gifts that are not taxed or are tax-deductible rather than gifts that are taxed or are not tax-deductible; and
6. the analysis of the impact that step-wise gift-tax and/or bequest-tax distortions in the profits yielded by gift/bequest-related decisions will have on the economic inefficiency that is generated by economically-inefficient decisions to make or not make particular gifts or bequests is complicated by the empirical difficulty of determining the "profits" or "losses" (net gains) that decisions to make gifts or bequests in general or decisions to make gifts or bequests to different sorts of recipients confer on the donor(s)/testator(s): the correct analysis would have to resolve a variety of troubling issues—(A) do gifts or bequests in general confer benefits on the donors/testators that at least equal the dollar value of the gift or bequest because the donor would not make the gift or bequest unless the dollar value to the donor/testator of doing so at least equals the dollar cost to it of doing so in which case (allocative transaction costs aside) monetary gifts or bequests would increase economic efficiency by at least the number of dollars transferred (if one assumes that the donee/beneficiary places a dollar value on the gift or bequest equal to its monetary magnitude and ignores any secondary economic-efficiency effects of the redistribution of wealth that gifts and bequests effectuate) or (at the other extreme) would it be accurate to assume that gifts or bequests would not generate any economic-efficiency gain if the redistribution

of wealth they effectuate has no indirect effect on economic efficiency because gifts and bequests impose dollar costs on the donor/testator equal to the number of dollars transferred (because the donor/testator obtained no equivalent-dollar benefits by making the gift or bequest) or would it be accurate to assume that donors/testators do obtain some equivalent-dollar gains from making gifts or bequests but still suffer a net equivalent-dollar loss from doing so (in which case on the above assumptions gifts or bequests would generate an increase in economic efficiency that was lower than their monetary magnitudes), (B) do some gifts or bequests to recognized charities or to relatively impecunious relative, friends, employees increase economic efficiency by changing the distribution of wealth, (C) do political gifts and bequests to political causes, political parties, and political candidates increase or decrease economic efficiency and would it be TBLE (even if it were morally acceptable) to take this last issue into account when analyzing the economic efficiency of taxing political contributions in general or to particular political cause, parties, or candidates when analyzing the economic efficiency of particular gift/bequest-tax regimes. I stop here. I suspect that many will conclude I should not have started.

The tenth set of taxes on the margin of income on which I will comment is wealth taxes. Such taxes will generate negative step-wise distortions in the "profits" (net gains) an individual or jointly-filing couple can earn by doing market labor or do-it-yourself labor that increases their wealth rather than producing leisure to the extent that they would not otherwise choose to consume the net wages they receive or the *desiderata* their non-market labor produces in the tax year in which they perform the market labor or do-it-yourself labor in question. Wealth taxes will also generate a negative step-wise distortion in the "profits" (net gains) generated by decisions to save and invest rather than consume and a positive step-wise distortion in the "profits" or net gain of giving gifts to others whose wealth-tax rates are lower.

The eleventh set of taxes-on-the-margin-of-income-related points I will make focuses on real-estate taxes, which can be levied on individual owners of real estate, couples that file joint ventures that own real estate, and businesses. I will limit myself to making three points:

1. real-estate taxes generate a negative step-wise distortion in the profits or net gain generated by decisions to improve the real property one owns;
2. to the extent that (put crudely) the real-estate taxes that would be levied on a given physical property in a high-real-estate-tax jurisdiction exceed the real-estate taxes that would be levied on the same property if it were located in a low-real-estate-tax jurisdiction by more than the sum of (A) the amount of the pollution/congestion/visual-aesthetic/olfactory/fire-and-disease-related external cost a relevant locator or locator family would impose on others if it located in the former jurisdiction exceed the amount of such externalities it would generate if it located in the low-real-estate-tax jurisdiction *plus* (B) the amount by which the allocative cost of supplying the relevant locator/locator family with police

and fire protection and medical and educational services if it located in the high-real-estate-tax jurisdiction exceeds the allocative cost of supplying the same services to the locator in question if it located in the low-property-tax jurisdiction, the operative real-estate-tax regime would generate a negative step-wise real-estate-tax/externality/social-service-supply-and-pricing distortion in the profits of constructing the relevant housing unit in the high-real-estate-tax jurisdiction rather than in the low-real estate-tax jurisdiction; and

3. if real-estate costs constitute a lower percentage of the total cost of operating an internet retail company than they do of operating traditional brick-and-mortar retail outlets and/or if the effective real-estate-tax rate that applies to the real estate of internet retail operations is lower than the effective real-estate-tax rates that apply to traditional brick-and-mortar distributive outlets (because of differences in their locations), real-estate taxes will generate a positive step-wise distortion in the profits yielded by allocations of resources from the creation and continued operation of brick-and-mortar distributive outlets to the creation and operation of internet retail companies.

The twelfth set of taxes-on-the-margin-of-income-related points I will make focuses on taxes on business income. I will limit myself to making seven sets of points. The first set is descriptive:

1. in most tax regimes, the profits that businesses earn are taxed twice: the business pays business-income taxes when it realizes taxable business income, and the business' shareholders pay taxes on the business profits when those profits are distributed as dividends to the shareholders or when those profits' retention by the business increases the value of the business' shares, and hence, the capital gains that shareholders who sell some or all of their shares in the company realize by doing so;

2. businesses do not have to pay taxes on the amount by which their expected profits in future tax-years have been increased by decisions they have made or events that have occurred in the tax-year in question—i.e., business taxes are levied on realized business profits, not on increase in expected business profits;

3. typically, the tax-rate that is levied on dividend income is higher than the tax-rate that is levied on the capital gains generated by the sale of shares;

4. in all business-income-tax regimes I know, the effective tax-rate levied on the profits yielded by different categories of investments varies from category of investment to category of investment because some relevant tax laws explicitly allow investments of some sorts to be depreciated for tax purposes more quickly than they depreciate economically (e.g., allow investments in research to be expensed—to be written off in the year in which they are made even when their economic life is 20 or 30 years), because it is difficult to determine the rate of economic depreciation of many types of assets and taxpayers take advantage of this difficulty by claiming that certain assets depreciate more quickly than they actually do, and occasionally because tax laws explicitly levy a lower tax-rate on the profits yielded by certain types of businesses or the sale of certain types of

assets (say, timber) than they levy on the profits yielded by other types of businesses or the sales of other types of assets—indeed, in extreme cases, the tax-law treatment of depreciation results in the tax law's levying a negative tax-rate on the profits yielded by certain types of businesses; and

5. tax laws allow businesses to carry forward the losses they sustain in one tax year for a limited number of years (say, 5 years)—i.e., to use the tax loss they sustained in 2018 to offset the profits they earned in all years up to 2023.

The remaining points I will make about business-income-tax policies focus on the step-wise distortions various features of such tax regimes can generate in the profitability of different categories of resource allocations.

Second, as I have already indicated when analyzing the consequences of some features of our unearned-income-tax policies, the facts that dividends are taxed, that dividends are taxed at a lower rate than capital gains, and that capital gains are not taxed until realized generate a positive step-wise distortion in the profits of leaving earnings under the control of the established company that realized them and in an oPp economy would cause economic inefficiency by making it profitable for shareholders to leave earnings under the control of the companies in which they currently own shares even if the investments those companies could make with those retained earnings would yield a lower supernormal profit-rate than would the investments that other companies could make with those earnings.

Third, tax laws that have the three features just referenced also generate a negative distortion in the "gains" shareholders can secure by substituting current consumption financed by dividends or capital-gain realization for future consumption.

Fourth, business-income-tax laws that do not require businesses to pay taxes on increases in their expected future incomes but do require them to pay taxes on their realized income generate a step-wise positive distortion in making investments that will tend to yield more future income as opposed to investments that will tend to yield more current income.

Fifth, business-income-tax laws that have accelerated depreciation and other provisions that result in their applying a negative tax-rate to the income generated by certain kinds of investments will generate a positive step-wise distortion in the profits yielded by such investments and, if the extant exemplars of all other types of Pareto imperfections the relevant economy contains do not jointly yield a step-wise distortion in any relevant choice's profitability and no relevant resource allocator ever makes any errors, will generate economic inefficiency by causing some investments to be after-tax profitable and made even though they were before-tax unprofitable and economically inefficient.

Sixth, business-income-tax laws that apply a lower effective tax-rate to the income generated by some categories of investment than to income generated by other categories of investment will generate a positive step-wise distortion in companies' whose shareholders want to retain their earnings making investments whose profit-yields are taxed at a lower rate rather than investments whose profit-yields are taxed at a higher rate even when the before-tax supernormal profit-rates of the lower-taxed investments are lower than the before-tax supernormal profit-rates of the higher-taxed investments: this conclusion is significant because companies often have financial constraints on the total amount of investments they can make that result in their rejecting investments that would be profitable for them to make if they did not have to reject other investments to do so for financial reasons.

Seventh, tax provisions that allow businesses to carry forward losses they incurred for a limited number of years will yield a positive step-wise distortion in the profits a company that cannot make use of a prior tax loss can realize by merging or allowing itself to be acquired by a company that can make use of that tax loss: if all the other exemplars of all types of Pareto imperfections the relevant economy contains jointly generate no step-wise distortion in the profits yielded by the relevant merger/acquisition choice and the relevant choosers do not make any relevant errors, this distortion would yield economic inefficiency if the assets of the company with the tax loss could be more efficiently employed by that company's managers than by the managers of the company that would result from the tax-loss-induced merger or acquisition and/or if the merger or acquisition in question generated allocative transaction costs that exceeded any increase in economic efficiency it would otherwise yield.

I want to close this discussion of the economic-efficiency effects of taxes on the margin of income with a point that should be obvious. Even if taxes on the margin of income would decrease economic efficiency in the various ways I have described (despite the fact that some of them might increase economic efficiency by internalizing externalities and reducing material inequality and property), they might not be economically inefficient overall because the revenues they yield the government may enable it to execute other policies that increase economic efficiency by more than the taxes would (otherwise) decrease economic efficiency.

8.4   The Step-Wise Resource-Allocator-Non-Sovereignty Distortions in the Private Benefits, Private Costs, and Profits that Exemplars of Various Functional Categories of Resource Allocations Respectively Confer on, Impose on, and Yield the Actors to Which These Resource Allocations Allocate Resources and the Effect that Resource-Allocator Non-Sovereignty Has on Economic Inefficiency by Causing Resource Allocators to Reject Profitable Resource Allocations and to Execute Unprofitable Resource Allocations

Resource allocators are non-sovereign to the extent that they do not possess all the information that would be relevant to their identifying the choices that would best satisfy their preferences. Thus, consumers are not sovereign to the extent that they have imperfect information about the dollar value to them of products they might choose to buy—*inter alia*, about the relevant products' physical attributes and performance capabilities, the dollar value to the buyer of the product's various performance capabilities, the dollar value or cost to the buyer of various product-image-related advantages and disadvantages, the relative dollar value to the buyer of future consumption *versus* current consumption, etc.—and about the cost to buyers of buying and owning various goods—i.e., *inter alia*, about the cost-per-ounce of different products or of given products sold in different quantities, about the maintenance and repair costs of different durable products, etc. Similarly, (1) unit-output producers may not possess perfect information about the relative cost of using different known production processes or about the demand curves they face, (2) QV investors may not possess perfect information about the private cost of creating and using particular QV investments, about the demand for the product or service that a particular QV investment would create, about the likelihood that an innovative product-R&D QV investment would yield a product discovery, about the length and breadth of the IP-law protection they could secure for their product discovery, about their ability to prevent others from using their product discovery without paying for the right to do so by keeping it secret, and/or about the buyer power of the actors to which they might want to sell any discovery-related patents or to license to use such patents; and (3) production-processes researchers may not possess perfect information about the cost of executing particular PPR projects, about the likelihood that particular PPR projects will yield various production-process discoveries, about the dollar value of such discoveries to their possible users, about the length and breadth of any IP-law protection they would obtain for their production-process discoveries, about their ability to keep such discoveries secret, and about the buyer power of the actors that might want to purchase production-process patents or licenses to use the production-process discoveries. Although most of the relevant information-imperfections are attributable to the fact that information is not freely available, some are attributable to what cognitive psychologists claim are human dispositions to behave in ways that do not conform with traditional economic models' assumptions that humans make the choices that maximize their utility from a stable set of "rational" preferences and make from their individual prospectives optimal investments in obtaining relevant information—more specifically, some information imperfections are attributable to the facts that humans tend to ignore low-probability possible outcomes that have not occurred recently and/or have not come to their attention, that humans tend to assign too high probabilities to low-probability outcomes that have recently eventuated and come to their attention, that humans have "bounded willpower"—tend to make decisions against their lifetime interest that sacrifice future benefits for present benefits (though humans also try to overcome these dispositions by obligating themselves to save and keeping certain foods and drinks out of the house), that humans place a higher value on keeping something they have than on obtaining that *desideratum* (for reasons unrelated to the attraction of the familiar)—the so-called endowment effect of possessing something, that humans seem to manifest what appears to be an irrational as opposed to non-rational aversion to sustaining losses, that humans tend to believe that bad outcomes are more likely to occur for them than for others when there is no factual basis for this assumption, that humans make decisions that manifest the fixed-cost fallacy, that humans who are concerned with the morality of the choices they make that will affect others tend to misperceive the morality of the choices available to them from their own normative perspectives in ways that lead them to conclude that the choice that is in their material interest is morally desirable.[5]

Imperfections in the information available to resource allocators can cause economic inefficiency both by generating step-wise distortions in the private cost and private benefits that particular resource allocations impose/confer on them and by causing resource allocators to make positive and negative resource-allocating choices that are not in their interest. Thus, imperfections in the information available to sacrificing resource-users can generate step-wise distortions in the private cost of actual resource-uses by causing the sacrificer to overestimate or underestimate the dollar value to it of resources that are allocated to another use—i.e., by generating positive or negative step-wise distortions in the private cost of the misvalued resources to their actual user. Imperfections in the information available to consumers that cause them to overvalue or undervalue the units of output they consume can generate step-wise resource-allocator-non-sovereignty distortions in the private benefits of producing units of extant products, in the private benefits of producing units of products created by QV investments (in the private benefits of using created QV investments), and in the private benefits of using production-process discoveries (in the private benefits a marginal-cost-reducing production-process discovery enables its user to obtain and hence in the private benefits the production-process researcher obtains by using its discovery itself or licensing others to do so.) Imperfections in the information available to actual resource-users can cause consumers, UO producers, QV investors, and production-process researchers to make choices that are not in their interest. Moreover, unless such results are prevented by the step-wise distortions that are generated by the interaction of the extant exemplars of all other types of Pareto imperfections the relevant economy contains, the non-sovereignty of both sacrificing resource-users and actual resource-users will cause inter-ARDEPPS and intra-ARDEPPS QV-to-QV misallocation, inter-ARDEPPS and intra-ARDEPPS UO-to-UO misallocation, inter-ARDEPPS and intra-ARDEPPS PPR-to-PPR misallocation, and conventional consumption-optimum misallocation. The State may be able to reduce resource-allocator non-sovereignty and the amount of economic inefficiency such non-sovereignty causes by grading products, banning certain low-quality products altogether, and subsidizing private companies that provide "consumer reports," though obviously the allocative efficiency of all such State interventions is contestable.

8.5   The Step-Wise Resource-Allocator-Non-Maximization Distortions in the Private Benefits, Private Costs, and Profits that Exemplars of Various Functional Categories of Resource Allocations Respectively Confer on, Impose on, and Yield the Actors to Which These Resource Allocations Respectively Allocate Resources and the Effect that Resource-Allocator Non-Maximization Has on Economic Inefficiency by Causing Resource Allocators to Reject Profitable Resource Allocations and Execute Unprofitable Resource Allocations

Resource-allocator non-maximization can yield step-wise distortions in the private benefits, private costs, and profits yielded by resource allocations in all the ways that resource-allocator non-sovereignty can do so. Resource-allocator non-maximization can also affect the amount of economic inefficiency that is generated by decisions to execute or not to execute the exemplars of a given category of resource allocations by leading the resource-users to which those resource allocations allocated/(would have allocated) resources to execute unprofitable resource allocations or to reject profitable resource allocations. More specifically, non-maximization by sacrificers can generate positive or negative step-wise distortions in the private benefits and profits a resource allocation will yield the resource-user to which it allocates resources by leading the sacrificer to accept offers for resources that do not compensate them for the revenue-loss the withdrawal of those resources will impose on them and to reject offers for resources that would have more than compensated them for the losses the withdraw of the relevant resources from them would have imposed on them. Non-maximization by resource-users to which resource allocations of interest would allocate resources can also affect economic efficiency by causing actual resource-users to accept allocations of resources that are unprofitable and to reject allocations of resources whose acceptance by them would have been profitable. Resource-allocator non-maximization can cut either in the same direction or in the opposite direction as resource-allocator non-sovereignty when the issue is their joint impact on the economic efficiency of resource allocations that are executed or not executed.

Resource allocators can fail to maximize either because they make resource-allocating decisions unthinkingly (because they suffer from what economists colorfully denominate "*acrazia*") or because they do their maths wrong. I have personally encountered many consumers whose purchasing-decisions were critically affected by their inability to calculate the relative price-per-ounce of options that contained different numbers of ounces of the product concerned and have taught many students who have found it difficult to calculate the present value of a stream of benefits or profits even when supplied with the relevant rate of discount. I have no systematic evidence to support this conclusion, but I suspect that workers, consumers, and businesses often make resource-allocating decisions that they would not have made had they done their maths right. The State can reduce such errors not only by providing better education but also by requiring retail distributors to post price-per-ounce information on their shelves or to include price-per-ounce information in their internet listings.

8.6 The Step-Wise-Buyer-Surplus Distortions in the Private Benefits, Private Cost, and Profits that Exemplars of Various Functional Categories of Resource Allocations Respectively Confer on, Impose on, and Yield the Actors to Which the Relevant Resource Allocations Allocate Resources

I have already considered many of the buyer-surplus distortions that will be TBLE to take into account when predicting or post-dicting the economic efficiency of a choice under other headings. Thus, I have attributed to imperfections in seller price-competition the negative step-wise distortions in the private benefits of producing units of output whose sales generate marginal revenue that is lower than the price(s) for which the unit(s) in question could have been sold because those sales increase the buyer surplus secured by buyers of the intra-marginal units of the good in question. When this negative step-wise distortion would have affected the private benefits that a sacrificing unit-output producer would have realized by selling the sacrificed units of its product, it will convert into an equal negative step-wise distortion in the private cost to the actual resource-user of the resources in question, hence a negative step-wise distortion in the private cost to the actual resource-user of the use to which the actual resource-user put the sacrificed resources (regardless of whether that use was increasing the output of an existing product, creating or using a created QV investment, or executing a PPR project), and hence, a positive step-wise distortion in the profits the relevant resource allocation yielded the actor to which it allocated resources. When this negative step-wise distortion affected the private benefits that the actor to which a resource allocation of interest allocated resources obtained by increasing its unit output, it will have generated a negative distortion in the private benefits of producing the additional units of an existing product to whose production the resource allocation in question devoted resources, a negative distortion in the operating profits that the use of a QV investment to whose creation a resource allocation of interest devoted resources conferred on the QV investor to which that resource allocation allocated resources, and a negative distortion in the private benefits that users of a marginal-cost-reducing production-process discovery yielded by a resource allocation of interest obtained by increasing their unit outputs and hence in the private benefits (and profits) that the relevant resource allocation yielded each such production-process researcher to which it allocated resources. Similarly, I have attributed to the relevant buyers' monopsony power the buyer-surplus-related step-wise negative distortion in the private benefits that (1) a QV investment created with resources allocated by a resource allocation of interest confers on the relevant QV investor or (2) a PPR project executed with resources allocated by a resource allocation of interest confers on the relevant production-process researcher that are generated by the price-concessions (i.e., buyer surplus that buyers of related product or production-process patents or buyers of licenses to produce patented products or use patented production processes are able to secure on the transactions in question). Obviously, if the analysis that is being executed has already taken account of buyer surplus under another heading, it would be incorrect to include that buyer surplus when calculating the step-wise-buyer-surplus-distortion component of the step-wise formula for the aggregate distortion in the profits yielded by the resource allocation in question: my protocol for economic-efficiency prediction/post-diction instructs the analyst to avoid such double-counting. However, not all buyer surplus that can yield step-wise distortions in the profits yielded by resource allocations of interest will be taken into account by analyses that focus on the buyer-surplus consequences of sellers' facing downward-sloping demand curves or buyers' in bilateral-monopoly situations being able to extract concessions because their prospective suppliers are dependent on their patronage. Some buyer surplus is generated because it would be prohibitively privately-transaction-costly for sellers to identify the demand prices of their potential customers even if that price were the same for each of the units that each of their customers might buy[6] and/or because sellers make mistakes when pricing their products. Buyer surplus that would have been generated by sacrificed sales or were generated by actual sales for these latter reasons will yield the same step-wise distortions in relevant private-benefit, private-cost, and profit figures for the same reasons that imperfection-in-seller-price-competition-generated or "monopsonistic"-buyer-generated buyer surplus would generate. Obviously, one should not count seller-error-generated-buyer-surplus step-wise distortions when calculating the buyer-surplus component of the step-wise distortion in the profits yielded by a resource allocation of interest if one has already taken account of the distortion in question when calculating the resource-allocator-non-sovereignty or resource-allocator-non-maximization step-wise-distortion components of the step-wise-distortion formula for the aggregate distortion in the profits yielded by any resource allocation of interest.

I want to close this buyer-surplus discussion with one more concrete point: in situations in which two or more new QV investments (of given size or two or more new PPR projects of given size) would be profitable if each were the only investment (project) of the relevant kind that was made (created) but no new QV investment (or no new PPR project) would be profitable if two or more investments (projects) were made (executed), buyer surplus will generate a positive step-wise distortion in the profits yielded by making the QV investment (executing the PPR project) whose use will generate less buyer surplus rather than more buyer surplus, and this distortion will cause the less-economically-efficient QV investment to be made (the less-economically-efficient PPR project to be executed) if (1)(A) the difference between the profit-yield of the QV investment (PPR project) whose use would generate less buyer surplus and the profit-yield of the QV investment/PPR project whose use would generate more buyer surplus was larger than (B) the number of dollars by which the profits that would be yielded by the former investment (project) exceeded the profits that would be yielded by the latter investment (project) and (2) the interaction of all exemplars that the relevant economy contained of all other types of Pareto imperfections did not render the lower-buyer-surplus-generating QV investment (PPR project) more-economically-efficient than the higher-buyer-surplus-generating QV investment (PPR project)—did not generate a negative step-wise distortion in the profits yielded by a resource allocation to the lower-buyer-surplus-generating investment (project) from the higher-buyer-surplus-generating investment (project) that exceeded the buyer-surplus difference *minus* the profit-difference for the two QV investments (PPR projects) in question.

*****

Section 1.4.4 of this study provided a somewhat-detailed but far-from-comprehensive account of the distortion-analysis protocol for economic-efficiency analysis that I believe is third-best-allocatively-efficient. As its name suggests, this protocol focuses to a significant extent on the aggregate distortion in the profits yielded by the exemplars of various functionally-defined categories of resource allocations whose execution was/would be elicited by the choice whose economic efficiency is at issue and the aggregate distortions in the profits that would have been yielded by the exemplars of various functionally-defined categories of resource allocations whose execution was/would be deterred by the choice whose economic efficiency is at issue (where "the aggregate distortion in the profits yielded by any resource allocation" equals the difference between the profits that resource allocation yields/would yield the resource-user to which it allocated/would allocate resources and the economic efficiency of that resource allocation that is generated by all exemplars of all types of Pareto imperfections the economy in question contains). Section 6.2 of this study distinguished two coincident formulas for the aggregate distortion in the profits yielded by any specified resource allocation—"onesy (1E)" formulas, which calculate the relevant difference "in one go," and "step-wise (SW)" formulas, which equate the aggregate distortion in the profits yielded by a specified resource allocation with the sum of the seven distortions in those profits that would be calculated to be yielded by all exemplars of each of the seven types of Pareto imperfections if the calculation of such individual-type-of-Pareto-imperfection-oriented step-wise distortions were based on the usually-counterfactual assumptions (1) that the exemplars of the other 6 types of Pareto imperfections the economy contained would not collectively affect the relevant aggregate-profit distortion and (2) that the exemplars of each type of Pareto imperfection that was the focus of one component of the step-wise distortion formula would not affect the relevant aggregate-profit distortion by affecting one or more exemplars of one or more of the other 6 types of Pareto imperfections. Section 6.7 explains why I believe it will be third-best-allocatively-efficient for economic-efficiency predictors/post-dictors to use step-wise rather than onesy aggregate-profit-distortion formulas. Chapters 7 and 8 have analyzed in considerable detail the step-wise formula for the aggregate distortion in the profits yielded by a wide variety of functionally-defined categories of resource allocations. By identifying the wide range of Pareto imperfections that will affect the aggregate distortion in the profits yielded by exemplars of various categories of resource allocations and the different ways in which given Pareto imperfections will affect the aggregate distortion in the profits yielded by different resource allocations, Chaps. 7 and 8 have revealed the complexity of the protocol that Sect. 1.4.4 outlined.

Three additional points need to be made. First, because the preceding analysis focused on the various distortions that are generated, respectively, by each type of Pareto imperfection, it did not pay attention to the possibility that a resource allocation could generate economic inefficiency by altering the amount of poverty and material inequality in the society in which it took place. I suspect that this possibility is most salient for resource allocations that devote or withdraw resources from PPR and for resource allocations that result from producers' choosing to substitute one known production process for another. The concern is that PPR that discovers more-capital-intensive production processes that are more profitable to use than their pre-existing, less-capital-intensive (less-automated) alternatives and choices to substitute lower-private-cost, known, more-capital-intensive (more-automated) production process for higher-private-cost, known, less-capital-intensive (less-automated) production processes may increase poverty and material inequality and economic inefficiency on that account by reducing the amount of labor hired by the producers that use the discovered or known more-capital-intensive production process in question and the skill, marginal physical products, and hence marginal revenue products and wages of the labor that the producers in question hire. Admittedly the resulting additional poverty and material inequality could be prevented by off-setting tax and/or social-welfare redistributive policies, but since as we have seen such tax policies or the financing of such social-welfare policies would themselves increase the amount of various categories of economic inefficiency that are generated the prospect of combining them with the production-process choices in question would not eliminate the poverty/material-inequality-related distortion in the profits yielded by relevant PPR and known-production-process choices even if it were realistic to assume that the relevant production-process-related choices would be combined with offsetting redistribution policies.

Second, because the protocol I am recommending is a protocol for third-best-allocative-efficiency analysis, it instructs the economic-efficiency analysis to execute those but only those theoretical and empirical research projects whose execution is *ex ante* economically efficient.

Third, because the data that is relevant to the prediction or post-diction of the economic efficiency of any choice will almost always be relevant to the prediction or post-diction of the economic efficiency of a wide variety of other choices, it will almost always be third-best-allocatively-efficient for analysts who are focusing on one choice to execute more extended and refined theoretical and empirical analyses than would be TBLE if the results of those analyses could not be used to analyze the economic efficiency of other choices.

Notes

1. This reality does not call into question the value of any approach that makes use of the notion of single-Pareto-imperfection-oriented step-wise private-figure distortions because each such step-wise distortion is calculated on the

assumption that the relevant economy contains the exemplars of all other types of Pareto imperfections that it actually does contain.

2. It is important to recognize that the fact that a buyer of labor must pay higher wages to attract workers of greater skill and assiduity does not make that buyer a monopsonist of the "facing-an-upward-sloping-supply-curve" type because the supply curve that that concept references is the supply curve for labor (or anything else) of a given quality. I want to take this opportunity to make a related (though admittedly only tangentially related) point. Currently, in the USA, there is considerable support for central-government (federal) legislation raising the minimum wage. One argument that is made against this policy is that it would not benefit the set of individuals it is intended to help because the increase in the minimum wage will lead to a reduction in the number of workers hired to do jobs for which the pre-legislation wage was lower than the proposed increased minimum wage. This argument has in turn been countered with empirical evidence that establishes that state legislation that increased the minimum wage in the state in question has not led to any or at least any significant reduction in the number of people hired to do the work whose pre-legislation wage was lower than the increased minimum wage. I am concerned that the researchers who did this empirical research did not take any or sufficient account of the possibility that the employers whose wage payments would be affected by any increase in the minimum wage might respond by replacing their original workers with more-skilled, more-assiduous workers who would be willing to work for them for the higher minimum wage but not for the lower wage these employers originally offered. If that is the case, the increased-minimum-wage legislation might harm its intended beneficiaries as a class even if it did not significantly reduce the number of workers doing "the jobs" that the intended beneficiaries did pre-legislation. I am concerned that the increase in the minimum wage may create an unnecessary permanent Lumpenproletariat—a class of individuals who will not be employed regardless of the general macro-economic situation (unnecessary because they would be hired at a lower wage though they will not be hired at the higher, increased minimum wage, given that the dollar value of their labor to employers is lower than the higher minimum wage though it equals or exceeds the lower wage they were original paid). Three final points: (1) I recognize that, if the only way to improve the welfare of low-paid workers were to increase the minimum wage, the desirability of increased-minimum-wage legislation would depend on facts that I have not provided (*inter alia*, on the percentage of the relevant class of workers that the increase in minimum wage would cause to lose their jobs and their ability to find loss-minimizing other work); (2) I am not opposed to redistributing income to the poor—to the contrary, I support such redistributions primarily because I think they are required by our commitment to a liberal conception of justice and because they promote the moral good as I envision it (justice-considerations aside) but also because (as I explained in Chap. 1) they increase economic efficiency; and (3) I believe that efforts to benefit low-wage earners by increasing the minimum wage are less desirable than efforts to do so

through negative income-taxes or welfare policies and belong to a misguided set of policies that seeks to improve the distributions of income and wealth by constraining market transactions rather than by complementing them with government redistributions.

3. Of course, a buyer's facing an upward-sloping supply curve will lower the price it pays for the monopsonized "good" (the monopsony will lower average kost of purchase to the monopsonist) at the same time that it generates a positive step-wise distortion in the kost the monopsonist incurs to purchase all but the first unit of the monopsonized good it might purchase (assuming that the monopsonist does not engage in perfect price discrimination when purchasing the monopsonized good from each of its suppliers).

4. For a more-detailed discussion of this reality, see note 7 of Chap. 7 and the text of Sect. 7.1.1.3 to which it is attached.

5. For the canonical law-and-economics article discussing these realities and their legal and policy implications, see Jolls et al. (1998). For more recent discussions of the relevant cognitive-psychology literature and/or its relevance for economics, see Cartwright (2018), Teitelbaum and Zeiler (2018), Wilkinson and Klaes (2018), Zamir and Teichman (2014), Dhami (2016), and Zamir and Teichman (2018).

6. I make this point because a seller's facing a downward-sloping demand curve would not result in its sales' yielding buyer surplus if it (1) could charge the demand price for each unit of its product it sold at non-prohibitive transaction cost and (2) did in fact do so.

References

Cartwright, E. (Ed.). (2018). *Behavioral economics* (3d ed.). London and New York: Routledge.

Dhami, S. S. (2016). *The foundations of behavioral economic analysis*. Oxford: Oxford University Press.

Jolls, C., Sunstein, C. R., & Thaler, R. (1998). A behavioral approach to law and economics. *Stanford Law Review, 50,* 1471–1547.

Teitelbaum, J. C., & Zeiler, K. (Eds.). (2018). *Research handbook on behavioral law and economics*. Cheltenham, U.K.: Edward Elgar Publishing.

Wilkinson, N., & Klaes, M. (2018). *An introduction to behavioral economics* (3d ed.). London: Macmillan Education.

Zamir, E., & Teichman, D. (Eds.). (2014). *The Oxford handbook of behavioral economics and the law*. Oxford: Oxford University Press.

Zamir, E., & Teichman, D. (2018). *Behavioral law and economics*. New York: Oxford University Press.

Some Negative and Positive Implications of the TBLE Distortion-Analysis Protocol for Economic-Efficiency Prediction/Post-diction

9

Abstract

Section 9.1 criticizes various first-best antitrust-related economic-efficiency-related arguments. Section 9.2 criticizes (1) the standard Law & Economics argument that holding tortfeasors liable in accident and pollution cases will equate the profitability and economic efficiency of all avoidance-move decisions and (2) the conventional first-best analysis of the economic efficiency of shifting from a negligence/contributory-negligence legal regime to a strict-liability/contributory-negligence regime on realistic assumptions about the prevailing legal and social realities. Section 9.3 criticizes the standard argument for the conclusion that too little R&D of all kinds is done from the perspective of economic efficiency, discusses the economic efficiency of various policies that have been proposed to stimulate R&D, and makes some preliminary comments on policies that might be adopted to reduce R&D-related misallocation. Section 9.4 criticizes various first-best-economic-efficiency public-finance-related arguments.

At many places in the first eight chapters of this study, I have attempted to maintain or stimulate reader interest by pointing out the importance of taking appropriate account of The General Theory of Second Best and the variety of ways in which economies use resources—i.e., by explaining why the TBLE variant of distortion analysis that I believe Second-Best Theory warrants both undermines conventional FBLE economic-efficiency analyses and the conclusions such analyses reach and generates defensible conclusions about the economic efficiency of various behaviors and policies that differ significantly from those yielded by first-best-economic-efficiency analysis. This chapter justifies these claims by executing (1) detailed critiques of canonical, FBLE economic-efficiency analyses of a variety of seller-competition-related issues, accident-and-pollution-loss-related tort-law issues, R&D-related issues, and tax-policy issues and (2) Second-Best-Theory-derived distortion analyses of such issues that are admittedly far-less-comprehensive-and-refined than would be TBLE in most policy-decision contexts.

© Springer Nature Switzerland AG 2020
R. S. Markovits, *Welfare Economics and Second-Best Theory*,
https://doi.org/10.1007/978-3-030-43360-4_9

9.1   Seller-Price-Competition-Related Economic-Efficiency Issues: Some Second-Best-Theory-Based Critiques of Canonical, FBLE Economic-Efficiency Analyses and Some Preliminary Second-Best-Theory-Derived Distortion Analyses of These Economic-Efficiency Issues

9.1.1   Second-Best-Theory-Based Critiques of Three Canonical, FBLE Analyses of Seller-Price-Competition-Related Economic-Efficiency Issues

9.1.1.1   The Deadweight Loss of Monopoly

The traditional economic-efficiency rationale for pro-competition policies focuses on the supposed tendency of each individual imperfection in seller price-competition an economy contains to generate economic inefficiency by causing the seller that faces that imperfection to produce fewer units of its product than would be economically efficient. Admittedly, if an individual imperfection in seller price-competition would always generate this outcome, that reality would not depend on the category or categories of use from which the resources that could be used to produce the additional units of the underproduced product whose production would be economically efficient would be withdrawn. However, in the context of this study, it is worth pointing out that economists who make these deadweight-loss-of-monopoly claims are implicitly assuming that the resources that would be used to produce the additional units of any underproduced good would be withdrawn exclusively from the production of units of other extant goods—that the misallocation that they are alleging would be generated by each imperfection in seller price-competition would in my terminology be inter-ARDEPPS UO-to-UO misallocation.

Diagram 9.1 illustrates the conventional, first-best argument for the conclusion that each imperfection in seller price-competition will cause the seller that faces it to produce fewer units of its product (say, X) than would be economically efficient. Diagram 9.1 contains three curves: the demand curve (DD_X) the seller in question faces—the curve that indicates the quantity of its product it will sell at various before-purchase-tax prices, the marginal revenue curve (MR_X) the seller in question faces, and the marginal-cost curve (MC_X) the seller in question faces. (Although Diagram 9.1's construction of DD_X as linear and MC_X as horizontal will usually not be realistic, its assumptions about the shapes of these curves play no role in the relevant first-best argument.)

Here is the traditional argument for the conclusion that each imperfection in seller price-competition causes the producer that faces it to produce too few units of its product from the perspective of economic efficiency: (1) the economically-efficient output of any good is the output at which the demand curve for it (DD_X in Diagram 9.1) cuts its marginal-cost curve (MC_X in Diagram 9.1) from above

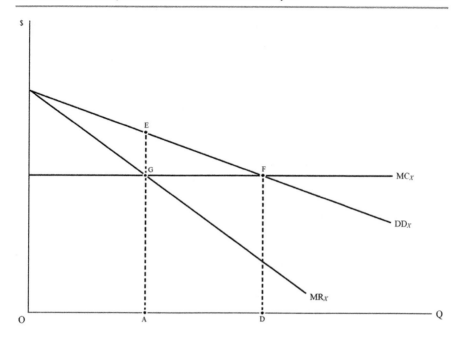

Diagram 9.1   The standard "deadweight loss of monopoly diagram"

(OD units in Diagram 9.1); (2) the actual output of any good is the output at which
the marginal-revenue curve its producer faces (MR_X in Diagram 9.1) cuts its
marginal-cost curve (MC_X in Diagram 9.1) from above (OA units in Diagram 9.1);
(3) the imperfection in seller price-competition that causes the relevant DD_X to be
downward-sloping and MR_X to be lower than DD_X will cause the actual output at
which MR_X cuts MC_X from above (OA) to be lower than the output at which DD_X
cuts MC_X from above (OD); and (4) the associated economic inefficiency (the
so-called deadweight loss of monopoly) is the area between the relevant DD_X and
MC_X curves between the relevant product's (X's) actual and economically-efficient
output (area EFG in Diagram 9.1).

Diagram 9.1 reflects two additional assumptions made by proponents of the
standard, first-best argument about the deadweight loss of monopoly: (1) that sellers
that face imperfections in seller price-competition will face demand curves that are
downward-sloping over the relevant range and (2) that sellers that face
downward-sloping demand curves will engage in single pricing (will set a single
per-unit price and allow all buyers to purchase as many units of the product they
respectively produce as they respectively wish to purchase at that price). (This
second assumption underlies the construction of the MR_X curve: for example, if the
seller sold each unit of its product for the highest price anyone would pay for that
unit, MR_X would coincide with DD_X.) Even if I accept these two empirical
assumptions, which are certainly not entirely unrealistic, the conventional

deadweight-loss-of-monopoly argument would be undermined by its first-best character—i.e., by the fact that it would be correct only if (1)(A) the DD curves for each relevant product coincides with the marginal-allocative-value curve (MLV) for that product—the curve that indicates the net dollar-gain generated by the consumption of successive units of the good in question—and (B) the MC curve for each product coincides with the marginal-allocative-cost curve (MLC) for that product—the curve that indicates the allocative value that the resources used to produce successive units of the good in question would have generated in their sacrificed uses—or (2) the actual deviations between the relevant DD and MLV figures on the one hand and the relevant MC and MLC figures on the other perfectly offset each other's tendencies to cause the actual output of the good in question to diverge from the economically-efficient output of that good. Although the first set of conditions just delineated will always be satisfied if the economy is oPp, it will be satisfied only rarely and fortuitously in economies that are realistically-Pareto-imperfect, and the second set of conditions just delineated will be satisfied only rarely and fortuitously when the first set of conditions is not satisfied.

   Section 6.3.5's analysis of the aggregate distortion in the profits yielded by allocations of resources to the production of the marginal unit of one product X from the production of less-than-one, one, or more-than-one just-extra-marginal units of another product Y reveals why in an economy in which the supra-competitive price of X is not the only relevant Pareto imperfection one cannot assume that, from the perspective of economic efficiency, too few units of any product X whose price is supra-competitive will be produced (even on the assumptions on which Diagram 9.1's construction is based)—viz., why even on those assumptions, in such a world, the aggregate distortion in the profits yielded by such a resource allocation may be zero or positive, not negative. Chapter 7's analyses of the step-wise distortions that all exemplars of imperfections in seller competition generate in the private benefits yielded by the use of QV investments and production-process discoveries and Chap. 8's analyses of the step-wise distortion that all exemplars respectively of each of the other six types of Pareto imperfections generate in these two private-benefit figures imply that this conclusion will be even more justified in cases in which the production of the marginal unit of X withdraws resources not only from the production of units of other extant products but also from QV-investment creation and PPR execution. When some of the resources devoted to producing units of any product X whose price is supra-competitive will be withdrawn from the creation of QV investments and/or the execution of PPR projects, any aggregate distortion in the private benefits that would have been generated by the use of such sacrificed QV investments or PPR projects will convert into equal distortions in the private cost of producing the marginal unit of X.

   But perhaps I have wandered too far from Diagram 9.1. The problem with using Diagram 9.1 to prove that the supra-competitive price of any product X will lead to few units of X being produced from the perspective of economic efficiency is that one cannot establish this conclusion by examining the difference between the heights of the DD and MC curves for the product in question between its actual output and the output at which the DD curve for it cuts its MC curve from above because the relevant analyses would focus on the MLV and MLC curves for the product in question not the DD and MC curves for that product and, in an otherwise-Pareto-imperfect economy, the MLV_X curve will usually not coincide with the DD_X curve, and the MLC_X curve will usually not coincide with MC_X curve. Thus, the MLV_X curve will tend to be higher than the DD_X curve to the extent that taxes are levied on the purchase of X, will tend to be higher than the DD_X curve if the consumption of units of X generates external benefits, will tend to be lower than the DD_X curve if the consumption of unit of X generates external costs, will tend to be higher than the DD_X curve if the buyer who paid the indicated price for the unit in question undervalued the unit or overestimated the cost of purchasing it, will tend to be lower than the DD_X curve if the buyer in question overvalued the relevant unit of X or underestimated the cost of purchasing it, and will tend to be higher than the DD_X curve if the buyer of X is a conventional monopsonist of X who does not engage in price discrimination when purchasing units of X. Similarly, the MLC_X curve will tend to be higher than the MC_X curve if the economy's extant Pareto imperfections generate a negative distortion in the private benefits that the resources used to produce the relevant unit of X would have conferred on the alternative resource-users from which the producer of the relevant unit of X bid away resources, will tend to be lower than the MC_X curve if the economy's extant Pareto imperfections generate a positive distortion in the private benefits that those resources used to produce the relevant unit of X would have conferred on the alternative resource-users from which the producer of the relevant unit of X bid away resources, will tend to be higher than the MC_X curve if the production of X generates external costs, and will tend to be lower than the MC_X curve if the production of X generates external benefits (to save space, I am not examining with more specificity all the possibilities analyzed in great detail in Chaps. 7 and 8).

In short, the traditional analysis of the so-called deadweight loss of monopoly must be rejected because that analysis is a first-best analysis whose implicit assumptions are clearly unrealistic. Although there may be good reason to believe that the supra-competitive pricing of extant products (and the fact that taxes are levied on market-earned income and on unearned income but not on leisure-production-and-consumption-generated benefits and do-it-yourself-labor-generated benefits) leads to the underproduction of market-produced products and the overproduction of leisure and overperformance of do-it-yourself labor from the perspective of economic efficiency and from that perspective to too few resources being devoted to UO production overall relative to the amount allocated to all alternative uses of resources combined, there is no good reason to conclude that the output of each good whose price is supra-competitive is too low from the per-spective of economic efficiency. The traditional analysis of the "deadweight loss of monopoly" is based on totally unrealistic assumptions, and the conclusions it generates are clearly false.

9.1.1.2 The Economic Efficiency of Preventing Mergers or Acquisitions that Would Convert a Perfectly-Competitive Industry Into a Pure Monopoly While Creating a Firm that Could Produce the Product in Question at a Lower Marginal and Average Total Cost

This section criticizes Oliver Williamson's canonical analysis of what he denominated "the welfare-trade-off" and I would call "the economic-efficiency trade-off or the economic-efficiency-effects analysis" that should be executed to determine the net economic efficiency of prohibiting a series of horizontal mergers and/or acquisitions (hereinafter M&As) that would convert a perfectly-competitive industry into a pure monopoly while creating a firm that faces a lower marginal-cost curve (and the same fixed costs) post-M&A than the participating firms would have faced at that time.[1] Like Williamson, I will ignore the allocative transaction costs of executing the mergers and acquisitions in question, the allocative transaction cost of generating and applying policies that respond to such mergers and acquisitions, the allocative transaction cost of the State's raising the revenues to finance the creation and application of such policies, and the economic-efficiency gains or losses that any decision to prohibit/allow any given series of such mergers or acquisitions would generate by deterring/eliciting future private conduct of the same kind and of related kinds. I will make two criticisms of Williamson's analysis: (1) it is first-best in character—i.e., it proceeds on the assumptions that the DD and MLV curves for the product involved coincide, that the pre-merger MC curve for the product involved coincides with the pre-merger MLC curve for that product, and that the post-merger MC curve for the product involved coincides with the post-merger MLC curve for that product—and (2) it ignores many categories of economic inefficiency and allocative costs whose magnitudes the M&As in question might affect, including but not limited to those I have indicated I will also ignore at this juncture.

Diagram 9.2 is devised to illustrate both Williamson's first-best "welfare-trade-off" analysis and the part of my critique of that analysis that focuses on its first-best character. To simplify the notation, I have not included any symbol in Diagram 9.2 to identify the product (say, product X) that is being produced by the firms that are participating in the mergers or acquisitions on which Williamson's analysis focuses. In Diagram 9.2, DD, MLV, MC, and MLC continue to stand respectively for "demand curve," "marginal-allocative-value curve," "marginal-cost curve," and "marginal-allocative-cost curve." The subscript "F" stands for "firm," the subscript "IND" stands for "industry," the subscript "B" indicates that the curve in whose symbolic representation it appears is the curve that prevailed before (hence "B") the execution of the mergers and/or acquisitions of interest, and the subscript "A" indicates that the curve in whose symbolic representative it appears is the curve that prevails after (hence "A") the execution of the mergers and/or acquisitions of interest. Since the mergers and/or acquisitions of interest convert the relevant industry from a perfectly-competitive-industry into a pure monopoly (in which only one firm is operating)—i.e., since the firm created by the mergers and/or

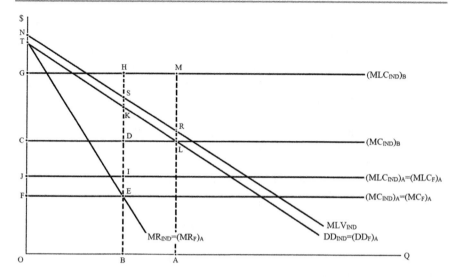

Diagram 9.2 A diagram that illustrates Williamson's "welfare-trade-off" analysis and part of my critique of it

acquisitions of interest constitutes the seller-side of the relevant industry after the mergers and acquisitions of interest have been executed, DD_{IND} is identical to $(DD_F)_A$, MR_{IND} is identical to $(MR_F)_A$, MC_{IND} is identical to $(MC_F)_A$, and $(MLC_{IND})_A$ is identical to $(MLC_F)_A$. Diagram 9.2 contains seven curves: DD_{IND} $(DD_F)_A$, $MR_{IND} \equiv (MR_F)_A$, MLV_{IND}, $(MC_{IND})_B$, $(MC_{IND})_A \equiv (MC_F)_A$, $(MLC_{IND})_B$, and $(MLC_{IND})_A \equiv (MLC_F)_A$. My use of Diagram 9.2 will assume that all costs of production are variable and that $(MC_{IND})_B$ and $(MC_{IND})_A$ are therefore the industry supply-curves respectively before and after the mergers and/or acquisitions of interest are executed. (Williamson also makes this assumption implicitly.) Diagram 9.2 assumes that $DD_{IND} \equiv (DD_F)_A$ is linear and that all the MC and MLC curves are horizontal. These assumptions are made solely for reasons of convenience: no important conclusion depends on these features of Diagram 9.2. Diagram 9.2's construction of $MR_{IND}=(MR_F)_A$ reflects Williamson's assumption that both before and after the series of mergers and acquisitions of interest X will be sold through single pricing: although this assumption significantly affects Williamson's analysis, it is not germane to my critique of that analysis (and will in any event often be realistic). Diagram 9.2 has been constructed on three additional empirical assumptions that do not play a critical role in my critique of Williamson's analysis, though they obviously will affect significantly the diagram's implications for the economic efficiency of the mergers and/or acquisitions whose consequences it illustrates. First, the MLC_{IND} curve in Diagram 9.2 is constructed to be 10% higher than its DD_{IND} curve: this assumption would be accurate if a 10% purchase tax were levied on the sale of X, no other Pareto imperfection affected the relationship between the marginal allocative value of any unit of X and the pre-purchase-tax price that the seller of that unit of X could obtain for it, and the income-effects of reductions of the price of X did not affect the allocative value of intra-marginal units of X. Second, both the $(MLC_{IND})_B/(MC_{IND})_B$ ratio and the $(MLC_{IND})_A/(MC_{IND})_A$ ratio in Diagram 9.2 equal 1.5: although I suspect that, for reasons that Chaps. 7 and 8 revealed, the MLC/MC ratio for almost products exceeds one, I doubt that it is often as high as 1.5. This assumption has been made for visual convenience. However, I see no reason to believe that the mergers and/or acquisitions will tend to change MLC_X/MC_X in any direction.

I will now use Diagram 9.2 to illustrate and criticize Williamson's analysis. According to Williamson, the mergers and acquisitions he describes will increase economic efficiency by reducing the allocative cost of producing the post-M&A output of X but will decrease economic efficiency by decreasing the unit output of X. Williamson assumes that the M&As of interest will reduce MC_{IND} firm CO to FO and, despite that fact, will reduce the output of X from OA to OB by converting the industry from a perfectly-competitive industry (whose output is determined by the intersection of MC_{IND} and DD_{IND}) to a pure monopoly whose output is determined by the intersection of MC_{IND} (which is changed by the M&As of interest) and MR_{IND}. Because Williamson's is a first-best-allocative-efficiency analysis that assumes that $DD_{IND} \equiv MLV_{IND}$, that $(MC_{IND})_B \equiv (MLC_{IND})_B$, and that $(MC_{IND})_A \equiv (MLC_{IND})_A$, Williamson concludes that the M&As whose economic efficiency he is analyzing will increase economic efficiency by reducing the total allocative cost of producing the after-M&A output of X by area CDEF (the M&A-generated CF reduction in per-unit marginal cost *times* the OB after-M&A unit output of X) and will decrease economic efficiency by reducing the output of X from OA to OB by the area between DD_{IND} and $(MC_{IND})_B$ between outputs OB and OA (i.e., by area KLD). For Williamson, then, the net economic efficiency of the M&As on which he is focusing depends on the difference between area CDEF and area KLD. My first critique of Williamson is that his analysis of both categories of economic-efficiency effects his M&As have is based on the unrealistic empirical assumptions of first-best-allocatively-efficient economic-efficiency analyses: if, for example, as Diagram 9.2 assumes, the other Pareto imperfections the relevant economy contains (which Williamson ignores) cause MLV_{IND} to be 10% higher than DD_{IND} rather than to coincide with DD_{IND} and the $(MLC_{IND})_B/(MC_{IND})_B$ and $(MLC_{IND})_A/(MC_{IND})_A$ ratios to be 1.5 rather than one so that the M&A-generated reduction in the *allocative cost* of producing the after-M&A output of X is 1.5 *times* the M&A-generated reduction in the *private cost* of producing that output rather than equaling the M&A-generated reduction in the private cost of producing that output, the increase in economic efficiency the relevant M&As will generate by reducing the allocative cost of producing the after-M&A output of X will be (area GHIJ) = 1.5 (area CDEF) and the M&As of interest will generate an increase in economic efficiency by reducing the output of X from OA to OB of area HMRS rather than a decrease in economic efficiency of area KLD by reducing X's output from OA to OB. Of course, these specific conclusions are artefacts of Diagram 9.2's assumptions about the relationship between MLC_X and MC_X and the relationship between MLV_X and DD_X. My point is not that Williamson's approach will always produce conclusions about the net effect that the M&As on which he is focusing will have on the two categories of economic efficiency on which he concentrates that are biased against the economic efficiency of such M&As (though I suspect that that is true) but that the first-best approach he takes is extremely inaccurate and almost certainly not TBLE.

Williamson's analysis is also deficient for reasons that Diagram 9.2 cannot be used to illustrate—viz., because it ignores the fact that the M&As whose economic efficiency he is analyzing will also affect the intensity of QV-investment competition in the industry in which they take place and because, in part but only in part for this reason, it ignores the fact that those M&As will also affect the amount of economic inefficiency the relevant economy generates by making economically-inefficient decisions to create or not to create QV investments and to execute or not to execute PPR projects. Contrary to the conventional assumptions that Williamson implicitly adopts, the fact that he is assuming that the industry in which the M&As of interest would be executed was originally "perfectly competitive" does not imply that the equilibrium quantity of QV investment in that industry is invariant: "industries" that are perfectly competitive can contain larger or smaller numbers of product variants and more or less capacity (can "deliver" the material product or service they supply faster or slower on the average throughout a fluctuating-demand cycle), and the M&As whose economic efficiency Williamson is analyzing will almost always affect the equilibrium quantity of QV investment in the industry or ARDEPPS in which they take place—(1) will tend to increase the equilibrium-QV-investment quantity in the relevant industry by raising prices at the industry's before-M&A QV-investment quantity and concomitantly both the (supernormal) rate-of-return that would be yielded by the before-M&A QV investments in the relevant area of product-space at the quantity of QV investment the industry would have contained after the date of the M&As' execution if the M&As did not change the industry's equilibrium-QV-investment quantity and the (supernormal) rates-of-return that would be yielded by additional QV investments in that ARDEPPS and (2) will tend to decrease the equilibrium-QV-investment quantity in the relevant ARDEPPS by substituting a situation in which no incumbent has a monopolistic (or natural-oligopolistic) QV-investment incentive to withdraw any of its QV investments in the relevant ARDEPPS for a situation in which the pure monopolist created by the M&As in question would have a monopolistic QV-investment incentive to withdraw one or more QV investments it would otherwise have found profitable to maintain or create. Whether Williamson's M&A would increase or decrease the equilibrium-QV-investment quantity in the industry in which they took place and whether any increase or decrease in the industry's equilibrium-QV-investment quantity would increase or decrease economic efficiency cannot be determined without knowing many facts that will vary from situation to situation, but it is clear that Williamson completely ignored those consequences of the M&As whose economic efficiency he was analyzing. Williamson also ignored the fact that the imperfections in seller price-competition and imperfections in QV-investment competition and possibly in PPR competition that would be generated by the M&As whose economic efficiency he was analyzing might also affect the amount of misallocation generated by economically-inefficient decisions to create and not to create QV investments in other ARDEPPSes and to execute and not to execute PPR projects in other ARDEPPSes by altering the aggregate distortion in the private benefits that would be generated by relevant allocations of resources to UO-producing, QV-creating, and PPR-executing resource-uses in the relevant M&As' "industry" and hence in the private cost and profit-yields of UO-producing, QV-creating, and PPR-executing resource-uses in other "industries" that would withdraw resources from one or more categories of use in the relevant M&As' industry. Finally, like everyone else, Williamson ignored the possibility that, by decreasing seller price-competition and QV-investment and PPR competition in the M&As' industry, the M&As in question might increase poverty and material inequality and thereby the various types of economic inefficiency that poverty and material inequality can cause.

9.1.1.3 The "Social"—I.e., Economic-Efficiency—Cost of Monopoly—I.e., of Imperfections in Seller Competition

Starting with the 1954 publication of Arnold Harberger's article *Monopoly and Resource Allocation*,[2] a large number of economists attempted to estimate the economic-efficiency loss (sometimes miscalled "the social cost") of imperfections in seller competition (usually inaccurately called "monopoly").[3] Many of the individual articles in this body of literature (1) focus exclusively on the alleged tendency of any imperfection in seller price-competition to cause any individual producer that faced it to produce too few units of its product from the perspective of economic efficiency (i.e., on "deadweight-loss-of-monopoly" claim), (2) assume implicitly (I state with non-quiet confidence) that the resources that would be devoted to producing the additional units of products whose production would be economically efficient would be withdrawn from the production of units of other extant products, (3) execute first-best analyses of the impact of an individual imperfection in seller price-competition on the category of economic inefficiency on which they focus, (4) implicitly assume bizarrely that, if all producers faced an imperfection in seller price-competition, all would produce too few units of their products from the perspective of economic efficiency (again, I am contending that these scholars believed they were analyzing the amount of what I call inter-ARDEPPS UO-to-UO misallocation the relevant economy contained), and therefore (5) overestimate the amount of misallocation the imperfections in seller price-competition an economy generates by causing its products to be produced in economically-inefficient proportions. Some of the articles in this literature focus on the fact that in one sense imperfections in seller competition could be said to cause economic inefficiency because the fact that any imperfection in seller competition a seller faces will enable it to obtain profits it could not otherwise secure will induce sellers to engage in economically-inefficient conduct to put themselves in a position in which they face imperfections in seller competition. The kinds of conduct that scholars who make this valid point have in mind include price-fixing, predatory conduct, efforts to secure tariff-protection, efforts to induce government to limit entry into their areas of product-space, the execution of mergers and acquisitions that would not have been profitable but for their tendency to reduce the absolute attractiveness of the best offers against which their participants would have to compete in the future, and efforts by individual sellers to differentiate their products so as to establish what I call competitive advantages over all their rivals when competing for the patronage of at least some buyers. Although as I have already stated this economic-efficiency objection to imperfections in seller competition is valid and should be seriously considered, the scholars who make it do not do a good job of analyzing the economic inefficiency of the behaviors in which firms engage to reduce the competition they face: (1) assume that the private transaction costs of those behaviors equal their allocative counterparts, (2) ignore the tendency of price-fixing and predatory pricing to generate intra-ARDEPPS UO-to-UO misallocation, (3) manifest a FBLE-analysis-based belief that any merger or acquisition that would have yielded its participants losses had it not benefitted them by reducing the absolute attractiveness of the offers against which they would have to compete would reduce economic efficiency by an amount equal to the losses they would have imposed on their participants had they not benefitted them in the above way, and peculiarly (4) in some instances assume that any effort that sellers make to differentiate their products through either advertising or packaging or by making what I call QV investments that create new products produce nothing of allocative value whatsoever. Moreover, more generally, this body of literature pays no attention to the existence of imperfections in QV-investment competition and imperfections in PPR competition or to the possibility that imperfections in seller price-competition and imperfections in QV-investment competition and PPR competition may cause what I call intra-ARDEPPS UO-to-UO, UO-to-QV or QV-to-UO, PPR-to-QV or QV-to-PPR, UO-to-PPR or PPR-to-UO, inter-ARDEPPS QV-to-QV, and inter-ARDEPPS PPR-to-PPR misallocation and may also cause various kinds of economic inefficiency by increasing poverty and material inequality. I find these omissions—which obviously bias the literature's conclusion about the amount of economic inefficiency caused by imperfections in seller competition in the opposite direction from the bias that results from the errors the literature makes when analyzing the amount of inter-ARDEPPS UO-to-UO resource misallocation that imperfections in seller price-competition generate—particularly regrettable because I believe that imperfections in seller competition cause far more of these ignored categories of economic inefficiency than of inter-ARDEPPS UO-to-UO misallocation.

   In short, the literature on the economic inefficiency generated by imperfections in seller competition manifests all the shortcomings that I claim applied-Welfare-Economics economic-efficiency analyses manifest more generally: (1) this literature ignores the fact that not only price-competition but also QV-investment competition and PPR competition can be imperfect for reasons that can cause economic inefficiency; (2) its analyses of inter-ARDEPPS UO-to-UO misallocation are first-best analyses that yield conclusions that are clearly unjustified and erroneous; (3) its assumption that private transaction costs equal allocative transaction costs is almost certainly false and manifests the relevant scholars' ignoring The General Theory of

Second Best; and (4) the literature fails to take account of most of the categories of economic inefficiency whose magnitudes imperfections in seller competition can affect and fails to say anything remotely-sensible about the effect of imperfections in seller competition on those categories of economic inefficiency it usually ignores when it makes some oblique reference to them. Enough (probably more than enough) said: *dayenu*.

9.1.2   Some Preliminary Analyses of the Economic Efficiency of Various Categories of Antitrust/Competition-Law-Covered Conduct

This section analyzes the economic efficiency of various categories of antitrust/competition-law-covered conduct. Because this section is not analyzing the economic efficiency of prohibiting these categories of conduct, it does not consider any such prohibition's allocative-transaction-cost effects, the allocative cost of imprisonments that would result from any such prohibition's enforcement, any allocative inefficiency that would be generated by any decisions the government made to finance the drafting, passage, and implementation of any such prohibition, or the allocative efficiency of any such prohibition's specific and general deterrence effects. The discussions that follow will proceed on the following assumptions:

(1) across all cases, increases in products' P/MC ratios will not tend to either increase or decrease inter-ARDEPPS UO-to-UO misallocation;

(2) from the perspective of economic efficiency, economies allocate too many resources to the creation of non-innovative QV investments relative to the amount they allocate to UO production and PPR execution;

(3) increases in poverty and material inequality increase economic inefficiency for a number of reasons and all tolled;

(4) from the perspective of economic efficiency, economies devote too many resources to the creation of QV investments that entitle their owners to obtain patents;

(5) from the perspective of economic efficiency, economies devote too few resources to PPR execution; and

(6) given the total amount of resources they devote to QV-investment creation, economies devote too many resources from the perspective of economic efficiency to QV-investment creation in ARDEPPSes whose economics-marginal QV investments' supernormal profit-rates are inflated by a higher amount by imperfections in seller competition and too few resources from the perspective of economic efficiency to QV-investment creation in ARDEPPSes whose economics-marginal QV investments' supernormal profit-rates are inflated by a smaller amount by imperfections in seller competition.

I recognize that, although I have provided arguments that favor each of these conclusions, the last three are contestable inter alia because their accuracy depends on facts I have not elicited about (1) the extent to which relevant product-R&D projects and relevant PPR projects reduce the probability that other projects that are competitive with them will make the discoveries each relevant project-set seeks to make (first), (2) differences in the average length and breadth of the legal protection that IP law gives respectively to product discoveries and production-process discoveries, and (3) the determinants of any differences in the legal protection that IP law gives to different product discoveries of various types and to different production-process discoveries of different types.

I want to emphasize at the outset that the point of this section is not to convince readers of the correctness of the preceding six claims or of any particular conclusions that I reach about the economic efficiency of the various categories of conduct on which it focuses. The point of this section is to reveal the differences between the concrete economic-efficiency analyses that the TBLE distortion-analysis approach to economic-efficiency analysis implies are TBLE and concrete, first-best economic-efficiency analyses.

9.1.2.1   Some Preliminary Comments on the Differences Between the Conventional, First-Best Analysis and the TBLE Distortion Analysis of the Economic Inefficiency of Horizontal Price-Fixing (Contrived-Oligopolistic Pricing) and the Differences Between the Conclusions About the Economic Inefficiency of Such Price-Fixing that These Two Categories of Economic-Efficiency Analysis Generate

In my terminology, a business is said to have initiated an oligopolistic practice if it made a move that it would not have found profitable but for its belief that its rivals' responses would or might be influenced by their realization that it would or might react to their responses. When the rivals' belief is attributable to their perception that the initiator would be given an opportunity to react to any non-cooperative response they made in a way that would render unprofitable for them those responses they would otherwise find profitable and that the initiator would find such a reaction inherently profitable, the oligopolistic conduct is said to be "natural." When the rivals' belief is attributable to the oligopolistic pricer's having communicated a threat to retaliate against their non-cooperation and/or a promise to reciprocate to their cooperation, the oligopolistic pricing is said to be "contrived." The conventional analysis of the economic efficiency of contrived-oligopolistic pricing (conventionally called horizontal price-fixing) initiator's having communicated an oligopolistic threat that it would retaliate against their non-cooperation and/or would reciprocate to their cooperation, the oligopolistic conduct is said to be contrived. The standard economic-efficiency analysis of contrived-oligopolistic pricing focuses on its alleged tendencies to yield economic inefficiency (1) by generating private transaction costs (the private transaction cost of arranging and enforcing the price-fix), which analysts assume equal the allocative transaction cost of doing so, and (2) by causing too few units of the price-fixed product to be produced from the perspective of economic efficiency relative to the amounts produced of other products in production. I will criticize these two claims and then explain why I think that horizontal price-fixing causes economic inefficiency.

I start with my two criticisms of the conventional analysis. First, although the conventional claim that price-fixing causes economic efficiency by generating transaction costs is correct, the conventional assumption that price-fixing generates allocative transaction costs equal to the private transaction costs it generates is almost certainly wrong: in my judgment, taken together, the aggregate distortions in the private benefits that the resources allocated to the arrangement and enforcement of horizontal price-fixes would have yielded in their sacrificed uses will virtually always be negative so that the allocative transaction costs that horizontal price-fixing generates will exceed the private transaction costs such price-fixing generates. Second, I am confident that price-fixing will not increase inter-ARDEPPS UO-to-UO misallocation by as much as the conventional analysis, which is based on the traditional, first-best "deadweight-loss-of-monopoly" analysis, concludes it will: indeed, although I suspect that horizontal price-fixing may tend to increase the amount of misallocation generated by the overproduction of leisure (despite the fact that individuals who create QV investments probably produce/consume too little leisure), with that exception I see little reason to believe that price-fixing will increase inter-ARDEPPS UO-to-UO misallocation (if I use the notation of Sect. 6.4, will increase the difference between the weighted-average P^*/MC^* ratios of relevant sets of products).

I also think that horizontal price-fixing will increase at least four categories of economic inefficiency that the conventional analysis ignores: (1) by leading to cheating or non-cooperative outbidding by competitive inferiors who never agreed to participate in the price-fix and derivatively to retaliation by price-fixers against worse-placed rivals that have beaten the price-fixers' contrived-oligopolistic offers and to defensive retaliation by non-cooperators that have been the targets of offensive retaliation, price-fixing will tend to cause intra-ARDEPPS UO-to-UO misallocation to the extent that the privately-worse-placed sellers that obtain sales by engaging in "cheating" and retaliation are also allocatively-worse-placed and will increase allocative transaction costs in a way that the conventional analysis ignores by causing firms to make allocative-transaction-costly cheating bids and retaliatory offers regardless of whether those bids yield the cheaters and retaliators any sales; (2) price-fixing will increase UO-producing and PPR-executing to QV-creating resource misallocation both (A) by increasing equilibrium QV investment in the ARDEPPSes in which the price-fixing is practiced by raising the prices charged in those ARDEPPSes at relevant QV-investment quantities (unless the price-fixing is combined with the erection of sufficient retaliation barriers to QV investment to offset or outweigh the effect of the price-rises on equilibrium QV investment) and (B) by increasing QV investment in other ARDEPPSes by decreasing the unit outputs of price-fixed products (i.e., by increasing the negative step-wise monopoly distortion in the private benefits that would have been yielded by the production of the units of the price-fixed products whose production the price-fix prevents); (3) price-fixing will increase the amount of economic ineffi-ciency generated by economically-inefficient decisions not to execute PPR projects by increasing the negative step-wise distortion in the private benefits that resources saved by production-process discoveries would have generated had they been used to produce the price-fixed products rather than the products to whose production processes the relevant PPR projects related and hence the negative step-wise monopoly distortion in the private benefits that the use of PPR projects confers on the researchers that execute them; and (4) price-fixing will increase the amount of economic inefficiency the economy generates because of poverty and material inequality by increasing the extent of poverty and material inequality in the society in which the horizontal price-fixing is practiced. Obviously, the TBLE distortion-analysis approach to analyzing the economic inefficiency generated by horizontal price-fixing (the approach that I think responds third-best-allocative-efficiently to The General Theory of Second Best) will focus to a TBLE extent on each of these four possibilities.

9.1.2.2 Some Preliminary Comments on the Differences Between the Conventional First-Best Analysis and the TBLE Distortion Analysis of the Economic Inefficiency of Predatory Pricing and the Differences Between the Conclusions About the Economic Inefficiency of Predatory Pricing that These Two Categories of Economic-Efficiency Analysis Generate

"Predatory conduct" (e.g., predatory pricing, advertising, or investing) is conduct perpetrated by an actor that would not have found it *ex ante* profitable but for the actor's perception that the conduct would reduce the absolute attractiveness of the best offers against which the actor would have to compete by driving a rival out and/or deterring the entry of a new competitor (in the case of predatory QV or PPR investments, when this effect would render *ex ante* profitable investments that would be *ex ante* economically inefficient in an otherwise-Pareto-perfect economy).[4]

My critique of the conventional first-best analysis of the economic inefficiency of predatory pricing is identical to its contrived-oligopolistic-pricing counterpart[5]: (1) the conventional analysis of the economic efficiency of predatory pricing makes the first-best assumption that the private transaction costs that predatory pricing causes the predator and its targets to incur (because predatory pricing involves predators' using resources to identify profitable predatory-pricing opportunities, to plan predatory-pricing campaigns, to make predatory offers to buyers for whose patronage they would not otherwise have bid, and to plan and make retaliatory offers to customers of predation-targets that have engaged in defensive retaliation against them and involves predation-targets' using resources to make rebids to reduce the losses that predatory pricing imposes on them and to execute defensively-retaliatory moves) equal the allocative transaction costs that predation generates; (2) it executes a FBLE analysis of the effect of the price-increases to which predatory pricing leads on inter-ARDEPPS UO-to-UO misallocation; (3) it ignores the possibility (indeed, the high probability) that predatory pricing and any retaliatory pricing to which it leads will generate intra-ARDEPPS UO-to-UO misallocation to the extent that it causes sales to be made by privately-worse-placed suppliers (that will generally by allocatively-worse-placed as well); (4) it ignores the impact that predatory pricing will have on the misallocation generated by economically-inefficient decisions to create or not to create QV investments and to execute or not to execute PPR projects; and (5) it ignores the fact that predatory pricing will also cause economic inefficiency by increasing the incidence of poverty and material inequality in the society in which it is practiced.

The Second-Best-Theory-warranted distortion-analysis protocol for analyzing the economic inefficiency of predatory pricing corrects all these errors of commission and omission just as its contrived-oligopolistic-pricing counterpart does. However, it is important to point out one difference between the economic-inefficiency effects of contrived-oligopolistic pricing and predatory pricing to which the approach I am recommending would call attention, a difference that is linked to the impacts that these two types of pricing respectively have on QV investment and PPR in the areas of product-space in which they are practiced. As Sect. 9.1.2.1 indicated, contrived-oligopolistic pricing will usually increase equilibrium QV investment in the ARDEPPSes in which it is practiced, and there is no reason to believe that such pricing will substitute one QV investment for another in the ARDEPPSes in which it is practiced. Neither of these conclusions applies to the QV-investment effects of predatory pricing. Predatory pricing will be profitable (and presumably, therefore, will often be practiced) only when the target it will eliminate will not be immediately replaced by a rival QV investment that is equally competitive with the predator's projects as were the target's product(s)—i.e., only when (1) barriers to entry or to incumbent QV-investment expansion will deter potential or actual competitors from replacing the QV investment the predation drove out, (2) the predation causes the firms that respond to the exit of the target by "replacing" the investment(s) that had been driven out with one or more projects that create one or more products that are less competitive with the predator's QV investments than the target's QV investment(s) was (were), or (3) the predator forestalls any rival from "replacing" the QV investment (s) its predation drove out by making one or more QV investments itself. In the first of these cases, the predatory pricing will reduce rather than increase equilibrium QV investment in the ARDEPPS in which it is practiced, and in the second and third of these cases, it will alter the identity of the QV investments located in the ARDEPPSes in which the relevant predatory pricing is practiced. Rather than revealing that the allocations of resources to the creation of the additional QV investments that horizontal price-fixing will cause to be made in the ARDEPPSes in which it is practiced will tend to be economically inefficient, the distortion-analysis protocol I think Second-Best-Theory warrants will reveal that any tendency of predatory pricing to reduce equilibrium QV investment in the ARDEPPSes in which it is practiced (or equilibrium PPR in those ARDEPPSes if the business of the ARDEPPS in question is the execution of PPR projects) will tend to be economically efficient and will instruct the analyst to examine whether any tendency of predatory pricing to induce the predator or some non-target rival to substitute its own QV investment(s) for the QV investment(s) the predator drove out will increase, decrease, or leave unchanged intra-ARDEPPS QV-to-QV misallocation in the ARDEPPSes in which predatory pricing is practiced.

9.1.2.3 Some Preliminary Comments on the Differences Between the Conventional, First-Best Analysis and the TBLE Distortion Analysis of the Economic Efficiency of Horizontal Mergers and Acquisitions (M&As) and the Differences Between the Conclusions that These Two Categories of Economic-Efficiency Analysis Generate

This section will use the symbol "M&As" to refer to "mergers and/or acquisitions." I should indicate at the outset that the conclusions that conventional, first-best analyses of the economic efficiency of particular horizontal M&As or specified subsets of such M&As differ from those that TBLE distortion analyses generate because the TBLE analysis would include more sophisticated and accurate investigations than would the conventional analysis both (1) of the effects that relevant M&As would have on the prices of the goods produced by the M&A participants, on the prices of the goods produced by the M&A-generated firm's product-rivals, and on the equilibrium quantities of QV investment in the ARDEPPSes in which the M&A participants' products are located if the M&As generated no static or dynamic efficiency and (2) of the impact that any static or dynamic efficiencies an M&A generates will have on the intensity of seller price-competition and QV-investment competition. More specifically, as I have demonstrated in great detail elsewhere,[6] conventional analyses of the impact of horizontal M&As on seller price-competition (1) fail to distinguish between situations in which sellers engage in individualized pricing and situations in which they charge across-the-board prices, (2) fail to define the concept of "oligopolistic conduct" or the related concept of the highest non-oligopolistic (individualized or across-the-board) price—HNOP—a seller could charge, (3) ignore many important determinants of the HNOP a seller could charge and hence of the impact of horizontal M&As on the HNOPs both of the M&As' participants and of the resulting firm's rivals (indeed, ignore entirely the reality that horizontal M&As can change the HNOPs of the product-rivals of the firm that results from the M&As), (4) fail to distinguish natural-oligopolistic pricing from contrived-oligopolistic pricing, (5) incorrectly analyze the determinants of whether a seller can obtain an oligopolistic margin naturally and the determinants of any contrived-oligopolistic margin a seller will find profitable to charge and hence incorrectly analyze the determinants of the impact of horizontal M&As on the natural and contrived-oligopolistic margins that their participants obtain and on the natural and contrived-oligopolistic margins that the product-rivals of the firm that results from the M&A obtain (indeed, ignore entirely the reality that horizontal M&As will affect the natural and contrived-oligopolistic margins that the rivals of the firm that results from the M&A will obtain), (6) assume incorrectly (A) that markets can be defined non-arbitrarily and (B) that the "best" way to predict the impact of a horizontal M&A on seller price-competition is to define the markets in which its participants are operating and base one's predictions in substantial part under the old approach on the shares that the M&A participants have of the sales made or of the assets located in those markets and on the pre-merger concentration of the seller-side of those markets (the percentage of the just-referenced sales/assets made/owned by the four or eight firms in the market that had the largest percentage of those sales/assets) and under the new approach on the pre-M&A HHI for the defined market and the M&A-generated increase in that HHI (where HHI equals the sum of the squares of the market shares of all firms placed in the market in question), (7) totally or virtually totally ignore the fact that horizontal M&As can affect the intensity of QV-investment competition as well as the equilibrium quantity of QV investment in the ARDEPPSes in which the M&A participants operate and consequently develop no conceptual systems or theories for predicting inter alia the impact of horizontal M&As on QV-investment competition and equilibrium QV investment in their participants' "markets," and (8) (A) have made no attempt to analyze the determinants of the impact that any static efficiencies or inefficiencies a horizontal M&A generates (which relate to the impact that a horizontal merger can have on the private cost of producing relevant quantities of its participants' pre-M&A products) or any dynamic efficiencies or inefficiencies a horizontal M&A generates (which relate to whether the firm the M&A creates faces higher or lower barriers to QV-investment expansion than its participants would have faced after the date of the M&A) will have respectively on the intensity of seller price-competition and the intensity of QV-investment competition in the M&A market and (B) do not recognize that horizontal M&As can also affect the intensity of QV-investment competition and equilibrium QV investment in the M&A market by affecting the retaliation barrier to expansion, the monopolistic QV-investment incentives or disincentives, and/or the natural-oligopolistic QV-investment disincentives faced by one or more rivals of the firm that results from the M&A.

Now that I have gotten that jeremiad off my chest, I will describe what I take to be the typical, conventional first-best analysis of the economic efficiency of horizontal M&As and the ways in which that analysis differs from the TBLE distortion analysis of such transactions' economic efficiency (which I think responds appropriately to The General Theory of Second Best). Let me begin by acknowledging that I am unaware of any actual "conventional, first-best analysis" of the economic efficiency of particular horizontal mergers or acquisitions and that the only published account by an economist who ignores The General Theory of Second Best of how the economic efficiency of a defined subset of horizontal M&As should be analyzed is the Oliver Williamson analysis criticized in Sect. 9.1.1.2. I am relying on my understanding of the implications of first-best-economic-efficiency analysis, on comments I have heard relevant economists make about the economic efficiency of horizontal M&As, and on proposals I have read by economists who ignore The General Theory of Second Best about the economically-efficient way to regulate horizontal M&As that create firms (now here is an ambiguity) that either will perform given R&D projects more proficiently or will do more R&D than their participants would have done.

On my understanding, economists who ignore The General Theory of Second Best (1) believe that any price-increase to which horizontal M&As lead will increase inter-ARDEPPS UO-to-UO misallocation by the amount that a first-best analysis of this effect would conclude such a price-increase would, (2) ignore the effect that horizontal M&As would have on equilibrium QV investment in the ARDEPPSes in which they take place if they did not yield dynamic efficiencies and more generally the impact that horizontal M&As would have on economic efficiency if they did not generate dynamic efficiencies by altering (I suspect in general by increasing) the total quantity of QV investment in the economy in which they take place and the total amount of economic inefficiency generated by economically-inefficient decisions to create or not to create QV investment, (3) ignore the fact that horizontal M&As that do not generate PPR-related dynamic efficiencies will tend to reduce the total amount of resources devoted to PPR in the economy in which they take place and hence the total amount of economic inefficiency generated by economically-inefficient decisions not to execute PPR projects in the economy in which they take place, (4) ignore the tendency of horizontal mergers to generate economic inefficiency by increasing the incidence of contrived-oligopolistic and predatory conduct in the ARDEPPSes in which they are executed and the misallocation that (as we saw in Sects. 9.1.2.1 and 9.1.2.2) such pricing generates, (5) ignore the tendency of horizontal mergers to generate economic inefficiency by increasing poverty and material inequality by reducing seller price-competition and QV-investment competition in the ARDEPPSes in which they are executed, (6) assume incorrectly that the economic-efficiency gain that will be generated by any static efficiency that a horizontal merger generates equals the private-cost saving it generates (when I suspect the relevant economic-efficiency gain exceeds the private-cost saving in question), (7) misanalyze the economic-efficiency effects of any dynamic efficiencies a horizontal M&A generates—(A) assume that the economic-efficiency gains that will be generated by dynamic efficiencies that result in the new firm's executing a more-economically-efficient project than would have been executed by one of its participants or one of their non-participant rivals will equal the number of dollars by which the relevant dynamic efficiencies increase the profits yielded by the project in question whereas (I suspect) a TBLE distortion analysis of this issue will yield the conclusion that the relevant economic-efficiency gain will exceed the referenced profit-increase, (B) assume that any additional QV investments/PPR projects that dynamic efficiencies cause to be created/executed in the ARDEPPS in which the relevant M&A takes place will increase economic efficiency by an amount equal to the profits the additional investment-projects yield their creators/executers whereas (I suspect) a TBLE distortion analysis of this issue will yield the conclusion that any additional QV investments M&A-generated dynamic efficiencies cause to be created will increase economic efficiency by less than the profits those investments yield their creators and may well be economically inefficient and that any additional PPR projects that M&A-generated dynamic efficiencies cause to be executed will increase economic efficiency by more than the profits they yield their executers, and (C) ignore the possibility (which admittedly may have no operational policy-relevance) that the dynamic efficiencies an M&A generates may reduce equilibrium QV investment or equilibrium PPR in the ARDEPPS in which the relevant M&A is executed by substituting for a situation in which one or more M&A participants and/or one or more rivals of the firm that results from the M&A faced non-prohibitive QV-investment disincentives a situation in which the firm that results from the M&A and one or more of its rivals face critical natural-oligopolistic QV-investment disincentives, and relatedly (8) misanalyze the economic efficiency of permitting horizontal M&As that would otherwise be deemed illegal on the ground that they would or did "lessen competition" in the sense of inflicting a net equivalent-dollar loss on the customers of the M&A participants and the customers of the product-rivals of the firm that results from the M&A "combined" by reducing the absolute attractiveness of the best offers they respectively received from any worse-than-privately-best-placed supplier if the firm that resulted from the M&A would either execute one or more of the R&D projects that would have been executed anyway more proficiently than they would otherwise have been executed by an M&A participant or by a non-participant rival of the M&A participants or increase the quantity of R&D done in the ARDEPPS in which the M&A took place—i.e., would misanalyze the economic efficiency of this proposal because it would misanalyze the economic inefficiency the mergers in question would generate by lessening competition, the economic-efficiency increase they would generate by increasing the proficiency with which given R&D projects are executed, and misanalyze the economic efficiency of any tendency of the M&As in question to increase the amount of resources devoted to product R&D and PPR. I have described the deficiencies of what I take to be the conventional, first-best analysis of the economic efficiency of horizontal M&As in ways that anticipate the TBLE distortion-analysis approach to these issues. To save space and to preserve interest in the forthcoming Springer book on the economic efficiency of various actual and proposed antitrust laws,[7] I will not delineate that approach to these issues here.

9.1.2.4 Some Preliminary Comments on the Differences Between the Conventional, First-Best Analysis and the TBLE Distortion Analysis of the Economic Efficiency of Some of the Pricing-Techniques, Contractual Arrangements, and Sales Policies that Are Surrogates for Vertical Integration and the Conclusions that These Two Categories of Economic-Efficiency Analysis Generate About the Economic Efficiency of Such Conduct

For two reasons, this section's analyses are particularly complicated: (1) the various surrogates for vertical integration on which it focuses perform a wide variety of functions whose respective performances have significantly different impacts on economic efficiency, and (2) the economic efficiency of any exemplar of any of these surrogates for vertical integration will often depend on the behavior that would be substituted for that surrogate if it were prohibited or not used for some other reason (depend on the answer that should be given to the "Compared to what?" question[8]—i.e., will often depend on whether the firm that employed the pricing-technique, contractual arrangement, or sales policy in question would respond to its prohibition by abandoning any attempt to achieve the objectives of the conduct in question, by trying to achieve the relevant goal(s) by engaging in different conduct other than vertical integration, or by vertically integrating.

I will focus separately on each of the surrogates for vertical integration just listed. I will begin by defining the surrogate in question, then state without fully explaining the functions that each such category of conduct can perform, after that execute a preliminary TBLE distortion analysis of the economic efficiency of the relevant category of conduct, next give the most-accurate account I can of the conventional, first-best analysis of the economic efficiency of the category of conduct in question, and finally point out the differences in the first-best and TBLE analyses of that category of conduct and the differences in the conclusions they reach about the economic efficiency of such conduct. I should emphasize at the outset that this section's functional and economic-efficiency analyses will be far less complete than those that will be provided in my forthcoming study of the economic efficiency of the conduct covered by US and EU antitrust law and of the various policies that could be applied to such conduct.[9]

I start with the pricing-techniques that firms that are not vertically integrated into the consumption of the goods they produce can employ when selling their outputs to independent distributors or final consumers. I refer to non-discriminatory single pricing, conventional inter-buyer price discrimination, perfect price discrimination executed either by charging different prices for each unit of the product in question that the relevant buyer purchases or by charging the relevant buyer a buyer-surplus-removing lump-sum fee for the right to purchase the output of the seller's product at which the buyer's demand curve for it cuts the seller's marginal-cost curve for it from above at a per-unit price equal to the price at which the relevant demand curve cuts the relevant marginal-cost curve from above, the mixed pricing-technique that combines lump-sum fees with per-unit prices that exceed the marginal cost of producing the marginal unit of output that would bring its total output to the quantity at which the buyer's demand curve for it cuts the seller's marginal-cost curve for it from above, those tie-ins that enable the seller that uses them to shift the locus of its supra-marginal-cost per-unit pricing, and those reciprocity agreements that enable the firm that uses them to convert some of its supra-marginal-cost per-unit pricing into the sub-marginal-cost per-unit pricing of one or more goods it buys. For the most part, these pricing-techniques are designed to enable their employer to increase its profits by converting into seller surplus what would otherwise be buyer surplus. However, (1) decisions to combine per-unit prices with lump-sum fees may also increase the seller's profits by reducing the sum of the risk costs it and its customers face because they do not know how many units of the seller's product the relevant buyers will purchase over a period of time that it is profitable for both to have their sale/purchase contract cover, (2) some tie-ins and reciprocity agreements are designed to reduce the amount by which a seller's supra-marginal-cost pricing of an intermediate product (an input) reduces the sum of its and its customer's profits by inducing the buyer to make jointly-unprofitable substitutions against the seller's intermediate product, and (3) some tie-ins and reciprocity agreements that are probably primarily designed to reduce the amount of transaction surplus (buyer surplus *plus* seller surplus) the seller will destroy when removing any given amount of buyer surplus through supra-marginal-cost per-unit pricing because such pricing reduces the buyer's quantity purchases below the quantity that is in the joint interest of the seller and buyer for the buyer to purchase also increase a manufacturer-seller's profits by reducing the loss that the manufacturer-seller's supra-marginal-cost pricing imposes on it by deterring a distributor-buyer from making demand-increasing expenditures that are in the joint interest of the manufacturer and the distributor for the distributor to make.

I will base my preliminary account of what I will contestably describe to be the seven "major" components of any TBLE distortion-analysis analysis of the economic efficiency of these pricing-techniques on the assumption that firms that are forbidden from using any pricing-technique other than non-discriminatory single pricing will respond to such a prohibition by engaging in such pricing—i.e., will not, for example, respond by engaging in forward vertical integration (to avoid having to sell their goods to others). First, TBLE distortion analysis will recognize that the substitution of any of the other pricing-techniques just referenced for non-discriminatory single pricing will generate private transaction costs and even higher allocative transaction costs. Second, TBLE distortion analysis will conclude that the use of any complicated pricing-technique will increase equilibrium QV investment in the ARDEPPSes in which it is employed and in the economy as a whole by raising the profits and supernormal profit-rates yielded by any given quantity of QV investment in the ARDEPPS in which the fancier technique is employed and on that account will decrease economic efficiency—i.e., the TBLE distortion analysis of any fancier pricing-technique will analyze the extent of the economic inefficiency it will generate by raising equilibrium QV investment in the relevant economy. Third, TBLE distortion analysis will analyze the reduction in private risk costs that some fancier pricing-techniques will effectuate because each dollar of private-risk-cost reduction will be associated with a one-dollar decrease in allocative risk costs. Fourth, any TBLE distortion analysis will estimate the economic-efficiency gains (or losses) that some fancy pricing-techniques that manufactures employ when selling their products to distributors generate by increasing the amount of demand-increasing expenditures (on promotional displays, shelf-space, in-store salesmanship and advice, door-to-door salesmanship, media advertising) the distributors make by predicting how the manufacturers would respond to any prohibition of their using these techniques. If it is determined that the manufacturers did or would respond by abandoning the goal of controlling their distributors' demand-increasing expenditures, the TBLE distortion analysis will proceed by investigating (1) the impact of the techniques in question on such expenditures, (2) the impact of the additional expenditures on the joint profits realized by the distributors and manufacturers in question, and (3) the distortion in those joint profits generated by the Pareto imperfections that distort the private cost of the expenditures in question, the private cost to the manufacturers of any additional units of output the expenditures enable them to sell, and/or the incremental revenue the manufacturers obtain on the additional sales the expenditures would enable them to make (by creating a gap between the before-tax-prices for which the units in question could have been sold and the marginal revenues their sales would have generated and/or by creating a gap between those before-tax prices and the marginal allocative values of the units in question [where the latter gap would most likely be generated by purchase taxes and/or buyer errors, whose magnitudes the demand-increasing expenditures in question could either increase by providing misleading information or decrease by providing information that is useful to buyers]). If it is determined that the relevant manufacturers did or would respond to prohibitions of the use of any relevant pricing-techniques by offering to pay that percentage of each of its distributors' demand-increasing expenditures that equals the percentage the manufacturer obtains of the benefits to it and the distributor that those expenditures generate, TBLE analysis will consider (1) the impact that the substitution of the subsidy policy for the pricing-techniques will have on the demand-increasing expenditures the relevant distributors make, (2) the economic-efficiency gain/loss that will result from any related increase/decrease in distributor demand-increasing expenditures, and (3) the additional private and allocative transaction cost that the subsidy-program would entail (of the manufacturers' calculating the appropriate subsidy-percentage, of the distributors' reporting their demand-increasing expenditures to the manufacturers, of the manufacturers' assessing the honesty and accuracy of those reports, and of the manufacturers' making the relevant subsidy-payments). If it is determined that the relevant manufacturers will respond to the prohibition of any relevant pricing-technique by including in their contracts with distributors provisions obligating them to make particular demand-increasing expenditures and/or a specified quantity of such expenditures, the TBLE analysis will focus on the extra allocative transaction costs of devising and enforcing those clauses and the economic-efficiency gain or loss the shift to such clauses will generate because they will result in the distributors' making demand-increasing-expenditure decisions that are not in their and the manufacturer's joint interest. If it is determined that the relevant manufacturers did or would respond to prohibitions of the use of any relevant pricing-techniques by vertically integrating forward into distribution, the TBLE efficiency analysis will proceed by estimating (1) the loss that the vertical integration would have generated had it prevented the manufacturer from suffering losses because its independent distributors did not make some demand-increasing expenditures that would have been in their and the manufacturers' joint interest and (2) the aggregate distortion in those losses. Fifth, TBLE distortion analysis will estimate the amount of inefficiency that the use of any fancy pricing-technique will generate by increasing poverty and material inequality by reducing buyer surplus and increasing seller surplus. Sixth, TBLE distortion analyses will examine the amount of conventional consumption-optimum misallocation that is generated by inter-buyer price discrimination. Seventh, TBLE distortion analyses will devote a third-best-allocatively-efficient amount of resources to predicting or post-dicting the impact of the relevant use of each such pricing-technique on the amount of economic inefficiency generated by economically-inefficient decisions to execute or not execute PPR projects whose execution would increase the total amount of resources the economy devotes to PPR execution, on intra-ARDEPPS and inter-ARDEPPS PPR-to-PPR misallocation, on inter-ARDEPPS and intra-ARDEPPS QV-to-QV misallocation, and on inter-ARDEPPS and intra-ARDEPPS UO-to-UO misallocation: I should acknowledge that I see no reason to believe that, taken together, all uses of any of these fancier pricing-techniques will either increase or decrease any of these categories of economic inefficiency and that, although the use of a particular fancy pricing-technique by all sellers in a given ARDEPPS could conceivably generate misallocation in one or more of these categories, I doubt that it will be TBLE to investigate these possibilities.

The TBLE distortion analysis of the economic efficiency of fancy pricing-techniques seems likely to differ in five ways from the conventional, FBLE analysis of the economic efficiency of the use of such techniques. First, the FBLE analysis but not the TBLE distortion analysis will assume that these techniques' impact on private transaction costs equals their impact on allocative transaction costs. Second, the FBLE analysis will conclude that the use of these techniques will increase economic efficiency by increasing the amount of resources devoted to QV-investment creation in the relevant economy while TBLE distortion analyses will conclude that any increase in the amount of resources the relevant economy devotes to QV-investment creation will decrease economic efficiency. Third, unlike the TBLE distortion analyses, FBLE analyses will claim that, to the extent that the use of these techniques would induce distributors to make additional demand-increasing expenditures, the prohibition of their use would decrease economic efficiency (1) by the same amount that it would reduce the relevant manufacturers' profits if they would respond to their prohibition simply by abandoning any attempt to control their distributors' demand-increasing expenditures, (2) by the sum of (A) any loss the prohibition would impose on the manufacturers by reducing their distributors' demand-increasing expenditures if they would respond to the prohibition by adopting a demand-increasing-expenditure-subsidy policy (which I will assume at the present juncture would not secure as high demand-increasing expenditures as would the pricing-technique) and (B) any additional private as opposed to allocative transaction costs the substitution of the subsidy-program for the pricing-technique generated, and (3) by the loss that any vertical integration forward into distribution the prohibition of the pricing-technique would induce the manufacturers to execute would have generated had it not prevented them from suffering losses because independent distributors would make too low demand-increasing expenditures from the perspective of the distributors' and the manufacturers' joint interest. Fourth, unlike TBLE distortion analyses, FBLE economic-efficiency analyses would ignore the negative impact that the pricing-technique in question would have on economic inefficiency to the extent that, relative to the conduct that the relevant manufacturers would substitute for the pricing-technique in question, its use would increase poverty and material inequality by reducing buyer surplus and increasing seller surplus. Fifth, and perhaps least importantly in this context, unlike TBLE distortion analyses, FBLE analyses would ignore the impact that the pricing-techniques in question and the behaviors that would be substituted for them would have on the extent of the various categories of resource misallocations on which the seventh component of the TBLE distortion-analysis approach I identified would focus.

I turn now to tie-ins and reciprocity agreements.[10] As I indicated in Sect. 9.1.2.4, some such contractual arrangements—in particular, tie-ins that are sometimes misdescribed as "full-line-forcing tie-ins"—are entered into to reduce the amount of transaction surplus that is destroyed in the process of removing a relevant given amount of buyer surplus by the charging of a supra-marginal-cost per-unit price for the so-called tying product (by such pricing's reducing the quantity of the tying product that is bought and the expenditures that the immediate buyers of the product that are its distributors make to increase the demand for it). Some tie-ins (and some functionally-analogous reciprocity agreements) are used to implement the pricing-technique in which a durable product or idea is sold for a combination of a lump-sum fee and a per-unit price for each use that exceeds the marginal cost of that use to the seller (which is usually zero). Thus, instead of selling a machine outright for a lump-sum fee, the seller may enter into an arrangement in which the buyer is obligated both to pay a (lower) lump-sum fee and to purchase its full requirements of a product it uses together with the machine (buttons if the machine is a button-fastening machine, salt if the machine is a salt-packing machine) for more than that second (so-called tied) product's market price: if the buyer uses one unit of the second product each time it uses the machine, the difference between the contractual price of the tied product and that product's normal market price is the operative "meter rate" for using the machine. Such meter pricing, which could also be implemented by installing a meter or charging the buyer end-product royalties—i.e., a fee for the sale of each unit of its final product it sells (which it used the machine to produce)—may increase the seller's profits more by enabling it to overcome its and/or the buyer's pessimism about the frequency with which it would use the seller's machine if the buyer could do so at no per-use charge and by shifting some of the risk of the buyer's using the machine less often or more often than was anticipated on the weighted average from the buyer to the seller (since, when the buyer is more risk-averse than the seller or the lack of predictability of individual buyers' usage creates more risk for each buyer than it does for the seller [which is interested in total usage, not in usage by individual buyers], such a shift in risk will reduce the sum of the buyers' and seller's risk costs than it will decrease those profits by increasing the private transaction cost of selling to the buyer in question). However, tie-ins and reciprocity agreements can also perform other functions—(1) reducing the private cost of controlling the quality and attributes of the complements that buyers combine with a seller's product or of controlling the quality of the ingredients (inputs) that a seller uses to produce a product a buyer is purchasing, (2) reducing the private cost of preventing buyer arbitrage when the seller is engaging in conventional, inter-buyer price discrimination or is charging some buyers lump-sum fees in addition to per-unit prices, (3) reducing the cost of practicing conventional price discrimination, and (4) concealing tax fraud, contract fraud, price-regulation violations, predatory pricing, and/or price discrimination that either is illegal or might be incorrectly perceived to be illegal.

I will now describe and compare the TBLE distortion analysis and the conventional, FBLE analysis of the economic efficiency of tie-ins and reciprocity agreements that perform these latter four functions. Sellers may find it profitable to control the complements that their customers combine with their products because (1) the buyer's use of an inferior or less-compatible complement would prevent the seller from making profitable repeat-sales to the buyer in question when that buyer's complement-choice was against the buyer's interest and the buyer attributed the resulting poor performance it experienced to the seller's product rather than to the complement the buyer combined with the seller's product, (2) the buyer's use of an inferior or incompatible complement would prevent the seller from making a profitable sale to one or more other buyers because the buyer's complement-choice was against the buyer's interest and the buyer mistakenly attributed the poor performance it experienced to the seller's product and bad-mouthed the seller's product to other potential customers of the seller, and/or (3) the buyer's use of an inferior, cheaper complement would prevent the seller from making profitable sales to other potential customers despite the fact that the buyer's complement-selection was in the buyer's interest in that the associated cost-saving exceeded the cost to the buyer of the reduction in performance-quality because other prospective buyers of the seller's product would observe the seller's product's worsened performance and mistakenly attribute that performance to the seller's product rather than to the low quality of the complement with which it was combined.

A seller can prevent its customers from combining inferior complements with its product by specifying the attributes of the complements its customers must use and legally enforcing the associated contractual obligation, by placing customers under a legal obligation to purchase specified complements from someone else and enforcing that legal obligation, or by placing its customers under a legal obligation to purchase their full requirements of suitable complements from it for their normal market price and enforcing that legal obligation. Sellers will choose this last, tie-in option when it is less-transaction-costly than its alternatives and/or is more efficacious in inducing buyers to use complements the seller wants them to use. The TBLE distortion analysis of the economic efficiency of such complement-quality-controlling tie-ins will focus on (1) the allocative-transaction-cost savings as opposed to the private-transaction-cost savings they generate and (2) the economic-efficiency effects of any change they make in the extent to which their employers succeed in controlling the complements that their customers combine with their products: the latter analysis is complicated by the fact that such tie-ins will reduce economic efficiency to the extent that they prevent buyers that would benefit by using inferior complements from doing so (though I suspect that when the profit-loss that the tie-in imposes on the seller because the tie-in obligation is against the interest of the buyers involved is smaller than the profit-gain the tie-in yields the seller by preventing actual buyers from mistakenly using inferior complements and prospective buyers from underestimating the quality of the seller's product, the tie-in will increase economic efficiency on these accounts on balance). To save space, I will omit the largely-analogous TBLE distortion analysis of the economic efficiency of reciprocity agreements in which buyers (say, retail food chains) seek to control the quality of the inputs (ingredients) their suppliers (say, food-product producers) incorporate into the products the buyers purchase from them. The conventional FBLE analysis of the economic efficiency of this functional type of tie-in or reciprocity agreement will differ in two important respects from its TBLE counterpart: (1) it will assume that the impact of any such agreement on allocative transaction costs will equal its impact on private transaction costs, and

(2) it will ignore both the possibility that any participant in any such agreement might otherwise have made a choice that was not in its interest and the probability that non-participant potential buyers could be misled by statements of participant-buyers and could draw wrong inferences about the quality of the seller's product from observations of its performance when that performance was worsened by the complement with which the product was combined.

I will now address the difference between the TBLE distortion analysis and the conventional FBLE analysis of the economic efficiency of tie-ins that function by increasing the profits the seller can realize by deterring its buyers from engaging in arbitrage. Buyers to which a seller is charging a discriminately-low per-unit price will have an incentive to resell their purchases to buyers to which the seller is charging a discriminatorily-high per-unit price and buyers that a seller is charging a lump-sum fee in addition to a per-unit or per-use price will have an incentive to resell their purchases or the right to use the machine they purchased to buyers from whom the seller has not extracted a lump-sum fee to the extent that such transactions are not rendered unprofitable by the sum of the private costs that the potential arbitrage-participants would have to incur to identify each other and negotiate a deal and the private cost of retransporting the good or machine-service in question. Sellers can prevent their customers from engaging in arbitrage by including anti-arbitrage provisions in their contracts of sale and enforcing the resulting legal obligations, by announcing and/or following sales policies of not continuing to supply buyers that engage in relevant arbitrage, by vertically integrating forward to bring inside their organization the buyers to which they would otherwise have charged discriminatorily-low per-unit prices or lump-sum fees, by ceasing to engage in conventional price discrimination or to charge lump-sum fees, or by obligating the buyers to which they want to charge discriminatorily-low per-unit prices or lump-sum fees to purchase at its normal market price the quantity of a second good that would be costly to cross-sell that they would use in their own businesses (or would consume) if they used all of the tying good they purchased from the seller themselves. The TBLE distortion analysis of the economic efficiency of such tie-ins would take TBLE account of the allocative-transaction-cost savings as opposed to the private-transaction-cost savings that the tie-ins would generate (say, if the seller would otherwise try to prevent arbitrage by including arbitrage-prohibiting clauses in its contracts of sale and enforcing the associated legal obligations). If the seller would respond to the prohibition of the relevant tie-ins by ceasing to engage in conventional price discrimination or lump-sum pricing, the TBLE distortion analysis of the tie-ins would include a TBLE analysis of the economic efficiency of the conventional price discrimination and lump-sum pricing in question, which would focus on (1) any extra allocative transaction costs their substitution for single pricing would generate, (2) the conventional consumption-optimum misallocation that conventional price discrimination generates, (3) the impact that lump-sum pricing has on the sum of buyer and seller risk costs, (4) impact that these pricing-techniques have on economic efficiency by increasing or decreasing poverty and material inequality, and (5) the economic efficiency of any tendency these pricing-techniques have to increase equilibrium

QV investment both in the ARDEPPSes in which such pricing is practiced and in the economy as a whole (that would probably conclude that any such increase in equilibrium QV investment would decrease economic efficiency). If the seller would respond to the prohibition of the relevant tie-ins by substituting sales policies that were less effective at preventing arbitrage, the TBLE distortion analysis of the economic efficiency of the relevant tie-ins would include a TBLE analysis of the economic efficiency of the additional arbitrage that would result (which I suspect would conclude that, holding constant the amount of conventional price discrimination and lump-sum pricing that is being practiced, any such additional arbitrage would increase economic efficiency, though the relevant Pareto imperfections would result in the profits that the arbitrage yielded its participants exceeding the arbitrage's economic efficiency by causing the private transaction cost of the arbitrage to be lower than its allocative transaction cost). In the unlikely case that the seller would respond to the prohibition of its tie-ins by acquiring or merging with the buyers to which it would otherwise charge discriminatorily-low per-unit prices or lump-sum fees, the TBLE distortion analyses of the economic efficiency of the relevant tie-ins would include a TBLE analysis of the economic efficiency of the vertical integration their prohibition would induce—inter alia, of the loss that integration would have generated had it not taken care of the arbitrage problem and of the aggregate distortion in that loss that would be generated by the interaction of all relevant Pareto imperfections. I could but will not provide additional detail.

The conventional FBLE analysis of the economic efficiency of such tie-ins will differ from its TBLE distortion-analysis counterpart in at least the following four respects: (1) it will assume that any private-transaction-cost effect equals its allocative-transaction-cost counterpart; (2) it will ignore any impact that conventional price discrimination and lump-sum pricing have on economic efficiency by increasing or decreasing poverty and material inequality; (3) it will assume that any tendency that price discrimination and lump-sum pricing have to increase QV investment both in the ARDEPPSes in which they are practiced and in the economy as a whole will increase economic efficiency by the profits the induced QV investments yield the QV investors that create them; and (4) it will assume that the losses that any induced vertical integration would have generated for the integrating firm had it not prevented arbitrage are associated with equal economic-efficiency losses.

Sellers can also enter into reciprocity agreements to prevent their trading partners from engaging in cross-selling—in particular, sellers of inputs can also use reciprocity to prevent customers to which they are charging discriminatorily-low per-unit prices or lump-sum fees from buying units not just to use them in their own operations but to resell them to other prospective users from which the input-producer in question wanted to obtain higher per-unit prices or lump-sum fees. The relevant reciprocity agreement would obligate the input-buyer to supply the input-seller with the quantity of the input-buyer's final product that the input-buyer would produce if it used all the units of the input-seller's product it purchased in its own operations. The components of the TBLE distortion analysis of the economic efficiency of such reciprocity agreements, the components of the conventional TBLE analysis of the economic efficiency of such agreements, and the differences between these two types of economic-efficiency analyses are respectively identical to their tie-in counterparts.

The next functional type of tie-in and reciprocity agreements I will discuss contains tie-ins and reciprocity agreements that increase the profitability of practicing conventional inter-buyer price discrimination. Section 9.1.2.4 has already discussed one variant of tie-ins that can perform this function—meter-pricing tie-ins. As I explained there, meter-pricing tie-ins enable producers of durable machines or ideas to reduce the private transaction cost of substituting for the outright sale of the machine or the outright sale of the right to use an idea for a lump-sum fee a more complicated pricing-technique in which the buyer is charged a lower lump-sum fee for the right to use the machine or idea for a supra-seller-marginal-cost per-unit price. At this juncture, the relevant point is that, although meter-pricing tie-ins may be profitable even when they do not result in the seller's engaging in conventional inter-buyer price discrimination, the basic pricing-technique whose transaction cost the meter-pricing tie-in reduces will tend to be more profitable when different potential buyers will use the machine or idea to different extents since when that is the case the meter pricing will be more likely to benefit the seller by helping the seller overcome its own ignorance about the frequency with which different prospective buyers are likely to use its machine or idea. Hence, in practice, meter-pricing tie-ins will sometimes—indeed, will usually—help their employers practice conventional price discrimination. Other sorts of tie-ins can also increase the profitability of conventional price discrimination for their employer. In particular, package-pricing tie-ins (in which individual units of two or more goods are sold together as a package) can reduce the cost of practicing price discrimination when the seller (1) realizes that those buyers that place a higher-than-average dollar value on one or more products it sells place a lower-than-average dollar value on one or more other products it sells (when the dollar value to all relevant buyers of a relevant package of two or more goods it sells is more homogenous than is the dollar value of each member of the relevant package to all such buyers) but (2) does not know which buyers place higher-than-average and lower-than-average dollar values on the individual goods in the package. In these circumstances, package-pricing tie-ins can reduce the cost of practicing price discrimination on each member of the package by obviating the seller's incurring the research cost of identifying the higher-dollar-valuing and lower-dollar-valuing potential buyers of each product in the package. Package-pricing tie-ins can also benefit the sellers that employ them by enabling them to practice price discrimination without appearing to do so (when they charge all buyers the same price for the package) or by reducing the apparent extent of their price discrimination (when they charge different buyers different prices for the package but the package-prices offered to different buyers vary less than would the prices those buyers would have been charged for the individual members of the package) in situations in which price discrimination is or might be perceived to be illegal or would manifest retaliation that would evidence the discriminator's practice if horizontal price-fixing or predatory pricing, which is illegal, and might if detected elicit further retaliation by rivals. I will restrict myself to pointing out what I take to be the most important difference between the TBLE distortion analysis of the economic efficiency of price-discrimination-effectuating package-pricing tie-ins and the conventional, FBLE analysis of their economic efficiency: unlike the FBLE analysis, the TBLE distortion analysis will not assume that the private-transaction-cost savings such tie-ins generate equal their allocative counterparts. Reciprocity agreements can also perform the function of reducing the market-research costs of practicing price discrimination in those rare instances in which an actor believes that potential customers that place a higher-than-average/lower-than-average dollar value on the input they produce will be willing to supply them with the final product the input-buyer uses the input to produce for a lower-than-average/higher-than-average price. The conventional FBLE analysis of the economic efficiency of such reciprocity agreements will differ from the TBLE distortion analysis of their economic efficiency in the same ways that their counterparts for package-pricing tie-ins differ.

The last functional category of tie-ins and reciprocity agreements whose TBLE and FBLE economic-efficiency analysis I will consider and compare are tie-ins and reciprocity agreements that function by concealing the extent and/or location of their users' predatory pricing, retaliation, maximum-or-minimum price-regulation violations, contract fraud, and/or tax fraud. For example, a seller that wants to charge a given buyer a price for a good that exceeds the maximum allowed price for that good and a discriminatorily-low price for another good may be able to conceal what it is doing or reduce the apparent extent of its price-regulation violation/price discrimination by selling the two goods in a package in which (in the ideal case in which the magnitudes of the price-regulation violation and price discrimination are equal) the former good is sold for its highest permitted price and the latter good is sold at a non-discriminatory price. Or a producer of two movies whose actors as a group are entitled to royalties equal to different percentages of the revenues generated by their distribution to exhibitors may effectuate contract fraud by renting the higher-royalty movie to exhibitors at a lower price than they would otherwise be charged for it on condition that the exhibitors rent the lower-royalty movie for a higher price than they would otherwise be willing to pay for it. Reciprocity agreements in which a firm lowers its price on a good it sells in exchange for its trading partner's lowering the price the former firm must pay for a good it buys can perform the same concealing function. I will restrict myself to making two points about the difference between the TBLE distortion analysis and the FBLE analysis of the economic efficiency of such tie-ins and reciprocity: (1) unlike the FBLE analysis, the TBLE analysis will not assume that the effect of such agreements on the private transaction costs that are generated by the firm's concealment efforts (which turn in part on their impact on the incidence of such concealment efforts) equals their allocative counterparts, and (2) the FBLE analysis and the TBLE analysis of the economic efficiency of the behaviors that such agreements attempt to conceal will be different (which is relevant to the extent that these tie-ins and reciprocity agreements affect the incidence of such behaviors).

I turn finally in this section to resale-price-maintenance (RPM) agreements (in which, typically,[11] manufacturers prohibit their independent distributors from reselling the manufacturer's product for less than some specified price) and vertical territorial restraints and customer-allocation clauses (which restrict respectively the geographic territories in which individual independent distributors may make sales and the non-geographic-location attributes of the customers to which they may make sales). A manufacturer may enter into minimum-price-setting RPM agreements and may restrict the territories in which and the buyers to which its independent distributors can make sales for a large number of legitimate reasons[12]:

(1)   to prevent its independent distributors' competition with each other (intra-brand competition) from reducing the prices its products' ultimate consumers pay for its products;

(2)   to prevent its products' quality-reputation or image from being damaged by its being resold for a low price;

(3)   to prevent intra-brand competition from deterring its independent distributors from making demand-increasing expenditures (in salesmanship, in-store promotion, advertising) that would be in the manufacturer's and its distributors' joint interest by creating the possibility that one distributor's expenditures would lead to a sale's being made by another distributor (note that the manufacturer is interested in the profits its independent distributors realize by selling its products [is interested in maximizing its and its independent distributors' joint profits] because their profits determine the lump-sum [franchise] fees they will be willing to pay the manufacturer for the right to distribute its product);

(4)   to prevent intra-brand competition from leading its independent distributors from making some demand-increasing expenditures that are against its and their joint interest to take customers away from each other;

(5)   to induce its independent distributors to provide sound warrantee-services to buyers of its product by making it more likely that buyers who are induced to make repeat-purchases by the warrantee and the warrantee-services with which they are provided will make their repeat-purchases from the independent distributor that provided the warrantee-services; and

(6)   to induce its individual independent distributors to make jointly-profitable communications conveying information the distributor obtains about effective sales-pitches or uses to which the manufacturer's product can be put by reducing or eliminating the possibility that this information will be used by other distributors of the manufacturer's product to compete against the communicating distributor.

As always, the effects of RPM clauses, vertical territorial restraints, and vertical-customer-allocation clauses will depend in substantial part on the responses any relevant manufacturer will make to its inability to include them in its contracts with its independent distributors—viz., on whether the manufacturer will respond to the prohibition of such clauses by doing nothing to achieve the objectives they can accomplish, by lowering the lump-sum fees and raising the per-unit prices it charges its independent distributors, by substituting for such clauses sales policies of not renewing the franchises of independent distributors that do not follow its instructions to behave in the way that is in its and all its distributors' joint interest, by subsidizing its independent distributors' demand-increasing expenditures, by ceasing to offer warranties to its customers or supplying warrantee-services itself, or by vertically integrating forward into distribution. I do not have the space here to work through and contrast the TBLE distortion analysis and FBLE analysis of the economic efficiency of RPM clauses, vertical territorial restraints, and vertical-customer-allocation clauses on varying assumptions about the responses that the manufacturers that would otherwise include them in their contracts would make to their prohibition. However, I will list and briefly discuss what I suspect are the four most important differences in these two categories of analysis of the economic efficiency of such prohibitions.

The first difference relates to the analysis of the economic efficiency of any increase or decrease the prohibition of these clauses causes in the price that consumers must pay for the goods in question: the prohibition will increase the prices consumers pay if it leads the manufacturer to increase the per-unit prices it charges its independent distributors and will decrease the prices consumers pay if the manufacturer responds to the prohibition either by doing nothing to reduce intra-brand competition or by adopting sales policies that are less efficacious at stopping intra-brand competition. The standard FBLE analysis will conclude that any such increase/decrease in prices to consumers will increase/decrease inter-ARDEPPS UO-to-UO economic inefficiency and will calculate the magnitude of these impacts on first-best assumptions, while TBLE distortion analysis will take third-best-allocatively-efficient account of the net distorting effects of the economy's other Pareto imperfections on the profits yielded by any related increase or decrease in the unit outputs of the products directly involved and will probably conclude that (leisure and do-it-yourself labor aside) the relevant increases and decreases in consumer-prices will across all cases have no impact on inter-ARDEPPS UO-to-UO misallocation but that any resulting increase/decrease in consumer-prices will decrease/increase economic efficiency by decreasing/increasing the total amount of resources the economy in question devotes to unit-output production.

The second difference relates to the analysis of the impact of such prohibitions on the allocative transaction costs that are generated by the manufacturer's attempts to control the conduct of its independent distributors. The prohibition of such restraint-implementing clauses may reduce the total private transaction costs that are generated by manufacturers' efforts to control their independent distributors if it leads the manufacturers to stop trying to control its distributors and will increase the total private transaction costs that such manufacturer-efforts at distributor-control generate if it leads manufacturers to substitute more-privately-transaction-costly methods of control—for example, subsidies for demand-increasing expenditures that require not only the making of payments but also the review of reported expenditures or sales policies that require monitoring of distributor conduct. The FBLE analysis will simply assume (implicitly) that any increase or decrease in private transaction costs equals the associated increase or decrease in allocative transaction costs whereas the TBLE distortion analysis will devote a third-best-allocatively-efficient amount of resources to examining the ratio of the allocative to the private transaction-cost effect.

The third difference relates to the two approaches' analysis of the economic efficiency of the demand-increasing expenditures that would not be made if the manufacturer replaced its RPM, vertical-territorial-restraint, and vertical-customer-allocation clauses with subsidies or sales policies that were less successful at eliciting them or simply acquiesced in its distributors' making lower demand-increasing expenditures than would be in their and its collective interest. The conventional FBLE analysis would simply assume that the elimination of any such expenditures would reduce economic efficiency by the same amount that it would reduce the profits of the manufacturer and its independent distributors combined. The TBLE distortion analysis would take TBLE account of the difference between the private cost and the allocative cost of the expenditures, the difference between the private cost and the allocative cost of producing the units of output whose sales the expenditures in question would effectuate, the possibility that some of the expenditures might mislead consumers rather than supply them with useful information, and various other Pareto-imperfection-related issues whose resolution might undermine the FBLE analysis' assumption that the expenditures' impact on economic efficiency equals their impact on the independent distributors' and manufacturers' joint profits.

The fourth difference relates to the conventional, FBLE analysis' and TBLE distortion analysis' analyses of the economic efficiency of any tendency of the prohibitions in question to induce the relevant manufacturers to vertically integrate forward either completely into the distribution of its own products or partially into the performance of some of the tasks that the prohibited clauses were designed to induce its independent distributors to perform—viz., to place advertisements aimed at final consumers in local media or to perform warrantee-services itself. The FBLE analysis of these effects would assume that any complete vertical integration the prohibition of these contractual clauses would engender would reduce economic efficiency by the same number of dollars by which it would reduce the manufacturer's profits if the vertical integration would not reduce the losses it sustained because independent distributors would not make the decisions that were in their and its joint interest and that the substitution of manufacturer advertising and warrantee-service provision for independent-distributor advertising and warrantee-services would reduce economic efficiency by the same amount that it would reduce the profits that the relevant advertising and warrantee-services yield the manufacturer. The TBLE distortion analysis of this economic-efficiency issue would take third-best-allocatively-efficient account of the distorting impact of the relevant economy's Pareto imperfections on the losses in question.

9.2 The Economic Efficiency of Various Legal Responses to the Generation of Possibly-External Accident and Pollution Losses: Differences Between the Conventional FBLE and the TBLE Distortion-Analysis Approaches to Two Salient Issues

The first-best character of the conventional Law & Economics analysis of the economic efficiency of various legal regimes that could be applied to actors whose conduct generated accident and/or pollution losses is manifest in two sets of assumptions that the conventional FBLE analysis implicitly makes: (1) the assumption that (A) the private cost to the avoider of any accident-and/or-pollution-loss avoidance-move the avoider makes equals its allocative cost and (B) that—if accident-and/or-pollution-loss victims are never contributorily negligent, all other-tort-law doctrines are first-best-allocatively-efficient, and the private benefits of avoidance to potential injurers that would be legally liable for any accident and/or pollution losses they were found at trial to have caused would not be distorted by law-related private transaction costs, victim errors, and/or judge and jury errors—the private benefits of avoidance to potential injurers will equal the allocative benefits their avoidance would generate and (2) the assumption that no relevant economic-efficiency conclusion is (critically) affected by (A) the non-first-best-allocatively-efficient components of tort-law doctrine, (B) the private transaction cost that victims, injurers, and the state must incur to make tort-law claims, to settle such claims, and to litigate and resolve such claims, (C) victim (or, for that matter, injurer) errors, or (D) judge and/or jury errors. The two sections of this section reveal respectively that the conventional Law & Economics analysis of the economic efficiency of tort law makes each of these errors—is on these accounts first-best-allocatively-efficient.

9.2.1 The Assumption of the Conventional Law & Economics Analysis of the Economic Efficiency of Various Tort-Law Regimes that the Private Cost of Any Avoidance-Move to the Avoider Equals that Move's Allocative Cost and that the Private Benefits that Any Avoidance-Move Would Confer on Any Strictly-Liable Potential Injurer Would Equal the Allocative Benefits that that Avoidance-Move Would Generate if Tort-Law Doctrine Were Otherwise FBLE, no Victim or Injurer Ever Made a Relevant Error, no Judge or Jury Ever Made a Relevant Error, and no Private Transaction Costs Were Generated by the Making of Tort-Law Claims, the Non-Litigative Resolution of Such Claims, or the Litigation of Such Claims

Conventional Law & Economics analyses of the economic efficiency of various tort-law regimes[13] all assume that the private cost of any avoidance-move to an injurer or victim equals the allocative cost that avoidance-move generated and that, if the conditions referenced in the heading of this section are fulfilled, the private benefits that any avoidance-move should be expected on the weighted average to confer on (legally-recognized) victims equal the allocative benefits the relevant avoidance-move should be expected on the weighted average to generate. These assumptions underlie the conventional Law & Economics claims that both strict liability and negligence as operationalized by the Hand formula will (on the assumptions articulated in the heading to this section) equate the profitability of avoidance to an avoider with its economic efficiency—inter alia, that both doctrines will render all economically-efficient avoidance-moves profitable and all economically-inefficient avoidance-moves unprofitable on the assumptions referenced in this section's heading.

However, as should by now be clear, none of these claims is correct: given the Pareto-imperfectness of the economies in which the relevant tort-law regimes are operative, (1) the private cost of any avoidance-move will equal its allocative cost only rarely and fortuitously, (2) the private benefits that any avoidance-move should be expected on the weighted average to generate for prospective victims will equal the allocative benefits they should be expected on the weighted average to generate for them only rarely and fortuitously, and (3) under both a strict-liability regime and a negligence regime, the profitability and economic efficiency of avoidance-moves will equal each other only rarely and fortuitously. The first of these claims reflects the fact that the economy's Pareto imperfections will almost always distort both (1) the private benefits that the resources that would be sacrificed to the execution of any resource-consuming avoidance-move would have generated (did generate) in their actually-sacrificed or (potentially-sacrificed) uses and (2) the private benefits that would be generated by the resources saved by avoidance-moves such as reducing unit output that saves resources. The second of these claims reflects the facts that (1) part of the private benefits that avoidance will confer on prospective victims are the wage-losses that avoidance will prevent some such victims from suffering by preventing them from being injured or becoming ill and (2) the other Pareto imperfections the economy contains will distort the net wages those victims would have earned had they not been injured or made ill by distorting the private benefits their labor would have conferred on their prospective employers. The third of these claims reflects the fact that there is no reason to believe that the private-cost distortions and private-benefit distortions the preceding two sentences discussed will perfectly offset each other. Even if the assumptions referenced in the heading to this section were true, the conclusions of the conventional Law & Economics analysis of the economic efficiency of various tort-law-liability regimes would be undermined by the first-best character of the analyses that generated them.

9.2.2 The Assumption of the Conventional Law & Economics Analyses of the Absolute and Relative Economic Efficiency of Strict-Liability, Strict-Liability/Contributory-Negligence, Negligence/Contributory-Negligence, and Comparative-Negligence Tort-Law-Liability Regimes that the Conclusions They Reach Will Not Be Affected by Components of Tort-Law-Liability Doctrine that Are Not FBLE, by Victim and Injurer Error, by Judge and Jury Error, and by the Private Transaction Cost of Making and Processing Tort-Law Claims

I will focus on the relevance of this assumption when the issue of interest is shifting from a strict-liability/contributory-negligence regime to a negligence/contributory-negligence regime.[14] I acknowledge the possible inaccuracy of any conclusion that the disposition of conventional Law & Economics scholars to execute first-best-allocative-efficiency analyses inclines them to underestimate the extent to which accident-and-pollution-loss-relevant tort law contains doctrines that are not FBLE, the incidence and seriousness of the relevant mistakes that accident-and-pollution-loss victims and (to a lesser degree) tortfeasors make, the incidence and seriousness of the mistakes that judges and juries in accident-and-pollution-loss tort-law cases make, and the magnitude of the private transaction costs that are generated by the making, non-litigative resolution of, and litigation of accident-and-pollution-loss tort-law claims (though these scholars' belief that first-best analyses yield accurate economic-efficiency conclusions clearly underlies their failure to take such non-first-best-economically-efficient doctrines, errors, and transaction costs into account when analyzing the economic efficiency of various accident-and-pollution-loss-liability regimes and may account for their failure to pay attention to realities that they think are irrelevant to their analyses).

In any event, I will now list a number of realities that the relevant conventional first-best analyses ignore to which a TBLE distortion analysis would pay significant, TBLE attention. I will also comment on how these realities affect the economic efficiency of shifting from a negligence/contributory-negligence (N/CN) to a strict-liability/contributory-negligence (SL/CN) accident-and-pollution-loss legal-liability regime.

I will begin by identifying the non-FBLE accident-and-pollution-loss-related tort-law-doctrine-application reality[15] that in my judgment has the biggest impact on the relative economic efficiency of N/CN and SL/CN tort-law-liability regimes —viz., the fact that in practice common-law courts assess for negligence the rejection of only a subset of the various types of avoidance-moves that injurers could make. For example, although common-law courts assess for negligence decisions by manufacturers to reject known, less-accident-and-pollution-loss-generating (hereinafter "safer") production processes (i.e., decisions to use a production process that generates more accident and pollution losses than would a known alternative), they do not assess for negligence the manufacturer's rejection of safer locations,[16] its rejection of the option of producing a product variant whose production (and consumption) is safer rather than producing a product variant whose production (and consumption) is less safe, its rejection of the option of producing fewer units of its product, or its rejection of the option of doing research designed to discover safer production processes, safer production-locations, and/or product variants whose production (and/or consumption) is safer. Obviously, in an oPp situation, this practice-reality favors the economic efficiency of shifting to a SL/CN regime from a N/CN regime since injurer-liability under SL liability does not depend on the nature of the avoidance-move that the injurer rejected or, for that matter, made.

I turn now to errors that accident-and-pollution-loss victims and injurers may make. Accident-and-pollution-victim non-sovereignty (and/or non-maximization) is relevant to the extent that unjustified distrust of the legal system leads relevant victims not to make or litigate claims that are justified and/or to accept settlements that are lower than the damage-awards to which they are entitled that they would receive. I suspect that in an oPp situation the non-sovereignly of victims would favor the economic efficiency of shifting from N/CN to SL/CN because that shift would render irrelevant one issue (the injurer's negligence) about whose resolution accident-an-pollution-loss victims tend to be unduly pessimistic. Accident-and-pollution-loss injurers may also be non-sovereign—for example, may not recognize the full range of avoidance-moves they could make, may overestimate the cost of such moves, and may underestimate the amount by which such moves would reduce the accident and pollution losses the injurers generate (perhaps because they underestimate the amount of such losses they would generate if they did not avoid). Although the SL/CN regime would provide injurers with less information about the avoidance-moves they could make than would a N/CN regime (in which the identity of the avoidance-moves available to them and the private cost and benefits of each such available move would be legally relevant), I suspect that this comparative advantage of N/CN regimes is outweighed by the comparative advantages that SL/CN regimes have because they provide potential injurers with more information about the losses they are generating both directly by leading to damage-awards and indirectly by affecting insurance-rates (in that under a SL/CN regime more claims will be made both because [as I argued previously] victim pessimism will be less of a deterrent and because [as I will argue below] private transaction costs will be lower). However, for current purposes, the important point is not the accuracy of my weighing of these offsetting considerations but the failure of conventional FBLE analyses of the relative economic efficiency of N/CN and SL/CN regimes to take victim and injurer errors into account.

The next set of realities that the relevant standard, first-best Law & Economics analysis ignores is judge and jury errors. My admittedly far-worse-than-TBLE-informed speculations are that (1) judges and juries tend to find injurers non-negligent when they were negligent, (2) judges and juries tend to give damage-awards that are lower than legally-recoverable losses (too much attention is paid to outlier cases in which jury damage-awards are too high), and (3) the percentage by which judges and juries underestimate legally-cognizable losses is higher in strict-liability cases (in which the plaintiff's lawyer finds it more difficult to put on evidence of injurer wrongdoing) than in negligence cases. It is not clear whether my speculations on these issues favor or disfavor the economic efficiency of shifting from a N/CN regime to a SL/CN regime. But once more, the relevant point for me is the probable TBLE of considering judge and jury errors when analyzing the relative economic efficiency of N/CN and SL/CN accident-and-pollution-loss legal-liability regimes.

It would be incorrect to claim that the conventional, first-best analysis of the relative economic efficiency of N/CN and SL/CN regimes ignores the private transaction cost of making, settling, and litigating accident-and-pollution-loss legal claims. To the contrary, its conclusion that the N/CN regime is more economically efficient than the SL/CN regime rests on the combination of (1) its FBLE-analysis-derived false conclusion that both the N/CN regime and the SL/CN regime will induce both potential injurers and potential victims to make all the avoidance-decisions they confront economic-efficiently and (2) its conclusion that the operation of the SL/CN regime will generate private transaction costs (which it assumes incorrectly will equal their allocative counterparts) since under it victims will be legally entitled to obtain compensation for their losses while the operation of the SL/CN regime will generate no private or allocative transaction costs since under it no potential injurer will be negligent, no victim will mistakenly make an incorrect legal claim, and (presumably) the obviousness of the fact that the injurer was not negligent (the fact that a summary judgment will be made against any plaintiff in an accident-of-pollution-loss case) will preclude victims who are not entitled to compensation from profiting by holding up non-liable injurers—from suing to induce their injurer to pay them off to avoid the cost of litigation.[17] However, the conventional, first-best analysis does ignore two effects of the private-transaction-costliness of making, settling, and litigating accident-and-pollution-loss-related tort-law claims: (1) the tendency of the transaction costs that victims must incur to make, settle, and litigate such claims to deflate the avoidance-incentives of potential injurers by increasing the percentage of entitled victims that does not make or pursue justified legal claims and (2) the tendency of the fact that it will usually be cheaper for injurers than for victims to litigate (as opposed to settling) accident-and/or-pollution-loss cases (because the injurers are more skilled than the victims at choosing lawyers and are more likely than victims to be repeat-players) to deflate the avoidance-incentives of injurers by increasing the difference between the settlements they can induce their victims to accept and the losses their victims were actually entitled to recover.[18]

9.3   The Economic Efficiency of the R&D Decisions that Would Be Made in an Economy Absent Legal Interventions and the Economic Efficiency of Various Proposed R&D-Related Government Policies: Differences Between the Conventional FBLE and the TBLE Distortion-Analysis Analyses of These Issues

9.3.1   The Analysis of the Economic Efficiency of the R&D Decisions that Would Be Made Absent Government Interventions: Differences Between the Conventional FBLE and the TBLE Distortion Analysis of This Economic-Efficiency Issue

The conventional FBLE analysis of the economic efficiency of the R&D decisions that would be made in an economy whose R&D decisions were not affected by any government policies (1) recognizes that the profits yielded by R&D will be deflated by any benefits that the relevant R&D confers on people who use the knowledge the R&D discovers without paying for the right to do so, (2) assumes that the associated deflation in the private benefits that an R&D project confers on "the researcher" equals the profits the use of the knowledge that the relevant R&D project discovers by non-paying users enables these unauthorized users to earn, (3) implicitly assumes that no Pareto imperfection other than the discovered-knowledge-unauthorized-use "external benefits" that R&D confers on the non-paying users of the knowledge it discovered distorts the profits yielded by individual R&D projects, relatedly (4) assumes that, absent government intervention, R&D-related misallocation would be generated solely by decisions not to execute economically-efficient R&D projects (ignores the possibility that R&D-related misallocation can also be generated by economically-inefficient decisions to execute economically-inefficient R&D projects), relatedly (5) implicitly assumes that the analysis of the economic inefficiency generated by decisions not to execute economically-efficient R&D projects (and, I would add, the economic inefficiency generated by decisions to execute economically-inefficient R&D projects) need not distinguish between product R&D and production-process R&D, and relatedly (6) assumes (A) that economically-inefficient R&D decisions will be made only when the discovered-knowledge-unauthorized-use external benefits an R&D project should be executed to generate exceed the project's *ex ante* economic efficiency and (B) that, in those cases in which the external character of the just-referenced external benefits renders an economically-efficient R&D project unprofitable, the resulting inefficiency will equal the profits the rejected project would have generated if all users of any knowledge it created had to pay a price for the right to use that knowledge equal to the value of that knowledge to them. The first-best character of this conventional analysis (1) is manifest directly in its assumptions that (A) the private benefits that a non-paying user of discovered knowledge secures by using it equal the net allocative-efficiency gains the non-paying user's use of the relevant knowledge generates and (B) the only Pareto imperfection distorting the profits yielded by R&D projects is the discovered-knowledge-unauthorized-use-related external benefits just referenced—i.e., is manifest directly in Items (2) and (3) in the preceding list—and (2) is manifest indirectly in Items (4), (5), and (6) in the preceding list.

The TBLE distortion-analysis analysis of the economic inefficiency that would be generated by an economy's economically-inefficient R&D decisions differs from its conventional FBLE-analysis counterpart in at least the following seven ways:

(1) it contains a TBLE distortion-analysis analysis of the distortion in the profits yielded by research that is generated by actors' using the knowledge the research discovers without paying for the right to do so, which takes TBLE account of the aggregate distortions in both the private cost and the private benefits of such "unauthorized" uses that are generated by the other Pareto imperfections in the relevant economy;

(2) it contains TBLE analyses of the aggregate distortion in the private cost of executing the relevant product-R&D and PPR project that is generated by (A) the different sets of Pareto imperfections whose interactions would have distorted the private benefits that the resources used to execute any relevant product-R&D and PPR project would have generated for the sacrificing users in the sacrificed uses from which they would be withdrawn and (B) any externalities generated by the execution of the product R&D or PPR in question;

(3) it contains TBLE analyses of the aggregate distortions in the operating profits that any relevant product researcher would realize by using its product discovery that would be generated by the interaction of the imperfections in seller price-competition and QV-investment competition a relevant product-R&D researcher would face when selling its discovered product or making the product-R&D investment, the imperfections in seller price-competition that would face any unit-output producer from which resources would be withdrawn when the created product was produced, the externalities generated by the production and consumption of the discovered product and the externalities that would have been generated by the production and consumption of the units of other goods' outputs sacrificed to the production of the discovered product, the purchase taxes levied on the sale of the created product, the monopsony power of any buyer to which the researcher sells any patent it obtains on its discovery or licenses the right to use its discovery, the external costs that individual product-R&D projects generate by reducing the probability that other projects aiming to make the same discovery will make that discovery (first), the external costs that individual product-R&D projects that discover new products generate by inflicting losses on owners of pre-existing projects who place a positive value on owning "the latest thing," and so on and so forth;

(4) it contains TBLE analyses of the aggregate distortions in the profits a production-process researcher will realize by using its discovered production

process itself, by selling any patents the research enabled it to secure, or by licensing others to use its discovery that are generated by the interaction of all the Pareto imperfections I previously showed would generate such distortions;

(5) it almost certainly yields the conclusion that the Pareto imperfections other than the unauthorized-use-of-discovered-knowledge external-benefit imperfection on which first-best analyses exclusively focus will inflate the profits yielded by product R&D and deflate the profits yielded by PPR so that policies will have to distinguish between these two categories of research if they are to be TBLE; relatedly

(6) it will analyze the economic efficiency of decisions to execute or not to execute particular R&D projects by comparing the profits or losses those projects would have yielded the researchers that did or could have executed them with the aggregate distortion in the profits they did or would have yielded that was generated by the interaction of all relevant exemplars of all types of Pareto imperfections not with the aggregate distortion in those profits that would be generated in an oPp economy by unauthorized-use-of-discovered-knowledge-generated external benefits; and relatedly

(7) it will recognize the possibility that, if the government of any relevant economy does nothing to influence R&D decisions, actors will cause economic inefficiency by executing R&D projects that are economically inefficient as well as by failing to execute R&D projects whose execution would have been economically efficient.

9.3.2   The Conclusions About the Economic Efficiency of Various Government Policies that Have Been Proposed to Reduce the Amount of Economic Inefficiency Generated by Economically-Inefficient Decisions to Execute or Not to Execute R&D Projects: Some Differences in the Conclusions Generated by Conventional FBLE Analyses and TBLE Distortion-Analysis Analyses

As I indicated in Sect. 9.3.1, FBLE analyses of the economic efficiency of the R&D decisions that prospective researchers would make absent government interventions conclude that, absent government interventions, too few resources would be devoted to both product R&D and PPR from the perspective of economic efficiency. Obviously, economists who ignore The General Theory of Second Best do take into account (1) existing IP law and existing tax-law provisions authorizing firms that do product and production-process research to expense their R&D investments and (2) the possibility that IP production may cause economic inefficiency by leading discoverers to price the right to use their discoveries in a way that causes the discoveries to be underutilized from the perspective of economic efficiency when considering the economic efficiency of other policies that would increase the amount of resources devoted to R&D. Although such scholars should therefore recognize the possibilities that (1) the existing IP protection and tax-incentives may fully offset or outweigh the tendency of the unauthorized-use-of-discovered-knowledge-generated external benefits of R&D that they correctly argue would lead too few resources to be devoted to R&D from the perspective of economic efficiency in an oPp economy and (2) any policy that increases R&D by lengthening or broadening IP protection might decrease economic efficiency more by leading to the underutilization of discovered knowledge than it increases economic efficiency by increasing the amount of resources devoted to R&D, the conclusions that their FBLE analyses yield seem to have led them to conclude that a wide variety of policies that would increase the amount of resources devoted to product R&D and to PPR would be economically efficient. This section executes very preliminary distortion analyses of the economic efficiency of three such policies.

The first is the proposal that the IP protection offered for both product discoveries and production-process discoveries be lengthened and broadened. I must be careful here: although the first-best character of the R&D-economic-efficiency analyses executed by economists who ignore The General Theory of Second Best almost certainly underlies their failure to see that the policies that would most reduce the economic inefficiency generated by economically-inefficient decisions to execute and not to execute product R&D will be quite different from the policies that would most reduce the economic inefficiency generated by economically-inefficient decisions to execute and not to execute PPR, the first-best character of their R&D-economic-efficiency analyses does not seem to account for their apparent belief that lengthening and broadening IP protection will increase economic efficiency more by stimulating the execution of additional "initial" R&D projects than it will decrease economic efficiency by reducing the extent to which the discoveries that R&D projects yield are used (including by researchers who want to build on the "initial" discoveries). Indeed, I suspect that first-best analyses will overestimate the economic-efficiency losses that IP protection generates by causing discoveries to be underutilized from the perspective of economic efficiency. Clearly, however, third-best-allocatively-efficient analyses of the economic efficiency of lengthening and broadening IP protection will analyze separately the economic efficiency of lengthening and broadening (and shortening and narrowing) the IP protection given respectively to product discoveries and production-process discoveries and may well conclude that, if nothing else could be done to affect the amounts of product R&D and PPR that are executed, it would be economically efficient to shorten and narrow the IP protection given to product discoveries while lengthening and broadening the IP protection given to production-process discoveries.

The second set of policies that many economists who ignore The General Theory of Second Best claim will reduce the amount of R&D-related economic inefficiency is tax policies that would reduce the effective tax-rate levied on the profits yielded by both product R&D and PPR (say, by lowering the effective tax-rate levied on the profits actually yielded by R&D of both sorts below the effective tax-rate levied on the profits actually yielded by the production of units of "old" products and on the profits yielded by new QV investments that do not discover technological or scientific knowledge) (say) by applying lower tax-rates to the tax-calculated profits yielded by R&D than to the tax-calculated profits yielded by non-R&D activities or by lowering the tax-law-calculated profits yielded by R&D below the actual profits yielded by R&D by allowing R&D investments to be expensed while requiring other sorts of investments to be depreciated at the rate at which their economic value declines through time. The TBLE distortion analysis of the economic efficiency of such tax-policies and the conclusions that such analyses reach about the economic efficiency of these tax-policies differ from their FBLE counterparts in precisely the same way that the FBLE distortion analysis of and conclusions about the economic efficiency of IP policies differ from their FBLE counterparts.

The third set of policies that economists who execute first-best economic-efficiency analyses recommend be adopted to reduce R&D-related misallocation is antitrust policies that firms be allowed to execute mergers and acquisitions (M&As) that would otherwise be deemed illegal because they would lessen competition despite their tendency to increase their participants' R&D expenditures and/or R&D-execution proficiency if the M&As in question are shown to increase their participants' R&D expenditures and/or proficiency. The economists who claim that this policy would be economically efficient have not executed thorough first-best analyses of its economic efficiency—i.e., have not analyzed on first-best assumptions either the economic-efficiency gains that M&As that increase their participants' R&D proficiency and/or R&D expenditures to any given extent would generate on this account or the economic-efficiency losses that such M&As would generate by lessening competition. In my judgment, had they executed such analyses, the erroneous assumptions that first-best analysis makes would have led them (1) to underestimate the economic-efficiency gains that would be associated by an M&A's reducing by any given amount the cost of executing a given product-R&D or PPR project, (2) to mistakenly assume that the economic-efficiency gain that would be generated by any additional product-R&D project an M&A would cause to be executed would equal the profits that project would yield its executer when (I believe) the associated economic-efficiency gain would be lower than those profits (indeed, when in fact many of the induced product-R&D projects would be economically inefficient though profitable), (3) to mistakenly assume that the economic-efficiency gain that would be generated by any additional PPR project an M&A would cause to be executed would equal the profits that project would yield its executor when (I believe) the associated economic-efficiency gain would be higher than those profits, (4) to overestimate the inter-ARDEPPS UO-to-UO misallocation that the relevant M&As would generate by decreasing seller price-competition, (5) to ignore the fact that any reduction in seller price-competition a relevant M&A would generate would increase UO-to-QV and

PPR-to-QV misallocation, (6) to ignore the fact that any reduction/increase in QV-investment competition a relevant M&A would generate would increase/decrease UO-to-QV and PPR-to-QV misallocation, (7) to ignore the fact that any effect a relevant M&A would have on the intensity of seller price-competition and/or QV-investment (or PPR) competition will also affect the amounts of inter-ARDEPPS QV-to-QV and inter-ARDEPPS PPR-to-PPR misallocation the economy generates, (8) to assume incorrectly that the private transaction costs of executing M&As equals their allocative counterparts when in fact they will do so only rarely and fortuitously —indeed, will (I believe) be lower than their allocative counterparts, (9) will ignore the tendency of M&As that lessen competition to generate economic inefficiency by increasing poverty and material inequality, and (10) will ignore the impact that the policy they are recommending will have on the amount of economic inefficiency the government generates when financing its operations by increasing/decreasing the cost to government of regulating M&As. Obviously, in my view, the TBLE distortion-analysis analysis of the economic efficiency of this M&A proposal would correct all these errors of commission and omission by executing TBLE analyses of the issues to which they relate.

9.4   The Economic Inefficiency that Taxes on the Margin of Income Generate by Affecting Market-Labor/Leisure-"Production" Choices and the Economic Efficiency of Using Tax Policy to Reduce the Magnitudes of Various Categories of Resource Misallocation: Differences Between the Conventional FBLE and the TBLE Distortion-Analysis Analysis of These Issues

As Sect. 2.3 acknowledges, public-finance economists have done a better job of taking account of the fundamental insights of The General Theory of Second Best than any other subset of applied welfare economists. Nevertheless, as Sect. 2.3 also argues, even those public-finance economists who have made important contributions to Second-Best Theory have not executed analyses that take full account of The General Theory of Second Best. Section 9.4 discusses one issue that the public-finance literature has misanalyzed because it has not responded fully to The General Theory of Second Best and one set of possibilities that the public-finance literature has not to my knowledge addressed because it has failed to respond to the multiplicity of uses to which resources can be devoted and the ways in which any economy's Pareto imperfections can distort the profitability of withdrawing resources from one or more categories of use and devoting them to a particular category of use.

9.4.1   The Difference Between the FBLE Analysis of and the TBLE Distortion-Analysis Analysis of the Economic Efficiency of the Tendency of Taxes on the Margin of Income to Induce Individuals to Substitute "Leisure Production" for Market Labor

Conventional FBLE analysis yields the conclusion that, because taxes on the margin of income generate what I denominate a negative step-wise tax distortion in the private benefits and "profits" of performing market labor, it causes prospective market laborers to make economically-inefficient decisions when choosing whether to "produce leisure" (or perform do-it-yourself labor) or to perform market labor. TBLE distortion analysis (1) recognizes that taxes on the margin of income are not the only Pareto imperfections that distort the profitability of performing market labor, (2) demonstrates inter alia that imperfections in seller price-competition generate negative step-wise distortions in the private benefits and "profits" of performing unit-output-producing and PPR-executing labor and positive step-wise distortions in the private benefits and profits of performing QV-investment-creating labor, (3) demonstrates that on that account taxes on the margin of income would generate more misallocation than the conventional first-best analysis concludes by affecting choices between "producing leisure" and performing unit-output-producing market labor and PPR-executing market labor and less misallocation than the conventional first-best analysis concludes by affecting choices between "producing leisure" and performing QV-investment-creating labor (indeed, may actually reduce the amount of economic inefficiency generated by economically-inefficient choices between producing leisure and performing QV-investment-creating market labor) if the other types of Pareto imperfections actual economies contain could be ignored. Obviously, the TBLE distortion-analysis analysis of the economic inefficiency that taxes on the margin of income generate by affecting choices among leisure-production and the performance of do-it-yourself labor on the one hand and the performance of market labor on the other hand differs from its conventional FBLE counterpart (1) by paying TBLE attention both to the just-referenced issues and to the extant exemplars of the monopsony, externality, resource-allocator-non-sovereignty, resource-allocator-non-maximization, and buyer-surplus Pareto imperfections that relevant economies contain and (2) almost certainly by yielding more complicated and different conclusions about the effect of taxes on the margin of income on the amount of misallocation generated by economically-inefficient choices between producing leisure or performing do-it-yourself labor on the one hand and performing different categories of market labor on the other hand.

9.4.2   The Difference Between the Conventional FBLE Analysis and the TBLE Distortion-Analysis Analysis of the Ability of Tax Policy to Reduce the Amount of Economic Inefficiency Generated by Economically-Inefficient Allocations of Resources Between UO-Producing and QV-Investment-Creating Uses, Between PPR-Executing and QV-Investment-Creating Uses, Between QV-Investment-Creating Uses in Different ARDEPPSes, and Between PPR-Executing Uses in Different ARDEPPSes

The failure of scholars who execute conventional FBLE analyses of the economic efficiency of non-government choices and government policies to devise tax policies to reduce the categories of economic inefficiency referenced in this section's heading is at least as much attributable to the conventional analysis' failure to focus explicitly on allocations of resources to QV-creating and PPR-executing uses as it is to the first-best character of those analyses. I will assume *ad arguendo* that the TBLE distortion-analysis analysis of these possibilities would conclude that in all or virtually all economies, from the perspective of economic efficiency, (1) too many resources are devoted to QV-investment creation relative to the amount that is devoted to UO production, (2) too many resources are devoted to the creation of both QV investments that do not make scientific or technological discoveries and QV investments that do make such discoveries relative to the amount that is devoted to PPR execution, (3) given the total amount of resources devoted to QV-investment creation in the economy as a whole, from the perspective of economic efficiency, too many resources are devoted to QV-investment creation in some ARDEPPSes and not enough to QV-investment creation in other ARDEPPSes, and (4) given the total amount of resources devoted to PPR execution in the economy as a whole, from the perspective of economic efficiency, too many resources are devoted to the execution of PPR projects that relate to the production processes used to produce the products produced in some ARDEPPSes and not enough resources are devoted to the execution of PPR projects that relate to the production processes used to produce the products produced in other ARDEPPSes. If these conclusions are accurate, they open up the possibility that economic efficiency would be increased by tax policies (1) that apply a higher effective tax-rate on the profits generated by the creation and use of new QV investments than on the profits generated by the production of "old" products and on the profits generated by the execution of PPR projects and the use of the discoveries they yield,[19] (2) that apply a higher effective tax-rate on the profits yielded by QV investments in individual ARDEPPSes whose total QV investment uses up an economic-inefficiently-high percentage of the resources the economy devotes to QV-investment creation than on the profits yielded by QV investments in individual ARDEPPSes whose total QV investment uses up an economic-inefficiently-low percentage of the resources the relevant economy devotes to QV-investments creation, and (3) if I place each PPR project in the ARDEPPS in which the products to whose production process it relates are located, that apply a higher effective tax-rate on the profits yielded by the execution and use of PPR projects in ARDEPPSes whose PPR projects use up an economic-inefficiently-high percentage of the resources the relevant economy devotes to PPR execution and a lower effective tax-rate on the profits yielded by the execution and use of PPR projects in ARDEPPSes whose PPR uses up economic-inefficiently-low percentages of the resources the relevant economy devotes to PPR execution. Obviously, I have not addressed the practicability of the above tax policies. My point is that, at least to my knowledge, public-finance economists have not recognized their possible economic efficiency.

*****

This chapter has sought to establish both the importance of The General Theory of Second Best and the gains that would be secured by the substitution of TBLE distortion analysis (or any other economic-efficiency-analysis protocol that would be equally or more TBLE) for conventional FBLE economic-efficiency analysis. This chapter attempts to achieve these objectives by pointing out the difference between these two protocols for economic-efficiency analysis and the difference between the conclusions they generate when the issues of interest are the economic efficiency of (1) competition-law-covered conduct and policy, (2) accident-and-pollution-related conduct and policy, (3) R&D-related conduct and policy, and (4) tax-related conduct and policy.

I acknowledge that some of the arguments this chapter makes were made or at least anticipated in earlier sections of this study. I hope that the cost of this chapter's repetitiveness is outweighed by the value it creates by providing a better grounding for this study's central conclusions.

Notes

1. Williamson (1968).
2. Harberger (1954).
3. For more-detailed critiques of and citations to individual articles on the "social cost of monopoly," see Markovits (2008), respectively, at pp. 283–286 and p. 466 notes 19–22.
4. The parenthetical is necessary to prevent from being classified as predatory investments made by investors that would not have found them *ex ante* profitable but for the investor's belief that the prospect of the investment's deterring a rival investment would critically reduce what would otherwise have been a critical monopolistic investment-disincentive the investor would otherwise have faced in relation to the investment in question without giving the investor a critical monopolistic investment-incentive to make the investment in question. Relatedly, an investment is correctly deemed to be predatory if *ex ante* the investor perceived itself to have a critical monopolistic investment-incentive to make it. For further explanation, see Markovits (2014a) at 582–595.
5. For current purposes, I will ignore the fact that many economists contend that predatory pricing (other than the variant of predatory pricing that is called "limit pricing") is rarely if ever practiced because it would rarely if ever be profitable. For a discussion of the articles in which this claim is made and an

explanation of why I reject the empirical assumptions on which the theoretical arguments for this conclusion are based, see Markovits (2014a) at pp. 519–530.

6. See Markovits (2014b) at 4–16 and 22–37.

7. Markovits (forthcoming).

8. To Americans of my generation, the question "Compared to what?" calls to mind the comedian Georgie Jessell, who famously posed it in response to his straight-man's question "How's your wife?" Although this riposte was no doubt sexist when made, it is intrinsically gender-neutral, and these days would be as likely to be made in response to the question "How's your husband (or boyfriend)?"

9. Markovits (forthcoming).

10. The text that follows will not fully explain the ways in which and the conditions under which tie-ins and reciprocity can perform the functions it references. For fuller discussions of these issues, see Markovits (2014b) at 276–325.

11. Admittedly, resale price maintenance sometimes involves a seller's setting the maximum price that its independent distributors can charge for its product. Sellers include such maximum-price constraints in their contracts with their independent distributors for two main responses: (1) to prevent their own supra-marginal-cost per-unit pricing from inducing their independent distributors to set resale prices that exceed the prices that are in their distributors' and their own joint interest and (2) in special cases in which the profits in which the seller can make by selling other goods or services increase with its unit sales of its basic product, to prevent its independent distributors from setting higher prices that will reduce the profits the manufacturer can realize on these other products by reducing the unit sales of the resale-price-maintenance-controlled good. The best example of the latter possibility is a newspaper's setting a maximum resale price that news agents may charge for its papers in order to increase the newspaper's circulation when the quantity of advertising the newspaper can sell for any given price increases with the newspaper's circulation. I have ignored these possibilities in the text to shorten the exposition.

12. In rare instances, such RPM agreements and vertical territorial and customer-allocation restrictions may be entered into/agreed to enable either the manufacturers they involve or (less frequently) the distributors they involve to implement horizontal-price-fixing arrangements or agreements to divide up a "market." The text ignores these possibilities both because I think they are remote and because the TBLE distortion-analysis and FBLE analysis of their economic efficiency have already been covered by Sects. 9.1.2.1's and 9.1.2.3's discussions respectively of horizontal price-fixing and competition-reducing horizontal mergers and acquisitions.

13. The regimes that have been analyzed include strict-liability/contributory-negligence regimes, strict-liability regimes without contributory-negligence, negligence/contributory-negligence regimes, and comparative-negligence regimes. The following accounts of these doctrines are simplified. In law, (1) an injurer is said to be strictly liable if the injurer is liable for any loss for which it was the "legal cause," regardless of whether the injurer was at fault for causing that loss; (2) in law, an injurer is said to be liable because it was

"negligent" if its causing the loss could be attributed to its failure to show "ordinary care"—on one account, if it failed to make an avoidance-move whose private dollar-cost to the injurer would have been lower than the amount by which the move would have reduced legal–victim weighted-average-expected accident-and/or-pollution losses. This formula (which fails to take account of the fact that avoidance will also affect the risk costs that the prospective injurer and victims face because of the accident-and/or-pollution-loss contingency [by amounts that depend on the operative legal-liability regime]) was first proposed by Judge Learned Hand—Hand (1947) at 173; (3) in law, a victim's "contributory negligence" is said to have caused a loss if its failure to show "ordinary care" was a legal cause of the loss—on Hand's formula, if the loss resulted because the victim failed to make an avoidance-move whose private cost to the victim would have been lower than the amount by which the move would have reduced weighted-average-expected accident-and/or-pollution losses: according to the traditional "contributory-negligence doctrine" (which still goes by that name in the United States), a victim's contributory negligence bars the victim from recovery when the injurer's liability is based on its negligence; and (4) in law, the most defensible variant of the "comparative-negligence doctrine" (which has many different variants) states that in cases in which the injurer is negligent and the victim is contributorily negligent, the loss is to be divided between them proportionate to their faults (measured by metrics that the law has done a poor job of specifying).

14. I recognize that in common-law countries the alternatives are (1) negligence/ contributory negligence or comparative negligence or (2) strict liability without contributory negligence. I focus on switching from negligence/contributory negligence to strict liability/contributory negligence despite this fact because it seems obvious to me that strict liability with contributory negligence is more economically efficient than strict liability without contributory negligence.

15. Specifically, I am ignoring various non-FBLE accident-and-pollution-loss-case-related doctrines that do not have much of an effect on whether economic efficiency would be increased by shifting from a N/CN to a SL/CN tort-law regime (though these doctrines may well affect the amount by which a shift from a N/CN regime to a SL/CN regime will increase economic efficiency)—e.g., the "scope of liability" ("proximate cause") doctrine, which relieves injurers that would otherwise be liable of liability on the ground that they were not the "legal cause" of a loss for which they were the "cause in fact," doctrines that deem unrecoverable certain categories of losses (e.g., the losses that observers of an accident sustain from observing an accident that put them at no physical risk, the risk costs that the potential victims of an accident-or-pollution-loss-generating event bear in relation to the contingency of its occurring even when it does not eventuate, the companionship-and-sympathy/empathy-related losses that the friends and family [other than the sponse, who can recover for the loss of consanguinity] of a victim sustains when the victim is injured or killed), the doctrine that deems a victim contributorily negligent for rejecting an avoidance-move that would have been first-best-allocatively-efficient if the

injurer did not avoid but was less first-best-allocatively-efficient than an injurer avoidance-move the victim's avoidance would have obviated, doctrines such as the "last clear choice doctrine," the "assumption of risk doctrine," and "the fellow-servant rule" that at least on some interpretations and applications create the possibility that injurers will be relieved of liability even when they would otherwise have been found strictly liable or liable because negligent.

16. Unlike economists, lawyers do not consider the location in which production takes place to be a component of the production process the producer uses. I acknowledge, of course, that when consumers value the location of distribution and goods are sold where they are produced, location is also an attribute of the product that is produced.

17. I should note that, in the real world in which injurers may behave negligently and victims may bring suits that are *ex ante* unprofitable for them to bring, a priori argument cannot establish that the SL/CN regime will be less-transaction-costly than the N/CN regime: although fewer suits will be brought in a N/CN regime than in a SL/CN regime, the average private and allocative cost of litigating a case under a N/CN regime will be higher than the average cost of litigating the "same" case under a SL/CN regime since under the former but not the latter regime the negligence issue will have to be tried.

18. The fact that injurers are more likely to be repeat-players than their victims will also tend to deflate the avoidance-incentives of injurers by increasing the amount by which the settlement-payments they make fall below their victims' losses because it renders it profitable for injurers to reject individual settlement-offers whose acceptance would otherwise be advantageous to establish a reputation for tough bargaining that will enable them to secure more advantageous settlement-agreements in the future.

19. Obviously, if TBLE distortion-analysis analyses would reach different conclusions about the economic efficiency of the amounts of resources that the relevant economy devotes to QV-investment creation relative to the amounts it devotes respectively to the production of old products and the execution of PPR, those conclusions would favor the economic efficiency of different tax policies.

References

Hand, L. (1947). United States v. Carroll Towing, 159 F2d 169 (2nd Cir. 1947).

Harberger, A. (1954). Monopoly and resource allocation. *American Economic Review, 44*, 77–87.

Markovits, R. (forthcoming). *The welfare economics of antitrust policy and U.S. and E.U. antitrust law*. Heidelberg, New York, Dordrecht, London: Springer.

Markovits, R. (2008). *Truth or economics: On the definition, prediction, and relevance of economic efficiency*. New Haven and London: Yale University Press.

Markovits, R. (2014a). *Economics and the interpretation and application of U.S. and E.U. antitrust law* Vol. I: *Basic concepts and economics-based legal analyses of oligopolistic and predatory conduct*. Heidelberg, New York, London, Dordrecht: Springer.

Markovits, R. (2014b). *Economics and the interpretation and application of U.S. and E.U. antitrust law* Vol. II: *Economics-based legal analyses of mergers, vertical practices, and joint ventures*. Heidelberg, New York, London, Dordrecht: Springer.

Williamson, O. (1968). Economies as an antitrust defense: The welfare trade-off. *American Economic Review, 58,* 18–36.

The Approach that Would Be TBLE for a Government to Take to Economic-Efficiency Prediction/Post-diction—The Rest of the Story

10

Abstract

This chapter indicates some of the non-analytic-protocol matters that a government must handle third-best-allocative-efficiently for its overall approach to economic-efficiency prediction/post-diction to be TBLE. The issues it references include (1) whether to legally obligate non-government actors to supply relevant information, whether and how to compensate them for doing so, how to evaluate the information they supply, (2) the criteria to be used to select relevant government employees, the training and supervision to give such employees, (3) the compensation to be paid such employees, the criteria to be used to decide whether to retain, promote, or fire them, (4) whether the employment-contracts of such employees should limit their ability to become employees of, do paid consulting work for, or give paid speeches to specified sets of non-government actors during and after their government service, (5) the identity of the non-government actors that should be entitled to provide information to economic-efficiency analysts and the time-constraints and page-constraints that should be imposed on any such entitled information-providers, (6) the obligations of economic-efficiency analysts to justify their conclusions, and (7) the nature of the process for reviewing economic-efficiency analysts' conclusions (including the rights of specified parties to challenge those conclusions, the duty of the analysts to respond to challenges, and the obligations of supervisors to justify their ultimate economic-efficiency conclusions).

In the not-too-distant past, I sometimes listened to a radio news program in which the presenter (Paul Harvey) gave two accounts of each story. His initial account provided what sounded like an accurate factual description of what had happened. He then proceeded to tell what he called "the rest of the story." Often "the rest of the story" provided information that cast a very different light on his initial account. I am glad to say that, in my judgment, "the rest of the story" that this chapter tells

© Springer Nature Switzerland AG 2020
R. S. Markovits, *Welfare Economics and Second-Best Theory*,
https://doi.org/10.1007/978-3-030-43360-4_10

does not cast doubt on the third-best allocative efficiency of the protocol for economic-efficiency analysis I am arguing is third-best-allocatively-efficient for economic-efficiency analysis to use. However, I think it is still instructive to raise and comment on the additional issues that a government would have to resolve third-best-allocative-efficiently to create the protocol that would be TBLE for it to use to generate economic-efficiency predictions/post-dictions.

I will now be somewhat more specific, though limitations of space and personal expertise will affect the quality and comprehensiveness of this chapter's comments. To start, I have no doubt that it would be TBLE for government to "assemble"— i.e., to require others to supply and/or to collect itself—data on the incidence and magnitudes of the Pareto imperfections in the government's own economy and, when appropriate, in other economies as well. Relatedly, government must make TBLE decisions about (1) the information that non-government resource allocators must supply about such matters as the contemporary dollar-value of their investments, the prices they charge for and sales they make of each product they produce, the pollution and accidents generated by their production of successive units of the various products they produce, by their creation of their respective QV investments, and by their execution of their various PPR projects,[1] (2) any compensation it will provide to such non-government information-providers, (3) the choices it will make to finance any such payments, and (4) the methods it will use to check the accuracy of any such information that non-government actors provide.

Government must also make TBLE decisions about the non-government actors that are not legally obligated to supply such information that should be entitled or allowed to provide information, about the amount of such information such actors may provide, and about the time they have to supply such information and/or to question the accuracy of information the government has collected itself or received from other non-government actors, about the responses that government economic-efficiency analysts must make to the information that non-government actors provide and to the requests that such actors make that additional possibilities be considered, and about the procedural protocols, decision standards, and remedies that will be TBLE for analysts and/or reviewing courts to follow, use, and provide.

In addition, the government must make TBLE decisions about (1) the criteria and decision-process it uses to select the civil servants and/or independent contractors it employs to do economic-efficiency-impact-relevant theoretical and empirical work and to make economic-efficiency predictions/post-dictions and (2) the training it gives such workers. Government must also do a TBLE job of providing the civil servants and independent contractors it hires to predict/post-dict the economic efficiency of non-government conduct or government policies appropriate incentives to do their work third-best-allocative-efficiently, must pay such individuals TBLE salaries, must put in place TBLE oversight regimes, must create and implement TBLE promotion schemes, must create and implement TBLE rules about whether those who have worked in any government economic-efficiency prediction/post-diction program can subsequently work for those who were benefited or harmed by the predictions/post-dictions to which the government worker in question contributed or give speeches or take university positions that are financed by affected actors.

Finally, government must put in place a TBLE system of reviewing the accuracy of the predictions/post-dictions "it" makes—must require its analysts to provide detailed explanations of the conclusions they reached, must make TBLE decisions about the actors that are entitled to comment on the conclusions reached and the arguments made for those conclusions (though I do not think it would be TBLE to require economic-efficiency analysts to address all evidence submitted by and all arguments made by any "entitled commentator"), and must establish a TBLE system for reviewing the economic-efficiency predictions/post-dictions that are made (though, given the current content of legal education and the nature of legal practice, I doubt that the review should be carried out by "normal" courts—for example, by any Court of Appeals in the U.S. federal court system).

Again, I recognize that this discussion of "the rest of the story" has been partial. I included it because I believe that readers should be reminded of the salience of the issues it raises, even if my treatment of them here has been superficial.

Note

1. I recognize that the analysis of the choices of this kind that will be TBLE is complicated by the facts that the public revelation of some of this information (1) will benefit its providers' rivals and (2) may facilitate its providers' and their rivals' practice of contrived oligopolistic and predatory pricing. However, unlike some, I do not think that the first of these realities gives the potential provider of such information a property-right to it—i.e., a constitutional right to be compensated for the cost of generating the information and the transaction and other costs of supplying it to the government and making it public.

Conclusion

11

Abstract

The Conclusion briefly summarizes the content of this study and expresses the hope that the economic-efficiency-analysis protocol it recommends or some superior variant of this protocol others develop will be used and will increase both the economic efficiency and the overall desirability of government decisions.

What has this study done? It has articulated the definition of "the impact of a choice on allocative/economic efficiency" that I believe is "correct" (that creates a concept that is consistent with popular and professional intuitive understanding and is most useful) and has explained why the alternative definitions that economists use are in the above sense "incorrect." It has stated the central conclusion of "The General Theory of Second Best" and pointed out that this General Theory undermines the "first-best" protocol that the vast majority of economists use to predict or post-dict the impact of non-government or government choices (involuntary conduct, and natural events) on economic efficiency. It has described and criticized the theoretical-Welfare-Economics literature on The General Theory of Second Best and argued that the vast majority of applied-Welfare-Economics analyses of the economic efficiency of various types of non-government conduct and government policies ignores both The General Theory of Second Best and many categories of economic inefficiency. It has argued that, although some applied-Welfare-Economics studies do execute analyses of the way in which exemplars of two Pareto imperfections of one or two types interact to cause or not cause one category of economic inefficiency that make useful contributions to the development of a protocol for economic-efficiency prediction/post-diction whose use would be *ex ante* economically efficient, taken together even this valuable literature is deficient in that it ignores most types of Pareto imperfections, most categories of economic inefficiency, and the fact that to be *ex ante* economically efficient an analytic protocol must take account not only of the allocative benefits but also of the

© Springer Nature Switzerland AG 2020

R. S. Markovits, *Welfare Economics and Second-Best Theory*,

https://doi.org/10.1007/978-3-030-43360-4_11

allocative costs of research. It has defined the concept of "a third-best-allocatively-efficient" (TBLE) protocol for economic-efficiency analysis (the protocol that is *ex ante* most economically efficient, given the allocative cost and inevitable inaccuracy of theoretical research, empirical research, and efforts to derive economic-efficiency predictions and post-dictions from such research and pre-existing knowledge and given as well as the allocative cost of the government's financing efforts to predict or post-dict the economic efficiency of non-government choices and government policies). It has defined the concepts of "a distortion in the private cost of a specified resource allocation to the resource-user to which that resource allocation allocates resource," "a distortion in the private benefits that a specified resource allocation confers on that resource-user," and "the distortion in the profits that a specified resource allocation yields that resource-user"—respectively, the difference between those private figures and their allocative-cost, allocative-benefits, and allocative/economic-efficiency counterparts. It has defined the concepts of "the aggregate distortion in any private-cost, private-benefit, or profit figure"—the distortion in that figure that is generated by the interaction of all exemplars of all types of Pareto imperfections the economy in question contains. It has identified the large variety of categories of resource allocations and associated categories of economic inefficiency: the list it provides reflects inter alia the facts that (1) economies devote resources not only to the production of units of extant goods but also to the creation of quality-or-variety-increasing (QV) investments and the execution of production-process-research (PPR) projects and (2) the amounts of various categories of economic inefficiency an economy contains are affected by the extent of poverty and material inequality in the relevant society. It has defined two categories of coincident formulas for the aggregate distortion in the private cost, private benefits, and profits yielded by any specified resource allocation, each of which takes full account of the different ways that all of an economy's Pareto imperfections interact to cause or not cause respectively each category of economic inefficiency the economy can contain. It has developed a third-best-allocatively-efficient protocol for predicting/post-dicting the impact of a choice on economic efficiency that instructs the analyst (1) to derive conclusions primarily from estimates or guesstimates of (A) the choice's impact on the amounts of resources devoted to various categories of resource allocations defined by the category (categories) of use(s) from which the respective allocations withdraw resources and the category of use to which they allocate resources and the area(s) of product-space from which the allocation withdraws resources and the area of product-space to which they allocate resources, (B) the profits that were/would be yielded by the resource allocations the choice did/would elicit and the losses that would have been yielded by the resource allocations the choice did/would deter, and (C) the post-choice aggregate distortion in the profits that were yielded by the resource allocations the choice did/would elicit and the post-choice aggregate distortion in the losses that would have been generated by the resource allocations the choice did/would deter and (2) to do that research and only that research into these issues that is TBLE. It has explained why this proposal is important by showing (1) that the protocol it recommends differs from the protocol that economists who ignore both The General Theory of Second Best and many categories of resource allocations and economic inefficiency use to analyze the economic efficiency of (A) various antitrust-policy-covered categories of conduct and many related antitrust policies, (B) accident-and-pollution-loss-generating conduct and some related tort-law doctrines, (C) product-R&D-related and PPR-related IP, tax, and antitrust policies, and (D) various other tax-policy issues and (2) that the protocol it recommends will almost certainly yield very different economic-efficiency conclusions from those yielded by the conventional, first-best analyses it criticizes. Finally, it touches on a variety of government-decision-making-process regulatory-issues that would have to be resolved third-best-allocative-efficiently to create the approach that would be TBLE for a government to use to predict or post-dict the economic efficiency of non-government conduct and government policies.

What do I hope? I hope that Welfare Economics students and scholars, some members of the policy audience, and some government decision-makers will read this book. I hope that readers will identify and correct the errors it contains. I hope that readers will improve the protocol it recommends in ways other than by correcting mistakes of commission I have made. I hope that applied welfare economists and government decision-makers will use the protocol this book recommends or some superior variant of this protocol it enables others to develop. Finally, I hope that the use of the TBLE distortion-analysis protocol I am recommending or of an improved variant of this protocol others develop will increase not only the economic efficiency but the moral desirability of government decisions.

My sophomore-year high-school English teacher gave our class the following instruction for executing any writing assignment: "Say you are going to say it. Say it. Say you said it." I have done my best to obey her command.

Appendix A
A Pedagogically-Valuable
Economic-Efficiency-Impact-Analysis Diagram

Abstract

Appendix A (1) delineates an economic-efficiency-impact-analysis diagram that students report helps them understand both the distortion-analysis protocol for economic-efficiency prediction/post-diction that I claim is TBLE and the relevance of some of the determinants of a choice's impact on the amount of economic inefficiency generated by the relevant economy's economically-inefficient decisions to execute or not to execute exemplars of a referenced fully-specified series of resource allocations, (2) uses that diagram to illustrate some of the relationships that underlie important components of the distortion-analysis protocol for economic-efficiency prediction/post-diction I claim is TBLE, and (3) explains why—despite its pedagogic and heuristic usefulness—this diagram plays no role in the protocol for economic-efficiency prediction/post-diction that I claim is TBLE.

A.1.1 The Resource-Allocation Marginal-Allocative-Product Curve: Its Definition and Symbolic Representation

In my terminology, a "resource-allocation marginal-allocative-product curve" is a curve in a diagram whose vertical axis measures dollars and whose horizontal axis measures in dollars the total allocative cost of the resources that were/might be devoted to a referenced fully-specified series of resource allocation—a curve that indicates the allocative benefits that successive batches of resources whose allocative product in their sacrificed uses in the ARDEPPSes from which they were/would be withdrawn was/would be (say) $1 did/would generate in a specified/to-be-specified category of use or functionally-related pair of uses in the specified/to-be-specified ARDEPPS to which the referenced fully-specified resource allocation did/would allocate them. Although I recognize that one could construct resource-allocation marginal-allocative-product curves for resource allocations from any individual category of use or any pair of related uses to any individual category of use or any pair of related uses, this appendix will focus

© Springer Nature Switzerland AG 2020

R. S. Markovits, *Welfare Economics and Second-Best Theory*,

https://doi.org/10.1007/978-3-030-43360-4

exclusively on the subset of such curves that provides information about three subcategories of three-to-one resource allocations (resource allocations from UO-producing-and-using, QV-creating-and-using, *and* PPR-executing-and-using resource-uses in one or [almost always] more-than-one specified ARDEPPS to a UO-producing-and-using, QV-creating-and-using, *or* PPR-executing-and-using resource-"use" [enquoted because the resources are actually being devoted to two related resource-uses] in a single specified ARDEPPS). The negative implication of the preceding sentence is that this appendix will not reference any resource-allocation marginal-allocative-product curve (or any resource-allocation marginal-allocative-cost curve or resource-allocation total-allocative-cost quantity [see below]) that is associated with (1) allocations of resources from the use of one known production process to the use of another known production process, (2) allocations of resources from the production and use (consumption) of one or more units of one product variant to the production and consumption of a different product variant in the same or in a different ARDEPPS, (3) allocations of resources from the creation and use of one QV investment in a given ARDEPPS to the creation and use of a different QV investment in the same or a different ARDEPPS, (4) allocations of resources from the execution and use of a PPR project in a given ARDEPPS to the execution and use of another PPR project in the same or a different ARDEPPS, (5) allocations of a unit of a final good from one to another of its potential consumers, (6) allocations of resources from or to pricing-techniques that are designed to increase the proficiency with which their employers convert potential buyer surplus into seller surplus, (7) allocations of resources from or to the commission of (liberal) moral-right-violative acts, (8) allocations of resources from or to non-governmental legal-claim-making or legal-dispute-resolving activities, (9) the allocation of resources from and to governmental dispute-resolution processes by non-government and government actors, (10) the allocation of resources by government and non-government actors to legislative/administrative-rulemaking/Presidential-decree-promulgating processes, (11) the allocation of resources from and to electoral/political-campaign processes, etc.

In this text, the symbol RAMLP$_{.../...}$ is used to refer to any referenced resource-allocation marginal-allocative-product curve. In this symbol, (1) "RA" stands for "resource allocation" (to distinguish *resource-allocation* marginal-allocative-product curves from conventional *factor* marginal-allocative-product curves—MLPs), (2) "MLP" for "economics-marginal allocative product," (3) the entry that replaces the first ellipsis in the subscript indicates the category of use or functionally-related pair of uses to which the referenced resource allocation devotes resources and the ARDEPPS to which the relevant resource allocation allocates resources, and (4) the entry that replaces the second ellipsis in the symbol's subscript indicates the category or categories of uses or functionally-related pairs of uses from which and the ARDEPPSes from which the referenced resource allocation withdraws resources. More specifically, the entry that replaces the first ellipsis in the subscript of the symbol will be "(C+U)UO...," "(C+U)QV...," or "(C+U)PPR...,": the "(C+U)UO..." symbol-component indicates that the referenced resource allocation did/would devote resources to the production (i.e., creation, hence "C") and use (hence "U") of a unit of output in the ARDEPPS that would be specified by an entry that replaces the ellipsis in the (C+U)UO… symbol-component; the "(C+U)QV…" symbol-component indicates that the referenced resource allocation did/would devote resources to the creation and use of a QV investment in the ARDEPPS that would be specified by an entry that replaces the ellipsis in the (C+U)QV… symbol-component; and the (C+U)PPR… symbol-component indicates that the referenced resource allocation did/would devote resources to the "creation" (i.e., execution) and use of a PPR project (discovery) in the ARDEPPS that would be specified by an entry that replaces the ellipsis in the (C+U)PPR… symbol-component. The entry that replaces the second ellipsis in the subscript of the RAMLP$_{\ldots/\ldots}$ symbol is "(C+U)UO…, (C+U)QV…, and/or (C+U)PPR…." These symbols identify the categories of use and ARDEPPSes from which the resource allocation in question withdraws resources. The "(C+U)," "UO," "QV," and "PPR" symbols in the entry that replaces the second ellipsis in the RAMLP$_{\ldots/\ldots}$ symbol have the same referents in this ellipsis as they did in the first ellipsis in the RAMLP$_{\ldots/\ldots}$ symbol. The entries that replace the ellipsis in the entry that replaces the second ellipsis in the RAMLP$_{\ldots/\ldots}$ symbol indicate the ARDEPPS(es) from which the referenced resource allocation did/would withdraw resources.

I acknowledge that, although the RAMLP$_{\ldots/\ldots}$ symbol just described is regrettably complicated, it does not indicate either (1) the proportions of the successive batches of resources whose allocative cost is $1 that were/would be devoted to a referenced category of use or pair of functionally-related uses in a referenced ARDEPPS that was/would be withdrawn from, respectively, UO-producing-and-using, QV-creating-and-using, and PPR-executing-and-using uses (when the resource allocation withdraws resources from multiple categories of use or multiple functionally-related pairs of categories of use) or (2) the proportions of each successive resource-batch that were/would be withdrawn from various ARDEPPSes. This omission is made more regrettable by the fact that both these proportions will usually differ from successive resource-batch to successive resource-batch.

A.1.2 The Resource-Allocation Marginal-Allocative-Cost Curve: Its Definition and Symbolic Representation

In my terminology, a "resource-allocation marginal-allocative-cost curve" is a curve in a diagram whose vertical axis measures dollars and whose horizontal axis measures in dollars the total allocative cost of the resources that were/might be devoted to a referenced fully-specified series of resource allocations that indicates the allocative cost of the successive batches of resources that were/might be devoted to the diagram-covered fully-specified series of resource allocations. I construct this curve to be horizontal because, for convenience, I assume that the successive batches of resources that were or might be allocated to the referenced fully-specified series of resource allocations all have the same allocative cost. I construct this curve to be horizontal at the height of $1 because, for convenience, I assume that the marginal allocative cost of each successive batch of resources devoted to any referenced series of resource allocations is $1—that each successive batch of resources covered by any economic-efficiency-impact-analyzing diagram I consider did generate/would have generated $1 in net allocative benefits in the uses from which the referenced resource allocation did/would withdraw them. In this text, the symbol $RAMLC_{.../...}$ is used to refer to any referenced resource-allocation marginal-allocative-cost curve. In this symbol, "RA" continues to stand for "resource allocation," "MLC" stands for "marginal allocative cost," and the entries that replace the ellipses that precede and follow the forward-slash in the subscript are perfectly analogous to their counterparts in the subscript of the $RAMLP_{.../...}$ symbol discussed in Sect. A.1.1.

A.1.3   The Economic-Efficiency-Impact-Analyzing Diagram

Section A.1.3 presents two economic-efficiency-impact-analyzing diagrams that contain $RAMLP_{.../...}$ and $RAMLC_{.../...}$ curves, explains how these diagrams can be used to analyze the impact of a choice whose economic efficiency is at issue on the quantity of economic inefficiency that is generated by economically-inefficient decisions to execute economically-inefficient resource allocations in a referenced fully-specified series and/or economically-inefficient decisions not to execute economically-efficient resources allocations in that series and uses the diagram to illustrate the relevance of the most important determinants of the impact of a choice on the amount of economic inefficiency generated by economically-inefficient decisions to execute or not to execute resource allocations in a referenced fully-specified series of resource allocations. The two diagrams Sect. A.1.3 discusses differ in only one salient respect: Diagram A.1 constructs the relevant $RAMLP_{.../...}$ curve to be linear, whereas Diagram A.2 constructs it to be convex to the origin.

   Diagram A.1 has two axes. Both measure what they measure in dollars. The horizontal axis measures in dollars the total allocative cost of the resources that could be allocated by exemplars of the referenced fully-specified series of resource allocations. This axis is labeled the $TLC_{.../...}$ (total-allocative-cost) axis where the ellipses in the $TLC_{.../...}$ subscript will be replaced by entries that are perfectly analogous to the already-explained entries that replace the analogous ellipses in the subscript of the $RAMLP_{.../...}$ and $RAMLC_{.../...}$ symbols. The vertical axis measures in dollars two "parameters." One is the marginal allocative cost of the successive batches of resources that a referenced fully-specified series of resource allocations could allocate. Although I could divide any $TLC_{.../...}$ figure into batches of resources whose allocative cost have any magnitude, for visual convenience, Diagram A.1 assumes that the allocative cost of each successive batch of resources that the individual exemplars of the referenced series of resource allocations allocate is $1: therefore, the $RAMLC_{.../...}$ curve in Diagram A.1 is constructed to be horizontal at the height of $1.

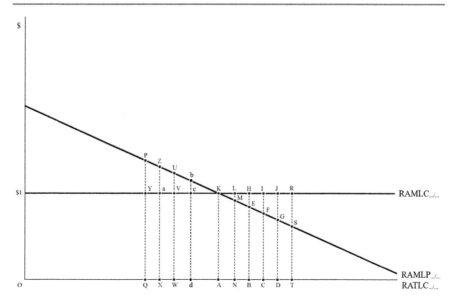

Diagram A.1 An economic-efficiency-impact-analyzing diagram that contains a linear RAMLP.../... curve

The RAMLP.../... curve in Diagram A.1 is the exemplar of that curve that I have already defined that would be accurate if (1) each successive batch of resources allocated by exemplars of the referenced series of resource allocations had an allocative cost of $1—i.e., if the allocative value that was/would be sacrificed when the resources in each successive batch of resources were/would be withdrawn was $1—and (2) the curve in question were downward-sloping and linear. For two reasons, the assumption that RAMLP.../... curves are downward-sloping will almost always be accurate—i.e., the allocation to any referenced use or pair of functionally-related uses in any ARDEPPS of each successive batch of resources whose allocative cost is $1 will almost always be lower than that of its predecessor: (1) even if each of the successive one-dollar-in-allocative-cost batches of resources whose devotion to the referenced use or pair of functionally-related uses in the referenced ARDEPPS were/would be physically equally-large and did/would have the same physical product in the use or pair of functionally-related uses to which they were/would be allocated as did all previous resource batches whose net allocative product in their alternative uses was $1, the allocative value of (A) the successive, equally-large increases in unit output that those resources' use would yield, (B) the successive QV-investment uses those batches of resources would effectuate when the relevant allocation of resources devoted them to a QV-investment-creating-and-using pair of functionally-related uses, or (C) the successive production-process-discovery uses those resource-uses would effectuate when the relevant allocation of resources devoted them to PPR-executing-and-using uses would decline, and (2) in reality, the successive batches of resources of an allocative cost of $1 that would be allocated by the successive exemplars of any referenced fully-specified resource allocation would be progressively physically-smaller because the alternative uses from which the physical resources in each successive one-dollar-in-allocative-cost batch of resources would be withdrawn would be progressively more-allocatively-valuable.

Diagram A.1's assumption that the RAMLP$_{.../...}$ curve it contains is linear is unlikely to be accurate. RAMLP$_{.../...}$ curves could be linear for an infinite number of reasons. The most-easy-to-articulate set of conditions under which an RAMLP$_{.../...}$ curve would be linear is (1) the allocative value of the successive units of the referenced ARDEPPS' products that could be produced, of the successive QV investments/QV-investment expenditures that could be created/made in a referenced ARDEPPS, or of the successive PPR projects/PPR expenditures that could be executed/made in a referenced ARDEPPS drop at a constant rate and (2) the marginal allocative products in their sacrificed alternative uses of each individual resource in the successive batches of resources of a total allocative cost of $1 that would be withdrawn from a referenced category of use or functionally-related pair of uses (the allocative value of the units of the products each such resource would otherwise have produced in the ARDEPPS[es] from which they would be withdrawn, the allocative value of the contribution each such resource would otherwise have made to the completion of one or more QV investments in the ARDEPPS[es] from which they would be withdrawn, or the allocative value of the contribution each such resource would otherwise have made to the completion of one or more PPR projects in the ARDEPPS[es] from which they would be withdrawn) rise at a constant rate. However, there is no reason to believe that RAMLP$_{.../...}$ curves will often be linear. I hasten to add that, at no point, will this appendix make and defend an argument that depends on any RAMLP$_{.../...}$ curve's linearity.

The preceding discussion focused inter alia on the definitions of the resource-allocation marginal-allocative-cost and resource-allocation marginal-allocative-product curves that appear in Diagram A.1. As previously indicated, the symbols for these curves were, respectively, RAMLC$_{.../...}$ and RAMLP$_{.../...}$. The text that follows also references particular points on these curves that indicate, respectively, the marginal allocative cost and marginal allocative product of the economics-marginal exemplar of the referenced series of resource allocations that brought RATLC$_{.../...}$ to the quantity at which the point in question is located. The symbols for these points are, respectively, RAMLC$_{\Delta.../\Delta...}$ and RAMLP$_{\Delta.../\Delta...}$: unlike the symbols for the curves, the symbols for these particular points on these curves include a "Δ" before each component of the symbol's subscript where the "Δ" indicates that the particular resource allocation that brought the relevant series of resource allocation's RATLC$_{.../...}$ quantity to the indicated quantity was an economics-marginal resource allocation.

I will now use Diagram A.1 to illustrate the protocol for predicting/post-dicting the impact of a choice on the amount of misallocation generated by the economically-inefficient choices to execute one or more economically-inefficient possible exemplars of the diagram-referenced fully-specified series of resource allocations or not to execute one or more economically-efficient exemplars of that series of resource allocations. I will begin by making five preliminary points.

First, if the economic actor who makes the relevant economics-marginal resource-allocation choice is a sovereign maximizer, no economies of scale apply over the relevant range to the series of resource allocations in question (so that, inter alia, the economics-marginal resource allocation is mathematics-marginal—i.e., is infinitesimally small), and the economics-marginal and first-extra-marginal resource-use or functionally-related pair of resource-uses to which resources are being allocated are inherently-equally-profitable (and presumptively inherently-economically-efficient)—i.e., if the rate-of-return that would be generated by the first-extra-marginal resource-use or functionally-related pair of resource-uses in the relevant series would equal the rate-of-return that was generated by the economics-marginal resource-use or functionally-related pair of resource-uses in the series in question if the former use or pair of resource-uses were substituted for the latter, $P\pi_{\Delta.../\Delta...}$ will be zero for the economics-marginal resource allocation in question. Second, and relatedly, if the above three conditions are fulfilled, the difference between the heights of the $RAMLC_{.../...}$ and $RAMLP_{.../...}$ curves at the equilibrium total-allocative-cost quantity for the referenced series of resource allocations will equal not only the amount by which the economics-marginal exemplar of the referenced series of resource allocations increased (or decreased) economic inefficiency but also the negative of the aggregate distortion in the profits yielded by that economics-marginal resource allocation: if $P\pi_{\Delta.../\Delta...} = 0$, the definition $\Sigma D(P\pi_{\Delta.../\Delta...}) \equiv P\pi_{\Delta.../\Delta...} - LE_{\Delta.../\Delta...}$ will imply that $\Sigma D(P\pi_{\Delta.../\Delta...}) = -LE_{\Delta.../\Delta...}$. Thus, in Diagram A.1, if the equilibrium $RATLC_{.../...}$ quantity is OX and the resource-use or functionally-related pair of resource-uses that brought $RATLC_{.../...}$ to OX yielded zero profits (supernormal profits), $\Sigma D(P\pi_{\Delta.../\Delta...}) = -\$Za$ and the $LE_{\Delta.../\Delta...}$ for the economics-and-mathematics marginal resource allocation that brought $RATLC_{.../...}$ to OX will be $+\$Za$. Similarly, in Diagram A.1, if the equilibrium $RATLC_{.../...}$ quantity is OB and the resource-use or functionally-related pair of resource-uses that brought $RATLC_{.../...}$ to OB yielded zero profits, $\Sigma D(P\pi_{\Delta.../\Delta...}) = +\$HE$ and $LE_{\Delta.../\Delta...} = -\$HE$. Third, and again relatedly, if the above three conditions are fulfilled, 100% *times* ([the difference between the heights of the $RAMLC_{.../...}$ and $RAMLP_{.../...}$ curves at the total-allocative-cost quantity associated with any economics-marginal resource allocation] *divided* by [the height of the $RAMLC_{.../...}$ curve at the total-allocative-cost quantity in question]) will equal the negative of the aggregate-percentage-distortion in the profits yielded by the relevant economics-marginal resource allocation. Fourth, and again relatedly, if the allocative efficiency of the economics-marginal exemplar of the referenced fully-specified series of resource allocations is zero, the aggregate distortion in the profits yielded by that allocation will also be zero: thus, if in Diagram A.1 the total allocative cost of the referenced fully-specified series of resource allocations is $OA, $LE_{\Delta.../\Delta...} = RAMLP_{\Delta.../\Delta...} - RAMLC_{\Delta.../\Delta...} = 0$ and $\Sigma D(P\pi_{\Delta.../\Delta...}) = 0$. And fifth, in Diagram A.1, the total misallocation generated by all allocatively-inefficient decisions to execute or not to execute exemplars of the referenced fully-specified series of resource allocations is the area between the RAMLP$_{.../...}$ and RAMLC$_{.../...}$ curves in that diagram between the total allocative cost of the resources devoted to the referenced fully-specified series of resource allocations in equilibrium and the amount of resources whose devotion to the relevant fully-specified series of resource allocations would have been economically efficient. Thus, if OB in resources is devoted to the referenced fully-specified series of resource allocations, the misallocation generated by the AB of economically-inefficient allocations in question will be area KHE, and if OX in resources is devoted to the referenced fully-specified series of resource allocations, the misallocation that will have resulted from the failure to devote an additional XA in resources to that fully-specified series of resource allocations will be area ZKa.

I will now use Diagram A.1 to illustrate how one could infer (1) the impact of a choice on the amount of economic inefficiency generated by the economically-inefficient choices to devote or not to devote resources to any diagram-covered fully-specified series of resource allocations from (2) accurate estimates of (A) the pre-choice $\Sigma D(P\pi_{\Delta.../\Delta...})$ figure for the economics-marginal exemplar of that series of resource allocations, (B) the post-choice $\Sigma D(P\pi_{\Delta.../\Delta...})$ figure for the marginal exemplar of that series of resource allocations, and (C) the RAMLP$_{.../...}$ curve for that series of resource allocations between the pre-choice and post-choice equilibrium RATLC$_{.../...}$ quantities for the referenced series of resource allocations if $P\pi_{\Delta.../\Delta...} = 0$ both pre-choice and post-choice and the choice did/would not affect the associated RAMLP$_{.../...}$ curve. Thus, if the analyst knows that the applicable RAMLP$_{.../...}$ curve was the curve represented in Diagram A.1 and that the two conditions articulated at the end of the preceding sentence were satisfied, the analyst (1) could infer from the accurate conclusions that $\Sigma D(P\pi_{\Delta.../\Delta...})$ was (−PY) pre-choice and (−Za) post-choice that the choice whose economic efficiency is at issue would reduce the amount of economic inefficiency generated by economically-inefficient decisions to execute or not to execute (in this case, not to execute) exemplars of the diagram-covered series of resource allocations by area PZaY from area PKY to area ZKa, (2) could infer from the accurate conclusions that $\Sigma D(P\pi_{\Delta.../\Delta...})$ was (−PY) pre-choice and (−UV) post-choice that the choice whose economic efficiency is at issue would reduce the amount of misallocation generated by economically-inefficient decisions not to execute economically-efficient resource allocations in the diagram-covered series by area PUVY from area PKY to area UKV, (3) could infer from the accurate conclusions that $\Sigma D(P\pi_{\Delta.../\Delta...})$ was (−Za) pre-choice and (−UV) post-choice that the choice whose economic efficiency is at issue would reduce the amount of misallocation generated by decisions not to execute economically-efficient resource allocations in the diagram-covered series by area ZUVa from area ZKa to area UKV, (4) could infer from the accurate conclusions that the choice whose economic efficiency is at issue would/did increase $|\Sigma D(P\pi_{\Delta.../\Delta...})|$, respectively, from $|{-}Za|$ to $|{-}PY|$, from $|{-}UV|$ to $|{-}PY|$, and from $|{-}UV|$ to $|{-}Za|$ that that choice would/did increase the misallocation generated by economically-inefficient decisions not to execute economically-efficient resource allocations in the diagram-covered series, respectively, by areas PZaY, PUVY, and ZUVa, (5) could infer from the accurate conclusions that $\Sigma D(P\pi_{\Delta.../\Delta...})$ was IF pre-choice and HE post-choice that the choice whose economic efficiency is at issue would reduce by area HIFE from area KIF to area KHE the amount of economic inefficiency generated by economically-inefficient decisions to execute economically-inefficient resource allocations in the diagram-covered series, (6) could infer from the accurate conclusions that $\Sigma D(P\pi_{\Delta.../\Delta...})$ was IF pre-choice and LM post-choice that the choice whose economic efficiency is at issue would reduce by area IFML from area KIF to area KLM the amount of economic inefficiency generated by economically-inefficient decisions to execute economically-inefficient exemplars of the diagram-covered series of resource allocations, (7) could infer from the accurate conclusions that $\Sigma D(P\pi_{\Delta.../\Delta...})$ was HE pre-choice and LM post-choice that the choice whose economic efficiency is at issue would reduce by area LHEM from area KHE to area KLM the amount of economic inefficiency generated by economically-inefficient decisions to execute economically-inefficient resource allocations in the diagram-covered series, (8) could infer from the accurate conclusions that the choice whose economic efficiency is at issue would increase $\Sigma D(P\pi_{\Delta.../\Delta...})$, respectively, from HE to IF, from LM to IF, or from LM to HE that the choice would increase the amount of economic inefficiency generated by the executed economically-inefficient exemplars of the diagram-covered series of resource allocations, respectively, by areas HIFE, LIFM, and LHEM, and (9) could infer from the unusual pair of accurate conclusions that the choice whose economic efficiency is at issue had altered the operative $\Sigma D(P\pi_{\Delta.../\Delta...})$ figure from $(-Za)$ to $(+HE)$—unusual because I suspect that few choices will change the sign of the relevant $\Sigma D(P\pi_{\Delta.../\Delta...})$ figure—that that choice will have changed the amount of misallocation generated by the economically-inefficient decisions (1) not to execute economically-efficient exemplars of a diagram-covered series of resource allocations and (2) to execute economically-inefficient exemplars of that series of resource allocations from area ZKa to area KHE (while changing the "character" of the economically-inefficient resource-allocation decisions that are executed from decisions not to execute economically-efficient resource allocations to decisions to execute economically-inefficient resource allocations).

I will now use Diagram A.1 to illustrate the relevance of three factors that influence the impact that a choice whose economic efficiency is at issue will have on the amount of economic inefficiency generated by the economically-inefficient exemplars of any decisions to execute or not to execute exemplars of any diagram-covered series of resource allocations. The analyses that follow are based on two assumptions. The first is that, both pre-choice and post-choice, $P\pi_{\Delta.../\Delta...}$ for the economics-marginal resource allocation in the diagram-covered category is zero.

As I have already indicated, the assumptions that both the pre-choice and the post-choice $P\pi_{\Delta.../\Delta...}$ equal zero imply that both the pre-choice and the post-choice $\Sigma D(P\pi_{\Delta.../\Delta...})$ for the economics-marginal exemplar of the diagram-covered series of resource allocations equals $(-LE_{\Delta.../\Delta...})$—the negative of the distance between the $RAMLP_{.../...}$ and the $RAMLC_{.../...}$ curves at the equilibrium $RATLC_{.../...}$ quantity: if $P\pi_{\Delta.../\Delta...} = 0$, the definition $\Sigma D(P\pi_{\Delta.../\Delta...}) \equiv P\pi_{\Delta.../\Delta...} - LE_{\Delta.../\Delta...}$ implies that $\Sigma D(P\pi_{\Delta.../\Delta...}) = -LE_{\Delta.../\Delta...}$. By way of contract, if $P\pi_{\Delta.../\Delta...} > 0$, the definition $\Sigma D(P\pi_{\Delta.../\Delta...}) \equiv P\pi_{\Delta.../\Delta...} -LE_{\Delta.../\Delta...}$ implies not only that $-LE_{\Delta.../\Delta...}$ = $P\pi_{\Delta.../\Delta...} -\Sigma D(P\pi_{\Delta.../\Delta...})$ but that the allocative efficiency of the economics-marginal exemplar of the diagram-covered series of resource allocations exceeds $-\Sigma D(P\pi_{\Delta.../\Delta...})$ by $P\pi_{\Delta.../\Delta...}$—that (1) when $\Sigma D(P\pi_{\Delta.../\Delta...})$ is negative, the allocative-efficiency gain generated by the relevant economics-marginal resource allocation (the amount by which the height of the RAMLP$_{.../..}$ curve exceeds the height of the RAMLC$_{.../..}$ curve at the equilibrium RATLC$_{.../..}$ quantity) exceeds $|\Sigma D(P\pi_{\Delta.../\Delta...})|$ by $P\pi_{\Delta.../\Delta...}$ and (2) when $\Sigma D(P\pi_{\Delta.../\Delta...})$ is positive, the allocative-efficiency loss generated by the relevant economics-marginal resource allocation (the amount by which the height of the RAMLC$_{.../..}$ curve exceeds the height of the RAMLP$_{.../..}$ curve at the equilibrium RATLC$_{.../..}$ quantity) will fall below $|\Sigma D(P\pi_{\Delta.../\Delta...})|$ by $P\pi_{\Delta.../\Delta...} > 0$: indeed, when $P\pi_{\Delta.../\Delta...} > 0$, the relevant economics-marginal resource allocation will generate an economic-efficiency gain (the RAMLP$_{.../..}$ curve will be higher than the RAMLC$_{.../..}$ curve at the equilibrium RATLC$_{.../..}$ quantity) despite the fact that $\Sigma D(P\pi_{\Delta.../\Delta...}) > 0$ if $P\pi_{\Delta.../\Delta...} > \Sigma D(P\pi_{\Delta.../\Delta...})$.

Thus, if $P\pi_{\Delta.../\Delta...} = (+\$2)$, $LE_{\Delta.../\Delta...}$ (the distance between the RAMLP$_{.../..}$ curve and the RAMLC$_{.../..}$ curve) will be $(+\$5)$ when $\Sigma D(P\pi_{\Delta.../\Delta...}) = (-\$3)$ where $|-\$3|$ is lower than the \$5 distance between the relevant RAMLP$_{.../..}$ and RAMLC$_{.../..}$ curves at the equilibrium RATLC$_{.../..}$ quantity. Similarly, if $P\pi_{\Delta.../\Delta...} = (+\$2)$, $LE_{\Delta.../\Delta...}$ will be $(-\$3)$ when $\Sigma D(P\pi_{\Delta.../\Delta...}) = (+\$5)$ and $LE_{\Delta.../\Delta...}$ will be $(+\$1)$ when $\Sigma D(P\pi_{\Delta.../\Delta...}) = (+\$1)$. In any event, this section's discussion will assume that $P\pi_{\Delta.../\Delta...} = 0$ and therefore that one can assume that $LE_{\Delta.../\Delta...} = -\Sigma D(P\pi_{\Delta.../\Delta...})$ and that one can determine the equilibrium RATLC$_{.../..}$ quantity from the $\Sigma D(P\pi_{\Delta.../\Delta...})$ figure and the RAMLP$_{.../..}$ curve. This assumption will eventually be relaxed.

The second assumption on which the discussion that follows is based is that the choice whose economic efficiency is at issue will not alter the RAMLP$_{.../..}$ curve for the referenced series of resource allocations. The possible TBLE of relaxing this assumption will also be considered below.

The discussion that follows will also take advantage of two features of the construction of Diagram A.1: the fact that the RAMLP$_{.../..}$ curve is constructed to be linear and the fact that QX = XW = Wd = AN = NB = BC = CD = DT. The combination of these two diagram-construction attributes and this section's assumption that $P\pi_{\Delta.../\Delta...}$ is zero for all economics-marginal exemplars of diagram-covered fully-specified series of resource allocations allows me to assume inter alia that (1) $|\Sigma D(P\pi_{\Delta.../\Delta...})|$ at any equilibrium at which RATLC$_{.../..} = 0Q$ exceeds $|\Sigma D(P\pi_{\Delta.../\Delta...})|$ at any equilibrium at which RATLC$_{.../..} = 0X$ by the same amount by which $|\Sigma D(P\pi_{\Delta.../\Delta...})|$ at any equilibrium at which RATLC$_{.../..} = 0X$ exceeds $|\Sigma D(P\pi_{\Delta.../\Delta...})|$ at any equilibrium at which RATLC$_{.../..} = 0W$ and (2) $\Sigma D(P\pi_{\Delta.../\Delta...})$ at any equilibrium at which RATLC$_{.../..} = 0C$ exceeds $\Sigma D(P\pi_{\Delta.../\Delta...})$ at any equilibrium at which RATLC$_{.../..} = 0B$ by the same amount by which $\Sigma D(P\pi_{\Delta.../\Delta...})$ at any equilibrium at which RATLC$_{.../..} = 0N$ exceeds $\Sigma D(P\pi_{\Delta.../\Delta...})$ at any equilibrium at which RATLC$_{.../..} = 0A$. I hasten to add, however, that no conclusion this discussion reaches will depend on these features of the diagram's construction. Indeed, I will explain why I have narrowed one of the conclusions I articulate to take account of the possibility that actual $RAMLP_{.../...}$ curves may not be linear.

I will now use Diagram A.1 and a second economic-efficiency-impact-analysis diagram that contains a $RAMLP_{.../...}$ curve that is convex to the origin—Diagram A.2 —to illustrate three points about the determinants of the impact of a choice whose economic efficiency is at issue on the amount of economic inefficiency generated by the economically-inefficient exemplars of decisions to execute or not to execute exemplars of a referenced fully-specified series of resource allocations. The first point is that, controlling for the pre-choice $|\Sigma D(P\pi_{\Delta.../\Delta...})|$ figure, the amount by which any choice whose economic efficiency is at issue that does not change the sign of the $\Sigma D(P\pi_{\Delta.../\Delta...})$ figure decreases/increases the magnitude of economic inefficiency generated by economically-inefficient decisions to execute or not execute exemplars of a referenced fully-specified series of resource allocations will increase with the amount by which the choice whose economic efficiency is at issue decreases/increases the operative $|\Sigma D(P\pi_{\Delta.../\Delta...})|$ figure. Thus, in Diagram A.1, if the pre-choice $|\Sigma D(P\pi_{\Delta.../\Delta...})|$ figure is PY, the choice will decrease the magnitude of the above quantity of economic inefficiency by area PZaY if it reduces $|\Sigma D(P\pi_{\Delta.../\Delta...})|$ by (PY−Za) from PY to Za, will decrease the magnitude of the above quantity of economic inefficiency by the larger area PUVY if it reduces $|\Sigma D(P\pi_{\Delta.../\Delta...})|$ by the larger amount (PY−UV) from PY to UV, and will decrease the magnitude of the above quantity of economic inefficiency by the still-larger amount area PKY if it reduces $|\Sigma D(P\pi_{\Delta.../\Delta...})|$ by the still-larger amount PY (from PY to zero). Similarly, if the pre-choice $\Sigma D(P\pi_{\Delta.../\Delta...})$ is LM, the choice whose economic efficiency is at issue will increase the magnitude of the above quantity of economic inefficiency by area LHEM if it increases $\Sigma D(P\pi_{\Delta.../\Delta...})$ by (HE−LM) and will increase the magnitude of the above quantity of economic inefficiency by the larger amount area LIFM if it increases $\Sigma D(P\pi_{\Delta.../\Delta...})$ by the larger amount (IF−LM) from LM to IF.

In fact, when the operative $RAMLP_{.../...}$ curve is linear and was not changed/would not be changed by the choice whose economic efficiency is at issue, the amount by which the choice whose economic inefficiency is at issue will decrease/increase the amount of economic inefficiency generated by the economically-inefficient exemplars of decisions to execute or not execute exemplars of the referenced fully-specified series of resource allocations will increase/decrease with that choice's impact on $|\Sigma D(P\pi_{\Delta.../\Delta...})|$ even if the choice does change the sign of the operative $\Sigma D(P\pi_{\Delta.../\Delta...})$ figure. Thus, in Diagram A.1, a choice that decreases the absolute value of the operative $\Sigma D(P\pi_{\Delta.../\Delta...})$ figure from $|{-}PY|$ to $|{+}LM|$ where PY > LM will decrease the amount of economic inefficiency caused by economically-inefficient decisions to execute or not execute the exemplars of the referenced fully-specified series of resource allocations by area PKY *minus* area KLM, a relevant choice that decreases the absolute value of the operative $\Sigma D(P\pi_{\Delta.../\Delta...})$ figure from $|{+}RS|$ to $|{-}UV|$ will decrease the above quantity of economic inefficiency by area KRS *minus* area UKV, a relevant choice that increases the absolute value of the operative $\Sigma D(P\pi_{\Delta.../\Delta...})$ figure from $|{-}UV|$ to $|{+}RS|$ will increase the above quantity of economic inefficiency by area KRS *minus* area UKV.

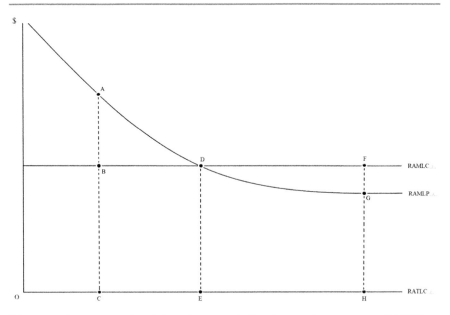

Diagram A.2 An economic-efficiency-impact-analyzing diagram that contains an RAMLP.../... curve that is convex to the origin

   I will use Diagram A.2 to illustrate the second point I will make at this juncture: as my statement of the first point indicates, the monotonic relationship the first point articulates between (1) the absolute magnitude of the impact of the choice whose economic efficiency is at issue on the quantity of economic inefficiency generated by the economically-inefficient exemplars of decisions to execute or not to execute exemplars of a referenced series of resource allocations and (2) the choice's impact on the absolute value of the $\Sigma D(P\pi_{\Delta.../\Delta...})$ figure for the associated set of resource allocations will not obtain when the choice in question changes the sign of the operative $\Sigma D(P\pi_{\Delta.../\Delta...})$ figure. As previously indicated, Diagram A.2 differs from Diagram A.1 in only one salient respect: the RAMLP.../... curve that Diagram A.2 contains is convex to the origin instead of linear. Diagram A.2 illustrates the second point because it reveals that when the operative RAMLP.../... curve is convex to the origin a choice that decreases the absolute magnitude of the relevant $\Sigma D(P\pi_{\Delta.../\Delta...})$ figure (say) from $|-\$AB|$ to $|+\$FG|$ may increase the amount of economic inefficiency generated by economically-inefficient decisions to execute economically-inefficient resource allocations in the referenced series or not to execute economically-efficient resource allocations in the referenced series (from area ADB to area DFG). Put crudely, this possibility reflects the fact that, when the relevant RAMLP.../... curve is convex to the origin, the amount of resources (measured by their allocative cost) that a smaller positive $\Sigma D(P\pi_{\Delta.../\Delta...})$ "cause" to be allocated economic-inefficiently from and to the referenced uses/ARDEPPSes ("causes" is enquoted because the actual causes are the Pareto imperfections that generate the relevant aggregate-profit-distortion figure) *exceeds* the amount of resources (measured by their allocative cost) that the absolutely-larger negative $\Sigma D(P\pi_{\Delta.../\Delta...})$ deterred from being allocated from and to the referenced uses/ARDEPPSes despite the economic efficiency of the foregone allocations of resources. Thus, in Diagram A.2, the Pareto imperfections that generated the absolutely-smaller post-choice $|\Sigma D(P\pi_{\Delta.../\Delta...})|$ figure of $|FG|$ caused EH resources to be allocated economic-inefficiently to the referenced category of resource allocations, whereas the Pareto imperfections that generated the absolutely-larger pre-choice $|\Sigma D(P\pi_{\Delta.../\Delta...})|$ figure of $|-AB|$ deterred only CE in resources from being devoted to economically-efficient resource allocations in the referenced category from and to the referenced ARDEPPSes where EH > CE.

I return to Diagram A.1 to illustrate the third point I want to make at this juncture: controlling for the amount by which a choice whose economic efficiency is at issue changes the absolute magnitude of the operative $\Sigma D(P\pi_{\Delta.../\Delta...})$ figure, assuming that the operative $RAMLP_{.../...}$ curve is both linear and unchanged by the choice whose economic efficiency is at issue, and assuming as well that $P\pi_{\Delta.../\Delta...}$ is zero both pre-choice and post-choice, the impact that the choice whose economic efficiency is at issue will have on the amount of economic inefficiency generated by economically-inefficient decisions to execute or not to execute exemplars of any fully-specified series of resource allocations will increase with the absolute value of the pre-choice $\Sigma D(P\pi_{\Delta.../\Delta...})$ figure. Thus, in Diagram A.1, (1) a choice that decreases $|\Sigma D(P\pi_{\Delta.../\Delta...})|$ by (PY−Za) from the larger absolute amount $|-PY|$ will increase economic efficiency by the larger area PZaY whereas a choice that decreases $|\Sigma D(P\pi_{\Delta.../\Delta...})|$ by the same amount (Za−UV) = (PY−Za) from the absolutely-smaller amount $|-Za|$ will increase economic inefficiency by the smaller quantity area ZUVa (which is smaller than area PZaY), (2) a choice that increases $|\Sigma D(P\pi_{\Delta.../\Delta...})|$ by (Za−UV) from the lower amount UV will increase economic inefficiency by the smaller area ZUVa whereas a choice that increases $|\Sigma D(P\pi_{\Delta.../\Delta...})|$ by the same amount (PY−Za) = (Za−UV) will increase economic inefficiency by the larger area PZaY, (3) a choice that increases $|\Sigma D(P\pi_{\Delta.../\Delta...})|$ by (HE−LM) from the smaller amount LM will increase economic inefficiency by the smaller quantity area LHEM whereas a choice that increases $|\Sigma D(P\pi_{\Delta.../\Delta...})|$ by the same amount (IF−HE) = (HE−LM) from the larger amount HE will increase economic inefficiency by the larger quantity area HIFE (which is larger than area LHEM), and (4) a choice that decreases $|\Sigma D(P\pi_{\Delta.../\Delta...})|$ by (IF−HE) from the larger amount IF will reduce economic inefficiency by the larger area HIFE whereas a choice that decreases $|\Sigma D(P\pi_{\Delta.../\Delta...})|$ by the same amount (HE−LM) = (IF−HE) from the smaller amount HE will reduce economic inefficiency by the smaller quantity area LHEM. These conclusions reflect, respectively, the facts that (1) the larger the absolute magnitude of any negative pre-choice $\Sigma D(P\pi_{\Delta.../\Delta...})$ figure, the more economically-efficient the exemplar of the referenced economics-marginal resource allocation and the more economically-inefficient choices not to devote additional resources of given allocative cost to the referenced series of resource allocations (until RATLC$_{.../...}$ reaches its economically-efficient quantity), (2) the larger the absolute magnitude of any negative pre-choice $\Sigma D(P\pi_{\Delta.../\Delta...})$ figure, the more economically-efficient the economics-marginal exemplar of the referenced series of resource allocations and the more economically-efficient decisions to devote additional resources of given allocative cost to the referenced series of resource allocations (until RATLC$_{.../...}$ reaches its economically-inefficient quantity), (3) the larger any positive pre-choice $\Sigma D(P\pi_{\Delta.../\Delta...})$ figure, the more economically-inefficient any decision to devote any given amount of additional resources (measured by their allocative cost) to the referenced series of resource allocations, and (4) the larger any positive pre-choice $\Sigma D(P\pi_{\Delta.../\Delta...})$ figure, the more economically-inefficient the economics-marginal exemplar of the referenced series of resource allocations and the more economically-efficient decisions to withdraw given amounts of resources (measured by the allocative value they would have generated in their sacrificed uses) from the referenced series of resource allocations.

A.1.4 The Relevance of the Facts That $P\pi_{\Delta.../\Delta...} > 0$ for Most Economics-Marginal QV-Investment-Creating-and-Using Resource-Uses, for Most Economics-Marginal PPR-Executing-and-Using Resource-Uses, and for Some Economics-Marginal UO-Producing-and-Using Resource-Uses to the Impact of Any Choice on the Quantity of Economic Inefficiency Generated by All Economically-Inefficient Decisions to Execute or Not to Execute Exemplars of a Referenced Series of Resource Allocations

Sections A.1.3's and A.1.4's analysis of the way in which Diagrams A.1 and A.2 can be employed to analyze the impact of a choice whose economic efficiency is at issue on the amount of economic inefficiency generated by decisions to execute economically-inefficient exemplars of or not to execute economically-efficient exemplars of a diagram-covered series of resource allocations assume that both pre-choice and post-choice $P\pi_{\Delta.../\Delta...}$ equal zero for the relevant economics-marginal resource allocations. In fact, this assumption will rarely be accurate for resource allocations that devote resources to QV-creating-and-using or PPR-executing-and-using uses and will sometimes be inaccurate for resource allocations that devote resources to UO-producing-and-using uses. $\Sigma D(P\pi_{\Delta.../\Delta...})$ will rarely equal zero for resource allocations to QV-creating-and-using/PPR-executing-and-using resource-uses because (1) the minimum (private or allocative) efficient scale of all relevant QV investments and PPR projects is significant, (2) it will usually not be possible to increase the magnitude of a QV-investment project or a PPR project once it has reached its minimum privately/allocatively-efficient scale without reducing the supernormal profits (and, I expect, usually the economic-efficiency gains) it yields, and (3) the successively-most-profitable/successively-most-economically-efficient QV investments/PPR projects that could be created/executed in a given ARDEPPS will usually be successively-less-profitable/successively-less-economically-efficient than each of their predecessors if one assumes as I will for simplicity that QV investments/PPR projects are created/executed in the order of their inherent profitability/inherent economic efficiency (I am also assuming for simplicity that the profitability-rank and economic-efficiency rank of QV-investment projects are the same and that the profitability-rank and economic-efficiency rank of PPR projects are the same), and (4) even if the economics-marginal QV investment/PPR project could be executed at a variety of different scales without changing the amount of supernormal profits it yields, it is unlikely that the economics-marginal QV investment/PPR project will yield zero profits (will bring $RATLC_{.../...}$ in the ARDEPPS in question to the quantity that will result in the economics-marginal project's yielding just a normal rate-of-return). Moreover, although it is plausible to assume that $P\pi_{\Delta.../\Delta...}$ equals zero for economics-marginal resource allocations to UO-production-and-use when the marginal cost of the economics-marginal unit of output is low (given that MR = MC for products whose marginal-cost curve is low at its equilibrium output), I suspect that the marginal revenue generated by the sale of the economics-marginal unit of a good whose marginal cost at its equilibrium output is substantial will often exceed that marginal cost (because the marginal revenue that would be generated by the sale of the first-extra-marginal unit of a product whose marginal cost is substantial will often be significantly lower than the marginal revenue generated by the sale of that product's economics-marginal unit)—i.e., that $P\pi_{\Delta.../\Delta...}$ will often exceed zero for products whose marginal cost is high at their equilibrium outputs.

I have already indicated one of the reasons why $P\pi_{\Delta.../\Delta...}$'s exceeding zero makes it more difficult to use the economic-efficiency-impact-analysis diagram to predict or post-dict the impact of a choice on the amount of economic inefficiency generated by economically-inefficient decisions to execute or not to execute any of the exemplars of a diagram-covered series of resource allocations—viz., when $P\pi_{\Delta.../\Delta...} > 0$ pre-choice/post-choice, one will have to know the value of pre-choice/post-choice $P\pi_{\Delta.../\Delta...}$ to determine, respectively, pre-choice and post-choice $LE_{\Delta.../\Delta...}$. $P\pi_{\Delta.../\Delta...}$'s exceeding zero also makes it difficult to use the economic-efficiency-impact-analysis diagram to predict/post-dict the impact of a choice on the economic inefficiency generated by economically-inefficient decisions to execute or not to execute exemplars of a diagram-referenced series of resource allocations for a second, related reason: when $P\pi_{\Delta.../\Delta...} = 0$, $\Sigma D(P\pi_{\Delta.../\Delta...}) = -LE_{\Delta.../\Delta...}$ (which equals the distance between the heights of the $RAMLP_{.../...}$ and $RAMLC_{.../...}$ curves at the equilibrium $RATLC_{.../...}$ quantity), one can infer the equilibrium $RATLC_{.../...}$ quantity from accurate estimates of $\Sigma D(P\pi_{\Delta.../\Delta...})$ and the $RAMLP_{.../...}$ curve (regardless of whether $\Sigma D(P\pi_{\Delta.../\Delta...})$ is positive, negative, or zero) since the equilibrium $RATLC_{.../...}$ quantity is the $RATLC_{.../...}$ quantity at which the difference between the heights of the $RAMLP_{.../...}$ and $RAMLC_{.../...}$ curves equals the accurately-estimated $(-LE_{\Delta.../\Delta...})$ figure whereas when $P\pi_{\Delta.../\Delta...} > 0$, $LE_{\Delta.../\Delta...} = -\Sigma D(P\pi_{\Delta.../\Delta...}) +$

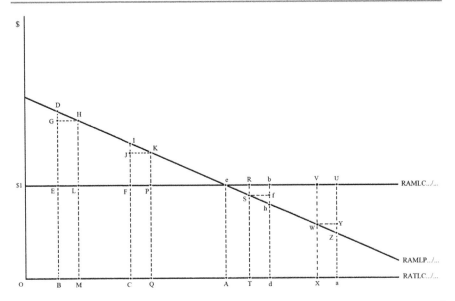

Diagram A.3 An economic-efficiency-impact-analysis diagram that illustrates the relevance of pre-choice $P\pi_{\Delta.../\Delta...}$ = post-choice $P\pi_{\Delta.../\Delta...} > 0$

$P\pi_{\Delta.../\Delta...}$ and one cannot determine the equilibrium $LE_{\Delta.../\Delta...}$ figure and hence the equilibrium $RATLC_{.../...}$ quantity perfectly accurately in any pre-choice and post-choice situation without estimating accurately not only the $\Sigma D(P\pi_{\Delta.../\Delta...})$ figure in the situation in question and the $RAMLP_{.../...}$ curve but also the $P\pi_{\Delta.../\Delta...}$ figure in the situation in question, regardless of whether the choice did not or would not affect the operative $RAMLP_{.../...}$ curve.

   Diagram A.3 can be used inter alia to illustrate this conclusion. Assume that $\Sigma D(P\pi_{\Delta.../\Delta...})$ has been accurately estimated to equal $(-HL)$ in Diagram A.3 and that Diagram A.3's $RAMLP_{.../...}$ curve has also been accurately estimated. If $P\pi_{\Delta.../\Delta...} = 0$, these accurate estimates would imply not only that $LE_{\Delta.../\Delta...} = (+HL)$ in Diagram A.3 but also that the equilibrium $RATLC_{.../...}$ quantity was OM (since, at $RATLC_{.../...} = OM$, the positive difference between the heights of the diagram's $RAMLP_{.../...}$ and $RAMLC_{.../...}$ curves equals $LE_{\Delta.../\Delta...} = [+HL]$). However, if $P\pi_{\Delta.../\Delta...}$ does not equal zero, one will not be able to infer equilibrium $RATLC_{.../...}$ for a diagram-covered series of resource allocations from accurate estimates of the prevailing $\Sigma D(P\pi_{\Delta.../\Delta...})$ figure and the operative $RAMLP_{.../...}$ and $RAMLC_{.../...}$ curves—i.e., one will not be able to infer equilibrium $RATLC_{.../...}$ without knowing in addition the prevailing $P\pi_{\Delta.../\Delta...}$. Thus, if we continue to assume that $\Sigma D(P\pi_{\Delta.../\Delta...}) = (-HL)$ in Diagram A.3 and that diagram's constructions of the operative $RAMLP_{.../...}$ and $RAMLC_{.../...}$ curves are accurate but assume that $P\pi_{\Delta.../\Delta...} = +DG$ rather than zero, the economic efficiency of the economics-marginal exemplar of the diagram-covered series of resource allocations will be DE = HL + DG rather than HL (since each dollar in profits the economics-marginal resource allocation yields will be associated with a one-dollar increase in its economics efficiency), and the equilibrium $\text{RATLC}_{.../...}$ quantity in Diagram A.3 will be OB rather than OM. Thus, any Diagram A.3-based analysis that ignored the fact that $P\pi_{\Delta.../\Delta...} > 0$ would overestimate the equilibrium $\text{RATLC}_{.../...}$ quantity and concomitantly underestimate the amount of economic inefficiency generated by economically-inefficient decisions not to allocate additional resources to the diagram-covered series of resource allocations (would yield the conclusion that in Diagram A.3 area HeI in misallocation would be generated by such decisions when the actual amount of misallocation generated would be the larger area DeE). Similarly, assume that $\Sigma D(P\pi_{\Delta.../\Delta...}) = +UZ$ in Diagram A.3. If $P\pi_{\Delta.../\Delta...} = 0$, one could infer from the fact that $\Sigma D(P\pi_{\Delta.../\Delta...}) = +UZ$ in Diagram A.3 that $\text{LE}_{\Delta.../\Delta...} = (-UZ)$, and one could infer from the combination of the fact that $\text{LE}_{\Delta.../\Delta...} = (-UZ)$ in Diagram A.3 and the accurately-estimated $\text{RAMLP}_{.../...}$ curve in Diagram A.3 that the equilibrium $\text{RATLC}_{.../...}$ quantity in Diagram A.3 was Oa. However, one could not infer the equilibrium $\text{RATLC}_{.../...}$ quantity for a fully-specified series of resource allocations from accurate estimates of its $\Sigma D(P\pi_{\Delta.../\Delta...})$ figure and $\text{RAMLP}_{.../...}$ curve if $P\pi_{\Delta.../\Delta...} \neq 0$. Thus, if $\Sigma D(P\pi_{\Delta.../\Delta...})$ has been accurately estimated to equal $(+UZ)$ in Diagram A.3 and that Diagram A.3's construction of its $\text{RAMLP}_{.../...}$ curve is accurate but $P\pi_{\Delta.../\Delta...} = +YZ$, the economic inefficiency of the economics-marginal exemplar of the diagram-covered series of resource allocations would be the smaller amount $(|-UZ| + |YZ|) = |VW|$ rather than the larger amount $|UZ|$ and the equilibrium $\text{RATLC}_{.../...}$ quantity would be the smaller quantity OX rather than the larger quantity Oa. Moreover, because any Diagram A.3-based analysis of a situation in which $\Sigma D(P\pi_{\Delta.../\Delta...}) > 0$ that ignored the fact that $P\pi_{\Delta.../\Delta...} > 0$ would overestimate the economic inefficiency of the economics-marginal resource allocation in the relevant series and overestimate the relevant equilibrium $\text{RATLC}_{.../...}$ quantity, it would overestimate the amount of economic inefficiency generated by economically-inefficient decisions to execute additional resource allocations of the diagram-covered series of resource allocations (in the preceding example, would yield the conclusion that area eUZ in such misallocation would be generated when the actual amount of misallocation generated would be the smaller area eVW).

I turn now to the question on which this section is focusing: How will the fact that $P\pi_{\Delta.../\Delta...}$ for a diagram-covered series of resource allocations exceeds zero affect the impact that a choice that has a known effect on the operative $\Sigma D(P\pi_{\Delta.../\Delta...})$ figure will have on the amount of economic inefficiency generated by the economically-inefficient decisions that were/would be made to execute or not to execute resource allocations of the diagram-covered series of resource allocations, given the associated pre-choice $\text{RAMLP}_{.../...}$ and $\text{RAMLC}_{.../...}$ curves, if the choice would not affect those curves (1) in cases in which the relevant $P\pi_{\Delta.../\Delta...}$ figures are both positive and equal and (2) in cases in which the pre-choice and post-choice $P\pi_{\Delta.../\Delta...}$ figures are different and one or both are positive?

I will start by using Diagram A.3 to illustrate the analysis of the first of these two cases. Diagram A.3 can be used to illustrate the impact of the fact that $P\pi_{\Delta.../\Delta...} > 0$ on a choice's effect on the amount of economic inefficiency generated by economically-inefficient decisions to execute and/or not to execute exemplars of a diagram-covered series of resource allocations in the special case in which the pre-choice and post-choice $P\pi_{\Delta.../\Delta...}$ figures are both positive and equal because, in Diagram A.3, DG, IJ, fh, and YZ (which are all positive) are constructed to be equal. Thus, Diagram A.3 reveals that, in the case in which the pre-choice and the post-choice $P\pi_{\Delta.../\Delta...}$ are, respectively, DG and IJ (where DG = IJ > 0), an analyst who assumes that both the pre-choice and the post-choice $P\pi_{\Delta.../\Delta...}$ figures are zero would mistakenly conclude that a choice that the analyst correctly surmised would change $\Sigma D(P\pi_{\Delta.../\Delta...})$ from (−HL) to (−KP) would change the equilibrium $LE_{\Delta.../\Delta...}$ from (+HL) to (+KP) and hence would change the equilibrium $RATLC_{.../...}$ quantity from OM (the quantity at which $LE_{\Delta.../\Delta...}$ = HD) to OQ (the quantity at which $LE_{\Delta.../\Delta...}$ = KP) whereas, in reality, given that both the pre-choice and the post-choice $P\pi_{\Delta.../\Delta...}$ equal DG = IJ, the choice will change $LE_{\Delta.../\Delta...}$ from (+DE) = (HL + DG) to (+IF) = (KP + IJ) (since the fact that $P\pi_{\Delta.../\Delta...}$ is positive will increase $LE_{\Delta.../\Delta...}$ dollar for dollar by the $P\pi_{\Delta.../\Delta...}$ figure) and the equilibrium $RATLC_{.../...}$ quantity from OB to OC. More to our current concern, Diagram A.3 illustrates the fact that, on the above assumptions about pre-choice and post-choice $\Sigma D(P\pi_{\Delta.../\Delta...})$, Diagram A.3's assumptions about the $RAMLP_{.../...}$ and $RAMLC_{.../...}$ curves, and our current premise that the choice whose economic inefficiency is at issue will not change the operative $RAMLP_{.../...}$ curve, any analysis that mistakenly assumes that both the pre-choice and the post-choice $P\pi_{\Delta.../\Delta...}$ figures equal zero when in fact they both equal DG = IJ will underestimate the amount by which the choice under review did/would reduce the quantity of economic inefficiency generated by economically-inefficient decisions not to execute additional economically-efficient exemplars of the diagram-covered series of resource allocations—in particular, would conclude that the reduction in economic inefficiency was/would be the smaller area HKPL when it actually would be the larger area DIFE. The associated qualitative conclusion about the sign of the error manifests the following relationship, which has already been established: ceteris paribus, the reduction in a relevant category of economic inefficiency that will be generated by a choice that reduces the absolute value of a relevant $\Sigma D(P\pi_{\Delta.../\Delta...})$ figure by a given amount without changing the sign of the relevant $\Sigma D(P\pi_{\Delta.../\Delta...})$ figure will increase with the difference between the pre-choice equilibrium $RATLC_{.../...}$ quantity and the economically-efficient $RATLC_{.../...}$ quantity (OA in Diagram A.3).

Diagram A.3 can also be used to illustrate the same abstract points in the case in which, both pre-choice and post-choice, the sign of the operative $\Sigma D(P\pi_{\Delta.../\Delta...})$ figure is positive. Recall that, in Diagram A.3, YZ is constructed to equal fh. Assume a case in which (1) pre-choice $P\pi_{\Delta.../\Delta...}$ = YZ > 0 and post-choice $P\pi_{\Delta.../\Delta...}$ = fh > 0 where YZ = fh and (2) pre-choice $\Sigma D(P\pi_{\Delta.../\Delta...})$ = UZ and post-choice $\Sigma D(P\pi_{\Delta.../\Delta...})$ equals the smaller amount bh. An analyst who mistakenly assumed that both the pre-choice $P\pi_{\Delta.../\Delta...}$ and the post-choice $P\pi_{\Delta.../\Delta...}$ equaled

zero would conclude that a choice that would reduce $\Sigma D(P\pi_{\Delta.../\Delta...})$ from UZ > 0 to
bh > 0, would reduce the absolute value of $|LE_{\Delta.../\Delta...}|$ from |UZ| to |bh|, would reduce
the equilibrium $RATLC_{.../...}$ quantity from Oa to Od, and would increase economic
efficiency by area bUZh whereas, in reality, the choice would reduce equilibrium
$|LE_{\Delta.../\Delta...}|$ from (|UZ| − |YZ|) = |VW| < |UZ| to |RS| = |bf| = (|bh| − |fh|), would
reduce equilibrium $RATLC_{.../...}$ from OX to OT, and would reduce the economic
inefficiency generated by all economically-inefficient decisions to increase the
amount of resources measured by their allocative cost devoted to the diagram-covered
series of resource allocations by the smaller amount area RVWS rather than by the
larger amount area bUZh. Once more, the associated qualitative conclusion about the
sign of the error reflects the fact that, ceteris paribus, the economic-efficiency gain
that will be generated by a choice that generates a given reduction in an absolute
$\Sigma D(P\pi_{\Delta.../\Delta...})$ figure without altering that figure's sign or changing any relevant
$RAMLP_{.../...}$ curve will increase with the pre-choice $RATLC_{.../...}$ quantity (since the
analyst's mistaken assumption that the pre-choice $P\pi_{\Delta.../\Delta...}$ was zero led the analyst
to overestimate the pre-choice equilibrium $RATLC_{.../...}$ quantity—e.g., in the
example under consideration, to conclude that it was Oa when it really was OX).

The preceding two analyses assumed that the choice whose economic efficiency is
at issue would reduce the absolute value of the relevant equilibrium $\Sigma D(P\pi_{\Delta.../\Delta...})$.
Obviously, one could also use Diagram A.3 to illustrate the analysis of the relevance
of the fact that the pre-choice $\Sigma D(P\pi_{\Delta.../\Delta...})$ and the post-choice $\Sigma D(P\pi_{\Delta.../\Delta...})$ are
both positive and equal to the impact on economic efficiency of a choice that would

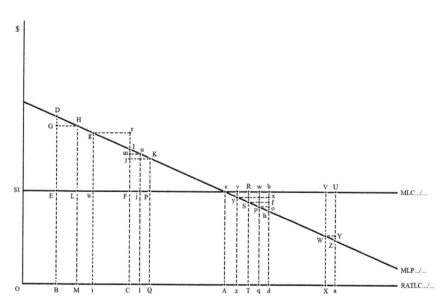

Diagram A.4 An economic-efficiency-impact-analysis diagram that illustrates the relevance of a
choice's increasing or decreasing equilibrium $P\pi_{\Delta.../\Delta...}$

increase the absolute value of the relevant equilibrium $\Sigma D(P\pi_{\Delta.../\Delta...})$ (e.g., that would increase $|\Sigma D(P\pi_{\Delta.../\Delta...})|$ from KP to HL or from bh to UZ).

I turn now to the relevance to a choice's impact of the amount of economic inefficiency generated by the economically-inefficient decisions to execute or not to execute exemplars of an economic-inefficiency-analysis-diagram-covered series of resource allocations of (1) the fact that the choice did/would increase the operative equilibrium $P\pi_{\Delta.../\Delta...}$ figure from a smaller positive number to a larger positive number (or, though I will not analyze an example of such a case here, from zero to a positive number) and (2) the fact that the choice did/would decrease the operative equilibrium $P\pi_{\Delta.../\Delta...}$ figure from a larger positive number to a smaller positive number (or, though I will not analyze an example of such a case here, from a positive number to zero). Diagram A.4 will be used to illustrate the relevant analysis. Diagram A.4 contains the same RAMLP$_{.../...}$ and RAMLC$_{.../...}$ curves as Diagram A.3 and all the points that Diagram A.3 contains. However, to enable it to illustrate the relevance of a choice's reducing or increasing equilibrium $P\pi_{\Delta.../\Delta...}$ to the choice's impact on the total amount of economic inefficiency generated by decisions not to execute economically-efficient exemplars of a diagram-covered series of resource allocations when pre-choice $\Sigma D(P\pi_{\Delta.../\Delta...}) < 0$, Diagram A.4 contains points m, r, n, j, l, g, u, and i, which Diagram A.3 does not contain, and to enable it to illustrate the relevance of a choice's reducing or increasing equilibrium $P\pi_{\Delta.../\Delta...}$ to the choice's impact on the total amount of economic inefficiency generated by decisions to execute economically-inefficient exemplars of a diagram-covered series of resource allocations when pre-choice $\Sigma D(P\pi_{\Delta.../\Delta...}) > 0$, Diagram A.4 contains points v, y, z, w, p, q, x, and o, which Diagram A.3 does not contain.

I will first use Diagram A.4 to address the case in which pre-choice $\Sigma D(P\pi_{\Delta.../\Delta...})$ < 0. As we saw previously, on the assumptions of Diagrams A.3 and A.4, the failure of an economic-efficiency analyst who accurately estimated pre-choice $\Sigma D(P\pi_{\Delta.../\Delta...})$ to be (−HL) and post-choice $\Sigma D(P\pi_{\Delta.../\Delta...})$ to be (−KP) (when $|{-}HL| > |{-}KP|$) to recognize that pre-choice $P\pi_{\Delta.../\Delta...}$ = DG and that post-choice $P\pi_{\Delta.../\Delta...}$ = IJ when DG = IJ would lead the analyst to conclude mistakenly that (1) pre-choice LE$_{\Delta.../\Delta...}$ was HL when it really was DE, (2) post-choice LE$_{\Delta.../\Delta...}$ was KP when it really was IF (since the positive equilibrium $P\pi_{\Delta.../\Delta...}$ figures would increase the economic efficiency of the economics-marginal resource allocation dollar for dollar), (3) the choice would raise equilibrium RATLC$_{.../...}$ from OM to OQ when it would actually raise it from OB to OC, and (4) the choice would reduce the economic inefficiency generated by all decisions not to execute economically-efficient exemplars of the diagram-covered series of resource allocations by the smaller amount area HKPL when the choice would actually reduce the above economic inefficiency by the larger amount area DIFE. The part of Diagram A.4 that covers RATLC$_{.../...}$ quantities zero to OA is designed to illustrate the analysis of the consequences of the separate error the analyst will make if— when pre-choice $\Sigma D(P\pi_{\Delta.../\Delta...})$ = (−HL) and post-choice $\Sigma D(P\pi_{\Delta.../\Delta...})$ = (−KP) —the analyst ignores either (1) the fact that the choice whose economic efficiency is at issue will reduce equilibrium $P\pi_{\Delta.../\Delta...}$ from DG = IJ to Im < IJ or (2) the fact that the choice whose economic efficiency is at issue will increase equilibrium $P\pi_{\Delta.../\Delta...}$ from DG = IJ to rJ > IJ. Thus, Diagram A.4 reveals that a choice that (1) reduces $|\Sigma D(P\pi_{\Delta.../\Delta...})|$ from $|-HL|$ to $|-KP|$ and (2) reduces equilibrium $P\pi_{\Delta.../\Delta...}$ from DG = IJ to mJ < IJ will (3) reduce $LE_{\Delta.../\Delta...}$ from DE to mF = nj rather than from DE to IF, (4) increase equilibrium $RATLC_{.../...}$ from OB to OI rather than from OB to OC (because at $RATLC_{.../...}$ = OI, $LE_{\Delta.../\Delta...}$ = IF − Im = nj [where Im is the amount by which the choice has reduced $P\pi_{\Delta.../\Delta...}$]), and (5) decrease the amount of economic inefficiency generated by decisions not to execute economically-efficient exemplars of the diagram-covered series of resource allocations by the larger area DnjE rather than by the smaller area DIFE (because, by reducing $P\pi_{\Delta.../\Delta...}$, the choice has reduced the economic efficiency of the relevant economics-marginal resource allocation). In other words, Diagram A.4 illustrates the fact that an analyst (1) who has (A) correctly estimated the operative $RAMLP_{.../...}$ curve, the pre-choice $\Sigma D(P\pi_{\Delta.../\Delta...})$ figure, and the post-choice $\Sigma D(P\pi_{\Delta.../\Delta...})$ figure but (B) has mistakenly assumed that the pre-choice $P\pi_{\Delta.../\Delta...}$ figure was zero when it actually was DG = IJ > 0 and has failed to recognize that the choice would reduce the equilibrium $P\pi_{\Delta.../\Delta...}$ figure from DG = IJ to mJ < IJ (2) will on the last account underestimate by a greater amount the economic-efficiency gain the choice generates by causing additional, economically-efficient exemplars of the diagram-covered series of resource allocations to be executed. In Diagram A.4, this conclusion reflects the "realities" that the fact that the choice will reduce $P\pi_{\Delta.../\Delta...}$ from IJ to mJ will cause it (1) to induce an additional Cl = mn of resources (measured by their allocative cost) to be devoted to the diagram-covered series of resource allocations and (2) to increase economic efficiency by area InjF on that account: thus, on the other assumptions I am now making, an economic-efficiency analyst who ignores the fact that the choice under review will reduce $P\pi_{\Delta.../\Delta...}$ from IJ to mj will underestimate the economic-efficiency gain the choice generates by area InjF. Thus, in cases in which pre-choice $\Sigma D(P\pi_{\Delta.../\Delta...})$ is negative, the error that an analyst who already assumed mistakenly that pre-choice $P\pi_{\Delta.../\Delta...}$ was zero when in actuality it was positive makes by ignoring the fact that the choice whose economic efficiency would render equilibrium $P\pi_{\Delta.../\Delta...}$ less positive will increase the amount by which the analyst's estimate of the economic efficiency of that choice underestimates its economic efficiency—in Diagram A.4, from the lower amount (area DIFE-area HKPL) to the higher amount (area DnjE-area HKPL).

   The left-hand side of Diagram A.4 can also be used to illustrate the relevance of a choice's increasing the positive value of the $P\pi_{\Delta.../\Delta...}$ figure for a diagram-covered category of resource allocations for the economic efficiency of a choice that reduces the absolute value of the negative $\Sigma D(P\pi_{\Delta.../\Delta...})$ figure for that series of resource allocations. For this purpose, continue to assume that the choice whose economic efficiency is at issue will reduce the absolute value of $\Sigma D(P\pi_{\Delta.../\Delta...})$ from $|HL|$ to $|KP|$ and that the pre-choice equilibrium $P\pi_{\Delta.../\Delta...}$ figure is DG = IJ but now assume that the choice will increase $P\pi_{\Delta.../\Delta...}$ from

DG = IJ to rJ = IJ + rI > IJ = DG. If post-choice $P\pi_{\Delta.../\Delta...}$ = rJ rather than pre-choice $P\pi_{\Delta.../\Delta...}$ = IJ, (1) post-choice $LE_{\Delta.../\Delta...}$ = gu = (KP + rJ) = (JF + rJ), (2) post-choice equilibrium $RATLC_{.../...}$ will be the smaller quantity Oi rather than the larger quantity OC, and (3) the choice will reduce the amount of economic inefficiency generated by decisions not to execute economically-efficient exemplars of the diagram-covered series of resource allocations (will increase economic efficiency) by the smaller area DguE rather than by the larger area DIFE. Diagram A.4 also illustrates the concomitant fact that an analyst (1) who has (A) accurately estimated the operative $RAMLP_{.../...}$ curve, the pre-choice $\Sigma D(P\pi_{\Delta.../\Delta...})$ figure, and the post-choice $\Sigma D(P\pi_{\Delta.../\Delta...})$ figure but (B) has mistakenly assumed that the pre-choice $P\pi_{\Delta.../\Delta...}$ figure was zero when it actually was DG = IJ > 0 and has failed to recognize that the choice would increase the equilibrium $P\pi_{\Delta.../\Delta...}$ figure from DG = IJ to rJ > IJ (2) will on the last account underestimate by a smaller amount the economic-efficiency gain the choice generates by causing additional, economically-efficient diagram-covered resource allocations to be executed. In Diagram A.4, this conclusion reflects the "realities" that the fact that the choice will increase $P\pi_{\Delta.../\Delta...}$ from IJ to rJ will (1) reduce the amount of additional resources (measured by their allocative cost) it causes to be devoted to the diagram-covered category of resource allocations by iC = gr and (2) will on that account reduce the economic-efficiency gain it generates by area gIFu. Thus, the left-hand side of Diagram A.4 can be used to illustrate the fact that, on our current assumptions, in cases in which pre-choice $\Sigma D(P\pi_{\Delta.../\Delta...})$ is negative, the errors that an analyst who already assumed mistakenly that pre-choice $P\pi_{\Delta.../\Delta...}$ was zero when it was actually positive makes by ignoring the fact that the choice whose economic efficiency is at issue would raise equilibrium $P\pi_{\Delta.../\Delta...}$ will decrease the amount by which the analyst's estimate of the economic efficiency of that choice underestimates its economic efficiency—will cause the underestimate to be the lower amount (area DguE–area HKPL) rather than the higher amount (area DIFE–area HKPL).

The right-hand side of Diagram A.4—the side that covers the part of the diagram at which $RATLC_{.../...}$ equals or exceeds OA—can be used to analyze situations in which (1) both the pre-choice and the post-choice $\Sigma D(P\pi_{\Delta.../\Delta...})$ figures for the choice whose economic efficiency is at issue are positive and (2) the pre-choice value of the relevant $P\pi_{\Delta.../\Delta...}$ figure is positive. I will use Diagram A.4 to analyze two related questions: when both pre-choice and post-choice $RATLC_{.../...}$ exceed OA because both pre-choice and post-choice $LE_{\Delta.../\Delta...}$ < 0, (1) how will the fact that a choice increases or decreases the $P\pi_{\Delta.../\Delta...}$ figure for a diagram-covered series of resource allocations affect the impact that the choice has on the amount of economic inefficiency generated by economically-inefficient decisions to execute economically-inefficient exemplars of the diagram-covered series of resource allocations and (2) how will the failure of an analyst who has mistakenly assumed that both pre-choice and post-choice $P\pi_{\Delta.../\Delta...}$ = 0 for the diagram-covered series of resource allocations to recognize that the choice will increase or decrease the $P\pi_{\Delta.../\Delta...}$ figure for that series of resource allocations when that figure is positive both pre-choice and post-choice affect the amount by which the analyst misestimates the quantity of economic inefficiency generated by decisions to execute economically-inefficient exemplars of that series of resource allocations. I will assume (as the analysis that Diagram A.3 illustrates assumes) that the choice in question will reduce $\Sigma D(P\pi_{\Delta.../\Delta...})$ from UZ to bh and that pre-choice $P\pi_{\Delta.../\Delta...}$ = YZ. However, rather than assuming (as the analysis that Diagram A.3 illustrates assumes) that the choice whose economic efficiency is at issue did/would not change $P\pi_{\Delta.../\Delta...}$—that pre-choice $P\pi_{\Delta.../\Delta...}$ = YZ = post-choice $P\pi_{\Delta.../\Delta...}$ = fh, the analysis that Diagram A.4 illustrates assumes that the choice whose economic efficiency is at issue will either reduce $P\pi_{\Delta.../\Delta...}$ from YZ to oh < fh = YZ or increase $P\pi_{\Delta.../\Delta...}$ from YZ to xh > fh = YZ.

The first question I will address is: How does the fact that the choice whose economic efficiency is at issue alters $P\pi_{\Delta.../\Delta...}$ affect its economic efficiency? As previously established, on the assumptions that Diagrams A.3 and A.4 share, a choice that reduces $\Sigma D(P\pi_{\Delta.../\Delta...})$ from (+UZ) to (+bh) while leaving $P\pi_{\Delta.../\Delta...}$ unchanged at YZ = fh will (1) change $LE_{\Delta.../\Delta...}$ from (−VW) to (−RS) = −bh + fh, (2) decrease $RATLC_{.../...}$ from OX to OT, and (3) increase economic efficiency by area RVWS. By comparison, a choice that reduces $P\pi_{\Delta.../\Delta...}$ from YZ = fh to oh < fh = YZ while reducing $\Sigma D(P\pi_{\Delta.../\Delta...})$ once again from (+UZ) to (+bh) will (1) alter $LE_{\Delta.../\Delta...}$ from (−VW) = (−UZ) + YZ to (−wp) = (−bo) = (−bh) + oh = (−RS − [fh−oh])—i.e., will reduce $LE_{\Delta.../\Delta...}$ by a smaller amount than it would have done had it not reduced $P\pi_{\Delta.../\Delta...}$ where the difference equals the amount by which the choice will reduce $P\pi_{\Delta.../\Delta...}$—viz., (fh−oh), (2) decrease $RATLC_{.../...}$ from OX to oq (the $RATLC_{.../...}$ quantity at which $P\pi_{\Delta.../\Delta...}$ = −wp)—i.e., will decrease $RATLC_{.../...}$ by less because it will reduce $P\pi_{\Delta.../\Delta...}$ and in so doing will decrease $LE_{\Delta.../\Delta...}$ and increase $RATLC_{.../...}$, and (3) will increase economic efficiency by the smaller amount area wVWp rather than by the larger amount area RVWS. Relatedly, a choice that increases $P\pi_{\Delta.../\Delta...}$ from YZ = fh to xh > fh = YZ while reducing $\Sigma D(P\pi_{\Delta.../\Delta...})$ once again from (+UZ) to (+bh) will (1) change $LE_{\Delta.../\Delta...}$ from (−VW) to (−vy) = (−RS + [xh−fh]), (2) decrease RATLC.../... from OX to Oz, and (3) increase the economic-efficiency gain the choice generates by area vRSy from area RVWS to area vVWy.

The second question I will address is: How will the mistake that an economic-efficiency analyst who has already made the error of assuming that pre-choice $P\pi_{\Delta.../\Delta...}$ = 0 when it is actually YZ = fh makes by assuming that the choice will not affect the equilibrium $P\pi_{\Delta.../\Delta...}$ figure when in reality it will either reduce $P\pi_{\Delta.../\Delta...}$ to a lower positive number or increase it to a higher positive number affect the accuracy of the analyst's prediction/post-diction of the choice's impact on the quantity of economic inefficiency generated by economically-inefficient decisions to execute economically-inefficient exemplars of the diagram-covered series of resource allocations? The starting point of the required analysis is the fact that the failure of the analyst to recognize that the pre-choice $P\pi_{\Delta.../\Delta...}$ was positive would cause the analyst to overestimate the economic-efficiency gain that a choice that reduced $\Sigma D(P\pi_{\Delta.../\Delta...})$ by a given amount to a lower positive figure would generate if the choice would not affect equilibrium $P\pi_{\Delta.../\Delta...}$. Thus, as I explained previously, on the assumptions of Diagram A.4 (and Diagram A.3), the error that an analyst who made no other mistake would make by assuming that (pre-choice $P\pi_{\Delta.../\Delta...}$) = (post-choice $P\pi_{\Delta.../\Delta...}$) = 0 when in reality (pre-choice $P\pi_{\Delta.../\Delta...}$) = YZ = (post-choice $P\pi_{\Delta.../\Delta...}$) = fh > 0 would cause the analyst to overestimate the amount by which a choice that reduces $\Sigma D(P\pi_{\Delta.../\Delta...})$ from UZ to bh would reduce the diagram-covered quantity of resource misallocation (by [area bUZh]−[area RUZS]).

I will start by using Diagram A.4 to illustrate the fact that the additional error that an economic-efficiency analyst who correctly estimates the relevant $RAMLP_{.../...}$ curve, the pre-choice $\Sigma D(P\pi_{\Delta.../\Delta...})$ to equal (+UZ), and the post-choice $\Sigma D(P\pi_{\Delta.../\Delta...})$ to equal (+bh) but mistakenly assumes that the pre-choice $P\pi_{\Delta.../\Delta...}$ = 0 when it was actually YZ > 0 would make if he or she incorrectly assumed that the choice would not affect equilibrium $P\pi_{\Delta.../\Delta...}$ when it would actually reduce $P\pi_{\Delta.../\Delta...}$ (say, from YZ = fh to oh < fh in Diagram A.4) would tend to cause the analyst to underestimate the economic-efficiency gain the choice in question would generate—to ignore the fact that, by reducing equilibrium $P\pi_{\Delta.../\Delta...}$ (in Diagram A.4 by reducing $P\pi_{\Delta.../\Delta...}$ from fh to oh), the choice would increase the economic-efficiency gain it generated (in Diagram A.4 by area RwpS) by decreasing equilibrium $|LE_{\Delta.../\Delta...}|$. When both pre-choice and post-choice $LE_{\Delta.../\Delta...}$ < 0, the failure of an analyst whose only other mistake was to assume that pre-choice $P\pi_{\Delta.../\Delta...}$ was zero when it actually was positive to realize that the choice whose economic efficiency he or she was analyzing did/would reduce $P\pi_{\Delta.../\Delta...}$ from a larger to a smaller positive number would reduce the amount by which he or she overestimated the diagram-covered category of economic-efficiency gain the choice did/would generate: in Diagram A.4, would cause the analyst's estimate of that gain —area bVWh—to exceed the actual gain—area wUZp—by a smaller amount than the amount by which the analyst's estimate would exceed the larger gain the choice would have generated had it not reduced $P\pi_{\Delta.../\Delta...}$ from fh to oh—area RUZS. Thus, in cases in which both pre-choice and post-choice $LE_{\Delta.../\Delta...}$ < 0, the error an analyst whose only other mistake was to assume that pre-choice $P\pi_{\Delta.../\Delta...}$ = 0 when it was actually positive makes by ignoring the fact that the choice whose economic efficiency is at issue did/would reduce equilibrium $P\pi_{\Delta.../\Delta...}$ from a higher to a lower positive number would partially counteract the impact of the former error—viz. would cause the analyst to overestimate the relevant economic-efficiency gain the choice did/would generate.

I will now use Diagram A.4 to illustrate the fact that the error that an economic-efficiency analyst whose only other error was to assume that pre-choice $P\pi_{\Delta.../\Delta...}$ = 0 when it actually was positive would make by assuming that the choice whose economic efficiency is at issue would not change equilibrium $P\pi_{\Delta.../\Delta...}$ when it actually would increase equilibrium $P\pi_{\Delta.../\Delta...}$ from a lower positive number to a higher positive number (in Diagram A.4, from YZ = fh to xh > fh = YZ) would tend to cause the analyst to underestimate the economic-efficiency gain the choice would generate—to ignore the fact that, by increasing equilibrium $P\pi_{\Delta.../\Delta...}$ (in Diagram A.4, by increasing it from fh to xh), the choice would increase the economic-efficiency gain it generated by area vRSy by decreasing equilibrium $|LE_{\Delta.../\Delta...}|$. Hence, the error that an economic-efficiency analyst makes by assuming that the post-choice $P\pi_{\Delta.../\Delta...}$ equals the pre-choice $P\pi_{\Delta.../\Delta...}$ when the post-choice $P\pi_{\Delta.../\Delta...}$ actually exceeds the pre-choice $P\pi_{\Delta.../\Delta...}$ will compound the error that the analyst makes by assuming that the pre-choice $P\pi_{\Delta.../\Delta...} = 0$ when it is positive: will increase the amount by which the analyst overestimates the economic-efficiency gain the choice in question generates. Diagram A.4 can be used to illustrate this conclusion. As we saw, Diagram A.4 reveals that an analyst who (1) correctly estimates the $RAMLP_{.../...}$ curve constructed in the diagram, (2) correctly estimates pre-choice $\Sigma D(P\pi_{\Delta.../\Delta...})$ to be UZ, (3) correctly estimates post-choice $\Sigma D(P\pi_{\Delta.../\Delta...})$ to be bh, but (4) incorrectly assumes that pre-choice $P\pi_{\Delta.../\Delta...} =$ post-choice $P\pi_{\Delta.../\Delta...} = 0$ when both equal YZ = fh will conclude that the choice will reduce the quantity of diagram-covered economic inefficiency generated by area bVWh, which equals area eVW *minus* area ebh, when, in fact, the choice would reduce the quantity of diagram-covered economic inefficiency generated by the smaller area RUZS, which equals area eUZ *minus* area eRS if the choice would not change $P\pi_{\Delta.../\Delta...}$—i.e., will overestimate the economic-efficiency gain the choice generates by (area bVWh−area RUZS). By way of contrast, although an analyst who correctly estimates (1) the $RAMLP_{.../...}$ curve, (2) the pre-choice $\Sigma D(P\pi_{\Delta.../\Delta...})$, and (3) the post-choice $\Sigma D(P\pi_{\Delta.../\Delta...})$ but (4*) incorrectly assumes that pre-choice $P\pi_{\Delta.../\Delta...} =$ post-choice $P\pi_{\Delta.../\Delta...} = 0$ when pre-choice $P\pi_{\Delta.../\Delta...} = YZ = fh$ and post-choice $P\pi_{\Delta.../\Delta...} = xh > fh$ will still conclude that the choice will reduce the quantity of the diagram-covered economic inefficiency generated by area bVWh when the choice will in fact reduce the quantity of that economic inefficiency generated by area vUZy from area eUZ to area evy (which is larger than the area—area RUZS—by which the choice would reduce the quantity of diagram-covered economic inefficiency if post-choice $P\pi_{\Delta.../\Delta...} =$ pre-choice $P\pi_{\Delta.../\Delta...} = fh$). Since the fact that the choice did/would increase $P\pi_{\Delta.../\Delta...}$ increases the amount by which it did/would decrease the quantity of diagram-covered economic inefficiency generated, an analyst's failure to take account of the fact that the choice increases $P\pi_{\Delta.../\Delta...}$ will tend to cause the analyst to underestimate the economic-efficiency gain the choice did/would generate—will counteract the tendency of the analyst's failure to recognize that $P\pi_{\Delta.../\Delta...} > 0$ to lead the analyst to overestimate the economic-efficiency gain the choice generated. Thus, is Diagram A.4, the amount by which an analyst who made no error other than the error of assuming that pre-choice and post-choice $P\pi_{\Delta.../\Delta...}$ equaled zero when both equaled YZ = fh would overestimate the reduction in the quantity of diagram-covered economic inefficiency that the specified choice did/would generate if post-choice $P\pi_{\Delta.../\Delta...} =$ pre-choice $P\pi_{\Delta.../\Delta...}' = fh = YZ$— area bVWh *minus* area RUZS—*exceeds* the amount by which an analyst who made no error other than the error of assuming that pre-choice $P\pi_{\Delta.../\Delta...} =$ post-choice $P\pi_{\Delta.../\Delta...} = 0$ when pre-choice $P\pi_{\Delta.../\Delta...} = YZ = fh$ and post-choice $P\pi_{\Delta.../\Delta...} =$

xh > fh = YZ—area bVWh *minus* area vUZy where area vUZy *exceeds* area RUZS by area vRSy.

A.1.5   The Relevance of the Choice's Changing the Operative RAMLP$_{.../...}$ Curve

So far, I have assumed that the choice whose economic efficiency is at issue would not change the operative RAMLP$_{.../...}$ curve. Obviously, if the choice under review does change the operative RAMLP$_{.../...}$ curve, that reality might affect the total economic-efficiency gain or loss generated by all exemplars of the diagram-covered series of resource allocations that are executed not only (1) by changing the economic efficiency of the exemplars of that series of resource allocations that the choice elicits or deters but also (2) by changing the economic efficiency of the exemplars of that series of resource allocations that would be executed regardless of whether the choice is made.

Section 1.4 of Chap. 1's outline of the protocol for analyzing the economic efficiency of a choice indicates that the protocol I am claiming is TBLE will take account of the way in which a choice will affect the economic-efficiency gain or loss generated by all exemplars of each category of resource allocations that are executed by altering the amount of poverty and material inequality the relevant economy generates. At this juncture, I want to acknowledge that, regardless of whether a choice affects the amount of poverty and/or material inequality generated by the economy in which it is made, it can affect the economic-efficiency gain or loss yielded by all exemplars of a relevant category of resource allocations by generating income and wealth effects that alter the allocative value of both the resource-uses to which the choice causes resources to be devoted and the resource-uses from which the choice causes resources to be withdrawn. The protocol I am recommending ignores this second possibility on the assumption that it would not be TBLE to consider it. I acknowledge that I have not justified this last assumption.

A.1.6   The Reason Why, Despite the Economic-Efficiency-Impact-Analysis Diagram's Pedagogic/Heuristic Usefulness, the Protocol for Economic-Efficiency Prediction/Post-Diction I Claim Is TBLE Does Not Make Use of It

I hope that the preceding sections of this appendix have established the pedagogic usefulness of the economic-efficiency-impact-analysis diagram on which it focuses. Nevertheless, the protocol for economic-efficiency prediction/post-diction I claim is TBLE does not use this diagram for two related reasons: (1) the diagram requires its employer to estimate the whole length of the relevant RAMLP$_{.../...}$ and

RAMLC$_{.../...}$ curves, which is useful if one is interested in the total economic-efficiency gain or loss generated pre-choice and post-choice by all exemplars of the diagram-covered series of resource allocations but is not necessary if one is interested solely in the economic efficiency of the exemplars of the diagram-covered series of resource allocations the choice under review elicits or deters and (2) although one could use a portion of the diagram that provides information solely on the segments of the operative RAMLP$_{.../...}$ and RAMLC$_{.../...}$ curves that cover the exemplars of that series of resource allocations that the choice under review elicits or deters to predict/post-dict the economic efficiency of the resource allocations the choice elicits or deters, it would not be TBLE to do so because, in order to do so, one would have to estimate the relevant pre-choice and post-choice RATLC$_{.../...}$ quantities—an allocatively-costly task one can avoid by focusing solely on the identity of the resource allocations the choice would/did elicit/deter, the profits/losses they yielded/would yield, and the distortions in those profits that were/would have been operative.

Appendix B
The Ability of a Sale to Generate Future Profits and the Step-Wise-Monopoly Distortion in Any Such Profits

Abstract

For simplicity, Chap. 7 (Sect. 7.1.1.1) ignored the realities that (1) for a variety of reasons, the sale of a unit of one product may increase the profits the seller makes in the future when selling that product and/or other products and (2) the imperfections in seller price-competition an economy contains can generate (SW[M]) distortions in these profits. Appendix B delineates five reasons why the sale of a unit of a product can increase the seller's future profits and executes partial analyses of the step-wise-monopoly distortions in any profits the sale of a unit of a product enables the seller to earn in the future when selling that product and/or other products for each of these reasons.

Section 7.1.1.1 assumed that the sale of a unit of output would affect the seller's profits only by generating conventional marginal revenue and marginal costs. In fact, for at least five reasons or sets of reasons, a seller's sale of a unit of its output may enable it to obtain benefits (in some instances, one should say "profits") without incurring any pricing-costs by altering the demand curve it faces on the product in question or on other products it sells (i.e., by raising the quantity of such products it will sell at a given price and/or the price it will obtain for units of those products it would have sold in any event). Appendix B delineates those reasons and executes partial analyses of the (SW[M]) distortion in any future profits that the sale of a unit of output enables the seller to realize for each of these reasons.

Here are the five reasons why the sale of one unit of one product may increase the profits the seller will earn in the future by selling that product or other products:

1. the immediate buyer may make repeat-purchases of the good in question when that buyer would not otherwise have purchased that good in the future or may pay a higher price for that good in the future than the buyer would otherwise have paid for it in the future (try it, you'll like it);
2. the sale of the unit of the good in question to its immediate buyer may cause other buyers to purchase it or increase the price they pay for it because the immediate buyer recommends it to them, because they observe and are positively impressed by its performance when used by the immediate buyer, and/or

R. S. Markovits, *Welfare Economics and Second-Best Theory*,
https://doi.org/10.1007/978-3-030-43360-4

because they want others to conclude that they have positively-valued characteristics that the immediate buyer possesses and believe that being seen to be a
consumer of the same product that the immediate buyer of the seller's product
purchased will lead others to conclude that they share these other
positively-valued attributes of the immediate buyer in question;

3. the sale of the unit of the good in question may increase the immediate buyer's
   demand for complements of the product in question or for other members of the
   product-line to which the product in question belongs because (in the latter case,
   for aesthetic of other reasons [as when all members of any given line of
   cooking-wares should be used in the same way and have the same performance-
   capacities but the proper method of use and performance-capacities of different
   product-lines differ]) a buyer's ownership of one member of a product-line
   increases the dollar value of other members of that product-line to the buyer in
   question;

4. the sale of the unit of the good in question may increase the demand curves for
   the seller's other products both of the immediate buyer and of other buyers who
   observe its performance for the immediate buyer or who are told by its
   immediate buyer that it performed well for that buyer by leading the other
   buyers in question to revise upwards their assessments of the seller's other
   products; and

5. the sale of the unit in question may increase the future demand curves for the
   good in question and for the seller's other products because the price that the
   seller charged for the unit in question (A) was "offensively" retaliatory against a
   rival that had beaten the seller's contrived oligopolistic offer and on that account
   will deter competitive inferiors from beating the seller's future contrived-
   oligopolistic offers, (B) was predatory and drove out its target when doing so
   decreased the absolute attractiveness of the best offers against which the
   predator will have to compete because the target was not immediately replaced
   by a rival that was as closely competitive with the predator as the target was, or
   (C) was "defensively" retaliatory (targeted either a contriver that had previously
   retaliated against the defensive retaliator's refusal to cooperate with the target's
   contrived oligopolistic behavior or a predator) and will reduce the absolute
   attractiveness of the offers against which the defensive retaliator will have to
   compete by deterring its rivals from directing offensive retaliation or predation
   against it.

I have no doubt that it will often be TBLE to take account of these ways in which
the sale of a unit of output can increase the seller's future profits when analyzing the
imperfections-in-seller-price-competition-generated (SW[M]) distortion in $PB_{(U)UO}$
and $P\pi_{UO}$. I will not attempt here to execute a full analysis of the impact of the
(SW[M]) distortion in these benefits and profits on the overall imperfections-
in-seller-price-competition-generated (SW[M]) distortions in $PB_{(U)UO}$ and $P\pi_{UO}$. In
particular, I will not take account here of the fact that the (SW[M]) distortion in
those benefits the sale of a unit of output confers on the seller by increasing its unit
output of the good in question or of other goods will be affected by the (SW[M])

distortions in the private benefits that would have been generated by the QV-investment-creating-and-using and PPR-executing-and-using resource-uses that were sacrificed to the production and sale of the additional units of any product of the seller in question that that seller produces that the sale of the relevant unit of the relevant product results in its producing and selling. However, I do want to make the following five points or sets of points:

(1) there is no (SW[M]) distortion in the private benefits that the sale of a unit of output yields the seller by enabling the seller to sell units of the product in question or any other product that it would have sold anyway for a higher price than it would otherwise have obtained for those units (assuming as I am that the sale of the unit of output in question does not reduce the price that the seller in question obtains for any other unit of its product it sells[1]);

(2) if the sale of the unit in question results in the seller's making additional future sales of the product in question or of other products, the imperfections-in-seller-price-competition-generated (SW[M]) distortion in the profits the seller makes on those sales (i.e., on the private benefits the immediate sale yields the seller by causing it to make other profitable sales) equals the relevant (SW[M]) distortion in the revenues it obtains from those additional sales—the difference between the sum of the before-tax prices that the buyers of those units could have paid for them and remained equally well-off and the sum of the marginal revenues it obtained on the sales in question (assuming once again that the sale of the unit in question does not alter the price[s] the relevant seller obtains for the units it would have sold in any event)—*minus* the relevant (SW[M]) distortion in the incremental (variable) cost the seller had to incur to produce the additional units of its product(s) the sale of the unit in question resulted in its selling, which equals the relevant (SW[M]) distortion in the private benefits that the resources used to produce and sell the additional units of the seller's product(s) would have generated in their sacrificed UO-producing-and-using, QV-creating-and-using, and PPR-executing-and-using uses [if I assume that it is TBLE to ignore the possibility that these resources might be withdrawn from one or more other categories of use], which depends on the (SW[M]) distortion in the private benefits of each such sacrificed use and hence inter alia on the percentages of the resources that would be used to produce the additional units of output that would be withdrawn, respectively, from UO-producing-and-using, QV-creating-and-using, and PPR-executing-and-using uses [which are important for among other reasons both because the step-wise-monopoly distortion in the private benefits yielded by QV-creating-and-using uses is positive whereas the step-wise-monopoly distortion in the private benefits yielded by the use of units of output and the step wise-monopoly distortion in the private benefits yielded by the use of production-process discoveries are negative and because there is no reason to believe that the weighted-average (SW[M]) percentage-distortion in the private benefits yielded by the use of units of output

is the same as the weighted average (SW[M]) percentage-distortion in the private benefits that PPR discoverers obtain by using their PPR discoveries]);

(3) if the sale of the unit of output in question benefits the seller by increasing the profits it will realize in the future by engaging in contrived-oligopolistic pricing because the sale is made as a result of the seller's retaliating against a privately-worse-placed rival that beat the retaliator's contrived-oligopolistic-price-containing offers to one or more buyers (because the sale will deter rivals from defeating the seller's future contrived-oligopolistic efforts), the associated increase in imperfections in seller price-competition will generate additional positive (SW[M]) distortions in the private benefits that the sale in question yields the offensive retaliator in that the additional contrived-oligopolistic pricing the sale causes to be practiced will decrease economic efficiency inter alia by creating additional positive (SW[M]) distortions in the private benefits of creating and using QV investments in the ARDEPPSes in which the additional contrived-oligopolistic pricing is practiced and additional negative (SW[M]) distortions in the private benefits of executing and using PPR projects in the ARDEPPSes in which the additional contrived-oligopolistic pricing is practiced[2];

(4) if the sale of the unit of output in question manifests the seller's engaging in predation and benefits the seller by driving out a target rival that will not be immediately replaced by a rival that is equally competitive with the predator as its target would have been and by increasing the profits the predator and contrived-oligopolistic conduct by strengthening its reputation for engaging in such: "strategic" conduct—i.e., manifests successful predatory conduct, the increases in imperfections in seller price-competition the sale will generate will yield additional positive (SW[M]) distortions in those private benefits in that at the same time that the resulting price-increases yield the predator private benefits, they will (on the assumptions of the SW-distortion analysis) decrease economic efficiency by causing additional positive (SW[M]) distortions in the private benefits of creating and using QV investments in the ARDEPPSes in which the predation in question and any additional predation and contrived-oligopolistic pricing to which it leads are practiced and by causing additional negative (SW[M]) distortions in the private benefits of executing and using production-process research in the ARDEPPSes in question[3]; and

(5) if the sale of the unit of output in question manifests the seller's engaging in defensive retaliation and benefits the defensive retaliator that makes the sale by deterring its target and others from engaging in contrived-oligopolistic conduct or predation that would inflict losses on the defensive retaliator, not only the magnitude but the sign of the (SW[M]) distortion in those private benefits will be uncertain because, although for reasons I have just discussed, any resulting decrease in contrived-oligopolistic conduct, offensive retaliation against firms that have undermined contrived-oligopolistic conduct, and predation will decrease the absolute magnitudes of the (SW[M]) distortions in the private benefits that various resource-uses yield the resource-users, one would need to have much more information than is currently available to determine whether—

even on the assumptions of (SW[M]) distortion analysis—any associated increase in economic efficiency would be larger or smaller than the private benefits the defensive retaliation yielded the defensive retaliator.

(6) Appendix B ignored the fact that, according to some consultants, increases in a firm's output can also yield it benefits by enabling it to learn things about producing its product that will cause it to face lower costs of production sooner than would otherwise be the case. I did not address this possibility because I doubt its significance. However, to the extent that extra current production does yield such "learning-by-doing" cost-reduction gains, the (SW[M]) distortion in those gains will depend on the (SW[M]) distortions in the private benefits the saved resources would have generated in their sacrificed alternative uses.

Notes

1. Moreover, when the sale of a unit of output increases the price that the seller can obtain for units of that product or other products it sells by increasing the accuracy of the relevant buyers' estimates of the dollar value to them of the relevant unit(s) of the relevant product(s), the sale of the unit of output in question will (ceteris paribus) reduce the resource-allocator-non-sovereignty step-wise negative distortion in the private benefits that the sale of the relevant units yielded the seller in question.

2. These two claims are explained, respectively, in Sects. 7.1.1.2 and 7.1.1.3. I should also note that, to the extent that the retaliators' being *privately-worse-placed* than their targets to supply the buyers to which the retaliators make their retaliatory sales is associated with the retaliators' being *allocatively-worse-placed* to supply the buyers in question, retaliatory sales will cause intra-ARDEPPS UO-to-UO misallocation. Indeed, even if a retaliatory offer does not result in the retaliator's making the sale (because the relevant buyer gives the target an opportunity to rebid and the target takes advantage of that opportunity), the retaliatory offer will yield economic inefficiency by inducing the buyer in question to make allocative-transaction-costly enquiries to the target about its willingness to beat the retaliator's offer and by inducing the target to make allocative-transaction-costly rebids. All the above points apply mutatis mutandis to predatory behaviors and to defensive retaliation against offensive retaliation and predation, though defensive retaliation almost certainly increases economic efficiency by deterring contrived-oligopolistic conduct and predation. I should note as well that, in legal regimes in which offensive retaliation and predation are prohibited, a full analysis of the economic efficiency of offensive retaliation and predation (and derivatively of defensive retaliation that deters them) would have to take account of the allocative transaction costs that the perpetrators and targets of offensive retaliation and predation generate when pursuing and defending related legal claims, the allocative transaction costs that the government generates when bringing and adjudicating related civil and criminal suits, and any allocative transaction costs

or economic inefficiency the government generates to finance its related legal activities.

3. The text focuses on the distorting effects of any decrease in seller price-competition that predatory conduct generates as opposed to any decreases in QV-investment competition or PPR competition to which such conduct may lead. The positive (SW[M]) distortions in the private benefits yielded by predatory conduct that lessens QV-investment competition in the ARDEPPSes in which the behavior in question is practiced. Will be associated with increases in economic efficiency while the positive (SW[M]) distortions in the private benefits yielded by predatory conduct that lessens PPR competition in the ARDEPPSes in which it is practiced will normally be associated with decreases in economic efficiency. For explanations, see the texts of Sects. 7.1.1.1 and 7.1.1.2.

Index

© Springer Nature Switzerland AG 2020

R. S. Markovits, *Welfare Economics and Second-Best Theory*,

https://doi.org/10.1007/978-3-030-43360-4

Printed by Printforce, the Netherlands